# Biological Warfare and Disarmament

## New Problems/New Perspectives

Edited by
Susan Wright

ROWMAN & LITTLEFIELD PUBLISHERS, INC.
Lanham • Boulder • New York • Oxford

ROWMAN & LITTLEFIELD PUBLISHERS, INC.

Published in the United States of America
by Rowman & Littlefield Publishers, Inc.
A Member of the Rowman & Littlefield Publishing Group
4720 Boston Way, Lanham, Maryland 20706
www.rowmanlittlefield.com

PO Box 317, Oxford, OX2 9RU, United Kingdom

British Library Cataloguing in Publication Information Available

**Library of Congress Cataloging-in-Publication Data**

Biological warfare and disarmament : new problems/new perspectives / edited by
Susan Wright.
     p.   cm. — (War and peace library)
   ISBN 0-7425-2468-X (cloth : alk. paper) — ISBN 0-7425-2469-8 (pbk. :
alk. paper)
    1. Biological warfare.  2. Biological arms control.  3. Disarmament.
I. Wright, Susan [DATE].  II. Series.
UG447.8 .B5645  2002
327.1′745—dc21                         2002009704

Printed in the United States of America

∞ ™ The paper used in this publication meets the minimum requirements
of American National Standard for Information Sciences—Permanence of
Paper for Printed Library Materials, ANSI/NISO Z39.48–1992.

# Contents

iii

# Acknowledgments

In the 1990s, biological warfare emerged as a multifaceted problem with no easy or obvious solutions in sight. Largely absent from Western efforts to address the issues at that time or since is an effort to understand the positions of non-Western countries except on Western terms. This book represents the outcome of an international collaborative project, *Forming a North-South Alliance to Address Current Problems of Biological Warfare and Disarmament*, designed to broaden the discourse on the biological warfare problem and to provide a space where non-Western perspectives could be seriously addressed.

The project was launched in July 1998 with a three-day conference held under the auspices of the UN Institute for Disarmament Research (UNIDIR) in Geneva. The conference brought together people from many backgrounds—scholars, journalists, industry representatives, members of nongovernmental organizations, and diplomats—and from many parts of the world to discuss issues related to biological warfare both before and after the Cold War. This book eventually required a sharper focus on the post–Cold War period. Nevertheless, all of the conference papers provided crucial reference points that have been valuable for the book's development.

As the project director, I acknowledge my debts with deep pleasure. I thank the participants in the initial conference and in later stages of the project. Without their insights and commitments, the book could not have been realized. I turned to many of these participants for advice and wish especially to acknowledge the role of Giri Deshingkar, who passed away in 2000 and is greatly missed by his colleagues. He left a rich legacy of scholarship on East Asia and on disarmament that includes his work on this book. As the principal advisor for the project, Richard Falk has played a special and extensive role. His deep understanding of the interplay of international law

v

and international relations has expanded my intellectual horizons not only during this project but also over the past twenty years.

Research and writing were carried out in two outstanding research centers: the Institute for Research on Women and Gender at the University of Michigan in Ann Arbor and the UN Institute for Disarmament Research (UNIDIR) at the United Nations in Geneva. Their directors, Abigail Stewart and Patricia Lewis, and members of their staffs provided supportive environments and highly professional assistance. I have a special debt to Kristin Blackburn, who took on the occasionally mind-blowing challenge of managing record-keeping on both sides of the Atlantic; Hazel Tamano, who turned her expert organizing skills in many creative directions in Geneva; and Romica Singh, Joseph Brunner, and Krista Nielson, who ably assisted with research in Ann Arbor. As the book evolved, I benefited greatly from many discussions not only with colleagues in Ann Arbor, Geneva, and elsewhere but also with the diplomats I interviewed during my stay at UNIDIR in 1998–99. They provided invaluable insights into the politics of disarmament negotiations, including those related to the Biological Weapons Convention. I also want to acknowledge the role of the students in my seminar on the politics of biological and chemical warfare and disarmament at the University of Michigan. Their probing questions transformed teaching into the reciprocal process that ideally it should always be.

The production of the book has benefited from the high standards and skills of many people. I thank David Akin and Paul Grams for their fine editorial work, Sandra duMonde for generously assisting with manuscript preparation at short notice, and Jo Ann Berg for preparing the index under major time constraints. I greatly appreciate the generative responses of the series editor, Mark Selden, and the professional support of Susan McEachern, Jehanne Schweitzer, and their colleagues at Rowman & Littlefield.

For making a project of this scope possible, I thank the New England Biolabs Foundation, the John D. MacArthur Foundation, the Ford Foundation, and the University of Michigan. The support of these institutions went far beyond funding to guidance and logistical support that was crucial for launching the project and for seeing it through to completion.

Special thanks are due to my son Jonathan, my sister and brother-in-law Rosemary and Thomas Hill, and many wonderful friends who helped me through a period of illness in 2000. Their encouragement meant far more than they know in enabling me to return to the project with health and energy fully renewed.

Finally, this book is dedicated to all those around the world who work tirelessly and often anonymously for peace and for a demilitarized world in which biological weapons, and all weapons, have no place.

# I

# THE GLOBAL CONTEXT

# 1

## Introduction

### In Search of a New Paradigm of Biological Disarmament

*Susan Wright*

In demonstrating the possibility of asymmetric warfare against the world's most powerful state, the September 11, 2001, attacks on the World Trade Center and the Pentagon introduced a radical new dimension to the problem of biological warfare. A powerful peaceful technology (civil aviation) was turned against the society it most benefits, revealing the disruptive fragility of industrialized and militarized nations. The attacks aroused deep fears that nuclear power plants or chemical factories or the highly pathogenic organisms originally developed as weapons by the United States and other industrialized countries would be future targets. It could also be inferred from al Qaeda's particular interest in weapons of mass destruction that such devices might not only be brandished but actually used. Although the mailing of anthrax-laced letters to American politicians and media personalities may be more properly classified as a "biocrime" rather than a terrorist action, it suggested how even a relatively small amount of a biological weapon could threaten indiscriminate killing and civil havoc.

In the fall of 2001, it appeared for a while that the attacks would unify most of the world in seeking cooperative approaches to protecting against biological warfare, including strengthening the principal legal barrier to biological warfare (BW), the 1972 Biological Weapons Convention (BWC). Yet in December 2001, the fifth review conference of the convention in Geneva was abruptly suspended after the United States proposed to terminate not

3

only the ongoing multilateral negotiations to strengthen the treaty but also their mandate. The American attempt to scuttle the BWC negotiations united representatives of virtually all other participating countries in stunned opposition. Evidently the goal of the Bush administration was to replace the multilateral effort, in which states participate on a formally equal basis, with a unilateralist emphasis on measures that would be determined and pursued by the United States either alone or with close allies.[1]

Before the September 11 attacks, the unilateralism of the Bush administration had become sufficiently obvious to have been named by a sympathetic journalist "the Bush doctrine": reject multilateral approaches to arms control as desirable in principle and deal, unilaterally if necessary, with perceived threats.[2] The administration's readiness to reject the Kyoto convention on climate change and ratification of the nuclear Comprehensive Test Ban Treaty and to scrap the Anti-Ballistic Missile Treaty heralded a stark unilateralist posture on a whole range of global issues. The Bush administration's rejection of the draft text of a new BWC inspection protocol several months before the fifth review conference suggested that its approach to the Biological Weapons Convention would be no exception.

For a while, the shock of the September 11 attacks appeared to temper this position as President George W. Bush turned to the United Nations for a condemnation of the attacks and sought to build an international coalition to fight terrorism. The United States accepted the assistance of a wide range of states—by no means confined to Western allies—for intelligence sharing, closing down the financial networks of al Qaeda, emergency aid for refugees, and negotiations to establish a new government in Afghanistan. But while cooperating with many states on these fronts, the United States also signaled its intention to fight the war in Afghanistan largely on its own terms.[3] "Either you are with us or you are with the terrorists," Bush declared to the U.S. Congress on September 21, 2001. Events since then have shown his determination that Washington alone would decide which countries fell into which camps.

In his State of the Union address to Congress on January 29, 2002, Bush insisted on accusing North Korea, Iran, and Iraq of "constitut[ing] an axis of evil, arming to threaten the peace of the world [with] . . . weapons of mass destruction." The threat of terrorist use of such weapons, including biological weapons, was thus conflated with the threats the United States perceives from countries seen as hostile to its interests. But the sharp rejection of such rhetoric by other states—and by no means only those accused—underscored the lack of global consensus regarding Bush's claims as well as the desire of many states, including Western allies, to seek peaceful solutions to other dimensions of the problems posed by weapons of mass destruction.

There is greater continuity in U.S. policy on biological warfare and disarmament than media coverage of the Geneva debacle might suggest. Fueling the Bush offensive against further multilateral negotiations for strengthening the Biological Weapons Convention is a view of geopolitics that has been maintained over the past three American presidencies. Since the end of the Cold War, American perceptions of security threats have shifted from the intense focus on the threat posed by Soviet weapons of mass destruction, especially nuclear weapons, to a fear of "proliferation" of weapons of mass destruction in the Third World. The threat of biological weaponry (often in tandem with chemical weaponry) is a prominent and particularly emotive element of this fear, justified by claims that biotechnology can overcome previous deficiencies of biological weapons and that the low cost and relative ease of production make them attractive to Third World countries. The sources of this threat are typically portrayed as "rogue" states and "terrorists," whose very characterization as such places them beyond the reach of "civilized" regimes of prohibition to which "responsible" states adhere.

America's closest ally, the United Kingdom, has generally shared these perceptions. Other Western allies have done so to varying extents. But certainly the September 11 attacks reinforced the widely shared Western perception that the source of the biological warfare problem lies outside the West and that the most appropriate response is to attack the perceived sources of the problem, either militarily or through economic and other means. It is not, of course, that there is no truth in the view that military interest in biological weapons has spread beyond the industrialized countries that were responsible for introducing modern forms of biological weapons in the twentieth century. In troubled regions of the world where nuclear weapons are overtly or covertly being developed or deployed, less powerful states may be tempted to contemplate a biological or chemical option, if only for deterrence purposes, and may therefore feel justified in remaining outside a biological weapons disarmament regime or, if within it, may maintain secret, undetectable programs that fall in the considerable gray area of this particular regime. With the notable exception of Iraq, however, whether Western perceptions of the intent of non-Western countries to develop biological weapons are accurate remains impossible to assess without access to intelligence reports, and perhaps not even then. Despite these qualifications concerning what is really known and what is possible to know about the BW interests of non-Western states, the Western orthodoxy on BW has become ever more entrenched, especially in the aftermath of the September 11 attacks.

Yet there are contradictions in this position. The United States intends to raise its level of spending on defense against biological terrorism to some $4.6 billion for fiscal years 2003 and 2004.[4] Much of this funding will support measures to defend against a BW attack and is broadly supported by the American people. But there are also disturbing indications that the biological defense effort will encompass the use of sophisticated techniques of genetic engineering and other forms of biotechnology to produce *modified* pathogens as weapons. Such plans could well destabilize the restraints on recourse to biological weaponry defined by the Biological Weapons Convention. It is ironic that a move to undermine the convention is being initiated not by the non-Western states that are regularly accused of violating the treaty, but by a powerful Western state that is also attempting to scuttle efforts to strengthen the BWC regime.

In spite of these indications that the most powerful Western state may well be contributing to the BW problem, Western perceptions of the problem are overwhelmingly dominated by the view that it emanates exclusively from non-Western states and terrorist organizations that harbor sinister intentions toward the West. The accuracy of these perceptions is hardly questioned, and certainly non-Western views of the problem are completely marginalized. The general purpose of the examinations of the BW problem given in this book is to reopen these questions by introducing alternative, and particularly non-Western, views on critical dimensions of the problem and on responses to it. But first, it is important to understand how the Western view of the BW problem has evolved in the post–Cold War period and how this view is linked to Western military policies, especially policies related to nuclear weaponry.

## EVOLVING PERCEPTIONS OF THE BW PROBLEM AND THE EMERGENCE OF THE ROGUE DOCTRINE IN THE WEST

The immorality of biological weapons has long been used in the West as an emotive subject, especially in relation to the intentions of non-Western countries that are seen as hostile or irresponsible. In Western parlance, these weapons are "the poor man's nuke." But there is some irony in this description. Biological weapons were developed as weapons of mass destruction before and during World War II by industrialized countries, notably the United States, the former Soviet Union, the United Kingdom, France, Germany, Japan, and Canada.[5] These programs were enshrouded in secrecy; few details about them emerged until many decades later.

After World War II, the West saw the problem of biological warfare largely in terms of the potential threat posed by the former Soviet Union. Indeed, the repeated policy reviews conducted by the U.S. Department of Defense in the late 1940s and 1950s reached substantially the same conclusion: The United States was unprepared to meet the Soviet BW threat and therefore had to expand its own offensive program. The presumed threat defined the imperative. At the same time, an undercurrent of Western concern about the potential threat of biological weapons as well as of chemical weapons[6] focused on their possible spread to less industrialized, non-Western countries. In the 1960s, with the exception of the use of chemical weapons by Egypt against Yemen, there was little evidence of such interest in either type of weaponry. Nevertheless, the United States and probably also the former Soviet Union were interested in preventing the potential spread of the very technologies of mass destruction that they were largely responsible for developing. Indeed, a key motive for America's abandonment of its own biological weapons program in 1969 and its endorsement of an international treaty to ban these weapons was that their spread would "not act as much to strengthen the big powers as it would to endow dozens of relatively weak countries with great destructive capability." As Han Swyter, a Defense Department advisor, explained in 1969: "The proliferation of chemical and biological capability would tend to reduce the world's balance of power, reducing ours. We would lose some of the advantages of nuclear and conventional capability which wealth gives to us and to the Soviets." A second motive, of equal geopolitical significance, was that the United States could rely for its defense on nuclear weapons, thus ensuring that the Biological Weapons Convention, completed in 1972, would be marked by the division of its parties into nuclear-possessor and nonpossessor states.[7]

During the Cold War, official concerns about a Third World biological weapons threat, which were in any case hypothetical, disappeared as tensions between the two superpowers escalated and the threat of a nuclear confrontation consumed attention. However, as superpower relations improved in the 1980s, official interest turned once again to the question of proliferation in the Third World. In June 1985, with concerns about the Soviet threat still in the foreground, President Reagan's Chemical Warfare Commission warned that "the Department of Defense does not have an adequate grasp of the biological warfare threat and has not been giving it sufficient attention. Both intelligence and research in this area, though improved after a virtual halt during the 1970s, are strikingly deficient. The Department should be devoting much more resources and talent to addressing the chemical and biological threats of the future as well as those of the present."[8] Iraq's use of chemical weapons in the Iran–Iraq war in the early 1980s was used to fuel such reemerging concerns. In 1985, a secret report of the U.S. Defense Science Board concluded that "the chemical and biological threats are increasing, Third World proliferation is getting worse, and the possible consequences are extremely serious."[9]

Such warnings were aired with increasing regularity in the late 1980s. Into the vacuum left by glasnost and the demise of the Soviet Union came an array of new enemies in the form of unruly Third World states intent on acquiring weapons of mass destruction and the means to deliver them and undermining the prevailing world order.[10] This view was foreshadowed in *Discriminate Deterrence* (January 1988),[11] the report of a prominent

Reagan administration commission charged with developing a long-term security strategy for the United States. The commission included such senior policy advisors as Henry Kissinger, Zbigniew Brzezinski, and Nobel Prize–winner and Defense Science Board member, molecular biologist Joshua Lederberg. Although the Commission still saw the power of the Soviet Union as an "extreme" threat, it also introduced the view that rising regional powers in the Third World, armed with nuclear or chemical weapons and ballistic missiles, could pose new threats to American security—a view that was soon taken up by Washington think tanks and various members of Congress. The Commission did not specifically mention biological weapons, but by the following year these weapons were figuring in security scenarios. In 1989, Senator John Glenn, chairman of the Senate Committee on Governmental Affairs, opened hearings on the "Global Spread of Chemical and Biological Weapons" with the claim that "a new part of the [security] equation is that weapons of mass destruction are no longer solely in superpower arsenals. Whatever our nonproliferation efforts, we may find that superpower-mass destruction-capability will now be in the hands of almost any nation that desires to possess it."[12] CIA Director William Webster claimed, ominously, that "at least 10 countries are working to produce both previously known and futuristic biological weapons."[13]

Official attention began to focus on a special category of countries deemed sufficiently immoral to use weapons of mass destruction or to employ terrorists to do so. "Maverick," "rogue," "backlash," and "outlaw" began to enter the security lexicon to denote countries believed to be developing such weapons and which had, in former president George H. W. Bush's words, "contempt for civilized norms."[14] Iraq under Saddam Hussein invaded Kuwait on August 2, 1990, and instantly became the leading symbol of the "rogue" state, a concrete embodiment of the post–Cold War threat. That Bush administration abruptly dropped its previous policy of "engagement" with Iraq. The Gulf War itself became seen as the first experience of combat against such a "rogue" threat and a model for future combat. As former Secretary of Defense (now Vice President) Dick Cheney told Congress in March 1991: "The Gulf War presaged very much the type of conflict we are most likely to confront again in this new era—major regional contingencies against foes well-armed with advanced conventional and unconventional munitions."[15] At the same time, Iran, Libya, and North Korea began to figure regularly in the "rogue" category.

Furthermore, a brief indication of interest in "engagement" with Iran on the part of the Bush administration was soon dropped in favor of a policy of "containment" with respect to Iran as well as Iraq.[16] Moves (discussed further elsewhere in this chapter) to impose export controls that would halt sales of military-related goods and technology to Iran, Libya, and North Korea as well as to Iraq underscored the extent to which all these countries were increasingly included in the "rogue" category. Such appraisals of the new threat were transmitted almost seamlessly to the incoming Clinton administration. "Rogue states" continued to feature as a core concept and containment as the best strategy to use against them. In contrast to U.S. policy for two decades before Iraq's invasion of Kuwait, which had attempted to "engage" Iran to "contain" Iraq, and, after the Iranian hostage crisis, vice versa, the Clinton administration pursued a policy of simultaneous containment of both countries, defining both as "rogues."[17] The most prominent articulation of this strategy was given by National Security Advisor Anthony Lake who, in an article in *Foreign Affairs*, called Iran and Iraq, along with Cuba, North Korea, and Libya "backlash states," characterized by authoritarian regimes, "radical ideologies," "siege mentalities," and the commitment to pursuing weapons of mass destruction.[18] Containment, according to Lake, required determined efforts to isolate these states, either multilaterally (in the case of Iraq) or unilaterally (in the case of Iran), and to prevent them from acquiring weapons of mass destruction.

By the mid-1990s, the "rogue doctrine," as Michael Klare has called it, was fully entrenched in Washington and in some London policy circles.[19] Moreover, as evidence that Saddam Hussein had acquired a biological arsenal was uncovered by the UN Special Commission (UNSCOM) in 1991–1995, and as defectors revealed that the former Soviet Union had pursued a huge offensive BW program that dwarfed the Iraqi one, the threat posed by potential rogue use of biological weapons came to the fore. With the airing of claims that use of biotechnology would produce more dangerous types of biological weaponry that would overcome past problems of control, biological warfare began to loom as a new threat, deemed comparable in power to that of nuclear weapons. The nerve gas attack on the Tokyo subway by the Aum Shinrikyo cult in 1995, along with the discovery that the cult had also attempted, unsuccessfully, to produce botulinum toxin and a strain of anthrax, was used to justify an expanded definition of the threat of biological and other weapons of mass destruction that included terrorist use and that also blurred differences between threats posed by "terrorists" and "rogue regimes." As former Defense Secretary William Perry wrote in 1996: "Terrorists operate in a shadowy world in which they can detonate a device and disappear, as the poison gas attack in Tokyo illustrates. Rogue regimes may try to use these devastating weapons as blackmail, or as a relatively inexpensive way to sidestep the U.S. military's overwhelming conventional military superiority. . . . The bottom line is, unlike during the Cold War, those who possess nuclear, chemical, and biological weapons may actually come to use them."[20]

In contrast to the intense American focus on "rogues," the Western allies of the United States were generally far less willing to think in such terms, let alone inscribe measures against such countries into their trading relations.

The European discourse tended to depict "proliferation" as a general trend without naming specific countries. As a report of a British conference attended by members of prominent Washington defense think tanks, Western government officials, and Western arms control organizations concluded in 1997: "In the recent past, biological weapons were not seen as a serious threat to international security. . . . This view is now widely challenged. Biotechnologies have become increasingly available around the world, and a significant number of states are known to have active [biological weapons] development programmes or weapons systems in place. . . . There is increasing concern that [these weapons] will be used by terrorist groups."[21]

For the remaining years of the century, government agencies and congressional committees, aided by the media, continued to fan fears of the use of biological and other weapons of mass destruction by unruly aggressors. As Defense Secretary William Cohen stated in November 1997: "As the millennium approaches, we face the very real and increasing prospect that regional aggressors, third-rate armies, terrorist groups and even religious cults will seek to wield disproportionate power by acquiring and using these weapons that can produce mass casualties. These are neither far-fetched nor far-off threats."[22] Such fears were intensified by sensational media coverage and a new genre of scary BW novels. *The Cobra Event*, by journalist Richard Preston, a terrifying story of biological warfare in New York City that blurred boundaries between fact and fiction, was said to have deeply impressed President Clinton.[23] In his 1998 State of the Union address, Clinton promised to address the dangers of biological and chemical weapons deployed by "outlaw states, terrorists, and organized criminals."[24] Amid escalating claims, a bipartisan congressional commission headed by former CIA director John Deutch released a massive report that portrayed "a dangerous world where hostile forces will seek to exploit WMD to their advantage and to threaten us."[25] Elsewhere, Deutch described the threat as "catastrophic," one that "spann[ed] the globe."[26] On the eve of the twenty-first century, official fear of weapons of mass destruction in the hands of rogues and terrorists, in which biological weapons were portrayed as playing an especially insidious role, had reached cataclysmic levels.

In contrast to the premonitions of the Clinton administration, when mass-casualty terrorist attacks came, they took a very different form, using the "low-end" technology of box cutters to turn the power of civilian jetliners into weapons. Nonetheless, in the aftermath of September 11 and the subsequent anthrax-laced mail to politicians and the media, American fears that biological weapons would be used directly in a future attack on the United States intensified.[27] President George W. Bush's fears of "rogue states" intent on developing biological and other weapons of mass destruction and what Bush called "their terrorist allies" were widely shared by politicians and disseminated by the mainstream media.

## IMPLEMENTATION OF
## NONPROLIFERATION POLICY

In Washington, the "rogue doctrine" was used rather consistently by successive administrations to justify a set of policies whose express purpose was to stem the spread of biological and others weapons of mass destruction. As President Clinton told the opening session of the United Nations in 1993:

> One of our most urgent priorities must be attacking the proliferation of weapons of mass destruction, whether they are nuclear, chemical, or biological. . . . [W]e know that many nations still believe that it is in their interest to develop weapons of mass destruction . . . More than a score of nations likely possess such weapons and their number threatens to grow. These weapons could destabilize entire regions. They could turn a local conflict into a global human and environmental catastrophe. . . . I have made nonproliferation one of our Nation's highest priorities. We intend to weave it more deeply into the fabric of all our relationships with the world's nations and institutions."[28]

Nonproliferation was woven into American relationships with other states through three main policies. In the first place, both the Bush and the Clinton administrations adapted the Cold War practice of technology denial to the proliferation threat through controls on exports of dual-purpose materials to states suspected of biological, chemical, or nuclear proliferation and sanctions against both noncompliant companies and the states themselves. A stream of legislation targeting states deemed to be "proliferants" issued from both administrations and from the U.S. Congress. These measures included the 1990 Enhanced Proliferation Control Initiative, which placed strict controls on exports of a variety of biological agents and equipment to twenty-eight states suspected of biological proliferation; the 1991 Chemical and Biological Weapon Control and Warfare Elimination Act, which provided for sanctions against firms deemed to be contributing to proliferation; the 1992 Iran-Iraq Arms Non-Proliferation Act, which extended sanctions already applying to Iraq to Iran; and the 1994 Iran-Libya Sanctions Act, which sanctioned foreign and domestic firms investing in the Iranian and Libyan energy sectors.[29]

Recognizing that export controls enacted by a single country, however influential, would not suffice to stem the dissemination of chemical and biological technologies to states around the world, both the Bush and the Clinton administrations actively supported the Australia Group, some thirty Western and Western-oriented countries formed in 1985 to encourage chemical companies in industrialized countries to deny relevant chemicals to Iraq. The Australia Group (AG) later expanded the scope of its efforts to include supplies that could be used for biological as well as chemical weapons programs and to extend its reach to countries deemed to be pursuing such programs. The group meets in private to share intelligence data about other states and to decide on the agents and equipment to be monitored and restricted. There is no public knowledge of the full range of states affected and no formal procedures available for affected countries to question the group's decisions.[30]

Furthermore, despite an understanding achieved by developing countries during the Chemical Weapons Convention (CWC) negotiations that the need for the Australia Group would be reviewed once the CWC entered into force,[31] the group has remained in existence and its operations have continued, even against non-Western countries that are parties to the BWC and the CWC in good standing. Although Australia Group members have claimed that the group's practices simply express and implement their commitments under the BWC and the CWC not to assist any state's efforts to acquire biological or chemical weapons, the fine structure of their actions suggests that the role of export controls is more than this. While states such as Iran, India, Pakistan, and China (all parties to the BWC and the CWC) have been targeted as "proliferators," Israel, which is widely understood to be a state with strong interests in biological and chemical weaponry and is not a party to either treaty, is described in an authoritative account of the AG as having "working relations" with individual AG members.[32]

As chapters 8 and 9 discuss, such forms of technology denial to non-Western countries pursued privately, outside the international regimes prohibiting biological and chemical weapons, have served as a serious source of North-South friction. "With the CWC already in force, the Australia Group is absolutely redundant, discriminating, and politically unacceptable," Ambassador Sha Zukang of China claimed in 1997.[33] Most fundamentally, the arrangement perpetuates the Western view that informs nonproliferation policy generally: that the real BW danger is associated with countries in the South, which are made subject to controls that are not relevant for countries in the North that do not need to import supplies, or if they do, are not subject to comparable levels of scrutiny.

By far the most forceful and determined form of technology denial was that practiced by UNSCOM against Iraq. The UN Security Council ceasefire resolution 687 gave UNSCOM extraordinary powers to investigate Iraq's weapons of mass destruction and to ensure that they were destroyed. This authority was backed up with economic sanctions that have had devastating effects on the Iraqi people and on the basic civil infrastructures of Iraq ever since. The treatment of Iraq surely stands as one of the most intrusive as well as the most punitive treatments of a defeated nation in history, a stark contrast with the Marshall Plan that supported the economic recovery of Germany after the devastation of World War II. The health and material resources of the Iraqi people have been severely weakened in the process, with over a million deaths attributed to the impact of sanctions, especially among children under the age of five.[34]

The treatment of Iraq is in striking contrast to the response of the United States to the discovery in the early 1990s that the former Soviet Union had committed massive violations of the BWC in pursuing a huge biological weapons program in the 1970s and 1980s (discussed in chapter 5). The Soviet program, the largest the world has ever known, employed some 65,000 people. The Iraqi program, encompassing some nine sites, was minuscule by comparison.[35] Under legislation originally proposed by Senators Richard Lugar and Sam Nunn and passed in 1991, the United States developed a "Cooperative Threat Reduction Program" designed to help ensure either the dismantling or the conversion of former Soviet weapons of mass destruction (WMD) programs, including its biological weapons program.[36] An important goal of the program was to stop the "brain drain" of skilled Russian scientists taking their expertise abroad, especially to "rogue" states. From the mid-1990s onward, some $3.5 million per year was spent on grants to encourage former biological weapons scientists to turn their expertise toward civilian applications and reduce the likelihood that they would sell their knowledge elsewhere.[37]

A second element of U.S. nonproliferation policy derives from American influence on and use of the international legal regimes banning chemical and biological weapons. The Chemical Weapons Convention, completed in 1992 during former president George H. W. Bush's term of office, included an intrusive inspection regime.[38] President Clinton professed support for ratifying the CWC and "putting teeth" in the Biological Weapons Convention through the negotiation of a protocol aimed at increasing compliance with the Convention's ban on biological weapons. According to Clinton in 1997: "The U.S . . . continues to play a leading role in the international effort to reduce the threat from biological weapons. We are an active participant in the Ad Hoc Group striving to create a legally binding protocol to strengthen and enhance compliance with the [Biological Weapons Convention]."[39]

However, Washington's commitments to protecting both its national security interests and industrial interests in biotechnology as well as to pursuing its nonproliferation goals have meant that it has tended to interpret the CWC and BWC selectively, exempting itself from requirements that applied to other states. When the United States ratified the Chemical Weapons Convention in 1997, it did so only on condition that it could impose three major conditions on on-site inspections that did not apply to any other party. A close observer of CWC developments has argued that "the United States has been the malignancy in the midst of the CWC" on the grounds that these conditions and the conduct of the United States during on-site inspections radically undermine the integrity of the treaty.[40] Similarly, far from working to "strengthen" the BWC by supporting a compliance protocol intended to enhance the transparency of military and civilian use of the biological sciences and biotechnology, the United States under the Clinton administration attempted to do the opposite, proposing measures intended to achieve a relatively high level of opacity for American industrial and military operations while requiring a higher level of transparency for other states.[41] The leverage exerted by the American pharmaceutical industry and the military not only created loopholes favorable to these sectors but more generally infected the Geneva negotiations with skepticism concerning the eventual outcome.

While the Clinton administration worked to achieve opacity for American defense and commercial activities *within* the multilateral process under the BWC, the Bush administration launched an offensive to close down the multilateral process entirely and to replace it with measures that were more susceptible to American influence. The loopholes in the proposed protocol achieved by the Clinton administration prepared the way. In July 2001, the Bush administration rejected the draft text of the compliance protocol on the grounds that the protocol "would put national security and confidential business information at risk, . . . [would not improve] confidence in compliance, and [would] do little to deter those countries seeking to develop biological weapons."[42] As noted previously, in December 2001 the administration went further, seeking to terminate the multilateral negotiations entirely. Under Secretary of State John Bolton indicated that the United States would prefer to develop measures for implementing the BWC under the authority of the UN Secretary-General. (Such procedures would then be controlled by the UN Security Council and subject to U.S. veto power rather than by an executive council of the BWC parties.) As Bolton observed at a press conference, such measures were intended to "break with the old [multilateral] approach" to strengthening restraints on recourse to biological warfare.[43]

Backing these technology denial and diplomatic nonproliferation strategies is a third element of nonproliferation policy, namely military programs that are specifically justified as defenses against "rogue" states and terrorists. Following the Gulf War, public questioning of the need for continued spending at Cold War levels was countered by Pentagon arguments that new types of munitions and defenses were needed to counter the rogue threat. Debate on military spending soon shifted from *whether* such new military capacities were really justified to *how many* such wars the United States should be prepared to fight simultaneously. Under Pentagon pressure, the

Clinton administration and Congress settled for two major wars, thereby ensuring that the threatened military budget was not substantially reduced. In contrast, the goal of the Bush administration has been a technological transformation and vast expansion of military capabilities designed to project U.S. power across the globe—a goal that Congress endorsed after September 11. Again, the ability to fight "rogues" and "terrorists" has framed public discussion.[44]

As former Secretary of Defense (now Vice President) Dick Cheney noted in 1991, the Gulf War was used as a precedent for future wars against rogue states in three main ways: first, preemption of "rogue" use of weapons of mass destruction through bombing designed to demolish WMD facilities; second, development of defensive measures for fighting in a combat environment contaminated by weapons of mass destruction; finally, should the need be necessary, the ability to threaten massive retaliation if weapons of mass destruction were used.[45] The Pentagon's "Counter-Proliferation Initiative," launched by former Secretary of Defense Les Aspin in December 1993, incorporated the dimensions emphasized by Cheney. It included in particular nonnuclear penetrating munitions for bombing underground installations; equipping U.S. forces to fight in environments in which nuclear, chemical, and biological environments would be used; and missile interception.[46]

These plans—which signified to some an American emphasis on preemptive strikes as opposed to an emphasis on arms control and export controls—aroused alarm elsewhere in the world. So also did the renewed support of the George W. Bush administration for a national missile defense (NMD). Initiated by the Reagan administration in the Cold War context as a defense against Soviet missiles, in the 1990s the NMD was forcefully revived as a defense against "rogue" states capable of launching long-range missiles armed with biological, chemical, or nuclear warheads. Sweeping aside worldwide fears that such a system would provoke a new arms race that could extend to outer space, the Bush administration withdrew from the Antiballistic Missile (ABM) treaty in determined pursuit of this new weapons system.[47]

In a similar manner, the Clinton administration in its final years and the Bush administration pursued a biological defense program that ran a serious risk of undermining constraints against biological warfare. As the salience of the BW issue increased in the United States in the 1990s, biological defense was deemed a high military priority. Under the Clinton administration, funding for both military and civilian programs skyrocketed. Funding for the Department of Defense's chemical and biological defense program increased steeply over the decade, to almost $800 million. Beyond this, responding to its own perception of a cataclysmic threat of a terrorist attack with weapons of mass destruction, the Clinton administration funded a large counter-terrorist initiative, committing a total of some $1.4 billion to launch a wide-ranging effort to develop vaccines, detection systems, and therapeutic drugs and to ensure a rapid emergency response in the event of an attack (see chapters 3 and 4).[48] In the aftermath of the September 11 attacks, the Bush administration and the U.S. Congress expanded this effort authorizing spending on defenses against bioterrorism to some $4.6 billion for fiscal years 2002 and 2003.[49]

Along with these large increases in funding, standards to ensure that American biological defense activities strictly complied with the letter and the spirit of the Biological Weapons Convention were relaxed. The treaty's vaguely defined boundary between permitted and prohibited development and production was exploited to allow a range of projects, uncovered by three *New York Times* journalists, that raised serious questions about commitment to the BWC. They also demonstrated the continuity between the Clinton administration, which launched them (apparently without presidential consent) and the Bush administration, which continued them.[50]

Beyond the American defense effort is the threat of massive retaliation should a rogue state use weapons of mass destruction. The Gulf War provided a precedent for such threats. On January 8, 1991, former President Bush threatened Saddam Hussein with "the strongest possible response" in the event that he used chemical or biological weapons. Although Bush did not specifically mention the use of nuclear weapons against Iraq, Secretary of State Baker later acknowledged that this possibility was conveyed to the Iraqi foreign minister, Tariq Aziz.[51] Secretly, however, President Bush and his advisors understood that they would *not* use nuclear weapons against Iraq.[52] This strategy of "calculated ambiguity"—threatening the use of nuclear weapons but secretly planning not to use them—was also adapted by the Clinton administration. In November 1997, the Clinton administration revised national policy for the targeting of nuclear weapons in a top secret directive, Presidential Decision Directive 60 (PDD 60). This nuclear policy not only retained options for nuclear strikes against Russia but also required general planning for nuclear strikes against "rogue states" such as Iraq in retaliation for use of weapons of mass destruction, including biological or chemical weapons.[53] At the same time, the Clinton administration was ambiguous about its intentions, both denying that it would use nuclear weapons against Iraq and refusing to rule out such use.[54]

There was no such ambiguity about the nuclear policy of Clinton's successor, however. The Bush administration's Nuclear Posture Review, leaked to the press in March 2002, shockingly broadened the conditions under which nuclear weapons might be used; beyond retaliation for an attack with nuclear weapons, the document listed retaliation for use of biological weapons, attacks on targets hardened to withstand a nonnuclear attack, and attacks in response to "surprising military developments." Once again, "rogue states" and biological weaponry were key elements in justifying the new policy.[55]

The bottom line for U.S. nuclear policy is clear: The United States does not restrict itself through a no-first-use policy and it keeps open the option of using nuclear weapons against states it defines as "rogues." As Richard Falk has argued, retention of nuclear weapons by the United States as a deterrent against selected states (which assumes willingness to use them) sustains a commitment "to weaponry of mass destruction by keeping the issues entirely outside the realm of serious political discourse."[56] The deep inequality in such practices is that Third World countries suspected of possessing biological and chemical weapons are threatened with use of weapons that have possibly far greater destructive power (see chapter 2).

## THE ROLE OF THINK TANKS AND NONGOVERNMENTAL ORGANIZATIONS

Although details of their responses have varied, Western think tanks and nongovernmental organizations (NGOs) specializing in arms control have largely absorbed and transmitted claims of a proliferation threat. At one end of the spectrum, Washington defense think tanks have promoted the "rogue doctrine." Hawkish Washington think tanks have even played with the idea of nuclear preemption of supposed WMD proliferation.[57] As a member of one of these organizations explained at a Western arms control conference in 1995, the weapons he had in mind would be "small"—a claim that elicited almost no critical response from the audience. At the other end of the spectrum, members of NGOs specializing in arms control have relied primarily on the general claim of proliferation to call for strong international regimes banning biological and chemical weapons.[58]

Despite such differences, a common thread runs through virtually all of these responses, namely, acceptance of a division of the world into two camps: "responsible" states that can be trusted with nuclear weaponry (and vast arsenals of conventional weapons) and "irresponsible" states that cannot be trusted with weapons of mass destruction and must be prevented from acquiring them. Arms control is seen as one element of a "web" of responses encompassing export controls, strong biological and chemical defenses, and, as one well-known article puts it, "determined and effective" military responses.[59] Finally, many Western arms control organizations are silent on the question of Western possession of nuclear weaponry and its use as a deterrent against "would-be proliferators" that contrasts with their active focus on the development and possession of biological and other WMD by non-Western states.

## THE CHALLENGE FOR THE TWENTY-FIRST CENTURY: THE SEARCH FOR AN ALTERNATIVE POLICY

The U.S.-dominated approach to global security is having the effect of polarizing Western and non-Western states, rendering a cooperative international search for security all but impossible. The Bush administration's response to the September 11 attacks, especially its conflation of the demonstrated threat of al Qaeda with the claimed threat of use of weapons of mass destruction by states it sees as hostile to American interests, has deepened the problem. Bush's strident accusations against Iraq, Iran, and North Korea as an "axis of evil" were strongly criticized around the world. Bush faced intense denunciations of his view of North Korea during his visit to South Korea; a warning from China that there would be "serious consequences" if the United States were to take action against Iraq; a warning from the United States' Arab allies, Jordan, Saudi Arabia, and Egypt, that a U.S. attack on Iraq would lead to instability across the Arab world and undermine the support of moderate Arab nations for the war on terrorism; a rebuke from Germany that the United States was treating its antiterror coalition partners like "satellites"; a reminder from Russia that the coalition had not agreed to target Iraq; a reminder from the Secretary-General of NATO that many European countries had good relations with Iran; and a lengthy warning from the European Union's foreign affairs commissioner that America's rapid success in Afghanistan was reinforcing some dangerous instincts: "that the projection of military power is the only basis of true security; that the US can rely only on itself; and that the allies may be useful as an optional extra but that the US is big and strong enough to manage without them if it must."[60] Such responses express growing fears concerning American geopolitics not only on the part of non-Western countries but also on the part of its close Western allies.

In view of these growing fears concerning America's own WMD policies as well as of the threat of international terrorism, this is an important moment to reassess the U.S.-dominated Western policies on biological warfare and the worldview that justifies them and to seek alternatives that support international cooperation in reaffirming the norm of biological disarmament. This book brings together authors from a wide range of backgrounds—international law, international relations, history, information science, medicine and public health, journalism, diplomacy, and the military—to take up this challenge. Particularly since approaches to the BW problem have been overwhelmingly dominated by a Western—and especially American—discourse on the problem, the book places special emphasis on introducing non-Western perspectives that are largely marginalized in the West.

First, the book examines the BW problem in the principal contexts in which it has been expressed since the Biological Weapons Convention entered into force. International lawyer Richard Falk surveys the global context, especially the nature of the present threats to international legal norms of prohibition of all weapons of mass destruction. Political scientist Laura Reed and science journalist Seth Shulman examine the rapid growth of the American biological defense effort over the past decade and draw attention to the risks this effort poses for "qualitative proliferation"—the spread of biogenetic technologies that could be used to construct novel and even more dangerous biological weapons. Physician Victor Sidel examines closely the social and ethical implications of one of the most significant elements of the American program, namely, reliance on vaccines. Russian specialist Anthony Rimmington examines the growth and impact of the huge secret Soviet biological weapons program pursued during the Cold War. Political scientist Laura Drake and historian and nuclear policy analyst Avner Cohen examine the BW problem as it occurs in one of its most intractable forms in the Middle East from the perspectives of the Arab states and of Israel respectively.

Second, the book addresses the political origins and purposes of the various international instruments that have been developed in various contexts to respond to particular dimensions of the BW problem. Political scientist and Middle Eastern specialist Amin Saikal and UNSCOM historian Stephen Black examine the history of the coercive disarmament of Iraq. Historian Susan Wright examines the geopolitical origins of the Biological Weapons Convention as revealed by the records of the government of the United Kingdom and of its closest ally, the United States. Political scientist Oliver Thränert examines the history of the negotiations for the BWC compliance protocol until the American move to terminate the negotiations in December 2001. The book also addresses two social conditions that proved influential for these negotiations. Susan Wright and information specialist David Wallace examine trends since the 1980s that have combined to veil the field of biotechnology in secrecy and their impact on the BWC protocol negotiations. Economist Biswajit Dhar examines the barriers posed by the growing global intellectual property regime to full implementation of article X of the BWC. Finally, the book includes perspectives on biological warfare and disarmament from two major non-Western countries, both of which are actively engaged in developing the biological sciences and biotechnology for peaceful purposes. Zou Yunhua, senior research fellow and professor at the Department of General Armaments of the People's Liberation Army of China, presents a Chinese perspective on the BW problem as it is viewed by a major state that is also one of a very few states to have suffered BW attacks. P. R. Chari, co-director of the Institute of Peace and Conflict Studies in New Delhi and a former member of the Indian Administrative Service, examines India's assessment of the BW problem from the perspective of a major regional state that perceives serious security threats internally as well as externally. Both chapters assess the efforts over the past decade to strengthen the BWC.

Third, the book addresses the political origins and purposes of the international instruments that have been developed in various contexts to respond to particular dimensions of the BW problem. Political scientist and Middle Eastern specialist Amin Saikal and UNSCOM historian Stephen Black examine the history of the coercive disarmament of Iraq (chapters 10 and 11). Historian of science Susan Wright examines the geopolitical origins of the Biological Weapons Convention as revealed by the records of the government of the United Kingdom and of its closest ally, the United States (chapter 12). Political scientist Oliver Thränert examines the history of the negotiations for the BWC compliance protocol until the American move to terminate the negotiations in December 2001 (chapter 13). The book also addresses two social conditions that proved influential for these negotiations. Susan Wright and information specialist David Wallace examine trends since the 1980s that have combined to veil the field of biotechnology in secrecy and their impact on the BWC protocol negotiations (chapter 14). Economist Biswajit Dhar examines the barriers posed by the growing global intellectual property regime to full implementation of Article X of the BWC (chapter 15). The concluding section of the book critiques the Western reduction of the BW problem to a single type of threat emanating from outside the West and argues for understanding and addressing the problem in terms of the varied geopolitical contexts in which it appears (chapter 16). New approaches to strengthening the regime of prohibition of biological warfare are proposed on this basis (chapter 17).

## NOTES

1. For accounts, see Jenni Rissanen, "Left in Limbo: Review Conference Suspended on Edge of Collapse," *Disarmament Diplomacy* 62 (January-February 2002), online: www.acronym.org.uk/dd/dd62/62bwc.htm; Susan Wright, "Bioweapons: U.S. Vetoes Verification," *Bulletin of the Atomic Scientists* 58(2) (March/April 2002), 24–26.

2. Greg Sheridan, "Bush Leads with Treaty Revolution," *The Australian* (16 August 2001), 11.

3. Ivo Daalder and James M. Lindsay, "Unilateralism Is Alive and Well in Washington," *International Herald Tribune* (21 December 2001), 4.

4. "Bill Approved to Boost Defenses against Terror," *Chicago Sun-Times* (24 May 2002), 31.

5. Erhard Geissler and John Ellis van Courtland Moon, eds., *Biological and*

*Toxin Weapons: Research, Development and Use from the Middle Ages to 1945* (Oxford: Oxford University Press, 1999).

6. The two categories tended to be addressed together for reasons related both to their promotion by the same or related military institutions and to the prohibition of their use under international law.

7. Matthew Meselson, review of *Tomorrow's Weapons, Chemical and Biological* by Jacques Hirshon Rothschild, *Bulletin of the Atomic Scientists* 20 (October 1964), 35–36; Han Swyter, "Political Considerations and Analysis of Military Requirements for Chemical and Biological Weapons," *Procedures of the National Academy of Sciences* 65 (1970), 266. For discussion of these motives on the part of the United Kingdom and the United States, see chapter 12.

8. United States, Chemical Warfare Review Commission, *Report of the Chemical Warfare Review Commission* (June 1985), 71.

9. United States, Defense Science Board Task Force, *Report on Chemical Warfare/Biological Defense* (1985), quoted in U.S. Department of the Army, Army Science Board, *Final Report of the Ad Hoc Group on Army Biological Defense Research Program* (July 1987), 6.

10. Michael Klare, *Rogue States and Nuclear Outlaws: America's Search for a New Foreign Policy* (New York: Hill and Wang, 1995), 26.

11. U.S. Commission on Integrated Long-Term Strategy (Washington, D.C.: U.S. Government Printing Office, January 1988).

12. U.S. Senate, Committee on Governmental Affairs and Permanent Subcommittee on Governmental Relations, *Hearings: Global Spread of Chemical and Biological Weapons*, 101st Cong., 1st Sess., 9 February 1989, 86.

13. Ibid., 10.

14. President George Bush, speech before the Commonwealth Club of San Francisco, February 7, 1990, quoted in Klare, *Rogue States and Nuclear Outlaws*, 237, n.54.

15. Secretary of Defense Dick Cheney, statement before the House Foreign Affairs Committee, Washington, D.C., March 1991; quoted in Michael Klare, *Rogue States and Nuclear Outlaws*, 63.

16. For a detailed account, see Robert S. Litwak, *Rogue States and U.S. Foreign Policy: Containment after the Cold War* (Baltimore, Md.: Johns Hopkins University Press, 1994).

17. The policy was articulated early in the Clinton administration by Martin Indyk, assistant secretary of state for Near Eastern affairs and a former executive director of the Washington Institute for Near East Policy. Martin Indyk, "The Clinton Administration's Approach to the Middle East," Soref Symposium, The Washington Institute for Near East Policy, 18 May 1993.

18. Anthony Lake, "Confronting Backlash States," *Foreign Affairs* 73(2) (1974), 46.

19. Klare, *Rogue States and Nuclear Outlaws*.

20. U.S. Department of Defense, Office of the Secretary of Defense, *Proliferation: Threat and Response* (Washington, D.C.: Government Printing Office, April 1996), iii.

21. Richard Latter, "Biological Weapons: The Growing Threat," Wilton Park

Paper 124 (January 1997). (Report based on Wilton Park Arms Control Seminar VII, 27–29 September 1996, "Deterring Biological Warfare: What Needs to be Done?") (London: HMSO, 1997), 1.

22. William S. Cohen, "In the Age of Terror Weapons," *Washington Post* (26 November 1997), A19.

23. Richard Preston, *The Cobra Event* (New York: Ballantine Books, 1997).

24. William J. Clinton, State of the Union Address, January 27, 1998, *Weekly Compilation of Presidential Documents* 34(5), 136.

25. U.S. Commission to Assess the Organization of the Federal Government to Combat the Proliferation of Weapons of Mass Destruction, *Combating Proliferation of Weapons of Mass Destruction* (14 July 1999), v–vi.

26. Ashton Carter, John Deutch, and Philip Zelikow, "Catastrophic Terrorism," *Foreign Affairs* 77(6) (November/December 1998), 80–94.

27. Significantly, the evidence concerning the source of anthrax used in the letters seemed to point to an American source, not a non-Western source. See William Broad and Judith Miller, "A Nation Challenged: The Investigation," *New York Times* (13 December 2001), A1; Rick Weiss and Joby Warrick, "Army Working on Weapons-Grade Anthrax," *Washington Post* (13 December 2001), A16.

28. U.S. White House, Office of the Press Secretary, Address by the President to the 48th Session of the United Nations General Assembly, September 27, 1993.

29. For discussion of these measures, see Litwak, *Rogue States and U.S. Foreign Policy*; U.S. Congress, Office of Technology Assessment, *Proliferation of Weapons of Mass Destruction: Assessing the Risks* (Washington, D.C.: U.S. G.P.O., 1993).

30. Amy Smithson, "Separating Fact from Fiction: The Australia Group and the Chemical Weapons Convention," The Henry L. Stimson Center, Washington, D.C., Occasional Paper No. 34 (March 1997).

31. Paul O'Sullivan, Statement on Behalf of the Australia Group, 629th Plenary Session of the United Nations Conference on Disarmament, UN Document CD/ 1164, 1–2.

32. Julian Perry Robinson, "The Australia Group: A Description and Assessment," in H. B. Brauch et al., eds., *Controlling Military Research and Development* (Amsterdam: VU University Press, 1991). For an account of Israel's BW program, see chapter 7.

33. Ambassador Sha Zukang, interview with the author, reported in Susan Wright, "Bioweapons: Cuba Case Tests Treaty," *Bulletin of the Atomic Scientists* (November/December 1997), 18–19.

34. John Mueller and Karl Mueller, "Rethinking Sanctions on Iraq," *Foreign Affairs* (May/June 1999), 43–53; Hans von Sponeck and Denis Halliday, "The Hostage Nation," *The Guardian* (29 November 2001), online: www.globalpolicy.org/ security/sanction/Iraq1/2001/1129hostage.htm (20 December 2001).

35. Amy Smithson, "Toxic Archipelago: Preventing Proliferation from the Former Soviet Chemical and Biological Weapons Complexes," The Henry L. Stimson Center, Washington, D.C., Report No. 32 (December 1999), 10; Milton Leitenberg, "Biological Weapons and Arms Control," *Contemporary Security Policy* 17(1) (April 1996), 6; Tim Trevan, *Saddam's Secrets: The Hunt for Iraq's Hidden Weapons* (London: HarperCollins), 346–47.

36. The Cooperative Threat Reduction Program began with the Nunn-Lugar Amendment to the Conventional Forces in Europe Treaty Implementation Act of 1991. James Clay Moltz, "Introduction: Assessing US Nonproliferation Assistance to the NIS," *The Nonproliferation Review* 7(1) (Spring 2000); Smithson, "Toxic Archipelago," 2–3.

37. Smithson, "Toxic Archipelago," 3–4, 91–94. Western concerns that former Russian bioweapons scientists were selling their skills to the Iranian government have been aired occasionally in the press; see, for example, Judith Miller and William Broad, "Iranians, Bioweapons in Mind, Lure Needy Ex-Soviet Scientists," *New York Times* (8 December 1998), A1.

38. Indeed, in 1984, then-Vice President Bush traveled to Geneva to propose extremely intrusive, "any time, anywhere" challenge inspections—at that stage a revolutionary idea—to the Conference on Disarmament.

39. William J. Clinton, "Message to the Congress on Weapons of Mass Destruction," *Weekly Compilation of Presidential Documents* 33 (12 November 1997), 1786.

40. Amy Smithson, "Still Rudderless: The Chemical Weapons Convention at Two," in Oliver Thränert, ed., *Preventing the Proliferation of Weapons of Mass Destruction: What Role for Arms Control?* (Bonn: Friedrich-Ebert-Stiftung, 1999), 67. The three conditions were (1) allowing the president to refuse a challenge inspection, (2) refusing to allow samples to leave U.S. territory, and (3) restricting the list of industry facilities subject to declaration and inspection.

41. See chapters 13 and 14.

42. U.S. Department of State, International Information Programs, Statement of Ambassador Donald Mahley, special negotiator for chemical and biological arms control issues, at the 24th session of the Ad Hoc Group of the BWC States Parties, 25 July 2001; available online at usinfo.state.gov/products/pdq/pdq.htm (archives) (20 December 2001).

43. U.S. Department of State, Statement of U.S. Under Secretary of State for Arms Control and International Security, John Bolton at Fifth BWC Review Conference, November 19, 2001; available online at usinfo.state.gov/topical/pol/arms/ stories/01111902.htm (20 December 2001); Under Secretary of State John Bolton, Press Briefing, Palais des Nations, Geneva, Switzerland, 19 November 2001; available online at usinfo.state.gov/topical/pol/arms/stories/01112001.htm (20 December 2001).

44. On the Clinton administration's defense policy, see Klare, *Rogue States and Nuclear Outlaws*, 97–168; on the Bush administration's policy, see Michael Klare, "Endless Military Superiority," *The Nation* (15 July 2002), 12–16.

45. Seth Carus, "Prevention Through Counterproliferation," in Ray Zilinskas, ed., *Biological Warfare: Modern Offense and Defense* (Boulder, Colo.: Lynne Rienner, 1999), 194–96.

46. Ibid., 200–203.

47. Litwak, *Rogue States and U.S. Foreign Policy*, 40–42; David Sanger with Michael Wines, "With a Shrug, a Monument to Cold War Fades Away," *New York Times* (14 June 2002), 11.

48. John Parachini, "Federal Funding to Combat Terrorism, Including Defense

Against Weapons of Mass Destruction, FY 1998–2001"; available online at cns.miis .edu/research/cbw/terfund.htm (20 December 2001).

49. U.S. White House, Office of Management and Budget, Budget of the United States, Fiscal Year 2003, "Mission Two: Enhancing Our Defense Against Biological Attacks"; available online at www.whitehouse.gov/omb/budget/fy2003/bud05.html; "Senate Rushes Bioterrorism Bill to White House," *USA Today* (24 May 2002).

50. Judith Miller, Stephen Engelberg, and William Broad, *Germs: Biological Weapons and American Secret War* (New York: Simon & Schuster, 2001), 287–314.

51. *New York Times* (13 January 1991), A9; James A. Baker, with T. M. DeFrank, *The Politics of Diplomacy: Revolution, War, and Peace, 1989–1992* (New York: Putnam, 1995).

52. William Arkin, "Calculated Ambiguity: Nuclear Weapons and the Gulf," *Washington Quarterly* 19(4) (Autumn 1996), 3–18; Stephen Schwartz, "Miscalculated Ambiguity: US Policy on the Use and Threat of Use of Nuclear Weapons," *Disarmament Diplomacy*, no. 23 (March 1998).

53. R. Jeffrey Smith, "Clinton Directive Changes Strategy on Nuclear Arms," *Washington Post* (7 December 1997), A1. This directive marked a major change in previous U.S. assurances that the United States would not use nuclear weapons against a nonnuclear party to the Nuclear Non-Proliferation Treaty unless attacked with nuclear weapons.

54. U.S. Department of State, Press Briefing by James P. Rubin, 5 February 1998.

55. Paul Richter, "U.S. Works Up Plan for Using Nuclear Arms," *Los Angeles Times* (9 March 2002), A1.

56. Richard Falk, "The Illegitimacy of the Non-Proliferation Regime," *The Brown Journal of World Affairs* IV(1) (Winter/Spring 1997), 76.

57. William Arkin and Robert S. Norris, "Tiny Nukes for Mini Minds," *The Bulletin of the Atomic Scientists* 48 (April 1992), 24–25.

58. See, for example, Marie Isabelle Chevrier, "Preventing Biological Proliferation: Strengthening the Biological Weapons Convention," in Thränert, *Preventing the Proliferation of Weapons of Mass Destruction*, 85–98; Julian P. Perry Robinson, "Chemical and Biological Weapons Proliferation and Control," in E. Clegg, P. Eavis, and J. Thurlow, eds., *Proliferation and Export Controls* (London: Deltac and Saferworld, 1995), 29–53.

59. Graham Pearson, "Prospects for Chemical and Biological Arms Control: The Web of Deterrence," *The Washington Quarterly* (Spring 1993), 145–62.

60. See, for example, Anon., "China Condemns Bush's 'Axis of Evil' Comments, *Agence France Presse* (31 January 2002); Anon., "North Korea Calls Bush a Moral Leper," *Agence France Presse* (1 February 2002); Anon., "Roundup: S. Korean Parties' Reactions Over Bush's Tough Stance Towards DPRK," *Xinhua General News Service* (2 February 2002); Toby Harnden, "British Official Criticizes Bush Rhetoric," *The Ottawa Citizen* (2 February 2002), A10; Harvey Morris and Richard Wolfe, "Bush Warned Against Attacking 'Axis of Evil': King Abdullah of Jordan . . .," *Financial Times* (1 February 2002), 7; Brian Knowlton, "U.S. Softens Tone on 2 'Axis' Nations," *International Herald Tribune* (18 February 2002), 1; David E. Sanger, "Bush Relishes the Reactions to 'Axis of Evil'," *International Herald Tribune* (18 February 2002), 1; Chris Patten, "Jaw-Jaw Not War-War: Military Success in Afghanistan Has Encouraged the US to Ignore European Doubts about Confronting the 'Axis of Evil'," *Financial Times* (15 February 2002), 16.

# 2

# The Challenges of Biological Weaponry

## A Twenty-First-Century Assessment

*Richard Falk*

The events of September 11 and their aftermath are reshaping the global political landscape, placing a renewed priority on security as defined by leading states, especially the United States. Concerns about weapons of mass destruction, including biological weaponry, are central elements of the American-led coalition against global terrorism. This sense of linkage between international terrorism and weapons of mass destruction was reinforced in late 2001 by the spread of anthrax through the U.S. postal system—resulting in widespread societal fears and producing five fatalities—despite the fact that the crime may well have been committed by an American citizen, not a terrorist organization. These developments provide a background for inquiry but should not obscure the continuity with the post–Cold War American stress on the vulnerability of the United States and other states to attack by the deliberate dispersion of toxic pathogens. Prior to September 11 such apprehensions were widely viewed apathetically or even suspiciously, but in recent months their credibility in the United States has hardly been questioned.

This chapter begins by considering how American perceptions of the nature of the biological warfare (BW) problem both before and after the September 11 attacks are related to U.S. military policies, especially nuclear policy. It acknowledges that in other parts of the world, especially in the countries of the South, September 11 is viewed very differently than it is in the United States. These states are called upon at this point, above all, to relate to a new call for total mobilization issued from Washington on the premise that either a country joins the U.S. campaign against global terrorism as an ally or it will be assumed to have chosen to side with the terrorist network.

## LOOKING BACK AT THE 1990s: AN ESCALATING CONCERN IN OFFICIAL WASHINGTON

Widespread confusion and controversy remain associated with the upgrading of biological warfare threats, especially by the U.S. government, that occurred during the decade after the end of the Cold War. According to U.S. intelligence sources, as many as twenty governments in the Third World had developed, to varying degrees, a biological weapons offensive capability. In addition, such weaponry was reported to be within reach of extremist political movements and religious cults. Part of the uncertainty associated with these issues arises from the inaccessibility of the facts, almost totally hidden behind walls of secrecy, associated with the weapons programs, the pharmaceutical industry, and the information attributed to intelligence agencies.

These inherent difficulties of assessment were and are compounded by suspicions that the BW threat was being deliberately or unwittingly manipulated by government officials and think tank wonks in the United States. The alleged motivations for these exaggerations range from a search for defense dollars to the wider effort to reformulate national security priorities in a convincing manner following the end of the Cold War. But, arguably, the most serious line of explanation for the pre–September 11 BW focus arises from the American-dominated effort to divert attention from its own retention of nuclear weaponry by arousing public anxieties in relation to nonnuclear weaponry of mass destruction. This diversion was then combined with a view that "rogue states" posed a sufficient threat to renew, in altered form, a deterrent role for nuclear weapons.[1] Such reasoning has been more aggressively expressed in the second post-Afghanistan phase of the response to September 11, during which a salient goal is to deter, and if necessary attack, those countries hostile to the United States that might be developing weapons of mass destruction and means for their delivery.

The strong U.S. push for a missile defense system was all along primarily linked to "rogue" states (three of which were recategorized and upgraded by George W. Bush in the 2002 State of the Union Address as the "axis of evil"), but also to terrorist networks and the overall need to avoid blackmail intimidation and even to defend against a possible missile attack. The international political effects of this technologically dubious American approach to its security remain uncertain, but there are a variety of dangers: further eroding respect for international law and arms control treaties, stimulating an expensive and destabilizing new cycle of arms rivalry, fostering an atmosphere of distrust and suspicion in international society, and leading major countries toward entering into defensive alliances and competitive arms races. The BW dimension is integral to the rationale for this line of American response to the rogue state/axis of evil/global terrorist threat, but it is only one element in a wider argument for rethinking, redesigning, and rehabilitating deterrence in the current global setting that lacks the sort of strategic rivalry among the most powerful states that existed during the Cold War era, and before that shaped the history of international relations for several centuries.[2]

Two main clusters of partisan responses have been generated by the security challenge associated with biological weaponry during the 1990s. The prevailing response, articulated by the U.S. government, emphasizes strengthening the existing nonproliferation regime to the extent possible with respect to all categories of weapons of mass destruction (WMD), and reinforcing the regime by passive and active deterrent and defense measures, including threatened retaliatory strikes with nuclear weapons. Nonproliferation accepts, at least in its public and rhetorical formulations, an abolitionist approach to biological and chemical weaponry, while retaining a nuclear weapons option. However, the Bush administration dramatically drew back from supporting six years of international negotiating efforts in Geneva to add a verification component to the Biological Weapons Convention (BWC) by way of a protocol on the ground that the proposed arrangements were insufficient to detect violations, and therefore worthless, or worse, would induce false confidence.[3] The U.S. position also emphasized its business- and national-security-oriented concerns that inspection and verification procedures would supposedly jeopardize valuable commercial and military secrets. It is difficult to avoid the conclusion that these self-interested reasons were the primary motive for refusing to go along with other countries on this matter of adding some verification procedures to the BWC.

The alternative response, articulated most clearly by transnational social forces and civil society organizations, is essentially based on an abolitionist approach directed at *all* weaponry of mass destruction, insisting especially on the elimination of existing stockpiles of nuclear weapons. These groups have opposed reliance on nuclear weaponry for decades, arguing that nuclear disarmament will promote human security for the peoples of the world far more effectively than will a combination of deterrence and nonproliferation. Abolitionists tend to ignore the BW threat, viewing it as diversionary, but are favorable to the establishment of a reliable, comprehensive regime of prohibition applicable to all WMD.[4] The preoccupation of abolitionists with nuclear weaponry has meant that there have been few mainstream challenges to the prevailing U.S. approach to biological weaponry.

The abolitionist attitude toward nuclear weapons has always had a dominant normative (law and morality) focus regarding such weaponry as totally unacceptable because it inflicts indiscriminate and catastrophic damage. This contrasts with the state-oriented prevailing view of big-power realists, which argues that peace and stability result best from maintenance of countervailing power. Such a geopolitical outlook is also convinced that "peace" depends on the deterrent impacts associated with the credible readiness of leading states to wage war successfully.[5] Most states do not conceive of their security in this manner, but rely on improvised arrangements designed to minimize their vulnerability to external attack, partly by defensive capabilities, partly by alliances, and partly by positive diplomacy.

This chapter considers some of the implications of this debate for current efforts to promote a more effective regime of prohibition for BW. At issue in the debate are both questions of efficacy (What approach has the best prospect of avoiding the development, threat, and use of WMD?) and fairness (What approach is most consistent with the goals of human security for a world community constituted of sovereign states having grossly unequal power and wealth?). On both counts, it is here maintained that it is more beneficial to fashion a comprehensive regime to prohibit all categories of WMD, including nuclear weapons. In contrast, the insistence by the nuclear weapons states on retaining a nuclear weapons option, one not even restricted by four of these states to a no-first-use commitment, undermines the argument that other states should renounce any reliance on WMD for security purposes. It also generates cynicism about the motives of the nuclear weapons states, especially with respect to their sanctimonious appeals on behalf of nuclear nonproliferation, their refusal even after the Cold War ended to attempt the negotiation of a nuclear disarmament treaty, and their simultaneous support for abolitionist regimes of unconditional prohibition for biological and chemical weapons. It seems evident that the pledge of these nuclear weapons states at the final hour of the 2000 Review Conference of the Nuclear Non-Proliferation Treaty (NPT) to work toward the elimination of nuclear weapons as an *ultimate* goal of national policy represented a rather disingenuous verbal concession with no expectations of substantive implementation. The pledge certainly did not, even at the time it was made, express any change of heart or commitment as to the continuing resolve to rely on, and further develop, nuclear weapons.[6]

Although this nuclearist posture is most pronounced on the part of the United States, it now seems to encompass the entire nuclear club, including its newest members, India and Pakistan. At this point, the nuclear weapons states do not even bother, as they did to varying degrees during the Cold War, to purport to seek nuclear disarmament, the very gesture seeming then to have at least propaganda value. Similarly, civil society has mostly abandoned the issue, partly out of a sense of futility and fatigue, given the refusal of these states to take specific steps that would reduce overall the role of nuclear weaponry in world politics and partly from a reduced sense of risk and public anxiety given the absence of strategic conflict between leading nuclear weapons states.

There is a disturbing issue hovering over this inquiry into efforts to prohibit biological weaponry. Assuming that the nuclear weapons states led by the United States sustain their adamant refusal to eliminate a reliance on nuclear weapons, should the ongoing processes that support the CW and BW regimes, as well as the nuclear nonproliferation treaty regime, be reevaluated, and possibly rejected? From the perspective of the equality of states, a fundamental norm of international law, are these regimes embodiments of the hegemonic structure of world politics that controls and deforms diplomatic practice? Put differently, is the current discriminatory approach to categories of weapons of mass destruction, and with respect to states in the North and South, preferable to an unrestricted admission that international law is no longer in a position to place any significant barriers in the paths chosen by governments of sovereign states to uphold their security by the acquisition of biological weapons? Arguably, this structure is less discriminatory toward the South since India and Pakistan crossed the nuclear threshold, but at the same time the expansion of the nuclear weapons club weakens whatever moral, political, and legal restraints can be attributed to the nonproliferation approach.

Such "subversive" questions should not occasion surprise, yet there is a tendency for each side in the debate about the utility of nonnuclear regimes to proceed as if the other side of the debate did not exist. Since the assumptions about human nature, the foundations and structures of international security, the weighing of risks, and the choice of policy options under conditions of radical uncertainty are so divergent, there is little to be gained at this point by a search for common ground. From an analytical viewpoint, it seems helpful at this time to make this cleavage clear to both sides, while acknowledging that many variations exist on either side of a paradigmatic divide.

At present, there are two diametrically opposed ways of addressing the dangers posed as a result of the alleged development of biological weaponry by an increasing number of states, and arguably by armed and militant substate actors, as well. On the one side is the mainstream approach that is being shaped by leading governments, their think tanks, and academic supporters. It is epitomized by the U.S. approach, which insists on delinking concerns about nuclear weaponry from the regulatory efforts relating to biological and chemical weaponry, dichotomously seeking prohibitory regimes for the latter and marginal adjustments of an essentially managerial character for the former.

On the other side are two groups of abolitionists in civil society. The first, and by far the largest, concentrates only on nuclear weapons, virtually neglecting other types of weapons of mass destruction. The second group insists on an integrated or linked regime of unconditional prohibition against all forms of weapons of mass destruction. The mainstream paradigm is geopolitically driven and dominant in intergovernmental circles, adheres to the postulates of political realism, and seeks to achieve stability primarily by reliance on military capabilities in a hierarchical world order. The alternative paradigm is normatively driven and mainly influential in civil society and Third World settings. It seeks to shape policy primarily by adherence to law and morality based on the grand norms of sovereign equality among states and the solidarity of humanity. It is committed to an ethos of disarmament and war prevention, as part of a wider commitment to achieve a peaceful, demilitarized, and just world order.[7] This chapter is written from the perspective of this alternative paradigm, and with an outlook that is committed to the establishment of an integrated regime of prohibition encompassing all weapons of mass destruction regardless of their classification as nuclear, chemical, biological, or radiological.

## THE CHANGING GLOBAL SETTING

As global leader and sole superpower, the United States exerts a disproportionate influence on the formulation of the global security policy, making a preoccupation with American assessments of threats and responses almost unavoidable. Nowhere has this observation seemed more accurate than in relation to the upgraded status of the challenge posed by the supposed advent of biological weaponry and the related prospect of biowar waged by rogue states or international terrorist networks. Since the Bush presidency, and especially after September 11, this generalization has become more evident and may yet provoke a series of counter-moves designed to check American hegemonic ambitions.

This American preoccupation with BW threats was taking shape even earlier. A few years ago President Bill Clinton apparently read Richard Preston's fictionalized account of biological terrorism, *The Cobra Event*, as if it were a policy memorandum on the dangerous vulnerability of American society to biological weaponry. Such a response to this best-selling novel, while not pretending to be based on evidence or rationality, contributed to a mood of growing public anxiety about biological warfare. This mood supported the widespread belief that the threat is real, and that its challenge should be treated as an urgent priority of national security policy. William S. Cohen, Clinton's secretary of defense, expressed such sentiments in the standard language of national security: "As the new millennium approaches, the United States faces a heightened prospect that regional aggressors, third-rate armies, terrorist cells, and even religious cults will wield disproportionate power by using—or threatening to use—biological weapons against our troops in the field or our citizens at home."[8] Significantly, even before the September 11 terrorist attacks, George W. Bush and Secretary of Defense Donald Rumsfeld repeated similar sentiments in articulating their more sweeping vision of the U.S. approach to defense and deterrence in the setting of the early twenty-first century.[9]

The secretary of the navy in Clinton's second term, Richard Danzig, converted this national anxiety about biowar into a full-fledged conceptual insistence that the world is poised on the threshold of a new era of warfare, epitomized by the acronym NEW, non-explosive warfare, which was sometimes also described in government and military circles as "asymmetric warfare." In Danzig's words, "[u]ntil now, explosive weapons have the attention of the military when it plans battles and of civilian agencies when they worry about the protection of airports, airplanes and government buildings. But the nation is under-protected against weapons that don't explode. Of particular concern are those that use biological agents or attack computer systems."[10] Such fevered contemplations of prospects of biological warfare by high government officials and the media would have been unthinkable as recently as a decade ago. The Bush administration invokes the BW threat in a more mechanical and routine fashion as part of the background for its view that America is faced with diverse threats to its security and that it must counter these by exploring innovative technological options, especially missile defense, and more slyly, moving ahead with its plans for new generations of nuclear weapons with more plausible battlefield roles and for an eventual weaponization of space.

The asymmetric war complementary analysis suggests that the United States is becoming vulnerable to well-calculated threats by much weaker, but elusive, enemies, and that cheap weapons of mass destruction epitomize this new security threat. Of course, such a line of thinking has become dogma in the months since the September 11 attacks and the apparently unrelated anthrax sequel.

As previously mentioned, the end of the Cold War led the security managers and the private sector infrastructure to put forward a range of threats to justify high budgets for the Pentagon. Indicative of this atmosphere were studies in the early 1990s calling for large appropriations to build defense systems designed to intercept meteors falling toward Earth. During the 1990s there was a revealing test of the imagination of national security managers to figure out ways to sustain societal support for weapons development and a large peacetime military capability in the absence of a strategic enemy such as the Soviet Union. Japan, China, the generic threat of "Islamic fundamentalism," and most persistently of all, "rogue states" (usually including Iraq, Iran, Libya, North Korea, and Cuba) were variously nomi-

nated by defense intellectuals and their allies in government and the private
sector to be dangerous enemies whose asymmetric challenges could only be
addressed by major investments in military technology and preparedness.
The claim of the U.S. government is that the threat of "rogue states" and
global terrorism is enhanced by the presumed efforts and ability of such
actors to gain access to biological weaponry, and more generally, to weaponry of mass destruction. Acquiring such capabilities would enable these
states to overcome their relative weakness and past impotence in a manner
that could allow them to threaten even the most powerful states at least
indirectly, yet frighteningly, via tactics of intimidation and a variety of terrorist attacks on soft targets. These apprehensions, of course, have been
confirmed for the entire American political establishment and mainstream
media by the September 11 experience. Such a dynamic is especially disturbing because there is no evidence linking Iraq, Iran, and North Korea to the
September 11 attacks, to the global terrorist network of al Qaeda, or to the
visionary anti-Americanism espoused by Osama bin Laden.

But the geopolitical anxieties have deeper roots that stretch back in time.
From this perspective, a chilling realization followed from confirmations
that the former Soviet Union had carried on a massive offensive biological
weapons program for many years subsequent to becoming a party to the
1972 Biological Weapons Convention. Either this pattern of Soviet noncompliance was not reliably established through intelligence efforts at the time,
or its existence was not disclosed until a much later time, perhaps to avoid
disrupting other areas of cooperation. Allegations of Soviet noncompliance
during the Cold War years tended to come from right-wing sources and
were dismissed as inflammatory ideological assaults on efforts to achieve
peaceful coexistence between the two superpowers. The impression was created, and remains, that almost any determined state can develop a major
offensive BW capability without much risk of detection.

Perhaps the most damaging conclusion drawn from the disclosures about
the Soviet program was that existing legal and moral prohibitions relating
to BW seemed to be of no significant value in inhibiting a government from
embarking on large-scale development of offensive BW capabilities and war
scenarios. These violations of the BWC continued well after the fall of the
Soviet Union and seemed to have been terminated only in the mid-1990s on
orders from the Russian government of President Boris Yeltsin. It is disturbing that a clandestine capability to wage large-scale biological warfare was
being developed under the cover of the existing BWC legal regime, and that
the flagrantly violative behavior was either not detected, or at least not effectively exposed by national intelligence capabilities. This experience is being
relied upon by confirmed opponents of arms control and disarmament
negotiations in the Bush administration to justify their skepticism about
constraining behavior of adversary states by reliance on treaties. Such an

attitude underlies the administration's unilateralism and undermines efforts to achieve international cooperation in general with respect to global problems, including such issues as global warming and regulating arms sales.

The U.S. attitude toward existing arms control treaties suggests that at any point constraints on policy can be repudiated for the sake of a new reading of national security priorities. This way of thinking and acting manifests a unilateralist insistence on regarding the most serious international legal commitments as provisional and not worthy of reliance by others. It is an extremely dangerous development that has been the signature approach of George W. Bush to any treaty move seeking to address global problems.

Such a conclusion is especially disturbing given the global leadership role and weight of the United States, its supposed enthusiasm for the Rule of Law, and the supposedly democratic character of its governing process. The degree of American democracy is contested due to the failures of the two-party system to present the electorate with meaningful choices and given the secrecy that exists with respect to defense policy and intelligence activities. Since September 11 the quality of American democracy has been further eroded by a mood of anxiety and a patriotic surge that allows the government to clamp down on the civil liberties and human rights of citizens and even more so of those residing in the United States as immigrants.

There exists in international society a widespread view that if even the United States is untrustworthy and unreliable in its formal international undertakings involving national security, then it is reasonable to assume that all other major states are similarly unreliable, or even more so. It has become well established that the U.S. government has often withheld the truth or denied truthful allegations when the subject matter bears on security issues. Several examples suffice to underscore the problem: the misleading reassurances given to allies, including Japan, that no nuclear weapons were stored on their territory during the Cold War; the denial for years of a massacre of Korean civilians by U.S. armed forces during the Korean War; and the air attack on retreating Iraqi soldiers after a cease-fire had been agreed upon in the Gulf War.[11] The American record on these matters is deeply troubling. Besides secret testing of weapons releasing radioactivity on its own citizens, the United States during World War II was guilty of firebombing Tokyo and several German cities, as well as dropping atomic bombs on Japanese cities. Perhaps most telling in the context of the apprehensions about Iraq was the intensive use of Agent Orange and other defoliants during the Vietnam War, which has led to widespread health hazards for large numbers of Vietnamese and no acknowledgment or apology.

Concerns about the reliability of international undertakings with respect to the elimination of BW were further magnified, and rendered plausible, by the perception that Iraq possessed the weaponry with which to wage substantial biological (and chemical) warfare in 1990 at the time of the Gulf

Crisis. Baghdad reportedly deployed anthrax weapons during the war, with intentions toward actual use that remains unknown.[12] Iraq, as the prime instance of a rogue state, had previously used chemical weapons in its devastating 1988 attack on the Kurdish village of Halabja in Iraq during the final stages of the Iran/Iraq War, giving the threat of a hostile CW or BW attack by Iraq added credibility. It is widely believed in the American policy community that it was only the presence of the American-led coalition of forces equipped with the means to retaliate in a devastating manner, possibly with nuclear weapons, that deterred Saddam Hussein from threatening, and possibly launching, an attack with biological and chemical weapons in 1991 during the Gulf War.[13]

Another aspect of the global setting relates to the erosion of the regime to prevent the proliferation of nuclear weaponry. In this regard the indirect impact of the mid-1998 nuclear test explosions by India and Pakistan on the entire spectrum of issues and concerns relating to weaponry of mass destruction needs to be reconsidered. These tests, and the U.S. reaction to them, raised obliquely two sorts of questions about the standard approach to WMD: first, concerns about the viability and ethics of the nonproliferation regime in the absence of a reciprocal disarming process by the nuclear weapons states;[14] and second, questions concerning why nuclear weapons should not be incorporated into a regime of prohibition, as has been the case for biological and chemical weaponry. How could one justify allowing the nuclear weapons states to retain and continue to develop nuclear weapons while denying other sovereign entities an equivalent option? And how can one reconcile a categorical rejection of biological and chemical weaponry with the deliberately ambiguous strategic posture adopted by the declared nuclear weapons states with respect to the threat or use of nuclear weaponry? Nuclear weapons states develop their policy toward the use of such weaponry in secret, thereby making it exceedingly difficult for the citizenry to challenge any disposition to rely on nuclear weapons if confronted by a national security crisis.

There are additional subsidiary reasons for concerns about a voluntaristic regime of self-restraint that arises from historical studies of past Japanese and American BW programs and applications.[15] The extent of this activity, especially on the American side, is not fully substantiated, and remains controversial. Nevertheless, these past programs are significant for an assessment of present risks in at least two respects: They show that these major political actors were secretive and deceptive about their BW activities, and that each was actively exploring the military utility of biological weapons. And, tellingly, such states were able to pursue biological weapons activities on a substantial scale without being reliably detected, or if detected, without occasioning any kind of strong response from external sources. These revelations also confirm the suspicion that leading states did not impose self-restraint with respect to investigating, and even in experimenting with and evaluating, the military potentialities of offensive biological weaponry.

The current concern about BW operates in a different setting. The earlier anxieties were associated with the possibility that one or another major state might introduce biological weapons as a battlefield weapon of choice. The present preoccupation relates to the threat or use of biological weaponry against a civilian society, especially as an instrument of terror used by an adversary too weak to wage war directly. It is this new context that gives rise to a focus on the supposed threats of asymmetric warfare.

Contemporary anxiety about BW seems mainly an American phenomenon at this point. It has been fostered by well-publicized American official efforts in recent years to prepare soldiers and citizens to take preventive action in response to a concerted use of biological weapons either against military forces, or more likely, against domestic society (see chapters 3 and 4). Such hypothetical BW attacks are generally presented as the work of an enemy of the United States, possibly occurring as a dimension of military combat but more likely as a result of a terrorist attack. In the last decade, a variety of high government officials have repeatedly claimed that American society remains dangerously "underprepared" to cope with these emergent challenges of biological weaponry and is hence vulnerable to attack. At the same time, due to the growing vigilance of the government, the United States is gradually becoming better prepared but also more "alarmed" at the plausibility of an attack. The anthrax postal dissemination, which appears to be an instance of biocrime rather than biowar, of course lent credibility to these worries and has led to rapidly increasing budgetary appropriations.

It remains difficult to know how to interpret this latest phase of the American public debate, especially in light of the September 11 attacks and the presentation of evidence that al Qaeda was interested in BW capabilities. Should this accentuated concern be understood as one more instance of fear-mongering in a political atmosphere in which the United States, in particular, continues to lack a traditional strategic enemy? Is this preoccupation with biowar a way to fashion new threats so as to build a post–Cold War case for a large defense budget in a period when increased fiscal discipline exerts downward pressure on all types of public spending? Or do these preparations represent a prudent reaction to intelligence warnings, terrorist incidents, and, of course, the revelations about the al Qaeda network?[16] What weight should be given to various indications that the U.S. government and American society continue to be viewed with extreme hostility by fanatical exponents of all-out war, attitudes conducive to anti-U.S. terrorist attacks by whatever means seem most effective? The success of the September 11 attacks has removed all doubts from American military planners, who are now in the process of prosecuting a global campaign against terrorism that involves military intervention in several countries that supposedly have links to al Qaeda or terrorist entities with similar worldviews.

An evidently increasing proficiency in the technical means to develop and disseminate biological weapons with maximum lethal effects contributes to the bleak picture advanced by those who believe that the United States continues to face a catastrophic BW threat from "rogue states" and terrorists. Developments in biogenetics create the impression that there is a growing mastery over the relevant technologies. Even certain countries opposed to biological weaponry on geopolitical grounds associated with counterproliferation priorities have invested in defensive programs that depend on simulated attacks with real agents of disease, generating as an inevitable by-product some sort of offensive capability, and with a certain ambiguity about future intentions in the event that some military advantage were to be identified in the course of such research and development activity. It is important to realize that realists in control of the security policy process of most governments accept the primacy of "military effectiveness" as the sole test of viability, tending to push aside moral and legal obstacles. The world-view of most political leaders remains Hobbesian in the sense of a war of all against all, with some accompanying sense of the irrelevance of legal and moral restraints on the pursuit of military goals in warfare. In addition, dual-use technology and the peaceful uses loophole in the BWC seriously blur the line between "development" and "renunciation" of biological weaponry. Protecting the secrecy of commercial and military activity further complicates the task of ensuring that legitimate undertakings are not being used, even unwittingly, to develop techniques and materials with important military applications.

Given the uncertainties surrounding questions concerning BW interests, public understanding of biological weaponry is dominated by arbitrary inferences, media hype, film portrayals, special interests, and bureaucratic ambitions. Navigating through such dark and treacherous waters is a difficult assignment for even the most concerned of global citizens. Such considerations might appear to justify preparing for the worst, which tends to be the sort of reasoning that prevails when a rich and powerful country's fundamental security is at risk. This reality suggests the importance of two features of governance that should be strengthened: first of all, the need in democratic societies for greater transparency of knowledge bearing on security policy, so that insider knowledge claims are less decisive; second, an ethos of responsibility on the part of political leaders so that threats to national well-being of the sort suggested by the darkest BW scenarios are not manipulated for short-term partisan gains. These imperatives take on added significance in the new political environment of war and intense patriotic fervor that translates into attitudes of extreme deference to governmental policy.

## IMPLICATIONS OF THE UNSCOM
## INSPECTION REGIME IN IRAQ

Approaching the problem of the biological weapons challenge from the perspective of international confidence in compliance with agreed standards indicates some consideration of efforts to verify compliance. In one sense, the massive Soviet era violations of the BWC, whether detected or not, do suggest the difficulty of relying on treaty commitments that are not reinforced by a means to verify compliance, especially in the face of suspicious events or evidence.[17] At the very least, this experience suggests that governments will be reluctant to rely too much on the mere existence of treaty commitments. Something more is needed. The something more involves a system of verification that is sufficiently intrusive and effective to give the international community confidence that major instances of cheating can be detected at an early stage, and further, that if such confidence exists it would likely deter a potential violator from embarking on such a route. The post–September 11 highlighting of Iraq as a potential threat has renewed a focus on reestablishing an intrusive inspection capability to provide reassurances about the nonpresence of weapons of mass destruction.

Due to the special circumstances of the Iraqi defeat in the Gulf War, it was possible to establish in 1991 an intrusive verification capability under the auspices of the United Nations that was entrusted with verifying Iraq's destruction of all weaponry of mass destruction, including components, and the abandonment of plans to acquire such weaponry. What makes this Iraqi experience instructive is that it represents the most extensive form of intrusive verification that has ever been established, and its operation was reinforced by a comprehensive sanctions regime. At the same time, the arrangement was vigorously resisted by the Baghdad government, whose noncooperation accentuated dependence on verified compliance. Iraq is a test case for addressing the problem of reliability in relation to the regime of prohibition associated with biological weaponry, as well as a yardstick by which to measure whether the proposed verification scheme that has been negotiated in recent years in the form of a protocol to be appended to the BWC is genuinely confidence-building or a dangerous form of false confidence.[18]

The activities of the UN Special Commission (UNSCOM) in Iraq during most of the 1990s brought recurrent high-profile media attention to the problems associated with verifying a claimed assertion by Iraq of its elimination of all categories of weaponry of mass destruction. What has become evident in Iraq is that even with an extraordinary array of intrusive prerogatives and resources over a period of years, the difficulties of verifying compliance or detecting noncompliance are formidable in the event that the government of the inspected country seeks to be elusive and defiant. It is also important to realize that the interaction between an inspectorate and a target society can itself become an independent source of tension, even of war-threatening gravity, as has recurrently occurred, reaching a climax during the 1998 standoffs and countdowns between Washington and Baghdad on the scope of UNSCOM access. Whether inspection, even when backed by intelligence capabilities, is an effective tool of verification is also a matter of controversy and throws doubt on what degree of confidence, if any, can be placed in a regime of prohibition that possesses only modest intrusive means to obtain verification of suspected violations, and where reasons for distrust abound.

In 1985, Michael Krepon cited the view prevailing among U.S. government specialists and advisors that "the US has never found anything that the Soviets have hidden successfully" and that "the possibilities of cheating were endless" in the setting of Cold War arms control arrangements.[19] In Iraq, despite the extensive probing by UNSCOM, undoubtedly backed by intelligence guidance from major Western countries, there seems to be a complete lack of confidence in the verification process on the part of U.S. officials. Secretary of State Madeleine Albright expressed her own skepticism by pointing out that Iraq has "a long history of elaborate deceptions and occasional confessions," in the latter case only when confronted by overwhelming evidence. Michael Krepon, in the same vein, adds that "the consensus in Washington is that one cannot close any book when we are talking about Saddam Hussein's ambitions." It is believed that Iraq could have produced biological weapons and have them produced and combat-ready in a matter of days and weeks even if the inspections, when in full swing, were accurately reporting the absence of such weaponry at a given time.[20] The highly intrusive UNSCOM inspections and other sources provided substantial evidence supporting the Commission's strong suspicions that Iraq had pursued an offensive BW program. But confirmation of these suspicions was made possible only by information resulting from the defection of high-level Iraqis who had previously administered Iraq's secret WMD programs (see chapter 11).

This reinforces the view that even highly intrusive verification procedures are unable on their own to provide reliable reassurance about compliance. The UNSCOM experience casts a shadow across efforts to strengthen the BWC by negotiating arrangements for verification. Even if a mechanism for verification can be agreed upon by the main participating governments in the Geneva negotiations, it is unlikely to build any degree of significant confidence that patterns of noncompliance are detected, or even deterred. And of what value is a rudimentary verification arrangement that can be evaded at will by a skillful violator? Does not this arms control search for some mechanism to be reached through consensus negotiations, even if it cannot solve the problems to which it is addressed, lend undue credence to those conservatives who oppose relying on treaty arrangements to protect sovereign rights, particularly with respect to security?

At a lower level of prominence, and moving somewhat toward an opposite conclusion, is the acknowledgment of the relatively smooth operation to date of the elaborate verification regime established by the Chemical Weapons Convention (CWC), pointing the way, perhaps, to a model of a more ambitious future verification arrangement in relation to the BW regime than is currently being considered at Geneva. But even with the CWC there are some disturbing signs that verification in practice is often watered down from what is prescribed by treaty.[21] There have been fewer inspections than required and a variety of reports of obstruction that limited the usefulness of the inspections that were made.[22] And it should be remembered that the United States diluted the obligatory character of the negotiated inspection arrangements for the BWC Protocol to protect the alleged industrial secrets of pharmaceutical firms (see chapter 14).

It is notable that verification even in its guise as a geopolitical tool for limiting the internal sovereignty of Iraq has had mixed results, despite Iraq's weakness after the Gulf War. Such an experience reinforces the central argument being made here that verification with respect to BWC is at most a holding operation, while the real work of control needs to be accomplished by disarmament, development (especially with respect to poverty), social and political justice, and norms and procedures designed to establish a comprehensive regime of prohibition directed at all WMD.

## WORLD ORDER CONCERNS

The more general relevance of world order must be considered against this background of regulatory efforts associated with the emergence of weapons of mass destruction, as well as in the context of the ongoing war on global terror being fought on multiple fronts. It is necessary to take account of the way in which the domestic and international security arrangements of dominant sovereign states have evolved to provide a sequence of justifications for the retention and development of some categories of WMD and the prohibition of other categories. The experience in this regard with nuclear weapons is especially significant, as well as discouraging from the perspective of viewing world order on the basis either of upholding the central idea of the law of war to prohibit indiscriminate weapons and tactics or the basic structural commitment of international law to the juridical equality of sovereign states. This latter commitment is written into the United Nations Charter in Article 2(1) as a basic principle of the organization and informs any legal order with the fundamental idea that equals should be treated equally. As such, it contrasts with geopolitical practices that are based on power inequalities.

The uneven renunciation of weaponry of mass destruction, as between countries, regions, and weapons systems, seems to be creating particularly dangerous problems in relation to unresolved regional conflicts. In this connection, one thinks immediately of the tensions and complexities of India and Pakistan in South Asia, North Korea and South Korea in Northeast Asia, China and Taiwan in Southeast Asia, and the Arab states and Israel in the Middle East. The competing explanations for the acquisition of and reliance on weaponry of mass destruction are usually related in some contextual way to deterrence, regional rivalry, and an ultimate retaliation option. An ambitious state may conceive of this weaponry, of course in its inner, secret counsels, as also useful for the exertion of diplomatic leverage, or possibly even as providing a valuable option to launch a surprise attack or gain a decisive battlefield advantage. And then there is the matter of geopolitical status and domestic prestige that is associated with entry into the nuclear weapons club of states, which was obviously important in the Indian and Pakistani case. The point here is that there has been an enhancement of military capabilities in regional conflicts within the South that seems to be increasing pressures on additional governments to acquire covertly or overtly some weaponry of mass destruction.

Several important issues of world public order are raised in a particularly strong manner by the dangers of biological warfare. First of all, the persisting relevance of sovereignty to the quest for security in the late 1990s bears heavily on how to think about the challenges posed by biological weaponry. The basic premise of the states system, which was itself legitimized in the Peace of Westphalia (1648) 350 years ago, is that a fully sovereign state enjoys an unrestricted and inherent right to acquire whatever military capabilities it needs and desires for security purposes. Without specific undertakings, international law imposes no limits on the rights of states to possess weaponry of choice in amounts decided upon by national policy. In the pursuit of its security a state must not violate explicit commitments of international law and not do harm to other states in some direct way. Of course, prudence may induce states to practice various forms of self-restraint with regard to tactics and weaponry, but the decision to do so is made on the basis of sovereign discretion, especially an evaluation of military effectiveness, not deference to a higher principle or through the application of international legal and moral norms.

There was an early hope that the advent of nuclear weaponry would be treated as a prelude to catastrophe for the human species unless some drastic steps were taken in unison to rid the world of this new menace. It was initially widely assumed that a renunciation of the option to possess or otherwise to make use of weaponry of mass destruction would exhibit a sense of responsibility on the part of political leaders of the countries victorious in World War II. After all, a horrified reaction to the large-scale battlefield recourse to gas warfare in World War I led to the adoption of the 1925 Geneva Protocol on the Prohibition of the Use of Poison Gases and Bacteriological Methods of Warfare. This was a small initiative that did not promise very much. It was an essentially declaratory and voluntaristic measure, but at least it represented a move in the direction of unconditional renunciation. The non-use of chemical and biological weapons in World War II, despite the notable exception of Japan's large-scale use of biological weapons on an experimental basis in China, was also on balance somewhat encouraging. It would also have seemed that if poison gas had been repudiated, at least partly for humanitarian reasons, then the pressure to repudiate nuclear weaponry would have been greater, considering its potential for catastrophic destruction. On this basis, a strong tradition of renunciation with respect to *all* categories of WMD would likely have been established, with moral, political, and legal underpinnings. Understanding why this did not happen is highly relevant to reducing the risks currently posed by biological weaponry.

The tendency to move away from such weaponry came to an abrupt halt in the aftermath of the use of atomic bombs against Hiroshima and Nagasaki. The use of these weapons was morally and legally aggravated by the fact that the targeted cities were heavily populated and without any particular military relationship to the war.[23] The fact that weapons of mass destruction were deployed to end victoriously a just war against the Japanese aggressors tended to shield these atomic attacks from critical scrutiny. It is notable that the official justification for using atomic bombs emphasized "saving lives"(both American and Japanese lives by bringing the war to a rapid end, obviating the need for an invasion of Japan's home islands) in the pursuit of war aims—a rationale that remains to this day the subject of intense controversy among historians as to whether it reflects the real or dominant reason for use. At any rate, such a justification makes no claim of ultimate necessity from the security perspective of the U.S. government at the time, a justification that the World Court considered in 1996 to be the only possible basis upon which a threat or use of nuclear weapons could be reconciled with international law.[24]

Arguably, by 1945 the grounds for using atomic bombs had been already morally and politically partially prepared by the earlier strategic bombing campaigns against German cities, by the German rocket attacks on English cities, and by unrestricted submarine warfare. This preparation was then extended after March 1945 to the firebombing of Tokyo and reached its climax when atomic bombs were dropped on Hiroshima and Nagasaki. Each of these belligerent practices was part of the embrace by both sides in World War II of the idea that a combination of technology, military doctrine, and ideology had substantially undermined the framework of "just war" providing rules of conduct. Associating "military necessity" with "total war" against the whole of the enemy society erased the key distinction between military and nonmilitary targets and converted the entire enemy society into a battlefield. The new reality of "total war," of all against all with no distinction between the civilian and military dimensions of the enemy society, removed many operative limits on tactical choices and converted the entirety of the enemy society into a battlefield. This character of warfare bears on whether it is feasible, or even reasonable, to cordon off particular categories of weaponry while leaving others available for use at the discretion of the richest and most powerful governments in the world in their willingness to absolutize the pursuit of their security goals. In the current setting, it also raises the question of whether there remains a meaningful distinction between "terrorism" and "war."

After a brief and superficial flurry of interest in nuclear disarmament in the years immediately after 1945, nuclear weaponry was quietly, but organically and sequentially, integrated into the national security policy of all five of the Permanent Members of the UN Security Council (although mainland China was not represented by the Beijing government on the council until 1971). At least three additional countries now possess an arsenal of nuclear weapons. There was never any subsequent, credible indication of a political will to eliminate the weaponry and renounce the option to threaten or even to use it, except briefly during the early period of Gorbachev's leadership of the Soviet Union in the years 1986–1988. The one moment of potential breakthrough occurred at the Reagan/Gorbachev mini-summit in 1986 at Reykjavik, Iceland. True, from time to time, vague nuclear disarmament commitments were endorsed by the superpowers and the other nuclear weapons states, even assuming legally binding forms, but these were never convincingly implemented or even seriously contemplated by the main nuclear weapons states. Indeed, over the years it has become increasingly evident that there is a political intention at the policymaking level of the states that possess nuclear weapons to keep nuclear disarmament off the global agenda to the extent possible. And although a disarmament motivation would be seemingly present for those nonnuclear weapons states not depending on the so-called nuclear umbrella, a serious challenge to nuclearism has never been effectively mounted.[25]

This absence of will became more manifest in the early 1990s as a result of the collapse of bipolarity and the related undermining of the deterrence rationale. The supposed Soviet superiority in conventional warfare, although probably exaggerated, gave nuclear weapons an indispensable role in the deterrent strategy of the West during the Cold War years and deflected criticism of such reliance. Furthermore, this perception of Soviet conventional superiority also persuaded European and Asian allies of the United

States to accept the deterrence role of nuclear weapons in situations other than in response to a prior *nuclear* attack.[26] The emergence of Russia as a friendly, severely weakened power in the 1990s revealed what had been the view of antinuclear critics all along, that nuclear weapons had been irreversibly and unshakably integrated into the strategic thinking of the states that possessed them. The Soviet threat functioned as a pretext for a policy that was over-determined, resting mainly on the belief that it was preferable to retain nuclear weaponry than to participate in disarming processes.

The end of the Cold War undermined the avowed security rationale for the retention of nuclear weaponry. Furthermore, the World Court in its historic Advisory Opinion *unanimously* confirmed the legal duty, derived from Article 6 of the Non-Proliferation Treaty, to pursue in good faith nuclear disarmament, and even more, to seek workable general disarmament arrangements via international negotiations. Yet even this combination of developments did little to stir a flicker of interest on the part of nuclear weapons states to initiate nuclear disarmament negotiations in a favorable international climate. Even without a strategic rivalry, a combination of inertia and vested interests discouraged any serious challenge to the nuclear weapons establishment. Civil society also backed off, sensing a diminished risk of nuclear war, given the Soviet collapse and Russia's new pro-West leanings.[27]

True, the Comprehensive Test Ban Treaty opened for signature in 1995, but not yet in force, precludes live nuclear tests in the future, which would certainly inhibit weapons development, especially by states that currently do not possess nuclear weapons. The treaty does not imply any disarmament, and it will only enter into force after all forty-four nuclear capable states have submitted their instruments of ratification, which never seemed likely and now seems impossible. A big blow to treaty prospects had already resulted from the 1999 refusal of the U.S. Senate to give its consent to ratification. In any event, simulated tests are apparently now technologically feasible, at least for the United States, to assess weapons' reliability and even to test proposed refinements and innovations. Such tests are not banned by the treaty. The prohibition on live testing of nuclear weapons, although welcome for a variety of reasons, would not have been tantamount to a renunciation of nuclearism. With the strong U.S. push for a missile defense system in the face of almost total international opposition, it is now quite likely that a new, expensive, and destabilizing cycle of competition will occur among nuclear weapons states to establish a balance between offensive and defensive modes of deterrence. The Bush administration has now made a formal commitment to abandon the 1972 Anti-Ballistic Defense Treaty by exercising its withdrawal rights. Such moves by the U.S. heighten a sense of uncertainty that could lead additional governments and even other nongovernmental political movements to acquire nonnuclear WMD. The United

States bears a heavy responsibility for this latest series of failures to strike a sustainable bargain with nonnuclear states based on its willingness to forego the pursuit of military advantages associated with its nuclear superiority.

In partial refutation of this dreary conclusion relating to nuclear weapons, it could be suggested that the successful negotiation and entry into force of an impressively far-reaching Chemical Weapons Convention, and the continuing interest of many states in strengthening the BWC, do represent steps in the direction of renunciation even in light of the exemption of nuclear weapons. These limited forms of renunciation in relation to WMD can be mainly understood from a geopolitical perspective as a commitment to overall prudence by most states, while not purporting to challenge the nuclear weapons status quo that rests on geopolitical realities. Evidence on the geopolitical origins of the BWC itself supports this view (see chapter 12). The main strategic effect of such nonnuclear regimes of prohibition is to ensure that the nuclear weapons states are not themselves subject to deterrence or possible attack by nonnuclear types of weapons of mass destruction, while themselves remaining free to deploy and threaten nuclear attack, or more relevantly, to rely on their superiority in conventional weaponry in pursuit of their global policy goals. It may be prudent for most states to cooperate with such an approach to avoid heightening catastrophic risks in relation to their search for regional security, but such a pragmatic adjustment does not alter a sovereignty-driven view of security arrangements. Leading and threatened states continue to treat their own sense of security as an absolute that takes precedence over legal and moral inhibitions on weaponry of mass destruction, as well as over the prudential and moral arguments of nuclear abolitionists.

The *political* preconditions for the principled renunciation of WMD have not been met at this stage of human history. In light of this, the *moral* case against the acquisition of biological weaponry is weakened for nonnuclear states whose security seems precarious. This moral case is further weakened by the unwillingness of the leading nuclear power to agree to *legal* arrangements that might create high confidence that a commitment to a regime of prohibition for biological weaponry was trustworthy. This combination of factors greatly complicates analysis of the prospects for meeting the emergent challenge of biological weaponry, especially given its seeming manipulation by the United States to mobilize support for the war against terrorism, an escalating defense budget, a potentially destabilizing missile defense system, and the overall militarization of space under exclusive U.S. auspices.

## HEGEMONIC REALISM AND WMD

The primacy of security is strongly reinforced by the predominance of realist traditions of statecraft that place a premium on doing whatever is perceived to serve the vital security interests of a state, contrary norms of morality and law notwithstanding. This realism tends to overshadow moral and legal considerations. A strong realist orientation was evident in the muted geopolitical reaction to Iraq's use of chemical weapons against Halabja.[28] At the time, neither superpower had any strategic interest in opposing Saddam Hussein's crimes against humanity, especially against a beleaguered people such as the Kurds, whose aspirations challenged the stability of several important states in the region, especially Turkey. Both the United States and the Soviet Union had stood by throughout most of the 1980s, virtually as cheerleaders, even in the face of Iraq's recourse to aggressive force in blatant violation of the United Nations Charter against Ayatollah Khomeini's Iran, resulting in a bloody war that lasted most of the decade.

This prevalence of realism is closely related to a preoccupation with biological weaponry during the 1990s in a number of respects. First of all, from such a perspective it makes it naïve, hypocritical, and discriminatory to berate a particular government for acting on behalf of its own security interests even if such action is seen by outsiders to be imprudent in some respects and destabilizing in others. The response pattern to prior acquisitions of and reliance on weaponry of mass destruction by the geopolitical leaders is so arbitrary and inconsistent that it undermines any claim of morality, weakening the argument for adherence to consistent norms of behavior. In some instances, nuclear weapons states have been silent or even complicit in the setting of proliferation, as with the earlier acquisitions by Britain, France, and Israel. With other states there has been a reluctant acceptance, as with the former Soviet Union and China, while with others there has been an initially hostile and coercive reaction, as with India and Pakistan, which is then abandoned in response to geopolitical opportunism. Such a pattern has been especially evident in the recent period as the United States dropped its concerns about Pakistani nuclear weapons, emphasizing its need for Pakistan as an ally in the struggle against the Taliban regime in neighboring Afghanistan. In relation to selected rogue states, renamed "the axis of evil," an interventionary threat in the form of preventive war is made on the basis of a so-called norm of nonproliferation. This threat and warning has been directed by President Bush against North Korea, Iraq, and Iran in the most alarming terms. It is itself a most controversial "doctrine" and is certainly a major and dangerous threat to use force in a manner not authorized by international law, but reflective of the post–September 11 U.S. approach to geopolitical risk management. Such an approach is arbitrary if compared to principled norms of restraint based on the UN Charter, but it possesses a rationality from the perspective of geopolitics. It embodies the priorities of the main hegemonic actor in this period, namely, the United States, and has been folded into the antiterrorist global campaign.

Second, it is a feature of the states system that political leaders are

expected to put their security interests ahead of all competing concerns, and
that an implicit willingness to disregard moral and legal factors must be
considered as part of the normal framework of diplomacy. What this has
meant in the wars of this century is that whatever weaponry (or tactics)
seemed militarily effective from the perspective of a "total war" mentality
was developed and then used (or not) and later justified on the basis of "military necessity" (will a given use, on balance, contribute to the war effort?),
notwithstanding applicable moral and legal inhibitions.[29] It is true that the
emergence of nuclear weaponry, and its possession by several states, has
induced an added dimension of prudence, but prudence has always been
treated as a virtue in Machiavellian realist traditions of statecraft.[30] To overlook this dominance of realism over the political and moral imagination is
to embrace sentimentality and false consciousness on a very serious
matter.[31]

The disregard of the 1996 World Court Advisory Opinion on the legal
status of nuclear weapons also offers a clear confirmation of "normative
deafness" on the part of all five Permanent Members of the UN Security
Council. It is a startling message to the world about the irrelevance of law
to matters of global security, given that this historic assessment was undertaken by what the Charter designates as the "judicial arm" of the United
Nations at the formal request of the General Assembly. To some extent this
geopolitics-first, sovereignty-second, international law-third character of
world order is written into the NPT in the form of the withdrawal provision, which acknowledges the primacy of the security dimension. It gives
treaty parties the right to withdraw with notice if the leaders of a state
believe that they need to withdraw to uphold the "supreme national interests," which, again revealingly, are left undefined and thereby are defined
subjectively. This acknowledgement of a similar primacy of security as
grounds for treaty withdrawal with notice is also embodied in the BWC,
article XIII and the CWC, article XVI. The interposition of geopolitics can
be vividly appreciated by the discretionary manner in which the U.S. government has invoked the withdrawal clause in the Anti-Ballistic Missile
Treaty and its refusal to allow North Korea to make a comparable exercise
of withdrawal in relation to the Non-Proliferation Treaty. In fact, North
Korea has the better case for withdrawal because its supreme national interests and security are under severe threat from the United States and others.

Third, for these reasons, *no* state, whatever its form of government, is
trustworthy when it comes to moral and legal undertakings that might at
some future time be seen by its leaders to impair its fundamental security. If
such guidelines pertain to the conduct of leading states, then it would seem
unacceptable from every viewpoint except geopolitical management to hold
smaller, weaker states to higher standards of accountability. Indeed, if the
latter were held to higher standards of accountability on a coercive or mana-

gerial basis, it would not be morally or politically inhibiting to any significant degree. Indeed, it might intensify the sense of an unjust world order, encouraging epithets such as "nuclear apartheid."[32]

These considerations apply to the American-led international effort to organize sanctions against India and Pakistan in an early response to their nuclear tests. It should be noted that despite developing nuclear weapons, both states were acting fully in accord with their legal obligations, never having signed the Non-Proliferation Treaty in 1968. They were both constitutional, civilian governments that were strongly and ardently supported in their controversial moves by the overwhelming tide of their respective domestic public opinions, including even the main opposition parties. Both were following through on previously announced political programs and were proceeding well within a reasonable conception of the security of the state in question. To impose punitive sanctions on these two states in response to their moves to acquire nuclear weapons seems wildly inappropriate except as a geopolitical countermove by a country that seeks to manage conflict throughout the world.

It is highly relevant to note that the main sanctioning state has consistently done on its own behalf, often with a less plausible security justification, what was being undertaken by India and, in reaction, by Pakistan. Such reasoning is not meant in any sense to endorse the substance of these decisions by India and Pakistan to embrace nuclearism, which seems irresponsibly provocative, highly risky for these states and their neighbors, and an embrace of morally and legally indefensible weaponry. It commits these states to a potential course of action in a highly unstable setting that threatens to ignite a regional war fought with nuclear weapons and likely to produce massive and indiscriminate forms of destruction with possibilities of huge casualties in these densely populated countries. The Afghanistan War to oust the Taliban and destroy the al Qaeda presence, combined with heightened tensions over Kashmir and with respect to the Hindu/Muslim clash, create a most dangerous set of circumstances for the peoples of the region. These dangers have been increased by the presence of nuclear weapons, but the self-appointed nuclear gatekeeping of the United States, which here proved ineffectual, finds no valid basis in either Westphalian logic of state equality or Charter logic concerned with the maintenance of international peace and security.

Fourth, disclosures since the end of the war relating to nuclear weaponry substantiate to a disturbing degree a suspected record of deception and misinformation. Even states with strong democratic procedures and credentials, such as the United Kingdom and the United States, hide unpleasant truths about nuclear weapons. There is no basis for supposing that such states, despite long constitutional traditions, are any less prone to conceal and lie, in the context of their security policy, than are states with a nasty authoritarian identity. These disclosures indicate that the U.S. government suppressed information about mishaps involving nuclear warheads that were stored in foreign countries, often so located in direct violation of agreements with the host governments. It also seems increasingly clear, thanks to the path-breaking and painstakingly careful scholarship of Stephen Endicott and Edward Hagerman, that sectors of the U.S. military bureaucracy contemplated the development for large-scale use of biological weapons as a weapon of choice late in the Korean War. These deliberations were taking place despite vigorous public protestations to the effect that the United States resented any allegation pertaining to use of such weaponry as false, as vicious propaganda, and as incompatible with American values and inconsistent with its dedication to military professionalism. There is considerable uncertainty as to whether the political leadership of the country would have implemented a military recommendation to rely on biological weapons had it been made. It should also be noted that most of the controversy was about whether such weapons were actually used in the Korean War, as alleged by communist countries, and as believed to be likely true to some extent on the basis of circumstantial and documentary evidence relied upon by Endicott and Hagerman.[33]

Fifth, the recalcitrance of a militarized bureaucracy is such that even when leaders make a decision to abandon covert programs involving weaponry of mass destruction, its implementation may be blocked and concealed for years within the deep structures of the security apparatus of the state. Leaders may not even realize that a forbidden program is continuing, possibly in a bureaucratic enclave operating within nonaccountable intelligence units of government, and even in violation of an internal directive. This seems to have been roughly the experience in the transitional period between the Soviet Union and Russia with regard to an extensive, concealed biological weapons program being carried on by a large, covert bureaucracy. The fact that such a large undertaking could persist in this manner is particularly worrisome, as it suggests the comparative ease with which a smaller program in violation of treaty obligations associated with the BWC could be concealed.

Sixth, states have very uneven technological knowledge and economic capacity and tend to deploy the most effective weaponry that is within their reach given their sense of perceived risks. In the aftermath of the Cold War there seems to be increased risks of exposure to attack on a regional level and intensifying intraregional rivalry for ascendancy and self-sufficiency in matters of defense. Unfortunately, the possession of weapons of mass destruction, whether nuclear, chemical, or biological, appears to have become more attractive to a series of governments, particularly in the Middle East.[34] In other words, with the collapse of the Soviet Union and the disappearance of global conflict, the stabilizing effects in regional settings of mutual deterrence and bipolarity have been eliminated. Part of that stabilizing impact of bipolarity on intrastate conflict was the result of bloc discipline associated with anxieties about the escalation of local conflicts into major wars. Without such anxieties there is far less incentive and capacity to impose constraints.

Seventh, with or without help from governments, the possibility that extremist political movements and apocalyptic religious cults will be able to obtain some capabilities to wage indiscriminate warfare with weaponry of mass destruction cannot be ruled out. Fortunately, until recently there has been little disposition to move in this direction, even by political actors that rely on terrorism to pursue their goals. The technology and resources needed to produce biological weapons may not be as accessible or as usable as was widely assumed in the feverish literature on the subject in the 1990s.[35] Nonetheless, given the anthrax scare and the disclosures of al Qaeda materials suggesting an intense interest in the acquisition of biological and chemical weaponry, and considering the launching of weapons of mass destruction at civilian targets on September 11, it is now accepted that global terrorist networks would acquire and use biological weapons if they could do so effectively. The indications that Aum Shinrikyo had made extensive efforts to disseminate lethal biological agents, as well as its partially successful attacks with sarin gas in the Tokyo subway system in 1995, have lent further support to the view that terrorist groups are now doing their best to acquire WMD.

## TENTATIVE CONCLUSIONS

This chapter has attempted to evaluate broad trends bearing on the effective renunciation of biological weaponry. It has considered the feasibility of establishing a treaty regime, adding a protocol on verification to the BWC that builds confidence in compliance. It adopts a rather skeptical view of these prospects due to the outlook of states that continue to be guided by realists preoccupied with achieving national security. This skepticism is reinforced by the reluctance of major countries, particularly the United States, to permit the sort of intrusive inspection system that might build confidence, and by the rather unsuccessful experiment in intrusive inspection carried out in Iraq during the course of much of the last decade. On the basis of this overall assessment, several conclusions with policy implications can be set forth. The intention is to stimulate both thought and action, avoiding the extremes of hysteria and complacency about biowar and bioterror dangers.

1. Despite the ending of the Cold War and bipolarity, the dangers of weaponry of mass destruction persist, although their form has changed.[36] Perhaps the two most important changes are a shift from the *global* menace of weaponry of mass destruction to that of *regional* menace and a deepening

realization that it will be difficult in such regional settings, especially in the
Middle East, to delink regimes of prohibition of chemical and biological
weapons from the existence of nuclear weaponry. As long as Israel is seen
as retaining a nuclear weapons option, it will be difficult, if not impossible,
to convince potential adversaries of Israel to forego attainable options relating to weaponry of mass destruction, regardless of widespread adherence by
countries elsewhere to regimes of prohibition. The nonadherence by several
Arab countries to the BWC and the CWC can be best understood in this
way.[37] Nevertheless, the U.S. approach to WMD poses a global threat that
outweighs the regional threat in the Middle East and the even more frightening threat in South Asia (India and Pakistan), as it is working to establish a
global structure of dominance (via space and WMD) that aims to control
the totality of political space on the planet.

2. A variety of developments, especially in light of the experience in Iraq
since the Gulf War, point to the difficulty of relying on negotiable verification arrangements as a hedge against noncompliance. Such difficulty is compounded by appreciating the continuing control of governmental
policymaking bearing on the security of the state by those who endorse
unrestricted sovereignty for their own state and adhere to realist styles of
statecraft.

3. Concerns about the danger of biological warfare are complicated by
the unavailability of information in the public domain that gives an accurate
and trustworthy sense of either the spread of biological weapons programs
or the likely utility of such weaponry in relation to combat or terrorist scenarios. These concerns are also made more difficult because of the overlap
of biological weapons activity with peaceful and commercial uses of the biological sciences and biotechnology. These issues are closely connected with
increasing contentions that secrecy at research and development stages is
needed to protect adequately valuable proprietary rights in private sector
pharmaceuticals and biogenetic engineering.[38] Thus, there is a symbiotic
relationship between secrecy on the part of government (for security policy)
and industry (for proprietary rights) that makes it difficult to attain high
and accurate levels of public awareness. This problem of assessment is compounded in the United States by the suspicion that the private and public
sector exaggerated the menace posed by biological weaponry so as to
increase support for higher defense spending. In the U.S. Congress, this suspicion has apparently dissolved in the wake of the September 11 attacks and
the anthrax episode.

4. Despite the tendency for its erosion by realist policy, geopolitical
opportunism, and regional tensions, it is important to appreciate that a significant framework of prohibition does still exist in relation to BW and is
reinforced by moral and cultural attitudes, as well as by treaty norms.
Despite its deficiencies, as discussed, such a regime deserves as much *responsible* support as possible. In this regard, it should be appreciated that sup-

port should not be achieved by delinking the nuclear problem from the biological warfare problem. Furthermore, the possibility of constructing a more effective regime of prohibition will depend on overcoming the resistance to transparency that is currently coming from military and commercial sources. To achieve this kind of result requires much more attention from "the new diplomacy," collaboration between moderate governments and transnational coalitions of voluntary citizens' associations. It may also require creating a stronger sense of obligation on the part of citizens, and especially relevant scientists and engineers associated with biological research, to monitor and report suspicious activities that seem to be incompatible with treaty obligations. There need to be safe havens for whistle-blowers with respect to BW activity and criminal accountability under both national and international law for violators and their political superiors.

5. Terrorist networks with global agendas are increasingly disposed to acquire weaponry of mass destruction by stealth or purchase through black markets. As al Qaeda and the worldview of Osama bin Laden exemplify, the ethos of such terrorism can be genocidal and its tactics designed to inflict maximum symbolic and substantive harm on innocent civilians.[39] The dangers associated with the possibilities of biological warfare now seem to relate to violent nonstate actors and movements at least as much as they do to states, and yet the only formal international undertakings are exclusively concerned with the behavior of states. The interplay between states and such organizations needs careful study, especially in light of the Afghanistan War and Pentagon plans for subsequent military undertakings by the United States. The antiterrorist campaign that is planned for a series of sovereign states cannot be reconciled with the regulation of the use of force by international law, the UN Charter, and the just war doctrine.

## NOTES

1. See Michael Klare, *Rogue States and Nuclear Outlaws: America's Search for a Foreign Policy* (New York: Hill and Wang, 1995). See also Steven Mufson, "Threat of 'Rogue' States: Is It Reality or Rhetoric?" *Washington Post* (29 May 2000), A1, A18; Philip Bowring, "'Rogue' States Are Overrated," *International Herald Tribune* (6 June 2000), 9.

2. For comprehensive analysis along these lines, adopting the more moderate and multilateral outlook of the Clinton presidency, see Jan Lodel, *The Price of Dominance: The New Weapons of Mass Destruction and Their Challenge to American Leadership* (New York: Council on Foreign Relations Press, 2001). The George W. Bush presidency, with its more unilateralist approach, its skepticism about treaty arrangements, and its enthusiasm for new weapons systems, accentuates these concerns.

3. See Michael R. Gordon and Judith Miller, "U.S. Germ Warfare Review Faults Plan on Enforcement," *New York Times* (20 May 2001), 1, 12.

4. See, for example, Robert Jay Lifton, "Illusions of the Second Nuclear Age," *World Policy Journal* 18 (Spring 2001), 25–30; see also the publications of the Nuclear Age Peace Foundation in Santa Barbara, especially those of its director, David Krieger. In some respects, there is a complementary relationship between nuclearists who emphasize the threat of biological weaponry and antinuclearists who exclusively focus their concerns on nuclear weapons.

5. See Jonathan Schell, *The Fate of the Earth* (New York: Knopf, 1982); Jonathan Schell, *The Abolition* (New York: Knopf, 1984); Jonathan Schell, *The Gift of Time: The Case for Abolishing Nuclear Weapons* (New York: Henry Holt, 1998); Robert Jay Lifton and Richard Falk, *Indefensible Weapons: The Political and Psychological Case Against Nuclearism,* 2d updated ed. (New York: Basic Books, 1991).

6. It is well known that "ultimate" is essentially a code word meaning "never." As such, it both pacifies antinuclear pressures while covertly reassuring the nuclear weapons establishment.

7. For articulation of this alternative paradigm see Richard Falk, *On Humane Governance: Toward a New Global Politics* (Cambridge, U.K: Polity, 1995); Richard Falk, *Law in an Emerging Global Village: A Post-Westphalian Perspective* (Ardsley, N.Y.: Transnational Publishers, 1998). It is being promoted most coherently by a civil society initiative called "Global Action to Prevent War: An International Coalition to Abolish Armed Conflict and Genocide." Its tactics and proposals can be found online at www.globalactionpw.org.

8. William Cohen, foreword to *Biological Weapons: Limiting the Threat,* ed. Joshua Lederberg (Cambridge, Mass.: MIT Press, 1999), xiii.

9. The most authoritative recent statement was made by President Bush in a major speech at the National Defense University, 1 May 2001, the substantial text of which is reprinted in *New York Times* (2 May 2001), A10.

10. Richard Danzig, "The Next Superweapon Panic," *New York Times* (15 November 1998), sections 14, 15.

11. See Seymour M. Hersh, "Overwhelming Force: Annals of War," *The New Yorker* 76, no. 12 (22 May 2000), 48–82.

12. See chapter 11.

13. Cf. the view of Abdullah Toukan, "Arab National Security Issues: Perceptions and Policies," in Shai Feldman and Abdullah Toukan, *Bridging the Gap: A Future Security Architecture for the Middle East* (Lanham, Md.: Rowman & Littlefield, 1997), 39–40.

14. Of course, the nonproliferation *treaty* regime includes a commitment by the nuclear weapons states to pursue nuclear disarmament in good faith; the nonproliferation *geopolitical* regime based on U.S. management contains no such commitment.

15. On the Japanese program prior to and during World War II carried out in China, see Sheldon Harris, *Factories of Death: Japanese Factories of Death 1932–1945* (London, 1945); on the U.S. program that operated during the first decades of the Cold War, see Stephen Endicott and Edward Hagerman, *The United States and Biological Warfare: Secrets from the Early Cold War and Korea* (Bloomington, Ind.: University of Indiana Press, 1998), esp. 1–87.

16. On attempted use of biological weapons by the Aum Shinrikyo sect, see John Steinbruner, "Biological Weapons: A Plague upon All Houses," *Foreign Policy* 109 (Winter 1997–1998), 85–96.

17. For a presentation of the Soviet program by one of its directors, see Ken Alibek, *Biohazard* (New York: Random House, 1999).

18. A consideration of these issues has become politically salient in 2001 as a result of the apparent refusal of the Bush administration to support the Protocol as negotiated allegedly because the verification scheme does not provide confidence that cheating can be detected in a timely fashion. For an analysis of the Protocol as an important step in the right direction with respect to verification, see Barbara Rosenberg, "U.S. Policy and the BWC Protocol," *The CBW Convention Bulletin*, no. 52 (June 2001), 1–3.

19. Michael Krepon, "The Political Dynamic of Verification and Compliance Debates," in *Verification and Arms Control,* ed. William C. Porter (Lexington, Mass: Lexington Books, 1985), 135–51.

20. These references and quotations are found in Barbara Crossette, "Iraq Approaches Clearance on Nuclear Weapons, Alarming U.S. Experts," *International Herald Tribune* (21 April 1998).

21. See evaluation of the CWC in "International: Just Checking," *The Economist* (2 May 1998), 42–44.

22. Amy Smithson, "Rudderless: The Chemical Weapons Convention at 1½," The Henry L. Stimson Center, Report No. 25, September 1998.

23. This assessment was reached by the only tribunal ever to assess the use of atomic bombs in response to a case for symbolic damages brought by six survivors in a Japanese court. For discussion see Richard Falk, "The Shimoda Case: A Legal Appraisal of the Atomic Attacks upon Hiroshima and Nagasaki," *American Journal of International Law* 59, no. 4 (1965), 759–93.

24. For discussion see Richard Falk, "Nuclear Weapons, International Law and the World Court: A Historic Encounter," *American Journal of International Law* 91, no. 1 (1997), 64–75.

25. Being under the nuclear umbrella meant an indirect acceptance of a security role for nuclear weapons to deter a nuclear or conventional attack and to enable a credible retaliation.

26. The most authoritative account of this role of nuclear weapons in the Cold War era is still probably that of Henry Kissinger in his influential book, *Nuclear Weapons and Foreign Policy*, A Westview encore ed. (Boulder, Colo.: Published for the Council on Foreign Relations by Westview Press, 1984).

27. This is the main argument developed in a Cold War setting in Lifton and Falk, *Indefensible Weapons.*

28. Or contrariwise, in the Western support for the legitimacy of the Khmer Rouge regime, despite its genocidal record, in the years after the Vietnamese intervention of 1979.

29. Such a generalization does not apply to "limited war" situations during the Cold War when fears of escalation beyond the nuclear threshold placed limits associated with geopolitical prudence on military tactics other than by reference to criteria of effectiveness.

30. See Raymond Aron, *Peace and War: A Theory of International Relations* (New York: Doubleday, 1966), 580–85, 609–11.

31. See chapter 6 for a comparable analysis of security issues.

32. See contributions of K. Subrahmanyam and Ali Mazrui to a volume based on the Nobel Jubilee Symposium celebrating the ninetieth anniversary of The Nobel Peace Prize, *Beyond the Cold War: New Dimensions in International Relations,* ed. Geir Lundestad and Odd Arne Westad (Oslo, Norway: Scandinavian University Press, 1993), 57–70, 85–94.

33. See Endicott and Hagerman, *The United States and Biological Warfare.* It should be admitted that their scholarship has been subject to severe criticism, and that my favorable view is based on a personal assessment of their analysis and supporting evidence.

34. The attempted and actual acquisition of WMD in the Middle East, as compared to other regions, reflects several distinctive conditions: Israeli possession of nuclear weapons, the turbulence of the region, resistance to hegemonic control by the United States, and dictatorial leaders seeking to maximize military capabilities at minimum cost.

35. For assessment of terrorist threats, see Bruce Hoffmann, "Change and Continuity in Terrorism," Lecture, Conference on "Terrorism and Beyond: The 21st Century," co-sponsored by Oklahoma City National Memorial Institute for the Prevention of Terrorism and the RAND Corporation, 17 April 2000; and Amy Smithson and Leslie-Anne Levy, *Ataxia: The Chemical and Biological Terrorism Threat and the U.S. Response*, Stimson Center Report No. 35. (Washington, D.C.: Stimson Center, 2000) and discussion in the section "World Order Concerns" in this chapter.

36. Instead of a danger of strategic nuclear war between superpowers, the new dangers are primarily associated with either regional nuclear warfare or "loose nukes," that is, the breakdown of command and control over the former Soviet nuclear weapons arsenal and the sale of nuclear know how and materials via criminal undergrounds.

37. See chapter 6.

38. This trend is clearly articulated in chapter 14. See also William Muth, "The Role of the Pharmaceutical and Biotech Industries in Strengthening the Biological Disarmament Regime," *Politics and the Life Sciences*, 18(1) (March 1999), 92–87.

39. This point is made by Walter Laqueur, *The New Terrorism: Fanaticism and the Arms of Mass Destruction* (Oxford University Press, 1998), 2–7, 254–82.

# II

## THE ROLES OF PAST AND PRESENT SUPERPOWERS

# 3

# A Perilous Path to Security?

## Weighing U.S. "Biodefense" against Qualitative Proliferation

*Laura Reed and Seth Shulman*

In the fall of 2001, the American public and the world were shocked and terrified by revelations about lethal anthrax bacteria sent via the U.S. mail. As a result of a few contaminated letters sent by a still-unknown person or organization, tens of thousands of postal workers and others were placed in danger and ultimately treated with a prophylactic course of antibiotics; millions of dollars were spent to decontaminate facilities including congressional office buildings; and new systems were introduced to irradiate mail in a number of high-volume postal facilities in the United States.[1] As frightening as this episode was, however, the sad truth, well-known by almost all biodefense experts, is that, with five people killed in the attacks and roughly a dozen treated for anthrax symptoms, this real-life scenario was about as benign as a biological weapon attack could be.

To appreciate the magnitude of the broader "biodefense" problem in human terms, consider the elaborate role-playing scenario held several years earlier, in February 1999, at a conference sponsored by Johns Hopkins University. In this exercise, in a hotel near Washington, D.C., more than 1,000 health professionals from the United States and Canada confronted a scenario in which an imaginary terrorist group unleashed smallpox on an unsuspecting U.S. public. Despite the participants' best efforts to implement an emergency response, they could not prevent a grim result: 15,000 projected deaths within two months and a total of 80 million lives lost within a year.

"We blew it," said Dr. Michael Ascher, a California health official who participated in the decision making as the scenario played out. "It clearly got out of control. Whatever planning we had . . . it didn't work. I think this is the harsh reality, what would happen."[2]

The Johns Hopkins scenario—one of several biodefense exercises conducted across the country over the past several years—was intended to underscore an almost unimaginably horrific threat posed by biological agents. Needless to say, with some 80 million projected casualties, it also highlights serious shortcomings in the government's ability to protect civilians in the event of such an attack.

But what conclusions should one draw from such a demonstration of the apparent vulnerability of populations to biowarfare in either the anthrax episode or the far more frightening exercise? The Bush administration, like the Clinton administration before it, has argued for a robust federal response, including vaccine stockpiles, emergency response training, and expanded technological research. In February 2002, Bush proposed $4.5 billion in new funding to defend the nation against biological terrorism, more than tripling existing funding levels.[3]

The fact is, though, that the decision to significantly augment biological weapons-related support came during the Clinton administration, long before any actual bioterror episode on U.S. soil. For example, the high-profile bioterror exercise mentioned above came on the heels of an announcement by then-President Clinton that his administration would seek a dramatic increase in spending on "biodefense" in the United States as part of a $10 billion program in FY 2000 to counter the potential terrorist use of weapons of mass destruction.[4]

To bolster support for the initiative, Clinton and many of his highest-ranking cabinet members, including Defense Secretary William Cohen and Secretary of Health and Human Services Donna Shalala, publicly and repeatedly voiced concerns about the vulnerability of the United States to a biological attack.[5] In March 2000, CIA Director George J. Tenet offered further justification for the Clinton initiative when he told a public session of the Senate Foreign Relations Committee that his agency believes one dozen states, including several hostile to Western democracies—Iran, Iraq, Libya, North Korea, and Syria—now either possess or are actively pursuing offensive biological capabilities. The biological threat, Tenet warned, "is growing in breadth and sophistication."[6]

The Clinton administration argued that a strong government response is merited because of dramatic advances in biotechnology; evidence of existing, offensive biological warfare programs; and heightened concern about "catastrophic terrorism."[7] As Clinton explained in an interview in 1999:

"[I]t would be completely irresponsible for us not to allocate a substantial investment in trying to protect America from threats that will be, in all probability, as likely or more likely in the future than the threats we think we face today."[8]

The Clinton administration's perception of the threat came on the heels of credible and high-profile revelations of a massive biological weapons program in the former Soviet Union that allegedly employed as many as 60,000 workers and scientists and spanned some one hundred facilities, with an annual budget of close to $1 billion.[9] In addition, by 1995 it had been established that U.S.-led coalition forces confronted a bona fide biological warfare (BW) threat in combat against Iraq in the 1991 Persian Gulf War: United Nations weapons inspectors later discovered that Iraq possessed at least 180 biological bombs and warheads containing anthrax and botulinum toxin, and the Iraqi regime had studied dozens more potential biological agents.[10] Equally unsettling, the Japanese cult Aum Shinrikyo attempted to develop deliverable forms of botulinum toxin and anthrax for use in terrorist attacks against Japanese civilians between 1990 and 1993.[11] Of course, in the aftermath of the terrorist attack on the World Trade Center in New York on September 11, 2001, the anthrax postal episode, and the subsequent Bush war on terrorism, the efforts of the Clinton administration to prepare for a biological weapons attack continue to be substantially augmented, as is shown by Bush's proposal to more than triple "biodefense" funding. Nonetheless, despite ample justification for augmented defense against terrorism in the current global climate, it is important to note that the Bush administration's current initiative—like that set in motion during the Clinton administration before it—runs counter to longstanding conventional wisdom that even a "substantial investment" cannot yield an effective civil defense against the BW threat.[12]

Most experts on biological weapons have long held that, short of issuing protective suits to the entire population, civilian defense against a surprise biological attack is virtually impossible due to the wide variety of biological agents and their inherent capacity for self-replication. Vaccines, for example, would only be useful in the highly unlikely event that the identity of the biological agent used was known with certainty. Even then, to be effective, the vaccine would have to be widely administered well in advance of the attack.[13] The same argument would prevent an effective defense against a biological attack directed at livestock, and it is unclear that any type of known protection or defense could be effectively mounted against an attack aimed at crops or other plant life.

To a large extent, this line of reasoning about the futility of civil biodefense has informed official U.S. BW policy for more than three decades.[14] Accordingly, the U.S. decision to unilaterally renounce its biological weapons program in 1969 remains one of the most significant developments in the history of this heinous class of weaponry. The move by the Nixon administration, which paved the way for the Biological Weapons Convention (BWC) of 1972, was publicly justified on the grounds that biological agents could have little or no military utility because they posed an unpredictable threat of disease that was likely to spread out of control.[15]

More specifically—and more important for our purposes—the calculation by the Nixon administration was threefold: (1) Because biological agents could initiate epidemics in civilian populations on either side of an armed conflict, they would never be militarily useful, and all but the most nihilistic state actor or terrorist group would be loathe to unleash them; (2) even in a war scenario, no effective civilian defense could be mounted and, given a nuclear deterrent, there would be no advantage at least to states armed with nuclear weapons to an in-kind retaliation to a biological attack; and (3) a continued biological weapons program would surely raise the specter of general and qualitative proliferation in the biological-weapons arena—something best avoided.[16]

In our view, the most meaningful way to evaluate the U.S. policy shift represented by the Clinton administration's biodefense initiative and now augmented under the directives of President Bush is to carefully subject it to this same well-established calculus. Specifically, we ask: First, has BW-related technology advanced significantly enough to make biological agents more controllable, and hence more conceivably useful as a military or terrorist weapon? Second, can an augmented biological weapons defense program now or in the foreseeable future offer any appreciable protection to civilians or enhance deterrence against an attack with biological agents? And third, to what extent does even a defensively oriented program risk spurring qualitative proliferation?

## THE CURRENT BIODEFENSE PROGRAM

Before we can evaluate the current U.S. biodefense program, we need to briefly review some of its key features. Several analysts have studied the program's funding in detail. Notably, John Parachini, formerly a security specialist at the Monterey Institute of International Studies and now at the RAND Corp., has compiled a detailed analysis of federal counterterrorist outlays including BW-related funding.[17]

What is immediately apparent is the phenomenal growth and breadth of the expanded biodefense program, a trend that began, as noted previously, during the Clinton administration. As the so-called Deutch Commission (named after the former CIA Director John Deutch) discovered when it reviewed the initial buildup in 1999, it is a daunting task to even trace the various funding components, not to mention analyzing the individual programs themselves. Calling it a "Gordian knot," the Deutch Commission found no fewer than ninety separate governmental agencies claiming some jurisdiction over the terrorist threat posed by weapons of mass destruction (WMD), including biological agents.[18]

According to Parachini's accounting, the U.S. government allocated more than $8 billion in FY 2000 to prepare against a terrorist attack on the United States with biological agents or other weapons of mass destruction, and requested $9.3 billion for FY 2001. Both are unprecedented amounts, especially in the context of the flat level of spending in the overall defense budget. Of this total, slightly more than half—roughly $5 billion—was spent by the U.S. military.[19] Although these figures include some efforts designed to defend against all WMD, they provide a sense of the scale of the overall initiative. The increases have continued in the Bush administration.

The press has tended to emphasize the emergency preparedness and training features of the initiative, such as the development of Rapid Response Teams by a number of agencies including the FBI and the National Guard. These programs have a significant component devoted to defense against biological weapons but are designed to respond to a variety of domestic terrorist attacks. And, in fact, some of these programs do exhibit among the largest increases. For example, across all agencies, funding for Rapid Response Teams (both in equipment and training) jumped more than six-fold between FY 1998 and FY 2000, according to Parachini's calculations.[20] And as some agencies worked to quickly institute such programs, the increases were often even steeper. For example, funding for the FBI's special response units increased more than fortyfold between FY 1998 and FY 2000, from $2.7 million to $120.9 million.[21]

Although a significant portion of the overall outlay of nearly $10 billion funded efforts to respond to a range of terrorist threats, some $1.4 billion is specifically earmarked for defense against weapons of mass destruction including biological agents, also an unprecedented total.[22] As with the overall initiative, slightly more than half of the total funds were overseen by the military. In FY 2000, the Defense Department's budget for its Chemical and Biological Defense Program totaled $791 million.[23] Here again, press accounts tended to stress the emergency response and preparedness components, such as teaching doctors to diagnose diseases like smallpox, Ebola, or Marburg viruses that the vast majority of clinicians have never seen firsthand. Effective or not, these efforts were motivated by a clear-cut defensive rationale that early diagnosis and medical response can significantly reduce the number of fatalities by establishing at an early stage a quarantine that could forestall some of the worst consequences of a biological attack.

But the initiative also included vast expenditures of a less clear-cut defensive nature. Almost no agency was left out. For instance, in FY 2001 the outgoing Clinton administration proposed to spend $19.2 million for laboratory infrastructure improvements at the Department of Agriculture and to initiate a $10 million program for basic research on potential biological agents. Similarly, the Department of Energy, a partner in the Human Genome Project, which recently produced a working draft of the human genome map, received dramatic increases in funding for basic research into biological agents. From $3 million in FY 1998, funding at the Department of Energy increased more than fourfold to $14 million for FY 2001, presumably leveraging their genetic sequencing research and technology to date.[24] Thanks to the investigative reporting of a team at the *New York Times,* we also now know that funding extended even to the CIA, which in the late 1990s undertook a secret project called Operation Clear Vision designed to build and test "bomblets" to dispense biological agents that had been pioneered first in the Soviet Union.[25]

Funding in almost all of these areas increased during the Bush administration. For instance, in 2002, Bush proposed spending $1.75 billion to conduct "basic and applied research" on a bioterrorism response at the National Institutes of Health, part of the Bush administration's proposed 2003 biological weapons research budget of $2.4 billion.[26]

Among the largest overall funding increases over the past several years has occurred at the Department of Health and Human Services (HHS). Here again, contrary to popular conception, much of the funding did not go to clear-cut defensive programs. The agency, which formerly had little jurisdiction in the area, is now spending more than $50 million annually to stockpile antibiotics and vaccines against a possible biological attack, while its research and development budget increased from $15.9 million in FY 1998 to $112 million in FY 2000. HHS spending on new vaccine research during this same period increased more than sixteenfold, from $2.9 million to $48.5 million,[27] reportedly in the hopes of developing improved vaccines against some of the most likely biological agents such as anthrax and smallpox.[28]

High-tech vaccine research, especially on this scale, is worrisome because of its potential to spur qualitative proliferation. As many experts have pointed out, vaccine research requires intimate knowledge of a given biological agent and is virtually identical in practice to the research needed to develop an improved offensive capability. Along these lines, perhaps most worrisome from the standpoint of qualitative proliferation are the significant increases in military spending related to biological weapons that tend to be obscured within the currently massive budgetary outlays.

Ever since the Persian Gulf War, the U.S. military has taken the threat of biological warfare extremely seriously, and concern has only increased as fear of bioterrorism has grown in the post–September 11 climate. Worried about the potential use of biological agents on the battlefield, the Defense Department has undertaken a major investment in detection, identification, and force protection measures. The Defense Department is also now vaccinating all of its 2.4 million troops against anthrax. While the crash vaccination program has attracted widespread headlines, of more geopolitical significance are the Defense Department's efforts to bring new technology into the field that is more likely to contribute to qualitative proliferation. The problem has plagued the program ever since the Nixon administration's renunciation of biological weapons in 1969. As Nixon's National Security Advisor Henry Kissinger put it, the United States needed to continue to research "offensive aspects" of biological agents "to determine what defensive measures are required."[29]

On the military research front, more than $25 million in federal funds continues to support the United States Army Medical Research Institute of Infectious Disease (USAMRIID), the U.S. Army biological weapons defense program at Ft. Detrick, Maryland.[30] Officially charged with developing vaccines and other drugs such as antibiotics that could be used to defend against a biological weapons attack, USAMRIID has long been criticized for secrecy and disproportionate attention to exotic biological agents and toxins, some of which are not even considered legitimate threats by the military's own intelligence data.[31] Even more troubling are recent revelations that, early in the Bush administration, a secretive Defense Intelligence Agency program code-named Project Jefferson undertook, despite the obligations of the Biological Weapons Convention, to make a genetically modified strain of anthrax. Program officials made the questionable argument that the small amounts of genetically modified anthrax they sought in the program indicated "a defensive intent" and would therefore comply with U.S. treaty obligations.[32] Yet such efforts clearly demonstrate the elusive line between defensive and offensive programs.

The problem is clearly illustrated in the cutting-edge research undertaken at the Defense Advanced Research Projects Agency (DARPA)—perhaps the most important current work for which unclassified information now exists. In contrast to the support for USAMRIID, DARPA's funding for defense against biological weapons more than doubled between FY 1998 and FY 2001, from $59 million to $162 million.[33] Further proposed increases are expected to boost DARPA's Biological Warfare Defense Program to more than $200 million by FY 2005.[34]

What is included in the DARPA research agenda? Some of the work involves research and development of strictly defensively oriented hardware such as biosensors and mobile detectors that might rapidly determine the presence of airborne biological agents. Other efforts include improved diagnostic tests that can swiftly determine the presence of disease. But DARPA will also spend at least $16 million on research "to exploit recent advances in high throughput genetic sequencers to obtain complete genetic information on a number of important pathogens and the non-pathogenic nearest neighbors."[35] According to DARPA literature, this research is designed to help develop an inventory of genes and proteins that can identify pathogenic markers in any guise, thereby enhancing capabilities to detect pathogens. But despite the stated defensive intent, this project produces much the same information one would seek to try to defeat detectors or increase the pathogenicity of a given biological agent. Although the information could theoretically be used to enhance detection capabilities, it could prove equally invaluable in trying to defeat an enemy's similar efforts. With such implications for offensive purposes, this project raises serious questions about qualitative proliferation.

Similar concerns are raised by DARPA's $16.5 million multipurpose program designed to "identify primary harmful immune responses to biological warfare agents."[36] This work is presumably targeted at better understanding the body's allergic or autoimmune response to certain agents; but this information could also theoretically aid in creating a biological agent that might trigger a deadly autoimmune response by sending a victim into anaphylactic shock. This is also true of DARPA's FY 2000 program to "use gene-shuffling techniques to generate molecules to be screened for superantigenic properties."[37] Here again, the work appears to seek a vaccine or treatment that could enhance the ability of the recipient's immune system to recognize pathogens, but the information could conceivably be used offensively as well.

On the whole, the most noteworthy features of the current expanded biodefense program are its breadth across the widest array of federal agencies and its scope, which encompasses efforts ranging from emergency response training and hardware development (including detectors and diagnostics) to an unprecedented increase in vaccine and basic research into many aspects of biological agents, their genetic makeup, and pathogenicity.

Notwithstanding the stated defensive intent, these latter efforts—especially those under military auspices—raise legitimate concerns about qualitative BW-related proliferation because of their potential offensive uses. DARPA literature justifies this work largely on the grounds that technological advances have significantly increased the threat posed by biological agents, noting that, "[t]he widespread availability of bacterial, viral, toxin and chemical stocks; minimal developmental cost and scientific expertise required; and abundance of weaponization potential comprises a sinister threat. The single largest concern, however, is from the exploitation of modern genetic engineering by adversaries to synthesize 'super pathogens.'"[38] Just how significant are these technological changes?

## TECHNOLOGICAL CONSIDERATIONS

Just past the cusp of the new millennium, our era is already being widely hailed as the biotechnology century. Ahead of schedule and under budget, the working draft of the human genome map, unveiled in March 2000, certainly gives the moniker some credence. There is little question that our understanding of the life sciences—and especially our growing grasp of genomics—has increased dramatically and promises tremendous advances to come. At this auspicious juncture, expert opinion diverges considerably about the implications of the advances in genetic engineering for the development of biological weapons.

On the one hand, in response to a near-hysterical level of concern on the part of the Department of Defense, many defense intellectuals, and the mainstream media, a number of experts have taken pains to note that it is not an easy matter to make biological weapons, especially for a terrorist group.[39] As some experts have noted, the creation of a mass-casualty biological weapon would entail scientific teams composed of persons highly trained in "microbiology, pathology, aerosol physics, aerobiology, and even meteorology."[40] In addition, as one analyst has pointed out, "finding trained and skilled personnel . . . who are willing to participate in mass murder, is a profound organizational roadblock, inherent to terrorist development of biological weapons, that is perhaps too readily discounted."[41]

Such a view, for example, was espoused by a blue ribbon panel tasked with assessing the U.S. response to potential terrorist activities, known as the Gilmore Panel. According to this panel's December 1999 report to the president and Congress, producing biological agents requires training, advanced techniques, and specialized equipment. In the case of *B. anthracis*, for example, transforming the bacterium into a spore suitable for use in a wide-scale terrorist attack necessitates a combination of skill and extreme care during a production technique that involves the application of heat or chemical shock. During all stages of the process *B. anthracis*, like all other biological agents, must also be continuously tested to ensure its purity and lethality and thus its utility for weapons purposes—a job requiring sophisticated, if not exotic laboratory equipment including fermenters, large-scale lyophilizers or freeze dryers, class II or III safety hoods, High-Efficiency Particulate Air (HEPA) filters, and centrifuges.[42]

In a similar vein, some analysts have stressed the difficulty of creating an aerosol cloud from biological agents and toxins. They have noted that most bacteria and protein toxins are fragile, unstable when heated, and sensitive to environmental factors like acidity and ultraviolet radiation from the sun. To be effective, a biological agent must overcome these environmental hurdles as well as the immune response of the human body, none of which are even remotely trivial matters.[43] As some have noted, for example, the Japanese terrorist organization Aum Shinrikyo had $1 billion in assets and counted talented graduate chemists among its members. Yet despite four years of trying, it could not make germ weapons work, so it turned to sarin nerve gas for its 1995 subway attack in Tokyo.[44]

Despite these difficulties, however, there is little question that advances in genetic engineering open up significant avenues for work on bacterial and viral agents over the next several decades. It is likely, in fact, that these techniques will lead to significant advances in four areas. First is facilitating the development of organisms that can be more stable for aerosol dispersal or that can withstand other adverse environmental factors. Second is increasing these agents' virulence, toxicity, and resistance to treatment (such as the Russian BW program's allegedly successful effort to create an antibiotic-resistant strain of anthrax).[45] Third is allowing researchers to alter immunological characteristics of a given organism to foil human immune resistance and detection. Fourth is providing the emerging ability to take benign microorganisms and splice a foreign gene into them to create an entirely new pathogenic agent.

Of these formidable new capabilities, undoubtedly the most significant effect is that advances in genomics and gene sequencing make it theoretically possible to design biological agents that could target particular ethnic groups by homing in on genetic differences, with the viral or bacterial agent activated only in the presence of a specific set of genetic "markers" known to exist with far greater frequency in a particular subpopulation. One report from the British Medical Association has warned that early versions of such weapons could exist by 2004.[46] Ominously, Malcolm Dando, who authored the report, warns that the increased precision and reliability that such sophisticated genetic engineering techniques can theoretically provide increase the chance that biological weapons might be used as "ethnic weapons."[47] One caveat to Dando's argument, as MIT biologist and BW expert Jonathan King has noted, is that because all humans belong to the same interbred species, no genetic markers will *exclusively* denote any one ethnic group; rather it will be a matter of a given group exhibiting a genetic marker with pronounced frequency above that of the general population. Nonetheless, King acknowledges that, in principle, given rapid advances in genetic engineering techniques, Dando's warning cannot be ignored.[48]

Concomitant with these dramatic technological advances is the increasing dissemination of genetic technology to a growing technically literate community, including techniques and infrastructure, that inevitably reduces existing hurdles to the creation of biological weaponry. As noted previously, the offensive BW program in the former Soviet Union allegedly employed at least 60,000 workers, at least a fraction of whom were highly trained in microbiology. Although little is known about technological transfer of genetic engineering techniques and materials among this population, worrisome inferences can be drawn from data in the United States. According to one report, for example, there are currently 1,308 U.S. companies now listed as actively commercializing biotechnology, employing well over 100,000 people, and this figure does not even include a significant highly trained graduate student population in the biological sciences. Along similar lines, a recent survey of 1,400 U.S. academic institutions found that 16 percent possessed human, animal, or plant pathogens that appear on the draft BWC list of biological agents.[49]

A decade ago, a strong case could be made that technological advances in the near term would *not* alter the traditional U.S. assessment of the military utility of biological agents.[50] Today, however, this argument is no longer supportable given the unprecedented pace of advances in genetic technology. Granted, policymakers would do well not to underestimate the difficulties involved in developing a usable and effective biological weapon (a factor specifically relevant to terrorist uses of biological agents), but there is little question that the technology to do so is rapidly advancing and becoming more accessible. In the medium term it is conceivable, even likely, that researchers will be able to draw on publicly available data from the human genome project and rapid advances in gene sequencing technology to design more targeted, controllable—and hence potentially more usable—BW agents.

In this sense at least, it seems that the Bush and Clinton administrations are justified in assuming that the traditional calculus about the potential military utility of BW has shifted. The question is, what, if anything, can be done to effectively combat the potential threat?

## ASSESSING THE EFFICACY OF A DEFENSIVE RESPONSE

Although the capability to make more effective biological weapons has undeniably improved and will likely increase through anticipated advances in genetic engineering, the same claim cannot be made for defensive capabilities, especially those directed at civil biodefense. As indicated previously, defensive activities tend to fall into three broad categories: training and equipment directed toward emergency preparedness; research, development, and production of defensive "hardware" including detection and diagnostics research and therapeutics; and finally, basic and applied research into biological agents aimed at vaccine development and increased understanding of emerging BW-related technology.

Of these activities, the domestic preparedness efforts are the most inherently defensive in nature. Many of these activities do stand a moderate chance of at least slowing the spread of disease, and there is certainly no harm in training professionals to attempt to respond to all types of crisis situations. But while it is difficult to argue against the notion of improved preparedness, it is also unclear how effective such efforts can hope to be against the threat posed by biological agents. Much of the current response planning assumes that attacks will be quickly detected and characterized. In fact, it may not be possible to characterize a biological attack quickly enough to provide an effective "rapid response." Furthermore, predictions about appropriate medical responses are based on very limited experience with civil incidents and epidemics and may prove unreliable in the face of a large-scale biological attack. And, of course, the tremendous uncertainty created by the ability to modify new weapons or strains of existing weapons significantly compounds these problems.

Consequently, much of the criticism of the current biodefense buildup has focused on the fact that even its substantial federal funding will yield relatively little defensive benefit. As John V. Parachini of the Monterey Institute of International Studies argued in 2000, the federal government should be "acting and spending smart and not just spending and talking big."[51]

Similar criticism has come from surprising quarters. For example, Larry Johnson, who served in the State Department and the CIA Office of Counterterrorism during the first Bush and the Reagan administrations, noted in 2000, "The problem with the money is right now every government bureaucracy in Washington is finding a mission in combating terrorism. This is utter nonsense. It is a misallocation of resources."[52] Jeff Simon, head of Political Risk Assessment, a security-consulting firm, emphatically agrees: "When there's so much money being poured around, every entity wants a piece of it, every government agency, every business, every consultant. It's almost like a runaway train—with no clear direction."[53]

Similar questions about efficacy are pertinent to all facets of the biodefense program. In the area of basic research and applied vaccine research, for instance, William C. Patrick III, who helped develop germ weapons for the United States before the country renounced its program in 1969, states the problem clearly. Patrick recently warned that vaccinations against particular germs can be easily countered by foes, making such safeguards potentially useless. As he put it: "It's a hell of a problem. Defensive measures are much more difficult than offensive ones. There's no easy way around it. You immunize against anthrax and then an enemy just tries something else."[54]

In essence, Patrick is describing a profound dilemma that is more serious than an ineffective program: If countermeasures are developed to overcome vaccines and other types of defense such as antibiotics, to at least some degree, defensively oriented measures have fostered qualitative proliferation.

## ASSESSING THE RISK OF QUALITATIVE PROLIFERATION

It is difficult, if not impossible, to accurately assess the risk of qualitative proliferation. On the one hand, it is clear that genetic technologies are advancing at an extraordinarily rapid rate. What is less clear is the extent to which defensively oriented research and development programs can reasonably be considered to push the pace of development even further.

Some analysts, like Milton Leitenberg, a biological weapons expert at the University of Maryland's Center for International and Security Studies, believe the risk of qualitative proliferation is high. Speaking about the initial Clinton administration buildup, Leitenberg noted: "My ultimate concern is the effect on proliferation. People here have gone nuts. They trumpet a perception of US vulnerability to chemical and biological weapons, whether or not that is the case, and they are likely to stimulate the interest of other states and terrorists in such weapons."[55]

Bolstering Leitenberg's concern is the fact that most proponents of the U.S. biodefense buildup would agree that fears of the BW program in the Soviet Union helped spur the call for an augmented biological defense program in the United States throughout the 1980s and to some extent continue to do so today. True, we now know that the covert program in the former Soviet Union was offensive in orientation, but a strong case can be made that any augmented research program will encourage other state actors to follow suit.[56]

Ultimately, any biological defense program must weigh the chances of its efficacy against the likelihood of spurring potential adversaries into a qualitative arms race. The key variable in such a calculation is the estimation of how much promise a defensively oriented program holds to provide a viable defense, military or civil.

Not surprisingly, DARPA takes a very optimistic tone about its ability to create a robust defensive technology, touting "revolutionary new approaches." According to DARPA's FY 2000 mission statement regarding its biological defense program, for instance: "Today there is a tremendous mismatch between the magnitude of the biological warfare threat and the Department's ability to adequately respond. . . . Recent dramatic developments in biotechnology, which this program will leverage, promise to eliminate this mismatch."[57]

In public statements, President Clinton appeared to philosophically subscribe to a similarly optimistic view about the potential for defensive technology to address this mismatch, or as he has put it, to close "the gap between the offense and defense"[58] in the biological weapons arena. As Clinton elaborated in 1999:

> If you look back through all of human history, people who are interested in gaining control or influence or advantage over others have brought to bear the force of arms. And what normally happens from the beginning of history is the arms work until a defense is erected, and then there's an equilibrium until there is a new offensive system developed, and then a defense comes up, going all the

way back to—well, even before it, but castle moats which were overcome by catapults.[59]

Unfortunately, however, the advent of nuclear weapons forever altered this view of the history of military technology. With the splitting of the atom, the calculus of defense effectively evaporated in the face of such a weapon of mass destruction, replaced only by the doctrines of deterrence and mutually assured destruction (MAD). Today, more than a half century since the advent of nuclear weapons, the problem of the limited efficacy of defensive measures against nuclear weapons has resurfaced in the United States as policymakers struggle to respond to the threat posed by ballistic missiles.

The ongoing debate over whether the United States should deploy a system of ballistic missile defense offers a particularly pertinent analogy to the quandary over qualitative proliferation in the BW arena. In the case of defense against nuclear weapons, the United States must weigh the chances of such a system's potential efficacy (especially in the face of easily adopted countermeasures) against the deterioration it will likely cause in relations with Russia, China, and other nations, as well as the prospect that it could prove destabilizing or even spark a renewed arms race.

As critics of a ballistic missile defense compellingly argue, there is little likelihood that such a unilateral, technologically mediated system will work given the reality that an attacker can easily foil such efforts.[60] Even dramatic technological advances cannot alter the inherent asymmetry between offense and defense: Attackers can always benefit from the fact that defenders must operate in an environment of uncertainty and incomplete information as they try to protect against all possible contingencies. Meanwhile, any systems that defenders deploy can be overcome by comparatively simpler countermeasures.

A similar calculus about the relative ease of adopting countermeasures to foil the defense holds for the offensive use of biological agents. As Steven Block, a biophysicist at Stanford University, has put it, biological weapons represent a "David and Goliath kind of warfare. . . . One guy in a garage can take down a giant."[61] Unfortunately, even though there are currently substantial technical obstacles to the development of viable biological weapons, the disturbing calculus put forth by Block and others makes them— theoretically at least—more easily within the reach of a wider range of state actors and potential terrorists. This potential for proliferation is inherent in the technology itself and is unlikely to change in the foreseeable future.

One analyst who fully appreciates the new threats posed by the power of genetic technologies is Bill Joy, cofounder and chief scientist of Sun Microsystems, and cochair of a recent presidential commission on the future of information technology. In a disturbing and widely read article, Joy argues that the confluence of our most powerful twenty-first century technologies—robotics, genetic engineering, and nanotechnology—will spawn a whole new class of accidents and abuses.[62] According to Joy, the destructive power of self-replication—a power he calls "the modus operandi of genetic engineering, which uses the machinery of the cell to replicate its designs"—presents the most worrisome challenge, especially when coupled with computer and robotic technologies. Added to the problem of uncontrollable self-replication, however, is the fact that, for the first time in history, such power will be widely within the reach of individuals and small groups. The democratization of the technology stands in contrast to the large facilities and rare and costly materials needed for success with nuclear technology. In the case of these new, cataclysmically destructive capabilities, Joy warns, "Knowledge alone will enable the use of them."[63]

Joy, a brilliant software programmer and avowed proponent of technological advances, probes the technological implications of these new advances with an unblinking eye, acknowledging the inherent imbalance between the myriad possibilities for accident and abuse presented in the new technologies compared with the minuscule chance of defending against the likely consequences. He became so troubled by the implications of these technological advances that he is now broaching among colleagues and professional groups the idea of a moratorium on research in these high-tech areas until safeguards against their misuse can be agreed upon and implemented. Joy's notion of a moratorium has yet to draw a critical mass of political support, but his thoughtful analysis should not be ignored.

## CONCLUSION

The specter of biological warfare or terrorism is surely terrifying. Especially vexing is the fact that advances in molecular genetics and biotechnology have yielded a variety of new techniques that might, to varying degrees, incrementally remove specific obstacles to the development of potentially more usable biological weapons. To be sure, significant technological hurdles remain, and the Biological Weapons Convention codifies a legal and moral barrier that is widely respected worldwide. Although it is difficult to imagine that technological advances could diminish the universal horror associated with the use of disease as a weapon, however, these advances cannot be ignored to the extent that their application can theoretically eliminate some of the unpredictability of biological agents in open warfare.

Despite the fear that these technologies naturally engender, however, the reality of a unilateral, technologically based biodefense is highly problematic and will remain so for the foreseeable future. To be sure, troops can be protected, at least in a crisis, by well-designed protective gear and reliable detection and diagnostic methods that can help to identify and thereby avoid, and even contain, the presence of hazardous biological agents. But even though a dramatic increase in federally sponsored vaccine research is currently underway, it has been frequently pointed out that vaccines are useful only in the face of positive intelligence with respect to the nature of the hostile agent; similarly, treatment with drugs such as antibiotics is useful only for bacteria and only after the isolation and testing of the organism.

Ultimately, as a defense against terrorism or against any type of unknown biological agent used in a military or paramilitary scenario, genetic engineering offers little chance in the foreseeable future to create an effective biological defense, despite government posturing to the contrary. Thus any defensive BW program must carefully weigh its inherently limited efficacy against its very real potential for escalating qualitative proliferation in the biological arena. Domestic preparedness efforts and research into detector and diagnostic technology show some promise to ameliorate the worst impacts of a biological attack, but the inescapable fact is that civil defense remains an elusive goal now and in the foreseeable future. Furthermore, although the direct causal link is unclear, there is little question that a dramatically augmented biological defense research program threatens to erode global norms against the development and use of biological agents.

To be sure, the imbalance between offensive and defensive capabilities presents a difficult quandary. Nonetheless, the current inclination among U.S. policymakers to expand a defensive program is misguided. It is imperative that we be clear-eyed in our assessment of the efficacy of such biodefense efforts. Taking into account the myriad options available to a would-be attacker using biological agents, whether terrorist or state actor, in our view, the current unilateral, technologically mediated biological defense program underway in the United States places the nation on a perilous path that offers little hope of enhancing security.

As unsatisfying as it may seem to those who seek a unilateral, technological fix to the problem, nations and their civilian populations are best protected by upholding and strengthening the international regime that outlaws this heinous class of weapons, including a verification protocol to provide monitoring and inspection machinery for the Biological Weapons Convention. Especially in the current geopolitical climate, with the United States focusing on a serious and ongoing terrorist threat to its security, any steps that threaten to even slightly weaken or otherwise undermine this international regime are likely to prove ill-advised, however domestically appealing they may appear.

## NOTES

1. See Lawrence K. Altman and Gina Kolata, "Anthrax Missteps Offer Guide to Fight Next Bioterror Battle," *New York Times* (6 January 2002), 1.

2. As quoted by Laurie Garrett, "Countries Lose Out in Germ Terror Test," *Newsday* (22 February 1999), 4A.

3. United States, White House, Office of the Press Secretary, Fact Sheet: "Defending Against Biological Terrorism," 5 February 2002.

4. See Eliot Marshall, "Bioterror Defense Initiative Injects Shot of Cash," *Science* 283 (26 February 1999), 1234.

5. In one incident that drew controversy for its sensationalism, Defense Secretary William Cohen appeared on the ABC News program *Nightline* with a five-pound bag of sugar, warning viewers that a similar amount of anthrax could kill half the population of Washington, D.C., although scientists familiar with anthrax later showed that amount was considerably exaggerated. For an example of statements by HHS Secretary Donna Shalala, see Ellen Beck, "U.S. Vulnerable, Unprepared for Age of Germ Terrorism," *Biotechnology Newswatch* (15 March 1999), 4.

6. Testimony, United States Senate Foreign Relations Committee, *Hearings: The Worldwide Threat in 2000: Global Realities of Our National Security,* 22 March 2000.

7. See, for instance, Ashton Carter et al., "Catastrophic Terrorism," *Foreign Affairs* 77(6) (November/December 1998), 80–94.

8. Interview with Judith Miller and William J. Broad of *The New York Times,* 21 January 1999, *Weekly Compilation of Presidential Documents* 35(4) (1 February 1999), 109–55.

9. Judith Miller, Stephen Engelberg, and William Broad, *Germs: Biological Weapons and America's Secret War* (New York: Simon & Schuster, 2001), 167. See also Ken Alibek with Stephen Handelman, *Biohazard: The Chilling True Story of the Largest Covert Biological Weapons Program in the World-Told from the Inside by the Man Who Ran It* (New York: Random House, 1999); chapter 5.

10. Tom Mangold and Jeff Goldberg, *Plague Wars: A True Story of Biological Warfare* (New York: St. Martin's Press, 1999), 291; R. Jeffrey Smith, "Iraq's Drive for a Biological Arsenal," *Washington Post* (21 November 1997); United Nations Security Council, "Note by the Secretary General," S/1995/864, 11 October 1995; United Nations Security Council, "Note by the Secretary General," S/1996/848, 11 October 1996; chapter 11.

11. David Kaplan, "Aum Shinrikyo" in *Toxic Terror,* ed. J. Tucker (Cambridge, Mass.: MIT Press, 2000), 208–26.

12. See, for example, Harlee Strauss and Jonathan King, "The Fallacy of Defensive Biological Weapons Programmes," in *Biological and Toxin Weapons Today,* ed. E. Geissler (Oxford: Oxford University Press, 1986). As reviewed in the following discussion, this view to some extent informed the U.S. renunciation of its offensive biological weapons program in 1969.

13. This argument is discussed in somewhat greater detail in Richard Novick and Seth Shulman, "New Forms of Biological Weapons?" in *Preventing a Biological Arms Race,* ed. S. Wright (Cambridge, Mass.: MIT Press, 1990), 103–20.

14. See, for example, George W. Christopher et al., "Biological Warfare: A Historical Perspective," *Journal of the American Medical Association* 278(5) (6 August 1997), 415.

15. Statement on Chemical and Biological Defense Policies and Programs, 25

November 1969, in *Public Papers of the President of the United States: Richard Nixon, 1969* (Washington, D.C.: Government Printing Office, 1970), 968. As James Leonard, Assistant Director of the U.S. Arms Control and Disarmament Agency (ACDA) during the Nixon administration and the head of that administration's efforts to negotiate the terms of the Biological Weapons Convention with the Soviet Union, has put it: "I can't stress this enough. The U.S. military did not think there was any military use for biological weapons. This was their main reason for allowing the BW ban to go ahead" (quoted in Mangold and Goldberg, *Plague Wars*, 55).

16. Mangold and Goldberg lend some credence to each of these arguments in a brief chapter on the history of the Biological Weapons Convention. Regarding the second argument, they offer Nixon's speech writer, William Safire, quoting the president as follows: "If somebody uses germs on us, we'll nuke 'em." (61). In an interesting discussion in their notes, they cite an interview with Alan Neidle, James Leonard's deputy at ACDA during the Nixon years, in which he reviews the administration's consideration of the proliferation issue (402, note 26).

17. See John Parachini, "Federal Funding to Combat Terrorism, including defense against weapons of mass destruction FY 1998–2001"; available online at cns.miis.edu/research/cbw/terfund.htm, which offers detailed breakdowns of federal funds by category and agency. See also U.S. Department of Defense, Chemical and Biological Defense Program, *Annual Report to Congress* (Washington, D.C.: Government Printing Office, March 2000), Annex E, "DOD Joint Service Chemical and Biological (CB) Defense Program Funding Summary."

18. Steve Goldstein, "Combating Terrorism Becomes Growth Industry; Fear of Biological Weapons Fuels Rising Budgets," *Philadelphia Inquirer* (26 November 1999).

19. Parachini, "Federal Funding to Combat Terrorism."

20. Ibid. According to Parachini, funding for equipment for "first responders" across all agencies increased from $15.1 million in FY 1998 to $95.2 million in FY 2000, while training and exercises for "first responders" increased from $13.3 million in FY 1998 to $90.4 million in FY 2000.

21. Ibid.

22. See Eliot Marshall, "Bioterror Defense Initiative Injects Shot of Cash," *Science* 283(5406) (26 February 1999), 1234.

23. Department of Defense, *Annual Report to Congress*, Annex E.

24. Parachini, "Federal Funding to Combat Terrorism."

25. Miller, Engelberg, and Broad, *Germs*, 292–306.

26. U.S. White House, Office of the Press Secretary, Fact Sheet: "Defending Against Biological Terrorism," 5 February 2002.

27. Ibid.

28. William Broad and Judith Miller, "Thwarting Terror: Germ Defense Plan in Peril As Its Flaws Are Revealed," *New York Times* (7 August 1998), A1.

29. See U.S. National Security Decision Memorandum 35 (25 November 1969).

30. For an overview of funding and other issues in the Clinton administration's response, see Ricki Lewis, "Bioweapons Research Proliferates," *The Scientist* 12(9) (27 April 1998). See also USAMRIID website at www.usamriid.army.mil.

31. See, for instance, Seth Shulman, *Biohazard: How the Pentagon's Biological*

*Warfare Research Program Defeats Its Own Goals* (Washington, D.C.: Center for Public Integrity, 1993). See also U.S. General Accounting Office, *Combating Terrorism: Need for Comprehensive Threat and Risk Assessments of Chemical and Biological Attacks* (Washington, D.C.: General Accounting Office, 1999).

32. Miller, Engelberg, and Broad, *Germs,* 309.

33. See U.S. Department of Defense, Department of Defense FY 2001 Budget Estimates: Research, Development, Test and Evaluation, Defense-Wide Vol. 1: Defense Advanced Research Projects Agency (DARPA), February 2000; available online at www.darpa.mil. See also Defense Authorization Bill, Fiscal Year 1998, Report Language Overview, 26 June 1998.

34. Miller, Engelberg, and Broad, *Germs,* 308. See also Defense Advanced Research Projects Agency (DARPA), RDT&E Budget Item Justification Sheet (R-1 Item Nomenclature Biological Warfare Defense PE 0602383E, R-1 #15); available online at www.darpa.mil/body/pdf/DARPAFY2001BudgetEstimates.pdf.

35. DARPA, RDT&E Budget Item Justification Sheet, 75.

36. Ibid., 79.

37. Ibid., 78.

38. Ibid., 74.

39. See, for example, Tucker, *Toxic Terror.*

40. Discussion quoting Gilmore Panel in Anthony H. Cordesman, *Counterproliferation, Counterterrorism, and Homeland Defense: A Threat Analysis* (Washington, D.C.: Center for Strategic and International Studies, 12 June 2000).

41. Ibid.

42. Advisory Panel to Assess Domestic Response Capabilities for Terrorism Involving Weapons of Mass Destruction (Gilmore Panel), *Assessing the Threat,* First Annual Report to the President and the Congress (15 December 1999), 24.

43. See Cordesman, *Counterproliferation, Counterterrorism, and Homeland Defense.*

44. See David Kaplan, "Aum Shinrikyo (1995)," in Tucker, *Toxic Terror,* 217.

45. See, for instance, Al J. Venter, "Keeping the Lid on Germ Warfare," *International Defense Review* 31(5) (May 1998), 26.

46. John Von Radowitz, "Biological Weapons Warning: Genetic Spin-Off May Create Arms For 'Ethnic Cleansing,'" *Birmingham Post* (22 January 1999), 8; see Malcolm Dando and Vivienne Nathanson, *Biotechnology Weapons and Humanity,* Report by the British Medical Association, January 1999.

47. Malcolm Dando, "Technological Change and Future Biological Warfare," unpublished paper presented at a conference on "Biological Warfare and Disarmament: Problems, Perspectives, Possible Solutions," UNIDIR, Geneva, 5–8 July 1998.

48. Jonathan King, interview with Seth Shulman, January 2001.

49. Cordesman, *Counterproliferation, Counterterrorism, and Homeland Defense.*

50. See Novick and Shulman, "New Forms of Biological Weapons?"

51. Quoted in Paul Richter, "Experts Assess Risk of 'New Terrorism' Threat," *Los Angeles Times* (7 February 2000), A16.

52. Larry Johnson, as quoted on the *News Hour with Jim Lehrer,* broadcast on PBS 6 June 2000. Johnson, now a consultant, served in the State Department and the CIA Office of Counterterrorism during the Bush and Reagan administrations.

53. As quoted in Goldstein, "Combating Terrorism Becomes Growth Industry."

54. As quoted by William Broad and Judith Miller, "Thwarting Terror: Germ Defense Plan." For further arguments on this theme, see also Wright, *Preventing a Biological Arms Race*, chapters 4–6.

55. As quoted in Clive Cookson, "Deadly Concerns: The US Government Has Over-reacted to the Threat of Bioterrorism," *Financial Times* (London) (27 August 1999), 14.

56. Along these lines, Jonathan Tucker has noted that the Soviets rationalized their program by the need to counter so-called black budget programs in the United States. Interview with Laura Reed, February 2001.

57. DARPA, RDT&E Budget Item Justification Sheet, 74.

58. Interview with Miller and Broad, 21 January 1999.

59. Ibid.

60. George Lewis, Theodore A. Postol, and John Pike, "Why National Missile Defense Won't Work," *Scientific American* 281(2) (August 1999), 36–41.

61. Pamela Hess, "CIA: Many Countries Making Bio-weapons," *United Press International* (3 March 1999).

62. Bill Joy, "Why the Future Doesn't Need Us," *Wired* (April 2000), online: www.wired.com/wired/archive/8.04/joy.html.

63. Ibid.

# 4

# Defense against Biological Weapons

## Can Immunization and Secondary Prevention Succeed?

*Victor W. Sidel*

### PREVENTIVE MEASURES AGAINST
### THE CONSEQUENCES OF USE OF
### BIOLOGICAL WEAPONS

Those concerned with the promotion and protection of health classify preventive measures in two basic categories: primary prevention and secondary prevention. Primary prevention consists of measures to prevent the health consequences of an illness or injury by preventing its occurrence. Prevention of scurvy by adequate intake of vitamin C–containing foods, of smallpox by elimination of the virus in the ecosphere, and of lung cancer by measures to prevent smoking are examples of effective primary prevention. Secondary prevention consists of measures to prevent or minimize the health consequences of an illness or injury or the spread of an infectious disease to others after the disease process has begun. Examples are treatment of scurvy with vitamin C and of smallpox by antiviral agents, and prevention of the consequences of lung cancer by measures to detect it early in its course and to respond promptly to excise it or to arrest its growth. In general, primary prevention is more difficult to accomplish because the causes of the disease may be unknown and, when they are known, the preventive methods may be difficult technically or politically to implement. Since measures for primary prevention are usually more effective and rarely have negative consequences, they are generally considered preferable to secondary prevention even when implementation is difficult or expensive. Secondary prevention is usually easier to implement politically and technically but, since such methods are often ineffective or only partially effective, they may create a false sense of security and encourage risk-taking, are usually more expensive than primary prevention, and are more likely than primary prevention methods to have adverse consequences.

A preventive method that bridges these categories is immunization. An immunization that prevents the occurrence of or arrests the progression of an infectious disease may be used for either primary or secondary prevention. Immunization as a preventive measure is generally effective and inexpensive, but repeat immunization may be required. Immunization under rare special circumstances may in theory lead to the total eradication of the cause of a disease, as will be discussed in the section on smallpox, but immunization generally does not eradicate the causative organism in the ecosphere. Immunization may fail for several reasons. First, it may not be offered to or accepted by everyone who is exposed to the infectious agent. Second, individuals exposed may have underlying conditions, such as immune deficiency, that prevent the immunization from being fully effective. Third, immunization may not be effective against the specific type of infectious agent to which the population is exposed. Finally the dose of infectious agent to which an individual is exposed may be large enough to overcome the protection offered by the immunization.

Applying these definitions to the use of biological weapons, primary prevention is prevention of use of such weapons. Strict adherence to the Biological Weapons Convention (BWC), which prohibits their development, production, stockpiling, and transfer, is an example. Secondary prevention is prevention of the biological weapon from reaching its target or prevention or minimization of the health consequences after the human target has been infected. Secondary prevention methods against purposeful disease or injury, such as those caused by weapons of mass destruction (WMD), may provoke specific enemy responses. First, an enemy may respond by increasing the number of weapons in its stockpiles to overcome the defense or even use the weapons preemptively because of suspicion that the defensive method is part of an offensive program. Second, an enemy may change the nature of the weapons or the method of attack so as to avoid or overcome the defensive method. These responses to secondary prevention may be particularly relevant to biological weapons.

Secondary prevention of the consequences of use of biological weapons is analogous in many ways to the methods advocated to prevent or minimize the consequences of the use of nuclear weapons. The Strategic Defense Initiative ("Star Wars") proposals of the 1980s were said by their advocates to be purely defensive efforts, but they have been viewed by potential adversaries as part of preparation for a "first strike" and have led to even greater arms buildups. The Anti-Ballistic Missile (ABM) Treaty was negotiated in 1972 to outlaw the implementation of large-scale ABM systems.[1] The ABM treaty was abandoned by the United States in June 2002 to permit it to deploy a new anti-missile system that would violate or would require amendment of the treaty. The proposal had been rebuffed in the United Nations General Assembly, which voted 80 to 4 against, urging all countries to maintain and respect the treaty.[2] The vote reflected concern that abrogating the treaty, even in the name of defense, may rekindle and destabilize the nuclear arms race. For example, the People's Republic of China announced that a U.S. missile defense program would be viewed as a threat to China's national security and would lead to countermeasures, including building more nuclear missiles.[3]

As noted elsewhere in this book (see chapter 3), U.S. support for biological warfare (BW) activities, confined to defensive activities by President Nixon in 1969, began to increase steadily in the 1980s. This growth was justified by growing tensions between the two superpowers and U.S. suspicions that the former Soviet Union was pursuing an offensive BW program. Boris Yeltsin's acknowledgment of that program in 1992 and the uncovering of evidence of Iraq's offensive BW program in the 1990s provided further reinforcement for American concerns, which in turn were used to justify further increases in support for biological defense. But it was the government's preoccupation with "bioterrorism"—the use of biological agents by individuals or subnational groups to advance social or political goals—that produced an extraordinary increase in biological defense activities and support for them in the 1990s. Beginning in 1995, when President Clinton announced a new policy against "super-terrorism," funding for biological defense began to soar. In 1997, a $52.6 million Domestic Preparedness Program was authorized to develop emergency response teams in leading cities, with special training for police, fire, and public health officials for combating biological and chemical terrorism. In January 1998, President Clinton proposed further antiterrorism initiatives and asked Congress to authorize $10 billion, including $1.4 billion for protecting the civilian population against biological and chemical weapons. The proposals aimed to create and strengthen urban emergency response teams, protect government buildings, improve the nation's ability to detect and diagnose disease outbreaks, and increase national stockpiles of vaccines and antibiotics. In doing so, the administration initiated a new and close relationship between the public health and national security systems. As Secretary of Health and Human Services Donna Shalala told the press in 1999: "This is the first time in American history in which the public health system has been integrated directly into the national security system."[4]

In June 2000 the National Commission on Terrorism, created by Congress in 1998, recommended that the U.S. military rather than civilian agencies lead the response in the event of a terrorist attack in the United States, and that the U.S. government begin surveillance of foreign students in the United States. In December 2000, a panel chaired by James Gilmore, the governor of Virginia, urged president-elect Bush to bolster U.S. preparedness against terrorist threats by the creation of a new counterterrorism agency and by loosening restrictions on CIA agents that prevented them from recruiting confidential informants who have committed human rights abuses.[5] The failure of the CIA, the FBI, and police forces locally, nationally, and internationally to detect preparations for and to prevent the attacks on September 11 has been used as an argument to increase the funding for and the powers of these agencies, just as the dissemination of anthrax has been used as an argument to increase the funding for biological defense and antibioterrorism programs. However, the attacks on September 11 and the anthrax dissemination may instead be an argument for a reexamination of the efficacy and the rise of the accepted "defenses."

The purpose of this chapter is to examine the policy and ethical implications of the biological defense and antibioterrorism programs approved in the 1990s and reinforced in 2001 and, in particular, their implications for public health.

## POLICY AND ETHICAL ISSUES RAISED BY EXPANSION OF U.S. BIOLOGICAL DEFENSE PROGRAMS

When the U.S. Biological Defense Program began to expand far beyond its focus on protective clothing in the 1980s, several analysts examined closely the implications of developing specific medical defenses such as vaccines. These analyses were drawn in part from earlier analyses of the military itself.[6] Several general criticisms of prophylactic defenses emerged from these and later analyses.

1. *Development of defensive measures will always lag behind offensive measures.* Charles Piller and Keith Yamamoto[7] and Richard Novick and Seth Shulman[8] have elucidated the potential of genetic engineering techniques and other biogenetic technologies to produce new "designer" weaponry. Recent publications suggest that genetic engineering techniques have already been used, in the former USSR and now in Russia, and perhaps in other countries as well,[9] to produce modified agents that may be more useful as biological weapons because of their stability, ease of delivery, infectivity, resistance to defensive measures such as immunization, or resistance to treatment once infection or toxicity has occurred. Thus it is likely that a determined adversary could circumvent the protection provided by immuni-

zation or an effective response through diagnosis and treatment following an attack. Indeed, it is alleged that the former Soviet Union accomplished this for anthrax and other pathogens by developing strains of organisms that could defeat the American anthrax vaccine or treatment of diseases caused by biological agents used as weapons.

2. *Military forces can knowingly conduct research on offensive use of biological weapons under the cover of defensive research since offensive and defensive research are inextricably joined for at least some phases of the work.* It is widely understood by military establishments that defensive dimensions of BW research and development are closely intertwined with offensive dimensions.[10] For example, in the course of defensive research, it is possible (indeed probable, if military researchers are conscientiously working to explore forms of organisms against which defenses might be needed) that new forms of organisms may be found or developed that would be more effective as biological weapons.[11] Indeed, it is difficult to imagine testing medical defenses against organisms not ordinarily found in nature except by producing such organisms. Furthermore, military scientists might be tempted, ostensibly in the interest of defense, to go further in the study of more virulent or more stable or more easily disseminated organisms. A recent history of U.S. biological weapons programs provides additional evidence of the close relationship between offensive and defensive biological weapons programs.[12]

3. *Biological weapons research, even if truly defensive in intent, can be viewed by a potential military adversary as an attempt to develop protection for a nation's military forces against an organism that the nation itself might wish to use for offensive purposes, thus permitting the nation to protect its own personnel in a biological first strike.* Although military researchers in a particular country may deny interest in offensive development, given the secrecy surrounding biological warfare activities, it is generally impossible for other states to assess such claims. A nation secretly preparing a stockpile of biological weapons for use in war (whether intended as deterrence, retaliation, or first use) would be likely to prepare vaccines and other defensive measures to protect its own troops and population. Indeed, the reason military leaders are likely to give for the preparation of any form of altered bacilli or viruses, to present the appearance of compliance with the BWC, is that these organisms are needed for preparation of defenses. However, particularly given the secrecy that shrouds BW activities, it may be impossible for adversaries to determine whether a nation's defensive efforts are part of preparations for offensive use of biological weapons or not.[13]

Even if BW research is relatively open, other nations may view with suspicion the intense interest of the U.S. military establishments (in contrast to civilian medical researchers) in vaccines or treatment against specific organisms, particularly organisms that are not found in nature or that cause few problems unless purposely spread. Similarly, the present program to build more high-containment facilities suitable for work with lethal pathogens may rekindle an arms race in BW agents.

Such fears about U.S. biological defense activities, as well as concern about defensive programs in other nations, could well feed a continuing arms race in the development of novel biological weapons. Just as the U.S. Army supported its requests for appropriation of funds in this area by citing suspicions and possible exaggerations of what others are doing, so the armies of other countries have tried to maximize their resources by casting not-unreasonable suspicions on the activities of the United States and its allies. In Japan it was Dr. Ishii Shiro's 1930 report, almost certainly untrue but unfortunately very plausible, that the most powerful Western countries were secretly studying biological weapons that led to Japan's embrace of biological weapons research and eventual use of such weapons.[14] Similarly, the former Soviet Union's BW program was maintained and expanded after the entry into force of the Biological Weapons Convention (BWC) because of suspicions that the United States was maintaining research on offensive weapons.[15] The public release in May 2001 of a recommendation by a Bush administration review panel that the United States not accept the draft agreement to strengthen the enforcement of the BWC[16] lends new credence to suspicions that the United States continues to work on offensive biological weapons under the cover of defensive research.

4. *The threat of biological weapons and of bioterrorism has been exaggerated.* The threat of bioterrorism, and probably of biological weapons in general, has been consistently exaggerated. This exaggeration has increased since the attacks of September 11 and the subsequent dissemination of anthrax through the U.S. postal system. Since there was no evidence of any use of biological weapons in the September 11 attacks and since the dissemination of anthrax caused a total of five deaths and a total of fewer than twenty cases of human anthrax, questions must be raised about the purpose of the exaggeration, which may be the expectation of gain in wealth, prestige, or power from policies that constitute a response to hyperbolic statements of the threat. Bioterrorism, for example, has been presented as a major threat to public health. Statements of some public officials and media imply that bioterrorism incidents have done serious damage and have increased dramatically in recent years.[17] Presentations on the topic generally open with "scenarios," fictional accounts of what "could" happen. At a recent annual meeting of the American Public Health Association, a panelist warned the audience that a hypothetical terrorist might at that moment be spreading deadly smallpox virus into the air, while in a companion video prepared by the Centers for Disease Control a shadowy fictional terrorist was shown with a parcel of deadly biological agents that could kill thousands or even millions.[18] In 1998, Secretary of Defense William Cohen held

up a five-pound bag of sugar on a national television broadcast and declared that if the sugar were anthrax, the organisms could kill half the population of Washington, D.C.

Presentations like these are designed to capture attention but contribute little to reasonable assessments of risk.[19] In fact, to date, documented examples of bioterrorism have been rare and have caused relatively few casualties compared with cases of terrorism involving explosives. Only one incident has occurred in the United States. In 1984 in Oregon a religious cult allegedly contaminated several salad bars with *Salmonella,* resulting in numerous cases of gastrointestinal illness but no deaths.[20] Outside the United States the well-financed Japanese religious cult, Aum Shinrikyo, used a nerve agent, sarin, that killed seven people in a Tokyo suburb, Matsumoto, in 1994 and used it again in 1995 in a Tokyo subway, killing twelve people and injuring a number of others.[21] The Aum also attempted to develop biological weapons but was unsuccessful despite years of preparation.[22] Although presentations about bioterrorism in the media, at conferences, and by government officials repeatedly refer to these episodes as "examples," they are the total sum of documented cases.

To make a reasonable estimate of the risk of a terrorist attack using biological weapons, it is useful to distinguish between very different types of potential incidents. The most frightening is the use of biological agents in a manner that would cause huge devastation and tens of thousands or even millions of casualties. Weapons using biological agents that could cause catastrophic casualties are extremely difficult to produce and still harder to deploy. Only nation-states with large military, scientific, and technical capacity may have the ability to carry out such an attack. International treaties and conventions prohibiting chemical and biological weapons proliferation and use would bring universal condemnation even from those who might otherwise sympathize with the cause. (Similar calculations apply to chemical weapons.)

As distinct from catastrophic events, smaller-scale incidents—similar to those that occurred in Japan or Oregon—could reasonably be considered within the capabilities of organizations or individuals. But it appears unreasonable to expect that terrorist organizations, in secret and without government support, could develop a capacity that only a limited number of nation-states have had the resources to acquire. Governments are unlikely to allow even allied political organizations access to weaponry that the governments themselves would not use because of fear of opprobrium or retaliation. Religious cults or doomsday fanatics that might use such weapons would not be expected to get any type of state assistance.[23] Furthermore, weaponization of chemical and biological agents is difficult and dangerous, and would-be weaponizers may be more likely to harm themselves rather than others.[24]

To demonstrate that the risk of bioterrorism is substantial and rising, some officials count "attempts" or "threats" of the use of biological or chemical agents as incidents.[25] Indeed, the number of anthrax hoaxes has climbed substantially in the last two years.[26] Authorities have responded to such hoaxes with emergency response teams that have caused enormous disruptions at substantial cost. But the increased number of hoaxes does not constitute evidence of increased risk of real incidents. Such phenomena are rather evidence of increased risk of hoaxes. The costs of these hoaxes may simply be adverse outcomes of the campaign against bioterrorism, since the scare scenarios and the extraordinary speculation about alleged dangers of bioterrorism have given such hoaxes a credibility they would not have received even a few years ago.

In conclusion, claims of "catastrophic bioterrorism" are unnecessarily alarmist, and alarmist claims bring their own costs. Although the risks of bioterrorism cannot be simply dismissed, neither should they be exaggerated.[27]

5. *Resources are being diverted from needed public health services.* Allocation of public funds for social well-being and for public health programs—which are essential to the health of the people of the United States and of the world—should not be a zero-sum game. But even in rich nations like the United States priority setting for public resource allocation among many urgent needs is usually required. The funds so far allocated to antibioterrorism projects may be small compared to the huge military budget of the United States, and even compared to the desperately underfunded public health and social welfare budgets of the United States and the world, but investment of these funds in programs to improve the education, nutrition, housing, and other measures for disease prevention for the world's peoples is needed. Such public health investment is also likely to be far more useful for prevention of health consequences if chemical or biological agents were ever used than are the specific secondary prevention measures being proposed.

The public health burden of the few dramatic and deplorable known incidents of bioterrorism pale in comparison with those of "ordinary" diseases and accidents. In the United States alone there are an estimated 76 million food-borne illnesses each year, with 325,000 hospitalizations and 5,000 deaths.[28] Each year in the United States there are approximately 60,000 chemical spills, leaks, and explosions, of which about 8,000 are considered "serious," with more than 300 deaths.[29]

Abroad, the need for increased support for public health is far more urgent. In India during 1999 there were two million new cases of tuberculosis, causing about 450,000 deaths. Effective treatment for tuberculosis in India costs about $15 U.S. per person treated. An investment of $30 million annually for a few years, compared to the current U.S. contribution to India of $1 million for this purpose, could virtually wipe out the disease and—by saving the lives of young people, who are frequent victims of the disease— could also be effective in combating poverty in India.[30] It is estimated by the United Nations that $10 billion invested in safe water supplies could cut by up to one-third the current four billion cases of diarrhea worldwide that result in 2.2 million annual deaths.[31] The billions of dollars committed to combating the so-far unrealized threats of bioterrorism could be used far more effectively to treat the very real threats of disease in other countries, especially developing countries.

6. *Preventive measures may be ineffective or dangerous.* Fear of bioterrorism may prevent activities or disclosure of information useful for protecting public health. With respect to hazardous industrial chemical sites, the U.S. Environmental Protection Agency, for example, has announced plans to limit public disclosure mandated by the Clean Air Act.[32] The policy change is claimed to address concerns that terrorists could use such information to attack the sites. It may be equally likely that the corporations that own these sites have lobbied for the policy change to prevent disclosures for commercial reasons and that antiterrorism has become a convenient excuse for dysfunctional secrecy. Similar secrecy might be applied in the future to hazardous biological sites.

A further new and dangerous effect of the bioterrorism initiative is the expansion of research facilities that study potential biological and chemical warfare agents. Known as Level IV facilities, highly lethal agents such as smallpox and ebola virus can be stored and studied in them. Until recently, such activities were known to have taken place at a Centers for Disease Control and Prevention (CDC) facility in Atlanta and at the U.S. Army's facility at Fort Detrick, Maryland. Under the new program, the public was informed that Plum Island, a Department of Agriculture laboratory on the edge of the New York metropolitan, area is being "upgraded" to Level IV, and an unknown number of other facilities are also being opened.[33] It is not impossible that these facilities may be used by researchers, with the best of "defensive" intentions, to attempt to genetically engineer new BW agents to evaluate their potential risk and to develop countermeasures.

These facilities pose other serious dangers. They are not immune to accidents and leaks either at the facilities themselves or during the transport of pathogens. Worldwide experiences with presumably fail-safe facilities such as nuclear power plants should remind us that accidents can and do happen. Increasing the number of Level IV facilities will tend to increase the chance that an accident could occur. The chance of an accident may be remote but may be more likely than the threat against which these facilities are designed to prepare.

7. *The benefit to public health programs of the "dual use" of antibioter-*

*rorism funding may be exaggerated.* Supporters of antibioterrorism programs have argued that they will make significantly more money and expertise available for medical and public health infrastructures, a so-called dual use of the funding.[34] However, spending patterns so far suggest that the programs will be dominated by military spending, with little left for meaningful health programs. Of the $10 billion allocated by the U.S. federal budget for fiscal year 2000 for the antiterrorism campaign, about $7 billion was allocated to the U.S. Department of Defense. Of the remainder, some $1.5 billion was earmarked specifically for nuclear, chemical, and biological antiterrorism programs.[35] Some funds would indeed support useful functions like basic surveillance of the incidence of infectious disease and computerization of essential public health data. But these funds do not necessarily represent new public health investment. An examination of FY 1999 budget proposals for the National Institutes of Health (NIH) suggests that "each institute's request level was reduced in order to pay for a new research initiative to combat bio-terrorism."[36] The 2003 budget submitted to Congress by the Bush administration in February 2002 proposed a major increase in spending to defend against bioterrorism but substantial cuts in the funding for other public health programs such as preventing chronic diseases and birth defects and controlling infectious diseases. Excluding funding for bioterrorism defense, the CDC would be cut by $340 million under the Bush administration proposal, bringing its nonbioterrorism budget to about $4.1 billion, down from more than $4.4 billion in 2002.[37]

8. *The risks of associating public health programs with military, intelligence, and law enforcement programs have been inadequately discussed.* The Clinton administration's call for the integration of the public health system into the national security system and its continuation under Bush raises fears that the goals of public health agencies will be subordinated to, or at least confused with, military, intelligence, and law enforcement objectives. Subordination of public health planning to military and police direction is already taking place. Many metropolitan areas are conducting emergency maneuvers in preparation for unconventional attacks and consequently stretching already limited municipal resources dedicated to public health and welfare. Military, intelligence, and law enforcement agencies and personnel have long histories of secrecy and deception that are contrary to fundamental public health principles of transparency and truthfulness. They may therefore be unsuitable partners for public health agencies that need to justify receiving the public's trust. The result of such partnerships in planning may be public cynicism and resistance to legitimate public health measures.

The U.S. Department of Defense has a long history of failure to adhere to public health principles. A recent example is the DoD's failure to obtain informed consent for the experimental use of the substance pyridostigmine bromide, even after being required to do so by the Food and Drug Administration.[38] American troops were ordered to take pyridostigmine bromide as possible protection against the nerve agent soman. A DoD-sponsored Rand Corporation study has reported that pyridostigmine bromide cannot be excluded as a potential factor in Gulf War Syndrome.[39] Although there was evidence that Iraq had used chemical weapons in the Iran–Iraq War and suspicion that Iraq possessed the agent sarin, no one believed Iraq had soman. Nonetheless an agent that was experimental even for protection against soman was used, with no evidence of actual use of any nerve agents and with no evidence of efficacy against nerve agents that might have been used, and no evidence for safety in widespread use under these conditions. Tens of thousands of cases of serious illness among Gulf War veterans may have resulted. In addition, the DoD also failed to keep adequate records of immunization of troops in the Gulf and in Bosnia and has since insisted, in the face of criticism from public health professionals[40] and from Congress, on maintaining its ill-considered mandatory Anthrax Vaccine Immunization Program.

Law enforcement agencies are no better partners for public health. Recently released information provides details about the FBI's "disinformation" campaign, through a double agent, Joseph Cassidy, to convince the USSR that the United States had developed a new chemical weapon called GJ. The object was to spur Soviet investment in trying to produce agents that the United States had been unable to produce. The ruse apparently backfired: The Soviets were able to produce a usable, much more toxic, and highly effective nerve agent called Novichok.[41] In another FBI-conducted clandestine operation a double agent named Dmitri Polyakov was used to convey information that the United States was undertaking a secret biological weapons program despite President Nixon's renunciation of biological weapons in 1969 and the U.S. signing of the BWC in 1972. It is now clear that in 1973, in part as a result of the disinformation campaign, the Soviets intensified the program for research and development of biological weapons. The results of these campaigns were summarized in the *Bulletin of the Atomic Scientists* in September 2000:

> [T]he U.S. disinformation and deception operations of the 1960s and 1970s, designed to stimulate Soviet interest and investment in CBW, were only too successful, leading to the development of effective chemical and biological munitions.

This is a disastrous outcome. Although there is little danger of Russia (or the United States) using CBW, there is the new danger that remnants of the vast U.S.-encouraged Soviet program may end up in "rogue states" or even in the hands of freelance terrorists.[42]

The FBI's deceptions in these areas and their provocative actions in others is evidence that the FBI is an unreliable and dangerous partner for public health, which must depend on the public's perception that truth will be told about health hazards.

Similarly, municipal police forces in many cities, including New York City and Los Angeles, are with good reason viewed with deep suspicion by the poor, immigrant, and nonwhite populations. Subordination of public health planning to military and police direction is already taking place, with many metropolitan areas conducting emergency maneuvers in preparation for unconventional attacks, with consequences that include the stretching of already limited municipal resources dedicated to public health and welfare.[43]

## VACCINES AS MAJOR COMPONENTS
## OF BIOLOGICAL DEFENSE

Much of the defensive work on biological agents supported by the United States has concentrated on vaccines. The word "vaccines" is used to denote a class of measures, including antibacterial and antiviral vaccines and toxoids and antitoxins, that are used to block infection by an organism or the toxic effects of a toxin in advance of or shortly after an organism or toxin has entered the body of the victim. "Vaccines" as defined in this chapter differ from "barriers," which attempt to keep the organism or toxic agent from reaching the body, and from "treatment" by antibacterial, antiviral, antifungal, or other agents that attempt to treat the infection after it is established. At first glance, vaccines appear to offer promise for defense against certain biological agents. If the biological agent or toxin that will be used to cause a harmful effect is known in advance, if a vaccine known to block the infection or toxicity is available, and if the cost of use of the vaccine in economic or health terms is reasonable, there would appear to be little argument about the defensive benefits of use of the vaccine.

However, major problems occur when the uncertainties involved in military calculations are examined. The precise nature of the biological agent or toxin that will be used, or if one will be used at all, is unlikely to be known with certainty in advance. Even if the agent is known in advance, the efficacy of a vaccine is rarely known in advance because of the difficulty of testing it adequately and because of the unpredictability of variables such as levels of exposure and the condition of the victims at the time of the attack. The cost of the vaccine in economic terms may be known, but the adverse health effects or adverse collateral effects of the use of the vaccine are likely to be largely unknown. Two examples of vaccines—one known in the past to be extremely effective and safe and one for which efficacy and safety have been questioned—will illustrate the problems posed by a defense strategy based on vaccines.

## Immunization against Smallpox

An excellent example of a vaccine that has been widely tested and is known to be effective against a strain of virus that might be used in a BW attack is vaccinia, the organism from which the word vaccine is derived. After an extraordinary international effort to effect the global eradication of smallpox, led by Donald Henderson, now the Dean Emeritus of the School of Hygiene and Public Health at Johns Hopkins University, the last known outbreak of smallpox occurred in Somalia in 1977, and smallpox was declared eradicated by the World Health Organization in 1980. At a major international meeting on emerging and reemerging infections held in Atlanta, Georgia, in March 1998, according to a report in the *Journal of the American Medical Association*,[44] Henderson discussed the use of smallpox vaccination in the face of the threat of the use of smallpox as a weapon in war or in an attack by terrorists. Henderson said the virus could once again devastate human populations if it were used as a weapon. He reminded his audience that the virus had in the past killed between 25 and 30 percent of unvaccinated victims, and he estimated that no more than 10 to 20 percent of the U.S. population have significant residual smallpox immunity.

Estimating that the United States has only some fifteen million doses of smallpox virus in reserve, Henderson warned that this supply would be quickly exhausted in the face of an outbreak and it would take many months to produce new stocks. He advocated the training of physicians and other medical personnel to recognize the effects of smallpox and of other potential BW agents and the preparation of stockpiles of vaccines and drugs to meet the emerging threat, noting that a national or international response would be needed for a large-scale attack. Preparation for such threats would require an improved capacity for surveillance at local, state, and international levels; stocking of vaccines and drugs; more effective diagnostic tools; and health care workers trained to promptly diagnose and contain an outbreak.

The threat of smallpox as a biological weapon gained credibility in 1998 when former Soviet biological weapons scientist Ken Alibek alleged that the Soviet Union had reproduced "scores of tons" of smallpox and plague viruses and had stockpiled "hundreds of tons" of anthrax organisms.[45] He also alleged that both smallpox, as well as anthrax, had been weaponized. Other informants reported that the Russians had developed vaccine-resistant strains of smallpox and tested them on prisoners.[46] Alibek's chilling response to a query on what he would use as a biological weapon was, "I'd use anthrax mixed with smallpox."[47] Although questions have been

raised about some aspects of Alibek's credibility, his allegations have clearly
had an important influence on biological defense policy.

No credible expert is currently advocating immunization of military
forces or civilian populations with vaccinia. Experts argue only that stockpiles of vaccine against smallpox be prepared. Such stockpiles would then
be available if an attack with smallpox virus was unleashed. These proposals fail to recognize the diversion of resources they require or the fact that
unused stockpiles may become outdated and useless. More important, they
ignore the contention that a genetically altered smallpox virus might overcome the vaccine. They also ignore the argument that preparation of stocks
of vaccine against the currently known strain of smallpox vaccine might
cause a potential bioweaponeer to engineer new strains of smallpox virus.
In addition, they ignore the risk of cases of generalized vaccinia following
vaccination and the progress being made in the development of antiviral
agents that might be used for treatment of smallpox.

Furthermore, those who call for production by the United States or its
allies of massive new stockpiles of vaccine against smallpox ignore the argument that another nation might be fearful that a potential aggressor nation
was preparing stockpiles of vaccine against a disease known to have been
eliminated from Earth to use it as a biological weapon itself. Such fears may
be magnified by the U.S. decision not to destroy its stock of smallpox virus,
which it had planned to destroy in accordance with requests by the World
Health Organization, the American Public Health Association, and other
groups.[48] In September 2001, the Centers for Disease Control and Prevention awarded a $343 million contract to a British company for forty million
doses of smallpox vaccine.[49] In July 2002, the U.S. government approved
vaccination of 500,000 "first responders." In view of the hazards involved
in diversionary and expensive preparation for a largely unsubstantiated
threat of attack by smallpox virus, the argument that "doing something is
better than doing nothing" may actually be counterproductive and hazardous.

## Immunization against Anthrax

In contrast to the anti-smallpox vaccine, which has worked effectively for
two centuries to protect those to whom it has been given, the vaccine being
used to protect against inhalation anthrax has not been proven to provide
reliable protection against it. Nonetheless, the U.S. Department of Defense
used that vaccine for immunization of some 150,000 U.S. troops in the Persian Gulf War and in 1997 announced that it would be required for all 2.4
million active duty military personnel and reservists.[50] As of December 7,
2000, almost two million individual doses had been administered to almost

500,000 active and reserve service members.[51] The efficacy, safety, and advisability of the program have all been questioned.

## Efficacy of the Anthrax Vaccine

The current vaccine, first tested in the early 1960s and approved for use to prevent cutaneous anthrax by the U.S. Food and Drug Administration (FDA) in 1970, two years before efficacy data were required for licensing, has only been clearly demonstrated effective against cutaneous anthrax. There is insufficient human evidence to believe that the current vaccine will be effective in protecting troops against airborne infection with anthrax, the pathway that would most likely be used by biological weapons. The only published human efficacy trial of an anthrax vaccine was a study in the late 1950s and early 1960s in a mill that processed raw imported goat hair contaminated with *Bacillus anthracis* and in which clinical anthrax infections occurred.[52] The vaccine was shown to provide some protection against cutaneous anthrax, but the number of cases of inhalation anthrax was not sufficiently large to reach definite conclusions about the efficacy of the vaccine in preventing inhalation anthrax. Testing of the vaccine by purposeful exposure of humans to inhalation anthrax would clearly be unethical. Trials with monkeys and guinea pigs have yielded contradictory results.[53] After reviewing the test data in 1994, the Senate Veterans' Affairs Committee concluded that "the vaccine should be considered investigational when used as a protection against [biological weapons]."[54]

Even if this particular strain of anthrax were shown to be effective, as later tests on monkeys were claimed to show,[55] there is still the question of whether the efficacy of *any* vaccine can be assumed for battlefield conditions, given the possibility that an adversary could either use a different strain or genetically engineer a new one. The anthrax case is particularly poignant since it is known that both of these possibilities already exist. There are several known strains of anthrax, and it is possible that a specific vaccine may not protect against the one that might be used. Furthermore, a particularly troubling use of genetic engineering—the alteration of biological agents to overcome the protection provided by vaccines or antibiotics— has been recognized for some time. Researchers in Russia disclosed in the British journal *Vaccine* in 1997 that they had genetically engineered a strain of anthrax that uses genes from *Bacillus cereus*. The new strain is apparently able to overcome the protection offered by the Russian anthrax vaccine and it is therefore likely to be able to overcome the protection offered by the Michigan Biologic Products Institute (MBPI) vaccine.[56] Recent analysis of tissue specimens from the bodies of victims of an explosion of a bioweapons factory in Sverdlovsk in the former Soviet Union in 1979 indicated that DNA sequences from four different strains of anthrax were present. It is possible that these strains may have been selected to overcome the protection offered by vaccines against anthrax.[57] Such evidence would seem to support claims that the former Soviet Union had developed genetically altered strains of anthrax to circumvent the use of vaccines against them.[58]

If so, the available evidence on anthrax underscores the claim that *no* vaccine against the organism can be claimed to be effective on the battlefield. As the Deputy Director for Science and Public Health of the CDC concluded in 1998: "Although the current anthrax vaccine has been shown to be effective in preventing the cutaneous form of anthrax, CDC is neither aware of definitive data that demonstrates the vaccine's ability to protect against the inhalation form of this disease in humans, nor are we aware of any data relative to the efficacy of this vaccine in humans exposed to genetically-altered *Bacillus anthracis* strains."[59]

## Safety of the Anthrax Vaccine

The possible risks of inoculating military personnel against anthrax are still largely unknown. The only previous experience with inoculation of large numbers of people with the anthrax vaccine was its use on some 150,000 troops during the Persian Gulf War, but the records of adverse events during this use have never been released. Both the Presidential Advisory Committee on Gulf War Veterans' Illnesses and the House Committee on Government Reform and Oversight were sharply critical of the failure to maintain adequate records. As the House Committee concluded: "DOD failure to adhere to record-keeping requirements should result in the presumption of service connection for any subsequent illness to service personnel to whom the drug . . . was administered."[60]

Furthermore, there were indications that the vaccine being used may have important defects. Inspections by the U.S. Food and Drug Administration of the supplier, the MBPI (which since its sale in 1998 to a consortium of private investors headed by Admiral William J. Crowe, a former chairman of the U.S. Joint Chiefs of Staff, has been known as the BioPort Corporation) revealed contamination of the vaccine, reuse of outdated vaccines, and relabeling of lots that originally failed in order to place them in use. These safety problems caused the FDA to halt production in December 1999.[61] Permission to resume production was granted by the FDA in February 2002 with the condition that the vaccine must carry a warning of rare severe side effects and of unconfirmed reports of causing birth defects.[62]

More than 1,500 Vaccine Adverse Event Reporting System (VAERS) reports have been submitted reporting reactions to the vaccine, with at least two hundred reactions described as "fatal, life-threatening, or resulting in hospitalization or permanent disability."[63] Furthermore, passive reporting systems often result in major underreporting of adverse reactions, whereas active reporting systems are likely to provide much more complete and accurate data. In a study at an airbase in Dover, Delaware, for example, it was found that only 20 percent of personnel with probable systemic reactions had actually filed VAERS reports.[64]

## Advisability of the Anthrax Immunization Program

The Governing Council of the American Public Health Association at its meeting in 1999 adopted a policy statement urging the Department of Defense "to delay any further immunization against anthrax using the current vaccine or at least to make the immunization voluntary." A congressional subcommittee investigation concluded in 2000 that the anthrax vaccination program was "a well-intentioned but overwrought response to the threat of anthrax as a biological weapon."[65] A report from the CDC Advisory Committee on Immunization Practices in December 2000 recommended routine use of the current vaccine only for persons engaged (1) in work involving production quantities or concentrations of *B. anthracis* cultures and (2) in activities with a high potential for aerosol production. It is of interest that the report does not comment at all on military use of the vaccine.[66]

Informed consent for use of the vaccine was not obtained from military personnel who received the vaccine even though its use for protection against inhalation anthrax has not been approved by the FDA and it should have been considered an investigational agent.[67] A recent detailed analysis of the approval status of the current vaccine by two judge advocate generals in the Air Force Reserve also argues that the vaccine should have been viewed as an investigational drug and that informed consent should have been obtained from each recipient.

Troops in a war zone face a more general danger against which vaccines provide no protection. If a vaccine is considered effective but actually provides little or no protection against a novel strain or high concentration of a biological agent, troops may be exposed to biological hazards that might have been avoided if a misleading impression of protection had not been generated. Furthermore, the troops themselves, with an illusion of protection, may take risks that they would otherwise avoid.

Concern about the safety of the current vaccine has caused a large number of military personnel to refuse inoculation with the current vaccine even though refusal has in many cases led to disciplinary action for disobedience of military orders to adhere to the U.S. Anthrax Vaccine Immunization Program. It is estimated that at least 450 military personnel have refused, although the number has never been publicly acknowledged.[68] Some refusers have been discharged under "less-than-honorable" conditions. The recent court-martial conviction of a U.S. Air Force physician for his refusal to take the vaccine is an example of military punishment of a knowledgeable and principled action in opposition to the program.[69]

## The Impact of Immunization on Control of Biological Weapons

Beyond the issues of the safety and efficacy of specific vaccines for military purposes, there is the question of their long-term impact on the control of biological weapons. As noted previously in this chapter, research and development for defenses against biological weaponry are highly ambiguous activities, and their pursuit may mislead other nations, particularly if they are conducted under conditions of high secrecy. The journalist Seymour Hersh reported in 1998 that one of the reasons the U.S. military became concerned about the use of anthrax in the Persian Gulf was the discovery that Iraqi soldiers captured in an American covert operation had immunity to anthrax. As Hersh comments: "Military planning had to assume the worst-case scenario—that Iraq was planning a BW attack."[70]

In the case of Iraq, later evidence showed that U.S. concern that the Iraqi military had weaponized biological agents was justified (see chapter11). But Pentagon preparations to vaccinate U.S. troops might engender precisely the same concerns with respect to U.S. intentions. In a world in which many nations are prepared to believe the worst about the military policies of other nations, information about immunization of the armed forces of a potential enemy may lead to destabilizing suspicions and unnecessary, costly, and risky countermeasures to possible bioattack. Action by the United States to immunize its troops might cause other countries to develop BW defenses, thereby sending ambiguous signals about their own intentions; even worse, immunization of American troops might provoke other states to develop biological weapons designed to overcome the protection provided to American troops, thereby initiating a dangerous biological weapons race.

## CONCLUSION

Effective defense against the potential threat of biological weapons must include several elements. Primary prevention against the use of these weapons, by strengthening the BWC and enforcing it effectively, is of course the only truly effective defense.[71] Negotiating a strong protocol to ensure compliance with the BWC would have contributed to this goal. Unfortunately, during the negotiations in the 1990s, the United States, Russia, and other major states pressed for provisions that were advantageous to them but weakened the regime as a whole (see chapter 13). Furthermore, in July 2001, the United States rejected the protocol entirely, on the grounds that it needed to shield its pharmaceutical industry and military from inspections and, ironically, that the protocol would be too weak to detect cheating.[72] At the fifth BWC review conference in December 2001, the Bush administration went further, moving to terminate further negotiations entirely, thereby effectively suspending the negotiations for at least a year, until the parties decide on a response to this move to scuttle any multilateral machinery to verify BWC compliance.[73]

The BWC has also been weakened in recent years by research undertaken in the United States, Russia, the United Kingdom, and a few other industrialized countries to explore the properties of genetically altered pathogens. Researchers at St. Mary's School of Medicine in London, for example, created a potentially lethal hybrid virus from hepatitis C and dengue virus in the course of work aimed at a vaccine against hepatitis.[74] Evidence has also been disclosed that the United States has attempted to produce a genetically engineered form of anthrax that resists the protection provided by a vaccine.[75] An essential approach to strengthening the BWC is to prohibit development of novel biological agents that do not have a peaceful purpose as their unambiguous justification, even if these activities are promoted for defense.

Beyond these measures, a strong political commitment to abolition of *all* weapons of mass destruction is needed to overcome resistance to a truly effective BWC. So long as the nuclear powers fail to recognize their obligations under the Nuclear Non-Proliferation Treaty, recently reinforced by a unanimous decision by the International Court of Justice, to move toward the elimination of nuclear weapons, biological and chemical weapons are likely to remain a threat, given the tendency of virtually all states to respond to perceived threats by relying on deterrence. If the United States wishes to protect its people against biological weapons, the best method would be to join in negotiating a Nuclear Weapons Convention and, in accordance with it, to dismantle the U.S. nuclear capability. Only then can the United States effectively argue that other nations should give up their weapons of indiscriminate mass destruction and only then will the world, and the United States and its troops, approach effective protection against biological weapons.

There is an essential role for civil society in this effort. Civil society organizations and individuals must advocate strengthening the BWC and its strict enforcement. Most governments are too constrained to exert decisive leadership by history, by international agreement, or by other priorities imposed by an uneducated electorate or by officials unwilling to adopt new modes of assuring disarmament or new ways of achieving peaceful resolution of conflict. Civil society can help provide that leadership. In addition, research organizations, professional societies, and individual scientists should pledge not to engage knowingly in research or teaching that furthers the development and use of BW agents.

If secondary prevention is needed, the most effective action, many public health experts agree, would be protection of all people of the world by raising their resistance against all serious infectious diseases, not just diseases caused intentionally. General secondary preventive methods provided by public health measures such as adequate nutrition and access to a safe water supply may protect the body's ability to defend itself against the onslaught of infections. Biological weapons may have as their goal overcoming the body's general resistance to infectious diseases as well as overcoming the specific protection offered by immunization. Use of antibiotics and other treatments of those infected can reduce morbidity and mortality but are usually less effective than prevention.

Immunization programs will indeed play an important role in this effort. As an example, it is possible for measles to be eliminated entirely from the world, but one million people needlessly die annually of this disease. The World Health Organization has estimated that routine immunization of infants reached a level of 80 percent in 1990 and has remained at that level although child health officials have set a goal of 90 percent immunization by the year 2000. As another example, an epidemic of meningitis began in West Africa in the mid-1990s, affecting Chad, Mali, Niger, Nigeria, and other countries, and has resulted in 300,000 cases, many with complications such as deafness, mental retardation, and death. A minimum of seven million doses of vaccine will be needed over the coming months to respond to the epidemic, but current stockpiles are about one million doses short of the needed amount. However, public health measures are just as essential for countering disease as immunization. This is as true for intentionally caused disease as for naturally caused disease.

As part of this effort, industrialized countries should enable developing countries to build capacity for detection, diagnosis, and treatment of all disease by providing technical information and needed resources. Article X of the Biological Weapons Convention, encouraging the exchange of information and materials for peaceful purposes, must be strengthened. In particular, nations that are in compliance with the BWC should receive equal treatment with respect to trade in the agents and equipment covered by the BWC.

Under extraordinary circumstances, such as a BW attack that has already occurred or is credibly imminent, short-term use of secondary prevention methods such as barriers or stockpiling of antibiotics to which the pathogen is known to be sensitive, or of immunization against the specific pathogen, may be justified. Although the United Nations Charter under Article 51 permits self-defense by an individual nation or a group of nations, when time permits there would be long-term benefit to the calling of enforcement action by a UN force authorized by the UN Security Council under Article 42. Such emergency actions do not negate the arguments against secondary prevention and "preventive" immunization given in this chapter; on the contrary, they reinforce the need to avoid such "defensive measures" unless they are indisputably needed.

## NOTES

1. Treaty between the United States of America and the Union of Soviet Socialist Republics on the Limitation of Anti-ballistic Missile Systems (1972); available online at www.acda.gov/treaties/abm2.htm (5 December 1999).

2. United Nations General Assembly News Service, "General Assembly Calls for Strict Compliance of 1972 ABM Treaty, As It Adopts 51 Disarmament, International Security Texts," 12 December 1999; available online at www.un.org/News/Press/docs/1999/19991201.ga9675.doc.html (6 December 1999).

3. E. Eckholm, "China Says Shield Proposed by U.S. May Force Buildup," *New York Times* (11 May 2000), A1.

4. U.S. White House, Office of the Press Secretary, transcript of press briefing by Attorney General Janet Reno, Secretary of Health and Human Services Donna Shalala, and Richard Clarke, president's national coordinator for security, infrastructure, and counterterrorism, 22 January 1999; Available online at www.fas.org/spp/starwars/program/news99/9901220 ht.html (18 August 1999).

5. David Vise, "Panel Calls for Creating Counterterrorism Agency," *Washington Post* (15 December 2000), A8.

6. Richard Novick and Seth Shulman, "New Forms of BW," in *Preventing a Biological Arms Race,* ed. Susan Wright (Cambridge, Mass.: MIT Press, 1990), 103–19; Charles Piller and Keith R. Yamamoto, "The U.S. Biological Defense Research Program in the 1980s: A Critique," in Wright, *Preventing a Biological Arms Race,* 133–68; Jonathan King and Harlee Strauss, "The Hazards of Defensive Biological Warfare Research," in Wright, *Preventing a Biological Arms Race,* 120–32; Susan Wright and Stuart Ketcham, "The Problem of Interpreting the U.S. Biological Defense Research Program," in Wright, *Preventing a Biological Arms Race,* 243–66; Erhard Geissler, "A New Generation of Vaccines against Biological and Toxin Weapons," in *Biological and Toxin Weapons Today,* ed. Erhard Geissler (Oxford: Oxford University Press, 1986), 36–65.

7. Charles Piller and Keith R. Yamamoto, *Gene Wars: Military Control over the New Genetic Technologies* (New York: Beech Tree Books, 1988).

8. Novick and Shulman, "New Forms of Biological Warfare," 103–19.

9. Judith Miller, Stephen Engelberg, and Stephen Engelberg, *Germs: Biological Weapons and America's Secret War* (New York: Simon & Schuster, 2001).

10. Wright and Ketcham, "Problem of Interpreting the U.S. Biological Defense Research Program," 243–66; Piller and Yamamoto, "U.S. Biological Defense Research Program in the 1980s," 133–68.

11. Piller and Yamamoto, "U.S. Biological Defense Research Program in the 1980s," 133–68.

12. Ed Regis, *The Biology of Doom: The History of America's Secret Germ Warfare Project* (New York: Henry Holt, 2000).

13. Wright and Ketcham, "Problem of Interpreting the U.S. Biological Defense Research Program," 243–66; Piller and Yamamoto, "U.S. Biological Defense Research Program in the 1980s," 133–68.

14. John W. Powell, "A Hidden Chapter in History," *Bulletin of the Atomic Scientists* 37(8) (1981), 45–49.

15. Ken Alibek, *Biohazard* (New York: Random House, 1999); Raymond L. Garthoff, "Polyakov's Run," *Bulletin of the Atomic Scientists* 56(5) (2000), 37–40.

16. Michael Gordon and Judith Miller, "U.S. Germ Warfare Review Faults Plan on Enforcement: Pullback from Pact Would Irritate Allies Trying to Limit Biological Weapons," *New York Times* (20 May 2001), 1, 12.

17. William Clinton, Remarks by the President on Keeping America Secure for the 21st Century, The White House, Washington, D.C., 22 January 1999; available online at www.whitehouse.gov/WH/New/html/19990122-7214.html (18 August 1999).

18. Training the Public Health Workforce in Issues Related to Bioterrorism, Session 1001, American Public Health Association Annual Meeting, Chicago, 8 November 1999.

19. Jeanne Guillemin, "Scare Campaign About Biological Weapons Is Itself a Threat," *Boston Globe* (2 December 1999), A27.

20. T. J. Torok et al., "A Large Community Outbreak of Salmonellosis Caused by Intentional Contamination of Restaurant Salad Bars," *JAMA* 278 (1997), 389–95.

21. Alan H. Lockwood, "The Public Health Effects of the Use of Chemical Weapons," in *War and Public Health*, ed. Barry S. Levy and Victor W. Sidel (Washington, D.C.: American Public Health Association and Oxford University Press, 2000), 84–97.

22. Robert Jay Lifton, *Destroying the World to Save It* (New York: Henry Holt, 1999).

23. J. B. Tucker, "Bioterrorism Is the Least of Our Worries," *New York Times* (16 October 1999), A19.

24. U.S. General Accounting Office, *Combating Terrorism: Need for Comprehensive Threat and Risk Assessments of Chemical and Biological Attacks.* (Washington, D.C.: General Accounting Office, 1999).

25. Robert M. Burnham, Statement for the record of Robert M. Burnham, Chief Domestic Terrorism Section, FBI, on threat of bioterrorism in America, 20 May 1999; available online at www.fbi.gov/preesrm/congress/congress99/bioleg3.html (8 December 1999).

26. Leonard A. Cole, "Anthrax Hoaxes: Hot New Hobby?" *Bulletin of Atomic Scientists* 55 (1999), 6–11.

27. Amy Smithson and Leslie-Anne Levy, *Ataxia: The Chemical and Biological Terrorism Threat and the U.S. Response,* Stimson Center Report No. 35 (Washington, D.C.: Stimson Center, 2000); H. W. Cohen, R. M. Gould and V. W. Sidel, "Bioterrorism Initiatives: Public Health in Reverse?" *American Journal of Public Health* 89(11) (1999), 1629–31.

28. P. S. Mead et al., "Food-related Illness and Death in the United States," *Emerging Infectious Diseases* 5(5) (September-October 1999), 607–50.

29. U.S. Government Printing Office, 1999, House hearings, "Internet Posting of Chemical 'Worst Case' Scenarios: A Roadmap for Terrorists."

30. Celia W. Dugger, "India Wins Battles in its War on TB, But It Has a Long Way to Go," *New York Times* (25 March 2000), A4.

31. "Price of Safe Water for All: $10 Billion and the Will to Provide It," *New York Times* (23 November 2000), A10.

32. U.S. Environmental Protection Agency, "EPA and DOJ Propose Regulations for Public Access to Risk Management Plans," Headquarters Press Release, Washington, D.C., 26 April 2000; available online at yosemite.epa.gov/opa/admpress.nsf/.

33. Judith Miller, "Long Island Lab May Do Studies of Bioterrorism," *New York Times* (22 September 1999), A1.

34. Michael R. Fraser and Donna L. Brown, "Bioterrorism Preparedness and Local Public Health Agencies: Building Response Capacity," *Public Health Reports* 115 (2000), 326–30.

35. U.S. White House, Office of the Press Secretary, transcript of press briefing by Reno, Shalala, and Clarke; Center for Nonproliferation Studies, Monterrey Institute of International Studies, Federal Funding to Combat Terrorism, including Defense Against Weapons of Mass Destruction, FY 1998–2001; available online at www.cns.miis.edu/research/cbw/terfund.htm.

36. Wrap-Up for the 2nd Session of the 105th Congress, 11 October 1998, 12; available online at www.uhsa.uh.edu/pages/UHS/Federal/1987011.html (15 August 1999).

37. Sheryl Gay Stolberg, "Buckets for Bioterrorism, But Less for Catalog of Ills," *New York Times* (5 February 2002), A20.

38. George Annas, "Changing the Consent Rules for Desert Storm," *New England Journal of Medicine* 326 (1992), 770.

39. Steven Lee Myers, "Drug May Be Cause of Veterans' Illnesses," *New York Times* (19 October 1999), A18.

40. Victor W. Sidel, Meryl Nass, and Tod Ensign, "The Anthrax Dilemma," *Medicine and Global Survival* 5(2) (October 1998), 97–104.

41. David Wise, *Cassidy's Run: The Secret Spy War Over Nerve Gas* (New York: Random House, 2000); J. Risen, "U.S. Dangled Poison Secrets Before Soviets, Book Reports," *New York Times* (5 March 2000), A16.

42. Raymond L. Garthoff, "Polyakov's Run," *Bulletin of the Atomic Scientists* 56(5) (September/October 2000), 37–40.

43. Sabin Russell, "Bay Area Cities Get Terrorist-ready," *San Francisco Chronicle* (26 February 1999), A1.

44. Joan Stephenson, "Emerging Infections on Center Stage at First Major International Meeting," *Journal of the American Medical Association* 279 (8 March 1998), 1055–56.

45. Tim Weiner, "Soviet Defector Warns of Biological Weapons," *New York Times* (25 February 1998), A1, A8.

46. Wendy Orent, "Escape from Moscow," *The Sciences* (May-June 1998), 26–31.

47. Richard Preston, "The Bioweaponeers," *The New Yorker* (9 March 1998), 52–65.

48. Judith Miller and William J. Broad, "Clinton to Announce That U.S. Will Keep Sample of Lethal Smallpox Virus, Aides Say," *New York Times* (22 April 1999), A12; Judith Miller, "U.S. Confirms It Will Keep Deadly Virus Cells," *New York Times* (23 April 1999), A3.

49. Jim Geraghty, "Smallpox Vaccine Purchase Spurs Homeland Defense Discussion," *Stars and Stripes* (26 April 2001), 1, 12.

50. Bradley Graham, "Military Chiefs Back Anthrax Inoculations," *Washington Post* (2 October 1996), A12; Steven Lee Myers, "U.S. Armed Forces to be Vaccinated Against Anthrax," *New York Times* (16 December 1997), A1, A22.

51. Jim Garamone, "Full-Scale Anthrax Vaccine Program May Restart in October," Armed Forces Press Service, 28 December 2000; available online at www.defenselink.mil/news/Dec2000200012281.html (9 March 2002).

52. Phillip S. Brachman, Herman Gold, Stanley A. Plotkin, et al., "Field Evaluation of a Human Anthrax Vaccine," *American Journal of Public Health* 56 (1962), 632–45.

53. P. C. B. Turnbull, "Anthrax Vaccines: Past, Present, and Future," *Vaccine* 9 (1991), 533–39; B. E. Ivins and S. H. Leppla, "Study of Immunization Against Anthrax with the Purified Recombinant Protective Antigen of *Bacillus Anthracis*," *Infect. Immunization* 66 (1998), 3447–49.

54. Committee on Veterans' Affairs, U.S. Senate, *Is Military Research Hazardous to Veterans' Health?* (Washington, D.C.: Government Printing Office, 1994).

55. B. E. Ivins, M. L. M. Pitt, P. F. Fellows, et al., "Comparative Efficacy of Experimental Anthrax Vaccines Candidates Against Inhalation Anthrax in Rhesus Macaques," *Vaccine* 16 (November/December 1998), 1141–48; A. V. Stepanov et al., "Development of Novel Vaccines Against Anthrax in Man," *Journal of Biotechnology* 44 (1996), 155–60.

56. A. F. Pomerantsev, N. A. Staritsin, Yu V. Mockov, and L. I. Martinin, "Expression of Cerolysine AB Genes in *Bacillus anthracis* Vaccine Strain Ensures Protection Against Experimental Hemolytic Anthrax Infection," *Vaccine* 15 (1997), 1846–50.

57. Paul J. Jackson et al., "PCR Analysis of Tissue Samples from the 1979 Sverdlovsk Anthrax Victims," *Proceedings of the National Academy of Sciences* 95(3) (3 February 1998), 1224–29; Nicholas Wade, "Anthrax Findings Fuel Worry on Vaccine," *New York Times* (3 February 1998), A6; Nicholas Wade, "Tests with Anthrax Raise Fears That American Vaccine Can Be Defeated," *New York Times* (26 March 1998), A24.

58. Ken Alibek with Stephen Handelman, *Biohazard* (New York: Random House, 1998); Richard Preston, "The Bioweaponeers," *The New Yorker* (9 March 1998), 52–65; William J. Broad, "Gene-Engineered Anthrax: Is It a Weapon?" *New York Times* (14 February 1998), A4.

59. Claire Broome, Deputy Director for Science and Public Health, Centers for Disease Control and Prevention, letter to author, 14 December 1998.

60. Presidential Advisory Committee on Gulf War Veterans' Illnesses, Special Report, 31 October 1997; U.S. House of Representatives, Committee on Government Reform, Subcommittee on National Security, Veterans Affairs and International Relations, *The Department of Defense Anthrax Vaccine Immunization*

*Program: Unproven Force Protection* (17 February 2000); online: www.house.gov/reform/ns/reports/anthrax1.pdf (24 July 2002).

61. Catherine Strong, "FDA Cites 30 Deficiencies in Anthrax Vaccine Production," Associated Press (15 December 1999); Elaine Sciolino, "Shortage Forces Pentagon to Cut Anthrax Inoculations," *New York Times* (11 July 2000), A14; Elaine Sciolino, "Anthrax Vaccination Program Is Failing, Pentagon Admits," *New York Times* (13 July 2000), A22.

62. "Troubled Company Is Allowed to Resume Making Vaccine," *New York Times* (1 February 2002), A13.

63. Thomas Williams, "Anthrax Vaccine Complaints on the Rise," *Hartford Courant* (2 June 2001), A3.

64. David Castellon, "Dover Airmen Report Myriad Ill Effects From Anthrax Shots," *Air Force Times* (17 April 2000).

65. U.S. House of Representatives, Committee on Government Reform, *The Department of Defense Anthrax Vaccine Immunization Program: Unproven Force Protection.*

66. Centers for Disease Control and Prevention, "Use of Anthrax Vaccine in the United States: Recommendations of the Advisory Committee on Immunization Practices (ACIP)," *Morbidity and Mortality Weekly Report* 49(RR15) (15 December 2000), 1–20.

67. George Annas, "Protecting Soldiers from Friendly Fire: The Consent Requirement for Using Investigational Drugs and Vaccines in Combat," *American Journal of Law and Medicine* 24 (1998), 245–60.

68. In March 2001 the Office of the Inspector General of the Department of Defense alleged that statements of Major General Paul Weaver, director of the Air National Guard, were "inconsistent with guidelines for honesty" when he testified in September 1999 at a congressional hearing: "We've had 10,700 people inoculated for anthrax in the Air National Guard, with one known refusal documented."; Dave Eberhart, "General's Anthrax Vaccine Testimony "'Inconsistent with Honesty,' Says Inspector," *Stars and Stripes* (11 May 2001).

69. Deborah Funk, "Anthrax Vaccine Refuser Avoids Jail Time, Air Force Doctor Is Restricted to Base, Must Forfeit $21,000," *Air Force Times* (2001); Reni Winter, "Buck Fined, Avoids Jail, Can Stay in Service," *Biloxi Sun Herald* (23 May 2001).

70. Seymour Hersh, *Against All Enemies: Gulf War Syndrome: The War Between America's Ailing Veterans and Their Government* (New York: Ballantine Books, 1998), 14; William J. Broad, "Book Says Pre-Gulf-War Discovery Raised Germ Warfare Fears," *New York Times* (7 June 1998), A6.

71. Richard Falk, "Inhibiting Reliance on Biological Weaponry: The Role and Relevance of International Law," in Wright, *Preventing a Biological Arms Race,* 241–66.

72. Elizabeth Olson, "U.S. Rejects New Accord Covering Germ Warfare," *New York Times* (26 July 2001), A7.

73. Susan Wright, "U.S. Vetoes Verification," *Bulletin of the Atomic Scientists* 58(2) (March/April 2002), 24–26.

74. Charles Arthur, "Scientists Made Virus 'More Lethal than HIV'," *The Independent* (London) (24 July 2001), 7.

75. Miller, Engelberg, and Broad, *Germs.*

# 5

# The Soviet Union's Offensive Program

## The Implications for Contemporary Arms Control

*Anthony Rimmington*

Throughout the 1970s and 1980s the Soviet Union was successful in developing an offensive biological weapons capability that gave it overwhelming superiority in these weapons over the United States and other Western countries. Its secret biological warfare (BW) network possessed the capacity for the wartime production of hundreds of tons of a range of biological agents that included plague, tularaemia, glanders, anthrax, smallpox, and Venezuelan equine encephalomyelitis. Most significantly, it developed specially adapted multiple-warhead intercontinental ballistic missiles for delivery of its biological weapons, designed to totally disrupt civilian activities in targeted countries. Following the collapse of the USSR, the dismantling of this vast program has been a major priority for Western governments, which have also invested heavily in initiatives to prevent proliferation of BW technologies and weapons systems from the former Soviet Union (FSU).

The apparent ease with which the Soviet Union was able to circumvent its international treaty obligations and pursue such an ambitious offensive BW program has profound implications with regard to the operation of the Biological Weapons Convention (BWC). The fatally flawed decision to omit mechanisms for verification via on-site inspections from the BWC presented the Soviet leadership with the opportunity to violate Article I with impunity. It is to be hoped that any future protocol to the BWC that seeks to establish a strengthened verification regime will incorporate mechanisms for highly intrusive inspections of known or suspected BW facilities. Given the primary role of ostensibly civil biotechnology and pharmaceutical facilities within the Soviet BW program, it is also highly desirable that any projected compliance regime not be confined to defense installations.

Close examination of the management structure of the Soviet BW program indicates that there may in fact be an extremely wide range of legitimate targets for intrusive inspections implemented under any future protocol to the Convention. This chapter provides new information about and analysis of a range of organizations that constituted the Soviet BW complex. It identifies a highly compartmentalized subprogram aimed at the development of biological weapons against economically valuable crops and livestock. In addition, it provides evidence that the Soviet security apparatus was both involved in the management of the overall program and executed long-term BW research of its own. The utilization within the BW program of scientific personnel and institutes belonging to the country's extensive network of anti-plague facilities is also described. From the analysis it becomes apparent that, in the case of the FSU at least, bioscience facilities subordinate to a wide range of organizations, including the Ministry of Defense, Ministry of Agriculture, Ministry of Health, and the state security services, are of legitimate proliferation concern.

The threat posed to the international community by the Soviet BW program continues despite the collapse of the USSR. The Russian Federation, which has inherited the bulk of Soviet BW facilities, has made encouraging moves toward the termination of its offensive BW effort. However, at the time of writing significant sections of the Russian biological weapons complex remain closed to the United States and its allies. Moreover, staff who managed the Soviet offensive BW program continue to occupy key administrative positions within the Ministry of Defense and within the civil conglomerate *Biopreparat* and its affiliated facilities. Such "Cold War warriors" may pose a serious obstacle to the reorientation of the BW complex to a civil profile, at least in the short term. In addition, there remains a serious risk that weapons scientists, agents, and technologies will be transferred to countries or terror groups pursuing their own biological weapons programs. International efforts to contain this threat have been slow to be initiated but are now a major funding priority for the United States and its allies. The process by which the vast BW infrastructure within the FSU is dismantled, and modern biopharmaceutical industries, which are fully under the control of civil bodies, are established is likely to be a long and difficult one. It will require Western input and monitoring for many decades to come.

A further dimension to the fallout from the collapse of the Soviet BW program concerns its ongoing environmental legacy, which could pose a severe threat both to local populations and the international community as a whole. The full extent of the environmental impact of the program has been largely ignored until now, but this chapter records serious cases of releases of military strains from BW facilities. It also reveals the locations of fifteen proving grounds where serious contamination of the environment may have occurred. International initiatives to monitor and make safe such sites are at early stages, but they may be viewed as complementing efforts being undertaken to prevent the migration of former weapons scientists elsewhere and the associated proliferation of the technologies.

The first part of this chapter focuses on the background of the launch of the major offensive program in the 1970s and identifies a number of parallels between this program and the early Soviet BW effort begun in the 1920s. The second part of the chapter provides an account of the Soviet BW program run by *Biopreparat* and affiliated agencies from the 1970s until the collapse of the USSR. A small number of original documents drawn from official Russian state archives are employed, and they appear to go some way toward authenticating information provided by recent defectors from the program and from published sources.[1] A description is also provided of important BW subprograms managed by the Ministry of Agriculture and the state security services. The final part of the chapter focuses on the aftermath of the Soviet BW program, especially the ongoing threat of proliferation and the environmental hazards posed by accidental releases of military strains and by heavily contaminated BW test sites.

## THE ORIGINS OF THE SOVIET BIOLOGICAL WEAPONS PROGRAM

The launch of the Soviet Union's first major BW program in 1928 was made against a background of genuine alarm within the Soviet leadership concerning the country's deteriorating international position and its lack of military and economic preparation for defense.[2] It constituted part of a wider effort undertaken at this time, including the publication of the first five-year plan, aimed at developing the Soviet Union's industrial capacity for the mass production of modern weapons and combat equipment. The basis for the new focus on biological weapons was a report commissioned in February 1928 by Kliment Voroshilov, the People's Commissar for Defense, on the Soviet Union's preparedness for biological warfare. This resulted in a document prepared by Yakob Moiseevich Fishman, Director of the Red Army's Military-Chemical Directorate, which would underpin Soviet BW efforts for the next decade. It asserted that "the bacterial option could be successfully used in war" and proposed a plan for the organization of Soviet military bacteriology. Fishman also outlined the measures that would have to be adopted for defense against bacteriological attack. One of his critical recommendations was that field tests be conducted to determine the viability of anthrax weapons, and that defensive preparations be strengthened, including the development of BW equipment.[3]

There are some extremely interesting parallels between the Soviet Union's early biological warfare program and that subsequently spearheaded in the early 1970s by *Biopreparat*. Both were launched against the background of the Soviet Union's ratification of major international treaties aimed at curtailing the development and use of biological weapons. The Soviet government launched its first major program for the development of biological weapons in 1928, the same year that it acceded to the Geneva Protocol[4]; later in a similar fashion the *Biopreparat* program was launched against the background of the Soviet Union's ratification of the Biological Weapons Convention. Both programs were supported at the highest levels of the political and military leadership.[5] As was later to be the case within the *Biopreparat* system, the early BW program was partially concealed within ostensibly civil organizations such as the Commissariats of Health and Education. In addition, in both programs the state security services played a pivotal role in the concealment and management of BW research and production.

Another major parallel between the 1928 program and that launched by *Biopreparat* in the 1970s is the sheer scale of the Soviet BW effort compared with the other major powers. The Soviet Union's early offensive program, with its network of dedicated facilities and proving grounds, easily outstripped that of the major Western powers.[6] By the mid-1930s the Soviet program incorporated a dedicated BW facility—the Red Army's Military Scientific-Medical Institute (*Voennyi nauchnyi meditsinskii institut RKKA*)—and also embraced research within the Military-Medical Academy (*Voenno-meditsinskoi akademii*) in St. Petersburg (then Leningrad) and a number of other civil and military facilities.[7] Furthermore, a number of BW proving grounds were established, including facilities on Gorodomyla Island in Lake Seliger (close to the town of Ostashkov in Tver, then named Kalinin-*oblast'*), an experimental test site on one of the Solovetskii islands in the White Sea,[8] and a 10,000-square-kilometer tract of land on Vozrozhdenie Island (*Ostrov Vozrozhdenie* or "Island of Rebirth") in the Aral Sea.[9] Vozrozhedenie would later become the primary test site for a new generation of biological weapons developed by the *Biopreparat* offensive program during the 1970s and 1980s.

A lack of archival and published sources renders it difficult to assess the degree of success attained by the early Soviet BW program in the period from 1928 to the end of World War II. A wide range of agents, including plague, tularaemia, leprosy, foot-and-mouth disease, cholera, dysentery, typhus, paratyphoid, and tetanus, were investigated both in the laboratory and in the field with a view toward their use as offensive battlefield weapons.[10] A number of long-range research programs were also initiated at this time that would bring about the development and application of a range of defense vaccines during the war. As a result, 8.5 million Soviet troops were vaccinated against plague, 90,000 against anthrax, and an unknown number against tularaemia.[11] Soviet scientists are also reported to have successfully developed a range of defensive apparatuses including portable kits for the defense of personnel against CBW attack and miniaturized laboratories for identification of bacteriological agents used in enemy attacks.[12] In 1938 Marshal Kliment Voroshilov provided what was probably the Soviet government's most public admission of its achievements in this field: "Ten years ago or more the Soviet Union signed a convention abolishing the use of poison gas and bacteriological warfare. To that we still adhere, but if our enemies use such methods against us, I will tell you that we are prepared—fully prepared—to use them also and to use them against aggressors on their own soil."[13] However, it should be noted that just four years earlier Stalin had been informed privately that the Soviet BW program was facing severe problems.[14]

Whatever the reality behind the purported successes of the early BW research, the Soviet program was to be massively undermined by two devastating blows in the late 1930s from which it would take decades to recover. The first was the mass repression (dubbed the Great Terror) instigated by Stalin, which began in 1936 and reached its culmination in 1937–1938.[15] During this period it is estimated that more than eight million people (5 percent of the population) were arrested, with some 800,000 (one in ten) probably executed.[16] Large numbers of biological scientists were arrested, often together with their entire research teams.[17] The most prominent victim of the security organs was Ivan Mikhailovich Velikanov, the scientist responsible for the coordination and management of the Soviet BW program, who was taken into custody in Vlasikha on July 6, 1937, and executed on April 8, 1938 (he was "rehabilitated" in 1956). The mass arrests of experts in microbiology and BW technology had an immediate impact on the country's development of biological weapons and on the quality of its military microbiological projects.

The second major blow, which would continue to have a negative impact for decades afterward, was Stalin's support of Lysenko and the concomitant political repression of Mendelian genetics.[18] As a result, biological sciences in the Soviet Union during and after World War II suffered a terrible slump, and this had a severe impact on the country's BW effort. Not until 1965 was Lysenko overthrown, and as late as the 1990s one study found that "genetics in the republics of the former Soviet Union . . . suffers from the effects of the Lysenko years. Young biologists struggling to resurrect the field in the 1970s, 1980s, and 1990s had difficulty finding role models among their elders, or sustaining traditions in their institutions."[19] The disastrous position in which the Soviet Union found itself with regard to molecular biology and genetics as a result of Lysenkoism eventually led the party leadership to unleash a massive military and civil program aimed at duplicating the progress achieved in the West.

## THE OFFENSIVE BIOLOGICAL WEAPONS PROGRAM AND THE ROLE OF *BIOPREPARAT*

The development of the Soviet BW program from the end of World War II through the late 1960s has not been well documented either in Soviet or more recent Russian publications. However, the expansion of the Ministry of Defense's BW network during this period reflected an emphasis in the economy as a whole on rearmament based on new weapons technologies, including atomic weapons, rocketry, jet propulsion, radar, electronics, and biological weapons themselves.[20] One of the key features of the program at this time, which was to be duplicated and amplified to an unprecedented degree in the 1970s and 1980s, was the utilization for BW projects of ostensibly civil facilities subordinate to the USSR Ministry of Health. Throughout the 1950s and 1960s institutes belonging to the anti-plague network focused their research and development on "Problem No. 5" (*"Pyataya problema"*) which was the code name then used by the Soviet authorities to obscure BW research.[21] The BW infrastructure established during this period was used as the foundation for the establishment of a much more powerful program that was to be launched with the support of the highest political authorities in the early 1970s. (See appendix 5A for a detailed chronology of events.)

The Soviet Union signed the Biological Weapons Convention on April 10, 1972, and deposited its instruments of ratification of the Convention on March 26, 1975, when the treaty came into force. However, despite the public destruction of stocks of biological weapons in the United States and the associated dismantling of the bulk of the American research apparatus and destruction of its production facilities, it was precisely at this moment that the USSR launched the most ambitious offensive BW research, development, and production program in its history. There has still been no entirely adequate explanation of the Soviet decision to focus massive resources on biological weapons, or why the program was surreptitiously retained for two decades. During this time the Soviet Union entered into a wide range of international treaties to limit stockpiles of strategic and conventional weapons; it also acknowledged the existence of its chemical weapons stockpiles.

Initially, at least, it appears likely that the main impetus for the launch of a new large-scale program was concern within the Soviet military leadership that rapid advances in molecular biology and molecular genetics in the West might have given the United States and its allies a substantive lead with regard to the creation of a new generation of biological weapons. In addition, Soviet assessments of the extent and success of the American CBW effort appear to have been influenced by U.S. deception and disinformation operations aimed at diverting resources from mainstream military programs.[22] Soviet concerns at the time are reflected in a decree issued by the Communist Party of the Soviet Union (CPSU) Committee and USSR Council of Ministers in May 1974, which noted that fundamental discoveries in this area had major theoretical and applied significance and that "the general level and scale of research in molecular biology and molecular genetics in our country is still not satisfactory."[23] The implementation of a massive BW effort was aimed at closing this gap and appears to have been conducted in the belief that Soviet violations of the BWC would remain undetectable. This attitude within the military is highlighted by Arkady Shevchenko, diplomat and personal advisor to Gromyko, who defected to the United States in April 1978:

> While the military strongly opposed any agreement on chemical or biological weapons, the political leadership, Gromyko in particular, felt it necessary for propaganda purposes to respond to a proposal by Great Britain to conclude a special separate convention to prohibit biological warfare as a first step. The military's reaction was to say go ahead and sign the convention; without international controls, who would know anyway? They refused to consider eliminating their stockpiles and insisted upon further development of these weapons. The Politburo approved this approach. The toothless convention regarding biological weapons was signed in 1972, but there are no international controls over the Soviet program, which continues apace.[24]

In August 1985 the CPSU Central Committee and the USSR Council of Ministers published a second decree that further promoted the BW program by calling for large-scale measures to accelerate the development of biology and biotechnology.[25] Although bureaucratic inertia was inherent within the Soviet defense sector, this cannot plausibly account for the continuation of the illicit program during the collapse of the USSR and beyond. One analyst has speculated that the policy resulted from the Soviet Union's inability to compete with the United States with regard to the Strategic Defense Initiative of the 1980s, due to major economic and technological problems. Against this background, the Soviet leadership viewed their sophisticated biological weapons capability as offering the only counterbalance to the threat of nuclear blackmail if the United States successfully developed an effective space-based laser defense system. Politburo member Valentin Falin made a reference to this line of thinking in 1987: "We won't copy [the United States] anymore, making planes to catch up with your planes, missiles to catch up with your missiles. We'll take asymmetric means with new scientific principles available to us. Genetic engineering could be a hypothetical example. Things could be done for which neither side could find defences or countermeasures, with very dangerous results."[26]

The major influence on Soviet decision makers with regard to BW policy in the early 1970s was Academician Yurii Anatol'evich Ovchinnikov. Ovchinnikov was one of only two scientific advisors to the Politburo and is reported to have represented the KGB on the Executive Committee of the USSR Academy of Sciences.[27] He was one of the key figures on a special commission established by the USSR Council of Ministers' Military-Industrial Commission (*Voenno-promyshlennyi kompleks* or *VPK*).[28] The *VPK* was the keystone of the entire Soviet defense complex, coordinating and controlling activities, and had close ties to both *Gosplan* and the Central Committee's Defense Industry Department.[29] It has been reported that the special commission assessed the ongoing research in the network of Ministry of Defense BW facilities under Smirnov and made a number of recommendations aimed at duplicating the biotechnological progress made in the West.[30] Ovchinnikov subsequently led the Soviet BW research effort within the USSR Academy of Sciences.[31]

As a result of the commission's report, decrees and orders were issued to establish a major new BW program, given the special code name *Fermenty* ("Enzymes"), which was abbreviated to "*F*." A key feature of the program was to be the establishment of a new system of BW facilities, to run parallel to that of the Ministry of Defense. It would focus on fundamental problems in molecular biology and genetics and the development of advanced technology for the military. Many other civil and military agencies were to participate, with their activities coordinated via a new interagency council. Major allocations of hard currency were to be provided for the new BW program for the procurement of equipment and reagents and for the construction of dedicated facilities. It has recently been estimated that the cost of creating and maintaining the system during the first fifteen years of its existence was at least 1.5 billion rubles. This made it an extremely cost-effective option relative to nuclear weapons research.[32]

The new BW network was incorporated within the Main Administration of the Microbiological Industry under the Council of Ministers (*Glavnoe upravlenie mikrobiologicheskoi promyshlennosti pri Sovete Ministrov SSSR* or *Glavmikrobioprom*). The latter organization was established in 1966 to manage the Soviet Union's nascent biotechnology industry and initially incorporated sixty-two research and production facilities. It provided an ideal civil cover for illicit BW activity.[33] The department within *Glavmikrobioprom* responsible for BW development and production was the All-Union Science-Production Association *Biopreparat* (*Vsesoyuznoe nauchno-proizvodstvennoe ob"edinenie "Biopreparat"*), which was officially established by Order No. 131 DSP on April 24, 1974.[34] On June 26, 1974, a number of facilities that would play a major role in the Soviet offensive BW program were transferred to *Biopreparat,* including the Berdsk Chemical Factory, the Omutninsk Chemical Factory, the "Progress" Factory, and the Special Design Bureau of Biologically Active Substances. Two newly created facilities were also incorporated within *Biopreparat* at this time: the All-Union Scientific-Research Institute of Especially Pure Biopreparations and the All-Union Scientific-Research Design Institute of Applied Biochemistry.[35]

A pivotal organization was now established under *Glavmikrobioprom* for the management of the new BW program: the Interdepartmental Scientific-Technical Council for Molecular Biology and Genetics. The Council, headed by Viktor M. Zhdanov, included representatives from a range of military and civil agencies participating in the new BW program, including Major-General Lebedinskii (USSR Ministry of Defense); A. A. Skladnev and S. I. Alikhanyan (*Glavmikrobioprom*); Burnazyan (USSR Ministry of Health); Yu. A. Ovchinnikov, G. K. Skryabin, and A. A. Baev (USSR Academy of Sciences); and a representative from the USSR Ministry of Agriculture. Also always present at the Council meetings were Vasilli Dmitrievich Belyaev, head of *Glavmikrobioprom*, and representatives from the Central Committee of the Communist Party, the *VPK*, and the KGB. In 1975 the Council was reorganized, with Belyaev replacing Zhdanov as chairman and Smirnov and Ogarkov being appointed as members.[36] Interestingly, the Ministry of Medium Machine Building (*Minsredmash*), which controlled the Soviet nuclear weapons network and had a significant input into developing the new BW network, does not appear to have been represented within the Council.[37] The Council had responsibility for the formulation of new scientific programs, the coordination of the many different agencies engaged in the BW effort, and the allocation of major sums of hard currency. Of the $10 million per annum of hard currency available in the 1970s, 40 to 45 percent went to *Biopreparat*, and around 30 percent to the USSR Academy of Sciences, with the Ministries of Defense, Health, and Agriculture each receiving around $1 million to $1.5 million for their BW projects. However, key decisions with regard to the BW program could only be implemented with the approval of the Central Committee and the *VPK*.[38]

Senior military personnel were assigned key positions in the *Biopreparat* network. Among these appointments was that of Kanatzchan Baizakovich Alibekov, a full colonel in the Soviet Army who became the first Deputy Director of *Biopreparat*. Alibekov, a pivotal figure in the development of the Soviet BW program from 1988 to 1991, left Russia for the United States in 1992, changing his name to Ken Alibek. Debriefed by the U.S. authorities for five years, he provided an authoritative account of the Soviet BW program.[39]

The *Biopreparat* network underwent rapid expansion in the 1970s with the construction of a number of huge new dedicated BW research and development facilities. The first facility to be commissioned in April 1974 under the terms of a CPSU decree was the All-Union Scientific-Research Institute of Applied Microbiology (*VNIIPM*), based in Obolensk one hundred kilometers to the south of Moscow. It was quickly followed by the creation in August 1974 of the All-Union Scientific-Research Institute of Molecular Biology (*VNIIMB*) at Kol'tsovo near Novosibirsk.[40] In 1980 *VNIIPM*'s Laboratory of Molecular Immunology was spun off from its parent facility to form the Institute of Immunology at Lyubuchany near Chekhov in the Moscow *oblast'*.[41] One of the key components of the new Soviet BW network was its "mobilization capacity," which comprised fully outfitted, tested, and ready to operate BW production plants with weapon-filling lines. Six such plants have been documented; they incorporated capacity for the wartime production of hundreds of tons of a range of biological agents including plague, tularaemia, glanders, anthrax, smallpox, and Venezuelan equine encephalomyelitis. Alibek reports that the Pokrov plant alone had sufficient capacity to manufacture up to one hundred tons of smallpox and forty to eighty tons of Venezuelan equine encephalitis.

According to Alibek and another high-ranking defector from *Biopreparat*, Vladimir Pasechnik, who left the FSU for the United Kingdom in 1989, the Soviet military developed a range of tactical and strategic weapons to deliver its biological weapons, including a small fleet of medium-range bombers carrying spray-tank delivery systems for tactical attacks, a strategic warplane carrying cluster bombs, and several SS-18 intercontinental ballistic missiles carrying multiple warheads.[42] It is also alleged that the Soviets were working on a tactical cruise missile system, each missile carrying a payload of multiple canisters that could be released at a number of preprogrammed targets. It was expected that the release of biological warheads from ICBMs would cause catastrophic epidemics that would lead to a total disruption of civilian activities in targeted countries.[43]

An indication of the scale of the Soviet program is provided by Smithson's recent report for the Stimson Center, which estimates that the Soviet Union employed around 65,000 people in its biological warfare complex, including 40,000 in *Biopreparat*, 15,000 in the Ministry of Defense, and an additional 10,000 in the Ministry of Agriculture's own facilities.[44] These figures, taken together with the large number of research and production facilities that have now been identified, offer strong support for the conclusions of a January 1991 U.S./UK inspection team describing the offensive program as "the largest such program that the world had ever known."[45] Certainly Leitenberg's assertion that the scale of the Soviet program was of an order of magnitude larger than that of the U.S. program when it incorporated an offensive component at its height in 1969 appears reasonable.[46] Taken in conjunction with the weapons and delivery systems that were successfully developed, it can be persuasively argued that the Soviet Union possessed overwhelming superiority with regard to these weapons of mass destruction over the United States and other Western countries.

## THE MINISTRY OF AGRICULTURE'S OFFENSIVE ANTI-CROP AND ANTI-LIVESTOCK BW PROGRAMS

The Soviet authorities utilized a further civil organization, the USSR Ministry of Agriculture, to conceal and manage a second major offensive BW program, aimed at economically important crops and livestock. According to Alibek the Ministry's program was code-named *Ekologiya* ("Ecology"). A special division, the Main Directorate for Scientific-Research and Experimental-Production Establishments (*Glavnoe upravlenie nauchno-issledovatel'skikh i eksperimental'no-proizvodstvennykh uchrezhdenii pri Ministerstve sel'skogo khozyaistva SSSR*), was established to research and manufacture anti-livestock and anti-crop weapons.[47] It is reported to have made a special request to the Ministry of Defense for assistance with the recruitment of trained military microbiologists, and a large number of military personnel appear to have been subsequently transferred to the Ministry of Agriculture.[48] Approximately 10,000 people are reported to have been employed in the Directorate's network of facilities.[49] The agricultural BW program is alleged to have been highly successful and is reported to have led to the development of weaponized variants of foot-and-mouth disease and rinderpest for use against cattle, African swine fever for use against pigs, and ornithosis and psittacosis for use against poultry. A range of anti-crop weapons was also created, including agents for the destruction of wheat, rye, corn, and rice.[50]

The Ministry of Agriculture's program had the potential to cause massive dislocation and economic damage in targeted countries. Foot-and-mouth disease, for example, can be spread by aerosol and in this way is capable of almost uncontrollable spread. A study conducted almost twenty years ago hypothesized the entry of foot-and-mouth disease into the United States, with the disease subsequently becoming endemic, and estimated that the damage would result in U.S. $27 billion (adjusted for inflation) in lost trade. Even a limited outbreak that actually occurred in Italy in 1993 cost U.S. $11 million to eradicate, with losses to the export trade tallying an additional U.S. $120 million. A further example is provided by the 1997 outbreak of foot-and-mouth disease in Taiwan, which led to the slaughter of more than eight million pigs, with losses to the economy estimated at between U.S. $15 billion and U.S. $25 billion.[51]

The launch of the *Ekologiya* program is closely connected with a decree for "strengthening work in the field of microbiology and virology" issued on August 7, 1958, by the Central Committee of the CPSU and the Council of Ministers. The decree is reported to have established six specialized research institutes and branches under the USSR Ministry of Agriculture (*Soyuzno-respublikanskoe Ministerstvo Sel'skogo Khozyaistva SSSR* or *Minsel'khoz*) to conduct anti-animal and anti-plant offensive BW programs.[52] The Ministry of Agriculture's anti-crop/anti-livestock BW program appears to have been subsequently expanded to incorporate a number of other facilities (see appendix 5C), including the Almaty Biocombine (Kazakstan) and the Pokrov Factory of Biopreparations (Vol'ginskii, Vladimir *oblast'*).[53]

The anti-crop and anti-livestock offensive BW program appears to have been mainly compartmentalized within facilities belonging to the Ministry of Agriculture. However, efforts were apparently made to create links to BW facilities belonging to the Ministry of Defense, *Biopreparat*, and other parts of the Soviet BW complex. Pivotal to this process was the appointment of the head of the *Ekologiya* program to the Soviet Interdepartmental Scientific and Technical Council for Molecular Biology & Genetics, which was formed in the early 1970s to coordinate advanced research in biological weaponry.[54] As a result, links were established to Ministry of Defense facilities in Ekaterinburg and Sergiev Posad.[55] Furthermore, *Biopreparat*'s research center *Vektor*, which includes experimental agricultural enterprises and its own farm, is reported to have tested BW agents developed by the *Ekologiya* program.[56] In addition, as detailed previously, the Ministry of Agriculture was allocated specific production tasks within the wider biological weapons program concerned with the development and manufacture of agents (such as smallpox) for use against human populations.

The heart of the Ministry of Agriculture's anti-livestock biological weapons program appears to have been located in the Vladimir *oblast'* to the northwest of Moscow. Two of its key research and development facilities and its most significant BW production plant were in this region. The All-Union Scientific-Research Foot-&-Mouth Disease Institute (*Vsesoyuznyi nauchno-issledovatel'skii yashchurnyi institut* or *VNIYaI*), renamed in 1992 the All-Russian Scientific-Research Institute of Animal Health (*Vserossiiskii nauchno-issledovatel'skii institut zashchity zhivotnykh* or *VNIIZZh*), occupies an 11.6-hectare site at Yur'evets (Vladimir *oblast'*) in conjunction with the Factory *Yur'evetsvetbiopreparat*. It also possessed branches in Yerevan and Dushanbe.[57] According to Alibek, the facility researched and developed a range of anti-livestock weapons including African swine fever, foot-and-mouth disease, and rinderpest.[58]

The Ministry of Agriculture's offensive BW facilities in the Vladimir *oblast'* had extremely close links with a major complex employing 400 people located at the Gvardeiskii military settlement, near Otar, Dzhambul *oblast'*, Kazakstan. It incorporated both the USSR Ministry of Agriculture's Scientific-Research Agricultural Institute (*NISKhI*) and a dedicated Ministry of Defense biological weapons proving ground (*poligon*). The latter was used for testing a range of anti-livestock weapons developed within the Ministry of Agriculture's offensive BW program. Together, the institute and the associated proving ground occupied a territory of nineteen hectares and incorporated fifteen laboratories, a vivarium, greenhouses, and a vaccine production facility.[59]

From its inception the ostensibly civil institute at Gvardeiskii was in reality dominated by military officers. As in the case of *Biopreparat,* key personnel at the Gvardeiski institute, including the director and deputy director, had strong military affiliations.[60] The precise role of *NISKhI* in the Ministry of Agriculture's offensive program is unknown. However, among the agents being investigated at the facility were those responsible for a number of economically important diseases including rinderpest, equine influenza, rabbit haemorrhagic fever, sheep and goat pox, fowl pox, Newcastle disease, African swine fever, blue-tongue, and Aujeszky's disease.[61]

Relatively little is known about the USSR Ministry of Agriculture's network of anti-crop facilities. The key research and development facility appears to have been the All-Union Scientific-Research Institute of Phytopathology (*Vsesoyuznyi nauchno-issledovatel'skii institut fitopatologii or VNII fitopatologii*), which was created in 1958 at Vyazemy, near Golitsyno, Moscow *oblast'*.[62] Alibek reports that *VNII fitopatologii* developed a range of anti-crop weapons, including agents for the destruction of wheat, rye, corn, and rice.[63] The Vyazemy institute may have coordinated the research and development, production, and testing programs of a number of subordinate facilities, including the Central Asian Scientific-Research Institute of Phytopathology (*Sredneaziatskii nauchno-issledovatel'skii institut fitopatologii*), which was created in 1958 in Durmen' (possibly now renamed Yukariyuz), near Kibrai, ten kilometers northeast of Tashkent. According to Alibek, this highly guarded facility, which encompassed laboratories, greenhouses, and an experimental farm as well as proving grounds for testing biological and chemical anti-crop agents, was engaged in both the development and testing of weapons.[64] A direct result of the work at this institute was a unique collection of fungal pathogens against wheat and rice described as "the world's largest."[65] Thousands of anti-crop chemicals were also developed and tested.[66] Very little is known of its research and development programs (see appendix 5A), but part of its research may have involved purification and production of mycotoxins.[67] Beginning in the 1970s, the Gvardeiskii complex in Kazakstan was also used for both the development and testing of anti-crop biological weapons.[68]

## THE STATE SECURITY APPARATUS AND SOVIET
## BIOLOGICAL WEAPONS PROGRAMS

The Soviet security apparatus played a prominent role in the development of the biological weapons programs, becoming involved as early as the 1920s in the management of the mainstream BW effort and establishing its own network of research laboratories focusing on assassination.[69] Alibek has recently claimed that the KGB First Main Directorate's Laboratory 12 was involved in a number of political assassinations in the 1970s and that more recently it had been conducting its own research into biological weapons, primarily against individual human targets.[70] He also claims that the USSR Ministry of Health's Third Main Directorate managed a special BW program with the code name *Fleyta* (or "Flute"), which developed nonlethal and lethal psychotropic and neurotropic biological agents for the KGB.[71]

The Soviet intelligence services also played a vital role in acquiring foreign BW technologies and related information for the offensive weapons program.[72] The best documented example of such activity concerns the case of Professor Marcus Klingberg, who emigrated from the USSR to Israel in the late 1940s and subsequently worked at the top-secret Israel Institute for Biological Research at Ness Ziona. This facility plays a pivotal role in Israel's BW program and probably possesses the capability to produce offensive biological agents.[73] Klingberg, who eventually became a world-renowned epidemiologist and Deputy Director of the Ness Ziona institute, was arrested by the Israeli authorities, secretly tried and convicted of passing BW secrets to the FSU, and sentenced to eighteen years' imprisonment.[74] In the absence of any release of information from Israel, the nature of the BW intelligence secured by the KGB and its impact on the Soviet Union's BW program remain unassessed.

Several reports link the intelligence services to the acquisition of strains for use in BW research and development. In the 1950s, for example, the Soviets were successful in obtaining, via a routine medical exchange with the United States, a severely infectious strain of tularaemia (Schu-4) with a high mortality rate.[75] Alibek claims that KGB agents in 1959 were also successful in procuring a strain of smallpox from India that subsequently became the Soviet Union's principal "battle strain" and was produced at the Ministry of Defense facility in Zagorsk.[76] Finally, in an interview in the summer of 1999, Lieutenant-General Valentin Evstigneev (head of the Ministry of Defense's Biological Defense Department) admitted that ebola strains maintained at his facility in Sergiev Posad were obtained by the intelligence services.[77]

It is not known whether the KGB's successor organizations, such as the External Intelligence Service (*Sluzhba Vneshenie Razvedaki* or *SVR*), continue to manage their own network of BW laboratories or sponsor BW research programs within other organizations. However, given the offensive nature of such work in the recent past, biological facilities belonging to the Russian state security services must be of proliferation concern. If they still exist, they represent legitimate targets for intrusive inspections under any future protocol to the Convention that seeks to establish a strengthened verification regime. The role of the security services in sponsorship of biological research within academic and industrial centers should also be closely monitored to ensure compliance with existing international commitments.

## THE LEGACY OF THE SOVIET BW PROGRAM

Following the collapse of the Soviet Union, the Russian Federation took control of most of the facilities associated with the offensive BW program. One of the key questions that has arisen since transition is the extent to which Russia has provided reassurance that this offensive BW effort has been terminated. In July 1992 Boris Yeltsin's government made a formal commitment to comply with the BWC when the Russian Supreme Soviet of the Russian Federation issued a decree "On Ensuring the Implementation of International Pledges in the Field of Chemical, Bacteriological (Biological) and Toxin Weapons."[78] Since then there have been encouraging indications that the government is succeeding in enforcing compliance with its new policy. For example, a senior staff member of the International Science and Technology Center (ISTC), an organization that provides funding for FSU weapons scientists to work on civil projects, has recently stated that the ISTC has established relations with all but two of an estimated thirteen to fifteen core biological weapons institutes.[79] In addition, a report from January 2000 suggests that one of the key Russian BW facilities, *Vektor* in Kol'tsovo, near Novosibirsk, is making substantive progress with regard to the demilitarization of its research programs.[80] The Russian government's effort to demilitarize has been bolstered by financial support from a range of U.S. and international agencies that aim to accelerate the transition to civil science and technology.

Nonetheless, despite a number of positive indicators, major sections of the Russian Federation's biological weapons complex have remained closed to the United States and its allies. The Russian Ministry of Defense has refused to allow access to four of the facilities that constituted the heart of the Soviet offensive program: the Scientific-Research Institute of Microbiology (Kirov), the Center of Virology (Sergiev Posad), the Center of Military-Technical Problems of Biological Defense (Ekaterinburg), and the Scientific-Research Institute of Military Medicine (St. Petersburg).[81] Further, there have been no reports of substantive contact with researchers working within the Ministry of Health's anti-plague facilities and the network of anti-plant and anti-animal BW facilities, and no access has been given to BW laboratories formerly subordinate to the KGB.[82] The immediate short-term obstacle to reorienting the network of Russian BW facilities toward civil projects is the retention of key administrative positions within *Biopreparat* and its affiliated facilities by staff who managed the Soviet offensive program.[83] As one analyst has indicated, it would appear that "these cold warriors want to perpetuate a weapons capability, the old way of life, and their own personal influence."[84]

Although the Russian Federation absorbed most of the facilities making up the Soviet Union's biological weapons program, several important BW installations are now located within a number of the newly independent states, including Belarus, Georgia, Kazakstan, and Uzbekistan. For example, key *Ekologiya* facilities formerly belonging to the anti-plant/anti-animal BW network are now located in the newly independent states of Kazakstan and Uzbekistan. Satellite research centers that were formerly subordinate to Russian agricultural BW facilities have been identified in Armenia and Tajikistan. Thus, as a result of the collapse of the USSR, there has been a significant increase in the number of countries in possession of technological capabilities associated with the development and production of offensive biological weapons. The newly formed governments of the FSU successor states initially had little knowledge of the installations they had inherited, and they were not in a realistic position to dismantle, convert, or absorb them into the commercial sector. However, the United States has acted quickly to assist Kazakstan with the demilitarization of its major BW facility in Stepnogorsk, and the ISTC is also channeling funding for demilitarization to BW researchers in the newly independent states.[85]

The combination of, first, a largely redundant BW complex with its huge network of facilities, and second, economic implosion resulting from the collapse of the Soviet Union, has led to a situation of serious risk that weapons scientists or agents and technologies will be transferred to countries pursuing their own biological weapons programs. American government officials have recently estimated that 7,000 biological weapons scientists possess critical knowledge and are of high-risk proliferation concern (some 6,500 of them are based in the Russian Federation and 500 in the newly independent states). Thus far, international efforts to support and monitor these researchers have been insufficient, and the ISTC is reported to have had only 1,000 FSU BW specialists on its grant payroll in 1998.[86] There may indeed have already been significant leaks. One recent report alleges that scientists from the N. F. Gamaleya Institute of Epidemiology & Microbiology (Moscow) undertook research in Iran in 1994. Approaches have also been made to anti-plant BW facilities, and Anatolii Makarov, the Director of the Institute of Phytopathology (Golitsyno), recently led a delegation of his scientists on a mission to Tehran.[87]

The collapse of central control of the Soviet Union's biological weapons network may also have led to a breakdown in security precautions at individual BW facilities. A number of incidents of unauthorized access to FSU biological weapons facilities have been documented.[88] It may also be the case that the security and accountability procedures that are in place are inadequate to prevent the theft or diversion of pathogenic strains or papers relating to weapons development and production. The vulnerability of FSU facilities is highlighted by the case of the USSR Ministry of Defense's BW facility in Ekaterinburg. This facility might be expected to have the highest level of security in the BW complex, but even here a military researcher was able to illegally procure an antibiotic-resistant strain of tularaemia in the mid-1980s and transfer it to his new laboratory in another institute.[89] Given concerns on the part of the United States and its allies that security at FSU facilities may still be deteriorating, the Cooperative Threat Reduction program is now funding a series of ISTC grants to enhance security at a number of institutes, including the Institute of Animal Health (Vladimir), *Vektor* (Novosibirsk), *Mikrob* Anti-Plague Institute (Saratov), the Institute of Phytopathology (Golitsyno), the Scientific Center of Applied Microbiology (Obolensk), the Kazak Anti-Plague Institute (Almaty, Kazakstan), and the Scientific-Research Agricultural Institute (Otar, Kazakstan).[90]

Another phenomenon with disturbing implications with regard to potential proliferation has been the rapid increase in recent years in the number of joint stock companies and other spin-offs created on the basis of organizations and facilities that provided critical input into the Soviet offensive biological weapons program. It is likely that the thirty or so companies thus far identified, many of which have established branches across the FSU, represent the tip of the iceberg. A good example of this trend is the Joint Stock Company "*Binom*," which in a recent advertisement detailed its role in the design and construction of a large number of BW facilities. These include the Berdsk Chemical Factory (Novosibirsk oblast'), the Omutninsk Chemical Factory (Kirov oblast'), *KNPK "Biomedpreparat"* (Stepnogorsk, Kazakstan), *Vektor* (Novosibirsk), and the State Scientific Center of Applied Microbiology (Obolensk).[91] Although new commercially based companies such as *Binom* are now undoubtedly playing a crucial role in the development of the civil pharmaceutical industry, they also represent a potential threat with regard to the proliferation of sensitive technologies and dual-use equipment from the FSU.[92]

Finally, a major legacy of the Soviet BW program that has been largely ignored in recent accounts is its full environmental impact. It would appear that the record of the military microbiologists with regard to contamination of the environment was no better than their colleagues in the civil sector who provoked nationwide protests following releases of microbial material into the atmosphere.[93] Leaks of military strains into the environment, which could potentially have a long-term impact on public health and the environment, may have occurred on a regular basis. Alibek alleges that a leakage of liquid anthrax from a reactor at the Ministry of Defense facility in Kirov in 1953 released the agent into the city's sewer system, where it was eventually detected in the rodent population. All subsequent attempts to eradicate the disease reportedly failed. In 1960, a wind-shift during a BW test on Konstantin Island in the Aral Sea led to widespread contamination and an emergency evacuation of the area.[94] A recent Russian report alleges that in the 1980s, *Biopreparat*'s Omutninsk BW production facility released a military strain of tularaemia into the environment. Rodents living in the forests surrounding the plant are said to have become infected, and again all attempts to eradicate the disease from local populations failed.[95] The best documented case of course concerns the release of an anthrax aerosol from Military Compound Number 19 in Ekaterinburg (formerly Sverdlovsk) on Monday, April 2, 1979, which has been the focus of intense local and international media attention over the past two decades. This incident led directly to the deaths of at least sixty-six people in Ekaterinburg itself and to cases of animal anthrax at a number of villages (Rudnii, Bol'shoe, Sedelnikovo, Maloe Sedelnikovo, Pervomaiskii, Kashino, and Abramovo) to the south-southeast of the city.[96] Given the absolute secrecy imposed on all aspects of the BW program, it is probable that there have been a number of other releases that have gone unreported in the Soviet media.

Appendix 5B provides details of the extensive environmental testing of biological weapons at more than fifteen sites across the former Soviet Union. It is likely that many of these will require extensive decontamination and subsequent monitoring for decades to come. It has recently been revealed, for example, that to avoid discovery by U.S. and UK inspectors, in the spring of 1988 the Soviet military transferred their stockpiles of anthrax from Ekaterinburg (formerly Sverdlovsk) to the Vozrozhdenie Island test site, where they were buried in a number of pits.[97] Despite the extensive use of bleach, it is alleged that live anthrax spores are still present at the site.[98] The existence of these deposits and other possible BW munitions is made all the more alarming by projections forecasting that the ongoing desiccation of the Aral Sea will lead within the next decade to the emergence of a substantial land bridge between Vozrozhdenie and the mainland.[99] In response to this threat, a number of U.S. agencies, in conjunction with the National Center for Biotechnology of Kazakstan, hope to establish a research station in Kazakstan to assess the future impact of the buried anthrax stocks and to produce data that might be utilized to limit the environmental hazard posed by the island.[100]

## CONCLUSION

The Soviet Union's success in illicitly developing and supporting a vast offensive BW program raises fundamental questions with regard to the operation of the Biological Weapons Convention. This article has demonstrated that the Soviet leadership cynically took the decision to violate Article I from the start, in the certain knowledge that they could cheat with impunity since the BWC had no mechanism for verification via on-site inspections. The present analysis may have important implications for any future protocol to the Convention that seeks to establish a strengthened verification regime. Certainly the ease with which the Soviet Union was able to violate the BWC suggests an urgent need to introduce highly intrusive inspections of known or suspected BW facilities. Furthermore, given the multi-organizational complexity of Soviet and Russian BW programs, it can be argued strongly that a compliance regime that omitted civil biotechnology and pharmaceutical facilities and included only military installations would make little sense. Indeed, given the wide-ranging extent of the Soviet effort and the existence of numerous subprograms, it may be that the criteria for selection of civil facilities for inspection should be widened to include laboratories subordinate to state security services and agricultural ministries. If progress is to be made in controlling biological weapons, it is essential that we learn the lessons from the massive Soviet violations of the BWC.

## APPENDIX 5A: CHRONOLOGY OF THE SOVIET UNION'S BIOLOGICAL WEAPONS PROGRAM

**1918** Establishment of a Central Veterinary Bacteriological Laboratory (*Tsentral'naya veterinarno-bakteriologicheskaya laboratoriya*) under the Red Army.[101]

**1921** In January the Central Veterinary-Bacteriological Laboratory is renamed the Central Microbiological Station.

**1924** The Central Microbiological Station is reformed as the Veterinary Microbiological Institute (*Veterinarnyi mikrobiologicheskii institut*) in St. Petersburg.

**1925** Yakob Moiseevich Fishman, Director of the Red Army's Military-Chemical Directorate (*VOKhIMU*), initiates the first Soviet BW research at one of its laboratories based in Moscow.[102]

**1928** The Soviet Union accedes to the Geneva Protocol.[103]

In February, Yakob Moiseevich Fishman prepares a report on BW preparedness of the Soviet Union for Kliment Voroshilov, Commissar for Defense. The Soviet Union's first major BW program is launched on the basis of the report's recommendations.[104]

The United State Political Administration (*OGPU*), a forerunner of the KGB, establishes a secret bacteriological laboratory for the

study of BW agents, headed by M. M. Faibich, at the Pokrovskii
Convent in Suzdal' (Vladimir *oblast*').[105]

Creation by the Red Army of a new BW facility, the Vaccine-Sera
Laboratory, in Vlasikha, close to the Perkhushkovo railway station in the Moscow *oblast*'. Professor Ivan Mikhailovich Velikanov (Head of the Department of Microbiology at Moscow State
University) is appointed Director of the Laboratory.[106]

The Veterinary Microbiological Institute is renamed the Red Army's
Veterinary Scientific-Research Institute.

**1931** Ivan Mikhailovich Velikanov decorated under the terms of the USSR
Revolutionary Military Council's Order No. 306.[107]

**1932** Ivan Mikhailovich Velikanov awarded the Order of the Red Star on
27 October.[108]

**1933** On April 16, the USSR Revolutionary Military Council issues an
Order amalgamating the Vaccine-Sera Laboratory with the Suzdal'
bacteriological laboratory to form the Red Army's Military Scientific-
Medical Institute (*Voennyi nauchnyi meditsinskii institut RKKA*)
at Vlasikha with Velikanov being appointed as its first Director.
The new facility, which is also known as the Biotechnical Institute
(*Biotekhnicheskii institut*), receives direct BW assignments from
the higher Soviet and party authorities and carries out a range of
tests on BW simulants at the existing Central Army Chemical
Proving Ground (*TsVKhP*) at Shikhany on the Volga.[109]

**1934** Establishment of a branch of the Biotechnical Institute known as the
Velikanov Institute or Institute No. V/2–1094 on Gorodomyla
Island (Lake Seliger) close to the town of Ostashkov in Tver (then
Kalinin) *oblast*'.[110]

**1935** On March 8 there is a conference of senior Soviet BW personnel in
Stalin's Kremlin Office. Besides Stalin himself, those present are
Ivan Mikhailovich Velikanov (Director of the Biotechnical Insti-
tute, Vlasikha), Demikhovskii (Vlasikha), Yaffe (Vlasikha), Yakob
Moiseevich Fishman (Head of the Chemical Administration of the
Red Army), and M.N. Tukhachevskii (Deputy Head of the Peo-
ple's Commissariat of Defense).[111]

**1936** The Soviet authorities select a 10,000-square-kilometer tract of land
on Vozrozhdenie Island (*Ostrov Vozrozhdenie* or "Island of
Rebirth") in the Aral Sea as a new BW proving ground.[112]

**1937** Arrest on July 6 of Ivan Mikhailovich Velikanov, chief architect of
the first major Soviet BW program.[113]

1938　Execution on April 8 of Ivan Mikhailovich Velikanov.[114]

1940　The threat of capture by German forces leads to the transfer of the Veterinary Microbiological Institute to a specially created base near Sergiev Posad (then Zagorsk).[115]

1941　Biotechnical Institute relocated to Saratov to prevent it from being captured by advancing German forces.
　　　Meeting on April 1 between M. M. Faibich (Biotechnical Institute), P. G. Mel'nikov (Head of the Administration of Military-Chemical Defense), and I. V. Stalin at the Kremlin. Subject of discussions unknown.[116]
　　　Biotechnical Institute evacuated from Saratov to Kirov in September in the face of a continuing German advance.[117]

1945　Soviet forces take possession in Berlin of the severely damaged Bacteriological Department of the Military Medical Academy's Institute for General & Military Hygiene (the "Kliewe Laboratory") which had been engaged in work on offensive use of biological weapons in combination with chemical weapons.[118]

1947　Construction of new military BW facility in Ekaterinburg (formerly named Sverdlovsk) based on designs developed for the Japanese biological weapons program.[119]

1953　Colonel-General Efim Ivanovich Smirnov is appointed head of the Red Army's Fifteenth Administration, which now manages Soviet BW facilities.[120]

1954　Veterinary Microbiological Institute in Sergiev Posad (formerly known as Zagorsk) used as the basis for the creation of a new military BW facility, then called the Scientific-Research Institute of Sanitation, for the study of viral and rickettsial agents.[121]
　　　Resumption of testing of biological weapons on Vozrozhdenie Island. A secret base, Aral'sk-7, with a population of more than 1,000, is established at the site.[122]

1958　Decree to establish a network of specialized anti-crop and anti-livestock BW facilities under the USSR Ministry of Agriculture issued in August by the Central Committee of the Communist Party of the Soviet Union (CPSU) and the Council of Ministers.[123]

1963　Rostov-on-Don Anti-Plague Institute is made lead facility for BW research within the civil anti-plague network. Among the projects underway at this facility are the production of an EV plague strain that is resistant to the majority of antibiotics in current use.[124]

**1964** USSR Ministry of Health establishes Specialized Anti-Epidemic Teams (*Spetsilizirovannye protivoepidemicheskie brigady* or *SPEB*) within the anti-plague network. The *SPEBs*, which remain in existence to this day in the Russian Federation, are mobile units comprising epidemiologists, bacteriologists, etc., that are capable of operating independently and are tasked with a specific BW role.[125]

**1967** On August 17 a top secret decree is issued by the Central Committee of the CPSU and the USSR Council of Ministers detailing the U.S. CBW program and calling for corresponding Soviet preparations.[126]

**1969** In September the Ministry of Defense's Institute of Military Medicine is established in St. Petersburg (then Leningrad). The Institute's Third Directorate (Bacteriology) is concerned directly with biological weapons.[127]

**1972** Soviet Union signs the Biological Weapons Convention on April 10.[128]

Viktor M. Zhdanov is appointed head of the Interdepartmental Scientific-Technical Council for Molecular Biology and Genetics, which has overall responsibility for the management of the Soviet BW program.[129]

**1973** All-Union Science Production Association *Biopreparat* is officially established on April 24. This is the lead organization of the new Soviet offensive BW program. General Vsevolod Ivanovich Ogarkov is appointed director.[130]

**1974** The All-Union Scientific-Research Institute of Applied Microbiology, *Biopreparat*'s most important bacteriological BW research center, is created in Obolensk (Moscow *oblast'*) on April 18 by a decree of the Central Committee of the Communist Party.[131]

A decree issued by the CPSU Committee and USSR Council of Ministers in May notes that "the general level and scale of research in molecular biology and molecular genetics in our country is still not satisfactory," and that fundamental discoveries in this area have major theoretical and applied significance.[132]

In August the All-Union Scientific-Research Institute of Molecular Biology (*VNIIMB*) is established at Kol'tsovo near Novosibirsk. The facility is *Biopreparat*'s premier BW center engaged in research on viruses.[133]

The All-Union Institute of Ultra Pure Biological preparations is established by *Biopreparat* in St. Petersburg (then Leningrad). The new institute researches and develops techniques for the testing and application of biological weapons.[134]

1975 Soviet Union deposits its instruments of Ratification of the BWC on March 26.[135]

1979 On Monday, April 2, there is an accident at a BW laboratory located within the USSR Ministry of Defense's Compound 19 in Sverdlovsk (now renamed Ekaterinburg), and an anthrax aerosol is released that is responsible for the deaths of at least sixty-six people. At the time, Soviet experts place the blame on ingestion of anthrax-infected meat, but this version of events is scientifically refuted by a Western team that gathers key evidence (including pathological samples of victims) during a visit to Ekaterinburg in 1992.[136]

Major General Yurii Tikhonovich Kalinin appointed Director of *Biopreparat*.[137]

1980 Establishment of the Institute of Immunology at Lyubuchany near Chekov. This facility is *Biopreparat*'s key center for the development of defensive medical preparations against BW agents.[138]

1982 Construction of the Scientific Experimental-Industrial Base in Stepnogorsk, Kazakstan, is initiated. This facility is scheduled to become the most important of *Biopreparat*'s mobilization facilities and possesses enormous capacity for the production of anthrax and other biological weapons.[139]

1983 Arrest in January of the alleged Soviet spy, Professor Marcus Klingberg, Deputy Director of the Israel Institute of Biological Research at Nes Ziona.[140]

1985 In August 1985 the CPSU Central Committee and the USSR Council of Ministers publish a second decree further underpinning the BW program by calling for the implementation of large-scale measures to accelerate the development of biology and biotechnology.[141]

1989 Vladimir Artemovich Pasechnik, Director of *Biopreparat*'s Institute of Ultra Pure Biological Preparations (St. Petersburg), defects to the United Kingdom and reveals extensive details of the Soviet offensive BW program.[142]

1991 As part of a new trilateral process, in January U.S. and UK inspectors visit four key *Biopreparat* BW facilities at Chekhov, Obolensk, Kol'tsovo, and St. Petersburg. The inspection team conclude in their report that "The Soviets had a massive, offensive biological warfare program run by Biopreparat and the military. It was the largest such program that the world had ever known."[143]

A reciprocal Soviet inspection of four BW sites in the United States begins on December 7, 1991.[144]

The USSR ceases to exist on December 31. The Russian Federation absorbs the bulk of the facilities that make up the Soviet BW program.

1992   Committee on Convention Problems of Chemical and Biological Weapons established in February.[145]

In April Boris Yeltsin issues decree "On ensuring the implementation of international pledges in the sphere of biological weapons."[146]

In September U.S. and UK policymakers arrive in Moscow to negotiate a memorandum of understanding on biological weapons, the Trilateral Agreement. This envisages, inter alia, a series of reciprocal visits to nonmilitary facilities.[147]

In October Kanatzhan Baizakovich Alibekov, First Deputy Director of *Biopreparat* from 1998 to 1992, defects to the United States and provides an authoritative account of the Soviet BW program.[148]

1993   On January 19 the U.S. Arms Control and Disarmament Agency notes that "the Russian offensive biological warfare program, inherited from the Soviet Union, violated the BWC through at least March 1992. . . . The status of the program since then remains unclear."[149]

As part of the Trilateral Agreement, in October a joint U.S./UK inspection team visits Russian BW production facilities at Pokrov and Berdsk.[150]

1994   On January 10 a second U.S./UK team begins another series of inspections under the terms of the Trilateral Agreement. The inspectors visit Russian BW facilities at Omutninsk and Obolensk.[151]

On February 11 a Russian team arrives in Washington for a Trilateral inspection of three sites in the United States.[152]

As part of the ongoing Trilateral process a Russian inspection team visits Evans Medical Laboratories, a vaccine facility in Speke, United Kingdom.[153]

1997   Searle invests $6 million in a new $32 million joint venture with *Biopreparat's* All-Russian Center for Molecular Diagnostics & Therapy.[154]

1998   On December 17 at a meeting in Tambov between Russian and U.S. representatives, it is agreed in principle that scientists from BW facilities belonging to the Russian Ministry of Defense will participate in a series of reciprocal visits to explore the terms of collaborative projects.[155]

**1999** On May 8 Lieutenant-General Valentin Ivanovich Evstigneev (at this time head of the Ministry of Defense's Biological Defense Department) is reappointed to the Council of Directors of *RAO Biopreparat*.[156]

On July 2 the Russian government issues a decree to establish the federal Pathogen Defense Programme, which aims, during the period 1999–2005, to restore and develop vaccine production at a number of key biotechnology facilities, including those belonging to *RAO Biopreparat* and the Ministry of Defense.[157]

In July and October reports appear in the local Kirov newspaper *Vyatskii nablyudatel'* of a cancer cluster at the Scientific-Research Institute of Microbiology's Kirov-200 station (Levintsy, near Strizhi).[158]

In August the Committee on Convention Problems of Chemical and Biological Weapons is disbanded and absorbed within the new Russian Agency for Munitions (Rosboepripasy).[159]

On November 20 a Center for Special Laboratory Diagnostics & Treatment of Highly Dangerous & Exotic Infectious Diseases is established under the Ministries of Health and Defense.[160]

**2000** On August 25 V. G. Mamigonov, Deputy Minister of the Ministry of Property Relations of the Russian Federation, signs Order No. 451-r relating to the transfer of cantonment No. 992 (the BW facilities at Levintsy near Strizhi) to the Vyatka State Technical University.[161]

**2001** In April Kalinin is replaced as head of *RAO Biopreparat* by a civilian public health expert, Dr. Ramil U. Khabriev.[162]

On December 21 the Russian government issues a decree to establish an Interdepartmental Commission on Biotechnology.[163]

**2002** On February 27 the Russian government announces that experts from the Russian Ministry of Civil Defense, Emergencies and Natural Disasters will conduct joint research with scientists from Kazakstan to assess the contamination of Vozrozhdenie Island.[164]

# APPENDIX 5B: BIOLOGICAL WEAPONS PROVING GROUNDS IN THE SOVIET UNION

| Location | Name | Institutional Affiliation | Period in Use | BW Activity |
|---|---|---|---|---|
| Chukotka | Proving ground of Centre of Military-Technical Problems of Anti-Bacteriological Defence | USSR Ministry of Defence | | Testing of attenuated BW combat strains |
| Durmen' (possibly now renamed Yukariyuz), Near Kibrai, Tashkent oblast', Uzbekistan | Proving ground of Central Asian Scientific-Research Institute of Phytopathology | USSR Ministry of Agriculture | 1958–1991 | Testing of anti-crop BW agents |
| Ekaterinburg (formerly Sverdlovsk), Russian Federation | Proving ground of Centre of Military-Technical Problems of Anti-Bacteriological Defence | USSR Ministry of Defence | | |
| Gvardeiskii settlement, Otar, Dzhambul oblast', Kazakstan | Proving ground of Scientific-Research Agricultural Institute | USSR Ministry of Agriculture | 1958–1991 | Testing of anti-crop and anti-livestock BW agents |
| Kirov, Kirov oblast', Russian Federation | Proving ground of Scientific-Research Institute of Microbiology | USSR Ministry of Defence | | |
| Kol'tsovo, Novosibirsk, Russian Federation | Proving ground of the Science Production Association Vektor | State Concern Biopreparat | | Testing of anti-crop and anti-livestock BW agents |
| Komsomol'skii Island, Aral Sea, Kazakstan | | USSR Ministry of Defence | | |
| Konstantin Island, Aral Sea, Kazakstan | | USSR Ministry of Defence | | |
| Kuzminki, Moscow oblast', Russian Federation | Kuzminki Proving Ground | People's Commissariat of Defence | 1918–1940 | Testing of anti-livestock BW agents including anthrax |

| Location | Facility | Organization | Dates | Description |
|---|---|---|---|---|
| Lake Peipus (Lake Chudskoe), Estonia Lake Peipus (Lake Chudskoe), Estonia | Unknown | Wa Prßf 9 (CW Defence Section of German Army Ordnancy Office) | 1942–1943 | Limited testing of foot-and-mouth disease virus |
| Nukus, Uzbekistan | | USSR Ministry of Defence | | Allegedly utilized for testing of BW simulants |
| Sergiev Posad (formerly Zagorsk), Moscow oblast', Russian Federation | Proving ground of Scientific-Research Centre of Virology | | | |
| Shikhany, Russian Federation | Central Army Chemical Proving Ground (TsVKhP) | People's Commissariat of Defence/ USSR Ministry of Defence | 1935 | Tests to develop reliable methods for the use of foot-and-mouth disease virus in combat operations |
| Solovetskii Islands | Solovetskii Prison of Special Significance | People's Commissariat for Internal Affairs (NKVD) | 1928–1942 | Research was conducted on Q fever, glanders, and melioidosis. |
| Unknown | Testing Ground East (Versuchsfeld Ost) or Bacteria Field East (B-Feld Ost) | Unknown (German control) | | A number of experiments with BW simulants, foot-and-mouth disease virus, arthropods, and weeds were planned at B-Feld Ost but no additional information concerning this work is available. |
| Verkhnyaya Pysma, Ekaterinburg oblast', Russian Federation | Proving ground of Centre of Military-Technical Problems of Anti-Bacteriological Defence | USSR Ministry of Defence | | Testing of BW simulants |
| Vozrozhdenie Island (Ostrov Vozrozhdenie or "Island of Rebirth"), Aral Sea, Uzbekistan/Kazakstan | Aral'sk-7 | People's Commissariat of Defence/USSR Ministry of Defence | 1936–1991 | Principal Soviet site for the testing of battlefield and strategic biological weapons |

# APPENDIX 5C: USSR MINISTRY OF AGRICULTURE ANTI-CROP AND ANTI-LIVESTOCK BW FACILITIES

| Soviet Name of Facility | Current Name | Location | Subordination (Soviet/Current) | Number of Personnel (Soviet/Current) | BW Activity |
|---|---|---|---|---|---|
| All-Union Scientific-Research Institute of Phytopathology | All-Russian Scientific-Research Institute of Phytopathology | Vyazemy, Near Golitsyno, 143050 Moscow oblast', Russian Federation | USSR Ministry of Agriculture/ Russian Academy of Agricultural Sciences | 1,200/276 | Developed anti-crop weapons, including agents for destruction of wheat, rye, corn and rice. |
| All-Union Scientific-Research Foot-&-Mouth Disease Institute | All-Russian Institute for Animal Health | p/o Yur'evets, Vladimir, 600900 Vladimir oblast', Russian Federation | USSR Ministry of Agriculture/Russian Ministry of Food and Agriculture | /1,000 | Researched and developed anti-livestock weapons including: African swine fever, foot-and-mouth disease, rinderpest, etc. |
| All-Union Scientific-Research Institute of Virology & Microbiology | All-Russian Scientific-Research Institute of Virology & Microbiology | Poselok Vol'ginskii, Pokrov, Petushinskii raion, 601120 Vladimir oblast', Russian Federation | USSR Ministry of Agriculture/Russian Ministry of Food & Agriculture | | Presumably engaged in the development of anti-livestock weapons. |
| Almaty Biocombine | Almaty Biocombine | Prospekt Abaya, 109, 480008 Almaty, Kazakstan | USSR Ministry of Agriculture/ National Centre for Biotechnology of Kazakstan | /577 | Reserve mobilization plant for production of biological weapons, primarily anthrax. |
| Central Asian Scientific-Research Institute of Phytopathology | Institute of Genetics | Durmen (possibly now renamed Yukariyuz), Near Kibrai, Tashkent oblast', Uzbekistan | USSR Ministry of Agriculture/Uzbek Academy of Sciences | /280 | Engaged in the development and testing of anti-crop weapons |
| Central Asian Branch of All-Union Scientific-Research Foot-&-Mouth Disease Institute | Unknown | Dushanbe, Tajikistan | USSR Ministry of Agriculture/ | | |

| | | | | |
|---|---|---|---|---|
| Factory of Bioprep-arations | Factory of Biopreparations | Poselok Vol'ginskii, Pokrov, Petushinskii raion, 601120 Vladimir oblast', Russian Federation | USSR Ministry of Agriculture/ Russian Ministry of Food & Agriculture | /1,000 | Mobilization facility for the manufacture of smallpox (up to 100 tons) and Venezuelan equine encephalitis (40 to 80 tons), as well as other viral weapons. Reserve facility for anti-livestock biological weapons. |
| North Caucasus Scientific-Research Institute of Phytopathology | North Caucasus Scientific-Research Institute of Phytopathology | Krasnodar raion, Russian Federation | USSR Ministry of Agriculture/ Russian Academy of Agricultural Sciences | | Presumably engaged in the development of anti-crop weapons. |
| Scientific-Research Agricultural Institute | Scientific-Research Agricultural Institute | Gvardeiskii settlement, Otar, 485444 Dzhambul oblast', Kazakstan | USSR Ministry of Agriculture/ National Centre for Biotechnology of Kazakstan | 400/210 | Tested anti-crop and anti-livestock biological weapons. |
| Transcaucasian Branch of the All-Union Scientific-Research Foot-&-Mouth Disease Institute | Armenian Scientific-Research Institute of Veterinary Medicine | Yerevan, Armenia | USSR Ministry of Agriculture/ | | |
| Central Russian Branch of the All-Union Scientific-Research Institute of Phytopathology | Central Russian Branch of the All-Russian Scientific-Research Institute of Phytopathology | Novaya zhizn' settlement, Tambov, Russian Federation | USSR Ministry of Agriculture/ Russian Academy of Agricultural Sciences | | |
| Research Institute of Phytopathology | Research Institute of Phytopathology | Federation | Agricultural Sciences | | |

## NOTES

1. The author wishes to express his gratitude to Mr. Christopher Joyce, a post-graduate student at the Center for Russian & East European Studies, University of Birmingham, for his assistance in the identification and retrieval of background documents relating to the Soviet BW program from the Russian State Archives.

2. J. Barber, M. Harrison, N. Simonov, and B. Starkov, "The Structure and Development of the Defense-Industry Complex," in *The Soviet Defense-Industry Complex from Stalin to Khrushchev,* ed. J. Barber and M. Harrison (London: Macmillan, 1999), 3, 39.

3. Ya Fishman, Rabota Bakteriologicheskoi Laboratorii *VOKhIMU,* Russian State Military Archive, (*RGVA*), Fond 33,987, Opis' 1, Delo 657, 141–45; V. Bojtzov and E. Geissler, "Military Biology in the USSR: 1920–45," in *Biological and Toxin Weapons Research, Development and Use from the Middle Ages to 1945: A Critical Comparative Analysis,* ed. E. Geissler and J. E. van Courtland Moon, SIPRI Chemical & Biological Warfare Studies (Oxford: Oxford University Press, 1999), chapter 8.

4. The Soviet Union acceded to the Geneva Protocol in 1928 with the reservations that: "1. The said Protocol only binds the Government of the Union of Soviet Socialist Republics in relation to the States which have signed and ratified or which have definitely acceded to the Protocol; and 2. The said Protocol shall cease to be binding on the Government of the Union of Soviet Socialist Republics in regard to any enemy State whose armed forces or whose allies *de jure* or in fact do not respect the prohibitions which are the object of this Protocol." Similar reservations had been made by France two years earlier. Stockholm International Peace Research Institute, *The Problem of Chemical and Biological Warfare: A Study of the Historical, Technical, Military, Legal and Political Aspects of CBW, and Possible Disarmament Measures, Volume II, CB Weapons Today* (Stockholm: Almqvist and Wiksell; New York: Humanities Press; London: Paul Elek, 1973), 161.

5. On 8 March 1935, for example, Stalin held a major conference of senior Soviet BW personnel in his Kremlin Office. Besides Stalin himself, those present were Ivan Mikhailovich Velikanov (Director of the Biotechnical Institute, Vlasikha), Demikhovskii (Vlasikha), Yaffe (Vlasikha), Yakob Moiseevich Fishman (Head of the Chemical Administration of the Red Army), and M. N. Tukhachevskii (Deputy Head of the People's Commissariat of Defense). "Posetiteli kremlevskogo kabineta I. V. Stalina, Zhurnaly (tetradi) zapisi lits, prinyatykh pervym gensekom. 1924–1953, Alfavitnyi ukazatel'," *Istoricheskii arkhiv,* No. 4 (1998).

6. However, Japan's BW program, initiated in 1930, appears to have subsequently surpassed in size and importance that of the Soviet Union. During the early 1930s it received massive military investment and subsequently underwent rapid development with the construction of the world's largest known biological warfare facility at Ping Fan, south of Harbin, in 1936. S. Harris, "The Japanese Biological Warfare Programme: An Overview," in Geissler and van Courtland Moon, *Biological and Toxin Weapons,* 127–52. See also chapter 8.

7. A note of caution should be added here since the main source of information concerning the role of the Military-Medical Academy and the utilization of the Solo-

vetskii Islands as a test site is K. Alibek and S. Handelman, *Biohazard: The Chilling True Story of the Largest Covert Biological Weapons Program in the World—Told from the Inside by the Man Who Ran It* (London: Hutchinson, 1999), 32–36. Alibek bases his account on "old reports of the Ministry of Defense" and "veterans in our program who had learned the facts in turn from older scientists." Geissler in his account confirms the use of the Solovetskii Islands for BW experiments. However, this version of the early history of the Soviet BW program is not corroborated by Hirsch (who is consistently reliable) or any of the more recent Russian sources. More important, some of Alibek's claims are in direct contradiction to the known facts. Vozrozhdenie Island was in use as a proving ground starting in the mid-1930s and therefore certainly did not come into use as a result of the evacuation of the BW test site based on the Solovetskii Islands. In addition a large number of well-documented sources indicate that it was the Biotechnical Institute (Vlasikha) that was relocated to Kirov in 1942 and took possession of an *Oblast'* Infectious Diseases Hospital. These and other relatively minor inconsistencies mean that we must remain extremely cautious about Alibek's historical account until verification is obtained via Russian academic publications or via archival research.

8. The main island of the group was the location of a biological station (*Biosad*), which remained operational until 1930. From 1934 to 1936 the laboratories of O. P. Florenskii were based here. Other islands included *Bol'shaya Muksolma*, location of a chemical laboratory in 1926, and *Malaya Muksolma,* which was used to hold a number of secret prisoners. Information was kindly provided by Mr. Christopher Joyce, postgraduate student at the Center for Russian & East European Studies, University of Birmingham.

9. According to a recent report, Komsomol'sk Island in the Aral Sea was also utilized by the Soviet Union as a BW test range. S. Pluzhnikov and A. Shvedov, "Ubiitsa iz probirki," *Sovershenno sekretno*, No. 4 (1998), 12.

10. The question of whether the Soviet Union was capable of deploying biological weapons in offensive operations during World War II remains unanswered. There is certainly no substantive evidence that any large-scale attacks were initiated, although captured German documents do contain a number of allegations concerning the use of BW in guerrilla and sabotage operations. A full analysis of German reports concerning such activities is contained in Bojtzov and Geissler, "Military Biology in the USSR: 1920–45."

11. The United States and the United Kingdom are reported to have failed to produce an anthrax vaccine suitable for human use during the war. Biological weapons scientists from the Biotechnical Institute also produced the Soviet Union's first industrial batches of penicillin in 1944 for use in hospitals at the front. The institute also developed technology for the production of bacteriophage, which were successfully utilized for the treatment of gas gangrene. V. A. Lebedinskii, T. G. Abdulin, V. I. Evstigneev, N. S. Garin, and E. P. Lukin, "Vklad nauchno-issledovatel'skii instituta mikrobiologii ministerstva oborony SSSR v razrabotku problem infektsionnoi immunologii," *Voenno-meditsinskii zhurnal*, No. 8 (August 1989), 67–69.

12. I. V. Darmov, I. P. Pogorel'skii, and V. I. Velikanov, "Nauchno-issledovatel'-skomu institutu mikrobiologii ministerstva oborony rossiiskoi federatsii–70 let," *Voenno-meditsinskii zhurnal* 320(2) (February 1999), 79–81; V. I. Velikanov, "K

60-letiyu sozdaniya nauchno-issledovatel'skogo instituta mikrobiologii ministerstva oborony rossiiskoi federatsii," *Voenno-meditsinskii zhurnal*, No. 12 (1993), 57.

13. The speech was given by Voroshilov on 22 February 1938. Stockholm International Peace Research Institute, *Problem of Chemical and Biological Warfare, Volume 1*, 287.

14. On 24 September 1934 Kaganovich wrote to Stalin, "On your instructions Comrade N. Kuibyshev reviewed the material relating to Yaffe's statement on military-bacteriological work. The situation there is very bad." Yaffe was employed at this time at the Red Army's BW institute in Vlasikha. *RGASPI*, Fond 558, Opus 11, Delo 742, II, 99–104.

15. Z. A. Medvedev, *Soviet Science* (Oxford: Oxford University Press, 1979), 32.

16. *The Cambridge Encyclopedia of Russia and the Former Soviet Union*, ed. A. Brown, M. Kaser, and G. S. Smith (Cambridge: Cambridge University Press, 1994), 109–10.

17. Bojtzov and Geissler provide an excellent account of the trumped-up charges and allegations of fictitious plots leveled against microbiologists and bacteriologists at this time. Bojtzov and Geissler, "Military Biology in the USSR: 1920–45."

18. Z. A. Medvedev, *The Rise and Fall of T. D. Lysenko* (New York and London: Columbia University Press, 1969); V. N. Soyfer, *Lysenko and the Tragedy of Soviet Science*, (New Brunswick, N.J.: Rutgers Universities Press, 1994); M. Popovsky, *The Vavilov Affair* (Archon Books, 1984); D. Joravsky, *The Lysenko Affair* (Chicago and London: The University of Chicago Press, 1970).

19. L. R. Graham, *Science in Russia and the Soviet Union: A Short History* (Cambridge: Cambridge University Press, 1993), 134.

20. B. Starkov, "The Security Organs and the Defense-Industry Complex," in Barber and Harrison, *Soviet Defense-Industry Complex*, 257

21. For example, in the early 1950s scientists at the *"Mikrob"* Anti-Plague Institute in Saratov worked on the development of an express method for detection of plague bacteria for the military. I. Domaradskii, op. cit., 42–43.

22. Garthoff, who was formerly employed at the CIA and then within the U.S. State Department in the Foreign Service, provides a detailed account of American attempts to use multiple channels to convey the misleading message to the Soviets that the United States was pursuing a clandestine biological weapons program in contravention of the 1972 BW convention. There has as yet been no verification of this version of events from other sources. R. L. Garthoff, "Polyakov's Run," *The Bulletin of the Atomic Scientists* 56(5) (September/October 2000), 37–40.

23. "V tsentral'nom komitete KPSS i Sovete Ministrov SSSR," *Pravda*, No. 20380 (21 May 1974), 1.

24. A. N. Shevchenko, *Breaking with Moscow* (New York: Alfred A. Knopf, 1985), 173–74.

25. "V Politbyuro TsK KPSS," *Pravda*, No. 24485 (16 August 1985), 1.

26. A. Venter, "The Invisible Threat: What Does Russia Have Up Its Biological Warfare Sleeve?" *International Defense Review* (9 January 1998).

27. A. Rimmington, *Who's Who in Russia & Republics Biotechnology* (Clifton, York: Technology Detail, December 1994), 214–16.

28. V. M. Zhdanov and O. V. Baroyan were identified by Domaradskii as members of the special commission. Alibek identifies Yurii Anatol'evich Ovchinnikov as the key member of the commission. Of considerable interest in relation to Ovchinnikov's role within the *VPK* is the fact that after his death from leukemia in February 1988 one of the principal signatures on his obituary was that of Igor' Belousov, then head of the *VPK*. I. Domaradskii, "Istoriya odnoi avantyury," *Znanie-sila*, No. 11 (1996), 63; Alibek and Handelman, *Biohazard*, 296; *Izvestiya* (20 February 1988).

29. T. Malleret, *Conversion of the Defense Industry in the Former Soviet Union*, Occasional Paper series No. 23 (New York: Institute for East-West Security Studies, 1992), 6–7; J. Cooper, "The Civilian Production of the Soviet Defense Industry," in *Technical Progress and Soviet Economic Development*, ed. R. Amann and J. Cooper (Oxford: Basil Blackwell, 1986), 31–33.

30. Domaradskii, "Istoriya odnoi avantyury," 58.

31. In September 1974 Ovchinnikov is reported to have summoned a group of biologists to the Presidium of the Academy:

> Without wasting words the vice-president informed them that they were confronted by a major political challenge. The Americans had stopped work on a superpowerful bacteriological weapon, and it was for Soviet scientists to make the most of this opportunity. A group of the ablest and most energetic specialists in various fields was being formed for the purpose—who would volunteer? It would be a storm troop, a force of marines, a biological commando, a crack division! All the money and equipment they wanted! No need for a higher degree! Even Jews were eligible! The one and only objective was to come up with a supervirulent type of virus or pathogenic microbe, and gene engineering was an excellent method to this end.

M. Popovsky, *Science in Chains: The Crisis of Science and Scientists in the Soviet Union Today* (London: Collins and Harvill Press, 1980), 229.

32. C. J. Davis, "Nuclear Blindness: An Overview of the Biological Weapons Programs of the Former Soviet Union and Iraq," *Emerging Infectious Diseases* 5(4) (July–August 1999). Mangold and Goldberg report that by the time of the Pasechnik defection in 1989 there was a yearly budget of several hundred million dollars for research, production, testing, and equipment design and that "co-ordinated military activities raised these totals to . . . nearly \$1 billion in annual spending." T. Mangold and J. Goldberg, *Plague Wars: A True Story of Biological Warfare* (London: Macmillan, 1999), 92.

33. A. Rimmington, Biotechnology in the USSR, Ph.D. thesis, Center for Russian & East European Studies, Birmingham: University of Birmingham, 1988, 306–7; Mikrobiologicheskaya promyshlennost', *Razvitie khimicheskoi promyshlennosti v SSSR 1917–1980*, Vol. 2 (Moscow: 1984).

34. *Biopreparat* was initially based within *Glavmikrobioprom*'s headquarters on Ulitsa Lestev, but in Autumn 1973 was transferred to a building formerly belonging to the Academy of Chemical Defense on Ulitsa Samokatnaya, 4a. Domaradskii, "Istoriya odnoi avantyury," 63.

35. These facilities were transferred to *Biopreparat* under *Glavmikrobioprom* Order No. 200 issued on 26 June 1974. Information on the origins of *Biopreparat* and its early organization can be found in the Russian State Economic Archive

(*RGAE*), Introduction to Fond 178, Opis' 1, Delo 5895 (*Glavmikrobioprom*, 1966–1985).

36. Domaradskii, "Istoriya odnoi avantyury," 59–65.

37. *Minsredmash* is reported to have transferred senior personnel for the management of *Biopreparat*'s program. In addition it was closely involved in the construction of new microbiological facilities at Aksu, near Stepnogorsk. A close personal friendship existed between Belyaev, head of *Glavmikrobioprom*, and Efim Pavlovich Slavskii, Minister of *Minsredmash*, and the latter made available *Minsredmash*'s excess construction capacity in Stepnogorsk to *Glavmikrobioprom*. E. I. Perov, Trudnye shagi "Progressa," *Stepnogorsk. Zdes' propisany nashi serdtsa. Stranitsy istorii goroda Stepnogorska Akmolinskoi oblasti*, Atamura, Almaty, 107–25; Perechen' predpriyatii Glavmikrobioproma, stroitel'stvo kotorykh vozlagaetsya na Mintyazhstroi SSSR, Minpromstroi SSSR, Minstroi SSSR, Minsel'stroi SSSR, Minenergo SSSR i Minsredmash, Prilozhenie, No. 8 k postanovleniyu TsK KPSS i Soveta Ministrov SSSR ot " " 1970g., Fond 178, Opis 1, Delo 953.

38. Oleg Ignat'ev is reported to have been the head of a BW department within the *VPK* during the 1970s. Domaradskii, "Istoriya odnoi avantyury," *Znanie-Sila*, 11(833), (1996), 67–68.

39. Alibekov provided an authoritative account of the Soviet BW program to the U.S. government. J. Langton, "A Plague on All Our Houses," *The Sunday Telegraph* (8 March 1998), 3.

40. L. Sandakhchiev, "Innovation Development Programme of the Association 'VECTOR' for 1995 and till 2005," State-Owned Concern "Biopreparat" Scientific-Production Association "Vector," *Novosibirsk* (1991).

41. Institut Immunologii, Lyubuchany, Moskovskaya oblast', SSSR, Chekhov, n.d., 12.

42. At present there is no means of independently verifying the existence of such tactical and strategic BW delivery systems. The account provided in this paragraph relies on the testimony of high-ranking defectors from the Soviet BW program and additional information provided in the open literature by Western intelligence sources. Until further information or testimony is forthcoming, this description of Soviet tactical and strategic capabilities should be treated with some caution.

43. Mangold and Goldberg, *Plague Wars*, 94–97. The text of this book is available with endnotes online at www.macmillan.co.uk.

44. A. E. Smithson, "Toxic Archipelago: Preventing Proliferation from the Former Soviet chemical and Biological Weapons Complexes," Report No. 32, The Henry L. Stimson Center, December 1999, 9.

45. Mangold and Goldberg, *Plague Wars*, 138. A referenced version of the text is available online at www.macmillan.co.uk.

46. M. Leitenberg, "Biological Weapons and Arms Control," *Contemporary Security Policy* 17(1) (April 1996), 6.

47. This Directorate is listed by *Veterinariya* and the Central Intelligence Agency as the Main Administration for Scientific-Research and Experimental-Production Establishments under the USSR Ministry of Agriculture. This organization is presumably the same as that referred to by Alibek as the Main Directorate for Scientific and Production Enterprises. P. P. Rakhmanin, "K 100-letiyu agrobiologicheskoi

promyshlennosti Rossii," *Veterinariya*, No. 8 (1996), 10; *Directory of Soviet Officials: National Organizations, A Reference Aid*, CIA National Foreign Assessment Center, CR81–11343, May 1981, 32–33; Alibek and Handelman, *Biohazard*, 37–38.

48. Some time around January 1960, for example, General V. Ya. Podalyan, the director of the closed USSR Ministry of Defense's Medical Institute (Sanitarnyi institut) in Moscow, is reported to have received a letter from the Ministry of Defense concerning the transfer of specialized personnel to the new Directorate that had been established by the USSR Ministry of Agriculture. A retired Russian military officer reports that the order confirming his transfer to the Ministry of Agriculture was personally signed by Marshall Malinovskii, the Minister of Defense. The majority of military personnel transferred from the Medical Institute to the Ministry of Agriculture remained based in Moscow. Excerpts from unpublished memoirs, 25 February 2000. These are scheduled to be published in 2001 as part of a new series of occasional papers by the Center for Russian & East European Studies, University of Birmingham.

49. J. Tucker, Biological Weapons Proliferation from Russia: How Great a Threat?, Remarks prepared for the 7th Carnegie International Non-Proliferation Conference, Washington, D.C., 11–12 January 1999; available online at ceip.org/programs/npp/tucker.htm.

50. Alibek and Handelman, *Biohazard*, 37–38.

51. C. Brown, "Agro-Terrorism: A Cause for Alarm," *The Monitor: Non-proliferation, Demilitarisation, and Arms Control* (Center for International Trade and Security) 5(1–2) (Winter–Spring 1999).

52. The facilities created at this time as a result of the decree were the All-Union Scientific-Research Institute of Phytopathology (Golitsyno, Moscow *oblast'*), the North Caucasus Scientific-Research Institute of Phytopathology (Krasnodar *raion*), the Central Asian Scientific-Research Institute of Phytopathology (Durmen', Tashkent *oblast'*, Uzbekistan), the All-Union Scientific-Research Institute of Virology & Microbiology (Pokrov, Vladimir *oblast'*), the All-Union Scientific-Research Foot-&-Mouth Disease Institute (Vladimir *raion*, Vladimir *oblast'*), and the Scientific-Research Agricultural Institute (Gvardeiskii, Kazakstan). The latter facility at Gvardeiskii is reported to have been attached to a Ministry of Defense Biological Weapons proving ground. L. Fedorov, "Khronika pamyatnykh dat 'khimicheskoi' zhizni TsK KPSS," *Posev*, No. 1 (1999). The Ministry of Agriculture was created in 1953 with its headquarters based at Orlikov pereulok, 1/11, 107139 Moscow. The Ministry was replaced by the All-Union State Agro-Industrial Committee (*Gosudarstvennyi agropromyshlennyi komitet* or *Gosagroprom*) in November 1985. *Gosagroprom's* headquarters remained based at Orlikov Pereulok. *Directory of Soviet Officials: National Organizations, A Reference Aid*, CIA National Foreign Assessment Center, CR81–11343, May 1981, 32–33; *Directory of Soviet Officials: National Organizations, A Reference Aid*, CIA Directorate of Intelligence, LDA87–1290, June 1987, 156.

53. The Soviet program appears to have run parallel to a U.S. program that included the testing, production, and stockpiling of anti-crop agents. Between 1951 and 1969, thirty-one anti-crop dissemination trials were conducted at twenty-three

different locations. Many anti-crop BW agents were screened, resulting in five standardized BW anti-crop agents. From 1951 to 1957, wheat stem rust spores and rye stem rust spores were produced at Fort Detrick and transhipped to Edgewood Arsenal, where they were classified, dried, and placed in storage. During 1962–1969, wheat stem rust spores were produced and transhipped to Rocky Mountain Arsenal, Denver, Colorado, classified, dried, and stored. Rice blast spores were also produced during this period under contract to Charles Pfizer and Company and shipped to Fort Detrick for classification, drying, and storage. The entire stockpile was destroyed as part of the U.S. biological warfare demilitarization program completed in February 1973. The U.S. Department of Agriculture took over the work from the Army Crops Division in the mid-1970s. N. M. Covert, *Cutting Edge: A History of Fort Detrick, Maryland 1943–1993* (Fort Detrick, Md: Public Affairs Office (HSHD–PA), Headquarters U.S. Army Garrison, September 1994), 27–33.

54. Alibek and Handelman, *Biohazard,* 37–38.

55. A recent interview with a former weapons scientist revealed that while working within the *Ekologiya* program his facility established close links with a laboratory based at the Center of Virology in Sergiev Posad (then Zagorsk). Interview with former anti-livestock weapons scientist, Ala-Acha, Kyrgyz Republic, 12 September 1999. A recent report published by the Center for Non-proliferation Studies suggests that joint work was also carried out in collaboration with the Center of Military-Technical problems of Anti-Bacteriological Defense in Ekaterinburg (then Sverdlovsk). G. Bozheyeva, Y. Kunakbayev, and Y. Dastan, *Former Soviet Biological Weapons Facilities in Kazakhstan: Past, Present, and Future* Center for Non-proliferation Studies Occasional Paper No. 1 (Monterey, Calif.: Monterey Institute of International Studies, June 1999), 16.

56. Under the terms of Decree No. 89 issued in 1989 by *Glavmikrobioprom,* the state-owned farm Iskitimsky (Morosovo, Iskitim *raion,* Novosibirsk *oblast'*), incorporating production buildings and 5,035 hectares of land, was transferred to *Vektor* for the construction of an Experimental Agricultural Production Enterprise. In 1988 *Vektor* also took possession of the village of Nizhny Koyon with adjacent land occupying 7,511 hectares, again in connection with the establishment of a new enterprise. *Vektor* established new animal-holding facilities at these sites for 440 cattle and an unknown number of pigs. These new facilities may have been connected with the agricultural BW testing program undertaken by *Vektor.* Lev Sandakhchiev, "Innovation Development Program of the Association "VECTOR" for 1992–1995 and Till 2005," 3, 18.

57. A. A. Gusev, "Gody stanovleniya i perspektivy nauchno-proizvodstvennoi deyatel'nosti," *Veterinariya,* No. 8 (1996), 31.

58. Alibek and Handelman, *Biohazard,* 301.

59. The BW complex was accessed via three security posts. Military guards remain on site to the present day since a large training center is maintained by the Kazak Ministry of Defense at Gvardeiskii. Bozheyeva, Kunakbayev, and Yeleukenov, *Former Soviet Biological Weapons Facilities in Kazakhstan,* 11–12.

60. Professor Khanduev originally graduated from the Military Veterinary Academy in Moscow. He was then appointed to a position at the Ministry of Defense's Sanitary-Medical Institute. In 1960 he was transferred to Gvardeiskii.

Interview with Academician Tsyren Khanduev, Kyrgyz Academy of Sciences' Institute of Biochemistry and Physiology, Bishkek, Kyrgyz Republic, 1100, 16 April 1999; Bozheyeva, Kunakbayev, and Yeleukenov, *Former Soviet Biological Weapons Facilities in Kazakhstan,* 12.

61. S. Mamadaliev, "The Detection of Probability of Bringing in Particularly Dangerous Infections to the Territory of the Republic of Kazakstan and the Development of Scientifically Based Measures of Control and Prophylactics," in *Conversion in the Framework of International Collaboration, Proceedings* (Almaty, Kazakstan, October 1996), 46–47; Bozheyeva, Kunakbayev, and Yeleukenov, *Former Soviet Biological Weapons Facilities in Kazakhstan,* 12.

62. *World of Learning 1994* (London: Europa Publications, 1994), 1256.

63. Alibek and Handelman, *Biohazard,* 301.

64. Ibid.; N. Rufford, "The West's Secret Weapon to Win the Opium War," *The Sunday Times* (28 June 1998). The institute appears to have focused on the development of fungal pathogens. There have been no references made to work on bacterial or viral phytopathogens.

65. Professor Abdukarimov Abdusattor (Director, Institute of Genetics) reported that pathogenic strains had been selected for resistance to fungicides. R. Carr, *Preliminary Report on DTI OSTEMS Visit to Uzbekistan* (November 1996), 13.

66. Information provided by Professor Abdukarimov Abdusattor, Director, to Dr. Anthony Rimmington (University of Birmingham), Uzbek Academy of Sciences' Institute of Genetics, Tashkent, 20 September 1996.

67. Ibid.

68. N. Khailenko, A. Sedlovski, and Sh. Roaliev, "Alloplasmatic Lines Genetic and Selectional Peculiarities for Spring Wheat Steady to Phytopathogens," *Conversion in the Framework of International Collaboration, Proceedings* (Almaty, Kazakstan, October 1996), 76–77; Alibek and Handelman, *Biohazard,* 301; Bozheyeva, Kunakbayev, and Yeleukenov, *Former Soviet Biological Weapons Facilities in Kazakhstan.*

69. A former assistant at the BW laboratory was interviewed in the Russian press in November 1992. A. Pasternak and O. Rubinkovich, "Taina Pokrovskogo monastyrya," *Nezavisimaya gazeta* (17 November 1992), 6. This facility appears to have in fact been a special prison laboratory, or *sharashka,* where approximately nineteen leading plague and tularaemia specialists were arrested and imprisoned by the *OGPU* and forced to work on the development of offensive and defensive biological weapons. The *OGPU* was the successor organization to the *Cheka* (the All-Russian Extraordinary Commission for Combatting Counter-Revolution and Sabotage). Both organizations were forerunners to the *KGB* (the Committee for State Security). The creation of the Suzdal' BW *sharashka* was part of a much wider process whereby the Soviet security organs tightened their grip over the defense industry and the development of new weapons and military-related production processes.

Other prison design and engineering bureaus and scientific complexes, for example, held the country's most prominent atomic physicists and the leading scientists from the aerospace industry, and there is also evidence to suggest that a *sharashka* was established in the prewar years for the development of chemical weapons.

Among those imprisoned and arrested by *OGPU* in the former convent were Professor Nikanorov (director of the *Mikrob* Scientific-Research Institute in Saratov), Dmitrii Golov (also employed at *Mikrob* and the first researcher in the USSR to succeed in isolating tularaemia), N. A. Gaiskii (head of the Anti-Plague Laboratory in Furmanovo), B. Ya. El'bert, and Suvorov, Darmov, Pogorel'skii, and Velikanov, "Nauchno-issledovatel'skomu institutu mikrobiologii ministerstva oborony rossiiskoi federatsii—70 let," *Voenno-meditsinskii zhurnal* 320(2) (February 1999), 79–80; *The Cambridge Encyclopedia of Russia and the Former Soviet Union*, ed. A. Brown, M. Kaser, and G. S. Smith (Cambridge: Cambridge University Press, 1994), 359; M. Popovsky, *Manipulated Science: The Crisis of Science in the Soviet Union* (New York: Doubleday, 1979), 156; M. Popovsky, *Science in Chains: The Crisis of Science and Scientists in the Soviet Union Today* (London: Collins and Harvill Press, 1980), 10, and text accompanying photographs 4 and 5; I. Domaradskii, "Perevertysh" (Rasskaz "neudobnogo" cheloveka) (Moscow, 1995), 27. One unsubstantiated report suggests that "thousands" of microbiologists were imprisoned within the *sharashka* system. S. Pluzhnikov and A. Shvedov, "Ubiitsa iz probirki," *Sovershenno sekretno*, No. 4 (1998), 12. Geissler suggests that a number of special laboratories run by the *NKVD* conducted BW research, but these additional facilities remain to be identified. Bojtzov and Geissler, "Military Biology in the USSR: 1920–45." The chemical *sharashka* was apparently based at what is now the State Scientific-Research Institute of Organic Chemistry & Technology in Moscow. L. A. Fedorov, *Khimicheskoe oruzhie v Rossii: Istoriya, ekologiya, politika* (Center of Ecological Policy of Russia, 1994). A useful account of the Soviet system of prison laboratories is provided in Medvedev, *Soviet Science*. Small teams of *OGPU* scientists are reported to have worked in collaboration with their military colleagues on the development of powdered and liquid forms of typhus for use in a primitive aerosol. Alibek has claimed that the security services strengthened their hold over the Academy's research when they transferred a number of its scientists and their equipment to an experimental test site on one of the Solovetskii Islands in the White Sea. The islands were already being used to house political prisoners and in February 1937 became the Solovetskii Prison of Special Significance, which was directly subordinate to *OGPU*'s successor organization, the *NKVD* (the People's Commissariat for Internal Affairs). V. Birshtein, Ya., "Eksperimenty na lyudyakh v stenakh NKVD," *Chelovek*, No. 5 (1997), 114–32; V. J. Birshtein, Beyond Doctor Mengele: Experiments on Humans and the Moral Dilemma of Soviet Scientists, unpublished manuscript; "A Stalin Prize for Murders," *Moscow News* 23(3427) (17–24 June 1990), 8–9. "Come Clean! Our Quest to Unlock the Secrets of Beria's Evil Labs," *Moscow News*, No. 18 (28 September–4 October 1990), 5.

70. Of considerable interest with regard to possible KGB biological weapons program are the continued reports in the Russian press that the then Chairman of the KGB, Yurii Vladimirovich Andropov, was infected with smallpox in Afghanistan during a visit in 1980 or 1982, which was after the World Health Organization had declared the disease eliminated. M. V. Supotnitskii and A. Vaganov, "Poshchadite natural'nuyu ospu!" *Nezavisimaya gazeta* (22 April 1999).

71. The KGB is also reported to have had a particular interest in a *Biopreparat* program called "Bonfire," which focused on regulatory peptides. Alibek and Handelman, *Biohazard*, 153–67.

72. An early example of such activities concerns the convicted Soviet spy Gordon Lonsdale. In his memoirs he claims that in 1954 he was assigned a number of tasks in the United Kingdom, the most important of which was to obtain information on developments in biological warfare at Porton Down. *Spy: Twenty Years in Soviet Secret Service—The Memoirs of Gordon Lonsdale* (New York: Hawthorn Books, 1965), 89–121.

73. See chapter 7; P. R. Kumaraswamy, "Has Israel Kept Its BW Options Open?" *Jane's Intelligence Review* 21(29) (3 January 1998); M. Lavie, "Reports of Israeli Biological Arms Center Around Secret Institute," *Associated Press* (25 October 1998).

74. It has recently been alleged that Klingberg's spying activity provoked alarm in the United States and the United Kingdom because Israel had access to secret information regarding both these countries' biological weapons programs. W. Barnaby, *The Plague Makers: The Secret World of Biological Warfare* (Bath: Vision Paperbacks, 1997), 115–16; P. R. Kumaraswamy, "Israel: An Embarrassment of Spies," *The Bulletin of the Atomic Scientists* 55(2) (March/April 1999). Israeli intelligence agencies are reported to view Klingberg as the spy who caused most damage to Israel's national security interests. Z. Schiff, "The Return of the Russian Intelligence," *Ha'aretz* (18 December 1995), B1, translated in FBIS-NES-95–244. Klingberg spent the first ten years of his sentence in solitary confinement. He was released because of his failing health. In March 1998 the State Attorney's Office requested that the Supreme Court return Klingberg to jail because of violations of the terms of his release. D. Izenberg, "State Moves to Reimprison Spy Klingberg," *Jerusalem Post* (8 March 1999); "Israel Frees Scientist Who Spied for Former Soviet Union," *Agence France Presse* (18 September 1998); B. Tsur, "Israeli Court Orders Release of Aging Spy," *Jewish Bulletin of Northern California* (11 September 1998); R. Shapira, "Klingberg to Be Moved to Open Prison Soon," *Ha'aretz* (9 February 1998); L. Collins, "Klingberg Parole Nixed," *The Jerusalem Post Internet Edition* (19 February 1997); N. Segal, "Spy Petitions Israeli Court, Says Illness Justifies Freedom," *Jewish Telegraphic Agency* (5 March 1995), 6. See also chapter 7.

75. L. Fedorov, "Voina iz probirki," *Novoe vremya*, No. 30 (20 September 1998), 17.

76. Alibek and Handelman, *Biohazard,* 112.

77. Valentin Evstigneev, "Shtamm Eboly v Rossiyu privezli razvedchiki," *Yadernyi Kontrol'*, No. 4 (July–August 1999), 24.

78. "Ob obeschenii vypolneniya mezhdunarodnykh obyatel'stv Rossiiskoi Federatsii v oblasti khimicheskogo, bakteriologicheskogo (biologicheskogo) i toksinnogo oruzhiya," *Postanovlenie Verkhovnogo Soveta Rossiiskoi Federatsii* (8 July 1992).

79. Smithson, "Toxic Archipelago," 49–50.

80. J. Miller, "United States Helps Russia Turn Germ Center to Peace Uses," *New York Times* (8 January 2000).

81. The Russian MOD facilities have recently expressed an interest in collaborating with the U.S. Army Medical Research Institute of Infectious Diseases. At a meeting in Tambov on 24 May 1999 it was agreed that scientists from the military institutes would participate in a series of reciprocal visits during which the terms of collaborative projects would be explored. Smithson, "Toxic Archipelago," 80.

82. Strenuous efforts to open up the anti-plant/anti-animal and anti-plague BW network are being made by the United States and international agencies. In May 1999, for example, four scientists from the Institute of Phytopathology were supported by the Department of Energy Initiatives for Proliferation Prevention (IPP) during a visit to the United States. The Russian researchers visited a number of universities and commercial laboratories as well as the Idaho National Engineering and Environmental Laboratory. Now Washington is expanding the number of FSU BW facilities supported by Cooperative Threat Reduction funds to include anti-plague centers such as the Stavropol' Anti-Plague Institute. J. Bohne, Russian Scientists Pay Visit to INEEL; available online at www.inel.gov/resources/news (16 December 1999), 1; Smithson, "Toxic Archipelago," 77.

83. A. Rimmington, "Fragmentation and Proliferation? The Fate of the Soviet Union's Offensive Biological Weapons Programme," *Contemporary Security Policy* 20, No. 1 (April 1999), 89–91.

84. Smithson, "Toxic Archipelago," 92.

85. Information on attempts at conversion of BW facilities within Kazakstan can be found in A. Rimmington, "Conversion of BW Facilities in Kazakstan," in *Conversion of Former BTW Facilities*, ed. E. Geissler, L. Gazsó, and E. Buder, NATO Science Series (Kluwer Academic Publishers, 1998), 167–86.

86. Smithson, "Toxic Archipelago," 49, 98.

87. N. Dmitriev, "Russkii uchenyi napugal New York Times," *Kommersant* 6(1650) (26 January 1999), 4.

88. Rimmington, "Fragmentation and Proliferation?" 86–110.

89. Ibid.

90. During the period 1997 to 1999 the Pentagon allocated $3 million to tighten security of FSU BW facilities. An additional $10 million was expected to be spent on security improvements by the Defense Department in 2000. Smithson, "Toxic Archipelago," 81–85.

91. "OAO 'Binom'—proektirovanie I stroitel'stvo ob"ektov po GMP," *Meditsinskii biznes* 10(64) (1999), 27.

92. A good example of the proliferation threat posed by such spin-offs is provided by the case of *VIVA*, which is based on the Almaty anti-plague facility. In 1995 the company produced a catalogue detailing twenty-nine strains of plague with resistance or sensitivity to a range of antibiotics. *VIVA* had already been linked by Indian officials to the outbreak of plague in India in 1994, a claim subsequently dismissed by the Kazak Ministry of Health. Rimmington, "Fragmentation and Proliferation?" 99–100.

93. The environmental crisis surrounding the civil biotechnology industry in the Soviet Union has been described by A. Rimmington, "Biotechnology and Industrial Microbiology Regulations in Russia and the Former Soviet Republics," in *Biosafety in Industrial Biotechnology*, ed. P. Hambleton, J. Melling, and T. T. Salusbury (London: Blackie Academic & Professional, 1994), 67–89

94. The Vozrozhdenie Island proving ground has also been linked to a number of environmental disasters in the Aral Sea area, but there is no substantive evidence of any major accident at this site. Bozheyeva, Kunakbayev, and Yeleukenov, *Former Soviet Biological Weapons Facilities in Kazakhstan*, 7.

95. L. Fedorov, "Death From the Test-Tube," *New Times* (20 September 1998).

96. An excellent overview of the Sverdlovsk anthrax disaster is given in M. D. Gordin, "The Anthrax Solution: The Sverdlovsk Incident and the Resolution of a Biological Weapons Controversy," *Journal of the History of Biology* 30 (1997), 441–80.

97. J. Miller, "Poison Island: A Special Report; At Bleak Asian Site, Killer Germs Survive," *New York Times* (2 June 1999).

98. The limitations of bleach with regard to the destruction of BW stockpiles are discussed by J.-L. Sagriplanti, "Anthrax, Disposal of Stockpiles—Russia (02)," *ProMED-Mail Post* (11 June 1999).

99. Rimmington, "Conversion of BW Facilities in Kazakstan," 175.

100. A. P. Zelicoff, "Anthrax, Disposal of Stockpiles-Russia (05)," *Pro-MED-Mail Post* (7 July 1999).

101. The Laboratory, which was renamed the Central Microbiological Station (*Tsentral'naya mikrobiologicheskaya stantsiya*) in 1921, was based on Ulitsa Arbat in Moscow. A branch of this facility was created in 1918 at a confiscated estate at Kuz'minki in the Volgograd *raion* of Moscow. The branch facility may have had links to the chemical weapons proving ground at Kuz'minki. The Institute of Experimental Veterinary Sciences also possessed a proving ground (*poligon*) at Kuz'minki that occupied an area of 1.7 hectares and was protected by a wooden stockade and guards. It was intended for "the study of especially dangerous infectious diseases of agricultural animals." The proving ground is known to have been utilized for experiments to determine the survival rates of horses when exposed to anthrax. It was in use until the beginning of the World War II, when it was presumably evacuated in the face of advancing German forces. The Central Microbiological Station was reformed as the Veterinary Microbiological Institute (*Veterinarnyi mikrobiologicheskii institut*) in St. Petersburg in 1924. The latter facility was itself renamed the Red Army's Veterinary Scientific-Research Institute (*Veterinarnyi NII Krasnoi Armii*) in 1929. The threat of capture by German forces led to the transfer of the institute to a specially created base near Sergiev Posad (then Zagorsk) in 1940. Stockholm International Peace Research Institute, *Problem of Chemical and Biological Warfare, Volume I*, 286; Yu Senatorov, "Yazva pod bokom," *Ogonek*, No. 46 (November 1996), 28–29.

102. This facility, managed by A. N. Ginsburg, was engaged in experiments aimed at increasing the virulence and stability of anthrax (*Bacillus anthracis*) and tests were also undertaken on *Clostridium botulinum*. However, Ginsburg's work is reported to have been limited by the lack of detonation chambers necessary for weapons development. In his memoirs Ipatieff reported that Fishman's chemical education was below average. E. Geissler, *Biologische Waffen-Nichts in Hitlers Arsenalen: Biologische und Toxin-Kampfmittel in Deutschland von 1915 bis 1945* (Munster: Lit Verlag, 1999), 584; V. N. Ipatieff, *The Life of a Chemist: Memoirs of V. N. Ipatieff*, The Hoover Library on War, Revolution, and Peace Publication No. 21 (Stanford, Calif.: Stanford University Press; London: Oxford University Press, 1946), 418–21; Stockholm International Peace Research Institute, *Problem of Chemical and Biological Warfare, Volume II*, 285.

103. See Stockholm International Peace Research Institute, *Problem of Chemical*

and *Biological Warfare Volume II*, 161, for the Soviet Union's reservations on acceding to the Geneva Protocol in 1928 (note 4, this chapter).

104. Bojtzov and Geissler, "Military Biology in the USSR: 1920–45."

105. A. Pasternak and O. Rubinkovich, "Taina Pokrovskogo monastyrya," *Nezavisimaya gazeta* (17 November 1992), 6; Darmov, Pogorel'skii, and Velikanov, "Nauchno-issledovatel'skomu institutu mikrobiologii," 79–80.

106. Vlasikha maintains its links to weapons of mass destruction to this day. It is now the location of the headquarters of the Strategic Missile Forces. *ITAR/TASS News Agency* (24 March 1997).

107. Darmov, Pogorel'skii, and Velikanov, "Nauchno-issledovatel'skomu institutu mikrobiologii," 57–59.

108. Ibid.

109. B. Starkov, "The Security Organs and the Defense-Industry Complex," in Barber and Harrison, *Soviet Defense-Industry Complex*, 256.

110. The proximity of the Vlasikha facility to Moscow meant that experiments with biological weapons posed a grave threat to the city's civil population. Hence the decision was taken to relocate to Gorodomyla. Institute V/2–1094 appropriated the laboratories and equipment of the Commissariat of Health's Foot-and-Mouth Disease Institute, which had been based on the island since 1930. The transfer of the main facility to Gorodomlya appears to have taken place in the autumn of 1937. Professor Nikanorov, a former prisoner in the Suzdal laboratory, was the director of the new facility, although Velikanov retained overall control of both institutes. G. F. Koromyslov, A. I. Lebedev, V. A. Shubin, and M. M. Gogolev, "Istoriya izucheniya problemy yashchura v VIEV(e) (1926–1976gg),"in *Problemy infektsionnoi patologii sel'skokhozyaistvennykh zhivotnykh: Tezisy dokladov konferentsii, posvyashchennoi 100-letiyu otkrytiya virusa yashchura, 27–31 oktyabrya 1997 goda*, (Vladimir, 1997); Velikanov, "K 60-letiyu sozdaniya nauchno-issledovatel'skogo instituta mikrobiologii," 57–59; W. Hirsch, *Soviet BW and CW Preparations and Capabilities*, Intelligence Branch, Plans, Training & Intelligence Division, Office of the Chief, Chemical Corps, Washington, D.C., undated, 157–58; M. C. Storella, *Poisoning Arms Control: The Soviet Union and Chemical/Biological Weapons*, Special Report, June 1984, Institute for Foreign Policy Analysis (Washington, D.C.: Corporate Press, Inc., 1984), 66, 82–83; Popovsky, *Science in Chains*, 156. Interestingly, as late as the 1960s Oleg Penkovskii claimed: "Near the city of Kalinin, on a small island in the Volga [presumably Gorodomlya] there is a special bacteriological storage place. Here they keep large containers with bacilli of plagues and other contagious diseases. The entire island is surrounded by barbed wire and is very securely guarded." See O. Penkovskiy, *The Penkovskiy Papers* (New York: Doubleday, 1965), 241. According to a recent Russian report, an institute for the study of foot-and-mouth disease was established on Gorodomlya before World War II. It records claims that a "top secret germ weapon was developed there." Interviews with local inhabitants confirm that biologists were at one time working on the island: "According to old-timers, some biologists or chemists came over, worked for a while, and then broke up camp and left." Currently a top-secret defense munitions plant, *Zvezda* (Ostashkov-3), is based on the island. There has reportedly been no admittance to Gorodomlya without a special pass since the 1930s, and guards are posted

on the main landing stage. See M. Shitz, "An Off Limits Island," *New Times International*, No. 32 (1993), 16–17.

111. "Posetiteli kremlevskogo kabineta I. V. Stalina, Zhurnaly (tetradi) zapisi lits, prinyatykh pervym gensekom. 1924–1953, Alfavitnyi ukazatel'," *Istoricheskii arkhiv*, No. 4 (1998).

112. Following the deportation of the resident population of Kulaks, Velikanov led the first expedition to the island in the summer of 1936. This comprised more than one hundred specialists and support staff from Institute No. V/2–1094. Rimmington, "Conversion of BW facilities in Kazakstan," 167–86. According to a recent report, Komsomol'sk Island in the Aral Sea was also utilized by the Soviet Union as a BW test range. S. Pluzhnikov and A. Shvedov, "Ubiitsa iz probirki," *Sovershenno sekretno*, No. 4 (1998), 12.

113. Velikanov, "K 60-letiyu sozdaniya nauchno-issledovatel'skogo instituta," 57–59.

114. Ibid.

115. Darmov, Pogorel'skii, and Velikanov, "Nauchno-issledovatel'skomu institutu mikrobiologii," 79–81.

116. "Posetiteli kremlevskogo kabineta I. V. Stalina."

117. Ibid.

118. The Department was evacuated to Giessen in 1944 and it is not known whether the Red Army succeeded in transporting any functional equipment from the Berlin facility back to the USSR. E. Geissler, Conversion of BTW Facilities: Lessons from German History, in Geissler, Gazsó, and Buder, *Conversion of Former BTW Facilities*, 58–59.

119. The Soviet armed forces overran a large number of Japanese BW facilities during their invasion of Manchuria in August 1945. This area has been described by one authoritative study of the Japanese BW program as "one gigantic biological and chemical warfare laboratory." Among the captured facilities was the vast BW complex at Ping Fan (in the suburbs of Harbin), which lay at the heart of the Japanese biological weapons effort. However, there was a systematic attempt to destroy all traces of the BW program and the facilities were leveled. Because of its sheer size, attempts to destroy the main building at Ping Fan failed, and the Soviet forces took possession of it relatively intact. In a recent interview Lieutenant-General Evstignneev, head of the Russian Ministry of Defense Biological Defense Department, claims that during Soviet military operations in Manchuria in 1945 samples of Japanese biological weapons were captured. However, he claims that these were loaded onto a ship bound for the USSR that subsequently disappeared without trace and thus "we received nothing from the Japanese in terms of biological weapons." Evstigneev also claims that the Soviet Union had no knowledge of any German BW program. L. Usacheva, "'Smert' pod shifrom 022," *Poisk* 50(85) (14–20 December 1990), 3; Alibek and Handelman, *Biohazard*, 37; Pluzhnikov and Shvedov, "Ubiitsa iz probirki," 12; "Valentin Yevstigneyev on Issues, Relating to Russian Biological Weapons," *Yadernyi Kontrol Digest*, No. 11 (Summer 1999); S. H. Harris, *Factories of Death: Japanese Biological Warfare 1932–45 and the American Cover-Up* (London and New York: Routledge, 1994), 3–5.

120. The Fifteenth Administration was also allocated a classified post box (*poch-*

*tovyi yashchik*, abbreviated to *p/ya*) number, A1968, which made no reference to its real location or street address. For a useful discussion of the special postal codes in use in the Soviet Union, see J. Cooper, K. Dexter, and M. Harrison, *The Numbered Factories and Other Establishments of the Soviet Defense Industry, 1927–67: A Guide, Part I. Factories and Shipyards*, Soviet Industrialisation Project Series (SIPS) Occasional Paper, No. 2, Center for Russian & East European Studies (Birmingham, Ala.: The University of Birmingham, 1999), i–ix.

121. It is alleged that this facility was subsequently utilized by the Soviet military for the production and storage of large quantities of smallpox. F. Smirnov, "Ukroshchenie virusov, Sozdan Tsentr spetsial'noi diagnostiki I lecheniya osobo opasnykh i ekzoticheskikh infektsionnykh zabolevanii," *Meditsinskaya gazeta*, No. 101–102 (29 December 1999), 10–11; V. K. Bulavko, "V pamyat' o E. I. Smirnove," *Voenno-meditsinskii zhurnal* 319(1) (January 1998), 89–90; Alibek and Handelman, *Biohazard*, 111–12.

122. It incorporated military unit No. 25484, which was based on the island but was part of, and subordinate to, a larger unit based in Aral'sk, Kazakstan, and a Scientific Field Testing Laboratory possessing its own P3 containment facility. The Laboratory, residential area, barracks, power station, air and sea ports, etc., were located in the northern part of the island. The open-air BW proving ground was based in the south of the island and was used for studies of the dissemination patterns of BW aerosols and tests of aerosol bomblets. S. Zeberkhanuly, "Aral Disaster," *Zhas alash* (23 May 1992), 2, translated in *JPRS*, JPRS-ULS-92-019 (2 July 1992), 3–5; R. F. Starr, *The New Military in Russia: Ten Myths That Shape the Image* (Annapolis, Md.: Naval Institute Press, 1996); V. Ponomarev, "Biological and Chemical Weapons in Kazakhstan," *Ecostan News: Ecological News from Central Asia* 2(9), online: stsfac.mit.edu/projects/leep /Ecostan/Ecostan209.html (12 January 1998); I. Nevinnaya, "Island of Degeneration," *Delovoi mir* 61(28) (March 1992), 1, translated in *JPRS*, JPRS-ULS-92-013 (1 May 1992), 1–2.

123. The Ministry of Agriculture was created in 1953 with its headquarters at Orlikov Pereulok, 1/11, 107139 Moscow. The Ministry was replaced by the All-Union State Agro-Industrial Committee (*Gosudarstvennyi agropromyshlennyi komitet* or *Gosagroprom*) in November 1985. *Gosagroprom*'s headquarters remained at Orlikov Pereulok. *Directory of Soviet Officials: National Organizations, A Reference Aid*, CIA National Foreign Assessment Center, CR81–11343, May 1981, 32–33; *Directory of Soviet Officials: National Organizations, A Reference Aid*, CIA Directorate of Intelligence, LDA87–1290, June 1987, 156.

124. Domaradskii, "Perevertysh" (Rasskaz "neudobnogo" cheloveka)," 42–43.

125. The *SPEB*s played an important role in clearing up outbreaks of cholera in Karapakalstan (1965), Astrakhan', Odessa and Kerch (1970), Novorossisk (1970), Vilkovo (1991), and Dagestan (1994). *Zhurnal mikrobiologii epidemiologii immunobiologii*, No. 3 (1996), Supplement, 14–18; Domaradskii, "Perevertysh" (Rasskaz "neudobnogo" cheloveka)," 50–51.

126. R. L. Garthoff, "Polyakov's Run," *The Bulletin of the Atomic Scientists* 56(5) (September/October 2000), 37–40.

127. S. I. Peymer, *Chemical Warfare and Radiation Research in the Former Soviet Union: The Military Medical Academy and Institute of Military Medicine (1979–1989)* (Alexandria, Va.: Global Consultants, Inc., 1992), 20.

128. M. Leitenberg, "Biological Weapons Arms Control," *Contemporary Security Policy* 17(1) (April 1996), 1.

129. In 1967 Viktor M. Zhdanov organized the donation of 140 million doses of vaccine per annum to the WHO campaign for the global eradication of smallpox. H. Bazin, *The Eradication of Smallpox: Edward Jenner and the First and Only Eradication of a Human Infectious Disease* (London: Academic Press, 2000), 172–73; W. Orent, "After Anthrax," *The American Prospect* 11(12) (8 May 2000).

130. Russian State Economic Archive (*RGAE*), "Introduction to Fond 178, Opis' 1, Delo 5895 (Glavmikrobioprom, 1966–1985)."

131. Rimmington, "Fragmentation and Proliferation?" 108.

132. "V tsentral'nom komitete KPSS i Sovete Ministrov SSSR," *Pravda*, No. 20380 (21 May 1974), 1.

133. Sandakhchiev, "Innovation Development Programme of the Association 'VECTOR' for 1992–1995 and till 2005."

134. J. Adams, *The New Spies: Exploring the Frontiers of Espionage* (London: Hutchinson, 1994), 270–83.

135. M. Leitenberg, "Biological Weapons Arms Control," *Contemporary Security Policy* 17(1) (April 1996), 1.

136. J. Guillemin, *Anthrax: The Investigation of a Deadly Outbreak* (Berkeley and Los Angeles: University of California Press, 1999).

137. I. Domaradskii, "Istoriya odnoi avantyury," *Znanie-sila*, Part II, No. 12 (December 1996), 56.

138. Rimmington, *Who's Who in Russia & Republics Biotechnology*, 332–34.

139. Ibid., 167–86.

140. Barnaby, *Plague Makers*, 115–16; Kumaraswamy, "Israel: An Embarassment of Spies."

141. "V Politbyuro TsK KPSS," *Pravda*, No. 24485 (16 August 1985), 1.

142. Adams, *New Spies*, 270–83.

143. Mangold and Goldberg, *Plague Wars*, 118–40.

144. Ibid., 144–57.

145. *Rossiskaya gazeta*, first edition, Moscow (28 February 1992), translated in *Summary of World Broadcasts*, Part 1, Former USSR, SU/1317, 29 (February 1992), C3/1.

146. *Izvestiya* (12 June 1992).

147. Mangold and Goldberg, *Plague Wars*, 170–76.

148. Alibek and Handelman, *Biohazard*, 241–56.

149. Quoted in the notes to chapter 19 (available only online) of Mangold and Goldberg, *Plague Wars*.

150. Mangold and Goldberg, *Plague Wars*, 196–99.

151. Ibid.

152. Ibid., 200–208.

153. Ibid., 207.

154. A. Rimmington, "Russia: Microbiological Conversion," *Oxford Analytica East Europe Daily Brief* (5 June 1997).

155. Smithson, "Toxic Archipelago," 49–50.

156. "Postanovlenie pravitel'stva rossiiskoi federatsii, No. 505," *Rossiskaya gazeta* (8 May 1999).

157. O federal'noi tselevoi programme "Sozdanie metodov i sredstv zashchity naseleniya I sredy obitaniya ot opasnykh i osobo opasnykh patogenov v chrezvy-chainykh situatsiyakh prirodnogo i tekhnogennogo kharaktera v 1999–2005 godakh," Predsedatel' Pravitel'stva Rossiiskoi Federatsii S. Stepashin, No. 737, Moscow, 2 July 1999, *Sobranie zakonodatel'stva Rossiiskoi federatsii*, No. 29 (19 July 1999), 6655–83.

158. V. Yakubovich, "V dome-ubiitse v Kirove-200 prodolzhayut zhit' lyudi," *Vyatskii Nablyudatel'* 27(2) (July 1999), online: www.ah.ru/ issue/viatsky/99/27/ 6.htm; "V 'rakovom korpuse' poyavilsya eshche odin bol'noi rebenok," *Vyatskii Nablyudatel'*, No. 43 (22 October 1999), online: www.ah.ru/issue/viatsky/99/43/ 25.htm.

159. "Kratko, no ponyatno," *Rossiiskaya gazeta*, (21 September 1999), 4.

160. F. Smirnov, "Ukroshchenie virusov," *Nauka*, No. 101 (1999), online: www.medportal.dn.ua/sef/2000/ 0669sef.htm.

161. Ministry of Property Relations of the Russian Federation Order No. 451-r, 25 August 2000.

162. J. Miller, "Russia: Germ-Warfare Expert Replaced," *New York Times* (5 April 2001).

163. "Russian Government Sets up Interdepartmental Biotechnology Commission," *Pravda On-Line* (24 December 2001), online: english.pravda.ru/politics/ 2001/12/24/24350.html.

164. "Russia Announces Plans to Participate in Research on Vozrozhdeniye Island, Monterey Institute of International Studies Research Story of the Week," *CNS* (19 March 2002), online: www.armscontrol.org/act/200111/uzbeknov01.asp.

# III

## MIDDLE EASTERN AND ASIAN PERSPECTIVES

# 6

# The Middle East

## Integrated Regional Approaches to Arms Control and Disarmament

*Laura Drake*

This chapter addresses the problem of biological warfare in the Middle East as it is interwoven into the region's larger political and military context. It highlights the interrelationships between the various types of weapons that exist in the Middle East rather than focusing on them individually. This requires that we deal with unconventional arms control and disarmament as a whole in its complete security context, from the perspective of the Middle East regional states involved, with an eye to their particular security dilemmas.

The state-security motive for biological armament is strong in this region, where it has recently become evident that even a formidable chemical arsenal is no deterrent against a nuclear-armed adversary, and where the development of nuclear weapons is technologically and economically unfeasible for most. For a Middle East regional arms control and disarmament effort to succeed, it must address these motivations and be based on the region's realities. Otherwise, efforts to eliminate biological and other weapons that threaten humanity will hold little interest for regional states and will fail. This chapter presents some broad, integrated concepts and questions regarding the nature and requirements of Middle East arms control and disarmament and lays out what is feasible and unfeasible.

First, in the Middle Eastern multipolar security environment, the most important differences in military deterrents, both conventional and uncon-

151

ventional, are not between categories of weapons, as during the Cold War, but rather across them. Marking certain weapons systems for control while leaving other equally dangerous systems alone makes no sense in a region such as the Middle East in which states possess different types of weapons. Any protocol targeting only some weapons would mean unilateral disarmament by some states while leaving their enemies fully armed.[1]

According to Philip Sabin, the most effective disincentive for using nuclear, biological, and chemical weapons is the fear that the enemy will respond in kind. Therefore, most uses of these weapons have been against enemies incapable of such retaliation.[2] According to this historical precedent, Israel's sole possession of unconventional weapons in the region makes their use more likely during some future crisis. The only realistic way to address the presence of biological weapons in the Middle East is within this larger regional context.

Second, meanings that applied to the superpowers in the Cold War take on a different cast when applied to regional powers. Those states advocating Middle East arms control are often more powerful than the regional states that are affected by such controls. Arms control can therefore take on coercive meanings that do not apply when the two strongest powers in the international system agree to mutual constraints on their own military capabilities.

The term "arms control" in the Cold War context referred to the voluntary installation of mutual restraints on the production and deployment of certain types of weapons. "Disarmament" meant the voluntary mutual reduction or elimination of similar types of weapons. Since the nuclear arsenals of the two superpowers differed only tactically, their security was affected by these procedures in a parallel and equivalent manner. If some power superior to both the United States and the Soviet Union had called for ceilings and reductions in only land-based nuclear warheads, with no cuts in submarine-launched or air-based warheads, the Soviet Union would have refused. Such a move would have undercut its security. The reverse is also true: had an arms control regime been imposed only on submarine-launched nuclear warheads; Washington would have been left at a severe disadvantage because this was the strongest part of the U.S. strategic triad. Arms control between the two superpowers therefore reflected their common national interests. Any serious arms control and disarmament effort in the Middle East will have to do likewise.

Israel has what appears to be a substantial arsenal of nuclear weapons, probably including thermonuclear capabilities, along with ample and diverse means to deliver them. It is likely that Israel also has biological and possibly chemical weapons capabilities. In any case, Israel, like Egypt and Syria, has not forsworn the option of producing biological munitions; none of these states has fully adhered to the 1972 Biological Weapons Convention (BWC). Israel has publicly forsworn chemical weapons, which it may have once produced, in its support (but not ratification) of the Chemical Weapons Convention (CWC). Israel's present and potential adversaries— certain Arab states and Iran—on the other hand, may have various mixtures of chemical and biological weapons capabilities, but no nuclear weapons. Syria, Egypt, and possibly non-Arab Iran have chemical weapons capabilities, while Iraq and possibly the other three may also have biological weapons capabilities. Egypt used chemical weapons during its intervention in Yemen in the 1960s, as did Iraq in its war with Iran and against the Kurds. Syria likely has the capability to mount chemical armaments onto its medium-range Scud-C missiles, and perhaps also onto the accurate short-range SS-21 missiles in its arsenal. Israel is developing defensive responses to these threats. The refusal of Egypt and Syria to sign the Chemical Weapons Convention and forswear chemical options parallels Israel's refusal to sign the Nuclear Non-Proliferation Treaty and forswear nuclear options.

From an internationalist ethical perspective, biological weapons are bad for humanity, as are nuclear weapons and indeed all types of weapons. But from a realist perspective it is necessary to ask *why* they exist rather than simply opposing their existence. So long as states live in an anarchic, Hobbesian international political order, they will acquire weapons to defend themselves against those rival states with which they compete for power, space, and control. Hence their security dilemma, leading to arms races and sometimes war.

## THE DEFINITION AND OBJECTIVES
## OF ARMS CONTROL AND DISARMAMENT
## IN THE MIDDLE EAST

Before we contemplate the control of biological weapons, other unconventional weapons, or any category of armaments, we must define such control in relation to the concept of disarmament. Generally, arms control refers to restrictions or reductions of numbers, types, locations, and categories of armaments, whereas disarmament means the divestiture of existing armaments.

Arms control can be mutual or unilateral. The former is voluntarily entered into, and hence, a form of peace; the latter is often coerced, typically by an enemy and under duress. In its unilateral form, arms control, paradoxically, is part of the methodology of warfare. By unilaterally divesting one party to a conflict of its security in a manner that favors its enemy's interests, coerced unilateral arms control is a euphemism for warfare by other means.

An a priori requirement of successful arms control, whether it be in the

Middle East or elsewhere, is a clear objective. Is the goal stability? Balance? Reduction of the likelihood of war, or limitation of its destructiveness? In the previous superpower equation the objective was the prevention of war, but that was only an intermediate objective. The larger objective was the prevention of *nuclear* war, of mass destruction, and since it was recognized that conventional war would likely escalate into nuclear war, the prevention of *any* war was deemed essential.

Conditions of bilateral nuclear balance do not prevail in today's Middle East. If the basic objective of arms control and disarmament in this region is the same objective as during the Cold War, namely, to prevent mass destruction of civilizations, then the immediate aim must be the prevention of unconventional war. If a MAD (Mutually Assured Destruction) Middle East does emerge, then there too the prevention of *any* war between such adversaries will be essential. What must be determined regarding any Middle East arms control equation are the goals of the parties involved: Is the proliferation of arms, conventional or unconventional, itself a cause of war? If so, then deproliferation (reduction by all states toward the direction of zero) rather than nonproliferation (prevention of further accumulation by selected states) might be the proper strategy. On the other hand, one might cite the domestic gun control slogan that "guns don't kill people, people kill people," and claim that what matters is who possesses the weapons. All states would probably agree with this perspective, although the identity of the problem state or states in each perception will vary, often quite dramatically. Each regional state or alliance will judge itself as benign and its enemies as having aggressive or "criminal" intentions.

As weapons systems become more destructive, states that lack mutual trust but exist in a condition of symmetrical balance will enter into arms agreements. They do so in the interest of self-preservation. In some cases, stronger states in asymmetrical power relationships seek to impose their perceptions on their enemies without realizing that they are doing so. They may wish to use arms control to further weaken their already weaker adversaries, while simultaneously adding to the destructive potential of their own superior arsenals. They may rationalize this by surreptitiously employing "objective" language to communicate their subjective perceptions. Here one might ask which security requirement is objectively more legitimate: to possess the types of weapons that unduly threaten others (by using them for deterrence) or to be safe from threat by those same types of weapons possessed by others? Clearly it is the latter, but in any case, states cannot expect to have it both ways.

States remain divided, however, on how the answers to these questions apply in the Middle East to their particular national interests, and perceptions surrounding these issues are as numerous as the number of states in the international system. Nevertheless, these are appropriate matters for arms control specialists to theorize about; in doing so, however, they must recognize the complex and divergent perceptions of the different states. They must put aside the perspectives of their own countries, if only temporarily, to be able to comprehend the interactions among these diverse national perceptions.

This approach raises a further question: In whose interest is arms control in a given area, or a certain type of arms control as opposed to another? Who benefits from adopting one procedure over another? In the case of the superpowers, there were no greater powers or international organizations mediating their bilateral arms control initiatives. The objective of arms control was the lowest common denominator of their interests: prevention of nuclear war and reduction in the size and instability of the combined nuclear threat. Their agreed means was preservation of the nuclear balance of terror. Mutually assured second-strike capabilities were deemed essential for offsetting the temptation to stage preemptive strikes. This was accomplished by banning all but token antiballistic missile systems on both sides. This precluded any possibility of defense and thereby made any offensive attack unthinkable. This ban on defense was accompanied by the control and gradual reduction of offensive nuclear armaments. The hope was to turn the arms race on its head and send it into a reverse spiral, one of reduction. It was hoped that someday the nuclear balance could be reduced to zero on both sides, eliminating the threat of nuclear terror. To lessen the probability of a conventional war that could escalate to the nuclear level, the two adversaries agreed to reduce their conventional force deployments to establish a situation of conventional, manageable parity.

These were the objectives of arms control in the superpower arena, but what should they be at the regional level in the Middle East? Should the goal be that of an external superpower, should it perhaps be the achievement of a global principle upheld by the totality of the world's states in the form of international organizations, or should it encompass the lowest common denominator of the security interests of the regional states? These goals are nowhere near the same.

1. *Great-Power Interests.* The United States is not impartial in the Middle East or anywhere else, but a nation-state with interests like any other. Its goals concerning arms control in other regions are based on its particular national interests in those regions, not on moral principles. America's goal, both before and after September 11, is the creation, preservation, or establishment of military balances favorable to some regional states and detrimental to others. According to Anthony Cordesman, arms control means "tailoring the flow of arms to *strengthen those countries* threatened by aggressor states" (emphasis added).[3] Similarly, Geoffrey Kemp unabashedly advocates the use of arms control as a "coercive element" against some regional states, while finding ways to "exempt [U.S.] friends and allies from

controls."[4] However, what the United States sees, or has been made to see, as best for itself is not necessarily best for the region or the world.

Some of the states disadvantaged by Washington's use of arms control as a strategic device do not see themselves as natural adversaries of Washington. Indeed, some of them would rather have normal or at least "proper" relations with the United States, on the basis of "live and let live." But they see their Israeli adversary as interfering in and deliberately poisoning their relationship with the United States. As William Hopkinson states, it is "doubtful whether the United States could contemplate an effective regime which operated against Israel, and to the extent that [the United States] did not, the reaction from Arab states would be all the stronger."[5] In the current context, American supervision of any arms agreement would likely ensure that the national security interests of those states hostile to Israel (although not necessarily to America) would be ignored or degraded in favor of those of Israel.

2. *Global Principle.* The second option is sponsorship of Middle East arms control by the international organizations, with a goal of global peace, justice, and cooperation, that would take place according to universal principles equally applied. In theory, at least, these organizations—particularly the United Nations—represent the lowest common denominator of national interests of all the participating states. For the international organizations, therefore, the objective of arms control is the "universal good," defined by what is common to the states collectively representing all humanity. Generally, this boils down to the prevention of the deadliest forms of warfare and the threat of such warfare. Regional security interests and hegemonic great-power interests will theoretically be marginalized by these organizations in pursuit of this broader goal. However, such organizations, because they are not states themselves but rather collections of states, are not international political actors in their own right. They cannot impose decisions; they lack the executive powers to enforce them. In short, they do not have the capacity to *act* independently of the balance of power among their respective member states.

3. *Lowest Regional Common Denominator.* In considering the third option, we must begin by recognizing that Middle Eastern states are divided on the nature of legitimate arms control. Nonetheless, we may suppose that the objective of the various parties in pursuing arms agreements is either to even out unfavorable military balances or sustain favorable ones. Their overall objective is to remove major threats to their security posed by other regional states. A good regional concept is that of the Israeli strategist Dore Gold, for whom arms control is "a component of national strategy" that seeks "to neutralize the strategic advantage of potential enemies through diplomacy."[6] The Arabs will see it in exactly the same way vis-à-vis Israel. Using the Cold War model as a guide, it is precisely the interaction of these

clashing sets of self-interest that should ultimately produce a balanced result, to the military advantage of neither side and yet to the ultimate benefit of all sides.

At more specific levels, the various regional states have widely divergent interests, but the lowest common denominator of these Arab, Iranian, and Israeli interests will differ from those of both the American superpower and international organizations such as the United Nations. A regional arms control objective will reflect the lowest common denominator of the interests of Israel, Iran, and the Arab tripolarity of Egypt, Syria, and Iraq. Saudi Arabia, in unique possession of Chinese CSS-II intermediate range missiles (of the range that was eliminated by the INF Treaty in Europe) and as the alleged partial financier of Pakistan's "Islamic bomb" program (along with Libya), will likely also have a say in any regional arms control process.[7]

For Arab states and Iran, a central objective of arms control is to eliminate the existing nuclear threat from Israel. For most of them, perhaps with the sole exceptions of Iraq and Iran themselves at this point, Iraq and Iran's respective potential biological and chemical capabilities have become less of an issue than they once were. The lowest Arab/Iranian common denominator is to prevent state civilian and military infrastructures from being threatened by any form of unconventional warfare. For Israel, the objective of arms control is, first, to prevent *conventional* war, since its adversaries cannot yet wage an assuredly successful unconventional war against it,[8] and second to rectify what it perceives as unfavorable conventional balances. This is probably because Israel sees conventional war as strategic (the primary game of survival and defense), whereas for the superpowers it was a primarily tactical exercise, acted out on third-party battlefields, to gain increments of advantage over the adversary. Arab states and Iran also perceive unfavorable conventional balances with Israel, but their problem is qualitative whereas Israel's is quantitative and spatial. The Arab states and Iran perceive a much more potent and therefore urgent threat coming from Israel's unconventional arsenal, however, and that will be their first priority.

In all cases, the purpose of arms control for any state is the same as the purpose of arms acquisition: to prevent one's own country from becoming a potential target of attack by another state using superior and/or highly destructive munitions. This singular objective can be carried out either by strategic neutralization (armament or arms control) or by physical elimination (counterforce warfare or disarmament). Even if one accepts the premise that the objective of arms control is the prevention of any war, the way this will be accomplished is through a kind of arms control that also preserves the basic concept of mutual strategic deterrence, although in a more stable form and at a lower overall level of destructiveness. This is as true now for the region as it was previously for the superpowers. Arms control and disarmament for sovereign states, like war itself, are means to an end, not ends in themselves.

## MULTILATERAL VERSUS
## INTERNATIONAL APPROACHES

Once the shared objectives of arms control and/or disarmament have been agreed upon, the nature of the negotiation process must be settled. Assuming that they act independently, Middle Eastern states will decide, perhaps with outside help and advice, on the nature of the negotiating arena that is in their interests to employ. This might be a multilateral negotiation forum like the long-defunct Arms Control and Regional Security (ACRS) section of the former Middle East peace process, in which multilateral arms control and disarmament treaties on the relevant issues would be signed subregionally. Or it might be an international forum such as the Conference on Disarmament used for negotiating such international treaties as the Nuclear Non-Proliferation Treaty (NPT), the Biological Weapons Convention (BWC), and the Chemical Weapons Convention (CWC). We shall refer to these as the multilateral and the international approaches, respectively.

Both approaches have advantages and disadvantages. The downside of the multilateral approach is that it is tied to the Arms Control and Regional Security (ACRS) format, which cannot cover all regional states. The ACRS was an official part of the multilateral peace track initiated during the 1991 Middle East peace conference in Madrid. Iraq, Iran, and Libya were not invited to participate, and Syria and Lebanon conspicuously absented themselves from multilateral processes of any kind that could have led to premature political relations with Israel. The boycotted multilateral committees included the infrastructure committees, the refugee committee, and most important for this discussion, the Arms Control and Regional Security Committee. These multilateral engagements signified premature or exaggerated forms of normalization of relations and addressed primarily Israel's political and economic interests. They were therefore tactically postponed by Damascus and Beirut until the more urgent security predicament of Israel's occupation of parts of Syria's national territory had been dealt with. The resulting lack of coverage of all but two of the region's formidable powers (Israel and Egypt) would have induced Israel not to involve the forum in nuclear-related issues. This is because the states by which Israel sees itself as most threatened—and which are therefore the primary targets of its strategic nuclear deterrent—are the same states that would not have been covered by an ACRS-based regime. It is therefore absurd to embrace an ACRS-type forum as the proper forum for Middle East regional arms control and disarmament efforts, for it would merely work to ensure that Israel and Egypt, already at peace for more than two decades, would not threaten each other militarily.

With only these two Middle Eastern polar powers participating in the ACRS, the forum predictably reached an impasse on the subject of whether to include nuclear weapons as subject to arms control and disarmament.[9] Since Israel refused to talk about reducing its nuclear weapons in that forum, the Arab participants just as adamantly refused to discuss reducing their forward force deployments, conventional or unconventional. The drafted statement of principle therefore contained no agreed language for dealing with unconventional weapons and their delivery systems. Washington's "bridging" proposals similarly failed to generate common ground on this issue. But even if the problem could have been glossed over to produce a written statement, it is not political declarations that matter but rather substantive accomplishments in limiting or destroying the most dangerous weapons.

The international approach is equally problematic, but for entirely different reasons. The major problem of the international arms control conventions is that of verification. The fundamental flaws of the NPT in particular have been repeatedly evident. Signature did not prevent Iraq from pursuing its nuclear program, nor is it now necessarily preventing Iran from pursuing its nuclear development. Indeed, as Avi Beker has noted, the NPT's very provision of access to fissile materials and nuclear reactors has the potential to turn its main objective on its head, into a "strategy for the acquisition of nuclear arms."[10] The NPT provides merely for bureaucratic forms of verification that fissile materials in the possession of any state other than the United States, Russia, China, Britain, or France are not being diverted to military use. This is relatively ineffective against a determined signatory state—perhaps slowing down the efforts of such a state but not stopping them entirely—and totally ineffective against the nonsignatory states such as Israel. Even though the International Atomic Energy Agency (IAEA) strengthened inspection procedures after its failure in Iraq, this has not so far made much of a difference in the efforts of the relevant Middle Eastern states and no difference at all with respect to Israel, which continues its rejection of the NPT as it pertains to its own nuclear arsenal.

Inspections under the NPT are carried out either by nationals of states without a direct stake in the agreement or by sympathetic nationals. Bureaucratic or sympathetic inspectors have no real incentive or enthusiasm for detecting treaty violations, regardless of their degree of objective professionalism, and they will therefore be easier to fool by states determined to produce prohibited weapons. For these reasons, and because adherence is supposedly universal yet simultaneously voluntary, the NPT is not a credible nuclear antiproliferation device. One writer characterizes Israel's attitude toward it as "contempt."[11] Israel in particular believes that to sign such a treaty would be to divest itself of the named weapons without any assurances that its adversaries have done the same, thereby imperiling its security. The Arab states and Iran have exactly the same fears regarding Israel.

Other global nuclear arms control treaties are equally problematic due to loopholes that defeat their very purpose. For example, the Comprehensive Test Ban Treaty allows for the withdrawal of participating states based on the emergence of an extraordinary event imperiling their security. Four of the five nuclear powers have already said that the loss of confidence in their nuclear arsenals (presumably due to the prolonged absence of testing) would constitute precisely such an event.[12] Thus, the mechanism's entire purpose is defeated: It makes the world's nuclear arsenals less predictable and hence more dangerous and unstable for a finite period of time. Unreliability of the nuclear arsenals will never lead to nuclear disarmament because states will react by withdrawing, even if only temporarily, from the treaty and resuming testing, rather than by destroying their nuclear arsenals.

The real value of all of the international conventions lies in their moral and other normative powers and in their attempt to influence the large-scale direction of world order through the use of macro-level socialization tactics. Their value is therefore political, not military; hence the description of the NPT by the Stockholm International Peace Research Institute (SIPRI) as a "political barrier" to nuclear proliferation.[13] What the Middle East needs is not another normative proclamation but a military agreement.

Another drawback to the international approach is Israel's long-standing cynicism and contempt for most international institutions, most notably the United Nations itself. Israel believes it has been treated unfairly in these forums due to the preponderance of adversarial members. For similar reasons, Israel resists entrusting any part of its security to others. Historically it has not done so even with its foremost ally, the United States. Therefore, it should not be surprising that Israel is equally averse to placing its security on a matter of this importance in the hands of uninterested international bureaucrats.

For Israel, the most reliable enforcer is not the ineffective international inspection regime of the IAEA, or even third-party (read American) sanctions of the type that were leveled against India and Pakistan, or even Iraq. Rather, it sees the best enforcer as being direct reciprocal accountability, both political and military. If a state violates an agreement, it suffers the consequences through the direct political or military action of the interested adversary state. This is indeed probably the best deterrent against a state that might consider a treaty violation. However, for Israel it also matters that the agreements be contractual; in Israel's view, states should make commitments to each other, not to third parties. This has been Israel's central premise in the peace process since its inception. This premise is consistent with the pattern of U.S.–USSR arms control agreements.

Israel's perspectives have emerged from the history of the Arab-Israeli conflict and Israel's problem of political normalization with Arab states. They also derive from Israel's early relations with the great powers and the involvement of those powers in trying to end the Arab-Israeli conflict by imposing pressure on the parties involved. Israel does not want to participate in a scenario in which it would be committed to discussing possible divestiture of nuclear weapons, perhaps then leading to pressure by a third party to actually do so. Such enduring perceptions are not easily changed; they have arisen out of the particular circumstances surrounding Israel's introduction into a region where it was unwanted.

Likewise on the Arab and Iranian sides. From their perspectives, an international collective security regime on disarmament that contains automatic triggering mechanisms will not work. This is because the Arabs suspect that if a U.S. ally like Israel were the treaty violator, Washington would use its superpower weight to intervene to ensure that penalties were not applied. They have seen Iraq severely punished in the name of the sanctity of UN resolutions, whereas when Israel violates UN resolutions on a massive scale, virtually across the board, Washington intervenes to block the world body from condemning it or applying supposedly mandatory penalties. Arab states and Iran have no conceivable interest in entering into such an enforceable "universal arrangement," one that they know in advance will not be truly universal but selectively applied against them. Although these countries have signed some of the existing agreements, these are not enforceable. Their signatures have not hindered them in pursuing those programs they see as necessary to counterbalance unconventional threats from their neighbors, especially Israel.

Arab states and Iran perceive the United States as incapable of separating its approach to regional and global arms control from its national alignment structures; this is even more true in the emotion-laden post–September 11 environment. For example, Arab states and Iran see that the United States has never pressed Israel to be a party to the NPT. They notice that Washington exempted Israel from the antiproliferation sanctions that were later leveled against Pakistan, even though these were supposed to be mandatory. They further saw Washington imposing even more severe sanctions on both India and the much more vulnerable Pakistan for conducting their 1998 nuclear tests, while neglecting to impose any sanctions on Israel whatsoever for conducting a nuclear test with South Africa in 1979. Arab states witnessed America's role in 1995 in pressuring Egypt to stop campaigning for Israel to sign the NPT, while simultaneously pressuring everyone else to agree to the document's indefinite extension. This seemingly contradictory behavior resulted in a pronounced loss of U.S. credibility on arms control issues.

A further example is Washington's continued effort to implement supply-side arms control at a time when the concept is obsolete even from a regional standpoint. Supply-side arms control is not relevant in a regional security environment where the most copious regional proliferator, Israel, has indigenous arms research, development, and production capabilities. Yet the United States continues to advocate supply-side arms control.

To prevent other Middle East states from acquiring the same indigenous capabilities that Israel has acquired (with U.S. complicity), Washington attempts to prevent these states from cooperating to pursue civil applications of "dual-purpose" technologies. The most important example is America's successful interference in the Egypt-Iraq-Argentina Condor II missile project, a cooperative indigenous production effort conceived by these three sovereign states. Equally notorious is the so-called Missile Technology Control Regime (MTCR), an American-initiated "gentleman's agreement" among some of the world's missile-supplier states not to send certain types of missiles or missile technologies to the Middle East.[14] The MTCR was designed as a nuclear arms control device,[15] but Washington continues to target the MTCR at nonnuclear capable Arab states and Iran while ignoring or even supporting the existence of the most dangerous long-range nuclear-armed missile arsenal, the Israeli Jericho II-B fleet, with ranges approaching 2,800 kilometers.[16]

Israel is, thanks to France and to some degree the United States, now capable of producing both missiles and nuclear warheads. Israel's Shavit three-stage rocket and space capabilities will soon considerably extend those already extensive ranges. This will enable Israel to produce nuclear-capable intercontinental ballistic missiles (ICBMs). If the United States is truly serious about supply-side arms control, then its own intensive contributions to Israel's research and development efforts, including Israel's participation in the Strategic Defense Initiative/National Missile Defense project, should be immediately halted as part of a larger arms control package. Unfortunately, this is a pipe dream. Yet the fact remains that the United States cannot hope to claim leadership over a supposed "universal good" if it so obviously sees that good as less than universal.

Thus the Arab states perceive the posture of the United States toward arms control as acutely and obviously self-contradictory. This perception is based on America's repeated statements that are meant to justify its arms control efforts in ethical terms. This has entailed the portrayal of arms control as a kind of universal value or norm in its own right, one that protects the interests of every nation and all humanity. Furthermore, the nonproliferation of unconventional armaments is implicitly and explicitly understood in the international community, via existing international arms control agreements, as a norm that is applicable to all but the great-powers themselves. Thus, what the Arabs see as contradictory is U.S. actions that seem to excuse Israel from what Washington then turns around and portrays to the rest of the world as a universal good and a universal interest. The only resolution to this contradiction, then, is that if Israel is to be exempted from a "universal" norm, then the Arab states and Iran must consider themselves to be exempt as well; this is for reasons of legal/moral consistency and, more important, to protect their own military security. Washington's refusal to be consistent in this regard thus renders the entire U.S. justification for any arms control empty in their eyes, as it appears no longer as a universal good but as a mere vehicle employed for the sole purpose of disarming Arab countries and Iran and thus weakening them strategically in front of their fully armed Israeli adversary. And it is precisely because U.S. arms control policy is self-interested but is justified outwardly in terms of the universal good that Arab states and Iran find U.S. exhortations about arms control hypocritical and unworthy of their support.

What Arab states and Iran do see are Israeli and American strategists, working together, engaged in semantic efforts to divide states (cynically, as they see it) into "objective" categories, such as "unstable and threatening states," states that carry out "radical and destabilizing actions,"[17] or "aggressor states" and "destabilizing states." The latter states are then placed in opposition to stable, peaceful, or "defensive states," in a *post-facto* effort to rationalize actions initiated by the selective would-be arms controllers.[18] The categorizations do not exist a priori but were added as a way to exclude the strongest Middle Eastern country from what is supposed to be a regionwide arms control process. The unspoken goal is the unilateral disarmament of states that are arming themselves in response to the threat they perceive coming from Israel, thus rendering these states even more vulnerable in the face of that threat. The fact remains that a "peaceful state" from one perspective is the "aggressor state" from another; that which is conceived as defense and deterrence by one state is perceived as offense and threat projection by another, and so forth. In a similar perceptual vein, there are many references in the American Middle East literature that characterize chemical and biological weapons as "particularly horrific weapons" but make no mention of nuclear weapons,[19] an omission that defies the imagination. These are not, then, objective categories, but rather subjective perceptions based on the agent's country of origin, political ideology, national sympathies, and state function.

Washington sees Israel as a "special case" for reasons of its own perceived national interest. However, when exceptions are created, universal declarations, principles, agreements, and so forth go out the window. But it is implausible to overtly argue for selectivity in front of the world at large. According to Frank Barnaby, "it is simply unconvincing to argue that nuclear weapons are good for some countries but not for others, and there are no grounds for stating that nuclear weapons deter war in Europe but will not deter war in other regions, like the Middle East."[20] Due to their high destructive potential, one cannot argue that one state has some inherent right to threaten an enemy with such a class of weapon and to simultaneously argue that the threatened state should not acquire the same weapon for deterrence. That which applies to one state must apply to all or else the enterprise will not be taken seriously. Logic dictates that selectivity in the global system must have some hidden purpose that differs from the declared purpose; this hidden purpose, however, is easily discernible by the targeted states whose security and national interests are placed in jeopardy by this type of selective arms control.

One cannot make recourse to arguments about universal moral, legal, or political principles if those principles are not meant to be universally applied. Some U.S. officials apparently do not think the Arab states are threatened by Israel.[21] This makes no sense to Syrians manning the defensive line in front of Damascus, facing the Israeli army less than fifty kilometers away. What matters most for arms control is the perspectives of enemy states toward each other, not those of third parties that are not under threat.

The most important result of "special cases" not universally seen as special is the loss of credibility of the third party that insists on exempting them from its intentions and, thereby, from its arms control or disarmament effort as a whole. Israel is not entitled to deluxe security while the Arab states and their combined populations of over 300 million people must continue to live under a colossal Israeli nuclear threat. The only possible conclusion is that, despite its constant declarations to the contrary, the United States is not serious about arms control and disarmament in the region, and that its statements on the topic should be dismissed as mere propaganda. This carries well beyond the region to other arms supplier states, which must also view American proddings to rein in the Middle East arms race as frivolous.

Whereas Israel does not take global arms control agreements seriously due to their verification problems, Arab states see them as ineffective because powerful parties are actively trying to de-universalize them. When the United States says "Middle East arms control" or "Middle East disarmament," Arab states hear "Arab arms control" and "Arab disarmament." An American president refers to "stopping proliferation of dangerous weapons in the Middle East"; Arab states see the United States providing Israel with unlimited quantities of dangerous weapons while going to extreme lengths to interfere with Arab arms-manufacture and acquisition. Similarly, the United States has been known to apply extraordinary pressures on a number of countries not to supply any kind of effective armaments, including conventional armaments such as tanks, to states in conflict with Israel, while continuing to supply Israel itself with world-class, cutting-edge weaponry. States so pressured in this one-sided arms control include the longtime friends and allies of Arab states and Iran, and also neutral states such as South Africa, China, North Korea, Argentina, Pakistan, and the former Czechoslovakia.

When high-handed diplomacy fails, Washington resorts to gunboat diplomacy in a manner that contravenes international laws regarding the freedom of the high seas. The U.S. government has taken to acts of naval interdiction bordering on piracy to interfere with internationally lawful and sovereign government-to-government military transactions. Recall the failed 1991 attempt by the U.S. Navy to hijack the lawful North Korean shipment of Scud-C missiles to the Syrian Arab Republic. These missiles were intended to become, and in fact became, the instruments of Damascus's new national security doctrine of "strategic deterrence," the post-Soviet replacement for its previous doctrine of "strategic parity." Arab states and Iran find they must act clandestinely even when breaking no international laws, hiding in the shadows like outlaws in their efforts to acquire the normal means of defense. This has gone so far that one can find informal discussion in U.S. and allied circles about the need to monitor or perhaps even restrict foreign nationals from visiting certain countries to study "dual-use" scientific subjects in overseas universities.[22]

In summary, if American arms control appears to be "for Arabs and Iranians only," it becomes just another sophisticated instrument of war, an elaborate form of strategic deception under the guise of promoting "world peace." This is even more the case in the aftermath of the September 11 attacks, in that Washington has since identified its position even more completely with Israel's—virtually taking the latter's positions off the shelf as its own—in the wake of the tragic event. In a real arms control scenario, one that is what it purports to be, "[n]o state is going to limit its own behavior unless the arms acquisition and deployment of its enemies are similarly and verifiably restricted."[23] In contrast, unilateral arms control or disarmament of another country is necessarily an act of war and hostility, not an act of peace. It renders the disarmed side relatively weaker, and hence more vulnerable to attack from the uncontrolled state. Indeed, mutuality is the only criterion that separates voluntary arms control from arms control as "war by other means." We can define this as arms control utilized by a state "to find a more advantageous military relationship."[24]

For arms control and disarmament processes to succeed, participating states must have an interest in them and must perceive that all participate equally. This means that the security they will gain by their participation must not be diminished and indeed should be increased. Even the unfinished document of the Arms Control and Regional Security committee in the multilateral track of the former peace process contains a point of agreement that "the arms control and regional security process should not at any stage diminish the security of any individual state or give a state a military advantage over any other."[25] Given the respective limitations of multilateral and international forms of arms control, it seems that the only viable form of arms control and disarmament, if indeed any is possible, is a strictly regional one, at least for the time being. That said, it is now necessary to deal with the problem of the place of arms control in the Middle East peace process.

## THE RELATIONSHIP BETWEEN ARMS CONTROL AND THE MIDDLE EAST PEACE PROCESS

The first acute question that arises regards sequencing: Which comes first, peace or arms control? Israel's stance has always been that it cannot even *discuss* its nuclear arsenal, much less put it on the negotiating table, until it has peace with all its regional enemies, including not only Syria but also the more distant and possibly unconventionally armed Iraq, Iran, and Libya.[26] Today Israel sees Iraq, Iran, and Syria as its primary external strategic threats; its nuclear deterrent is therefore aimed mostly at them (for a time it was also aimed at Moscow and the southern Soviet Union). Israel views its thinly veiled nuclear ambiguity as a strategic asset, not only vis-à-vis these powers but also in its relations with the United States.[27] For Israel to agree to negotiate its nuclear arsenal is to formally admit that it exists. This shroud of ambiguity will not be lifted unless Israel deems it in its interest to do so for other reasons, or unless there is a regionwide peace embracing its distant regional enemies, one that Israel believes might enable it to negotiate nuclear disarmament as part of a larger arms control package. The Arab states and Iran do not demand nuclear transparency from Israel, for fear of unalterably and directly catalyzing the legitimization of Israel's nuclear arsenal.

Indeed, Israel's insistence that confidence and security building measures should be the first element in any sequence reflects these same concerns. Israel's preference is that "operational arms control" designed to build confidence should take place first, perhaps in the context of multilateral ACRS-type negotiations, while "structural arms control" should be postponed until it can include Iraq, Iran, Libya, and Syria.[28] This serves Israel's purpose by providing a considerable time-delay to cushion discussions of nuclear disarmament. From the perspective of Israel's adversaries, the entire "confidence-building" concept serves Israel's interests by bringing about normalized relations with them through the back door. Some of the regional states may not want war with Israel, but they do not necessarily want to cooperate with it, either.

Furthermore, "confidence-building measures," especially of the communications type, are not necessarily viable and could even be harmful in the volatile, post–September 11 Middle East security environment of today. Such measures as prior notification of military exercises and exchanges of military information could be used for strategic deception by a state determined to wage war. Such a state could take advantage of confidence-building measures to create in the enemy a sense of false security. Such measures, by relaxing a state's level of alertness, can thereby reduce rather than increase its security.[29]

For the Arabs and the Iranians, the problem of Israel's nuclear program and its placement on the table comes first in the appropriate sequence, since it is the most destructive element in any current regional arsenal. (Of course, calling for the elimination of the program is different from demanding transparency of an existing arsenal, which is not in the Arab interest.) The Egyptians tried to pin down the Israelis along these former lines, suggesting that they agree to a precise timetable for signing the NPT.[30] The lack of the NPT's credibility among Israeli security elites, as well as in an objective sense, is an equally potent factor. Eventually, Arab strategists will have to take this lack of credibility into account when formulating their proposed options for controlling the region's present and future nuclear arsenals.

The most promising approach would seem to be negotiation of a nuclear, biological, and chemical disarmament program for the entire region, including even Israel's most distant enemies. Everyone in the area, Israel included, would have an interest in this. This is a concept that all sides in the Middle East have endorsed in principle.[31] It differs from the Latin American regime in that it would mutually prohibit all kinds of unconventional weapons, while omitting moralistic, politicized language. Such language is well suited to Latin America but not to the present-day Middle East. The program would also lack the regional institutional framework of the Latin American zone, for the same political reasons. Instead of referring disputes to a regional institution—since no such regional institution can be built due to Arab normalization concerns—they could be referred to an impartial international body such as the International Court of Justice, although necessarily in a nonbinding capacity limited to recommendation and the giving of advice. Israel would never tolerate this arrangement otherwise, due to its historical hostility to international organizations. The basic agreement could proceed instead along the lines of the U.S.–USSR model, complete with timetables that would be negotiated as hard military agreements by strictly military representatives. It could begin with arms control (a Middle East SALT agreement), move on to deproliferation (a START agreement), and ultimately, disarmament (a ground-zero agreement like the INF accord in Europe).

The severe limitations of including Middle East arms control under the heading of a future Middle East peace process have already been discussed. More important, doing something to prevent the emergence of a MAD Middle East is simply too vital to be blocked by the absence of major unconventionally armed parties or the chronic uncertainties of Middle East peace processes. Middle East arms control should not have to wait for the emergence of yet another Middle East peace process that may or may not succeed. Most Israelis, with the notable exception of former Israeli Likud Defense Minister Moshe Arens, believe that peace must come before arms control, but it is also true that this position gives Israel leverage in promoting the urgency of the political process itself. If the Israelis were faced with a real unconventional arms reduction proposal to consider, however, one that was consistent with their national interests and did not endanger state security, there is no reason why they could not embrace it.[32] Cold War precedent has demonstrated that directly negotiated arms control arrangements depend neither on mutual trust nor on the resolution of chronic political and security disputes between signatories.

It is wrong to assume that Syria's absence from the former ACRS implies that Damascus agrees with Israel on the sequence of peace before arms control.[33] The only way to determine this is to find out if Syria would favor initiating *military* arms control talks in delegations headed not by diplomats but by military strategists, prior to the conclusion of the bilateral peace talks. In other words, these talks would be designed in such a way that they would not be linked to and would not imply the normalization of political relations. Indeed, indications are that even if a comprehensive Middle East peace settlement is reached at some future date, it will usher in unprecedented demands from some of the participants for American and other weapons. They will want these to compensate for the loss in immediate security that peace with Israel will inevitably cause. This is the established pattern of Middle East peacemaking, and there is no reason to believe the next time will be any different. As Stephanie Neuman writes: "Should current peace negotiations in the Middle East be successful, weapons transfers are bound to be a political outcome."[34]

That states need not maintain normal or friendly relations or security cooperation and that even archenemies can find it in their security interests to undertake arms control and disarmament was amply demonstrated by the SALT I and SALT II agreements of the Cold War, and the later START and INF agreements. These processes were initiated or continued during the intense hostility that characterized U.S.–USSR relations during the Reagan years of the 1980s. Indeed, states in a condition of friendly peace as in Western Europe do not need arms control or disarmament, for the same reason that they do not need arms races. It is precisely among states whose relations are hostile, when the risk of war is at its highest, and where the threat of mass destruction hovers heavy over an area, that arms control and disarmament are most needed.

The negotiation of Arab-Israeli military agreements prior to the advent of any peace process is hardly unfamiliar; a precedent was set in 1948–1949 with the four Arab-Israeli armistice agreements. This has subsequently been repeated several times, the 1974 and 1975 Israel–Egypt military disengagement agreements and the 1974 Israel–Syria separation of forces agreement being cases in point. Other cases are the Israel–PLO cease-fire agreement of 1981 which lasted almost a year; the unofficial 1976 Israel–Syria "red lines" agreement that demarcated respective spheres of interest in Lebanon; and the Israel–Syria–Lebanon understandings of 1996, which constrained Israel and the Hezbollah from targeting immediate noncombatants on either side during the final phase of Israel's occupation of Lebanon (1978–2000). The approach of negotiating arms control and disarmament as strictly military talks on the Cold War model will allow all the proliferating regional states to arrive at military arrangements. They can then adhere to these without necessarily participating in an ACRS-type forum or other elements of a future peace process, which truly concern only those states that face or have faced Israeli occupation of some or all of their territory.

What will be necessary, however, is the lifting of the sanctions against Iraq, so that Iraq may participate in the region's arms control. Iraq's agreement to restrict the arms race in the national interest, entered into of its own free will but subject to strict mutual verification procedures, will last far longer than any agreement coerced by UNSCOM, the stillborn UNMOVIC, or any successor agency. From the moment the tainted UNSCOM organization lost Iraqi cooperation (by that point the agency was seen as doing intolerable harm from Iraq's perspective), Iraqi rearmament was free to resume. A future form of regional arms control on the model recommended here will not contain within its structure any agency ripe for espionage, since it will be based on first- and second-party verification, nor will it be judged based on whether it contributes to the lifting of sanctions, since under this formula the sanctions would have already been lifted. It will last longer because it will be in Iraq's interest to participate in it—which is not the case with UNSCOM or UNMOVIC—and not for any other reason.

In general, disarmament freely entered into is far more stable and long-lasting than that applied by outside force. As long as a state retains its sovereignty it will have access to the manpower, logistics, and financial resources—not to mention the motivation—to contravene forced attempts to disarm it. One must only recall the results of the last major attempt at such coercive disarmament against pre–World War II Germany in Versailles. Iraqi disarmament as it exists today is patterned on the model of Versailles. The next Iraqi generation, currently growing up under the carnage of long-term sanctions, will likely produce a future leadership that will vow to never allow Iraq to become vulnerable to such a thing again. Since this hostility came from a superpower, there is now a powerful motive for Iraq to acquire the means to deter a superpower, which can only mean unconventional weapons. The memory of the sanctions will pervade Iraq long after President Saddam Hussein is gone; indeed, the sanctions, now more than a decade old, are defining the political mindset of an entire Iraqi generation. The threat of an Iraqi biological weapons attack against the United States may become a self-fulfilling prophecy if Iraq is pushed too far. It would have been inconceivable for Baghdad to so threaten the United States but for the U.S.-led Gulf War and the monumentally destructive and apparently indefinite character of the sanctions that followed. If the sanctions were to be lifted as a part of an Iraqi entry into a Middle East region-wide arms control and disarmament procedure, one in which Iraq would participate like any other state, the result would be much more stable over the long-term.

In summary, what is required is a Middle East forum outside a peace process framework that covers not only the cordon states (the direct confrontation states adjacent to Israel's borders) in the Arab-Israeli conflict but also what Israel often refers to as the "long-distance threats" of Iraq, Iran, and Libya. It must do so without binding them politically in ways unacceptable to them. Arms control and disarmament are needed not only between these states and Israel, but also among themselves. Suitable balances must be found throughout the region, balances within which every state can feel secure. The stark imbalances between Iraq and Iran on the one hand, and the southern Gulf monarchies on the other, cannot be totally rectified. But the threat to the weak southern Gulf states can be reduced through the redeployment of Iraqi and Iranian large-scale forces away from their front lines. In this theater, in contrast to the Arab-Israeli theater, the distances are sufficient to allow for such redeployments. This eventuality might also allow the Americans to disengage militarily from the Gulf subregion, which is clearly in their long-term interests at this point.

For Iraq and Iran, conventional military redeployments away from their mutual frontier are not possible, however, because of the close location of Baghdad to the Iranian border coupled with the relative distance of Tehran from the Iraqi border. Since Iraqi and Iranian military capabilities are relatively equal, the threat they pose to each other can be reduced by mutually agreed prohibitions on unconventional weapons: Iraq and Iran would have to agree to scrap their biological and chemical capabilities, and both states, together with Israel and Syria, would have to forswear both of the above, in addition to any nuclear option. In a separate conventional package, the two Gulf powers could institute mutual conventional force reductions along with the other parties in the region, namely, Israel, Turkey, Syria, and Egypt. Thus, as Iraq and Iran proceed to reduce the potential destructive threat they pose to each other, they will, along with Israel, reduce the threat they may pose to other states in the region.

## CONCLUSION: ARMS CONTROL IN
## THE NATIONAL INTEREST

To sum up, it is not necessary for all the Middle Eastern states to have normal relations to conduct arms limitation and reduction agreements among themselves, provided the agreements are purely military agreements conducted by generals and not politicians. By way of comparison, the Cold War adversaries may have had diplomatic relations, but those relations were anything but normal. The two states viewed communism and capitalism, respectively, as illegitimate political systems, just as most states in the Middle East region, including some of those that have recognized Israel in peace treaties, continue to view Zionism—based as they see it on racialism and the displacement of indigenous peoples—as an illegitimate political system.

Furthermore, the issue of formal recognition would be neither necessary nor sufficient to allay Israel's concerns about the region's level of unconventional armament. These concerns derive from the fear that hostile countries, whether or not they recognize Israel formally, might still choose to wage unconventional war against it one day if there were no threat of massive retaliation. This embodies a variation on the concerns the United States and the Soviet Union expressed in their first- and second-strike debates. Had the two states not already recognized each other when the USSR was established, there is no reason to believe that this would have made nuclear war (and hence the motive for arms control) any more or less likely. Today the mutually recognized states of India and Pakistan face each other as fully armed adversaries, flirting with nuclear confrontation. They would not have been any less in need of nuclear disarmament had they not recognized each other.

Israel's primary motive in arming itself is to deter its enemies, whether those enemies recognize its legitimacy or not. Once deterrence reaches a point where it is considered unstable or insufficient to meet the unconventional weapons threat, states—Israel included—will have an inherent motive to pursue unconventional arms control to reduce the likelihood of an unconventional attack against themselves. This day of reckoning is not far away in Israel, due to the counterdeterrent unconventional advances of its enemies.

In the Arab-Israeli case, the concept of "trust" is often raised. That is, Israel does not trust countries that fail to recognize Israel as legitimate. Similarly, the Arab states and Iran do not trust Israel. India does not trust Pakistan. The Americans did not trust the Soviets. States do not need to trust each other to enter into mutually verifiable arms control agreements. If they did trust each other they would not require formal and verifiable arms control agreements. In fact, mutually hostile states will only enter into arms control agreements whose success is *not* dependent on the "goodwill" of the other party (in which they do not believe). More important is the condition that the results should be objectively and independently verifiable, and that the agreement makes the parties to an agreement more secure than they would be if an uncontrolled arms race were allowed by these actors to continue unabated.

Like Israel, Arab states and Iran sometimes refer to the outstanding political problems (e.g., the Palestinian situation) as barriers to arms control. The reason for this is twofold. First, they fear that the details of arms control will be imposed upon them by outside powers such as the United States, and that the agreement will be unbalanced, favoring one side, and therefore detrimental to their primary security interests. For this reason, the recommendation presented here is for the regional actors themselves, perhaps with outside expert advice from former U.S–Soviet arms control and disarmament negotiators, to change that formulation to one that more closely mirrors the U.S.–Soviet model of arms control. That way, regional states will not have to worry about unfavorable agreements being imposed upon them from outside.

Second, they fear that Israel might try to use arms control as a back door to the normalization of relations (economic cooperation, tourism, embassies, mandatory cultural exchanges, etc.). Arab states have not, however, shied away from concluding strictly military agreements with Israel when it was in their interests to do so, despite the presence of those very same outstanding political issues. Israel can obviate this Arab fear, as it has done in its previous military agreements with its Arab adversaries, by not trying to link arms control with other issues. In the U.S.–Soviet precedent, it should be mentioned, arms control was not linked by either side to outside issues.

The challenge, then, is for the regional actors themselves, perhaps with the aforementioned outside technical advice from Cold War–era disarmament experts, to construct arms control in such a manner that participation serves the primary security interests of all parties, along the U.S.–Soviet model. Cold War arms limitation and reduction was accomplished without resolving any of the outstanding political-military conflicts between the superpowers, which revolved around nothing less than the nature, security, and leadership of the world order and the legitimacy of the two protagonists' respective political systems. The incentive for participation, then as now, depends on the stability or instability of the military balance, as well as calculations about the ability of those states to rationally wage war. These incentives will remain regardless of the apparent state of political relations, which can be deceptive, especially in the fiercely multipolar Middle East.

As to whether something more is needed before arms control can be tried, this is the most important aspect of the Cold War analogy, since the Middle Eastern situation likewise represents a totalistic conflict between powers that fully distrust one another. U.S.–Soviet arms control worked because (1) the two states entered it willingly, as it was in their national interests to make it a high priority; and (2) the agreements were based not on trust but on hard first- and second-party verification. There is no reason why a Middle East agreement should be any different.

Some have suggested that a free trade or other type of economic agreement should precede regional arms control. In fact, a regional economic agreement will likely be the very *last* thing agreed to in the Middle Eastern context. This is because, first, it is perceived to be the very stuff of normalization, and the Arab countries and Iran are particularly wary of Israel's intentions in this area. Unlike arms control agreements, good economic relations *do* depend on trust, something that currently is and probably always will be lacking. The second reason for their opposition, generally led by Arab civil society and the professional/trade sectors, is the fear that Israel will use its First World status to infiltrate their economies, their resources, and their political systems, and will thereby eventually dominate them. This feared outcome is known popularly in the region as "Middle Easternism." Even in states that have made formal peace with Israel (i.e., Egypt and Jordan), it has been the educated sectors of civil society that have applied the brakes on economic cooperation and other forms of normalization with Israel. They have gone so far as to expel individual members of professional associations who have pursued cooperation on their own. It should also be noted here that there was no free trade agreement between the United States and the Soviet Union during the Cold War.

Most important of all is that friendly countries that enjoy peace and normal relations with one another do not need arms control. It is precisely at a conflict's hottest and most unstable point—when it threatens to escalate out of control and pose the danger of mass destruction—that arms control is most needed. In contrast, arms control between friendly states living in stable situations and enjoying economic cooperation and so forth (Israel and Turkey, or the United States and France, for instance), could not be considered meaningful. Therefore, reassurances are not what are required. Certainly the United States and the USSR did not have reassurances from each other, or from anyone else, before they set out to control the mutual threat of mass destruction.

There is an unfortunate Orientalist stereotype that everything in the Middle East is about psychology. This derives from a second Orientalist stereotype that holds that rationality in that region is not at a premium. In reality, Middle Eastern geopolitics is based on the same primary factors as it is everywhere: the cold calculation of what constitutes the national interest at any given time.

For this same reason, democratization of the Arab and Iranian political systems is not a prerequisite to arms control, as some might believe. This formulation was first used by Benjamin Netanyahu as an excuse to avoid peace negotiations with Syria and the Palestinians. These same negotiations thereafter reached an advanced status despite the authoritarian political systems characterizing some of the participants. Similarly, the United States conducted successful arms control with its Soviet enemy, even though it was well aware that the USSR was a totalitarian state. Once again there is no reason, except in Orientalist argumentation, why the Middle East should be any different.

The bottom line is that if and when the Israelis believe their military security would be enhanced by a military arms control agreement, as they have in previous bilateral military agreements entered into with individual regional adversaries such as Syria, they will seek to enter into one. The agreement would have the effect of reducing the military threat of enemy states. For Israel this is currently a conventional threat (which is objectively minuscule by military standards) but it could soon become a quite serious unconventional one. Israel could become interested in a specifically unconventional arms control program in order to *prevent* Arab states and Iran from further pursuing unconventional armaments, particularly if they appeared likely to succeed in obtaining them. A further inducement would be verification conducted not by an international organization but by the contending states themselves, perhaps with international escorts to mollify the security concerns of both Israel and its enemies. States like Iraq, Iran, and Syria might likewise be induced to enter into unconventional arms limitation or reduction with Israel provided that such negotiations were not linked to an Arab-Israeli peace process, which some of these states oppose. More important, and this also applies to present-day Syria, Israel's adversaries could potentially be induced to enter into an unconventional arms limitation process with Israel if the agreement were not perceived as a deception designed to bring about normalization of relations or "security co-operation" with Israel. Finally, they might be persuaded to participate if they thought it would increase their military security vis-à-vis Israel by diminishing the unconventional threat Israel poses to their homelands.

What is needed is not more Orientalist psychobabble, but rather a hard-edged awareness on the part of regional states that unconventional arms control is vital to their national survival. It must be made a high priority on this basis. The most productive contribution the international community can make is to increase this awareness.

One might ask: "Who could act as an honest broker?" Of course, the United States and the Soviets did not have one, yet their work succeeded. Still, a mediator might play a role. In the Middle East we encounter a multipolar environment, nonrecognition among some regional states, and a consequent need (as a result of that nonrecognition) for secrecy. For these reasons the introduction of outside mediation might be helpful, provided all parties consented. The parties might be inclined to accept the presence of Norway or the UN Secretary-General or some other mutually acknowledged impartial state or actor whose neutrality is not compromised by a direct stake in the outcome.

Rather than a regional conference on the Latin American model, one could envision a series of private bilateral and multilateral meetings among the participants held in neutral locations in the company of neutral mediators. If agreement were reached, it could then be announced publicly; in other words, after the fact. It is possible that some variation on this multipolar model could also be useful in the India–China–Pakistan relationship.

Should a Middle East military arms control and disarmament program covering nuclear, biological, chemical, and possibly conventional weapons systems develop, it will need effective mechanisms for intraregional verification if it is to be durable. Enforcement must be internal to the region, for no one outside the region is capable of such enforcement, nor is there anyone who could be relied upon by all parties to impartially apply enforcement sanctions. Furthermore, in the past, Arab states and Iran have perceived external enforcement mechanisms to be disproportionately targeted against them, even when objective considerations would require that their enemies be similarly targeted.

A few examples illustrate why Israel's geopolitical adversaries would be unlikely to trust the United States or an international organization dominated by it as an outside enforcer. When Israel invaded and occupied Beirut and half of Lebanon for three years, no sanctions resulted. However, when Iraq invaded and occupied Kuwait for five and one-half months, the result was an American-led international war against Iraq, followed by the indefinite application of sanctions at America's behest, and now topped off by the post–September 11 Bush administration threat of a new and unprovoked invasion of Iraq. The Iranians might note that when their intelligence service conducts assassinations abroad, Iran is threatened with sanctions, yet when the Israeli Mossad and Shin Bet conduct assassinations abroad and within the territories they occupy, respectively, there is no mention of sanctions. The problem extends beyond the Middle East. When India and Pakistan conducted their nuclear tests, they were met with sanctions. However, when Israel conducted its nuclear test with South Africa, a specific exemption was constructed for it, negating what would have been mandatory sanctions. The list could go on. Arab states and Iran are unlikely to enter into any arrangement that contains mechanisms of the sort that have historically targeted them disproportionately and, from their perspective, arbitrarily.

A realistically viable Middle Eastern arms control and disarmament arrangement would be mutually self-enforcing. That is, it would be enforced by reciprocal inspections and national verification measures negotiated and conducted by the parties to the agreement. The international community could be invited to offer ideas and suggestions. Because such agreements would be freely entered into, they would be valid only so long as participation remained in the interests of all the relevant states. If a state were to violate the agreement and try to conceal its activities, the violation would be uncovered by the mutual verification measures. At that point the state would have the choice of reversing the treaty violation or living without the agreement, since the other states would now also be free to carry out their own treaty violations. The potential breakdown of the arrangement, along with the loss of hard-earned benefits of arms control and disarmament, is perhaps the most effective penalty of all, for the approach is based on a political-military version of the market principle. If a state has deemed it in its national security interest to enter into such an agreement in the first place, the specter of its breakdown should provide the best possible deterrent to potential treaty violators.

## NOTES

An earlier version of this chapter was published by the Emirates Center for Strategic Studies and Research in Abu Dhabi, United Arab Emirates, as Emirates Occasional Paper 32, entitled "Integrated Middle East Regional Approaches to Unconventional Arms Control and Disarmament."

1. The perception is that of the Syrian Foreign Minister Farouq El-Sharaa, in the form of a 1989 statement cited in Shai Feldman, *Nuclear Weapons and Arms Control in the Middle East* (Cambridge, Mass: Massachusetts Institute for Technology Press, 1997), 211; and in Charles Flowerree and Brad Roberts, "Chemical Weapons Arms Control," in *Arms Control and Confidence Building in the Middle East,* ed. W. Seth Carus and Janne E. Nolan (Washington, D.C.: United States Institute for Peace, 1992), 102.

2. Once this response threshold was crossed by the Soviet Union, the fear in the United States was of the absolute damage that the Soviet Union could cause even if only a few of its warheads got through, something that even a "defeated" Soviet Union could accomplish. Philip Sabin, "Restraints on Chemical, Biological, and Nuclear Use: Some Lessons from History," in *Non-Conventional Weapons Proliferation in the Middle East: Tackling the Spread of Nuclear, Chemical, and Biological Capabilities,* ed. Efraim Karsh, Martin S. Navias, and Philip Sabin (Oxford: Clarendon Press, 1993), 13, 15.

3. Anthony H. Cordesman, "Current Trends in Arms Sales in the Middle East," in Shai Feldman and Ariel Levite, eds., *Arms Control and the New Middle East Security Environment* (Boulder, Colo.: Westview Press, 1994), 58.

4. Geoffrey Kemp, "The Bush Administration's Arms Control Agenda for the Middle East," in Feldman and Levite, *Arms Control and the New Middle East Security Environment,* 187. The explicit reference to "coercion," not intended for

Israel's nuclear program, is also in Lewis A. Dunn, "The Nuclear Agenda, the Middle East in Global Perspective," in Feldman and Levite, *Arms Control*, 241.

5. William Hopkinson, "Arms Control and Supplier Restraints: A UK Perspective," in Karsh, Navias, and Sabin, *Non-Conventional Weapons Proliferation*, 232.

6. Dore Gold, "Evaluating the Threat to Israel in an Era of Change," in Feldman and Levite, *Arms Control*, 95.

7. Frank Barnaby, *The Invisible Bomb: The Nuclear Arms Race in the Middle East* (London: I. B. Tauris, 1989), 101, 122–23.

8. For example, Address of Israeli Prime Minister Yitzhak Shamir to the United Nations General Assembly, 7 June 1988, cited in Feldman, *Nuclear Weapons and Arms Control*, 291. One of Shamir's criticisms of the NPT is that it has not prevented conventional wars between its signatories. This criticism is irrelevant because that was not the purpose of the NPT, which was concerned with the prevention of nuclear war.

9. Feldman, *Nuclear Weapons and Arms Control*, 15.

10. Avi Beker, "A Regional Non-Proliferation Treaty for the Middle East," in *Security or Armageddon: Israel's Nuclear Strategy*, ed. Louis Rene Beres (Lexington, Mass: Lexington Books, 1986), cited in Barnaby, *Invisible Bomb*, 150–51.

11. Barnaby, *Invisible Bomb*, 123.

12. Feldman, *Nuclear Weapons and Arms Control*, 166.

13. SIPRI, *The NPT: The Main Political Barrier to Nuclear Weapon Proliferation* (London: Taylor and Francis Limited, 1980).

14. From the perspective of Israel, the MTCR is inadequate because Israel is threatened strategically by missiles of a much lesser range than the 300 kilometer minimum it covers, for instance those positioned in nearby Syria. From the perspective of Arab states threatened by Israeli short- and long-range missiles, the MTCR seems aimed at the only delivery system they have that could possibly serve as a deterrent. The MTCR commits the additional sin of leaving the indigenous Israeli nuclear-armed missile threat completely intact and capable of future development.

15. Hopkinson, "Arms Control and Supplier Restraints," 231; Hartman, "Controlling the Proliferation of Missiles," in Feldman and Levite, *Arms Control and the New Middle East Security Environment*, 213. Those who now advocate tampering with the objective of the MTCR and extending the coverage to nonnuclear capable missiles will alarm the Arab states and Iran even further, giving the impression that it is their deterrent effort and not Israel's existing nuclear threat that is to be targeted. For the suggestion to denuclearize the MTCR's purpose, see Kathleen C. Bailey, "Can Missile Proliferation be Reversed?" *Orbis* 35(1) (Winter 1991), 10.

16. Gerald M. Steinberg, "Middle East Space Race Gathers Pace," *International Defense Review* (October 1995).

17. Senator John McCain, "A U.S. Congressional View on Arms Control," Transcript of a World Net Dialogue of the United States Information Agency and the Jaffee Center for Strategic Studies, reproduced in *Arms Control in the Middle East*, ed. Dore Gold (Boulder, Colo. and Tel Aviv: Westview Press and the Jaffee Center for Strategic Studies, Tel Aviv University, 1991), 54–55. At times the characterizations are almost comical: The reference to "unstable states" presumably includes Syria, Iraq, Libya, and Iran. The regimes in Syria, Iraq, and Libya have been in

uncontested power since 1970, 1978, and 1969, respectively, while post-revolutionary Iran enjoys a relatively stable and democratic presidential and parliamentary election system.

18. The perfect example of this can be found in Cordesman, "Current Trends in Arms Sales in the Middle East," 53, 55.

19. Posen, "Military Lessons of the Gulf War," in Feldman and Levite, *Arms Control and the New Middle East Security Environment*, 61.

20. Barnaby, *Invisible Bomb*, 148.

21. For instance, ignoring the siege mentality that is now being deeply felt in Syrian defense circles as a result of being enclosed on two fronts by a threatening Israeli-Turkish alliance, Senator McCain writes: "I do not believe that Syria is threatened by Israel or anyone else." McCain, "A U.S. Congressional View on Arms Control," 63. The problem is widespread in the United States, whose officials cannot seem to grasp the reciprocity of threat perception that characterizes "security dilemmas" in an anarchic international system.

22. Hopkinson, "Arms Control and Supplier Restraints," 234.

23. Gerald M. Steinberg, "International/Regional Verification Options in Nuclear Arms Control," in Gold, *Arms Control*, 92.

24. Posen, "Military Lessons of the Gulf War," 64.

25. Draft Statement on Arms Control and Regional Security, Tunis, Tunisia, December 1994, reproduced in Feldman, *Nuclear Weapons and Arms Control*, 323.

26. For Israel's fear that mere discussions could "slip" into unwanted negotiations, see Feldman, "Israel's National Security," 26.

27. Geoffrey Kemp, "Arms Control and the Arab-Israeli Peace Process," in Karsh, Navias, and Sabin, *Non-Conventional Weapons Proliferation*, 247; Feldman, "Israel's National Security," 17; Shai Feldman and Abdullah Toukan, "Bridging the Gap: Resolving the Security Dilemma in the Middle East," in Shai Feldman and Abdullah Toukan, *Bridging the Gap: A Future Security Architecture for the Middle East* (Lanham, Md.: Rowman & Littlefield, 1997), 77; and Feldman, *Nuclear Weapons and Arms Control*, 113, 191, 202, 249. In the latter work Feldman raises the additional interesting point that some American elites see Israel's nuclear program as being in their own interest, since it seems to free the United States from providing the ultimate guarantee for Israel's survival.

28. For the difference between operational and structural arms control, see Shai Feldman and Abdullah Toukan, "Background for Peace," in Feldman and Toukan, *Bridging the Gap*, 4–5. Briefly, operational arms control is about mechanics, intent, deployment, and early warning; structural arms control is about arms reduction or disarmament. For Israel's sequencing preferences, see Feldman, *Nuclear Weapons and Arms Control*, 243; and Abdullah Toukan, "Arab National Security Issues: Perceptions and Policies," in Feldman and Toukan, *Bridging the Gap*, 64.

29. Geoffrey Kemp makes this same point in "Arms Control and the Arab-Israeli Peace Process," 246.

30. Perhaps two years after the completion of the remaining Syrian and Lebanese tracks of the smaller-scale Arab–Israeli bilateral peace talks, for instance. Feldman, *Nuclear Weapons and Arms Control*, 13.

31. Israel, Egypt, and prerevolutionary Iran have all advocated nuclear weapons-

free zones: Israel's proposal is regionalist and independent of the NPT, whereas Egypt's is a NWFZ established on an internationalist NPT foundation. For reference to these proposals, see the Addresses of Israeli Prime Minister Yitzhak Shamir and Egyptian Foreign Minister Esmat Abdel Meguid to the United Nations General Assembly, 7 and 13 June 1988, respectively, reproduced in Gold, *Arms Control*, 141–46 and 147–55, respectively.

32. For the standard Israeli position that peace must come before arms control, see Kemp, "Arms Control and the Arab-Israeli Peace Process," 260. The contrary position of Moshe Arens is cited in Dore Gold, "Introduction," in Gold, *Arms Control*, 7.

33. Such an assumption is found in Feldman, *Nuclear Weapons and Arms Control*, 208.

34. Stephanie Neuman, "Controlling the Arms Trade," in Karsh, Navias, and Sabin, *Non-Conventional Weapons Proliferation*, 276.

# 7

# Israel

## *Reconstructing a Black Box*

*Avner Cohen*

No region reflects more acutely the intricacy and difficulty related to control and disarmament of biological weapons than the Middle East. All major powers in the region—Egypt, Iraq, Israel, and Syria—are widely believed to have pursued covertly one or another form of offensive BW program.[1] Yet details about these programs—their size, status, and strategic rationale—have been shrouded in secrecy. Apart from Iraq, no country in the Middle East has ever admitted to pursuing an offensive biological warfare (BW) program. In the context of the Middle East biological weapons are by far the least known, hence the least studied, category of weapons of mass destruction (WMD).

Tight secrecy is not the only obstacle to addressing the question of BW in the Middle East. The other difficulty—related to secrecy although distinct from it—is the linkages that strategically and politically tie BW to the two other categories on the WMD spectrum, chemical and nuclear weapons. Although biological weapons, like chemical weapons, are often referred to as "the poor man's bomb," the mortality that could be produced by a few kilograms of well-dispersed anthrax, unlike chemical weapons, might approach that of a single atomic bomb. Investment in offensive BW programs, then, might be justified as a strategic response to acquisition or development of nuclear weapons by a rival state. Iraq's pursuit of an offensive BW program suggests such a view of the strategic role of biological weapons.

Israel is the most significant player in the Middle East in the area of nonconventional weaponry. Its dominance is associated with its opaque nuclear weapons capability—the world's "worst-kept secret"—assumed to be sizeable in quantity and advanced in quality. Official secrecy notwithstanding, the "big picture" of Israel's nuclear capabilities and thinking is by now known. This is not the case, however, with Israel's chemical and biological warfare (CBW) capabilities. The biological field, more even than the chemical field, has remained Israel's biggest "black box."

This chapter attempts to penetrate this "black box." Following an overview of the evolution of Israeli attitudes toward and perceptions of nonconventional weaponry, it briefly traces and assesses Israeli attitudes and activities in the area of biological warfare. Most of the chapter tries to place the BW issue within the broader context of policy, deterrence, and arms control.

## ISRAEL AND NONCONVENTIONAL
## WEAPONRY: AN OVERVIEW

In a letter to Ehud Avriel, one of the Jewish Agency's operatives in Europe, in April 1948, David Ben Gurion, Israel's founding father, ordered Avriel to seek out and recruit East European Jewish scientists who could "either increase the capacity to kill masses or to cure masses; both things are important."[2] In 1948 this language meant developing a BW capacity, but it underlines a more general imperative: In its pursuit of survival Israel could not avoid exploring nonconventional weapons; the new nation could not afford *not* to research and develop indigenous nonconventional capabilities. This remains the essence of Israel's pursuit of nonconventional weapons ever since.

To understand why Israel committed itself so early to pursuing nonconventional weaponry one must understand fundamental Israeli attitudes about matters of security and survival. Ben Gurion had witnessed firsthand the genocide of the Armenian minority in Turkey during World War I. This might have been an early lesson that small minorities that cannot protect themselves in a hostile environment face a real threat of genocide. But it was the Holocaust that forced him to realize that such a catastrophe did happen, the world did not intervene to save the Jews, and it could happen again to the Jewish people. Israel must be strong enough to ensure that it would never happen again. Israel as a nation-state was founded in 1948 in the shadow of the Holocaust.

The determination not to be helpless again—a commitment to the idea that Jews should control their own fate—characterized Ben Gurion's campaign for Jewish statehood after World War I. Imbued with the lessons of the Holocaust, Ben Gurion was always consumed by fears for Israel's security.[3] Those fears stemmed from his understanding of the geopolitical realities of the Arab-Israeli conflict. As the War of Independence concluded in 1949 with an impressive Israeli victory, Ben Gurion was already convinced that the cessation of hostilities would not lead to a lasting peace but would be only a temporary pause before the next round of Arab-Israeli military conflict.[4] Ben Gurion saw Arab hostility toward Israel as deep and lasting. To have peace with Israel required that the Arabs accept their losses as final.[5]

Israel's pursuit of nonconventional weaponry was a direct answer to Ben Gurion's security anxiety.[6] His conviction that the Holocaust might not be a single and unique event in Jewish history but a reminder of Israel's enemies' ultimate desire became engraved in Israel's collective psyche and embedded into its idea of national security. As long as the Arab-Israeli conflict remains unresolved, Israel's ultimate threat remains an Arab war coalition aimed at the total destruction of Israel as a sovereign state. Ever since the early 1950s Israeli military planners have always considered a scenario in which a united hostile (Arab) military coalition would launch a war against Israel with the aim of liberating Palestine and destroying the Jewish State (known as *mikre ha-kol,* the "everything scenario"), the scenario of a major Arab war coalition against Israel.[7]

## Israel's Biological Warfare Program

Israel's quest for nonconventional weaponry started in its War of Independence in 1948. It was then that Israel's BW program was born. The scientists who surrounded Ben Gurion in 1948—especially Professor Ernst David Bergmann and the Katzir (Katchalsky) brothers—came from the fields of chemistry and microbiology. Their outlook reinforced Ben Gurion's conviction that Israel's leading edge in its struggle with its enemies depended on investing in science and technology. These scientists were the founders of the Science Corps within the Israeli Defense Forces (IDF), known as HEMED.[8]

When Ben Gurion instructed Ehud Avriel, his operative in Europe in April 1948, to find those Jewish scientists who could "either increase the capacity to kill masses or to cure masses," this was apparently weeks after he had approved the establishment of a new secret unit within HEMED dedicated to BW. Dr. Alexander Keynan, then a new Ph.D. in microbiology, was the leader of a small group of life science researchers from the Hebrew University who urged Ben Gurion—with the strong support of Katchalsky and Bergmann—to create the new unit. Bergmann and the Katchalsky brothers gave their full blessing to the proposal, and Ben Gurion probably easily endorsed it.[9] The small unit, soon called HEMED BEIT, was founded in February 1948 and was located first in Jaffa and later in a desolate grove outside the town of Ness Ziona. With the trauma of the Holocaust fresh in mind, a commitment was made to do everything necessary to establish a Jewish state. The creation of HEMED BEIT was an additional translation of this commitment into action.[10]

As Israel's War of Independence ended in 1949, a period of reorganization began at both the IDF and the Ministry of Defense (MOD).[11] As part of this organizational overhaul, HEMED was converted into MOD-sponsored civilian research centers ("Machons"). IIBR was founded in 1952, as a merger of two HEMED research centers, one the continuation of HEMED BEIT. From its very birth the IIBR evolved with a dual identity. For security and other bureaucratic purposes it was regarded as a highly classified research center ("Machon 2") run and funded by the Division of Research (EMET) at the MOD. For representative-scientific functions it was a civilian research center, named the Israel Institute for Biological Research (IIBR), under the jurisdiction of the Prime Minister's Office.[12]

Archival documentation about the birth of IIBR is unavailable, but it is known that Bergmann insisted that Israel must, as a matter of national security commitment, set up a national laboratory to be in charge of all biochemical research and development relevant to the national interest, in particular CBW capabilities.[13] Given the fact that the Arab states had no CBW programs in the early 1950s and HEMED BEIT's activities during the war, it is safe to speculate that Bergmann and his colleagues, like their contemporaries in the United States, the United Kingdom, and France, thought primarily about "offensive" capabilities.[14] Although the justification for establishing IIBR was presumably made in terms of providing the defense establishment with CBW capabilities, it appears that the research mandate Bergmann sought for the new institute was broader than merely satisfying those needs.

In addition to these motivations, both security and academic considerations may also have contributed to Bergmann's insistence on creating a *civic* identity, with a broad research mandate, for IIBR. It appears that Bergmann thought that the civic mandate of the IIBR would provide a legitimate cover, a kind of security shield, for the scientists involved in the projects undertaken there. From the outset Bergmann recognized the intrinsic "dual use" ambiguity involved in CBW research. There were also scientific-academic considerations. By maintaining a civic-legitimate structure and rationale, IIBR was able to attract top scientists by offering them the kinds of intellectual and material benefits available in similar academic environments: publishing research in scientific journals, attending scientific conferences, taking Sabbatical leaves, and the like.[15]

In 1952 Ben Gurion approved Bergmann's ideas regarding the reorganization of HEMED BEIT as a civilian state research institution. Almost five decades later, it is remarkable to realize how much of Bergmann's founding concept has survived the passage of time and changes in both science and politics. The current public mission statement of IIBR, as it appears in an elaborate IIBR website, reflects the broad scientific mandate, built on the ambiguity of dual use, with which Bergmann sought to color IIBR activities in the 1950s. In accordance with this philosophy IIBR's specialties are broadly defined as follows: "Backed by close to five decades of experience, the Israel Institute of Biological Research—IIBR—specializes in applied research, development and production in the fields of biology, chemistry, ecology and public health, in addition to basic research studies emanating from IIBR's applied projects."[16]

The national capabilities and expertise of IIBR are consistent with a full array of activities associated with a sophisticated CBW program, both on the defensive and offensive sides. Yet the website carefully avoids the issue of policy motivation and intent involved in the research of IIBR.

Although the elaborate IIBR website demonstrates how scientifically advanced Israel is in terms of its CBW capabilities—possibly as a deliberate way to project deterrence[17]—these capabilities and the intentions behind them are hardly a subject of public discussion among Israelis. By and large, Israeli activities in the area of CBW are treated as a national taboo, very much like, and perhaps even more than, the nuclear taboo. In a sense, this oddity, too, is the result of Bergmann's fundamental dual identity/dual use approach.

IIBR's website notwithstanding, the Ness Ziona facility—like Israel's nuclear facility at Dimona—is one of the nation's most guarded and most secretive installations. It has been treated by the security establishment not as a civic laboratory but rather as a most sensitive defense installation. Over the years the single building hidden in the orange grove at the outskirts of Ness Ziona has grown into many acres of a well-secured campus surrounded by a six-foot-high concrete wall topped with electronic sensors that reveal the exact location of any intruder. For security reasons the complex is deleted from aerial survey photographs and maps of the town; orange groves are inserted instead.[18]

Ever since the birth of IIBR Israel has erected a thick wall of secrecy, reinforced by strict military censorship, to conceal virtually all activities taking place within it.[19] Until the early 1990s the secrecy surrounding the Ness Ziona facility was so pervasive that its existence was rarely publicly acknowledged. A combination of events and developments has made the Ness Ziona facility more visible since the early 1990s.

In addition to global developments, such as the discovery of the massive clandestine BW program of the Soviet Union, the discoveries of the Iraqi BW program, and the concern over biological terrorism, Israeli-based developments, for the first time, brought IIBR into the headlines. First and foremost was the publication of the Klingberg espionage case, which involved IIBR secrets. In 1983, professor Avraham Marcus Klingberg, a world-

renowned Israeli epidemiologist who had emigrated to Israel from the
Soviet Union in 1948 and who subsequently was IIBR deputy director for
many years, was secretly arrested and convicted as a Soviet spy. Klingberg's
sentence was even harsher than that of Mordecai Vanunu, Israel's nuclear
whistleblower. Klingberg was sentenced to twenty years and, being considered a security risk even in jail, was kept in solitary confinement. Klingberg's
case is commonly viewed as Israel's worst espionage case.[20]

Later, in the late 1990s, after many years of anxious silence, the residents
of Ness Ziona started to ask questions and to raise concerns about the
potential impact of IIRB on their lives.[21] In August 1998, *Yediot Ahronot*,
Israel's leading newspaper, published a long exposé on IIBR, referring to it
as "Tel Aviv Metro's most severe environmental hazard," and raising questions about what the Israeli public can and cannot ask about IIBR and the
"conspiracy of silence" surrounding its activities.[22] The article revealed,
based on disclosure at the Knesset Science Committee, that four serious accidents had occurred at IIBR, with three fatalities and twenty-two injuries, in
the last fifteen years. No details were given about the circumstances of those
accidents, but the British *Foreign Report*, citing unnamed Israeli sources,
claimed that one of the accidents was so serious that the authorities were on
the verge of evacuating the entire town of Ness Ziona, before IIBR scientists
concluded that the threat had passed.[23]

In October 1998, Israel finally confirmed that DMMP, a chemical component used in the manufacture of sarin nerve gas, had been aboard the El-Al
Boeing 747 cargo aircraft that crashed over Amsterdam in October 1992
while carrying a shipment for Ness Ziona. The Israeli confirmation came
after six years in which Israel refused to provide a full account of what the
plane was carrying, claiming that it carried only "commercial cargo."[24] In
contrast, a Dutch parliamentarian called the plane "a chemical ware-
house."[25] If Israel conducted those cover-up efforts to shield the involvement of IIBR, the outcome was the opposite.

The same sense of hesitancy, ambivalence, and taboo that characterizes
Israeli attitudes toward the nation's secret nuclear program also typifies
Israeli attitudes toward the secret facility at Ness Ziona. Although it is true
that there is a noticeable change in societal attitudes of Israelis on these sensitive issues—certainly there is more willingness to ask tough questions, in
particular about potential environmental hazards and safety procedures—
this attitude is still very hesitant. As in the case of the Israeli nuclear program, at best Israelis are ambivalent about opening the "secrets" of Ness
Ziona. Most Israelis prefer not to know too much about what is going on
behind the fenced walls of the Institute in Ness Ziona.[26]

## Assessing IIBR

In the absence of public historical data about IIBR, there are many sensa-
tionalist rumors and speculations and few cautious inferences and recon-

struction. Given the Israeli taboo on the subject, it was a Dutch journalist—not an Israeli one—who conducted the most extensive investigation into the IIBR's unclassified history and its research activities. Applying methods of Internet-based bibliographical review (e.g., using Medline and UnCover) of hundreds of scientific publications written by some 140 scientists affiliated with IIBR over nearly fifty years, and aided by eminent experts on CBW (such as the British chemist Julian Perry Robinson), journalist Karel Knip reconstructed a crude history of the unclassified research conducted at Ness Ziona.[27]

Knip's overall conclusion is that the IIBR, since its establishment in the early 1950s, has been involved in a diversified array of unclassified research activities which, when put together, make sense *only* in the context of research into chemical and biological weapons.[28] In Knip's words: "The many hundreds of articles prove beyond doubt that the IIBR is Israel's main center for research into both chemical and biological weapons. The research conducted at the Institute consists of a bizarre combination of activities which acquire significance within one specific context, that of chemical and biological warfare."[29]

Such a broad-based bibliographical survey is certainly a great tool for reconstructing the institutional research interests of IIBR, but it tells us virtually nothing about the scope of the *classified* side of IIBR: issues related to development and weaponization. It cannot identify the proportion of classified and unclassified activity at IIBR, and such a survey in itself does not tell us whether or not Israel has offensive BW or chemical warfare (CW) programs. It is one thing to conduct extensive research into disease-causing viruses, bacteria, and fungi, the kind of basic research that takes place not only in BW programs but also in medical and agricultural research institutions worldwide. It is another to make claims about Israeli intentions and motivations—defensive or offensive—in the area of CBW. The latter simply cannot be inferred from the former.[30]

The fact that much of the research activities and findings of IIBR's researchers could be reported in scientific journals—which means, of course, that Israeli security authorities treat these publications as unclassified—highlights the notorious ambiguities regarding "dual" or "simultaneous" use involved in much of BW research. First, much basic research relevant to offensive BW programs is *inherently* "dual use" and has "legitimate" applications in medicine and agricultural research as well. Second, even in biological research that can be easily suspected as BW offensive research, such as research on some specific bacterial and viral pathogenesis mechanism, it is often difficult, and at times even impossible, to distinguish by the scientific research itself whether its underlying motivation is to create "defensive" (e.g., vaccine development) or "offensive" (e.g., engineering more virulent strains) capabilities.[31]

Still, Knip's report supports and confirms what has been presumed all along, and what the IIBR web site seems also to suggest: that Israel has substantial research *capabilities* relevant to both defensive and offensive CBW. But to make judgments about Israeli intentions, motivations, and strategy in the CBW areas—and especially regarding weaponization—one needs to know much more.

Assessing Israel's BW program and capabilities remains problematic. Any such effort is inevitably tentative and speculative. Although there is a near consensus among experts, based on anecdotal evidence and intelligence leaks, that Israel developed, produced, stockpiled, and perhaps even deployed chemical weapons at some point in its past (see the next section), this is not the case with biological weapons.[32] Although there is near agreement that Israel has maintained offensive BW capabilities, it is difficult to characterize exactly what those capabilities are and their specific status.[33]

It is probable that Israel has maintained some sort of production *capability*, but it is highly doubtful that Israel engages in production or stockpiling of biological weapons. On the issue of weaponization it makes sense that Israel has acquired expertise in aspects of weaponization, with the possible exception of testing.[34] One could speculate that a primary Israeli motivation for studying BW weaponization is to re-engineer the BW capability Iraq developed, or is said to have developed, to assess its effectiveness.

## STRATEGY, DETERRENCE, AND POLICY

### Chemical Weapons, Biological Weapons, and the Atomic Bomb: A Brief History

To reconstruct the development of Israeli strategic perceptions and attitudes regarding BW one must place the BW issue in a broader context of policy, deterrence, and arms control, including its strategic linkages with the two other categories of nonconventional weaponry, chemical and nuclear weapons.

Although Ben Gurion firmly supported Bergmann on the establishment of the IIRB in 1952 and monitored its development under his office, it is highly doubtful that he (or Bergmann) ever considered biological weapons as Israel's ultimate strategic weapons.[35] A variety of practical and military considerations, as well as diplomatic and moral considerations, made them the least-suited deterrence weapons. Indeed, all indications are that from early on Ben Gurion settled on the atom bomb, not biological weapons, as the answer to Israel's strategic predicament.[36]

Yet in the early to mid-1950s an Israeli nuclear project still seemed far in the future. When Ben Gurion returned to power in 1955 he immediately initiated a parallel effort, both short- and long-run, to provide Israel with options of last resort.[37] For the short run, in the spring of 1955 he initiated a crash project to develop "a cheap non-conventional capability." This "cheap non-conventional capability, which preceded the nuclear option," was a chemical not a biological capability.[38] For long-run needs, Ben Gurion initiated a national nuclear project. By 1955–1956 MOD Director-General Shimon Peres and Bergmann were exploring whether and how it would be possible for Israel to build the technological infrastructure for a nuclear weapons option. In October 1957 Israel signed a secret agreement for nuclear cooperation with France, and within months Israel had secretly started the construction of its nuclear facility in Dimona.

But the new nuclear commitment did not lessen Israeli commitment to chemical and biological weaponry. Bergmann's original arguments, which had led to the establishment of IIBR in 1952, were even stronger in the early to mid-1960s. While the timeline of the Dimona project remained uncertain, Israel had to counter Egypt's growing nonconventional capabilities. Dimona was never meant to be a substitute for Ness Ziona, only an addition to it.

Chemical weapons had been used in the Middle East in the 1920s and 1930s by various European countries, but Egypt was the first Arab country to develop, produce, deploy, and use them.[39] Egypt used chemical weapons in three different periods during its military involvement in the Yemen civil war (1963–1967). It was in 1967, in various episodes from January to July (including an incident on May 10, just four days before Egypt started to amass troops in the Sinai) that Egypt demonstrated both extensive and effective use of chemical weapons against the civilian population.[40] Some have suggested that the Yemeni war provided an opportunity for Egypt to test the chemical weapons in its arsenal.[41]

In 1959–1960 Egypt also initiated a secret program to develop and produce ballistic missiles with the assistance of German scientists who had worked on the V-2 rockets during World War II. In July 1962, on the tenth anniversary of the Egyptian revolution, Egypt test launched four of those prototypes and displayed twenty of them in a parade in Cairo. Israel was stunned by the revelations about the German-assisted Egyptian missile program, not realizing initially that those prototypes had no electronic guidance system. Israel's initial concerns were heightened by reports that Egypt was also planning, again with the aid of German scientists, to equip those missiles with radiological waste or chemical warheads. Those concerns and uncertainties remained active on the eve of the 1967 war.[42]

Details are not available, but there are indications that Israel upgraded its own offensive CW capability in the early to mid-1960s to counter Egyptian capabilities. There were CIA reports that Israel collaborated with France in 1960 on CW matters, including visits by Israelis to the French testing range at Beni Ounif in the Algerian Sahara where France experimented with CW.[43] In 1963, as Julian Perry Robinson pointed out, one of IIBR's publications disclosed "all but the last step" of the formula for the VX nerve gas.[44] This suggested that IIBR scientists were engaging in developing VX-related nerve gases (the chemical structure of VX was not known outside the United States).

Given the information about Egypt's use of CW in Yemen in 1967, Israel was concerned on the eve of the June War about the possibility that Egypt would resort to chemical warfare either on the battlefield or against the civilian population. It was apparently in response to these concerns that Israel purchased and shipped tens of thousands of gas masks from Europe (primarily Holland and Germany) days before the war. There are indications that on the eve of the 1967 war, Israel made its rudimentary nuclear capability operational due to concerns over the possibility of an Egyptian CW attack on its population centers.[45] There are also indications that Israel made its CW capability battle-ready. According to an Israeli analyst, "Egypt did not resort to chemical warfare because it feared Israeli retaliation in kind."[46]

Notably, senior Israeli military officers considered chemical and biological weapons quite differently in the 1960s, even though both were prohibited weapons under the 1925 Geneva Protocol. Chemical weapons were considered "nasty" but still usable military weapons, especially after it became known that Egypt had deployed and used them in Yemen. Biological weapons were perceived as a different category altogether. Apparently biologial weapons were considered morally "stinky" and militarily unusable. The case against biological weapons was formulated apparently more in military terms than in moral terms: Since wars in the Middle East are short-lived and decisive—terminated within days—no military use could be found for such uncertain weapons with a long incubation time. It was concluded that such "dirty" and prohibited forms of warfare lacked both the political credibility required for strategic deterrence and the military utility required for situations of last resort. At best, the use of biological weapons was thought to be limited to special covert operations. All estimates are that Israel did not have operational biological weapons on the eve of the 1967 war.

Regarding the nuclear issue, as the development stage approached completion in the mid- to late 1960s, Israeli strategists began to systematically articulate Ben Gurion's intuitive rationale for the nuclear program. In particular, Israeli strategists conceived certain "last resort" scenarios, that is, situations that could trigger demonstrations or even use of nuclear weapons. Each of these scenarios was defined as a threat to the very existence of Israel against which the nation could defend itself by no other means than the use of atomic weapons. One of these situations referred to the exposure of Israeli population centers to chemical or biological attacks.[47] This scenario may have been in the mind of the handful of Israeli decision makers who, on the eve of the Six-Day War, took emergency steps to make Israel's rudimentary nuclear capability operational and placed it on alert.[48] By 1970 Israel's status as a nuclear-weapons-capable state had become known worldwide.[49] Since then all Israeli governments have reaffirmed the commitment to maintain, preserve, and modernize the nation's nuclear weapons option.

The 1973 war was the first war in the Middle East in which both sides possessed some strategic WMD to be used as a last resort. Although it is well reported (but never confirmed) that Israel armed its nuclear weapons for concerns of last resort, it is less known that Egypt apparently prepared chemical weapons for use if Israel continued its military offensive to reverse Egypt's early achievements in the war.[50] In 1975, still under the veneer of ambiguity, Egyptian chief of staff General Abdel-Ghani Gamasi publicly warned that Egypt would employ nonconventional weapons if Israel resorted to the nuclear option.[51]

The period from 1970 to about 1990 was the golden age of Israel's policy of nuclear opacity. Israelis have come to view that policy as a great success story, providing their nation with the best of all possible worlds. Israel enjoys the benefits of deterrence but hardly pays a price for it. Furthermore, many Israelis believe that this low-profile policy played a constructive role both in making peace (especially in the Egyptian case) as well as deterring regional war (in the case of Iraq). The notion that the Arab-Israeli conflict cannot be settled by means of a large-scale war—the conclusion President Anwar Sadat drew after the 1973 war that led him to seek peace—was reached in the shadow of the bomb. In 1981, when Israel bombed the Iraqi Osiraq reactor, Iraq did not retaliate.

The role of chemical and biological weapons seemed to diminish under the Israeli opaque nuclear monopoly. Since the 1980s the Arab countries had made the argument that these weapons might become the Arabs' strategic weapons vis-à-vis the Israeli bomb, the so-called "poor man's bomb." Israelis, on the other hand, found quiet satisfaction in the emerging status quo.[52] In the 1970s Egypt supplied Syria with CW agents, and in the 1980s, after the peace with Israel, it closely cooperated with Iraq in the CW area (as the latter was at war with Iran).[53] Even after Iraq used chemical weapons in the Iran–Iraq war in the mid-1980s, Israelis still hardly viewed them as posing a threat to nuclear-armed Israel. It seems significant, however, that Israel supported the international efforts to ban chemical weapons, although without ratifying the Chemical Weapons Convention (CWC) itself. The Israeli participation in the Paris meeting on CW in 1989 demonstrated that Israeli interests converged with the interests of many countries in establishing stronger international norms against CW. There was a growing view in the Israeli strategic community that Israel's strategic situation would favor the CWC. As for BW, Israel maintained total silence on the subject.

## Nuclear vis-à-vis CBW Deterrence: The Uncertain Lessons of Iraq

By 1990–1991 Iraq had lost its strategic complacency. More than any other country in the world Iraq elevated—and ultimately blurred—the value of chemical and biological versus nuclear weapons. It was the Iraqi deployment and use of chemical weapons that revitalized the old but little-used phrase "weapons of mass destruction," combining all three categories of nonconventional weapons into a new bureaucratic (and muddy) category, WMD. The Iraqi experience with WMD created an intricate web of possible linkages—couplings and decouplings—among the three kinds of nonconventional weapons, in the context of deterrence, last resort use, and arms control. Ultimately, the 1995 revelations regarding the nature, scope, and rationale of the Iraqi BW program led some analysts to revisit the role of biological weapons as a strategic deterrent, especially against the use of nuclear weapons. They also led to reexamination of the effectiveness of nuclear weapons as a deterrent against the use of biological weapons. These issues are now central to the Israeli strategic predicament.

During the last stages of the Iran–Iraq war Saddam elevated the role of chemical weapons to both tactical weapons of terror and a strategic deterrent.[54] But on April 1, 1990, four months prior to the invasion of Kuwait, he threatened "to make fire burn half of Israel," using what he referred to as "binary chemical weapons," should Israel strike "at some Iraqi industrial installation."[55] The threat signaled Saddam's interest in projecting a deterrence posture vis-à-vis Israel: A large arsenal of advanced chemical weapons, along with their ballistic delivery means, implies that "strategic parity [has] practically [been] achieved by Iraq," and this constitutes a form of "balance of terror" between the two states.[56] Chemical weapons, associated with ballistic missiles, were portrayed as providing Iraq with the military means to confront a nuclear-armed Israel.

The specific context and purpose of Saddam's threat was to deter Israel from a military action against Iraq's nuclear program. In doing so Saddam enhanced the role of chemical weapons to the level of a strategic deterrent, or at least as a strategic protector of Iraq's nuclear program through its vulnerable period. Saddam's warning signaled Israel that an attempt to destroy Iraqi nuclear installations, as it had done in 1981, would be an Iraqi casusbelli that would lead to military retaliation.[57] Israel took Saddam's deterrent threats seriously; the Israeli government realized that attacking Iraq's nuclear program would mean an all-out Israeli–Iraqi war that could easily escalate to the nonconventional level.

Chemical weapons–tipped ballistic missiles were the central pillar of Iraq's deterrence strategy toward the United States and Israel after its invasion of Kuwait.[58] Both the United States and Israel lacked concrete knowledge regarding the Iraqi biological weapons program, but even so they took Saddam's threats seriously. Without ignoring defensive measures, both nations issued the sternest counterthreats. Secretary of State James Baker warned Iraqi Foreign Minister Tariq Aziz that escalating the conflict to the WMD level would be utterly unacceptable to the American people and would invoke awesome punishment. Baker's carefully worded message avoided explicating what the American response might be, but it was written in a manner that excluded nothing, including nuclear reprisals. Israeli Prime Minister Yitzhak Shamir pushed the policy of nuclear opacity to its limits when he issued a solemn warning to Iraq, promising to inflict "terrible and awful" pain on Iraq, yet without ever using the n-word.[59]

By the war's end some forty Iraqi Scud missiles had attacked Israel, most of them aimed at Israel's population centers. Israel was under constant fear that Iraq might escalate its Scud attacks to the CBW level, a move that would have left Israel with an extremely difficult dilemma. Given that Iraq did not launch chemical or biological weapons at Israel, many believe that Israel's veiled nuclear deterrence was effective in preventing Saddam's use of nonconventional capabilities.[60] This may be true, but it is only one of several competing explanations. It also leaves open some nagging questions: Can nuclear weapons effectively deter the use of lower-level WMD? Are there situations in which nuclear weapons simply cannot deter a nonnuclear adversary equipped with chemical or biological weapons? In fact, it is possible—even highly consistent with what was learned about Iraq's BW program—that Saddam's CBW strategic capabilities had been kept as strategic reserves for use in extreme situations of last resort. Viewed from this perspective, Iraqi deterrence was sufficiently effective to serve as a limitation on American and Israeli uses of their military power.

Still, facing the specter of Iraqi CBW attacks on Israel, Israeli leaders and strategists could not fail to recognize the profound limitations of nuclear weapons vis-à-vis CBW. Under almost any circumstances Israel could not use nuclear weapons in retaliation against an Iraqi CBW attack. To justifiably use nuclear weapons Israel must face a true last resort situation; the utility of nuclear weapons as reprisal is limited to extraordinary situations. Notwithstanding the uncertainty, it is very unlikely that CW attacks could constitute a scenario of existential peril to the integrity of Israel. Could Israel then use nuclear weapons in retaliation? Could Israel make a demonstrative nuclear use over Iraq's territory as a final act of deterrence?

There were those in Israel who worried, before and during the Gulf War, about a situation in which Saddam called the Israeli bluff by launching a limited CW strike on Israel, in a deliberate effort either to show the emptiness of Israel's nuclear deterrence vis-à-vis CW or to provoke an Israeli nuclear reprisal. Indeed, some worried that Saddam might be precipitating circumstances that would trap Israel into a nuclear demonstration. Such an event could be seen as Saddam's best chance to break down the American-led war coalition, to end the war, and to present Israel—not Iraq—as the real nuclear threat to the region. Indeed, in a response to this kind of scenario, and apparently concerned about escalation that could potentially provoke an unjustifiable nuclear use, Israeli Minister of Science Professor Yuval Ne'eman openly suggested in July 1990 that if Iraq used chemical weapons against Israel, Israel should retaliate in kind, "with the same merchandise."[61]

The atomic bomb was undoubtedly Saddam's most desired WMD, but biological weapons (and not chemical weapons) were his second choice. Biological weapons were Iraq's ultimate and most secretive WMD. But only in 1995, after the defection of Saddam's son-in-law, Hussein Kamal Hassan, did Iraq admit for the first time to having had an offensive BW program. By Iraq's own disclosures—which were still self-serving—after its invasion of Kuwait it initiated crash efforts to weaponize its BW program and to render it operational for military use. Baghdad regarded its biological weapons as ultimate strategic weapons to be used in situations of "last resort." Weeks prior to the war—in the wake of the United Nations Security Council's November 29, 1990, vote authorizing war against Iraq if it did not withdraw from Kuwait—Iraq filled and armed twenty-five Scud warheads with biological agents and stored them in distant airfields, whence they were to be fired at targets in Israel and Saudi Arabia if the allies marched on Baghdad and the regime fell.[62] Furthermore, Iraq invoked the specter of the Israeli bomb as a justification for its secret BW program, explaining its program as "a viable deterrent in answer to the possible attack by Israel using nuclear weapons."[63] Although the linkage of the Iraqi BW program to the Israeli nuclear program is politically self-serving and historically inaccurate, it does shed light both on the motivation and the strategy that guided Iraq's BW program.[64]

Iraqi use of Scud missiles tipped with biological weapons against Israel would have brought into being the scenarios discussed previously. The postwar discoveries about Iraq's BW capabilities allow us to revisit the war itself. By Iraq's own admissions, in extreme desperate situations, when Saddam's own survival might have been in danger, it is likely that he would have resorted to the use of the most Satanic weapons—weapons of sheer vengeance—at his disposal.[65] A threat of nuclear reprisal, even if perceived as credible, may not be effective in deterring a desperate BW vendetta. It seems that in such situations of last resort an Iraqi BW deterrent may be more effective as a deterrent than an Israeli nuclear counter-deterrent. In fact, Iraq does not even need to have fully operational BW systems to produce deterrent effects. The very uncertainty in itself creates deterrent effects.

Iraq's dealings with UNSCOM regarding its BW program in the period 1995–1998 have raised new concerns. Even though the BW program is the easiest of Iraq's WMD programs to reconstitute, Iraq is believed to have kept a substantial portion of its BW stockpile hidden from UNSCOM, claiming that it had destroyed it on its own. Iraq could have turned over most of its stockpile to UNSCOM while keeping a small seedstock, then claimed it no longer had any BW program. But it chose not to do so. Some analysts, such as Seth Carus and Laurie Mylroie, have suggested that a possible explanation for Iraq's behavior in this regard is maintaining a future option for state-sponsored biological terrorism without revealing its origins.[66]

Decades ago Israeli leaders made a strategic choice in favor of nuclear deterrence. They concluded that acquiring nuclear capability would allow Israel to secure its survival by establishing stable deterrence against its Arab neighbors; they hoped it could even force the Arabs to recognize the futility of the conflict and to bring it to an end. Israel has devised an inhibited nuclear posture, designed to project deterrence and at the same time to be the least provocative. The lessons of the Iraqi WMD case, and particularly its BW program, shed doubt on Israeli calculations. Nuclear deterrence may not be the most effective deterrent against state-sponsored BW terrorist attacks, especially if these leave no return address.

## The ACRS Experience

Many hoped that the end of the Gulf War would create a historical turning point in the effort to eliminate WMD. This expectation was loosely embodied in the text of the UNSC Resolution 687 of April 1991 which, in addition to the establishment of UNSCOM as the vehicle to disarm Iraq of its WMD, also called upon the region's states to negotiate and establish a regional zone free of all WMD. The formation of the Arms Control and Regional Security (ACRS) multilateral working group under the framework of the Madrid Peace Conference was viewed by many as the proper mechanism to negotiate such disarmament measures.[67]

To understand the unprecedented nature of ACRS one must review briefly the pre-Gulf War situation. The general pattern since the 1970s was for Arab states to call for regional nuclear disarmament and to point to Israel's refusal to sign the Nuclear Non-Proliferation Treaty (NPT), while Israel insisted on the establishment of peace as the prerequisite for negotiations on arms control and disarmament. Notably, the focus of those declarations was solely the nuclear issue; there was virtually no reference (or linkage) to other categories of WMD.

The most well advertised nuclear disarmament idea that has been circulated for years is the establishment of a nuclear-weapon-free zone (NWFZ) in the Middle East. Iran and Egypt cosponsored such a resolution at the UN in 1974, and since then the General Assembly has annually renewed it with slight yearly variations.[68] During the 1970s Israel abstained, but in 1980, after the peace treaty with Egypt, Israel joined in supporting the NWFZ resolution. This apparent regional consensus, however, went nowhere and meant little; the prerequisites that each side has stipulated for its support of a regional NWFZ were patently unacceptable to the other. The Egyptian proposal stipulated, as a precondition for the establishment of a NWFZ, that all parties adhere to the NPT. For Egypt, the NPT/International Atomic Energy Agency (IAEA) safeguards regime was an indispensable mechanism for the establishment of a NWFZ in the region.

Israel, which has refused to sign the NPT, emphasized in its own NWFZ proposal the difference between the regional and the global, or universal, approaches to nonproliferation. Israel proposed the NWFZ as a way to highlight its nuclear nonproliferation interests, despite its specific objections to the NPT. For Israel, a NWFZ was meant to be an alternative for NPT/IAEA mechanisms, which Israel considers deficient on the grounds that nuclear disarmament must take account of regional politics, which the NPT does not do. Behind the appearance of a regional consensus there persists a deadlock built on opposing interests.[69]

In the mid-1970s this difference over the NWFZ was immaterial. Until the Arab states were ready to recognize Israel and negotiate peace and security with it, the NWFZ proposal was purely theoretical. Israel, still a de facto nuclear power, had no great difficulty in proposing a NWFZ, recognizing that nothing practical would be achieved by those diplomatic exercises in the absence of fundamental political change, while tacitly refusing to accept external restrictions on its freedom of action in the nuclear field. Such a position was consistent with Israel's posture of nuclear opacity and did not require any debate in Israel. For their part, the Arab states' linkage of the NWFZ issue with the NPT was intended to embarrass Israel for its refusal to sign the NPT.[70]

The linkage between the nuclear issue and other WMD issues came later. By the late 1980s, in the wake of Iraq's use of chemical weapons, an international campaign to ban these weapons was under way. Its theme was that without a strong international action to eliminate chemical weapons altogether, they would continue to spread. On April 8, 1990, days after Saddam Hussein threatened to "burn half of Israel" with chemical weapons, Egyptian President Hosni Mubarak called on all the region's states to ban *all* chemical, biological, and nuclear weapons. Egypt submitted Mubarak's initiative to the UN as a formal proposal to establish a zone free of all WMD in the Middle East.[71]

The politics underlying Mubarak's initiative were obvious: It allowed Mubarak to side with the international community effort to ban chemical weapons while providing credence to the Arab claim of the close linkage between Israel's acquisition of nuclear weapons and Arab acquisition of chemical and biological weapons. Ever since Mubarak's initiative, Arabs have used the nuclear-CBW linkage in two distinct contexts: deterrence and disarmament. In the former, Arabs have presented Israel's nuclear program as the cause, rationale, and justification for Arab CBW programs: Arab CBW programs are a deterrent against Israel's nuclear weapons. In the latter, Arabs have maintained that, due to the deterrence linkage, there must be disarmament linkage as well. That is, it would be (normatively) wrong and (politically) impossible to disarm one category of WMD without linking it to the disarmament measures of the others.

In 1991, the American-led victory in the Gulf, the temporary neutralization of Iraq as a destabilizing regional power, and the establishment of UNSCOM as a UN disarmament agency created a widespread sentiment that there was a chance to depart from the patterns of the past and introduce a measure of arms control and regional security to the Middle East. The Bush administration hoped that the American victory in the Gulf could reignite the Arab–Israeli peace process along two parallel—but coordinated—tracks. The first is a bilateral track devoted to direct negotiations between Israel and its immediate Arab neighbors; the second is a multilateral track devoted to promoting multilateral and regional issues that affect all states of the region.

The creation of ACRS was the highlight of this vision. It was conceived as the common institution in which exchanges, discussions, and ultimately negotiations over all matters of regional security and arms control would take place. In two important respects the founding of ACRS seemed a departure from past Arab–Israeli exchanges. First, it implied implicit recognition of Israel and its right to exist by all its Arab members, including those who had no diplomatic relations with Israel. Second, it implied that its members, the Arab states and Israel, shared certain security issues, particularly the proliferation of WMD, and hence accepted the notion of a regional forum to discuss common concerns of "regional security."

However, the short history of ACRS suggests how premature the founding vision was. During the early discussions in the ACRS group it became clear that Arabs and Israelis maintain diametrically opposed interests, approaches, and priorities on matters of regional arms control and disarmament, in particular on the issue of WMD. The appearance of consensus about the long-term objectives of the ACRS process—in particular the objective of establishment of a zone free of all WMD—disguised the reality of sharp divisions as to how to render these objectives into a joint arms control and disarmament blueprint. For a while the ACRS co-sponsors made efforts to put those differences aside and focus instead on less divisive confidence-building measures. However, from 1994 to 1999, since Egypt and Israel were sharply divided over the issue of Israel and the NPT extension, it became apparent that the ACRS process had reached a point of real impasse. At the heart of the impasse was Israel's nuclear program.[72]

Egypt, along with other Arab states, pressured Israel to declare its nuclear weapons program and to place it openly on the ACRS agenda. Egypt sought to promote Mubarak's 1990 initiative to establish a weapons-of-mass-destruction-free zone (WMDFZ) in the Middle East. Evidently, the Egyptian effort aimed to force Israel to give up its opaque nuclear deterrence posture. For Egypt, bringing an end to Israel's nuclear superiority was probably the single most important interest on its national arms control agenda. Egypt insisted on entering into negotiations as early as possible, primarily through existing international treaties and organizations.[73] Beyond the official Egyptian position, Egyptian analysts have repeatedly made the point that to discuss the establishment of a WMDFZ in the Middle East, Israel must first ease its official policy of nuclear ambiguity and accept some measure of transparency for its nuclear capability.[74]

Israel vehemently opposed Egypt on this issue. For reasons outlined previously, Israel insists on maintaining and preserving its opaque nuclear monopoly, at least until regional comprehensive peace, including full Arab and Iranian recognition of Israel in recognized borders, is firmly established. Most Israelis maintain that their nation must keep their nuclear chip untouched and in play until the peacemaking process is complete, insisting that the establishment of a NWFZ ought to be the last stage of the arms control process. For Israel, the nuclear issue must be the very last stop on the long path of Arab–Israeli peacemaking. If anything, the nuclear program should be the guarantor that it would be unwise to revive the conflict.[75] As long as Israel still faces threats to its existence—including Iraqi and Iranian WMD threats—Israel has no intention of making any changes in its nuclear posture, not even to make the nuclear program more transparent. Until lasting peace is achieved, and until the Arab–Israeli conflict is resolved, Israel is committed to preserving and modernizing its nuclear posture. Given both the Israeli and Arab positions, and as long as the Arab–Israeli conflict does not reach finality and closure, no feasible way exists to address the CBW issue in a regional fashion.

## Israel and Global Arms Control Regimes

Another modality for addressing the spread of WMD is through global control regimes. Over the last four decades the international community has negotiated and devised three separate and distinct disarmament treaties addressing each of the three categories of WMD: nuclear weapons (the NPT), chemical weapons (the CWC), and biological weapons (the Biological Weapons Convention, the BWC).

Israel's traditional approach to *global* arms control and disarmament treaties has been a skeptical one. The reasons are intimately bound to the reasons that led Israel to explore nonconventional weaponry almost since its establishment, namely, the Israeli geopolitical predicament vis-à-vis the Arabs. As long as Israel's legitimacy as a state has not been accepted by its Arab neighbors, Israel is still committed to maintaining the deterrent capabilities needed to ensure its survival. For this reason, Israel has been generally reluctant to join universal disarmament and arms control instruments. Instead, as noted previously, Israel has advocated the *regional* approach, namely, that progress on control and elimination of WMD in the Middle East must be made in a manner that links the political issues of recognition, legitimacy, and peace with measures of arms control and disarmament.

On the nuclear issue—Israel's most critical issue—Israel has insisted that the NPT as a universal treaty cannot address Israel's security concerns. In 1968, the year the NPT was signed, Israel resisted strong American pressure to join the NPT, explaining that given its security predicament—including a Soviet threat—it simply could not renounce its nuclear option. A year later, Israeli Prime Minister Golda Meir explained to President Richard Nixon why Israel had developed nuclear weapons, why it could not sign the NPT, and why a low-profile posture of nuclear "opacity" would best serve both countries. Israel pledged not to test nuclear weapons or publicly admit to possessing them, while the United States—recognizing that the Israeli bomb was already a fait accompli—ended its pressure on Israel to sign the NPT. This became the basis of the Israeli posture of nuclear opacity.

The creation of ACRS in 1991–1992 was consistent with the basic Israeli regional approach. The Israelis hoped that ACRS could establish new measures of confidence-building and cooperative goodwill among the parties in the security arena, and side by side with the peace process. It was in this context that the Rabin government concluded in 1993 that the CWC presented the best WMD issue to demonstrate a new Israeli attitude to arms control. Given Israel's uncompromising position on the nuclear issue, signing an international treaty to eliminate chemical weaponry was thought to be a preferred option to not signing, whether or not the Arab states followed suit. In the eyes of Prime Minister Rabin, signing the CWC was a "net benefit" (some even considered it a win-win situation). Guided by these considerations, and pressured by the United States, Israel signed the CWC on January 13, 1993, the very day the treaty was opened for signature.[76]

Israel, however, postponed the decision on ratification for further review. As long as the U.S. Senate kept its ratification of the CWC uncertain, it was convenient for Israel to delay the issue as well. But when the United States finally ratified the CWC in 1997, and in the wake of the treaty's entry into force, the issue of ratification resurfaced in Israel as a priority policy issue. A top-level ad hoc ministerial committee, headed by Prime Minister Netanyahu, was formed to revisit thoroughly the entire Israeli position on the CWC.[77] After a series of meetings the ministerial committee quietly decided to take a "wait and see" attitude, that is, not to ratify the treaty at that time while keeping the issue pending a future review.[78] As of this writing, Israel has not made a new decision on the matter.

Informally, however, it is clear that Israeli thinking regarding the CWC has changed profoundly. The CWC is no longer seen as a "net benefit" to Israel, as Rabin considered it in 1993. A series of WMD-related external developments in recent years have raised serious concerns and doubts regarding the ratification issue. First, the ACRS process reached an impasse in the mid-1990s. Second, most of the significantly CW-related Arab states—Egypt, Iraq, Syria, and Libya—have not signed the CWC, linking their signing of the CWC with Israel signing the NPT. Third, since 1998 Iraq is no longer under an inspection regime, and it is reconstituting those programs. Finally, Iran, which ratified the CWC and even admitted some past CW-related activities, is believed to be producing and stockpiling chemical weapons.[79]

These developments returned Israel to its traditional cautious attitude. Two related areas of concern have reemerged: security and deterrence. If in 1993 Prime Minister Rabin's government concluded that Israel should, and could, live with the security risks entailed in the CWC's intrusive verification system, by the late 1990s, the security professionals had voiced their opposition louder. One specific point has been openly raised, that is, that the right under the CWC for any country to demand "challenge inspection" could be abused and threaten "the sanctity of Dimona."[80] However, not less important (and much more realistic) is the point—which was never made in public by Israeli strategists—that the verification provision of the CWC could surely infringe the sanctity of Ness Ziona.[81] All indications are that in the wake of the revelations about the Iraqi BW program Israel has even more reasons now to protect the secrecy of Ness Ziona than it had in 1992–1993.

Regarding the deterrence issue, in 1993 Rabin concluded that the benefits of joining the global effort to delegitimize and eliminate CW outweighed the benefits of projecting "chemical ambiguity" as a deterrent. This view may no longer prevail. The claim that Israel must retain ambiguity about its CW capabilities as a strategic deterrent, a strategic view that seemed to be passé in the early 1990s, has certainly gained new support.[82]

And finally, there is the never-discussed issue of the BWC. The limited public debate in Israel about the CWC is striking for its total lack of reference to the BWC. Not only did Israel not sign the nonverifiable 1972 BWC, which Egypt and Syria signed in 1972 (but never ratified) and Iraq in 1991,[83] but it apparently has never explained clearly its position on the BWC. Israel seems to maintain silence not only on its activities and capability in this field but also on its diplomacy. It is worth noting that the Israeli public—legislators, press, and citizen groups—has not raised questions about Israel's positions on these matters.[84]

## EPILOGUE: POST–SEPTEMBER 11

The events of September 11, 2001, the subsequent discoveries of al Qaeda's pursuit of CBW as the terrorist's ultimate WMD, concerns over Iraq, and the deteriorating situation with the Palestinians have dramatically awakened Israeli decision makers to the gravity of the CBW threat in Israel. In particular, two kinds of CBW scenarios have become nightmares to Israeli strategic planners and policymakers after September 11.

First, there is the possibility that an unidentified terrorist organization could execute a major CBW attack against Israeli population centers. The events of September 11 have clearly demonstrated that small terrorist groups may have the means to plan and execute a massive suicide attack inflicting unprecedented loss of life. The attacks demonstrate the vulnerability of a democratic and open society to such "asymmetric" attacks. They also suggest that the way deterrence works vis-à-vis nation-states may be utterly irrelevant to the context of suicide terror. Given the intensity of the military escalation between the Palestinians and Israelis, there is a real concern in Israel that Palestinian terrorist groups may resort to bioterrorism as their ultimate weapon.

Second, there is the possibility that Iraq, if attacked by the United States, would retaliate against Israel with CBW. Israeli decision makers take this scenario very seriously; they are convinced that Saddam would respond to an all-out American attack on his regime by playing the Israeli card. For Saddam, BW may be not only his ultimate form of deterrence but also his ultimate Samson option. Such an attack may even be designed to provoke Israel to retaliate with nuclear weapons, hence engulfing the entire region in a total war.

These post–September 11 scenarios strengthen those in Israel who insist that Israel should not change an iota in its posture of CBW ambiguity. If before September 11 there was even a small chance that Israel would ratify the CWC anytime soon, by now the ratification issue is dead. The more Israeli strategists recognize that nuclear weapons do not—and cannot—provide fail-safe deterrence for all nonconventional threat scenarios, in particular deterring subnational terrorist groups, the more reluctant they become to renounce the residual deterrence Israel may have by retaining a CBW option. If Israel abandoned its posture of CBW ambiguity, it could lose a deterrent against a CBW attack. Furthermore, some even quietly argue that if Israel were ever attacked by massive bioterrorism, a response in kind—without ever acknowledging it—might be the only retaliatory option left for Israel.

This author believes this thinking is both misleading and unfortunate. Although it is true that nuclear deterrence cannot provide fail-safe deterrence for all nonconventional threat scenarios, it would be a mistake to conclude from this that Israel must preserve a CBW offensive option. It would be tragic if the events of September 11 were to lead Israelis to give credence to the notion of a "chemical option" or "biological option" as an applicable strategic concept. Those Israeli strategists who suggest that Israeli nuclear weapons do not provide a credible means to deter the first use of CBW by an Arab state—let alone by subnational terrorist groups—could well be proved correct. Still, that does not mean that an Israeli CBW capability for retaliation in kind would provide a credible deterrent either. This author believes that even under the posture of CBW ambiguity, it is extremely doubtful that Israel could ever retaliate in kind if it were attacked with CBW.

This assertion is based on two considerations. First, Israel has powerful conventional military capabilities that would enable it to retaliate harshly against nearly all CBW attacks without the need to resort to nonconventional weaponry. Second, Israel has no interest in legitimating CBW and therefore has good reason *not* to retaliate in kind. The most effective and credible way for Israel to deter the use of CBW by its enemies is not by retaining a residual CBW option but rather by making clear that Israeli retaliation would be certain and many times more damaging than the effects of the CBW attack itself. The bottom line is that a nuclear-armed Israel, like the United States, has no strategic need to maintain a posture of "CBW ambiguity" on top of its nuclear posture. Only in the extreme case of a devastating CBW attack would Israel consider launching a nuclear reprisal, yet from the Arab perspective such an option exists and must be considered.

There are also domestic reasons why strengthening the resistance to renouncing CBW ambiguity is unfortunate. Israeli ratification of the CWC has implications for the health of the country's democracy, an issue that has hardly ever been discussed in this context. As already noted, Israel has employed extraordinary secrecy measures to protect its activities and policies in the CBW field. The Israeli government has never issued an official statement to the citizenry describing its activities in that area. From the normative perspective of democratic governance, a situation of total secrecy reinforced by a societal taboo is disturbing. That the citizens of a democratic country have been denied the right to know about their government's choices in a critical area of national policy and to debate them freely is detrimental to the spirit of democracy. The *total* lack of transparency in the CBW area in Israel has had many harmful effects, including a lack of democratic oversight, a lack of informed public debate, and concerns over possible harm to public health and the environment.

In the BW field, more than any other area of nonconventional weaponry, secrecy can be easily abused to weaken democratic oversight. Because of the inherent ambiguity between defensive and offensive BW activities, which are distinguished largely by intent, secrecy could allow an ostensibly defensive BW program to "drift" into the offensive mode. In the Israeli context, when the Knesset has virtually no independent means of parliamentary oversight and is fully dependent on information from the executive branch, the lack of democratic oversight over CBW activities is particularly serious. During the recent Israeli intragovernmental debate over ratification of the CWC, excessive secrecy reportedly prevented informed discussion even within the closed walls of officialdom. Defense officials claimed that many of the arguments against CWC ratification were too sensitive to be shared even with their bureaucratic counterparts in other agencies. Lacking access to information, the Israeli general public was completely excluded from the policy debate. Finally, the combination of official secrecy and societal taboo makes it easy for the Israeli defense establishment to conceal or cover up safety hazards, accidents, program mismanagement, and environmental damage associated with CBW activities.[85]

## POLICY PROPOSALS FOR ISRAEL

The following policy proposals, even though unrealistic given the current political situation in the Middle East, should be carefully considered for the longer term. Israel should seek the politically appropriate moment to convey a new and clear message unequivocally denouncing a CBW posture. Such a message would in effect involve partially abandoning its current policy of total secrecy and silence, and would therefore require substantial diplomatic preparation. A new Israeli policy on CBW, however, should be an integral component of a larger regional arms control initiative, including the nuclear issue. The following are the basic tenets of such an initiative.

First, although the Arab states have insisted on linking their own WMD programs to the Israeli nuclear program, Israel should reject this linkage. On the nuclear issue, Israel has made clear repeatedly that its nuclear capability is linked with the end of the Arab–Israeli conflict. Ever since the 1967 war Israel has proved itself a responsible de facto member of the nuclear club. Although Israel has yet to find ways to state this de facto reality, by now most of the world has come to understand and accept it. On the CBW issue, Israel should join the international effort to delegitimize and ban both CW and BW.[86] The fact that some Arab states condition their position on chemical and biological weapons to Israel's possession of nuclear weapons should not be an excuse for Israel not to be part of the effort to ban CBW.

Second, as a matter of principle, Israel should state—somewhat akin to

President Nixon's statement on BW in 1969[87]—that it does not view chemical and biological weapons as legitimate weapons or instruments of deterrence and thus has no need to retain offensive CBW programs of its own. In line with this message, Israel would ratify the CWC, regardless of its neighbors' actions. If the Israeli government concludes that the Iraqi threat precludes it from acceding to the BWC for the time being, it should at least issue a policy statement explaining its position. These steps would also create new and beneficial norms for Israeli society with respect to transparency and democratic oversight.

Third, Israel should continue to retain a strong scientific and technological infrastructure in the CBW area, devoted to defensive purposes. As an important function of its defensive mandate, such infrastructure should be the national body in charge of scientific monitoring, analyzing, and assessing intelligence relating to CBW programs in hostile countries, as well as new threats of bioterrorism.

Fourth, Israel should make publicly clear that it has the means and the will to retaliate in the most devastating way against any CBW attack. Whoever might use such weapons against Israel would be punished many times over.

## NOTES

1. The author would like to thank Milton Leitenberg, Jonathan Tucker, and Susan Wright for comments and suggestions made on previous versions of this chapter. Further details of the history of Israel's biological and chemical warfare programs are given in Avner Cohen, "Israel and Chemical/Biological Weapons: History, Deterrence, and Arms Control," *The Nonproliferation Review* 8(3) (Fall-Winter 2001).

2. Quoted in a letter to Ehud Avriel, 4 March 1948, in Michael Keren, *Ben Gurion and the Intellectuals* (in Hebrew) (Sede Boker, Israel: Ben Gurion University Press, 1988), 32.

3. "There is a saying, 'the dead will not praise God,'" he wrote in a letter to a noted Israeli scientist, "and if we face the threat of destruction—and unfortunately we do, and Hitler's Holocaust was only the most extensive and terrible of the attempts to destroy us during our history—to a certain extent this is the most fateful of our existence" (letter, David Ben Gurion to Shmuel Sambursky, 17 March 1963, David Ben Gurion Archive, Ben Gurion Research Center, Sede Boker, Israel (DBGA)).

4. David Ben Gurion, *War Diaries, 1948–1949* (in Hebrew), vol. 3 (Tel Aviv: Misrad Habitachon, 1982), 852–53.

5. David Ben Gurion, Diaries, Ben Gurion Research Center, Sede Boker, Israel, 26 April 1949; 23 October 1950. For a detailed analysis of Ben Gurion's view, see Zaki Shalom, *David Ben Gurion: The State of Israel and the Arab World 1949–1956* (in Hebrew) (Sede Boker, Israel: Ben Gurion University Press, 1995).

6. This is one of the central themes in Avner Cohen, *Israel and the Bomb* (New York: Columbia University Press, 1998).

7. Personal communication, Professor Yuval Ne'eman, head of the Planning Division of the IDF from 1953 to 1954, May 1997.

8. Ephraim Katzir, "The Beginning of Defense Research: Ben Gurion and the HEMED" (in Hebrew), in *David Ben Gurion and the Development of Science in Israel* (Jerusalem: Israel National Academy of Science, 1989), 37.

9. Sara Leibovitz-Dar, "Haydakim Besherut Hamedinah" ("Microbes in State Service"), *Hadashot* (13 August 1993), 6–10.

10. Ibid.

11. Munya M. Mardor, *Refa'el* (Tel Aviv: Misradha-bitahar, 1981), 53–66, 78–79, 104–6; Shlomo Gur, interview by author, Tel Aviv, June 1993.

12. Bergmann designed and implemented a similar arrangement for HEMED GIMMEL, the historical predecessor of Israel's nuclear program. In 1951–1952 HEMED GIMMEL was transferred from the military to become a state-sponsored nuclear research center. The new entity also had a double identity, as a classified research institute within the Ministry of Defense (Machon 3) and also, primarily for public and international convenience, as the Israel Atomic Energy Commission.

13. Interviews with former senior Israeli officials. Although we do not have hard historical documents, the context is clear. Bergmann's views should be seen against the background that (1) most Western countries had some kind of BW and CW programs within their defense R&D infrastructure in those days, and (2) Bergmann had a strong personal interest in these fields and was close to Prime Minister Ben Gurion.

14. It was not illegal for states to develop such capabilities; establishing national CBW programs was not at odds with international norms. All three major Western (and NATO) powers—the United States, the United Kingdom, and France—had significant CBW programs. Bergmann was well aware of the activities of those programs. Although the Geneva Protocol of 1925 prohibited first use of chemical and biological weapons, it said nothing about developing, producing, or even using those weapons in strict retaliatory fashion. For the historical context, see Barton Bernstein, "Origins of Biological Warfare Programs," in *Preventing a Biological Arms Race*, ed. Susan Wright (Cambridge: MIT Press, 1990), 9–26; Susan Wright, "Evolution of Biological Warfare Policy," in Wright, *Preventing a Biological Arms Race*; Brian Balmer, "The Drift of Biological Weapons Policy in the U.K. 1945–1965," *The Journal of Strategic Studies* 20(4) (December 1997), 115–45.

15. Interviews with close associates of Bergmann in Israel, 1992–1996.

16. See www.iibr.gov.il/profile.htm.

17. One cannot escape the thought that this impressive website—whose only reference to defensive aspects of CBW is to protective garments and detectors—is in itself a strong piece of Israeli deterrence. Without saying so explicitly, it demonstrates that Israel possesses powerful capabilities, defensive as well as offensive, in the area of CBW.

18. Shlomo Abramovitz and Mordechai Allon, "The Place Where Oranges Are Not Growing," *Yediot Ahronot Weekly Magazine* (7 Days) (14 August 1998), 16–20.

19. As a matter of ongoing policy, IIBR employees, including its director-general,

are strictly prohibited from speaking with the media. The IIBR has no spokesperson, and the spokesperson of the prime minister's office is the only individual who is authorized to respond to press queries regarding the IIBR. Recently it became known that the Israeli state comptroller criticized the government for unnecessary efforts to keep the issue of the BW threat outside the public debate. This policy illustrates how sensitive and secretive the BW issue is in the eyes of government officials.

20. Virtually all details regarding the Klingberg case are treated by the Israeli security establishment as classified, including the circumstances that led to his capture outside Israel. Klingberg was secretly sentenced in 1983 to a twenty-year jail term, but only in 1993 did the Israeli public learn about his case. For years both the security establishment and the judiciary firmly opposed humanitarian requests for early release due to his age and his deteriorating health. In September 1998, after a long legal struggle, Klingberg was released from jail and placed under strict conditions of house arrest. The security establishment still treats him as a very serious security risk. His release term prohibited him from having any contact with the outside world. On the Klingberg case, see "L'espion qui venait du Yiddishland," *Le Nouvel Observateur* (6 January 1994); Clyde Haberman, "Israeli Lifts Secrecy Veil from Spy Convictions," *New York Times* (4 May 1995); P. R. Kumaraswamy, "An Embarrassments of Spies," *The Bulletin of the Atomic Scientists* 55(2) (March–April 1999), 14–15, 61.

21. To be sure, the Ness Ziona residents' protests are not about Israel CBW policy; most residents assume Israel has CBW program and they still do not want to know too much about it. Rather, the subject of the protest is whether the center of Ness Ziona should be the home for such activity. As the town's attorney, Shay Segal, put it, no one disputes that Israel needs such a research center, "but far away from here—not in a residential area where people live." "Israel Town Assails Bio Building," *Associated Press* (8 October 1998). For more sources see note 22.

22. Abramovitz and Allon, "The Place Where Oranges are not Growing," 16–20; Peter Hirschberg, "Inside the Low White Buildings," *The Jerusalem Report* (21 December 1998), 18; Aliza Marcus, "In Israeli Town, Rare Challenge to Arms Plant," *The Boston Globe* (November 24, 1998); "Israelis Dice with Danger at Germ Warfare Plant," *The Guardian* (12 October 1998). Due to censorship requirements, there was virtually no Israeli-based material about the IIBR itself; the references to CBW activity were strictly based on "foreign sources."

23. "Israel's Secret Institute," *Foreign Report* (20 August 1998).

24. Peter Hirschberg, Harms van den Berg, and Herman Stall, "The Fatal Fallout from El-Al Flight 1862," *The Jerusalem Report* (21 December 1998), 16–21. To this day, a full twenty tons of cargo, some or all of it apparently being shipped by the Israeli Defense Ministry, has yet to be fully identified. And El-Al's lawyer in The Hague, Robert Polak, has told the Dutch government these details will never be forthcoming, because of what he terms "state security reasons."

25. Hirschberg, van den Berg, and Stall, "The Fatal Fallout."

26. The issue is still a near taboo for Israeli-based think tank and academic strategists. Although there has been some public discussion of the chemical issue recently by defense journalists and academic strategists—in the context of Israel and the CWC—there has been virtually no strategic discussion of the BW issue. The most

Israeli strategists are willing to say publicly regarding Ness Ziona is that the critical issue, as far as deterrence is concerned, is that in Arab eyes Israel possesses all weapons of mass destruction, including biological weapons.

27. Karel Knip's detailed exposé was published as a series of articles in February 1999 in the Dutch daily newspaper, *NRC Handelsband*. The articles in Dutch can be found at the NRC website, www.nrc.nl/w2/Lab/Ziona. Karel Knip generously provided this author with a nine-page English translation of the exposé. All citations appearing here are quoted from the English document Mr. Knip provided.

28. Interestingly, Knip found virtually no IIBR publications about the classical and renowned biological weapons that Iraq produced, such as anthrax and the botulinum toxin, even though it is quite "inconceivable" (in Knip's words) that the IIBR has not conducted considerable research into these areas.

29. Knip translation.

30. If there is, however, additional relevant information regarding weaponization or agent production, it could alter the significance of the same basic research.

31. For this reason Article I of the BWC says nothing at all about research, even though the preamble of the treaty disavows any research directed toward development of biological weapons. The problem is that it is impossible to "prove" the intent from the research itself. What constitutes the difference, of course, is research and development related directly to the weaponization process, but such research and development is by its nature highly classified and is not likely to be exposed via scientific publications. On these ambiguities see Marc Lappe, "Ethics in Biological Warfare Research," in *Preventing a Biological Arms Race*, ed. Susan Wright (Cambridge: MIT Press, 1990), 78–99.

32. For example, in 1974, U.S. military officials testified in Congress that they knew (from conversations with their Israeli counterparts) that Israel had an offensive CW capability. But when asked about Israel's BW capability, the Americans professed ignorance. U.S. Senate Armed Forces Committee, FY 1975 DoD Authorization Hearings, Part 5 (R&D), 7 March 1974, 4931.

33. U.S. Congress, Office of Technology Assessment, *Proliferation of Weapons of Mass Destruction: Assessing the Risk*, OTA-ISC-559 (Washington, D.C.: Government Printing Office, 1993), 65, 80. On the CW issue, the OTA report cites eleven public sources (government and NGO arms control experts as well as media) on the CW issue; 100 percent of the sources refer to Israel as "having undeclared offensive chemical warfare capabilities" (table 2-A-1, 80). On the BW issue, the report cites six public sources, of which four (67 percent) refer to Israel as "having undeclared offensive biological warfare programs" (table 2-B-1, 82).

34. The four aspects considered tantamount for complete weaponization are research, development, testing, and evaluation.

35. Interviews with former senior Israeli officials. There are persistent rumors that Ben Gurion's successor at the MOD in 1954, Pinhas Lavon, proposed using biological weapons in 1954 for some special operations. These proposals apparently created havoc among the handful of officials who knew about them, including Prime Minister Moshe Sharett. Veiled references to such proposals can be found in Sharett's diaries.

36. Cohen, *Israel and the Bomb*, especially chapters 2 and 3. We do not know if

and to what extent the biological option was actually weighed in the 1950s by Ben Gurion, Bergmann, and Peres in comparison to the nuclear option.

37. There is evidence to suggest that, in late 1954, Ben Gurion was preoccupied with the nuclear project. See Cohen, *Israel and the Bomb*, chapter 3.

38. Aluf Benn, "The Project That Preceded the Nuclear Option" (in Hebrew), *Ha'aretz* (2 March 1995).

39. SIPRI, *The Problem of Chemical and Biological Weapons*, vol. 1, *The Rise of CB Weapons*, 86–87, 159–61, 336–41 (New York: Humanities Press, 1971); SIPRI, *The Problem of Chemical and Biological Warfare*, vol. 5 (New York: Humanities Press, 1971), 227.

40. In those two incidents hundreds of civilians died. In the first attack, on 5 January 1967, nine Egyptian bombers dropped twenty-seven bombs on the village of Kitaf. According to eyewitness accounts, "some 95 percent of the people occupying the area up to two kilometers downwind had been seriously or fatally gassed. A quarter of the population had apparently been killed, and another quarter severely injured, some 250–300 casualties in all, and all apparently suffering from lung injuries." SIPRI, *Problem of Chemical and Biological Warfare*, vol. 5, 228–37.

41. W. Andrew Terril, "The Chemical Warfare Legacy of the Yemen War," *Comparative Strategy* 10(2) (1991), 109–19; Dany Shoham, "Chemical and Biological Weapons in Egypt, " *The Nonproliferation Review* 5(3) (Spring–Summer 1998), 48–58.

42. The story of the Egyptian missile program has not yet been told in full. For bits and pieces on the subject, see M. Navias, "Ballistic Missiles Proliferation in the Middle East," *Survival* (May/June 1989); Dan Raviv and Yossi Melman, *Every Spy a Prince* (New York: Houghton Mifflin, 1990); and Meir Amit, *Rosh Be-Rosh* (Or Yehudah, Israel: Hed Artzi, 1999).

43. Seymour Hersh, *The Samson Option* (New York; Random House, 1991), 63–64.

44. Julian Perry Robinson, "Behind the VX Disclosure," *New Scientist* (9 January 1975), 50.

45. Interviews with former senior officials in the United States and Israel.

46. Shoham, "Chemical and Biological Weapons in Egypt," 49.

47. Cohen, *Israel and the Bomb*, chapter 12.

48. Ibid., chapter 13. See also Yuval Ne'eman, "Israel in the Nuclear Weapons Age" (in Hebrew), *Nativ* 8(5) (September 1995), 38.

49. Hedrick Smith, "U.S. Assumes the Israelis Have A-Bomb or Its Parts," *New York Times* (18 July 1970), 1.

50. President Anwar Sadat and Defense Minister Abdel-Ghani Gamasi hinted this after the war. See Shoham, "Chemical and Biological Weapons in Egypt," 49.

51. Cairo Radio, 5 July 1975, cited in Shoham, "Chemical and Biological Weapons in Egypt," 50.

52. It is worth recalling what limited attention Israeli strategists had given to the CBW issue when they discussed nuclear issues until the Gulf War. See, for example, Shai Feldman, *Israeli Nuclear Deterrence* (New York: Columbia University Press, 1981); Yair Evron, *Israel's Nuclear Dilemma* (Ithaca: Cornell University Press, 1994).

53. Shoham, "Chemical and Biological Weapons in Egypt," 51.

54. Thomas McNaugher, "Ballistic Missiles and Chemical Weapons: The Legacy of the Iran-Iraq War," *International Security* 15 (Fall 1990).

55. "President Warns Israel, Criticizes U.S.," FBIS-NES-90–064, Daily Report, 3 April 1990; see also Alan Cowell, "Iraqi Chief, Boasting of Poison Gas, Warns of Destruction if Israel Strikes," *New York Times* (3 April 1990); cf. Karen Eliot House, "Iraqi President Hussein Sees New Mideast War Unless America Acts," *Wall Street Journal* (28 June 1990). In fact, Iraq did not have binary chemical weapons.

56. "Arab Power for Regional Peace," Iraqi News Agency, FBIS-NES-90–108, Daily Report, 17 April 1990. In his address to the Islamic conference in Baghdad on 18 June 1990, Saddam explained that his threat to burn half of Israel was just a way to signal deterrence resolve, not a reflection of interest to strike first. FBIS-Nes-90–118, Daily Report, 19 June 1990.

57. For this author's broader analysis of the Israeli–Iraqi deterrence "dialogue" about the nuclear issue see Avner Cohen and Marvin Miller, "Nuclear Shadows in the Middle East," *Security Studies* 1(1) (Autumn 1991), 54–77. For somewhat different readings see Shai Feldman, "Israeli Deterrence and the Gulf War," in *War in the Gulf: Implications for Israel*, ed. Joseph Alpher (Boulder, Colo.: Westview Press, 1992); and Amatzia Baram, "Israeli Deterrence, Iraqi Responses," *Orbis* 36 (Summer 1992).

58. Avigdor Haselkorn, *The Continuing Storm* (New Haven: Yale University Press, 1999).

59. Avner Cohen, "The Israeli Press Covers, and Then Covers Up, the Bomb," *Deadline* 6 (Summer 1991), 17–19; Shai Feldman, "Israeli Deterrence and the Gulf War," in Alpher, *War in the Gulf*; Haselkorn, *The Continuing Storm*.

60. Gerald M. Steinberg, "Parameters of Stable Deterrence in a Proliferated Middle East: Lessons from the 1991 Gulf War," *The Nonproliferation Review* 7(3) (Fall–Winter, 2000), 43–60; Shai Feldman, "Israeli Deterrence and the Gulf War."

61. "Israelis See Chemical Option Against Iraq," *New York Times* (28 July 1990). Ne'eman proposed to the Israeli cabinet that in facing the threat of Iraq's chemical weapons, Israel should issue a credible chemical threat of its own, hence not being compelled to cross the nuclear threshold in responding to Iraqi chemical attack. Ne'eman made his proposal public, but it was not endorsed officially. Apparently there was no great desire to qualify or even diminish the effect of Israel's nuclear deterrence, that is, by announcing in advance that use of chemical weapons would not provoke an Israeli nuclear response.

62. The United Nations Special Commission (UNSCOM) on Iraq and the International Atomic Energy Agency (IAEA) had investigated Iraq's pursuit of WMD since April 1991, but it was only in the period 1995–1998—after the defection of General Hussein Kamal Hassan—that UNSCOM analysts were in a position to identify, clarify, and assess many aspects of Iraq's vast BW program. In the wake of Kamel's defection, Iraq withdrew its third Full, Final, and Complete Disclosure (FFCD) on its BW program and admitted a far more extensive BW program that included weaponization. In the spring of 1998, UNSCOM experts concluded that Iraq's latest FFCD was deficient in all areas related to the Iraqi BW program, including history, organization, acquisition of raw material, R&D, agent production,

weaponization, and deployment. For a comprehensive account (including references to UNSCOM reports) of the Iraqi BW case, see Raymond A. Zilinskas, "Iraq's Biological Warfare Program: The Past as Future?" in *Biological Weapons: Limiting the Threat*, ed. Joshua Lederberg (Cambridge: MIT Press, 1999), 137–58; Milton Leitenberg, "Deadly Unknown About Iraq's Biological Weapons Program," *Asian Perspective* 24(1) (2000), 217–23; Stephen Black, "Investigating Iraq's Biological Weapons Program," in Lederberg, *Biological Weapons*, 158–64; and Richard Butler, "Inspecting Iraq," in *Repairing the Regime*, ed. Joseph Cirincione (New York: Routledge, 2000).

63. In a lecture in Israel on 17 July 2000, former UNSCOM executive director Richard Butler revealed that Iraqi Deputy Prime Minister Tariq Aziz had told him that Iraq's biological weapons were "to deal with the 'Zionist entity.'" Etgar Lefkovits, "Iraq Brags of Biological Weapons to 'Deal with Zionist Entity,'" *Jerusalem Post* (18 July 2000).

64. Haselkorn suggests, ironically perhaps, that Saddam's "germ in the basement" posture mirrors Israel's nuclear posture: establishing a secret arsenal of weaponized BW for situations of last resort while using ambiguity to invoke deterrence by uncertainty. However, biological weapons are radically different from nuclear weapons. The predictability, visibility, and immediacy of a nuclear blast makes it the ultimate deterrent; indeed, a self-deterred weapon. The unpredictability, invisibility, and belatedness of germ dispersal renders it less a deterrent weapon and more an ultimate terrorist weapon.

65. Haselkorn even suggested that the last Scud Iraq launched at Israel on 25 February, tipped with a concrete warhead, was meant to be a BW deterrent warning aimed at the United States and Israel against moving into Baghdad itself.

66. Their argument is that bioengineered BW agents could be traced by their DNA signature. After a BW terrorist attack, if authorities had some samples of the stockpile from which the agents came, they might be able to determine who was behind the attack through the DNA signature. But without any of the original stockpile, such identification would be very difficult. Personal communication with Seth Carus and Laurie Mylroie.

67. For a comprehensive historical review of the ACRS process, see Bruce Jentleson, "The Middle East Arms Control and Regional Security (ACRS) Talks: Progress, Problems, and Prospects," Institute on Global Conflict and Cooperation, Policy Paper No. 26, 1996; Peter Jones, "Arms Control in the Middle East: Some Reflections on ACRS," *Security Dialogue* 28(1) (1997), 57–70; and Joel Peters, *Pathways to Peace: The Multilateral Arab-Israeli Peace Talks* (London: Royal Institute of International Affairs, 1996).

68. For a detailed history of the Iranian-Egyptian NWFZ proposal, see Mahmoud Karem, *A Nuclear Weapon-Free-Zone in the Middle East: Problems and Prospects* (Westport, Conn.: Greenwood Press, 1988), 91–117. Karem made the point that the Iranian–Egyptian proposal was born in response to the reports that Israel armed nuclear weapons during the 1973 war. See also the UN report to the secretary general, *Establishment of a Nuclear Weapon-Free Zone in the Region of the Middle East* (New York: United Nations, A/45/435, 10 October 1990), 6–7.

69. On this impasse see *Establishment of a Nuclear Weapon-Free Zone in the Region of the Middle East*, 23–25.

70. Ibid.

71. United Nations, S/21252; A/45/219, 18 April 1990.

72. See references cited in note 67.

73. The Egyptian stance was strongly expressed by the Egyptian foreign minister, Amre Mussa, during his visit to Israel in early September. Mussa urged Israel to sign the NPT and dismantle its nuclear capability. He also suggested that Egypt would not sign the Chemical Weapons Convention if Israel continued to remain outside the NPT (see *Ha'aretz,* 31 August and 1 September 1994).

74. Some Egyptians have privately proposed that the timeline for establishing such a zone could be stretched to as long as fifteen or twenty years, but insist that, in the end, "all Israeli nuclear weapons must be dismantled." This is based on private communications with Egyptian specialists, mostly senior diplomats and academics, at various meetings during the past two years. On this issue, see also Shai Feldman, "Israel," in *Nuclear Proliferation after the Cold War,* ed. Mitchell Reiss and Robert S. Litwak (Washington, D.C.: The Woodrow Wilson Center Press, 1994), 80–82.

75. This kind of posturing was already evident during the first two rounds of the bilateral talks on arms control in Moscow in January 1992 and in the Washington "seminar" in May 1992. See Ruth Sinai, "Mideast Arms Talks," *Associated Press* (11 May 1992).

76. Gerald Steinberg, "Israeli Policy on the CWC," *OPCW Synthesis* (November 2000), 9–31.

77. The ad hoc committee included also Defense Minister Yitzhak Mordechai, Commerce Minister Natan Sharansky, and National Infrastructure Minister Ariel Sharon. Steve Rodan, "Bitter Choices: Israel's Chemical Dilemma," *Jerusalem Post* (18 August 1997); David Makovsky, "Israel Must Ratify Chemical Treaty," *Ha'aretz* (8 January 1998).

78. As then Minister of Defense Mordechai put it: "I think that we have to wait and see how things develop. The problem is that some of the states in the region are not signing, and there is no way of inspecting those who are [not signing]. We had discussion in the cabinet, and we decided to postpone a decision for a certain period. We will discuss it again." Ze'ev Schiff, "An Interview with Yitzhak Mordechai," *Ha'aretz* (16 April 1998). See also Steinberg, "Israeli Policy on the CWC."

79. Aluf Benn, "A Difficult Choice: The Chemical Weapons Convention," *Ha'aretz* (29 November 2000).

80. Ibid.

81. A veiled reference to the security of Ness Ziona may be found in Benn's article. Benn cites security sources who express strong opposition to the transparency provisions under the CWC, and in particular the requirement "to hand in a detailed report of all its activities for the development and production of chemical weapons in the past, and if in fact there were such activities, it must show the inspectors the installations themselves."

82. Steinberg, "Israeli Policy on the CWC," 31.

83. Iraq ratified the BWC following the adoption of UN Security Council Resolution 687, which, in addition to establishing UNSCOM, also "invited" Iraq to ratify the 1972 Convention (Paragraph 7). S/RES/687 (8 April 1991).

84. This author recalls not a single occasion when Israeli citizens publicly questioned why Israel has not signed the BWC.

85. Eileen Choffnes, "Germs on the Loose," *Bulletin of the Atomic Scientists* 57(2) (March–April 2001), 57–61.

86. It was recently reported that Israel will reconsider its refusal to sign the BWC. The impetus for the reconsideration appears to be bureaucratic. The Israeli Foreign Ministry wants to get involved in the negotiation of the verification and inspection protocol for the BWC. Since the early 1990s the Foreign Ministry took the position that Israel ought to participate in international negotiation of weapons control mechanisms, as long as these do not endanger its nuclear posture. The Foreign Ministry, however, argues that if Israel refuses to sign, it will not be able to influence formulation of the agreement's protocol. It was reported that the Defense Ministry still opposes signing the BWC but has agreed to deliberate the issue. Indeed, in accordance with this position, Israel has never publicly explained its refusal to sign the BWC. Israel has traditionally sought a regional weapons inspection agreement that will permit mutual checks by neighboring countries. Aluf Benn, "Israel Reviews Decision Not to Sign BW Pact," *Ha'aretz* (2 January 2001).

87. For the historical context of President Nixon's decision to end U.S. offensive biological and chemical warfare programs, see Robert A. Wampler, ed., *National Security Archive Electronic Briefing Book*, no. 58, 25 October 2001; available online at www.gwu.edu/~nsarchiv/NSAEBB/NSAEBB58/

# 8

## China

### Balancing Disarmament and Development

*Zou Yunhua*

Biological weapons have been a serious international concern since their introduction into the arsenals of several industrialized states in the twentieth century. Although international agreements, notably the 1925 Geneva Protocol and the 1972 Biological Weapons Convention (BWC), have been designed to ban the use, development, production, stockpiling, and transfer of biological weapons, there have been major violations of these agreements. Indeed, the Chinese people are among the very few to have suffered greatly from biological weapons attacks that violated the ban on use affirmed by the Geneva Protocol as a principle of international law.

Since the conclusion of the BWC, many new biotechnologies for modifying and producing living things have been developed. These may yield important benefits, but they may also be used to create novel organisms that could cause new human, animal, or plant diseases that resist conventional approaches to protection or treatment. Thus, they increase considerably the range of biological agents and bacterial toxins that might be used for biological warfare, and this means that increasing numbers of countries are obtaining technological capabilities to produce biological weapons. Particularly in view of the past violations of international law, the international community urgently needs to strengthen the 1972 Biological Weapons Convention and increase its universality.

As a developing country with strong interests in biological fields, China believes that both biological disarmament and peaceful biological development should be pursued as complementary goals. This chapter addresses

213

three dimensions of the biological warfare (BW) problem of particular importance to China: China's experience as a victim of biological warfare, China's interest in developing biotechnology for peaceful purposes, and China's commitments to disarmament and development and how they guide its positions on strengthening the prohibition of biological weapons.

## CHINA, A VICTIM OF BIOLOGICAL WARFARE

Since the 1930s, biological weapons have been used in two wars. During World War II, Japanese troops conducted germ warfare in more than twenty provinces and cities in China, killing more than twenty thousand people. The Chinese government also believes that there is conclusive evidence that the United States used biological weapons in northeastern China during the Korean War, disseminating by air a variety of biological bombs and containers that caused large-scale unprecedented plague, rat pestilence, cholera, and other epidemic diseases. These attacks by Japan and the United States are rare cases of biological weapons use in modern history. They constituted serious violations of international law and moral principles and caused vast suffering among the Chinese people.

### Japanese Biological Warfare in China

Details of the Japanese biological warfare program, described by one analyst as "astounding in its scale and cruelty," have been documented by Chinese, American, British, and Japanese scholars.[1] From 1931 to 1945, Japan developed and produced biological weapons on a large scale, and Japanese troops used these weapons across China, except in a few provinces such as Xinjiang, Tibet, and Qinghai. According to Sheldon Harris, "A conservative estimate is that the Japanese biological warfare program killed at least 10,000 people in its laboratory experiments and perhaps as many as several hundred thousand others in military field operations."[2]

Northeastern China became the major site of the development of Japanese biological weapons. The main center was a complex called Unit 731 located at Ping Fan, near Harbin, under the direction of General Shiro Ishii of Japan's Kwantung Army. At this site, numerous pathogens, including plague, anthrax, dysentery, typhoid, paratyphoid, and cholera, were studied for military purposes, and biological bombs were developed and manufactured. It is estimated that some 3,000 men, women, and children were killed in horrifying ways in experiments at Unit 731 alone. In 1949 a former Unit 731 official declared that during his five years in Ping Fan he witnessed approximately six hundred deaths from experiments annually.[3] The live experiments on humans were cruel and deadly. For example, a captured serviceman from Unit 731 later testified about an experiment he had witnessed being conducted on five Chinese in May 1941. Four of them first received injections of four different vaccines, and then a week later they were injected with rat plague. Three days later three of them died.[4]

Ishii's army and other biological warfare units conducted extensive BW field experiments against Chinese people, releasing biological agents directly into the open environment. These actions were not limited to the northeast; they were also carried out in north, south, and central China, and in Shandong Province. Numerous epidemics resulted. Various dispersal mechanisms were used in these human experiments, ranging from rats, to airdropped bombs, to liquid concoctions poured into reservoirs, wells, and rivers.[5] The Khabarovsk War Crimes Trial, conducted by the former Soviet Union in Siberia in 1949, recorded some of the atrocities committed in Japanese laboratories against Chinese people between 1931 and 1945. For example, one witness testified:

> In January 1945 I saw experiments in inducing gas gangrene conducted under the direction of the Chief of the 2nd Division, Colonel Ikari, and researcher Futaki. Ten prisoners were tied facing stakes, five to ten meters apart. The prisoners' heads were covered with metal helmets, and their bodies with screens, only their naked buttocks being exposed. At about 100 meters away a fragmentation bomb was exploded by electricity. All ten men were wounded and sent back to prison. I later asked Ikari and researcher Futaki what the results had been. They told me that all ten men had died of gas gangrene.[6]

The Japanese Army continued committing heinous crimes against the Chinese until the day they surrendered.[7] Unfortunately Japan has not acknowledged these crimes or issued an apology for them to this day.

## U.S. Biological Warfare against China and North Korea

China also holds that the United States used biological warfare against China and North Korea during the Korean War. The brief account that follows draws on several restricted (*neibu*) publications, in particular a history written by members of the Chinese Academy of Military Science and published in 1988, *The History of the War to Resist U.S. Aggression and Aid Korea.* Its authors had access to the China State Central Archives and the Archives of the People's Liberation Army. In 1999, the claims made in these publications received further support from two Canadian authors, Stephen Endicott and Edward Hagerman, who have provided evidence based on extensive interviews; recently declassified U.S., British, and Canadian documents; and documents from the Chinese central archives.[8]

In December 1950, while retreating south from a joint counterattack by Chinese and North Korean forces, the U.S. Air Force disseminated smallpox viruses at Pyongyang, Huanghaidao, and other places in North Korea. Then, in January 1952, the U.S. Army secretly committed germ warfare on a large scale. On January 28, the Chinese People's Volunteers first found insects released by the U.S. Army at Tieyuanjun and Longzhaodong in North Korea, and in the following weeks insects, rats, and sparrows carrying bacteria were found in several other places in China. Experiments revealed that among them these creatures carried the bacteria of ten diseases, including rat plague, cholera, typhoid fever, dysentery, meningitis, and encephalitis. The U.S. Army also used planes and artillery to disseminate bombs containing bacteria-treated tree leaves, cotton, food, and propaganda material.[9]

The bacteriological warfare committed by the U.S. Army generated new outbreaks of diseases that had long been eradicated in Korea, such as rat plague and cholera. On February 22, the North Korean government released a statement protesting this criminal use of bacteriological warfare and a supporting statement from the Chinese government quickly followed.[10]

In the spring of 1952, the Chinese government organized a team known as the "Investigation Team for the Crime of U.S. Imperialism Using Germ Warfare," composed of members of the Chinese Red Cross Society, representatives of various nongovernmental organizations, and scientific experts and scholars, to investigate these crimes in North Korea and northern China. Two other investigative groups, the International Association of Democratic Lawyers and the International Scientific Commission for the Investigation of the Facts Concerning Bacterial Warfare in Korea and China, also conducted investigations. All three groups concluded that the U.S. Army had indeed used germ warfare.[11] Some of the U.S. methods appeared to have been further developments of those used by the Japanese army during World War II.

Meanwhile, exhibitions were held in Beijing and Shenyang of photos and material objects related to the U.S. Army's use of germ warfare. In the face of this conclusive evidence, U.S. Secretary of State Dean Acheson defended the U.S. Army in the United Nations, providing testimony by biological experts and other evidence purporting to show that the claims against the United States were fraudulent.[12] In 1952, the Xinhua News Agency published confessions by twenty-five captured U.S. pilots stating that they had taken part in bacteriological attacks, and including restricted information about official U.S. policy concerning bacteriological warfare. These confessions contradicted the U.S. government denials.[13] It is important to note the view of two Canadian historians, Stephen Endicott and Edward Hagerman, who have argued in response to recent criticism from American analysts that "there is . . . good reason to conclude that the [American] flyers created their own statements and did so under stress and duress that was tough but not unbearable."[14] Endicott and Hagerman have also presented substantial evidence concerning the American BW attacks that draws on extensive archival research in the Canadian, Chinese, and U.S. government archives and on interviews with Chinese officials and scientists involved in investigating the attacks.

In conclusion, the evidence for the American BW attacks on North Korea and China is overwhelming, notwithstanding recent American criticisms of parts of this evidence. These U.S. attacks constituted a severe threat to the Chinese and Korean people and a violation of a well-established principle of international law: the general prohibition of the use of biological and chemical weapons affirmed in the Geneva Protocol. Demonstrations and meetings were held in many countries condemning these acts.[15]

## BIOTECHNOLOGY RESEARCH AND DEVELOPMENT AND ITS INDUSTRIALIZATION IN CHINA

Developing biotechnology for agriculture and industry is an important goal for China's high-technology industry program. Because China strongly believes that disarmament and arms control should not hinder, but rather promote, peaceful uses of science and technology, and also because of the dual-purpose nature of many biologically based activities, it is essential to understand the importance of the development of new biotechnologies to China.

Biotechnology research in China started in the early 1970s when research institutes of the Chinese Academy of Sciences initiated a study of enzyme fixation. After the first national symposium on enzyme engineering in April 1978, the work spread to other institutes, universities, and factories. Genetic engineering began in the late 1970s and was mainly conducted in agencies within the Chinese Academy of Sciences, the Chinese Medical Academy, and the Chinese Ministry of Education. There, scientists began to take part in the biotechnological developments that were being pursued elsewhere, such as basic work in genetic engineering.

In August 1982, the State Science and Technology Committee included genetic engineering in the National Research and Development Plan and began supporting research on a genetically engineered hepatitis B vaccine, genetically engineered interferon, and plant gene engineering. By 1983, the development of biotechnology was attracting considerable attention in government, scientific, and industry circles. In March of that year, enzyme and fermentation engineering were added to the National Research and Development Plan, and thereafter, programs were expanded to cover the full field of biotechnology. In 1983, the State Science and Technology Commission

*Zou Yunhua*

established the China Biotechnology Development Center. At the same time, biotechnology groups and expert committees were formed in the Ministry of Agriculture, the Ministry of Health, the State Medical Administration, the Chinese Academy of Sciences, and elsewhere. In 1987 a high-technology research and development project, the "863 Project," was begun, in which biotechnology has been earmarked as one of seven key areas. These projects have resulted in substantial growth in personnel working in biotechnology. By 1991 an estimated 31,500 scientific personnel were engaged in biotechnology.[16]

Biotechnology in China is being developed only for peaceful purposes, including biological defense. The "State Policy on the Development of Biotechnology" was drawn up in 1985 and put into practice in 1988.[17] The general goal for development of biotechnology is to address important problems in the areas of food production, medical treatment, health care, energy, resources, and environment for China's 1.2 billion people. Biotechnology is regarded as a key to fully and effectively using recycled resources, meeting the needs of the growing population, and improving nutritional standards. China has thus given priority to three areas for development: (1) agriculture, forest industries, and production of livestock and fish, particularly for breeding plants and animals, increasing the quality and output of economic crops; (2) medical treatment and health, developing new drugs and vaccines, and developing genetic cures for diseases that have proved incurable or difficult to treat by other means; and (3) food.[18]

Research and development in medical biotechnology has made important progress. China has successfully completed its work on hepatitis B and interferon, and both a genetically engineered dysentery vaccine and an Epstein Barr virus vaccine have been approved for testing in humans. Experimental research on more than ten genetically engineered multipeptide medicines has been completed, laying the foundation for clinical tests.[19]

China expects to take part in exploring the frontiers of international biotechnology and to participate, exchange, and compete with others working in this field around the world.[20] Nevertheless, despite state commitment to expansion of biotechnology, there are still problems in policy implementation that have posed difficulties for biotechnological development. One is a low level of funding from the state. For instance, the average annual budget for biotechnology research from the state's "863 Project" was only about 100 million RMB *yuan* (about U.S. $12 million) during the 8th Five-year Plan (1991–1995). This was supplemented to some degree by state and local governmental departments, but there remains a funding shortage.[21] Obviously it is very difficult to meet the enormous requirements of biotechnology research work with such limited support.

Despite the high government priority given to biotechnology, the industry remains underdeveloped, scattered among various government agencies responsible for agriculture, health, and medicine. It remains but a small part of China's biotech industry. Traditional bioindustry, supported by brewing technology, remains at a low technological level both in terms of product quality and production efficiency. Even in the rapidly developing and well-equipped bioindustry field, which emphasizes antibiotics production based on microorganism fermentation, China trails far behind more industrialized countries. For example, China's total annual sales of genetically engineered drugs are less than those of one U.S. company.[22]

Although China's bioindustry is embryonic, it is expanding and shows promise. For example, in the last five years the Chinese pharmaceutical industry has shown remarkable achievements in applying modern biotechnology and genetic engineering technology toward developing new drugs. By July 1998, fourteen biopharmaceutical drugs and vaccines had started production. The total industry output was worth roughly 2,000 million RMB *yuan*. Yet a large gap remains between China and other developed countries. China's new biodrugs and vaccines represent only one-third of those in the world, and total sales, about U.S. $250 million, are less than one-thirtieth of global sales.[23]

International cooperation in the biological sciences will inevitably confront the issue of intellectual property protection. As China has become more open, its economic and scientific systems have integrated with global systems. China's scientific community must observe global rules of competition—such as those protecting property rights—if it wishes to fairly compete internationally.[24] Further, its legal system must be compatible with those of other countries. On March 12, 1984, the first Chinese patent law was adopted at the fourth session of the Standing Committee of the Sixth National People's Congress. Late that year China acceded to the Paris Convention for the Protection of Industrial Property as amended at Stockholm in 1967. However, items suitable for patents, and the duration of patents, were limited under the 1984 law. In pharmaceuticals, for example, only production methods, not products themselves, were eligible for patent coverage. The situation changed as China's reforms progressed. In 1992 the Chinese government modified the 1984 law to provide patent rights for inventions of biotechnological medical products. Breeds of animals and plants, however, remain unpatentable.

In the biotechnology field, the 1992 law gives patent protection for invented microorganisms.[25] Foreign companies could apply for pharmaceutical product patents in China, and if granted, illegal production would be prohibited for twenty years.[26] For some circumstances China has adopted a dual-track protection system to strengthen intellectual property protection. For instance, in addition to patent coverage, China offers administrative protection to eligible American biotechnological pharmaceutical products according to a Sino–U.S. memorandum of understanding signed January

17, 1992.[27] In this context, the Chinese science and technology community and pharmaceutical community began paying more attention to issues of foreign patent protection.

Because different countries are at different developmental levels, and because they have diverse cultural, political, and legal systems, it is understandable that there are differences in national patent systems. Differences exist even among developed countries. For example, the European Patent Convention does not protect new animal and plant breeds, but many European countries have also joined the International Union for the Protection of New Varieties of Plants, signed in 1961 and subsequently amended, which specifically protects new plants. It should be pointed out that patent protection in the United States, Japan, and Australia is quite broad; patents are granted to all new animal and plant varieties that pose no public danger.[28] Given these national variations in patent coverage, the argument that biotechnology transfer can only take place after advanced intellectual protection systems are established is unrealistic; it cannot be used by some developed countries to justify shirking their responsibilities to transfer technology.

## CHINA'S COMMITMENT TO PROHIBITING BIOLOGICAL WEAPONS

The efforts of the People's Republic of China's to ban biological warfare go back to its foundation in 1949 when all international agreements and treaties signed by its predecessor were reexamined and treated differently according to their contents. Some were recognized, and others abolished, modified, or renegotiated. The Geneva Protocol of 1925 was one of the earliest agreements to be recognized. On July 13, 1952, then–Foreign Minister Zhou Enlai stated that the Chinese government was bound by the accession to the Protocol in the name of China on August 7, 1929, and that it would comply with and carry out the Protocol under the premise of mutual adherence by all state parties.[29] explained that "the protocol is beneficial to the consolidation of international peace and security, and conforms with the principles of humanitarianism"(author's translation). China's having suffered from biological attacks motivated its early support for effective prohibition of the use of biological as well as chemical weapons.

Although the 1925 Geneva Protocol was an important step toward banning biological weapons as well as chemical weapons, its authority was undermined by repeated uses of these kinds of weapons. One of the purposes of the 1972 Biological Weapons Convention (BWC) was to strengthen the prohibition against biological weaponry. From 1971 to 1979, following the recovery of China's seat in the United Nations, China did not join the

BWC. This should be understood not as a lack of commitment to the complete elimination of biological and chemical weapons but rather as a response to the geopolitical context of that period. The Cold War tensions were intense, and the United States and the Soviet Union were engaged in a ferocious arms race that China firmly opposed. China urged the two superpowers to reduce their arsenals as a precondition for universal disarmament.[30] China did not support the BWC because, like so many other arms control agreements during the Cold War, it was developed mainly by the two superpowers. China tended to regard such agreements as swindles when draft agreements were opened for discussion only after undisclosed bargains between the two superpowers had been made. China strongly defended and strictly adhered to the Geneva Protocol of 1925. Regarding the BWC, the Chinese government placed great importance on the question of prohibition of use. China consistently called for a "genuine and effective prohibition of the use of chemical and biological weapons" and stated that "prohibition of use is crucial for a comprehensive ban and elimination of chemical and bacteriological weapons." "But," Chinese delegates noted, "the BWC evaded the question and this would leave the door open for the superpowers to use this type of weapon of mass destruction in the future."[31] In addition, China refused to accept the accession of the Taiwan authority to the convention, on the grounds that "the Taiwan authority's signing of the convention was illegal and invalid."[32]

The implementation of China's open-door policy in 1978 allowed it to play a growing role in world affairs. The Chinese government began to stress the importance of arms control and disarmament work and to make it an important component of its overall diplomacy and defense policy. It actively attended multilateral negotiations and international conferences on arms control and disarmament. China first sent a delegation to the Conference on Disarmament in 1980, and in 1982 put forward its proposal for "three stops and one reduction" at the Second Special Session on Disarmament of the United Nations (SSOD II). It stated that the United States and the Soviet Union should stop testing, improving, and producing nuclear weapons and take the lead in drastically reducing all types of such weapons. This proposal played a positive role in promoting negotiations between the two countries and producing actual progress toward disarmament.[33] In this atmosphere, China acceded to the BWC in October 1984 and ratified it on November 15.

China took this step for several reasons. The Chinese government sees the BWC's prohibition of biological weaponry as consistent with its commitments to safeguarding world peace, protecting people, and preventing aggression. In 1984, former Vice Foreign Minister (now Vice Premier) Qian Qichen explained to the Standing Committee of the People's Congress that because China would never produce, manufacture, or use biological weapons, its commitment to the BWC would not be burdensome; nor would it harm China's defense. On the contrary, the BWC would constrain those states with biological weapons capabilities, especially the two superpowers. Qian Qichen also stated that China's joining the convention would allow it to participate in reviewing BWC-related issues such as compliance and that China would welcome a setting in which it, along with Third World countries, could expose BWC violations by superpowers. Finally, the BWC could prevent other states from developing such weapons and thus benefit world peace and security.[34]

Of course, China's accession to the BWC does not mean that it sees the convention as free of problems. The government saw this forum as an opportunity to address and try to remedy the BWC's shortcomings.[35] As Foreign Minister Wu Xueqian said at the time of ratification, "China's government regards the convention as imperfect. For example, the convention does not clearly prohibit the use of biological weapons, has not stipulated concrete effective measures of supervision and verification, and has no forceful sanctions against violations. China's government hopes these defects will be remedied and improved at a proper time."[36]

## CHINA'S SUPPORT FOR STRENGTHENING THE REGIME PROHIBITING BIOLOGICAL WEAPONS

China's policy for biological disarmament is determined by its fundamental interests and should be understood in terms of its history, culture, and tradition, particularly its own experience as a victim of biological warfare. China needs a peaceful and stable international environment to concentrate on economic construction. The prohibition on biological weapons is in the fundamental interests of the Chinese people as well as all other people.

China's policy on biological warfare has been repeatedly explained in international forums, and it is therefore incomprehensible that Western media and some Western countries often describe China as possessing chemical and biological weapons capabilities. Setting aside what their real intentions may be, several problems require discussion.

First, "capability" is a rather ambiguous concept. Take Japan, for example: How do we assess Japan's nuclear capability? Japan has the industrial and technological means to build a nuclear bomb and has claimed the ability to build nuclear weapons. However, if we judge "capability" only according to whether a country actually possesses nuclear weapons, we can say that Japan has none since it has never made a nuclear bomb. Furthermore, the meaning of "capability" in biological contexts differs from its usage in the Comprehensive Test Ban Treaty (CTBT). There, forty-four states are classified as having actual or potential nuclear capability based on a list of "world nuclear reactors" edited by IAEA in 1996. There is no standard definition of biological weapons "capability," and constructing one will be difficult.

A second problem is that defining "chemical and biological weapons" is even more difficult because of the intrinsic characteristics of such weapons. A pesticide factory may be capable of manufacturing chemical weapons, or a hospital researching epidemic viruses might be able to produce biological weapons. In other words, if we judge biological weapons capability according to vague criteria, we can say that *most* countries, including China, have such capabilities. A third problem is that, based on political biases and hostilities, American and some other mainstream Western media have confused public opinion by censuring China for possible offensive biological and chemical weapons programs. This has nothing to do with China's actual compliance with the biological and chemical weapon conventions. According to the solemn declaration of the former foreign minister, Wu Xueqian, at the time of ratification: "China has never and will not produce and possess biological weapons."[37]

## General Policy on Nonproliferation of Biological Weapons and Related Technologies

Preventing the proliferation of weapons of mass destruction is essential for safeguarding international peace and security and for pursuing the goal of a world free of weapons of mass destruction. China maintains that the final objective of nonproliferation is to eliminate weapons of mass destruction and improve the environment of global peace and security, while at the same time protecting the social and economic development interests of all states.[38]

The end of the Cold War offered an opportunity to consolidate the nonproliferation regime, and some progress was indeed made in arms control and disarmament, but some recent developments have undermined this progress. The large biological weapons program pursued in secret by the former Soviet Union and Iraq's extensive BW program, finally uncovered in 1995 following the Gulf War, have undermined confidence in the BWC. In addition, terrorism is also a concern. In March 1995, the Japanese sect called Aum Shinrikyo unleashed a chemical weapons attack against commuters in the Tokyo subway, in which twelve people died and 5,500 were injured. The Aum Shinrikyo was also developing biological weapons.[39]

The Chinese government has consistently advocated the complete prohibition and destruction of biological weapons. It opposes the production of biological weapons by any country and their proliferation in any form by any country.[40] Although China, unlike the United States, does not perceive a major increase in the threat of biological warfare, we do need to find ways to prevent the spread of these dangerous weapons.

China's general approach to achieving nonproliferation objectives was discussed by Sha Zukang, former Ambassador for Disarmament, in a series of presentations in the late 1990s. Sha argued that "while strengthening the nonproliferation regime, efforts to enhance scientific and technical cooperation should be intensified: they are two sides of the same coin, and if handled properly, can be mutually promotive."[41] For this reason, China opposes the discriminatory export control groups that have been created by a small number of Western countries and that establish a monopoly on certain forms of technology. Such arrangements will not be effective in ensuring nonproliferation. They can only deepen resentment among excluded countries and are likely to be abused by group members for their own purposes. Therefore, China believes that these groups should be either modified or abolished altogether and replaced by global arrangements grounded in universal participation.[42]

The Chinese government takes a prudent and responsible approach to the transfer of technology related to weapons of mass destruction, including biological weapons.[43] In particular, China has attached great importance to controlling exports of militarily sensitive materials and has adopted a series of regulations on transfers of these materials.

China recognizes that export controls are an essential means for ensuring nonproliferation. With respect to transfers of nuclear material, in May 1997, the Chinese government published the Circular on Questions Pertaining to the Strict Implementation of China's Nuclear Exports Policy, which explicitly stipulates that no nuclear materials, facilities, or related technologies exported by China may be supplied to or used by nuclear facilities that have not accepted safeguards of the International Atomic Energy Agency (IAEA). The circular also contains strict provisions regarding exports of dual-use nuclear-related materials. In September 1997, the Chinese government issued the Regulations of the People's Republic of China on Nuclear Export Control, banning any kind of assistance to nuclear facilities not accepting IAEA safeguards. In October 1997, China formally joined the Zanger Committee, one of the main international nuclear export control regimes. On June 10, 1998, China promulgated the Regulations on the Control of the Export of Dual-Use Nuclear Materials and Related Technology, imposing strict control on the export of nuclear-related dual-use materials and related technology.[44] For historical reasons (the export control regime was formed by a small group, lacking in impartiality and universality), China has not yet joined the Nuclear Suppliers Group, but it supports the Group's nonproliferation objectives and has incorporated its control lists, in their entirety, into its own national regulations.[45]

The Chinese government views India's criticism of nuclear cooperation between China and Pakistan as based on misunderstanding and unfounded suspicion. According to the Chinese ambassador to India, Zhou Gang, the program "aims only at peaceful use of nuclear energy, and it is under the safeguards of the International Atomic Energy Agency. Such cooperation is not directed against India."[46] With respect to defense, China once sold small quantities of conventional weapons to Pakistan, in response to Pakistan's request for assistance in strengthening its defensive capabilities and promoting stability and peace in South Asia. In contrast, India has purchased much larger quantities of conventional weapons from other countries. In this area, Pakistan is no match for India.[47]

With respect to transfers of chemicals and related technology, China supports normal international cooperation in its chemical industry and exchanges of related scientific and technological materials in accordance with the Chemical Weapons Convention (CWC). It opposes any export-control mechanisms that conflict with the purpose of the convention. In September 1990, the Chinese government drafted measures for strict control of the export of chemicals, their production technologies, and equipment. After signing the CWC, China issued a series of legal instruments to further enhance and perfect the supervision and control of chemicals. In December 1995, the Chinese government issued the Regulations of the People's Republic of China on the Supervision and Control of Chemicals, and, in accordance with these regulations, in June 1996 issued the List of Chemicals Subject to Supervision and Control and the Bylaws for the implementation of the regulations. The latter stipulated that the import and export of related chemicals are under the centralized management of the chemical industry under the State Council, and special companies designated by it.[48] More specifically, to ensure that chemicals and related technologies and equipment, if exported, are not used in the production of chemical weapons, a detailed list of chemicals subject to export control has been drawn up in accordance with the Verification Annex of the convention. Import and export of chemicals on this list and technologies and equipment used in their manufacture are under the centralized management of the Ministry of Chemical Industry (MCI). Business related to such imports and exports is handled by specialized enterprises designated by MCI and the Ministry of Foreign Trade and Economic Cooperation (MOFTEC). MCI, MOFTEC, and the General Administration of Customs (GAC) take joint responsibility for examining and approving imports and exports, issuing licenses, and making inspections. China insists that the governments of importing countries provide assurances that the relevant goods imported from China not be used to manufacture chemical weapons or be retransfered to a third country.[49]

In harmony with its general policy on export controls, China, together with other non-Western countries, has strongly opposed the current role of the Australia Group. The specific objection is that the Group imposes discriminatory controls, decided in secret, on normal trade in chemical and biological agents and equipment by states that are parties to the CWC and the BWC.[50] The relationship between the CWC and the Australia Group became a thorny issue during the CWC negotiations. Since the CWC contains clear restrictions on the export of sensitive chemicals, the continuation of the Australia Group has created a dual legal system that applies to CWC parties. According to Sha Zukang, such a system "inevitably causes confusion and affects the normal international trade of chemicals. This problem is compounded by the seemingly irresistible inclination of certain countries to impose their own standards or even their own domestic legislation onto other countries, thus giving rise to unnecessary international disputes. All this has seriously undermined the authority of the CWC. . . . There must be a single standard rather than two."[51] China has also criticized the Australia Group's export controls on biological agents and equipment.

## China's Position on Strengthening the Biological Weapons Convention

Since its accession to the BWC in 1984, China has supported the purposes and objectives of the Convention and has conscientiously fulfilled its obligations as a state party.[52] In particular, China has supported the development of "appropriate and feasible" verification measures for the Biological Weapons Convention. In fact, as noted earlier, at the time of its accession, China expressed a reservation that the BWC lacked an effective regime to implement its basic prohibition.[53]

In the 1980s, China supported the development and implementation of confidence-building measures (CBMs) in the form of information exchanges among the state parties. It participated in drafting these measures at the Ad Hoc Meeting of Scientific and Technical Experts in 1987.[54] Since 1987 China has annually reported to the United Nations on convention-related information and data in accordance with the decisions of the Review Conferences of the convention.[55] For instance, in response to CBM F, China declared that its small-scale defensive research program had started in 1958 and that its research foci included the study of characteristics of biological and toxin warfare agents, sampling, identification of biological agents, and rapid diagnosis. The program has also been involved in the development and applications of medicine and equipment for large-area sterilization and for killing insects and rats.[56]

China actively participated in the negotiation of the Protocol to the BWC by the Ad Hoc Group of States Parties initiated in 1995. In general, China holds that the verification system for the BWC should be guided by principles of fairness, appropriateness, and effectiveness. It must also address the specific nature both of biological weapons and of the biological sciences and biotechnology, as well as the wide application of the latter in industry, agriculture, and medicine.[57] Ambassador Sha Zukang has noted that verification mechanisms for the CWC or the CTBT are "not quite suited or hardly applicable for the verification of biological weapons."[58]

With respect to the specific nature of verification for the BWC, China holds that effectiveness and deterrence should be optimized.[59] That is, the scope of verification should not be so wide as to impose excessive burdens on parties, interfere with normal economic life, or even impair commercial secrets; on the other hand, if verification is too narrow, effectiveness will be harmed. The problem of balancing these two dimensions of verification should be the focus of the negotiations in the Ad Hoc Group. From a technical point of view, two extremes must be avoided in negotiating lists and thresholds of biological agents and toxins for declaration purposes, because an excessively narrow list will leave loopholes for verification and compliance, whereas an excessively extensive list will provide opportunities for abuse of verification.

The Chinese government holds that the verification regime should formulate concrete steps to prevent abuse of verification measures and improper interference with peaceful activities and to protect commercial secrets. It is important to protect the pursuit of normal civil production, scientific research, and commercial trade in the course of establishing a verification mechanism. The rapid growth of biotechnology over the past twenty years suggests that the field will play an increasingly important role for developing countries in addressing urgent problems of population, disease, food, energy, and the environment, and as a key to ensuring a strong and prosperous future. Strict constraints and excessive interference in the name of verification could impede the development of this promising field.

It is important to emphasize the dual-purpose character of biological activities. It is often difficult to distinguish between civilian and military applications or between offensive and defensive applications. These uncertainties could complicate negotiations by widening the scope of verification. For instance, in agriculture, research and development of pesticides, bactericides, and disinfectants are needed to combat insect pests and pathogenic bacteria that are harmful to animals and plants. Furthermore, a country's development of preventive vaccines and other defensive measures requires a process of research, trial-production, production, testing, stockpiling, training, and use. Yet this process is quite similar to that of producing biological weapons. Regarding the means of delivery, civil planes for transporting pesticides and city watering carts may serve to deliver biological warfare agents after refitting. Likewise, chemical plants, microorganism fermentation plants, and breweries may be refitted and enhanced to produce biological warfare agents.[60]

To sum up, China supports the enhancement of the effectiveness of the

BWC in a comprehensive manner. The Chinese government holds that to strengthen the effectiveness of the BWC, a necessary verification mechanism should be established. In view of the complexity of biological weapons and biotechnology, the verification mechanism to be established must be rational, just, and feasible. China also stresses that there should be concrete measures to promote international cooperation and exchanges among state parties in the field of biotechnology for purposes not prohibited by the BWC. These measures will be conducive to enhancing the universality of the BWC and the future Protocol.[61]

### China's Approach to the Negotiations for a Protocol to Strengthen the Effectiveness of the Biological Weapons Convention

With respect to the details of the negotiations for a BWC Protocol, initiated in 1995, China supports the consensus position of the state parties that declarations, visits, and investigations are fundamental elements of the future instrument. China accepts the need for detailed declarations and has proposed a text for declarations of biological defense programs.[62] It also holds that declaration and verification measures should be formulated according to objective, just, and scientific criteria instead of the prejudiced or subjective judgment of a few countries.[63]

On the question of visits, the Chinese have argued that any visit regime to be established should be aimed at strengthening the effectiveness of the BWC. Implementation of other disarmament agreements has shown that random visits that focus on high-risk facilities such as defense facilities are fair, effective, and feasible. The Chinese government believes that the purpose of clarification visits can be fully achieved through other measures contained in the Protocol and is still not convinced that the concept of clarification visits, as proposed, for example, by the United Kingdom in 1999,[64] should be incorporated in the Protocol, although this concept was discussed for some time. The Chinese government holds that there is no need for clarification visits. Moreover, clarification visits have inherent problems, such as a discriminatory effect on different state parties and a high risk of abuse. As for transparency visits, as proposed, for example, by Germany, the Chinese delegation considers that they appear to be nothing more than a mere formality. With vague purpose, poor feasibility, and huge financial waste, such visits make little contribution to the strengthening of the effectiveness of the BWC.[65] Ambiguities or uncertainties concerning declarations should be addressed primarily through processes of consultation, clarification, and cooperation.[66] In other words, visits should not be surrogate investigations.

A further issue concerns the focus of investigations. The parties have contemplated two approaches: investigations focusing on facilities, and "field investigations" focusing on outbreaks of disease. China is particularly concerned about the latter, as are India, Iran, and Pakistan. Their concerns are twofold: First, field investigations are more likely to occur in less-developed countries that are more susceptible to disease outbreaks. Second, investigation teams might be granted powers to move too easily from field to facility investigations, thus providing access to sensitive facilities.[67]

In general, the Chinese government believes that investigations should maintain a balance between building a rigorous and effective investigation regime aimed at preventing and punishing noncompliance, thereby genuinely strengthening the effectiveness of the BWC, and preventing the abuse of the right of requesting an investigation with a view to protecting the rightful security and commercial interests of state parties.[68] For these reasons, China welcomed several working papers on visits and investigations submitted to the Ad Hoc Group by the group of states known as the Non-Aligned Movement (NAM) and accepted many of its proposals.[69]

One issue that remained undecided during the negotiations is the nature of the decision-making process of the Executive Council of the implementing organization. Borrowing from the CWC and Comprehensive Test Ban Treaty (CTBT) negotiations, members of the Ad Hoc Group have considered alternative decision-making procedures: "red light," in which an inspection/investigation challenge request is carried out automatically unless the Executive Council countermands it, and "green light," in which no inspection/investigation challenge may proceed unless specifically authorized by a majority Council decision.[70] For the BWC Protocol, China and several nonaligned states favor the "green light" approach, as they did in the negotiations of the CWC and of the CTBT, on the grounds that inspections and challenge investigations need to be protected from abuse. China has argued that concrete provisions should be formulated accordingly in the following stages of the investigation mechanism: request for investigation, approval by the Executive Council, conclusion on investigation, and punishment of abuse.[71]

## Support for Development of Biological Fields for Peaceful Purposes

I mentioned previously that China, as a populous country with insufficient per capita energy and mineral resources, must pursue peaceful uses of new technologies on a large scale to achieve its economic goals. The Chinese position is that Article X should be understood as an integral part of the BWC and implemented as completely as the other articles.[72] This will increase the universality and effectiveness of the convention by encouraging developing countries to accede to it.[73] Furthermore, as a developing country with scientific resources in biological fields, China could be a provider as well as a receiver in biotechnology transfer. The Chinese government supports strengthening international biotechnological cooperation and exchange with numerous developing countries and hopes that scientific achievements will benefit all humankind.

China actively participates in many forms of international cooperation for the development of biotechnology. For example, China has continuing cooperative relations and projects with the World Health Organization, the United Nations Children's Fund (UNICEF), the United Nations International Center for Genetic Engineering and Biotechnology (ICGEB), and the Global Human Genome Project. On January 12, 2000, Chinese scientists announced that they had become the first in the world to determine the genetic makeup of a fatal prawn virus, which has been responsible for a drastic reduction in prawn production in China and other parts of Asia over the past few years. (The sequencing of the virus's genome, or its genetic map, will help scientists develop diagnostic tools and drugs to fight the leukodermal bacilliform virus, the largest known animal virus. Information available in China has shown that Chinese scientists are far ahead of their international counterparts, who have sequenced only 1 percent of the virus's genome.[74]) China and the European Community established the China-European Community Biotechnology Center in Beijing in 1991, and China and the Rockefeller Foundation have initiated a major cooperative research project on rice biotechnology. China also collaborates with various Western corporations.[75]

Article X of the BWC requires that implementation of the Convention avoid "hampering the economic or technological development of States Parties to the Convention or international cooperation in the field of peaceful bacteriological (biological) activities, including the international exchange of bacteriological (biological) agents and toxins and equipment for the processing, use or production of bacteriological (biological) agents and toxins for peaceful purposes." China places great emphasis on the significance of this article on the grounds that disarmament and arms control treaties should not hinder but rather promote the development of science and technology for peaceful purposes.[76] Biological disarmament and peaceful biological development should be seen as complementary, not antithetical, goals.

For this reason, throughout the negotiations for the BWC Protocol, China has consistently supported the position that article X should be implemented as effectively as those articles that provide measures aimed at strengthening the prohibition of biological weapons. In this connection, the draft of article VII, which addresses the conditions for scientific and technological development for peaceful purposes, involves one of the most sensitive questions for BWC state parties: the relationship between technology sharing, trade, and export controls.[77]

Underlying the Ad Hoc Group's discussions of scientific and technological cooperation for peaceful purposes is the continuing struggle over the future of the Australia Group. This has become a major problem for the Ad Hoc Group, and as long as the Western position remains unchanged, it will remain so. Despite an understanding during the CWC negotiations that the future of the Australia Group would be reviewed once the treaty entered into force, the group continues and, so far, there has been no sign of Western willingness to discuss phasing out or limiting its operation. Since the Group imposes export controls on biological and chemical agents and equipment, the question of its continuation has resurfaced in the context of the negotiations over the BWC Protocol. China's position is that export controls coordinated by the Australia Group must be superceded by national export controls coordinated through mechanisms or guidelines developed within the framework of the Protocol. Unfortunately, some Western countries refuse to discuss the issue for fear of further eroding the raison d'être of the Australia Group.[78] As Hu Xiaodi, China's Ambassador for Disarmament to the United Nations, explained China's position at the United Nations in October 2000: "The countries concerned should undertake to abolish those export control cartels that are incompatible with the BWC or its protocol. This issue relates to the equal rights for state parties and future universality of the protocol, therefore, its proper settlement will have decisive impact on whether the Protocol can be concluded."[79]

## The Failure of the Protocol Negotiations

Following six and one-half years of negotiations on the verification and compliance mechanism for the BWC, hopes for a successful outcome were dashed on July 25, 2001, when the United States announced its rejection not only of the composite text of a draft Protocol prepared by the chair of the negotiations, Tibor Toth, but also of further efforts to negotiate such an agreement. According to the head of the U.S. delegation for the BWC Protocol negotiations, Ambassador Donald Mahley, the composite text was not acceptable to Washington and there was no way to "fix" the text. To the shock of many, the United States also rejected the entire concept of a legally binding Protocol to the BWC.[80]

Mahley argued that "no nation" was more committed to combating the biological weapons threat than the United States. The United States had completed its review both of the Protocol text and of the current and emerging threat from biological weapons and had concluded that "the current approach to a Protocol" was not "capable of strengthening confidence in compliance with" the BWC. It would not improve the ability to verify compliance and would "do little" to deter countries seeking biological weapons. He also noted that the United States would "develop other ideas and different approaches that . . . could help to achieve our common objective of effectively strengthening the [BWC]."[81]

China joined Canada, Cuba, Japan, and South Africa in expressing serious concerns about the U.S. rejection of the Protocol. Ambassador Hu Xiaodi complained that the joint efforts of the parties to the BWC over many years had been made in vain. He stated that the Chinese government "expresses regret over the matter" and mentioned that the United States "is a big bio-tech power and has huge bio-defense programs and it is extremely vital for its participation in any efforts aimed to strengthen the effectiveness of the BWC." He urged other countries to make further efforts to persuade the United States to join with others in pursuing measures that could practically strengthen the effectiveness of the BWC in a manner acceptable to all. He also noted the U.S. claim that it had not abandoned its commitment to strengthening the BWC in the multilateral framework. China would "wait and see" whether "such rhetoric [would] soon be translated into concrete actions."[82]

## THE EMERGENCE OF A NEW THREAT OF BIOLOGICAL TERRORISM

One month after the September 11 terrorist attacks on the United States, that country feared a further attack with biological weapons after anthrax-contaminated letters were sent to media offices and to the office of U.S. Senator Thomas Daschle. By October 18, 2001, some twenty-nine cases of anthrax exposure had been confirmed.[83]

The September 11 attacks and the later dissemination of anthrax have indicated that terrorism could threaten all nations in the twenty-first century. Facing such threats is a common and long-term task for all countries. China staunchly opposes terrorism, including acts involving biological and chemical weapons. Chinese officials are working to protect China from such threats and have reiterated their call to eliminate biological and chemical weapons once and for all. China's exit and entry quarantine departments have been urged to conduct strict inspections of living things and materials entering the country, including plants, animals, international mail, and travelers' luggage. Goods that are determined to be infected with bacteria will be rejected.[84]

The Asia-Pacific Economic Cooperation (APEC) Economic Leaders' Meeting on October 21, 2001, in Shanghai, which was attended by President Jiang Zemin and President George W. Bush, produced a strong statement on counter-terrorism. Leaders of the APEC countries unequivocally condemned in the strongest terms the terrorist attacks on the United States on September 11, 2001. They considered the murderous deeds as well as other terrorist acts in all forms and manifestations as a profound threat to the peace, prosperity, and security of all people, of all faiths, of all nations. They also deemed it imperative to strengthen international cooperation at all levels in combating terrorism in a comprehensive manner. According to Chinese President Jiang Zemin, who spoke at this meeting: "A peaceful and stable environment is indispensable for sustained economic growth. Terrorism is a scourge that undermines stability. It is therefore a common task for people throughout the world to fight terrorism."[85]

## CONCLUSION

Today, international relations are going through complicated and profound changes, and elements of uncertainty are becoming increasingly salient in international situations. In the field of international arms control and disarmament, the integrity and authority of a well-established international disarmament legal system is being undermined. In the BW field, the U.S. rejection of the draft Protocol to the BWC led the almost seven-year-old talks into a serious impasse.

The Chinese have always maintained that the conclusion of a balanced and effective protocol through multilateral negotiations is the only feasible way to comprehensively strengthen the effectiveness of the BWC. With bioterrorism already becoming a real threat, one of the most effective ways to combat it is to work within the multilateral framework and conclude through negotiations a reasonable, feasible, and effective protocol on the basis of the existing mandate to strengthen the effectiveness of the BWC and enhance international cooperation.[86]

The conclusion of a protocol through negotiations to strengthen the effectiveness of the BWC is the common objective and long-standing aspiration of the international community. We have already covered a long and tortuous road in reaching our common goal, but there is still a long way to go.

Efforts to strengthen the Biological Weapons Convention by all state parties remind me of an ancient legend in China: "Hou Yi shoots down the suns."[87] According to this legend, once upon a time there were ten suns in the sky, and all the fields, forests, and grassland were scorched. An archer named Hou Yi valiantly shot down the nine unnecessary and harmful suns, leaving but one. From then on, crops, trees, and grass grew normally. As a party to the Biological Weapons Convention, China will act in the spirit of Hou Yi and contribute to a world free from all weapons of mass destruction.

## NOTES

The opinions expressed in this article are those of the author and do not represent positions of any official bureau.

1. This account draws on Lu Hui, *The Past and Future of Nuclear, Biological, and Chemical Weapons* (Beijing: Military Science Press, 1991); and Sheldon Harris, "The Japanese Biological Warfare Programme: An Overview," in *Biological and Toxin Weapons: Research, Development and Use from the Middle Ages to 1945,* ed. Erhard Geissler and John Ellis van Courtland Moon (New York: Oxford University Press, 1999), 12,752.

2. Harris, "Japanese Biological Warfare Programme," 127.

3. Ibid., 137.

4. Lu, *Past and Future of Nuclear, Biological, and Chemical Weapons,* 413.

5. Harris, "Japanese Biological Warfare Programme," 141–42.

6. Wendy Barnaby, *The Plague Makers: The Secret World of Biological Warfare* (London: Vision Paperbacks, 1997), 103–4.

7. Lu, *Past and Future of Nuclear, Biological, and Chemical Weapons,* 413.

8. *The History of the War to Resist U.S. Aggression and Aid Korea,* ed. Shen Zonhong and Meng Zhaohui (Beijing: Military Science Press, 1988); Lu, *Past and Future of Nuclear, Biological, and Chemical Weapons,* 205–9; Qi DeXue, "Great Contributions Made by Zhou En lai in Guiding the War to Resist U.S. Aggression and Aid Korea," *China Military Collected Works* (Beijing: Military Science Press, 1997), 876; Stephen Endicott and Edward Hagerman, *The United States and Biological Warfare: Secrets from the Early Cold War and Korea* (Bloomington: Indiana University Press, 1998).

9. *History of the War.*

10. *People's Daily* (China) (25 February 1952).

11. *History of the War.*

12. Professor Stephen Endicott kindly provided me with the following references for official U.S. denials of the use of biological warfare in the Korean War. U.S. Secretary of State Dean Acheson denied that U.S. or UN forces had used or were using bacteriological warfare, *New York Times* (5 March 1952), 3, col. 6. On 11 March 1952, General Matthew Ridgway, head of the U.S. Far East Command, stated that Communist charges that the United States was using biological warfare lacked "scientific truth," *New York Times* (11 March 1952), 1, col. 3.

13. For example, the navigator of the 8th Bomb Squadron 5th Bombing Group, 3rd Bomb Wing, Lieutenant Enoch, and the pilot of the 8th Bomb Sqaudron 3rd Bomb Group, 3rd Bomb Wing, Lieutenant Quinn, confessed that the U.S. Armed Forces on 1 January 1952 initiated biological warfare in North Korea on the territory of which they themselves dropped bacteria bombs on January 3 and January 10 respectively; see Jiang Siyi, ed., *The Big Event Dictionary of the PLA* (Tianjin: Tianjin People's Publishing House, 1992), 1170–71.

14. Stephen Endicott and Edward Hagerman, Response to Milton Leitenberg, "New Russian Evidence on the Korean War Biological Warfare Allegations: Background and Analysis," 5 July 1999; available online at www.yorku.ca/sendicott/ ReplytoMiltonLeitenberg.htm (30 March 2002). This article originally appeared on the Internet Cold War International History Project of the Woodrow Wilson International Center for Scholars in response to the article by Milton Leitenberg, at cwihp.si.edu.

15. The countries were the Soviet Union, German Democratic Republic, Czecho-

slovakia, Poland, Romania, Bulgaria, Hungary, Albania, Vietnam, Mongolia, India, Pakistan, Burma, Japan, Indonesia, Iran, Lebanon, Australia, United Kingdom, France, Holland, Italy, Switzerland, Belgium, Denmark, Sweden, Finland, Norway, and many South and Central American countries.

16. Xu Qingyi, "Review and Prospect of the Development of Biotechnology in China," *Progress in Biotechnology* 15(1) (1995), 5.

17. Ibid., 3.

18. See Guideline to the 9th Five Year Plan of National Science and Technology Development and 2010 Long Range Perspective.

19. Xu Qingyi, "Review and Prospect of Biotechnology Developments in China," *Progress in Biotechnology* 16(1) (1996), 2.

20. Ibid., 4.

21. Ibid.

22. Mang Keqiang, "Grasping Chance, Catching up with the Trend," *Progress in Biotechnology* 19(5) (1999), 5.

23. Hong Lang, "The Development and Production of Biotechnology in the Pharmaceutical Industry," *Progress in Biotechnology* 15(2) (1955), 3.

24. Meng Guangzhen, "On Strategic Programme for the Development of Biotechnology toward the Year of 2000," *Progress in Biotechnology* 15(2) (1995), 3.

25. Ren Dequan, "The Protection of Intellectual Property of Pharmaceutical and Biotechnological Products," *Progress in Biotechnology* 13(5) (1993), 53.

26. Ibid., 54.

27. Wang Lianqin, "The State of Affairs of Patent Protection of Abroad Bio-technological Drugs in China," *Progress in Biotechnology* 15(2) (1995), 48.

28. Ren, "Protection of Intellectual Property of Pharmaceutical and Biotechnological Products," 53.

29. *Foreign Affairs Documents, P. R. China,* 2 (13 July 1952), 77.

30. Information Office of the State Council of the People's Republic of China (IOSC), *China: Arms Control and Disarmament* (Beijing: IOSC, November 1995), 26.

31. Statement by the Chinese delegation at 27th UN Assembly in 1972.

32. Ibid.

33. IOSC, *China: Arms Control and Disarmament,* 26–27.

34. Vice Foreign Minister Qian Qichen's explanation in the Standing Committee of the People's Congress of China's accession to the BWC, 15 September 1984.

35. Ibid.

36. Foreign Minister Wu Xueqian's letter, 15 November 1984, to the foreign ministers of the United States, USSR, and United Kingdom on China's ratification of the BWC.

37. Ibid.

38. Working paper presented by China to Expert Meeting of P5 Arms Control Meeting, February 1992.

39. Barnaby, *Plague Makers,* 34.

40. IOSC, *China: Arms Control and Disarmament,* 191.

41. Sha Zukang, "The Future of Multilateral Arms Control," paper presented at 8th International Arms Control Conference on "New Horizons and New Strategies in Arms Control," 3 April 1998, Albuquerque, New Mexico.

42. Ibid.

43. Information Office of the State Council of the People's Republic of China, *China's National Defense* (Beijing: IOSC, July 1998), 40–42.

44. Ibid., 46–47.

45. Sha Zukang, "Some Thoughts on Non-Proliferation," paper presented at 7th Annual Carnegie International Non-Proliferation Conference on Repairing the Regime, 11–12 January 1999, Washington, D.C.

46. "India Urged to Stop Slandering China: Chinese Ambassador to India Zhou Gang in an Interview with Four Major English Newspapers in New Delhi on July 17," *China Daily* (20 July 1998), 4.

47. Zou Yunhua, *Chinese Perspectives on the South Asian Nuclear Tests* (Stanford, Calif.: CISAC, Stanford University, January 1999).

48. IOSC, *China's National Defense*, 48.

49. IOSC, *China: Arms Control and Disarmament*, 191.

50. China's Positions on Issues of Arms Control and Disarmament; available online at www.fmprc.gov.cn.

51. Sha, "Some Thoughts on Non-Proliferation."

52. Hou Zhitong, Statement at Third Review Conference of the Parties to the Biological Weapons Convention, Geneva, 12 September 1991; Sha Zukang, Statement at the Fourth Review Conference of the Parties to the Biological Weapons Convention, Geneva, 26 November 1996.

53. Sha, Statement at the Fourth Review Conference.

54. Ibid.

55. IOSC, *China: Arms Control and Disarmament*, 191.

56. Report to the UN by Chinese government on Seven Confidence Building Measures, 15 March 1992.

57. Sha, "Some Thoughts on Non-Proliferation"; Sha, Statement at the Fourth Review Conference.

58. Sha, Statement at the Fourth Review Conference.

59. Ambassador (to UN) Qin Huasun, speech at an informal BWC meeting of foreign ministers sponsored by Australia, 23 September 1998.

60. Lu, *Past and Future of Nuclear, Biological, and Chemical Weapons*, 460–61.

61. Information Office of the State Council of the People's Republic of China, "Arms Control and Disarmament," in *China's National Defense in 2000* (Beijing: IOSC, October 2000), 66.

62. BWC Ad Hoc Group of the States Parties to the BWC, Working Paper Submitted by China, "Declaration Formats," 3 July 1998, BWC/Ad Hoc Group/WP.291.

63. Speech by Ambassador Hu Xiaodi of the Chinese Delegation at the First Committee of the 55th UN Assembly, 3 October 2000.

64. BWC Ad Hoc Group of States Parties, Working Paper Submitted by the United Kingdom, BWC/AD HOC GROUP/WP.347, 19 January 1999.

65. Statement by Mr. Gu Ziping, Deputy Director-General of Arms Control and Disarmament Department, Ministry of Foreign Affairs of China, in the Ad Hoc Group of States Parties to the BWC, Geneva, 10 July 2000.

66. BWC Ad Hoc Group of the States Parties to the BWC, Working Paper Sub-

mitted by China, "Clarification Procedures and Voluntary Visit," BWC/Ad Hoc Group/WP.338., 7 January 1999.

67. Henrietta Wilson, "Strengthening the BWC: Issues for the Ad Hoc Group," *Disarmament Diplomacy* 42 (December 1999), 32–33.

68. Statement by Gu Ziping in the Ad Hoc Group of States Parties to the BWC.

69. Ad Hoc Group of the States Parties to the Biological Weapons Convention, Working Paper Submitted by the NAM and Other States, BWC/AD HOC GROUP/ WP.402, 22 September 1999.

70. Zou Yunhua, "China and the CTBT Negotiation," Stanford (Stanford, Calif.: CISAC, 1998), 19.

71. Statement by Gu Ziping in the Ad Hoc Group of States Parties to the BWC.

72. IOSC, "Arms Control and Disarmament," 66.

73. Sha, Statement at the Fourth Review Conference of BWC.

74. "Virus Genetic Map Cracked," *Weekly Watch of Beijing Review* 43(4) (24 January 2000), 4.

75. Xu Qingyi, "Retrospect and Prospect of China's Biotechnology Development," *Progress in Biotechnology* 15(1) (1995), 3; Wang Qinnan, "China Participates in Global Human Genome Program," *Biological Engineering Research* 15(1) (1995), 16.

76. Statement by General Qian Shaojun of the Chinese delegation at the NTB Ad Hoc Committee, 26 January 1996.

77. Henrietta Wilson, "Strengthening the BWC: Issues for the Ad Hoc Group," *Disarmament Diplomacy* 42 (December 1999), 28.

78. Sha Zukang, "Non-Proliferation at A Crossroads," address at Wilton Park Conference, 14 December 1999.

79. Speech by Ambassador Hu Xiaodi of the Chinese Delegation at the First Committee of the 55th UN Assembly, 3 October 2000.

80. Jenni Rissanen, "A Turning Point to Nowhere? BWC in Trouble as US Turns Its Back on Verification Protocol," *Disarmament Diplomacy* 59 (July/August 2001), 12.

81. Ibid.

82. Ambassador Hu Xiao Di, speech presented at the 24th Session of the BWC Ad Hoc Group, 17 August 2001.

83. "Washington: 29 Cases of Anthrax Exposure Confirmed," *China Daily* (18 October 2001), 1.

84. Jiang Zhuqing, "Nation on High Alert for Anthrax," *China Daily* (17 October 2001), 1.

85. Xinhua, "Chinese President Delivers Speech at APEC Economic Leaders Meeting," *China Daily* (21 October 2001), 1.

86. Statement by Ambassador Sha Zukang, Head of Delegation of the People's Republic of China at the Fifth Review Conference of BWC, Geneva, 19 November 2001.

87. Yuan Ke, *Dragons and Dynasties—An Introduction to Chinese Mythology*, trans. Kim Echlin and Ni Zhixiong (New York: Penguin Books, 1993), 74–79.

# 9

## India

### Straddling East and West

*P. R. Chari and Giri Deshingkar*

### THE CONFLICTING PARADIGMS

Rudyard Kipling's much-quoted aphorism "Oh, East is East, and West is West, and never the twain shall meet"[1] underscored his conviction that a civilizational chasm divided the Orient from the Occident, and a similar gulf characterizes differences between developing and developed nations. These generalizations are of limited applicability to India, however, since India does not conform to the stereotype of a developing country. India lies astride the developed and developing worlds. Its achievements in advanced technologies such as atomic energy, space research, aerospace, information systems software, and biotechnology underlie its approaches to global issues such as environmental problems, economic liberalization and globalization, and disarmament. Its pursuit of a nonaligned foreign policy after Independence was designed to further its national self-interest. Nonalignment has enabled India to balance its foreign policy between the Eastern and Western blocs and has shaped its stands on international issues.

When considering arms control and disarmament issues, we must recognize three crucial differences between India and the developing world. First, India has unique security concerns that set it apart from either the West or developing countries. Western nations are greatly concerned with the threat from weapons of mass destruction (WMD). More recently, their focus has shifted from nuclear weapons to the prospect of fissile materials leaking out of the former Soviet Republics and to the threat of chemical and biological

239

weapons. According to U.S. Under Secretary of State for Arms Control and International Security John Holum, although chemical weapons (CW) are more suitable for terrorist activity, biological weapons are "better classified closer to nuclear weapons in terms of their massive destructive potential."[2] Biological weapons are cheap, easy to manufacture, and spectacular in their destructive capabilities; they could become the weapons of choice for "rogue" states, and nonstate actors like religious terrorists who are not constrained by social responsibilities.[3]

Western perceptions of national security have become more sensitized to nonmilitary threats in recent years, notably those associated with terrorism. These perceptions have greatly heightened after the devastating attacks on the World Trade towers in New York and the Pentagon building in Washington on September 11, 2001. The use of the postal service to mail anthrax spores has dramatically added to fears and anxieties regarding biological weapons all over the world, especially with regard to their possession by religious terrorist organizations such as the Taliban and al Qaeda. These threats stem from resurgent subnationalist assertions of ethnic distinction and autonomy and religious fundamentalism.

Internal challenges to Western political structures are small because their polities have stabilized over the centuries since the Treaty of Westphalia was signed in 1648. The same cannot be said of developing countries. These came into existence when the colonial system unraveled, but they mainly remain in various stages of national and state consolidation. They are under siege from within due to historical, ethnic, religious, and tribal tensions that were papered over during colonial rule. A "decompression" effect exacerbated these dormant internal conflicts after independence. Nonetheless, the ruling elites of these countries often remain fixated on external military threats, even though internal and nonmilitary sources of insecurity such as financial instability, ethnic strife, terrorism, drug smuggling, small arms proliferation, environmental degradation, climate change, migration, and crises of governance are now more relevant to their national security.[4] Weapons of mass destruction are seen by them as a relatively minor threat. India is somewhat unique among decolonized countries in its deep concern with a nuclear threat, from Pakistan, especially given the ongoing Indo–Pak conflict in Kashmir.

India's differing perceptions of the major threats to its national security have influenced its choice of instruments for addressing these concerns, and this is a second area in which India is unique. Neither Western nor Third World countries have hesitated to use military force to ensure their national security. But the readiness of the Western nations to use their arms superiority against developing countries—as was dramatized by the NATO air war over Kosovo and the attempts to destroy Osama bin Laden and disrupt his al Qaeda organization in Afghanistan and elsewhere in the Muslim world—

predisposes developing countries toward acquiring WMDs to redress the gross military imbalance. The assiduous efforts by Iraq and several Middle Eastern countries to acquire chemical, biological, and nuclear weapons to neutralize the military superiority of the United States and Israel illustrates this. India, too, subscribes to such thinking. One reason it originally pursued development of nuclear capabilities, culminating in the "peaceful" nuclear explosion of 1974, was the nuclear threat embodied in the American Task Force, led by the USS *Enterprise*, which entered the Bay of Bengal during the Indo–Pak war in 1971. This was seen as an act of gunboat diplomacy.

Third, India is unique in its perspective on nonproliferation initiatives and policies. The nonproliferation policies of the Western nations are implemented by technology control/denial regimes like the Nuclear Suppliers Group, the Missile Technology Control Regime, the Australia Group, the Wassenaar Arrangement, and the European Union (EU) dual-use regulations. The last of these "creates a legal framework under which EU member states could be exempted from licensing and reporting requirements under the CWC and establishes an export control regime for all countries irrespective of whether or not they are a party to the CWC."[5] These regimes prohibit the export of sensitive technologies and regulate the flow of dual-use technologies. The United States in particular supplements these regimes with a coercive "counter-proliferation" policy premised on intelligence gathering, which includes National Technical Means (that is, satellite-based intelligence), interdiction of suspect technology and materials transfers, as well as use of military force to dissuade aspirant nations from acquiring WMDs.

Developed countries believe this approach will slow down WMD proliferation, but there are at least three reasons to think that it may fail. First, a determined aspirant nation can always acquire prohibited materials, equipment, and technology if it is willing to make the necessary financial and political sacrifices. Commercial greed, often in connivance with government agencies, can motivate private entities in technologically advanced nations to facilitate such acquisition, and this has contributed greatly to WMD proliferation in the past.

Second, the inexorable global diffusion of technology makes it progressively easier for WMD aspirants to acquire prohibited technologies, either through indigenous efforts or the importation of dual-use items. There have been several cases of sensitive technologies leaking. Furthermore, nations like North Korea, Pakistan, and China have no qualms about either stealing or exporting sensitive technologies, despite their obligations and commitments to the international nuclear regime.[6]

Third, technology denial cannot address the factors that compel nations to acquire hi-tech weapons, including WMDs. These factors cannot be dismissed as contrived since they are largely driven by security concerns and only marginally by prestige considerations. Suspected linkages between Pakistan and China in the nuclear and missile areas, for instance, have molded India's nuclear security concerns.[7] Pakistan's actions are similarly informed by the nuclear threat it perceives from India.[8]

India's policy toward technology-denial and control regimes elsewhere is ambivalent because of its differing interests and reservations concerning them. Lax export controls in some countries have enabled Pakistan to acquire its nuclear capabilities. However, strict export controls in other countries have deprived India of access to dual-purpose technologies for its own developmental purposes. India's record in not transferring sensitive technologies remains impeccable.

From an Indian perspective, there is an anomaly in the efforts of the Nuclear Five countries (N-5) to prohibit weapons of mass destruction: They insist upon the elimination of biological and chemical weapons, although their own record here is hardly inspiring. Furthermore, they are unwilling to commit themselves to eliminating their own nuclear arsenals within any foreseeable time frame. On the contrary, their policy declarations suggest they would continue to possess nuclear weapons in perpetuity, despite the obligations accepted by them under the Nuclear Non-Proliferation Treaty (NPT).

For instance, the North Atlantic Treaty Organization's Strategic Concept, which was declared on the organization's fiftieth anniversary, states that its "nuclear forces no longer target any country. Nonetheless, NATO will maintain, at the minimum level consistent with the prevailing security environment, adequate sub-strategic forces based in Europe which will provide an essential link with strategic nuclear forces reinforcing the transatlantic link."[9] A semi-official American report also declares that nuclear weapons are required to meet the WMD threat from state and nonstate actors. It adds: "By 2018 the United States will presumably have destroyed all its chemical and biological stocks; therefore, the right mix [of weaponry] would be a robust nuclear force useful for retaliatory purposes, plus precision-guided conventional weapons plus, perhaps, a doctrine of No First Use (NFU) of WMD that has political value."[10] The commitment to nuclear weapons to preserve its deterrent value is clear from the Bush administration's determination to deploy the National Missile Defense (NMD) and to take unilateral action and withdraw from the long-standing Anti-Ballistic Missile Treaty, to achieve this end.

In contrast, India has traditionally supported the demand for comprehensive and complete disarmament, and this position has remained unchanged even after its nuclear tests in May 1998 and its proclaiming itself thereafter to be a nuclear-weapons power. At the same time, India's nuclear policy has also been influenced by the Western nuclear powers, resulting in a policy characterized by considerable ambivalence. This question is discussed further below.

In sum, India's disarmament postures straddle those of the developed and developing countries. This chapter considers first how India's approach to disarmament has been shaped both by its larger security framework and its commercial interests. Second, the chapter examines India's approaches to the negotiation of the Chemical Weapons Convention (CWC) in the late 1980s and early 1990s and how these approaches have influenced its later approach to the negotiations, initiated in 1995, for a Protocol to ensure compliance with the Biological Weapons Convention (BWC). Finally, India's positions on specific issues during the negotiation of the BWC Protocol are examined.

## INDIAN TRADE AND SECURITY INTERESTS

India's position on Trade Related Intellectual Property Rights (TRIPS) changed radically during the GATT negotiations. It initially opposed the Western position but later supported it. The reversal reflected Western pressure and India's realization that it was isolated within the developing world. The TRIPS concept was unveiled in 1986 during the Uruguay ministerial meeting of the GATT contracting parties; it was designed to promote free trade, open markets, and ease the global flow of goods and services. The developing countries, however, saw it as a device to force open their economies to Western exploitation by eroding Third World restrictions on foreign investments, by erecting nontariff barriers, and by reducing farm subsidies.

India, along with Brazil, made concerted efforts to delay this dispensation, but failed to stem the Western, particularly American, pressure on the developing countries. The collapse of the Soviet Union and disarray within the G-77 countries ensured that the concerted assault of the G-7 nations would ultimately succeed in securing passage of the TRIPS agreement. India was one of the last countries to succumb.[11] This explains India's change of policy during the negotiations: It had shared the concerns of the developing countries earlier but caved in later to join the developed nations.

The interests of India's pharmaceutical industry, situated within both its private and public sectors, significantly shaped India's position on TRIPS. Generally, firms with foreign collaborations, and also the Indian scientific/industrial research community, favored TRIPS and a more rigorous patenting regime, but indigenous companies vehemently opposed this. Generally speaking, again, the Indian private sector has, with some exceptions, invested little in research, which is largely carried out in state-financed laboratories. "In the field of plant biotechnology, for instance, the major innovations have arisen from work in the public sector. For example, the development of the particle bombardment approach to transgenesis, the gene markers used to study or obtain genetically engineered plants, the development of Restriction Fragment Length Polymorphisms (RFLP) to enhance genetic mapping, have all emerged from laboratories and concepts in the public domain funded by taxpayers."[12] In this milieu, the state-financed laboratories and their umbrella organization, the Council on Scientific and Industrial Research, strongly favored a strict patent regime that would ensure them credit and royalties for their effort and enterprise. These general attitudes of the scientific bureaucracy strongly influenced the Indian government's position on TRIPS.[13]

Indian perceptions of and positions on major security issues, similarly, do not fit the stereotypes of either developed or developing countries. The Indian security community increasingly realizes that the real threats to national security arise from internal causes. Yet its external dimensions—principally the threat from Pakistan and China—claim greater attention from policymakers. The adversaries are nuclear-weapons states. Had the Indo–Pak conflict in the Himalayas (May–July 1999) and the subsequent confrontation between the Indian and Pakistani armed forces along the border in 2001–02 not been defused, escalation to the nuclear level was not inconceivable. India perceives a nuclear threat from state entities, but it sees a chemical and biological warfare (CBW) threat primarily from nonstate actors like religious and political terrorist groups.[14] Islamic terrorist groups have conducted attacks with bombs and explosives in different parts of India. These include spectacular attacks on the State Legislative Assembly in Kashmir in October 2001 and the Indian Parliament itself in December 2001. Terrorists might also use biological and chemical weapons to promote their cause as these become progressively easier to manufacture or procure.

The United States believes a CBW threat exists because, in the words of former U.S. Energy Secretary Bill Richardson, the "Chemical Weapons Convention and the Biological Weapons Convention remain ignored by some countries we suspect of having offensive chemical and biological capabilities—including regimes believed to support terrorism."[15] Besides, "It is possible, however, that groups, especially extremist groups with no ties to a particular state, could acquire and attempt to use such weapons in the future. The March 1995 attack on the Tokyo subway by the religious group Aum Shinrikyo using the nerve agent sarin . . . crossed a psychological boundary and showed that the use of [nuclear, biological and chemical] weapons was no longer restricted to the traditional battlefield."[16] This perception has dispelled the earlier notion that the use of chemical and biological weapons by political extremists, especially religious terrorists, was unthinkable. It has also shifted attention from the earlier fixation on nuclear weapons to the other types of weapons of mass destruction, chemical and biological weapons. According to a report in 1999, al Qaeda had obtained biological and chemical weapons and planned to use them, not only against Israeli and American targets but also against targets in India.[17] These extremist groups were active in Kashmir during and after the Kargil conflict.

India and the United States have jointly identified international terrorism to be a major threat to their security, and this may explain why India shares U.S. views on the CBW threat from terrorists acting in concert with states inimical to India.[18]

In 2000, India and the United States established a consultative mechanism to counter international terrorism and finalized a draft convention against terrorism for presentation to the millennium summit of the United Nations.[19] Like the United States and other developed countries, India has been the victim of "anthrax mail" attacks, currently being employed by unidentified criminal or terrorist groups. Several of them have proved to be hoaxes, but their intention is obviously to cause alarm and disruption. The resulting erosion of public confidence in the ability of the government to counter this form of biowarfare is, perhaps, the true intention underlying these attacks.

On the question of nuclear policy, India's position shifted somewhat after its five nuclear tests in May 1998; it now conforms largely to that adopted by the Western nuclear countries, while still genuflecting toward the developing and nonaligned nations. On the one hand, India has a long history of support for nuclear disarmament, and elements of its policy continue that tradition. For example, India has declared a moratorium on nuclear testing and a no-first-use policy. In 1999, India called for "an international conference to prepare a plan of action before the start of the new millennium for the complete elimination of nuclear weapons and the conclusion of a global Nuclear Weapons Convention."[20] It also tabled a resolution in the UN General Assembly for "de-alerting" nuclear weapons in national inventories. Such proposals stand in sharp contrast to the refusal of NATO countries to contemplate a no-first-use declaration, their decision to continue possessing nuclear weapons, and their stress on the centrality of nuclear deterrence in their strategic doctrine.[21]

On the other hand, India has embraced the goal of establishing a "credible minimum nuclear deterrent" that echoes the present NATO policy. Despite the commitment to pursue negotiations aimed at halting the nuclear arms race and achieving nuclear disarmament made in the Nuclear Non-Proliferation Treaty and also expressed in other nuclear arms control agreements such as the Limited Test Ban Treaty (1963), the Threshold Test Ban Treaty (1974),[22] and the Comprehensive Test Ban Treaty (1996),[23] the revised NATO doctrine notes that the Alliance will "maintain adequate nuclear forces in Europe. These forces need to have the necessary characteristics and appropriate flexibility and survivability, to be perceived as a credible and effective element of the Allies' strategy in preventing war. They will be maintained at the minimum level sufficient to preserve peace and stability."[24] Such a formulation resonates with India's own officially declared nuclear doctrine, which states: "Ours will be a minimum credible deterrent, which will safeguard India's security, the security of one-sixth of humanity, now and in the future. The National Security Council, with the assistance of its subsidiary bodies . . . will make important contributions to elaborating these concepts."[25] India's own declared credible minimum deterrent posture thus closely resembles NATO's minimal deterrent stance. This resemblance supports the view that although Indian security policy encompasses elements characteristic of both the nuclear and the nonnuclear powers, the positions of the nuclear powers have been more influential. No doubt there are important exceptions here, as, for example, with respect to no first use, discussed above.

## THE CWC AS PRELUDE TO
## THE BWC PROTOCOL

India actively participated in the negotiations of the Conference on Disarmament that yielded the Chemical Weapons Convention in 1993, and cosponsored the draft text in the UN General Assembly. It was an original state party to the CWC, which it ratified on September 3, 1996, ahead of Pakistan and China. This was despite strong opposition from its armed forces, which were convinced that Pakistan and China had chemical weapons stockpiles and manufacturing facilities that they would not admit to. India also exhorted Pakistan and other countries to join the CWC,[26] and it established a national authority under the cabinet secretary to collate information and fulfill its obligations under the CWC. India became the first Chair of the Executive Council of the Organization for the Prohibition of Chemical Weapons (OPCW) in May 1997 and was elected to the Executive Council for two consecutive two-year terms.

According to the Indian Ministry of External Affairs, "India believes that by agreeing to this unique disarmament treaty, the international community confirms its serious commitment to laying down the foundations of a new global security framework that is based on goodwill, understanding and cooperation. This is consistent with India's position in favor of the elimination of all weapons of mass destruction on the basis of multilaterally negotiated, nondiscriminatory agreements which provide for equal rights and obligations of all parties involved."[27] These broad principles have also guided India during the ongoing negotiations on the BWC Protocol, although the perception among its negotiators is that the intrinsic nature of, and therefore the verification problems associated with, the BWC and CWC are very different.

During the CWC negotiations, India initially sought to balance the CWC's transparency and confidentiality provisions but eventually accepted its highly intrusive verification provisions because they constituted a universal nonproliferation and disarmament regime. India recognized the need for transparency and effective national implementation of its obligations under the CWC. The BWC and CWC contain similar provisions, so one can assume that India's negotiating experience with the CWC influenced its views on negotiating the BWC Protocol. Yet it would be simplistic to assume that the two Conventions are identical, and India believes that "it would not be possible for the verification regime laid down in the Chemical Weapons Convention to be replicated in the BWC."[28]

An important difference between the contexts of the two conventions is that the chemical industry is older and more established than the biotechnology industry; it is less likely to witness radical discoveries or changes in its manufacturing processes. The biotechnology industry, on the other hand, is new, dynamic, and fast-growing, and industry leaders have "argued that [it] is more vulnerable to loss of proprietary information than the chemical industry."[29] A further difference is that, unlike chemical weapons, biological materials intended for military purposes can be rapidly produced and easily destroyed. These essential differences came to influence India's rethinking on the CWC's highly intrusive verification provisions, and the ease with which "challenge" inspections could be launched under it. India now believes this could prejudice the confidentiality of proprietary information about pharmaceutical products while doing nothing to detect illegal activity. Nevertheless, India does appreciate the need for transparency and for effectively implementing statutory commitments accepted under the BWC.

An explanation is necessary for India's declarations regarding its stocks of chemical weapons and old or abandoned chemical weapons, as well as its chemical weapons production facilities. Article III mandated such declarations within thirty days of the CWC entering into force. India's declarations to the Organization for the Prohibition of Chemical Weapons (OPCW) in mid-1997 admitted to the possession of chemical weapons and manufacturing facilities, and the OPCW inspected a chemical weapons facility at Gwalior run by the Defense Research and Development Organization (DRDO) in July and a laboratory at Ozra in August 1997.[30] But India requested that this information be excluded from the OPCW inspection report to the first Conference of the States Parties.[31]

India had issued a joint declaration with Pakistan in August 1992 on the complete prohibition of chemical weapons and had agreed to discuss a similar declaration on biological weapons.[32] Under this joint declaration both countries would never "develop, produce or otherwise acquire chemical weapons; or . . . use chemical weapons; or . . . assist, encourage or induce, in any way, anyone to engage in development, production, acquisition, stockpiling or use of chemical weapons."[33] Understandably, India's admission to possessing chemical weapons and its production facilities in 1997, five years after the joint declaration, led to alarm and derision in Pakistan. The Pakistani Foreign Office spokesman declared: "This revelation raises serious questions about [the] sincerity of India's commitment solemnly undertaken in its bilateral agreement with Pakistan and the international conventions."[34] We might add that it also raised doubts globally about India's commitment to the nonproliferation goal.

India's official explanation was that "Our declarations have been complete and in keeping with our commitment to the CWC. We are an original signatory and original State Party. Many other countries that had declared their intention to be an original State Party held back their ratifications. Our approach was to lead through example and it is encouraging that Pakistan has followed us. We can only hope that Pakistan's declaration is made with the same degree of commitment as is reflected in the Indian declaration."[35] Informal inquiries reveal that bureaucratic ineptitude—not unknown in governments—was responsible for this faux pas. Despite several inter-ministerial consultations, the DRDO did not inform other agencies about its chemical weapons program, nor was it specifically consulted before the External Affairs Ministry committed India to the joint declaration with Pakistan in 1992 or when India joined and ratified the CWC in 1996. Why the DRDO did not destroy its stocks of chemical weapons at any stage before India ratified the CWC in 1996 remains a mystery.

India derived some satisfaction from the knowledge that its confession of a chemical weapons program, despite knowing that considerable opprobrium would greet its declaration, was much appreciated by the international community.[36] OPCW Director General Jose Bustani held this out as an example worthy of emulation by other countries.[37] When judging India's conduct, remember that in addition to the United States, Russia, and Iraq, which had publicly admitted to possessing chemical weapons, six other countries, including India, China, and South Korea, also declared that they had chemical weapons and possessed production facilities.[38] Indeed, the United States was in violation of the CWC after ratifying it, as it had not promulgated guidelines for U.S. chemical industries to comply with the Convention's data declarations and inspections.[39] The general lesson from this episode is the need for complete transparency to allow for discovery of past infractions of the provisions of the CWC and for establishing national organizations to oversee future compliance. Effective verification and implementation procedures are essential for ensuring the regime's credibility.

Two further aspects of the CWC's implementation processes may influence India's approaches to the BWC Protocol. First, India has noted that "national implementing legislation containing provisions which undermine the Convention hold out the prospect of leading to matching responses by other states parties thereby leading to an unnecessary dilution to [sic] the spirit of confidence reposed in the CWC by a great majority of countries party to the CWC."[40] This circumlocutory language expresses India's concern over the approach taken in U.S. legislation to implement the CWC. That legislation ensured limits to the number of annual inspections, required testing of U.S. samples only in the United States, and empowered the U.S. president to block inspections for national security reasons.[41]

Article VII of the CWC requires that "Each State Party shall, in accordance with its constitutional processes, adopt the necessary measures to implement its obligations under this Convention." In other words, the CWC requires state parties to enact domestic legislation that will strengthen its implementation. But the U.S. legislation instead weakens its execution and thus erodes faith in the CWC's verification regime. This will adversely influence negotiations to enact similar provisions in the Protocol to the BWC now consigned to limbo and will set a bad precedent for other countries and other arms control negotiations. All this could also unravel the basic features of the Chemical Weapons Convention. As noted by one U.S. expert, "U.S. national security interests will be best served by the full and effective monitoring of the CWC's prohibitions. Congress and the Clinton Administration cannot lead the fight against chemical weapons proliferation by undermining the CWC's crucial monitoring provisions."[42]

Second, India has noted that "the existence of technology denial regimes such as the Australia Group (AG) remains an aberration when seen against the large number of ratifications the Convention has enjoyed so far."[43] The Australia Group, comprising some thirty developed nations, constitutes a self-appointed body to control the transfer of precursors to chemical weapons and equipment for producing CBW agents. Their "warning list" of chemicals differs from and expands upon the list of "scheduled chemicals" in the CWC and hence its export control system supercedes the CWC requirements.

The continuance of the Australia Group after the CWC's passage has been justified on the grounds that it provides its members with a joint forum to coordinate their export control policies and check CBW proliferation. It is further claimed that the two regimes (CWC and AG) are mutually reinforcing[44] and that the AG "signal(s) to a potential proliferator that it will not be able to play off one Australia Group member against another."[45] Furthermore, it is claimed that the possession of both chemical and biological weapons by Iraq and the Aum Shinrikyo calls for great caution in the export of chemical and biological precursors, especially since there are no verification mechanisms in the BWC.[46] Finally, it has been pointed out that several NAM members have yet to pass enabling domestic legislation to implement the provisions of the CWC—although apparently NAM members are slowly passing the required domestic legislation. Nevertheless, it is argued that some states might neglect to implement the BWC Protocol after it is completed.

Those outside the AG remain unconvinced by such arguments, seeing them as special pleadings to perpetuate a state of "technological apartheid." Part of India's objections to technology control and denial regimes arises from its unhappy experience with them; for example, it was once denied importation of a fertilizer plant based on the specious logic that it could be used to produce heavy water for use in a nuclear weapons program.[47] More generally, India sees the AG as both ineffective, for the reasons indicated previously, and unjustified in its application to members of the CWC in good standing. Subjecting parties in good standing with the CWC to further scrutiny of their requests by the Australia Group will only erode the value of the CWC; such dual scrutiny implies that Australia Group members have no faith in the CWC's verification and inspection procedures, to which they are adherents. Parallel arguments apply to the AG's coordination of export controls for biological agents and toxins that are permitted by the BWC for peaceful purposes.

## ISSUES IN NEGOTIATING THE BWC PROTOCOL

The negotiation of the BWC Protocol began in 1995, following a special conference of the state parties that established an Ad Hoc Group of the parties to the convention with a mandate to "consider appropriate measures" to strengthen the Convention, including a legally binding instrument. The negotiation of the BWC Protocol has raised several issues of particular importance to India and that are also fundamental for the implementation of the BWC.

### Access to Technology (BWC Article X)

Like the NPT and the CWC, the BWC encompasses both rights and obligations where access to technology is concerned. Whereas article III formulates an obligation on the part of each state party not to assist any state to manufacture or otherwise acquire biological weapons or their means of delivery, article X formulates the right of each party to "participate in the fullest possible exchange" of materials, equipment, and technical information for peaceful purposes. There is an inherent tension between these divergent objectives, and the emphasis could easily shift from the promotional to the regulatory aspects of these agreements. For the developed nations, nonproliferation is the dominant objective; for the developing countries, the assurance of developmental assistance is of prime significance. The bargain embodied in the NPT, CWC, and BWC is that developing countries would gain assured access to technology from developed countries in return for giving up their right to acquire WMDs. This bargain requires that both sets of countries honor their commitments. India's position is that this is not happening.

As discussed previously, the developed countries have established a web of technology control regimes whose prohibitions lie outside the NPT, CWC, and BWC schema, and it is realistic to assume that their prohibitions would mostly affect the least developed countries. Furthermore, the establishment of monopolies or oligopolies that achieve complete control over the production of pharmaceutical products (through, for example, patent regimes operating on purely commercial considerations) means that life-saving drugs may be priced out of the reach of developing countries.

With respect to the BWC, India recognizes the need to balance articles III and X, but it has consistently affirmed that article III should not be interpreted in a manner that impedes implementation of article X for parties in good standing. In the background is India's strong view that the Australia Group will lose validity and should be disbanded if the BWC Protocol ever enters into force and is replaced by multilateral export controls agreed upon within the framework of the BWC Protocol. Similar positions are supported by Iran, Pakistan, China, and Russia.[48] Also relevant is that in the 1990s access to new biological technologies became a particularly important issue because the availability of information about them has decreased in the decades since the BWC entered into force. This is due to increased commercial interest and increasingly stringent protection of proprietary information (see chapter 15). In this way the gap between the developed and developing countries has widened. Consequently, India emphasizes the need to promote "institutional ways and means of assuring cooperation between developed and developing countries . . . in such areas as medicine, public health and agriculture."[49]

Representatives of India also believe that the tension between the regulatory role of article III and the promotional role of article X should not be resolved at the expense of developing countries in good standing. According to Ambassador Arundhati Ghose: "The promotional aspects of article X are, we believe, a crucial element in strengthening the Convention and even perhaps in achieving universal adherence . . . It is essential that any control of dual use materials and technologies should not affect the socio-economic development of countries adversely, especially the development of developing countries."[50] In March 1997, India developed this view in a working paper submitted to the BWC Ad Hoc Group. To strengthen the implementation of article X, India proposed such measures as making available equipment and technologies developed by a state participating in the compliance regime for biological defense, collaborative research and development projects, joint ventures for biological defense including development of vaccines and diagnostic systems, and transfers of technology for the peaceful use of genetic engineering and biotechnology.[51]

Simultaneously, India accepted the need for "strengthened implementation of the provisions of article III [to] ensure that the cooperation envisaged under article X is not abused."[52] Ambassador Ghose stated at the Fourth

Review Conference: "We believe that [exports of biological materials and equipment] need not only to be monitored through declaration of exports, but regulated on the basis of guidelines to be negotiated and accepted by all States Parties, guidelines which should be multilaterally binding though nationally implemented, and which should be nondiscriminatory among States Parties." These guidelines would also "prohibit transfers to non-State political parties altogether," and "not only regulate the transfers of dual use products and technologies but also serve the promotional aspects of Article X."[53] In July 1997, India followed up on these ideas with a proposal to the Ad Hoc Group for guidelines regulating transfers of dual-use agents and equipment. Such transfers would require a declaration by the recipient to the exporting country providing information about the purpose of the transfer, the source of the materials, the quantity required, the final destination, intended use, and an end-use certificate, including information on secondary transfer, if any.[54]

## Commitment to Transparency

No verification procedure can ever be foolproof in ensuring compliance with the BWC, but strengthening such procedures can deter violations. The challenge lies in devising verification measures strong enough to discourage noncompliance but mild enough to gain the acceptance of the state parties. India is committed to ensuring a rational degree of transparency, including intrusive on-site verification measures that would simultaneously allow the protection of proprietary information. However, the BWC's implementation should not become an instrument for harassment. India participated in the Second and Third BWC Review Conferences (1986 and 1991), which led to the establishment of substantial confidence-building measures (CBMs), notably information exchanges on high-risk research laboratories, unusual outbreaks of disease, publications of relevant research, past biological warfare activities, human vaccine production, and legislation to implement the BWC.[55]

Over the years India's national interests have increasingly come to resemble those of Western nations in giving precedence to commercial secrecy over transparency to protect its pharmaceutical industry, especially manufacturers of traditional medicines. This is why India supports Japan's position that confidentiality should be maintained at all times by the establishment of a Confidentiality Commission, as was done in the case of the CWC. This would equally apply to all countries.[56] The industry's universal concerns regarding on-site inspections relate to "over-sampling and analysis of samples. But just as important are access to information, people, facilities, specific equipment, computer and written documents and the interest of the inspecting team to photograph and/or videotape various portions of the facility or perhaps even the entire visit."[57] National security considerations enter here. Concern that inspections may become "fishing expeditions" for military and industrial secrets has shaped India's views on intrusive verification measures. UNSCOM's Iraq experience shows that the problem of detecting prohibited activities and ensuring that state parties are in compliance with the BWC is not easy and can become highly controversial.

To address these divergent goals India joined Indonesia and Mexico in submitting a working paper to the Ad Hoc Group proposing that requests for dual-use agents, toxins, equipment, and technologies should be accompanied by detailed information as to their purpose, the location of the facility requiring them, and end-use certificates.[58] India also supported a verification regime that emphasizes declarations; it proposed submission of information on present and past bio-offence facilities, past bio-defense facilities, and other related facilities.[59] Declarations are essential to gain the basic information needed to monitor national biological weapons capabilities. Indeed, as the former director of the British Chemical and Biological Defense Establishment, Graham Pearson, says, "Mandatory declarations should be made for all facilities with high containment, all facilities using listed organisms, and national biological defense programs. These declarations should be underpinned by a low-key process to allow for further clarifications on declared items without the need for high-profile political or diplomatic activity."[60] According to John Steinbruner, a Senior Fellow formerly at the Brookings Institution, strong rules of disclosure would also ensure that "documenting compliance with those standards would provide continuous positive reassurance that relevant activities were being safely managed and exclusively devoted to legitimate purposes."[61]

Declarations, of course, need to be verified. A view still held by many Western states is that "an effective regime must accommodate a package of different types of visits, including some form of mandatory visits, which may be random and infrequent and still effective, to provide assurance that declarations are complete and accurate."[62] India is skeptical about this modality but not averse to such visits if a prior consultation process is established.[63] Most usefully, these visits could follow a random pattern, familiarize inspectors with the layout of sensitive facilities, and clarify the contents of declarations made. However, the United States is lukewarm toward such visits due to the strong opposition of its pharmaceutical and biotechnology industries. It would want them to be undertaken in only the most circumscribed manner to clarify specific ambiguities in the declarations made.[64] The United States is also averse to mandatory visits and random selection of facilities, for that matter, to any form of intrusive verification. This goes to the heart of the compliance system envisaged by the BWC Protocol. The exclusion of the United States from this dispensation is obviously not the answer, since this would eviscerate the Protocol altogether. To effect a compromise, the United Kingdom suggested "transparency visits" in the nature of "briefing tours," in addition to randomly selected visits. India joined the NAM (Non-Aligned Movement) group in proposing a different compromise, which envisions visits being initiated by the state party concerned, for clarification purposes. The NAM working paper was included in the rolling text.[65]

The primary Indian concern is that "visits" could be transformed into "investigations"; hence the modalities become important. There is a further Indian interest in the need to "protect sensitive commercial proprietary information and legitimate national security concerns."[66] India supports the idea that "visits should take place on the basis of proportionality—that is, the visits should be focused mostly on those countries with the most facilities."[67] As noted previously, the influence of private companies in the pharmaceutical and biotechnology sectors is steadily growing with the liberalization and globalization of the Indian economy. Their interests, coupled with those of the concerned scientific community, are influencing the government's approach to the BWC negotiations. These diverse interests could be reconciled by the technique known as "managed access" that is used for CWC inspections. According to the U.S. Arms Control and Disarmament Agency, this "allows for the negotiation between the inspection team and the States Party industrial site team to find the means to satisfactorily answer the questions posed by the inspecting team . . . [which] would presumably also be appropriate for the inspection of national defense facilities as they have similar concerns over loss of sensitive national security information."[68] It is possible that India might find such a procedure acceptable.

In contrast to visits, challenge inspections are intended to investigate specific complaints of noncompliance; they involve inspections of suspect facilities or field visits to investigate suspicious outbreaks of disease. They could also be used to discover undeclared sites or activities. BWC adherents are divided about what should be the triggering mechanism to launch challenge inspections. The "red light" procedure in the CWC requires three-fourths of the state parties to vote against a challenge inspection going ahead. The "green light" modality requires three-fourths of the state parties to vote in favor of the challenge inspection. India favors a "green light" procedure to check frivolous requests, with the qualification that decisions are reached within a specified time frame.[69] It is assumed that decisions would be taken by an executive council elected by the parties to the Protocol.

On a practical level, there should be greater awareness that illicit biological warfare activities can be easily concealed within legitimate industrial enterprises and can be quickly destroyed to avoid detection. Continuous surveillance of suspect facilities, coupled with drawing of samples on a real-time basis to assay by different technical means, may satisfy absolute verification requirements, but this requires a degree of intrusiveness that will never gain acceptance. This conclusion offers cold comfort to those who believe that it is possible to devise a verification system that could detect illegal activities under the BWC with complete certitude. Complete verification may not be possible in absolute terms, but support is needed for efforts to put in place the verification means that *are* possible but are currently absent in the BWC.

There is much sensitivity in India to foreign teams investigating "unusual" outbreaks of diseases, given the fact that epidemics occur regularly due to the country's inadequate public health services and sanitation conditions. Some of this sensitivity also stems from the possibility that "field investigations might provide a quicker and easier access to sensitive facilities than a facility investigation."[70] India therefore believes that such investigations should properly lie within the domain of other specialized bodies like the World Health Organization and the Centers for Disease Control in the United States. Toward this end, India, along with China, Cuba, and Indonesia, submitted a working paper arguing that "All natural outbreaks of disease do not pose a compliance concern to the Convention and therefore shall not be a cause for an investigation of a noncompliance concern. The diseases which are endemic in the region and present the expected epidemiological features shall not be considered as a unusual outbreak of disease."[71] However, the affected state party would expeditiously investigate such outbreaks in accordance with prescribed guidelines.

## CONCLUSION

The essence of India's concerns with regard to the Verification Protocol was expressed in a summation of its position to the fifth BWC review conference in November–December 2001. According to India's Ambassador Rakesh Sood,

> We believe that the provisions of Article I should be interpreted in the widest possible manner, to take into account any further developments in science and technology which can be seen to be in violation of the general prohibition in the article . . . We attach equal importance to the strengthening of both Articles III and X, which provide the two mutually inseparable aspects of any disarmament agreement that deals with a dual-use technology. We believe that transfer of dual-use materials for medical, diagnostic and treatment purposes should be regulated on the basis of guidelines to be negotiated and accepted by all State Parties. Such guidelines should, we further believe, prohibit transfers to non-

State actors. The promotional aspects of Article X are, we believe, a crucial element in strengthening the Convention and even perhaps in achieving universal adherence.[72]

India also expressed its apprehensions that the rejection of both the rolling text and the chairman's "Composite Text" by the United States in July 2001 has effectively stalled the negotiations to finalize the Verification Protocol.

At the review conference, the U.S abrogated this entire exercise by proposing on the last day that the Ad Hoc Group and its mandate to negotiate the Verification Protocol to the BWC be terminated. Instead, the U.S. proposed that the conference hold annual meetings, starting in November 2002, to "consider and assess progress by state parties in implementing the new measures adopted at the Fifth Review Conference" and to "consider new measures or mechanisms for effectively strengthening the BWC."[73] Coerced in this manner and to prevent the complete failure of the Conference, the state parties decided to adjourn the BWC for one year as a "cooling off" period. The irony in this situation cannot be missed; just when the need for verifying the BWC has been accentuated by the anthrax attacks and an increased awareness of terrorists gaining access to biological weapons, the U.S. effectively disrupted these negotiations.

In summary, it may be concluded that India perceives a nuclear threat primarily from its traditional adversaries, Pakistan and China. This perception has heightened since the India–Pakistan nuclear tests in May 1998 and the Kargil conflict in summer 1999. India is troubled by the Western emphasis on stemming biological weapons and chemical weapons proliferation while ignoring their obligations to achieve nuclear disarmament. Still, the fact remains that biological weapons do resemble nuclear weapons in their destructive potential. They are easy to manufacture and conceal but difficult to detect. Hence India cannot ignore the dangers presented to its national security by the proliferation of these weapons.

India is especially sensitive to the biological weapons threat from nonstate actors, and this possibility has intensified in view of the recurring terrorist outrages perpetrated in many parts of the country in recent years. This is largely a reflection of international terrorism emerging as the greatest threat to the comity of nations. India has become the target of several prominent religious-extremist terrorist groups acting in conjunction with states that have displayed a penchant for aberrant moral behavior. So far, no terrorist group has used biological weapons against Indian targets, but the Indian policy elite perceives this possibility as a threat. Apart from their danger to human beings there are worries that biological weapons could be used against livestock and agricultural crops. India's fears here have been strongly influenced by those of the United States and further enhanced by the cooperative relationship the two countries have forged to meet the

threat from terrorism after the September 11 attacks and heightened awareness of the WMD threat emanating from Afghanistan.

India is not indifferent to the question of the finalization of the BWC Protocol. On the contrary, its approach to the draft Protocol was always proac-
tive. Indian negotiators strenuously deny allegations to the contrary and
point to India's deep involvement in discussions of the Protocol among non-
Western countries, along with South Africa and China. They often question
Western positions, but only regarding deficiencies in the arguments. These
officials also note that they have fully participated in the meetings of the Ad
Hoc Group, have supported the negotiations by providing a Friend of the
Chair on National Implementation and Commitment, and have submitted
working papers on practically all the key issues under discussion. India is
committed to achieving a Protocol but believes that real progress is best
achieved through mutual accommodation of basic positions, not by being
stampeded into meeting artificial deadlines. India's basic position on the
essence of the BWC Protocol has not changed over the several years of its
negotiation. It supports a strengthened Convention through an effective
Protocol, with a transparent compliance regime that also facilitates the
transfer of biotechnology for developmental purposes.

The issues involved in the nonproliferation of biological weapons, like the
growing threat from international terrorism, go far beyond the negotiation
of a Verification Protocol to the BWC. Post–Cold War realities inform us
that international cooperation is crucial to meeting the new dangers from a
likely proliferation of WMDs in general and biological weapons in particular. Completing the BWC Verification Protocol is an important part of the
future agenda for international cooperation.

## NOTES

1. Rudyard Kipling, "The Ballad of East and West," *The Everyman Dictionary
of Quotations and Proverbs* (London: Chancellor Press, 1988), 140.19.

2. "Holum Outlines Arms Control Concerns before Senate Panel," *USIS Official Text* (29 June 1999).

3. *Strategic Assessment 1998: Engaging Power for Peace, Institute for National
Strategic Studies, National Defense University* (Washington, D.C.: Government
Printing Office, 1999), 203–4.

4. This contention is argued in P. R. Chari, "Newer Sources of Insecurity: The
Crisis of Governance in India," *RCSS Policy Studies* 3 (January 1998) (Regional
Centre of Strategic Studies, Colombo).

5. Ian Anthony and Jean Pascal Zanders, "Multilateral Security-related Export
Controls," in *SIPRI Yearbook 1998: Armaments, Disarmament and International
Security* (Oxford: Oxford University Press, 1998), 391.

6. U.S. House of Representatives, Select Committee, *U.S. National Security and*

*Military/Commercial Concerns with the People's Republic of China* (Cox report), 3 January 1999; unclassified version available online at www.house.gov/coxreport/; and reports on cooperation between Pakistan and North Korea in the nuclear and missile areas, for example C. Raja Mohan, "Pak Nuclear Exports to North Korea," *The Hindu* (11 July 1999).

7. See text of prime minister's letter to President Clinton after India's nuclear tests, *The Hindu* (14 May 1998).

8. See Prime Minster Nawaz Sharif's broadcast to the nation following Pakistan's nuclear tests, *IPCS Newsletter* (November 1998), 1.

9. "The Alliance's Strategic Concept—Approved by the Heads of State and Government participating in the meeting of the North Atlantic Council in Washington, DC on 23 and 24 April 1999," *Programme for Promoting Nuclear Non-Proliferation Newsbrief* 46 (Second Quarter 1999), 29.

10. National Defense University, Institute of National Strategic Studies, *1998 Strategic Assessment: Engaging Power for Peace*, chapter 12; online, www.ndu.edu/inss/sa98/sa98ch12.html (24 July 2002).

11. For an early history of India's positions on the GATT negotiations, see Devinder Sharma, *GATT to WTO: Seeds of Despair* (Delhi: Konark Publishers Pvt. Ltd., 1995), 3–7.

12. Sharma, *GATT to WTO*, 90.

13. Based on personal interviews with Indian officials involved in the GATT negotiations.

14. Based on personal interviews with Ministry of External Affairs officials.

15. USIS, "Energy Secretary Richardson on Nonproliferation," *Official Text* (22 July 1999).

16. USIS, "Energy Secretary Richardson on Nonproliferation." See also "The Transnational Threat," in *Proliferation: Threat and Response*, 1997, www.defenselink.mil/pubs/prolif97/trans.html.

17. "Bin Laden's Group Has Deadly Weapons," *Indian Express* (New Delhi) (20 April 1999), citing a Cairo report by the Deutsche Presse Agentur.

18. Based on personal interviews with Ministry of External Affairs officials.

19. Jyoti Malhotra, "India and US Agree to Agree on Terrorism," *The Indian Express* (6 April 2000).

20. Government of India, Ministry of External Affairs, Annual Report, 1998–99, 75.

21. C. Raja Mohan, "NATO's Nuclear Doctrine," *The Hindu* (30 May 1999).

22. The text of these treaties can be found in *Arms Control and Disarmament Agreements: Texts and History of Negotiations*, 1996 ed. (Washington, D.C.: Arms Control and Disarmament Agency, 1977).

23. The text of this treaty can be found in *Arms Control Today* 27(2) (April 1997).

24. NATO, Press Release, *The Alliance's Strategic Concept* (24 April 1999); online, www.nato.int/docu/pr/1999/p99-065e.htm.

25. Cf. Prime Minister's Statement in Parliament on 15 December 1998 on "Bilateral talks with the United States."

26. "India Urges Pakistan to Ratify CWC," *The Hindu* (29 May 1997).

27. Government of India, Ministry of External Affairs, Annual Report 1997–98, 91–92.

28. Government of India, Ministry of External Affairs, Annual Report 1997–98, 92.

29. Chapter 14.

30. Jean Pascal Zanders and John Hart, "Chemical and Biological Weapon Developments and Arms Control," in *SIPRI Yearbook 1998: Armaments, Disarmament and International Security* (Oxford: Oxford University Press, 1998), 460, citing *Agence France-Presse* (26 June 1997); *Times of India* (27 June 1997); and R. Bedi, "Indian Chemical Bases Come Under Scrutiny," *Janes Defence Weekly* 28(6) (13 August 1997), 5.

31. Zanders and Hart, "Chemical and Biological Weapon Developments and Arms Control," 461.

32. Government of India, Ministry of External Affairs, Annual Report 1992–93, 21.

33. The text of the Joint Declaration on the Complete Prohibition of Chemical Weapons can be found in *Crisis Prevention, Confidence Building, and Reconciliation in South Asia*, ed. Michael Krepon and Amit Sevak (New Delhi: Manohar, 1996), 260–61.

34. "Pakistan's Concern," *The Hindu* (22 August 1997).

35. Statement by Ms. Savitri Kunadi, Ambassador/PR of India to the United Nations Offices in Geneva at the Conference on Disarmament, 19 March 1998.

36. Based on personal interviews with concerned officials in the government of India.

37. "India Can Keep Its Chemical Weapons," *The Pioneer* (18 August 1997).

38. The Henry L. Stimson Center, *The CBW Chronicle* 2(4) (May 1998), 7.

39. Ibid. 2(3), 12.

40. Government of India, Ministry of External Affairs, Annual Report 1998–99, 76.

41. *New York Times* (23 May 1998). A summary of the Senate Resolution on Ratification embodying these reservations can be found in *Arms Control Today* 27(2) (April 1997).

42. The Henry L. Stimson Center, *The CBW Chronicle* 2(4) (May 1998), 12.

43. Embassy of India, Washington, D.C., Policy Statements, "India and Disarmament," (n.d.); online: www.indianembassy.org/policy/Disarmament/noteindiadisarmament.htm.

44. This argument, and others to support this conclusion, are made in Amy E. Smithson, *Separating Fact from Fiction: The Australia Group and the Chemical Weapons Convention*, The Henry L. Stimson Center, Occasional Paper no. 34, March 1997, v–vii.

45. Ian Anthony and Jean Pascal Zanders, "Multilateral Security-related Export Controls," in *SIPRI Yearbook 1998: Armaments, Disarmament and International Security* (Oxford: Oxford University Press, 1998), 388.

46. Anthony and Zanders, "Multilateral Security-related Export Controls," 392.

47. Based on personal interviews with Ministry of External Affairs officials.

48. Jenni Rissanen, "BWC Update: The BWC Protocol Negotiations, 18th Ses-

sion: Removing Brackets," *Disarmament Diplomacy* 43 (January/February 2000), 22; Jenni Rissanen, "Protocol Ad Hoc Group Enters Deeper into Consultations," *Disarmament Diplomacy* 48 (July 2000), 2–3; Jenni Rissanen, "BWC Update: Hurdles Cleared, Obstacles Remaining: The Ad Hoc Group Prepares for the Final Challenge," *Disarmament Diplomacy* 56 (April 2001), 9–12.

49. Statement by Ambassador Prakash Shah at the Third Review Conference of the Parties to the Convention on the Prohibition of the Development, Production and Stockpiling of Bacteriological (Biological) and Toxin Weapons and on Their Destruction, 1 September 1991.

50. Statement by Ambassador Arundhati Ghose to Fourth Review Conference, 1996; also see Statement of Ambassador Prakash Shah at Third Review Conference, 1991.

51. Working Paper by India, Measures to Strengthen Implementation of Article X of the BTWC, BWC/AD HOC GROUP/WP, 131, 10 March 1997.

52. Ibid.

53. Statement by H. E. Arundhati Ghose, Plenary Session, Fourth Review Conference of the States Parties to the Convention on the Prohibition of the Development, Production and Stockpiling of Bacteriological (Biological) and Toxin Weapons and on Their Destruction, 26 November 1996.

54. BWC Ad Hoc Group, Rolling Text of a Protocol to the Convention on the Prohibition of the Development, Production and Stockpiling of Bacteriological (Biological) and Toxin Weapons and on Their Destruction, 30 July 1997, 29–30.

55. U.S. Arms Control and Disarmament Agency Fact Sheet, Biological Weapons Review Conference, 1996; available online at www.acda.gov, November 1996, 1.

56. Based on interviews with Ministry of External Affairs officials.

57. William Muth, "The Role of the Pharmaceutical and Biotech Industries in Strengthening the Biological Disarmament Regime," in Symposium: Responding to the Challenge of Biological Warfare—A Matter of Contending Paradigms of Thought and Action, ed. Susan Wright and Richard Falk, *Politics and the Life Sciences* 18 (March 1999), 92–97.

58. Working Paper by India, Indonesia and Mexico: Measures to Strengthen the Implementation of Article III of the Biological and Toxin Weapons Convention, BWC/AD HOC GROUP/WP. 232, 3 October 1997.

59. BWC/AD HOC GROUP/WP. 318, 30 September 1998.

60. Graham S. Pearson, "Forging an Effective Biological Weapons Regime," *Arms Control Today* 24(5) (June 1994), 16.

61. John D. Steinbruner, "Biological Weapons: A Plague Upon All Houses," *Foreign Policy* 109 (Winter 1997–1998), 93.

62. Henrietta Wilson, "The BTWC Protocol: The Debate about Visits," *Disarmament Diplomacy* 40 (September/October 1999), 23.

63. Based on personal interviews with MEA officials.

64. The increase of secrecy with an attendant decrease in transparency regarding activities in the United States that come within the ambit of the BWC is perceptively described in chapter 14.

65. BWC Ad Hoc Group, NAM and Other States, Working Paper: Proposed Text for Visits, UN Document BWC/AD HOC GROUP/WP.402, 22 September 1999;

Henrietta Wilson, "Strengthening the BWC: Issues for the Ad Hoc Group," *Disarmament Diplomacy* 42 (December 1999), 33–34.

66. Government of India, Ministry of External Affairs Annual Report 1997–98, 92.

67. Jenni Rissanen, "The BWC Protocol Negotiation 18th Session: Removing Brackets," *Disarmament Diplomacy* 43 (January/February 2000), 23.

68. U.S. Arms Control and Disarmament Agency Fact Sheet, Biological Weapons Review Conference 1996; online: www.acda.gov, November 1966, 1.

69. P. R. Chari and Giri Deshingkar, "Putting Teeth into the BWC: An Indian View," in Symposium: Putting Teeth into the BWC: An Indian View, ed. Susan Wright and Richard Falk *Politics and the Life Sciences* 18 (March 1999): 89 (citing interviews with Government of India official).

70. Wilson, "Strengthening the BWC," 32.

71. BWC/AD HOC GROUP/WP.339, 6 January 1999.

72. India, Statement of Ambassador Rakesh Sood, Head of Delegation to the Fifth Review Conference of the States Parties to the Biological Weapons Convention, 20 November 2001.

73. United States, Proposal on Article XII, Fifth Review Conference of the Biological Weapons Convention, 7 December 2001. For an account of the proposal and response to it, see Jenni Rissanen, "Anger After the Ambush: Review Conference Suspended After US Asks for AHG's Termination," *BWC Review Conference Bulletin, The Acronym Institute,* 9 December 2001, online: www.acronym.org.uk/bwc/revcon8.htm.

# IV

## DISARMING IRAQ

# 10

## The Coercive Disarmament of Iraq

*Amin Saikal*

The history of forced disarmament involving weapons of mass destruction—nuclear, biological, and chemical weapons—in general has been a sorry one. With the exception of Germany and Japan, which following World War II were subjected as defeated powers to successful military limitations, the efforts made by major powers since then in this respect have failed to achieve their desired objectives. Whether in the form of comprehensive or partial arms control or disarmament, conducted within or outside the framework of the United Nations, all measures have inevitably been circumvented by the complexity of enforcing such measures and preventing states from finding ways of getting around the measures and manipulating them to their individual geopolitical interests. In recent times, no case has illustrated this so starkly as that of Iraq. The failure of the UN to enforce a coercive process of disarmament of Iraq following the Kuwait war of 1991 has not only caused immeasurable suffering for the Iraqi people but also has led to a long period of tension and conflict between Iraq and the UN, or more specifically two of its powerful members, the United States and the United Kingdom. It has also generated a major split among the five permanent members of the UN Security Council (UNSC). The process has now reached a worrisome impasse, setting Iraq, the United States and United Kingdom, and for that matter the UN, on a prolonged course of military confrontation, at the cost of making the region more unpredictable and volatile than has been the case historically, and imperiling the chances of creating a stable post–Cold War world order.

This chapter has three aims. The first is to outline the background to the crisis leading to UN involvement in a process of coercive, selective disarma-

*Amin Saikal*

ment of Iraq. The second is to discuss the process and its successes and failures. The third is to explore alternative approaches for a peaceful resolution of the present impasse.

## BACKGROUND

The end of the Gulf War in February 1991 produced mixed results. On the one hand, the U.S.-led international coalition succeeded in reversing the August 1990 Iraqi invasion of Kuwait and in degrading the military capacity of the Iraqi leader Saddam Hussein so that he could no longer be an immediate danger to Iraq's neighbors and America's interests in the region. On the other, the United States found it expedient not to prosecute the war to the point either of securing a sympathetic regime in place of that of Saddam Hussein[1] or eliminating Iraq's capacity to produce and possess weapons of mass destruction (WMD), which had become a source of utmost concern to the United States and its allies in the region, especially Israel.

The reason that the United States did not venture beyond the liberation of Kuwait was not necessarily what the Bush administration at the time implied, namely the lack of a UN mandate. It is worth stressing that Washington subsequently displayed no qualms over the lack of any specific UNSC authorization to repeatedly take military action against Saddam Hussein's regime, as in the cases of the U.S. missile strike in June 1993 and the ongoing U.S.–U.K. air campaign against Iraq since November 1998. Again, since the deplorable terrorist attacks of September 11, 2001, on the United States, the administration of President George W. Bush has persistently been threatening massive military actions to remove Saddam Hussein's regime from power for possessing chemical and biological weapons and supporting "international terrorism."

What constrained the United States in the wake of the Gulf War were four geopolitical considerations: the danger of a politically unacceptable level of American casualties; the lack of an obvious viable alternative to Saddam Hussein and his regime; the concern that in the absence of a central power Iraq could break up into several ethnic-sectarian enclaves, with each linked to and supported by a neighboring state; and the view that in the wake of such developments the state that could gain wider influence would be the U.S. arch enemy in the region, the Islamic Republic of Iran, given the country's sectarian affiliation with Iraq's Shi'ite majority. These concerns were shared by America's regional Arab allies, especially Saudi Arabia, which despite its dislike of Saddam Hussein's regime was reluctant to see its Sunni minority control of Iraq crumbling in favor of the predominantly revolutionary Shi'ite Islamic Iran.

It was also these very reasons that restrained Washington from acting in support of the Iraqi Kurdish and Iraqi Shi'ite uprisings following President Bush's public call on the Iraqi people to rise up in the wake of Desert Storm. Washington's failure to act enabled Saddam Hussein to crush those uprisings brutally, creating such tragic situations in northern and southern Iraq that the United States and its Western allies were ultimately forced to declare a "safe haven" for the Kurds and an air exclusion zone for the Shi'ites.

The survival of Saddam Hussein, with his tightly knit administrative-party-security apparatus and Republican Guard (which formed the backbone of his dictatorship) as well as his WMD remaining almost intact, quickly proved a source of major embarrassment and policy dilemmas for Washington. This more than anything else was to have a defining impact not only on U.S. policy toward Iraq but also the UN's treatment of the country. In addressing the issue of Saddam Hussein and his WMD capabilities, Washington now apparently found it imperative to use the UN as the main vehicle through which it could secure the final demise of Saddam Hussein's regime and the transformation of Iraq into a compliant state.

As the sole superpower in the emergent post–Cold War era, the United States successfully persuaded the UN Security Council to adopt the unique Resolution 687 of April 3, 1991, in support of and in addition to all the previous UNSC resolutions pertinent to the case of the Iraqi occupation of Kuwait. The Resolution, passed under Chapter VII of the UN Charter, was enforceable by military action if required, and formally established the conditions for the cease-fire that the United States had already signed with the Iraqis. While reinforcing UN economic and political sanctions, which had been imposed on Iraq under UNSC Resolution 661 shortly after its invasion of Kuwait on August 2, 1990, it not only provided for the demarcation of the Iraq–Kuwait border, the deployment of a UN observer group, the return of Kuwaiti property, compensation for loss and damage, and the repatriation of Kuwaiti prisoners of war, but also sanctified a process of coercive but selective disarmament of Iraq. It required that Iraq "unconditionally accept the destruction, removal or rendering harmless" of all its nuclear, chemical and biological weapons and "all ballistic missiles with a range greater than 150 kilometres," and under paragraph 22 made it clear that the sanctions against Iraq would be maintained until the provisions of Resolution 687 had been implemented to the satisfaction of the Security Council. To implement the resolution, a United Nations Special Commission (UNSCOM) for Iraq was to be established, in charge of destroying all of Iraq's WMD and eliminating its capacity to produce any more.

As could have been expected, Baghdad objected to the resolution on the grounds that it "constitutes an unprecedented assault on the sovereignty" of Iraq, and bitterly complained that it singled out Iraq with respect to WMD and "did not deprive the other countries in the region, particularly

Israel, of the right to possess weapons of this type, including nuclear weapons." Iraq pointed out that it was a party to the Nuclear Non-Proliferation Treaty and the Geneva Protocol on poisonous gases and bacteriological methods of warfare and supported the elimination of all weapons of mass destruction in the Middle East.[2] However, while in a state of shock and disarray from its humiliating defeat, Baghdad had no choice but to accept the resolution. It did so with an unspoken but obvious proviso that it would cooperate with the UN only in so far as doing so did not threaten the existence of Saddam Hussein's regime, leaving no doubt that its cooperation would not come easily. Within weeks of the passage of the resolution, UNSCOM was established, headed by an executive chairman who was responsible for the overall operation of the organization and the reporting of its findings directly to the UN Security Council.

Initially, UNSCOM's operations went fairly smoothly, and the Iraqi regime appeared to be cooperating to the extent necessary for the Commission to intensify its work. But this did not remain the case for long. In accepting Resolution 687, Iraq had agreed to a number of provisions, including the right of UNSCOM and the International Atomic Energy Agency (IAEA) to conduct no-notice inspections with complete access, and the right of UNSCOM to remove any document and to photograph or videotape whatever it considered relevant. However, once the threat of further American military action had subsided and the regime had regained its composure, by late June 1991 the Iraqis found it opportune to embark upon a process of deception and obstruction.[3] They denied access to an IAEA team, led by David Kay, to two sites, firing shots at the team, a development that the UN Security Council immediately condemned. Following the report of its High Level Mission, which investigated the incidents, the Security Council passed Resolution 707 on August 15, 1991, demanding that Iraq comply fully with Resolution 687 by providing "full, final and complete disclosure . . . of all aspects of its programs to develop weapons of mass destruction and ballistic missiles," and by allowing UNSCOM and the IAEA to have immediate and unrestricted access to whatever areas, facilities, equipment, and records they deemed relevant to their work.

In effect Resolution 707 provided UNSCOM with far-reaching powers to conduct intrusive inspections to enable it to meet the objectives of disarmament defined in Resolution 687. And as with Resolution 687, Resolution 707 was passed under Chapter VII of the UN Charter and its provisions could therefore be enforced if necessary.

## UNSCOM: AN EVALUATION

The organizational and operational difficulties confronting UNSCOM from the start could not be underestimated. This was the first time that the United

Nations had set up such a body and taken responsibility for the enforcement of a UNSC resolution in an area of arms control that had historically proven to be difficult to accomplish. In outlining on April 18, 1991, the organizational structure and concept of operations of UNSCOM, the UN Secretary-General presented the Commission as largely a specialized, technical body whose functions would be exclusively confined to finding, verifying, and eliminating Iraq's weapons of mass destruction.

However, such a description of UNSCOM soon proved to be misleading. The Commission's biggest problem was that its objectives from the start were intertwined with America's twin geopolitical goal of securing a compliant Iraqi regime. The fact that the Saddam Hussein regime turned out to be more deceptive, irritating, resilient, and uncooperative than could have originally been envisaged (as may have been the case with any regime of that nature under the circumstances) only added to the complexity of the situation. The regime's resistance to UNSCOM's mission caused the United States to become increasingly determined to attempt to influence the work of UNSCOM in pursuit of its own geopolitical goals. UNSCOM was influenced by the United States in three main areas.

In the first place, the United States could exert leverage on UNSCOM by virtue of its role as the organization's largest source of financial support. In its first five years the Commission led virtually a hand-to-mouth existence. Its direct cash annual running costs amounted to $25 million, which was supplemented by an additional annual operating cost of about $50 million coming from contributions in kind from UN member-states (including such items as inspectors' salaries, supplies of equipment, and helicopter flights). Although UNSCOM has never published a breakdown of financial contributions to its budget, the United States was throughout the largest donor. Without Washington's injection of funds, the Commission could not effectively either commence its work or maintain its operations. However, the United States would provide sufficient funds only for about six months' operations at a time, making it very difficult for UNSCOM to operate within reasonable budgetary expectations and to undertake forward planning confidently.[4] This was recorded in the November 1994 report of its first executive chairman, Rolf Ekeus, as well as in the Commission's April 1995 and April 1996 reports, which stated that "funds have only been identified for the first half of 1995 and are being received piecemeal," and that the financial situation of the Commission remains "precarious."[5] In fact, UNSCOM did not achieve a degree of financial independence until late 1997 when funds started flowing as a result of UNSC Resolution 986 under which Iraq was allowed to sell "oil for food."

The financial predicament in which UNSCOM was placed made the Commission vulnerable to a considerable degree of pressure from UN members and ultimately open to influence by its largest donor. In fact, Ekeus

confided a number of times to UNSCOM staff about the amount of time he
had to spend on fund-raising and the manner in which he had to be careful
not to offend the Americans as the main funding source. On one occasion
in late 1995 when Ekeus went to Washington to request more funds, the
State Department made a request with which Ekeus was not happy. But
without disclosing the nature of the request he told one of his staff that he
reluctantly agreed to it: "What could I do, we need their support." According to the same source:

> Even the contributions in kind were not always given without strings. We
> sometimes had to take equipment that we did not really want, but it was
> pushed on us for various purposes, e.g. sensors to detect the operation of plant
> equipment—the United States wanted to trial the use of this to test the feasibility
> of remote monitoring. On another occasion they gave us a biological labora-
> tory for installation at the Baghdad Monitoring and Verification Centre
> (BMVC). We had already decided that we could not safely perform biological
> analyses in Baghdad, but we installed the lab anyway (it was only used on a few
> occasions and then only for packing biological weapons' samples for transit to
> overseas labs).[6]

This clearly underlined the conflict between the need of the Commission to
operate as an independent, technical UN body and America's leverage to
influence the work of the Commission in a direction that would be conducive to the achievement of U.S. political objectives.

Second, the composition of UNSCOM as a multinational, highly specialized Commission also made it particularly vulnerable to the influence of the
United States and its allies. Since its administrative staff and specialist
inspectors came from different UN member-states and since only the United
States and some of its advanced allies, most importantly Israel and Great
Britain, had the necessary expertise, UNSCOM was left wide open from the
beginning to penetration by the United States and its allies. It was not surprising that the Commission rapidly found itself entangled in both cohabita-
tion and conflict with the American and Israeli intelligence networks. As has
now been widely reported and to some extent documented, not only did the
Americans and Israelis plant their agents in the organization, but they also
rivaled one another in terms of the information that they obtained and the
way they used UNSCOM for their own individual espionage purposes.[7]

At least two key posts of the Commission were continuously filled by
American officials. One was the post of deputy chairman, which was occupied by an official on secondment from the U.S. State Department, at first
Robert Gallucci and later Charles Duelfer. Another was the position of
director of operations, which was always occupied by an American who had
usually been a serving military officer from the Defense Department.
Although the incumbents were distinguished professionals and there is no

direct evidence to paint them as American agents in the Commission, it would have been difficult for them to be entirely independent if they wanted future careers in the U.S. government. Their presence, together with the occupation of some of the other senior positions by Americans from time to time in the Commission, provided the United States with considerable potential to influence UNSCOM policymaking and mission planning.

A third factor that bolstered the U.S. position in UNSCOM was the U.S. control of intelligence. Although UNSCOM set up its own Information Assessment Unit, it was dependent on intelligence supplied by member-states for data other than those collected by its own inspections and inquiries to suppliers. In practice, most of these data came from the United States, or more specifically the CIA.[8] The latter was secretly involved in helping UNSCOM interpret findings from the start of the Commission's work in 1991, but with an agenda different from that of UNSCOM. "Its goal," as was subsequently authorized by President Bill Clinton, "was to work with Iraqi dissidents, in Saddam's Special Security Organization and elsewhere, to overthrow the regime, by any means possible."[9] It is difficult to assess how selective the CIA was in the information it supplied to UNSCOM. Once a month the UNSCOM inspectors were visited in Bahrain by a team of predominantly CIA specialists from Washington to brief the inspectors on the imagery from U2 flights and at the same time to collect the inspectors' assessments. Ekeus always attended these meetings, although the same could not be said of his successor from mid-1997, Richard Butler. There was very little restriction on what could be passed back to the United States; for example, inspection reports which were confidential to the executive chairman would be handed over, as well as copies of documents inspectors may have collected in Iraq. To some degree Ekeus turned a blind eye to some of this, but there is no question he knew about it and approved, as Butler probably did also. In the words of one inspector: "The rationale for all of this is that the United States would help us analyze this material, and in some cases did so, but the offers of help were not entirely altruistic."[10]

The United States often attempted to direct, sometimes successfully, UNSCOM's collection and analysis effort. The American visitors would urge the inspectors to conduct inspections at certain locations, interview particular Iraqis, or make inquiries of certain companies. This was mainly at the working level, and since Ekeus and Butler left this to UNSCOM experts, the inspectors would sometimes resist if it did not suit their program. In some cases, however, the CIA appealed to the executive chairman, in which case the inspectors would have to argue their case. Beyond American influence on UNSCOM's data collection, there is considerable evidence that American intelligence also used UNSCOM's long-range monitoring equipment which, with Iraq's consent, had been placed in Iraqi facilities. Unbeknownst either to UNSCOM or the Iraqis, U.S. intelligence operatives installed tiny listening devices that intercepted Iraqi military communications and beamed them to Washington. This use of UNSCOM for espionage was not, ultimately, denied by Washington.[11]

Similarly, the Commission could not be rendered immune from penetration by those U.S. allies that had serious security and political interests in influencing its working. No actor was more bold and active in this respect than Israel. It is claimed that it was Ekeus who made contact with Israeli intelligence early in 1994,[12] but at least one senior inspector believes that it was actually the other way around: The Israelis approached UNSCOM. Certainly by late 1994 Israeli military intelligence was supplying UNSCOM with a lot of raw intelligence. This was far superior to what the Commission had been supplied by the CIA, which did not trust UNSCOM enough to give it anything but sanitized summaries. The raw data were mainly intercepts of Iraqi acquisitions, enabling UNSCOM to follow up on leads; the sudden burst of visits by UNSCOM inspectors to European suppliers in late 1994 and throughout 1995 was because of this information. It was partly through the Israeli information and partly through the information supplied by Saddam Hussein's son-in-law, Hussein Kamal Hassan, who defected in August 1995 to Jordan only to be killed by Saddam Hussein's forces upon his return to Baghdad within six months, that UNSCOM finally obtained leads that proved pivotal to the uncovering in mid-1995 of Iraq's biological weapons program and Iraq's final admission to that effect.[13]

The importance of the Israeli information gained saliency in all aspects of UNSCOM's work. Israeli intelligence officers commenced regular visits to New York, and UNSCOM inspectors were soon authorized to visit Tel Aviv. They were told by Ekeus to be "cooperative" because the Israelis, he felt, had a right to know what Iraq had been up to as they were likely to be a target. The inspectors interpreted this instruction to mean that they were allowed to provide the Israelis with any information that they had (imagery excepted, since this was controlled by the United States), and this is what they did. In return UNSCOM received more data from the Israelis. However, the Israeli connection started to die by late 1996 and was completely cut in April 1997. According to Scott Ritter, a key member of UNSCOM's intelligence unit, the Information Assessment Unit, this was because the United States had stepped in.[14] In sum, the Israeli connection played a major role in UNSCOM successes, but at a high political cost for UNSCOM.

In the meantime, Iraqi counterintelligence was able to detect the American and Israeli intelligence involvement in UNSCOM's planning and operations. It accused the Commission of having become a nest for American and Israeli spies, designed to help Washington in achieving its political goals rather than focusing on the technical task of disarming Iraq of its WMD and enabling the UN to lift its sanctions against the country. The Iraqi complaints were of course constantly dismissed as nonsense by UNSCOM,

Washington, and Jerusalem. There is no doubt that from late 1996 the Iraqi leadership began to harden its attitude toward UNSCOM more than ever before, and there was a major escalation in Iraq's efforts to obstruct the work of UNSCOM, including stalling and harassing inspectors as much as possible. In the middle of 1996, Saddam Hussein also moved to break up a major CIA operation, which had been set up in the Kurdish "safe haven" of northern Iraq to engineer the overthrow of his regime. He forged a temporary alliance with the Kurdish Democratic Party of Massoud Barzani to defeat the rival Patriotic Union of Kurdistan, led by Jalal Talabani, and in the process succeeded in overrunning the CIA base of operation, forcing the United States to repatriate about 2,000 Iraqis who were closely associated with their project.[15]

This development seriously hindered UNSCOM's operations. Despite all the difficulties, until mid-1996 UNSCOM had achieved some important successes in its mission. Its disarmament achievements had been twofold in nature. First was the actual elimination of weapons and related systems. UNSCOM has reported an impressive list of achievements, including the destruction of over 22,000 chemical munitions, 480 tonnes of chemical agent, almost 2,000 tonnes of precursor chemicals, 48 SCUD missiles, 32 launch pads, and an entire biological production plant.[16] Little of this was originally declared by Iraq, and it was only through the persistence of UNSCOM, via its inspections and other investigations, that Iraq even admitted their existence.

Most of the above items were destroyed in the first five years of UNSCOM's operations, and very little actual disarmament occurred after that. The last major disarmament was the destruction of a biological weapons plant and associated materials and equipment in June 1996. In the chemical area, a specialist Chemical Destruction Group (CDG) was established early in 1992,[17] which had completed its work by April 1994.[18] Very little in the chemical field was destroyed after 1994; for example in the last two years, 1997–1998, only 197 pieces of chemical glassware and a dozen mustard gas shells were destroyed.[19]

The second area of achievement in the disarmament field was the objective assessment of Iraq's declarations. This allowed UNSCOM to confirm those areas of Iraq's declarations that could be substantiated and alternatively enabled UNSCOM to identify those sections that were untrue or could not be verified. Many of UNSCOM's inspections in Iraq, its inquiries to suppliers, and the collection of other information had been to this end. UNSCOM had collected tens of thousands of documents, photographs, and videotapes and had an extensive computer database against which Iraqi declarations could be tested. This gave UNSCOM a comprehensive understanding of Iraq's weapons programs and helped define the scope of the disarmament work remaining.[20]

Although UNSCOM was unable to eliminate Iraq's remaining capabilities, the benefit of its work was that at least the extent of the threat, including its nature, was better understood, enabling regional powers and others to take defensive countermeasures. UNSCOM's achievements substantially slowed down as the Iraqi regime became more and more suspicious of its operations and decided to pursue a more confrontational course of behavior. By early 1997, it wanted UNSCOM to provide a timetable as to when its work would be completed and, for that matter, when the UN would end its economic sanctions against Iraq.

Iraq's growing suspicion of UNSCOM's operations and U.S. involvement in them caused a serious setback for U.S. policy, imperiling its efforts to achieve its political goals. It must have made the Clinton administration feel that its Iraq policy was rapidly unraveling and that Saddam Hussein was continuing to strengthen the longevity of his rule, at the cost of growing embarrassment and security anxiety for the United States. Washington thus needed to review and overhaul its policy approach, and required UNSCOM to become more assertive than ever in its dealings with Saddam Hussein's regime. This coincided with the decision of the first executive chairman of UNSCOM, Rolf Ekeus, to leave his position in July 1997 to become Swedish ambassador to the United States. Ekeus's move could not have come at a better time for the United States. He was succeeded by the Australian ambassador to the UN, Richard Butler, who brought a different approach and style to the running of UNSCOM, which coincidentally proved to be more in tune with what the United States wanted to achieve.

Rolf Ekeus was, in many ways, a typical Swedish diplomat: aloof, subtle, diplomatic, and suspicious of the United States and wary of other Europeans. His quiet manner and slow lilting style of speech made people listen and commanded respect. He was "the master strategist,"[21] and conscious of the fact that UNSCOM's credibility depended very much on the Commission being independent, and for this he often seemed to be at odds with what the United States wanted UNSCOM to do—a point which has been confirmed by Scott Ritter's description of Ekeus as being "his own man."[22] However, as mentioned previously, given America's leverage with UNSCOM, he was willing up to a point to compromise when necessary to maintain the support of the United States. The fact that he did not have a good relationship with UN Secretary-General Boutros Boutros-Ghali,[23] who was also not liked by Washington, helped Ekeus in his relationship with the United States.

In his dealings with the Iraqi side Ekeus would often be stubborn and insistent, although he would compromise over some issues, especially if he decided that they did not fundamentally undermine the working of UNSCOM. In his meetings with senior Iraqi officials he encountered considerable tensions from time to time, but he remained calm and in control.

According to those close to him, the Iraqis respected him. On his visits to Baghdad he would always have private "chats" with Iraqi Deputy Prime Minister Tariq Aziz, with no other staff present. At these meetings he may have at times reached confidential, informal agreements with Aziz, with minimal risk of being seen to be negotiating away powers given to UNS-COM by the Security Council. For example, he had an understanding that UNSCOM inspectors would not fly helicopters over Baghdad or presidential palaces. This could add considerable flight time if, for instance, they were going to Mosul (the helicopters being based at Rashid airfield south of Baghdad), although it is not clear what Ekeus obtained from the Iraqis in return. When he returned from these secret meetings he would simply indicate that they were successful or unsatisfactory. This would sometimes cause problems for inspectors, as Iraqi officials would tell the inspectors that Ekeus had agreed to something of which the inspectors were unaware, and they would have to refer the matter back to New York for confirmation.[24]

In sum, Ekeus was a pragmatist and a skilled operator who was able to balance the various pressures on UNSCOM. He appeared to be well aware of the problems of coercive disarmament of Iraq and was prepared to compromise with all parties to try to achieve the impossible. He was not a particularly good manager, as he left day-to-day running to the head of administration or chief of operations. A French officer described his management style as "blob management."[25] But this did not diminish his capacity to move the work of UNSCOM forward, enabling it to achieve a great deal during his tenure of office.

The style of Richard Butler, who took up office on July 1, 1997, was very different. Although a professional with a fairly impressive diplomatic career, his reputation as Australian ambassador to the UN was, in the eyes of at least some of those who worked for him, marked by "egotism and bombast." He brought these traits to UNSCOM with him. Almost from the start he was reportedly in conflict with his senior staff: "He demanded respect but did not listen to his experts." It is also reported that he kept much to himself and was distrustful of some of his senior staff. He rarely met with his inspectors on their return from missions and only occasionally discussed the progress of their work.[26] He seemed to consider these to be technical matters best left to them, whereas his work was on a higher political plane. In the words of one inspector, "in fact, he has very little appreciation of the technology of weapons of mass destruction and little interest."

His attitude in this regard was to have some embarrassing consequences. This was illustrated best in his meeting with Tariq Aziz on June 11–15, 1998, in which, as recorded in the video of the meeting released by the Iraqis, he kept referring to his staff even for some of the basics.[27] For example, he attempted to present his concept of disarmament for Iraq as beginning at the top and working down. In explaining this model he could recall that weapons were on top of his pyramid but had to refer to his staff for each of the next two layers: agents and materials. Although the model may have appeared to be intellectually appealing, it made little practical sense. For example, it is the materials and agents that are used to make the weapons, and in that sense they are of equal importance to the weapons. The "top down model" later became a source of jokes among senior UNSCOM inspectors. At the same time, it represented a clash of perceptions between what constituted disarmament to Butler and what it meant to the Iraqis.[28] At the June 1998 meeting, Tariq Aziz indeed showed that he had a far superior understanding of the issues. Butler eventually became irate and started to lecture the Iraqi deputy prime minister in a most undiplomatic manner. In the end it was Tariq Aziz who proposed a program of work to which Butler agreed.

A great deal has been speculated in the media about Butler's relations with the Americans. Although there is no hard evidence available to substantiate any suggestions that he was acting on behalf of the Americans, his approach was one from which Washington could take much comfort. UNSCOM staff have suggested that in his discussions Butler seemed to be constantly referring back to what the Americans might be thinking rather than what was best for the disarmament process. This was in contrast to Ekeus's approach: "Well, how do we convince the Americans to support us on this?" On one occasion, Butler confided that on his first day in office he was visited by "a very senior State Department official" who told him not to even think of listing outstanding issues with the Iraqis, "because they will pick them off one by one until all issues are satisfied." Butler said he waited for a year and then, when he detected a change in U.S. thinking, produced his "road map," which he asserted was really a de facto list of outstanding issues. This seems very much like acquiescing to U.S. demands.[29]

Some have even suggested that Butler was largely out for his own aggrandizement. He wanted international attention focused on what he was doing and to this end approached many of the issues head-on in his usual blunt and confrontational way. He also initially gave a free rein to one of the most controversial American inspectors, Scott Ritter, the former U.S. Marine Corps Intelligence officer, who had previously served in Operation Desert Storm, performing battle damage assessment for the Central Command in Riyadh, Saudi Arabia.[30] Ritter had been chosen by Ekeus to join a special UNSCOM intelligence team and be involved in only certain types of inspections. However, while Ritter apparently exceeded his mandate, his efforts began to pay off by 1997–1998, when he succeeded in cracking Saddam Hussein's most "closely protected communications," enabling him to uncover the Iraqi leader's elaborate system of signals concealing his weapons and protecting his own movements, information the CIA desperately wanted to be able to eliminate Saddam Hussein. This caused an intense tug-of-war between the CIA and Ritter for control of the information and placed Butler in an awkward position of choosing which side to support. According to one account, he was finally persuaded by Washington to resolve the issue in its favor as the main source in charge of intelligence.[31] Although this account has been disputed by Butler, Ritter did become harshly critical of Butler after leaving UNSCOM in a storm. Ritter has now alleged that Butler was all along informed of the CIA involvement in UNSCOM but did nothing to stop it,[32] an allegation that Butler has denied.

Whatever the nature of Butler's relations with Washington, which very strongly backed him in the way he was running UNSCOM and dealing with Iraq, one thing is clear: Throughout his tenure he stumbled from one crisis to another with the Iraqis. He was not trusted by Baghdad, which accused him of doing Washington's bidding and turning UNSCOM into a nest of American and Israeli spies. For his part, there is no doubt that Butler waved the stick a lot more than the carrot at Baghdad. Whenever he set out for a round of negotiations with the Iraqis, he preconditioned his visit by a veiled or open threat of going back to the Security Council to ensure Iraq's full compliance. He never failed to point out in some form to the Iraqi leadership the dire consequences that its noncompliance would entail. This characterized his approach to the crisis over the Iraqi decision in late 1997 to bar the American members of UNSCOM as hostile to Iraq, only to back down the following February under the threat of American military retaliation and the personal intervention of UN Secretary-General Kofi Annan, whose success in brokering a deal left Butler quite high and dry.[33] It also marked his handling of subsequent crises, which essentially led to Baghdad declaring in early October 1998 the end of its cooperation with UNSCOM on the ground that it was riddled with American and Israeli spies, and that Butler was working for American political objectives and therefore deliberately prolonging the work of UNSCOM and the UN sanctions against Iraq.[34]

Butler's report to the UN Security Council on October 15, 1998, which was eagerly awaited by Washington, marked a turning point in the whole UN process of disarming Iraq of its WMD. Its damning condemnation of Iraq for its lack of cooperation and disclosure of information about its WMD provided the trigger for the United States, supported strongly by the United Kingdom, to launch a massive air campaign against Iraq a little more than a month later. Ritter has even claimed that what Butler did in the report was a "set up" between him and Washington to justify the latter's bombing campaign.[35] The campaign, which was transformed into a war of attrition, was intended this time to spell the end of Saddam Hussein's rule. But as the Iraqi dictator survived it, it was clear that it actually destroyed the prospects for both UNSCOM and its executive chairman to resume their functions. With three permanent members of the Security Council—France,

Russia, and China—opposed to the American–British air strikes and highly critical of Butler's approach, and Iraq vowing not to accept any further UN inspections, it may have also marked the end of the coercive disarmament of Iraq.

Subsequently, Butler bitterly attacked Kofi Annan, and France, Russia, and China, of which he identified the last two as Iraq's "closest allies" on the Security Council, for allegedly destabilizing his mission. He accused Annan of undermining the work of UNSCOM by being too lenient toward Saddam Hussein in pursuit of a short-term diplomatic solution,[36] and blamed Iraq's Security Council allies for an "attempt to absolutely, finally kill UNSCOM." He even went so far as to claim that the former Russian Prime Minister Yevgeny Primakov was on the payroll of the Iraqi government to protect it.[37] Of course, his allegations were dismissed as an excuse for his own failures.

Although Butler cannot entirely be blamed for the downfall of UNSCOM, his confrontational approach and oversights almost certainly played a critical role in bringing about the Commission's early demise. This also has meant the end of any American approach to secure a change of regime in Iraq through the use of UNSCOM, economic sanctions, and military threat. It is not surprising that since the start of the second round of major military confrontation with Iraq in late 1998, the United States has been openly advocating the overthrow of Saddam Hussein's regime as its pronounced goal. Supported by the United Kingdom, it has remained determined to maintain the UN sanctions against Iraq as a means to secure a receptive regime in Baghdad. This it has done despite knowing that the sanctions have so far mainly hurt ordinary Iraqis rather than Saddam Hussein's regime.[38] However, the international community has shown declining interest in such an American approach. Russia, China, and France along with many Arab and non-Arab countries have declared their opposition to the continuation of the sanctions. Some of them have already broken the sanctions, a development that has played into the hands of the Iraqi leader for propaganda purposes but has brought little tangible benefit to the Iraqi people.

Meanwhile, the failure of UNSCOM has proved disastrous for the UN. It has not only deprived it of an on-site inspection body and enabled the Iraqi regime to recommence a rearmament program but has also thrown the UN into policy disarray as to how to deal with Iraq. After much soul-searching and incriminatory rifts among the UNSC permanent members and various proposals put forward (especially by France, Great Britain, and the Netherlands) to work out a replacement for UNSCOM, the UNSC finally adopted Resolution 1284 in March 2000 to set up the United Nations Monitoring, Verification and Inspection Commission, or UNMOVIC. While Hans Blix, a Swedish diplomat and a former head of the International Atomic Energy, was appointed to head this new body, UNMOVIC was to be financed from the "oil for money" deal with Iraq. However, UNMOVIC has thus far remained defunct, for one simple reason: The Iraqi government has not agreed to its creation and has refused to allow it to operate in Iraq. Baghdad has argued for a clear UN commitment to end the sanctions on a mutually agreed date before it will agree to any more inspections. Given the history of the Iraqi regime's opposition to any form of inspection, it is doubtful that UNMOVIC will become operational in Iraq soon. At the same time, the change of administration in Washington from Democrat Bill Clinton to the Republican George W. Bush in February 2001 has not helped the situation. President Bush has treated Iraq as "unfinished business" that he has inherited from his father's presidency, and he has vowed to do everything possible to contain Saddam Hussein's regime and possibly to secure an acceptable replacement for it.[39]

## PEACEFUL ALTERNATIVES

The current impasse calls for a new approach to solving the problem. Alternatives such as UNMOVIC, which essentially recast UNSCOM in a different mold and fail to provide clear endgames and timetables for ending the sanctions, are unlikely to receive Iraq's full cooperation. What is now required is a bold new initiative that would take the regime of weapons inspection out of the hands of the Security Council's permanent members and disentangle its objectives and operations from U.S. political goals. Such an initiative should aim at establishing an independent UN Commission that would be constituted by the UN Secretary-General and whose head would be directly responsible to him and report only to him. Its entire administration and operations should be exclusively financed from the UN's central budget, with no foreign cash donation or assistance in kind allowed to support any of its activities. The Commission's inspectors should be selected through a competitive process by its head, with help from a small UN team of expert advisors, from various countries. And the process should be conducted in such a way as not to enable any particular country to gain dominance. The UN Secretary-General would be responsible for briefing the Security Council about the Commission's findings through periodical reports. The Security Council may be given an opportunity to make suggestions for consideration by the Secretary-General and the head of the Commission, but without having the right to veto any of its findings.

A clear road map should be drawn up to show how and at what point the Commission's work will be considered completed and UN economic sanctions ended. One of UNSCOM's biggest problems was its lack of a clearly defined endgame. Indeed, it is never easy to declare a completely satisfactory end to any process of weapons inspections, especially ones dealing with biological weapons, which can be hidden away in small quantities from any regime of inspection. Ultimately, subjective judgment will need to be applied and an arbitrary line of some kind drawn as the only way of terminating the process. Without a clearly defined endgame, the goal post can easily be changed, as the United States did repeatedly for Iraq in the 1990s, and the process of inspection can easily be drawn out indefinitely, a prospect that will not be acceptable to any regime, let alone that of Saddam Hussein.

An alternative approach would be to manage the disarmament of Iraq as part of a regionwide regime of arms control and democratization. These were the very objectives that President George Bush promised in the wake of the Gulf War, but nothing came of them. Democratization in the Middle East is one of those goals to which Washington has not been able to pay more than lip service. This has been largely because the friendly Arab regimes on which it has needed to rely for geopolitical reasons are reluctant by their nature to accommodate democratic change. However, it is in the area of arms control that in a twist of irony Washington and Baghdad have expressed a common interest. Saddam Hussein's regime has endorsed the value that Washington has often attached to arms control in the Middle East, provided that Washington is not selective in its approach: one standard for Israel and another for the Arabs and Iran. Baghdad has often pointed to Israel's possession of WMD to justify its own acquisition of them. Yet at the same time it is clear to Baghdad that Washington will not subject Israel to a coercive process of arms control or disarmament, partly because Israel is always able to point its finger at an Arab country like Iraq to justify its own WMD capabilities. Consequently, no state in the Middle East has been really serious when it has publicly spoken in support of elimination of WMD in the region as a whole. Each side has only used such a proposal for its own propaganda purposes.

If Washington is adamant about eliminating Iraq's WMD capabilities, then it must not be discriminatory in its approach. It should press for the transformation of the entire Middle East into a "zone free of WMD" as proposed in Resolution 687. It is only in this way that a genuine regime of arms control could be established in the area and that Iraq could be persuaded to give up its programs of WMD altogether. Otherwise, irrespective of whether Saddam Hussein or someone else is in power in Baghdad, there would always be many other Arab and Iranian nationalists who would share his conviction for as long as Israel remains armed with WMD. However, since a regionwide elimination of WMD is not really on the U.S. agenda at present, the best alternative is to embrace the proposal outlined above: Allow the UN to set up a genuinely independent Commission, with a clear goal post and endgame, to deal with the present impasse confronting its relations with Iraq.

The UN's attempt to set up UNSCOM in charge of disarming Iraq of its weapons of mass destruction was novel and pioneering. But what made its creators confident that it would be able to achieve its objectives effectively is something very puzzling, indeed almost mind-boggling. The Commission's central, and for that matter most devastating, problem from the start originated from the fact that the United States wanted to use it for its unspoken political objectives rather than allow it to achieve the goals for which it was publicly established. Whereas the Commission's job was to eliminate Iraqi WMD, Washington wanted to control the Commission to the extent that it could help it with achieving its goal of destroying the Saddam Hussein regime. It had the necessary resources and leverage to do so, and UNSCOM was vulnerable, given its financial dependence, composition, and highly specialized methods of operations. The fact that the Iraqi authorities proved uncooperative, with a determination to conceal as much about their WMD as possible, could have been expected. The American and Israeli espionage involvement in UNSCOM simply provided them with the ammunition they needed. The choice of Richard Butler as the executive chairman of UNSCOM from July 1997 did not appear to help the situation either. His approach and style of operation seemed to be more agreeable to Washington's objectives than to UNSCOM's formal mandate.

A combination of these self-interested initiatives was in the end largely responsible for the discrediting and demise of UNSCOM and the very method of coercive, selective disarmament that the UN had undertaken. Yet the problem of Iraq continues to remain unresolved. There is now an urgent need for a bold and innovative alternative. The one which may be the best under the circumstances is the establishment of a UN body that would be directly responsible to the UN Secretary-General and independent of the permanent members of the UN Security Council. For the body to have the cooperation of Iraq, it must establish an appropriately defined endgame, leading to the lifting of the UN sanctions against Iraq within a specific period of time. Anything short of this is unlikely to enable the UN and the international community to reach a satisfactory and permanent resolution of the problem posed by Iraq's WMD.

## NOTES

1. For a discussion of Saddam Hussein's survival and its consequences, see Lawrence Freedman and Efraim Karsh, *The Gulf Conflict* (London: Faber and Faber, 1994), chapters 29–30.

2. United Nations Security Council (UNSC), *Identical Letters Dated 6 April 1991 from the Permanent Representative of Iraq to the United Nations Addressed*

Respectively to the Secretary-General and the President of the Security Council, S/ 22456, 6 April 1991.

3. For a detailed discussion, see Tim Trevan, *Saddam's Secrets: The Hunt for Iraq's Hidden Weapons* (London: HarperCollins, 1999), chapter 3.

4. Confidential sources.

5. UNSC, *Report of the Executive Chairman of the Special Commission*, S/ 1995/284, 10 April 1995; *Report of the Executive Chairman of the Special Commission*, S/1996/258, 11 April 1996.

6. Confidential sources.

7. For a detailed account, see Seymour M. Hersh, "Annals of Espionage: Saddam's Best Friend, How the CIA Made It a Lot Easier for the Iraqi Leader to Rearm," *New Yorker* (5 April 1999), 34–41.

8. Russia provided some valuable information on the Iraqi intermediate-range SCUD missiles that it had sold to the country, but nothing more than that.

9. See Hersh, "Annals of Espionage," 34–41.

10. Confidential sources.

11. Barton Gellman, "U.S. Spied on Iraqi Military Via U.N.," *Washington Post* (2 March 1999), A1. For an analysis of U.S. use of UNSCOM for espionage purposes, see Susan Wright, "The Hijacking of UNSCOM," *Bulletin of the Atomic Scientists* 55(3) (May/June 1999), 23–25.

12. See Peter Boyer, "Scott Ritter's Private War," *New Yorker* (9 November 1998), 63; Hersh, "Annals of Espionage," 37.

13. Trevan, *Saddam's Secrets*, 330–45.

14. Boyer, "Scott Ritter's Private War," 73.

15. Tim Weiner, "Iraqi Offensives into Kurdish Zone Disrupts U.S. Plot to Oust Hussein," *New York Times* (7 September 1996).

16. UNSC, *Report of the Executive Chairman of the Special Commission*, S/ 24984, 17 December 1992; *Report of the Executive Chairman of the Special Commission*, S/25977, 21 June 1993; *Report of the Executive Chairman of the Special Commission*, S/26910, 21 December 1993; *Report of the Executive Chairman of the Special Commission*, S/1994/750, 24 June 1994; *Report of the Executive Chairman of the Special Commission*, S/1996/848, 11 October 1996.

17. UNSC, S/24984, 17 December 1992.

18. UNSC, S/1994/750, 24 June 1994.

19. UNSC, *Report of the Executive Chairman of the Special Commission*, S/ 1998/920, 6 October 1998.

20. Personal communications.

21. Trevan, *Saddam's Secrets*, 144.

22. Hersh, "Annals of Espionage," 40.

23. Personal communications.

24. Confidential sources.

25. Confidential sources.

26. Confidential sources.

27. UNSC, S/1998/920, 6 October 1998.

28. Amin Saikal, "At the Heart of Iraq's Standoff, a Clash of Perceptions," *International Herald Tribune* (9 November 1998).

29. Confidential sources.

30. Boyer, "Scott Ritter's Private War," 61.

31. Hersh, "Annals of Espionage," 34–41.

32. "U.S. Used UNSCOM for Attack: Ritter," *South News* (Sydney) (7 January 1999).

33. Amin Saikal, "A Minefield of Diplomacy," *The Australian* (30 January 1998).

34. Brian Knowlton, "Iraq Assails Washington as Buildup Continues," *International Herald Tribune* (13 November 1998).

35. "Butler's UNSCOM Report a 'Set-up'—Scott Ritter," *New York Post* (18 December 1998).

36. Judith Miller, "Annan 'Wanted to Destroy UNSCOM': Butler Hits Out," *Sydney Morning Herald* (2 August 1999).

37. For a detailed account of Butler's views, see Richard Butler, *Saddam Defiant: The Threat of Weapons of Mass Destruction, and the Crisis of Global Security* (London: Weidenfeld & Nicolson, 2000), 2, and the book as a whole.

38. See, e.g., John Mueller and Karl Mueller, "Rethinking Sanctions on Iraq: The Real Weapons of Mass Destruction," *Foreign Affairs* (May/June 1999), 43–53.

39. For example, "Case of Unfinished Business in Iraq?" *Business Times* (Malaysia) (20 February 2001), 6.

# 11

## UNSCOM and the Iraqi Biological Weapons Program

### *Technical Success, Political Failure*

*Stephen Black*

The discovery in 1995 of an enormous, diverse biological weapons program in Iraq sparked new interest in development of a verification regime for the Biological Weapons Convention (BWC). The investigation of Iraq's BW program also provides the first case history of an international BW arms control verification effort. The inquiry undertaken by the United Nations Special Commission (UNSCOM) demonstrates both the inherent political difficulties of such an investigation and the possibilities of success.

The United Nation's actions in Iraq have made use of nearly all of the verification processes envisaged for the BWC, including information monitoring, remote sensing, inspections, on-site measures, and continuous monitoring. The UNSCOM case provides examples of the real-world implementation of BW verification techniques, including their accomplishments and failures. Specifically, the Commission's efforts in Iraq have shown the value of a process or systematic approach to BW verification, rather than a reliance on discrete verification tools.

Using a multifaceted verification strategy UNSCOM has also proven the possibility of detecting a covert, well-hidden biological weapons program—albeit in a coercive, postwar environment. Following the detection of the Iraqi BW program, UNSCOM attempted to determine the full scope of the program in order to eliminate it. Despite constant Iraqi claims to the contrary, the Commission repeatedly proved that Iraq never fully or accurately disclosed its biological weapons program or the fate of the actual weapons.

Despite its technical and investigative triumphs, UNSCOM eventually fell victim to political forces beyond its control. Although the Commission enjoyed numerous technical successes in its efforts to uncover Iraq's biological weapons program, it was never expected to be the enforcer of the cease-fire agreement. From the outset the enforcement of the disarmament process was the exclusive purview of the Security Council, as a whole.

By 1998 the Council was no longer united in its desire to see the coercive removal of weapons of mass destruction (WMD) from Iraq. The disarmament regime controlling Iraq—consisting of both the Commission and the Security Council— collapsed due to changing national objectives and political neglect of the deteriorating disarmament situation in Iraq. In December 1999 UNSCOM was disbanded by the Council and replaced with the United Nations Monitoring, Verification and Inspection Commission (UNMOVIC), an organization with a similar mandate but a starkly different modus vivendi.

The investigative experiences of UNSCOM show that multilateral BW verification can be made to work. However, the behavior of the Security Council, specifically in the late stages of the disarmament regime, carries troubling precedents for implementation and enforcement of other arms control efforts.

## UNITED NATIONS SPECIAL COMMISSION

In the spring of 1991 the United Nations Security Council adopted Resolution 687 (1991), which established the conditions of the cease-fire following Iraq's expulsion from Kuwait that year. A major condition of the cease-fire was the elimination, under international supervision, of Iraq's nuclear, chemical, and biological weapons and their ballistic missile delivery systems.

Resolution 687 specifically requires Iraq to declare its holding of and "unconditionally accept the destruction, removal, or rendering harmless, under international supervision, of: (a) All chemical and biological weapons and all stocks of agents and all related subsystems and components and all research, development, support and manufacturing facilities."[1] Iraq is further required to "unconditionally undertake not to use, develop, construct or acquire any of the items specified."

Resolution 687 also calls for the "forming of a Special Commission, which shall carry out immediate on-site inspection of Iraq's biological, chemical and missile capabilities, based on Iraq's declarations and the designation of any additional locations by the Special Commission itself."[2] This second category of sites allowed UNSCOM to conduct challenge or no-notice inspections. As a consequence, the Commission had the ability to both verify specific Iraqi declarations as well as to conduct investigative missions for the purpose of uncovering undeclared activities or items.[3]

The disarmament requirements of Resolution 687 are imposed on Iraq by two means. First, in creating the resolution the Council was acting under Chapter VII of the UN Charter, which allows it to take "action with respect to threats to the peace, breaches of the peace, and acts of aggression."[4] Actions taken under this chapter can include coercive policies such as economic sanctions and direct military action. The Council, using the mandate given to it by the Charter, first declared Iraqi actions in Kuwait to be a threat to international peace and security.[5] Then, as an integral part of the cease-fire Resolution 687 ending the Gulf War, the Council required the elimination of Iraq's WMD capabilities. Because Resolution 687 constitutes a cease-fire agreement, any breach can cause the political situation to revert to its pre-April 1991 state, that is, authorization of use of all necessary force to restore international peace and security.

Resolution 687 also explicitly includes a provision for compelling Iraqi disarmament.[6] An embargo on the sale of Iraqi petroleum products was put in place by Resolution 661 (1990) at the outset of the Iraq/Kuwait crisis. The drafters of Resolution 687 directly, and exclusively, linked the sale of Iraqi oil to Baghdad's compliance with the disarmament provisions of the cease-fire. Paragraph 22 of Resolution 687 notes that when the Security Council agrees that Iraq has completed all actions contemplated under the disarmament provisions of the resolution the oil embargo "shall have no further force or effect."[7] It seems apparent that in 1991 the Allies assumed that the multi-billion-dollar carrot of oil sales would be enough to ensure Iraqi compliance. This was not to be the case.

At the outset, the Special Commission was given sweeping powers to implement its mandate, including

"unrestricted freedom of movement without advance notice within Iraq,"

the "right to designate any site whatsoever for observation, inspection or other monitoring activity,"

the "right to unimpeded access to any site or facility for the purpose of the on-site inspection . . . whether such site or facility be above or below ground,"

the right to "conduct interviews,"

"the right to request, receive, examine and copy any record, data or information . . . relevant to the" Commission's activities,

the "right to install equipment or construct facilities for observation, inspection or other monitoring activity,"

"right to take photographs whether from the ground or from the air," and

the "right to take and analyze samples of any kind as well as to remove and export samples for off-site analysis."[8]

The nature of the information that Iraq must supply to the Special Commission on its proscribed WMD programs was later refined to a "full, final, complete, disclosure . . . of all aspects of its programs to develop weapons of mass destruction and ballistic missiles . . . and of all holdings of such weapons, their components and production facilities and locations."[9] The requirement for a full description of WMD activities is intended to provide a basis for evaluation of the extent of Iraqi compliance with the disarmament requirements.

Both UNSCOM's mandate and Iraq's obligations were clearly set forth in these binding Security Council resolutions.[10] First and foremost, Iraq is required to yield for elimination all of its weapons of mass destruction and certain ballistic missile systems. Iraq is further required to provide full, final, and complete disclosures of its WMD and missile programs. The Special Commission had two complementary tasks. First, UNSCOM was to determine the accuracy of Iraq's declarations as to the disposition of proscribed items and disclosures on its prohibited activities. Second, the Commission undertook investigative actions (inspections) to resolve concerns about the accuracy of Iraqi declarations and disclosures, specifically addressing the possible existence of undeclared proscribed weapons or missiles and undisclosed information about the WMD programs.

## THE BW INVESTIGATION

At the outset of its work, the Special Commission was faced with two mutually exclusive views of the BW situation in Iraq. First, as demanded by Resolution 687, in April 1991 Iraq made an initial declaration about its BW activities—that it had none: "Iraq does not possess any biological weapons or related items as mentioned" in Resolution 687.[11]

The second view consisted of a variety of concerns about the Iraqi BW program held by the members of the Security Council. While supporting governments had access to additional information, very little of it was shared, at least at the outset of the investigation, with the Special Commission.[12]

The Special Commission's seven-year biological weapons investigation was carried out in three, only slightly overlapping, periods. Initially UNSCOM sought to resolve concerns about a possible Iraqi BW program, something that Iraq strenuously denied. The Commission then moved to develop a system for monitoring Iraqi biological facilities and industries. Finally, after 1994 UNSCOM returned to the issue of Iraq's BW program and saw both significant increases in its knowledge of that program but also more tightly focused concerns about what might still remain.

To assess the scope of Iraq's BW program, including the types and number of proscribed biological weapons in Iraq, the Commission had to first verify Iraqi declarations and conduct limited searches for hidden weapons. From August 1991 until 1993 UNSCOM attempted to understand the extent of the Iraqi program. Given the flat Iraqi denial of any BW program, limited information on Iraqi BW efforts, and the technical complexities inherent to BW arms control, UNSCOM achieved little progress in this phase.

In August 1991 UNSCOM conducted its first BW inspection (BW-1) at the Salman Pak site. It was during this inspection that Iraq first admitted an offensive BW program. Iraqi scientists told the inspection team that from 1986 to August 1990 Iraq had engaged in military biological research, with both offensive and defensive purposes. Iraq acknowledged investigation of *Clostridium botulinum*, *Clostridium perfringens*, and *Bacillus anthracis*. However, the Iraqis maintained that their work had never moved beyond the research stage and that all BW activities had ended in August 1990. They also stated that all of the stocks of their BW agents had been destroyed at that time.[13]

Near the end of the first inspection Iraq presented the team with seed stocks of BW-relevant agents, including *Brucellus abortus*, *Brucella melitensis*, *Francisella tularensis*, and a number of additional strains of *Clostridium botulinum*. Iraq also turned over seed stocks of three biological warfare agent simulant organisms: *Bacillus subtilis*, *Bacillus cereus*, and *Bacillus megaterium*. Iraq's possession of these agents indicated a diverse and detailed BW research effort.

In hindsight it seems clear that Iraq's failure to declare these stocks initially was not the result of a misunderstanding of the terms of Resolution 687, but rather the first overt steps in its efforts to conceal the true BW program. Iraqi authorities knew, at that time, that the seed stocks were part of a full-scale offensive BW program and were therefore proscribed by Resolution 687.

Despite the existence of the seed stocks, which contradicted Iraq's initial declaration of no biological weapons or related items, UNSCOM could not yet prove a full-scale BW program. The official UNSCOM status report to the Security Council later in 1991 simply noted that, "No biological weapons or evidence of weaponization was found."[14]

If an Iraqi offensive BW program did exist, agent production and weaponization would be integral components. Two months after the first visit to the BW research facility at Salman Pak, the second UNSCOM biological inspection team examined a range of possible BW research or production facilities. The ten sites included pharmaceutical plants, a blood bank, vaccine production facilities, research sites with fermentation capability, and facilities specially designed to work with hazardous organisms. One of the sites investigated by the team was a remote industrial facility, which Iraq explained was intended for the production of single cell protein animal feed. The plant, soon to become famous, was called Al Hakam.

Following the inspection UNSCOM could only report that BW-2 had found no "biological weapons or facilities for filling weapons."[15] However, several of these sites had significant "dual-capability." Although it appeared that these sites had not been uniquely constructed to only conduct proscribed BW activities, some were capable of prohibited activities.

The dual-use nature of the BW-2 sites caused a dilemma that would plague the biological investigation: Suspicion and capacity do not necessarily prove proscribed activity. Despite concerns based on data provided by supporting governments and a clear Iraqi technical capacity, UNSCOM could not prove that Iraq had a BW program that included the production of BW weapons. In the face of consistent and strenuous Iraqi denials of anything beyond a limited research program, the Commission was stymied.

Throughout 1992 and most of 1993, the UNSCOM BW inspections progressed only as a component of the chemical weapons inquiry. In fact, for most of the early history of the Commission, the same individuals at the UNSCOM New York headquarters conducted the BW and CW investigations. Many on-site inspections aimed at uncovering hidden chemical and biological weapons were conducted during this period. Although the missions covered a large number of ammunition storage bunkers and related facilities, inspectors found no concealed chemical or biological weapons. The Commission continued to report that it was unable to locate any biological weapons or related weaponization facilities.[16]

## Ongoing Monitoring and Verification

In 1991 Iraq had rejected the concept of long-term monitoring as an affront to its national sovereignty. It was not until the fall of 1993, following years of Security Council pressure, that Iraq reluctantly agreed to abide by the Council's decision to implement UNSCOM's plan for continuing compliance monitoring, Resolution 715 (1991). Following Iraq's acceptance of long-term monitoring in November 1993, UNSCOM began to work toward development of information and procedures for ongoing monitoring and verification (OMV).

The purpose of OMV is to ensure that a biological warfare capability is not *reestablished* in Iraq, or that efforts to reestablish are detected. Thus the development of a system for future compliance monitoring, while clearly mandated by Council resolutions, was not a direct effort to uncover, and eliminate, an existing offensive BW capability. Of course UNSCOM maintained its interest in a possible concealed Iraqi BW capability, but from 1993 to the fall of 1994 no progress was realized in the search for an offensive Iraqi BW program.[17]

The implementation of OMV, across all disciplines, required a significant reallocation of Commission resources. The investigation of proscribed activities came to a near standstill as all capabilities were directed toward monitoring of the dual-use materials, equipment, and facilities in Iraq. To prepare implementation of biological OMV, the Commission reinforced the existing CBW staff with additional expert BW personnel. Concurrently, the biological investigation separated from the chemical group and became an independent effort within the organization.

Once complete, the UNSCOM regime for the long-term monitoring of Iraq's biological capabilities became a set of independent, interlocking, investigative capabilities and mechanisms. Using aerial surveillance, on-site inspections, materials and equipment tracking, real-time monitoring cameras, regular declarations of dual-use activities and materials by Iraq, and data from external sources, the Biological OMV Plan is intended to monitor Iraq sufficiently to detect future proscribed activities.

### Renewed Interest in the Offensive Program

Having established the BW OMV regime, the Commission refocused its attention on the lingering, still relevant, suspicions about a larger BW program than Iraq had admitted in 1991. Suspicions about the scale of Iraq's BW activities, which had only grown in the intervening three years, were ominous given what was known about Baghdad's nuclear and chemical weapons and ballistic missile programs. Iraq's declarations on the scope and scale of the other three fields of investigation had grown dramatically since 1991. Many worried that this was also to be the case with the BW program.

Beginning in 1994 UNSCOM investigators began a concerted effort to marshal their evidence and arguments in an effort to prove what had long been suspected. By April 1995 Commission experts still had no smoking gun for the Iraqi BW program. They did, however, have three incontrovertible pieces of evidence that pointed to the production of biological weapons.

### Complex Growth Media

In 1993 and 1994, as part of the requirements of OMV, Iraq submitted declarations on its legitimate biological activities and industries. These declarations covered a wide range of dual-capability facilities and activities, including breweries, vaccine production, and bio-pesticide production sites. The disclosures, and other related data from supporting governments, listed the importation and consumption of biological materials and equipment, including activities prior to 1991. Of specific interest to investigators was information on Iraq's import of thirty-nine tons of complex growth media by the Technical and Scientific Materials Importation Division (TSMID) under the Military Industrialization Commission.[18]

Iraq declared that this growth material had been used in hospital laboratories for disease diagnosis. Hospitals use only small quantities of media, and the material is acquired in small packages to reduce waste due to spoilage. The TSMID purchases, however, were in 25–100 kg drums. Of further concern were the types of media that had been imported, which were not well suited for health care purposes but were ideal for production of biological materials, including warfare agents.

Iraq was also unable to explain the fate of seventeen tons of TSMID media that could not be located. Iraq provided a number of stories to resolve this concern, but all explanations collapsed on investigation. For example, in one exchange Iraq claimed that the missing media had been distributed to hospitals in 1989, in their original packaging. It further claimed that the media, and all related documentation, were subsequently destroyed by rioters in the aftermath of the Gulf War. Curiously, growth media were only distributed to those provinces in which riots occurred. According to Iraq, no efforts were made to replace the media or compensate the hospitals for the loss, even though additional media were available elsewhere in the country.

When confronted with these discrepancies Iraq presented accounts of incompetent managers, loss, theft, fires, and a host of other reasons to explain away the missing materials. But all the Iraqi claims were either totally unsupported by evidence or did not hold up under scrutiny. UNSCOM's biological investigators spent a year establishing that various Iraqi assertions on the possible use or destruction of the growth media were not credible. By the spring of 1995, seventeen tons of media remained unaccounted for and unexplained by Iraq.

## Al Hakam

The Commission was also concerned about the purpose of a remote biological materials production facility called Al Hakam, which Iraq had declared to be a single cell protein (SCP) animal feed production facility. Al Hakam was initially visited by the second biological inspection team in 1991 and had troubled the Commission ever since. Although the team had not found conclusive evidence of proscribed activities at the site, the inspection report reflects the team's unwillingness to give the facility a clean bill of health. The BW-2 team, and later other experts, found that the site had design features that were superfluous for an SCP plant but would be highly advantageous in a biological weapons production facility.[19]

UNSCOM learned that the Hakam site was constructed in great secrecy, at a remote desert location, with extensive security and military fortifications. The site included sophisticated air filtration systems (using HEPA filters) on some buildings, for both incoming and outgoing air. These features all implied a use inconsistent with the facility declaration. Yet these indicators were only circumstantial, and Iraq maintained its assertions that the site was intended solely for the production of single cell protein animal feed.

## Weaponization

In addition to the bacterial growth media and Al Hakam, UNSCOM had learned of other equipment and materials in Iraq highly relevant to biological weapons production. Iraq had purchased four filling machines, which could be used to fill BW munitions, for a "bio-pesticides" project at the Salman Pak research site. However, until the Commission inquired about the machines Iraq had never mentioned any bio-pesticides research at Salman Pak. Iraq was also unable to provide any evidence for its claim that these machines had been destroyed during the war.[20]

UNSCOM also discovered that the Salman Pak site had acquired a spray dryer used to dry the bacterial slurry product of fermenters. Iraq claimed that the spray dryer was acquired for a "bio-pesticides" project, but experts found that the machine had a capability to produce dry particles in the 1- to 10-micron size. Particles of this size are optimal for biowarfare purposes but ineffective for bio-pesticides delivery.

Finally, the Commission discovered that Iraq attempted to procure particularly virulent strains of pathogenic microorganisms, including specific non-vaccine strains of anthrax. The requested organisms were known to be particularly effective as BW agents. Despite confirmation from the potential supplier, Iraq pointedly refused to admit the procurement attempt.

UNSCOM pressed the issues of unaccounted-for growth materials, a possible biological weapons production facility, and weaponization related materials for months without realizing any change in the Iraqi position. Every question and Commission assertion was met by denials, and a range of weak explanations and deceptions. On several occasions Iraq refused to meet with the Commission's BW experts and even produced forged documents in an effort to explain media destruction.

In April 1995 the Commission was able to fully express its suspicions and concerns. For the first time UNSCOM felt that the weight of circumstantial evidence, compounded by Iraq's inability and unwillingness to establish legitimate activities, could prove the existence of a concealed offensive BW program in Iraq. In its six-month report to the Security Council, UNSCOM stated:

> The Commission assesses that Iraq obtained or sought to obtain all the items and materials required to produce biological warfare agents in Iraq. With Iraq's

failure to account for all these items and materials for legitimate purposes, the only conclusion that can be drawn is that there is a high risk that they had been purchased and in part used for proscribed purposes—the production of agents for biological weapons.[21]

## IRAQ'S FIRST DISCLOSURE OF ITS BIOLOGICAL WEAPONS PROGRAM, JULY 1, 1995

Since 1991 Baghdad had maintained that its BW program was limited to civilian-run, defensive research, and employed the skills of only ten Iraqi experts.[22] Following four years of steadfast denials, in 1995 Iraq presented a significantly different portrayal of its biological weapons efforts.

Although the full range of reasons for Iraq's change of position in the BW investigation is unclear, it is likely that the threat of continuing investigation and a resulting prolongation of sanctions contributed to the fundamental change in Baghdad's attitude. The Commission also made it clear to Iraq that the BW investigation would not be suppressed.

On July 1, 1995, Iraq presented a new report on its BW efforts to UNSCOM investigators. In a brief oral statement Iraqi experts admitted that the program, offensive in nature, had run from April 1986 to September 1990. They further revealed that Iraq had indeed produced large quantities of anthrax and botulinum toxin at the Al Hakam site. Despite these revelations, Iraq continued to firmly deny weaponization of these or any other biological warfare agents.[23]

The July disclosure exposed many areas in which Iraq's statements were inconsistent with the Commission's information or where information was absent or vague, notably in the area of weaponization. Commission experts believed that Iraq was attempting to conceal information that would either "provide evidence of weaponization or reveal military connections with the biological weapons program."[24] Iraq refused to admit any link between the production of bulk BW agents and military requirements or intentions. This denial appears to have been yet another effort to limit UNSCOM's understanding of the full scope of the biological warfare program.

On August 7, 1995, General Hussein Kamal Hassan al-Majid, a major player in the Iraqi WMD programs and son-in-law of Saddam Hussein, fled to Jordan. His departure threatened the release of significant new information about the BW program and other areas of UNSCOM's work. This event prompted Iraq to release to UNSCOM a vast collection of previously hidden documentation related to proscribed weapons activities and to significantly revise its full, final, complete, disclosures on past proscribed activities in all weapons areas.

Just ten days after Hussein Kamal's flight, Iraq presented UNSCOM with a vastly different account of Iraq's past biological warfare program. The new disclosure, the second "full" story in as many months, included weaponization, additional agents, more production activities, research, and weapons storage sites. The report presented to UNSCOM also contained a different and more detailed account of the history and activities of the Iraqi biological warfare program.

## The Iraqi Biological Weapons Program Revealed

The late August 1995 disclosures stated that in 1974 the government of Iraq had adopted a policy to acquire biological weapons.[25] Although initial attempts to start a BW research program in the late 1970s failed, by 1985 the Muthanna State Establishment, Iraq's primary facility for chemical weapons research and development, production, and weaponization, fostered the full-scale commencement of a biological weapons program. According to Iraq, research at Muthanna concentrated on the characterization of *Bacillus anthracis* (anthrax) and *Clostridium botulinum* (botulinum toxin) to establish pathogenicity, growth and sporulation conditions, and storage parameters.

In 1987, the BW program was transferred from Muthanna to the Salman Pak facility, later inspected by BW-1. The work at Salman Pak included the acquisition of additional materials, equipment, and staff. The program also began to focus its attention on the use of various BW agents as weapons. The effects of BW agents on large animals, such as dogs, sheep, and donkeys, were tested in both laboratory inhalation chambers and in the field, and production scale-up studies for anthrax and botulinum toxin were started. Anthrax production allegedly began at Salman Pak around March 1989. Research on additional agents such as *Clostridium perfringens* (gas gangrene), aflatoxin, and trichothecene mycotoxins, including T-2 and DAS, was also conducted at Salman Pak.

As the result of a high-level decision to move ahead with a full program, in 1988 a new site for biological weapons production was created: Al Hakam. The design concept of the facility was drawn from Iraq's main chemical weapons site and included extensive perimeter security and widely dispersed buildings. Iraq claimed that production of botulinum toxin and anthrax for weapons purposes had begun at Al Hakam by 1989. In total, about 6,000 liters of concentrated botulinum toxin and 8,425 liters of anthrax were declared to have been produced at Al Hakam.

In 1989 aflatoxin production was established at a facility near Fudaliyah. Iraq declared that the facility was used for aflatoxin production in flasks from April/May 1990 to December 1990. A total of about 1,850 liters of toxin in solution was declared to have been produced at Fudaliyah.

The toxin ricin was investigated by Iraq in 1988. Following initial toxicological tests in conjunction with the chemical weapons program at Muthanna, ten liters of concentrated ricin were prepared. The ricin was placed in artillery shells and a field trial conducted. Iraq declared that the test was a failure, and the project was abandoned.

The Iraqi program expanded to include viral research in 1990. After initial activities at Salman Pak, the BW program acquired a foot-and-mouth disease vaccine production facility for additional BW efforts. Work on viruses for biological weapons purposes was said to include hemorrhagic conjunctivitis, a rotavirus, and camel pox. Iraq stated that little progress had been made and that no viral agents had been produced in bulk.

Weaponization efforts were initially conducted in concert with the existing, and well-established, chemical weapons program. From 1988 to 1990, weaponization efforts allegedly included field trials of aerial bombs, artillery rounds, and unguided artillery rockets. Trials were declared to have been conducted with both actual BW agents and agent simulants like *Bacillus subtilis* (instead of anthrax).

At the end of 1990 Iraq allegedly initiated a BW spray tank project. Iraq intended to mount the tank on either a piloted or remotely piloted aircraft and spray up to 2,000 liters of anthrax over a target area. Field trials of this system were purportedly conducted in January 1991 and considered a failure. However, a total of four tanks were modified and readied for use. Iraq claimed that all of the tanks were either destroyed during the war or destroyed unilaterally in 1991, in its effort to conceal the offensive BW program.

Iraq stated that BW agent had been loaded into both operational R-400 aerial bombs and Al Hussein ballistic missile warheads. These weapons were then deployed in January 1991 and were considered ready for use. Iraq claims that, in the summer of 1991, it unilaterally destroyed all of these filled munitions. All remaining bulk agent was allegedly destroyed at Al Hakam in the summer of 1991.

By October 1995 Iraq had declared the production of at least 19,000 liters of concentrated botulinum toxin, using almost 10,000 liters in munitions; 8,500 liters of concentrated anthrax, with about 6,500 liters loaded in munitions; and 2,200 liters of concentrated aflatoxin (allegedly 1,580 liters were filled into munitions).

## CONTINUING CONCERNS, CONTINUING INVESTIGATION

Iraq's July 1995 disclosures about its BW program not only validated the suspicions held by the Commission since 1991 but also opened wide a new field of inquiry. UNSCOM experts shifted to a verification of the scope of Iraq's newly declared offensive BW program. The Commission faced the "new" problem of conducting a quantitative investigation of Iraq's accounting for its produced BW weapons and agent. This quantitative assessment—also known as a mass or materials balance—involved checking the amount of material (agent, bombs, or even raw ingredients) procured or produced by Iraq against the amounts already destroyed to ensure that none remained. If the material balance did not sum to zero then UNSCOM would monitor or verify the destruction of the remaining proscribed items.

From 1995 to 1997 dozens of BW verification inspections were conducted, most of which resulted in uncertainties or clear inaccuracies in various parts of previous Iraqi declarations. When enough of these errors had been identified Iraq would produce a new "full, final, complete disclosure" (FFCD), and the process would start again. In total Iraq presented three "final" versions of its BW FFCD and four "drafts." The most recent FFCD was presented by Iraq on September 11, 1997.[26]

In response to continuing UNSCOM findings that it had not fully disclosed its biological weapons program, Iraq began calling for an independent (i.e., not UNSCOM) assessment of the BW declaration. In 1997 and 1998 UNSCOM convened three panels of international experts in biology, biotechnology, and biological weapons to examine Iraq's September 1997 FFCD.[27] The panels included a small number of UNSCOM experts and a far larger number of outside personnel. In all three cases the panels found the FFCD to be lacking in substance and accuracy.[28]

The third of these panels, termed a technical evaluation meeting (TEM), was held in March 1998 in Vienna. The panel concluded that a multitude of issues were incompletely described, inaccurate in their presentation, or missing entirely.[29] The assembled experts determined that a wide range of Iraqi BW activities required still further disclosure and clarification before Iraq's description of its program would be acceptable.

The TEM found that documented information on the origins, purpose, and current status of the offensive BW program was absent from the FFCD. Iraq failed to provide the rationale, justification, and requirements for organizations and sites involved in the BW program, including those for weapons tests, research and development, production, storage, weapons production and filling, deployment, and destruction sites for weapons, documents, and agents.

Some of the most startling problems involved the central issue of materials balances. The FFCD does not sufficiently explain acquisition of supplies, materials, munitions, and equipment. This gap includes the omission of substantial quantities of microbial growth media, which remain undeclared. The numerical accounting for growth media consumption is flawed and is based in large part on Iraqi estimates, many of which are themselves based on still other estimates. None of the estimated values is supported by documentary evidence. In summary, the TEM found that the declared quantities of BW agent produced were not credibly established.

Weaponization, weapons production, and unilateral destruction issues raised still more concerns. Iraq has not provided a complete disclosure on the numbers, types, and detailed accounting of individual BW systems. Declarations by Iraq on the alleged unilateral destruction of Al Hussein missile warheads filled with BW agents do not match the physical evidence available. Iraq's description of its aircraft spray-tank project is deficient in all areas, including planning, procurement, testing, and production. Because of limited data in the FFCD, no confident assessment can be made of the scale of production of BW-filled aerial bombs or their fate. The technical sophistication of Iraq's aerobiology research is also not adequately explained. The results of Iraq's BW research efforts were similarly unclear to the TEM.

The TEM expressed further apprehension over the concealment and discontinuation of the BW program. Despite the fact that the BW program was hidden from the Commission until 1995, there is no description in the FFCD of the rationale for this concealment, the actions taken to conceal the program, or the organizations involved. Iraq states that the BW program was "obliterated" in 1991, yet facilities, growth media, equipment, and core groups of experts at Al Hakam were retained.

Iraq maintains that it has provided a full and complete account of its BW program; however, UNSCOM's most recent assessment, supported by three panels of independent outside experts, is quite different. In April 1998 the Commission reported to the Security Council that:

> The disclosure provided by Iraq in September 1997 "still does not cover the entirety of the BW program." Iraq's FFCD is judged to be incomplete and inadequate and to contain major mistakes, inconsistencies and gaps in information. The FFCD does not provide a clear understanding of the current status of the BW program nor whether, nor when, it was terminated.[30]

## POLITICAL COLLAPSE

While UNSCOM was making significant advances in its understanding of the Iraqi BW program, the effort needed to continue this progress also increased. Each new detail about the Iraqi program required even more effort to extract. Iraq was increasingly willing to elevate technical and procedural issues to the high political arena. In the early 1990s Iraq was rebuked every time disarmament issues came before the Council. But by the latter half of the decade Baghdad no longer feared such criticism. In fact, given the growing split between the United States and the United Kingdom on one side and the French, Russians, and Chinese on the other, the response of the Council was sometimes not even unanimous.

This drop in international political support for strict verifiable elimination of Iraqi WMD capabilities coincided with heightened intrusiveness on the part of UNSCOM. As the Commission's knowledge of the Iraqi weapons programs grew, so did its understanding of Baghdad's process for hiding weapons and weapons-related information.[31] Iraqi documents seized by inspectors, deductive analysis of gaps in the material-balance of all WMD programs, and small pieces of data provided to UNSCOM by supporting governments all indicated the existence of a coordinated program for hiding information and materials from the UN. In late 1994 UNSCOM began to investigate the Iraqi concealment mechanism with the same intensity given to the industrial and scientific side of the proscribed weapons programs.[32]

Two organizations held the lead role in concealing materials and information from UNSCOM: the Special Security Organization (SSO) and the Special Republican Guard (SRG). By the summer of 1996 UNSCOM teams had gathered enough information—from previous inspections, Iraqi documents, Iraqis no longer in Iraq, open sources, and numerous supporting governments—to attempt to inspect numerous facilities containing SSO and SRG offices and barracks. Inspection of these facilities was blocked by Iraq, citing national security and sovereignty concerns.[33] The SSO and SRG are also the lead organizations responsible for protection of the Iraqi president and its other senior leadership.

Over the course of 1997 and early 1998 Iraq and UNSCOM moved through a series of crises, all related to the search for hidden proscribed materials and data. Because of their proximity to presidential facilities the SSO and SRG sites offered Iraq a convenient excuse for denial of access: UNSCOM was trying to inspect Saddam's palaces. In fact the teams had focused on SSO, SRG, and other facilities that, in some cases, happened to be located near the palaces.

The "palaces" crisis came to a head in January 1998 when Iraq refused to allow an UNSCOM team to conduct any inspections.[34] As tensions escalated the United Nations Secretary-General, Kofi Annan, joined the fray. At the conclusion of a highly publicized visit to Baghdad on February 23, the Secretary-General signed his Memorandum of Understanding (MOU) with the government of Iraq.[35]

With Iraq's pledge to allow disarmament to move forward, the MOU appeared to end the persistent problem of access to sensitive, presidential-level sites. The MOU also established special procedures for the inspection of the eight presidential sites. A new leadership structure for the visits—they could not be called inspections—was implemented. Diplomatic observers were also included in the process.

Despite its initial smooth implementation, the impact of the presidential site issue was to be profound. The effect was not on the Commission's technical assessments, investigative activities, or inspection operations. Rather the MOU was the first significant case of obvious political compromise on the disarmament aspects of the cease-fire agreement.

By seeking and then supporting the MOU, the Security Council members created a political dynamic of disarmament regime change. The implementation of the disarmament provisions was no longer strictly an UNSCOM/ Iraq affair, as the Secretary-General was now directly involved. In essence this dynamic of change meant that negotiations had begun. The belief that the provisions of Council Resolutions 687, 707, and 715 were written in stone was dead.

## Return to Work

Following the close of the presidential sites episode, UNSCOM operations returned to much the same state they had been in prior to the crisis. Monitoring teams inspected industrial, academic, research, and commercial facilities. Visiting disarmament teams held discussions and inspected sites declared by Iraq, primarily sites used to hide weapons in 1991 and unilateral destruction locations. However, an important component of the Commission's work, the unilateral search for hidden weapons, materials, equipment, and documents, was absent.

Within the new political reality UNSCOM found it difficult—even impossible—to conduct search inspections. By their very nature these inspections have uncertain outcomes, a risk that was no longer acceptable. Furthermore, the Commission leadership could no longer be certain of full Council support in the case of a standoff at an inspection site. With a few exceptions UNSCOM made little progress in its investigation of the Iraqi biological weapons program in 1998. As a direct consequence, there was no substantive change in Iraq's declaration from that of September 1997.

On August 5, 1998, following a tense series of meetings between the executive chairman of UNSCOM and the Iraqi deputy prime minister, the Revolutionary Command Council (RCC), Iraq's highest decision-making body, announced that it would no longer cooperate with the Special Commission on issues of disarmament. Iraq would no longer work, it said, with inspection teams and would provide no further data or disclosures on its proscribed activities.[36] In its statement the RCC asserted that "the Commission has been turned into a disgraced instrument for implementing the criminal American policy against Iraq either by finding pretexts and fabricating crises with a view to maintaining the sanctions or by spying over Iraq and threatening its national security and sovereignty."[37] Claiming that Iraq had completed all of the disarmament requirements, the RCC demanded that the Security Council immediately release the embargo on the sale of Iraqi oil.

The Command Council also called for the reorganization and relocation of UNSCOM. The near-term impact of the RCC decision was to end disarmament work by the Commission.

The Security Council made its views known in Resolution 1194. The Council condemned Iraq's actions and demanded that Iraq rescind its decision of August 5. To exert pressure on Iraq, the Council took the limited step of suspending its sixty-day reviews of the sanctions regime, which had only ever been viewed as a pro forma event. Iraqi maintained its decision.

After three months of allowing UNSCOM to conduct monitoring, and waiting for the Council to lift the oil embargo, on October 31 Iraq announced its decision to suspend, stop, or cease all activities of the Special Commission, including ongoing monitoring. The Security Council responded with a resolution (1205) condemning Iraq's decision. The resolution deemed Baghdad's new policy a "flagrant violation" of the cease-fire resolution. Again the Council offered a weak response to a pointed assault by Iraq on the cease-fire terms. Iraq was not simply blocking access to a single site, or refusing to hand over a document; it was now totally obstructing all disarmament aspects of the cease-fire agreement. The political environment in the Council, specifically the five permanent members, no longer supported a stringent, no-compromise implementation of the Council's own laws.

On November 14, as a result of military threats by the United States and the United Kingdom, involvement of the Secretary-General, and assurances from pro-Iraq members of the Council, Baghdad rescinded its August 5 and October 31 decisions. In a curious dismissal of its earlier position, Iraq agreed to allow UNSCOM and the IAEA to resume the full breadth of their activities.

With the resumption of its monitoring activities, the Commission also renewed its requests for relevant documents and additional information on Iraq's biological and chemical weapons activities.[38] Although for the most part Iraq cooperated with the monitoring teams, it maintained its refusal to turn over documents or supply new information. In mid-December the Commission's 258th inspection team entered Iraq to conduct searches for hidden documents and materials. The team experienced the same access limitations, delays, and sanitized sites that teams had experienced numerous times on a number of earlier inspections.[39]

As requested by the Council, the chairman reported on December 15, 1998, that Iraq was not adequately fulfilling the requirements of the relevant resolutions.[40] Early the next day, under expectations of unilateral military action, he ordered all UNSCOM personnel out of Iraq for the last time. Late on December 16, U.S. and UK military forces attacked facilities in Iraq. Although the Security Council had no position on the December attacks, several of the members—particularly Russia—strenuously opposed any use of force to compel Iraqi compliance.

Following the December military strikes UNSCOM has been unable to conduct any work in Iraq. The Security Council has remained divided as to its next steps. In late January 1999, in hopes of bridging their differences, the Council established a set of panels to examine the Iraq issue. One of the panels examined the disarmament problem.

In February and March 1999 the disarmament panel received briefings on the status of UNSCOM's work and debated ways to move forward. On March 27 the panel passed by consensus its report to the Council.[41] Most notable is that the Panel, consisting of a small number of UNSCOM staff, a host of outside arms control experts, and a few political representatives, fully supported UNSCOM's assessments of the state of the arms investigations, including the existence of significant unresolved issues.

By December 1999 the members of the Security Council thought they had closed ranks enough to vote on a new resolution covering disarmament in Iraq. After months of negotiations the permanent members had come up with a new formula for the inspection process, principally the replacement of UNSCOM with a new body, UNMOVIC. The new Commission would have the same mandate but would operate under increased Council and Secretariat oversight. Yet even with the changes to the disarmament regime in draft form, Russia, France, China, and Malaysia all abstained from voting for the resolution.[42]

From its very beginnings UNMOVIC found itself abandoned by the very body that created it. The new Commission has spent its time reviewing old UNSCOM files and training.[43] Iraq still totally opposes any return of inspectors and is unlikely to change its position given the exceedingly weak policies of the Security Council.

Even after the terrorist events of September 2001, both hijackings and anthrax attacks, the basic Security Council dynamic did not change. Following almost two years of low-level discussion and debate, the Council remained divided on the Iraq problem. Renewed U.S. demands for inspections, and an associated buildup of military threats, seem to have only generated a new Iraqi stalling campaign. In response to the Secretary-General's efforts to bridge the impasse, Iraq in March 2002 presented its own list of requirements.[44] By demanding to know how long further inspections will last and seeking guarantees that the confrontations of the past will not be repeated, Baghdad appears to favor the status quo. Despite optimistic projections by UNMOVIC about the speed with which it might be able to complete its task, it is unlikely that the Commission will ever get the chance without significant international political realignment.

## INEVITABLE CONFLICT

Some observers have suggested that the goal of designing a BW verification mechanism that can detect noncompliance is unattainable. The Special Commission has proven—in a specialized case to be sure—that it is not impossible to detect a concealed BW program, even when it is carefully hidden. With several years of significant effort supported by a highly intrusive inspection regime, UNSCOM was able to build a case that could have only one outcome: Iraq's admission of an offensive BW program. UNSCOM has also shown that such verification may require a highly intrusive, prolonged investigation, backed by threats of sanctions and military force.

To uncover the Iraqi program, UNSCOM used small pieces of circumstantial evidence that individually did not seem significant but together created a damning picture of Iraq's activities. This portrait was then used to highlight elements of investigative data that did not fit Iraq's declarations, anomalies that further developed and confirmed UNSCOM's theories.

UNSCOM demonstrated the value of a system approach to biological arms verification, rather than looking for single elements and discrete actions. The all-pervasive problem of dual-capability in BW arms control was addressed by looking not at single pieces of equipment nor specific materials but at the whole of the capability. It was the combination and obvious direction of Iraq's dual-use capabilities that convinced the world of Iraq's deceit.

Beyond the technical investigation many other factors have affected the outcome of disarmament in Iraq. In addition to UNSCOM and the government of Iraq, there is the critical role played by members of the Security Council. Initially the Council was responsible for creating the international law under which the disarmament investigations operated, but increasingly the Council was called upon to act as enforcer of those laws.

### Iraq

The policies of Iraq, UNSCOM, and the Security Council developed over time, but showed in all three cases consistent trends. The government of Iraq held to a constant policy of concealment of proscribed items and materials and a retention of technical and industrial capabilities. While UNSCOM had its successes, and Iraq its losses, the fundamental policy in Baghdad never changed.

Baghdad was pressed to destroy the long-concealed Al Hakam biological weapons production plant and was forced to admit BW-related technical and industrial capabilities that it initially sought to conceal. Yet these defeats did not change Iraq's fundamental desire to retain a WMD capacity, and where possible an extant capability. The discoveries made by UNS-COM, and related destruction actions, also served to shrink the pool of materials that Iraq wished to hide. As the pool shrank, Iraq's resolve increased. The political capital and national resources necessary to conceal the smaller cache of hidden items also decreased, thus allowing Iraq more successes for the same effort.

## UNSCOM

The mandate of the Special Commission remained constant. Throughout its history the Commission had only one instruction: Eliminate all WMD from Iraq. Over the eight years UNSCOM worked to attain this objective, it developed arms control verification tools and capabilities that were unimaginable in the spring of 1991. These techniques matched well with the need for ever-increasing intrusiveness. As Iraq buried its WMD capabilities deeper and deeper and worked harder to conceal them, UNSCOM followed close behind, by prying into Iraq's national security apparatus and even presidential offices.

The inspection techniques began in 1991 as a continuation of then-existing arms control treaties and conventions still in negotiation. At the outset UNSCOM interpreted its mandate to be only a small measure more intrusive than then-accepted cooperative arms control verification. But in the face of Iraqi deception, obstructions, and concealment, the Commission soon developed a more robust verification process. UNSCOM became increasingly willing to inspect sites connected with the Iraqi military, security services, intelligence organizations, and facilities owned by the Iraqi Presidency. Even the headquarters of Iraqi government ministries were eventually inspected.

The inspection tools and techniques used by the teams also improved. In the initial investigations the bulk of the inspectors' work involved visual inspection of industrial plants and storage sites (literally counting bombs). However, as the paucity of data available to the Commission became clear, interviews and close questioning of Iraqi scientists, military personnel, high government officials, and even presidential bodyguards became a standard.

Similarly, the U-2 reconnaissance aircraft became a central participant in surprise inspections. Initially the U-2 was used to collect images of Iraqi facilities for monitoring and inspection planning purposes. But as UNS-COM investigations began to directly target Iraqi concealment activities, specifically evacuation of sites immediately prior to inspection, the U-2 was put to a new and more invasive use. As inspection teams approached the site on the ground, a U-2 would fly in circles overhead collecting a record of activity in and around the facility. These photos of Iraqi vehicles fleeing sites minutes before inspectors arrived would be used to demonstrate the existence of a concerted, organized concealment mechanism. Other sensational techniques like highly sensitive forensic chemical and biological sampling, ground penetrating radar, and communications intercept systems were similarly brought into use to deal with Iraqi intransigence.

Thus UNSCOM and Iraq were each on the path to inevitable conflict. As the investigation progressed, the Commission became increasingly focused and intrusive. It had no choice given the remarkably plain language of its mandate. For its part Iraq never wavered from its desire to maintain a WMD capability. Iraq accepted a number of stinging defeats in its competition with UNSCOM, but the basic policy of concealment never changed. These two policy paths did not directly conflict through most of the early days of the disarmament regime. But in the late stages, from 1996 to 1998, the two sides were locked in a near-constant standoff from which neither could extricate itself.

## The Security Council

Given the irreconcilable conflict between UNSCOM and Iraq, the burden of resolving the standoff was elevated to the Security Council. In contrast to its resolutions, the Security Council members did not hold consistent views regarding the importance of the disarmament regime. The Council's initially strict, unanimous enforcement of the cease-fire requirements drifted to ambivalence and then to cases of open hostility toward the Special Commission. The rapid, forceful international condemnation of Iraqi noncompliance in 1991, 1992, and 1993 had faded by 1997, when a number of Council members actually abstained from voting on a resolution condemning Iraq's blockage of an inspection team.[45]

In general the Council showed a steady decline in resolve to enforce the cease-fire requirements. The trend in the Security Council was simply an adjustment of policy priorities on the part of the international community. Other objectives overtook the removal of weapons of mass destruction from Iraq. Some members, previously staunch supporters of strict disarmament, found that regional strategic issues and general inattention sapped their ability to convincingly lead the Council. Other countries, full supporters of Resolution 687 at the time of its passage, fondly recalled their prewar trade with Iraq and sought an environment that would allow them to economically reengage Baghdad. By 1998 one such country was called, by many, the "Iraqi Interest Section of the Security Council." Still other nations were swayed by the effects of the sanctions regime. The suffering of the Iraqi people, both real and that fostered by incessant fraudulent Iraqi propaganda, found many sympathetic ears.

When UNSCOM departed Iraq at the end of 1998, the members of the Security Council no longer considered Baghdad's weapons of mass destruction to be their most pressing policy concern. Without the single-minded focus of 1991 on full Iraqi compliance with the cease-fire terms, the Council members found it increasingly easy to compromise on or to ignore the incomplete state of disarmament in Iraq.

## ENFORCING DISARMAMENT

Forced disarmament is inherently problematic as it inevitably creates a state of tension. The process requires constant effort, for it cannot be achieved without pressure on the targeted state.

If the inspectors are capable and the inspected party has a depth of resistance, then continuing Security Council support and enforcement is required. Failing such support the inspected state will always be able to outlast and overcome the inspectors. It is after all a contest between hundreds of inspectors and tens of thousands of cheaters.

Outlawing biological weapons and creating a BWC Protocol, presumably with some form of international "Organization for the Prohibition of Biological Weapons," are only the first steps in eliminating the BW threat. Enforcement of the regime is also required.

What will the Security Council do when a treaty signatory hinders an authorized BWC team, whether it is called an inspection, a visit, or a consultation? Perhaps the state will unilaterally declare a certain category of facility off-limits to foreigners. Or perhaps the country could refuse to answer the BWC team's questions about an unusual outbreak of disease caused by a classic BW-related organism. In such cases of obstruction, the international community must look to itself, not the implementing organization, for maintenance of the regime.

The world's experience with Iraq's biological weapons program should demonstrate that if a country has a compelling reason to retain or develop a strategic WMD capability, it will pursue that goal despite international opinion. Iraq's actions of August 5, 1998, make this case in stark terms. The international community, and arms controllers in particular, should not underestimate the capabilities of nation states with such overriding national interests, nor should they overlook the perishable nature of international resolve.

## NOTES

This chapter is adapted from Stephen Black, "UNSCOM and the Iraqi Biological Weapons Program: Implications for Arms Control," *Politics and the Life Sciences* (March 1999). Relevant United Nations Security Council resolutions and documents and UNSCOM photographs are available online at www.un.org/depts/unscom.

1. United Nations Security Council Resolution 687, 1991.
2. Ibid.
3. UNSCOM's disarmament investigations and monitoring operations ceased in December 1998. The organization itself ended with the passage of resolution 1284 on December 17, 1999.
4. *Charter of the United Nations*, chapter VII.
5. United Nations Security Council Resolution 678, 1990.
6. The resolution also includes a more general ban on exports to Iraq of all goods other than food and humanitarian items. This restriction, covered by paragraph 21 of Resolution 687, is dependent on general Iraqi compliance with all aspects of the cease-fire and other Council decisions, including return of Kuwaiti property, recognition of boarders, repression of minority groups in Iraq, and war reparations.
7. United Nations Security Council Resolution 687, 1991, Paragraph 22.
8. Javier Perez de Cuellar, Secretary-General of the United Nations, Letter to His Excellency Ahmed Hussein, Minister for Foreign Affairs of the Republic of Iraq, 6 May 1991, unpublished.
9. United Nations Security Council Resolution 707, 1991.
10. Although UNSCOM ceased to exist in 1999, the disarmament requirements of Resolution 687 were reiterated in Resolution 1284, 1999, which created UNMOVIC.
11. Government of Iraq, letter addressed to the Secretary-General of the United Nations (Initial disarmament declaration), 18 April 1991, unpublished.
12. See, for example, the Gulf Link collection of U.S. government documents on the Iraqi BW program declassified as a result of the Gulf War Syndrome investigation, available online at www.gulflink.osd.mil.
13. United Nations Security Council, "Note by the Secretary-General," S/23165, 25 October 1991.
14. Ibid.
15. Ibid.
16. United Nations Security Council, "Note by the Secretary-General," S/23993, 22 May 1992.
17. United Nations Security Council, "Report of the Secretary-General on the Status of the Implementation of the Special Commission's Plan for the Ongoing Monitoring and Verification of Iraq's Compliance with Relevant Parts of Section C of Security Council Resolution 687 (1991)," S/1994/1138, 7 October 1994.
18. United Nations Security Council, "Note by the Secretary-General," S/1995/284, 10 April 1995.
19. Ibid.
20. Ibid.
21. Ibid.
22. United Nations Security Council, "Note by the Secretary-General," S/1995/864, 11 October 1995.
23. Ibid.
24. Ibid.
25. The information in this section is drawn from United Nations Security Coun-

cil, "Note by the Secretary-General," S/1995/864, 11 October 1995. This portrayal of the Iraqi BW program is probably accurate only in broad terms. This description of the program is illustrative, but not verified in specifics or scope.

26. United Nations Security Council, "Note by the Secretary-General," S/1997/774, 6 October 1997.

27. United Nations Security Council, "Letter dated 8 April 1998 from the Executive Chairman of the Special Commission established by the Secretary-General pursuant to paragraph 9 (b) (I) of Security Council Resolution 687 (1991) addressed to the President of the Security Council," S/1998/308, 8 April 1998.

28. United Nations Security Council, "Note by the Secretary-General," S/1998/332, 16 April 1998.

29. UNSC, "Letter dated 8 April 1998 from the Executive Chairman of the Special Commission . . . to the President of the Security Council."

30. UNSC, "Note by the Secretary-General," S/1998/332, 16 April 1998. This assessment is reiterated and further explained in United Nations Security Council, "Letter dated 27 January 1999 from the permanent representatives of The Netherlands and Slovenia to the United Nations addressed to the President of the Security Council," S/1999/94, 29 January 1999.

31. UNSC, "Letter dated 27 January 1999 from the permanent representatives of The Netherlands and Slovenia . . . to the President of the Security Council."

32. United Nations Security Council, "Note by the Secretary General," S/1996/848, 11 October 1996.

33. Ibid.

34. Curiously, the team's first and only day of inspections took it nowhere near any of Saddam's palaces.

35. United Nations Security Council, "Letter dated 25 February 1998 from the Secretary-General addressed to the President of the Security Council," S/1998/166, 27 February 1998.

36. United Nations Security Council, "Letter dated 12 August 1998 from the Executive Chairman of the Special Commission established by the Secretary-General pursuant to paragraph 9 (b) (I) of Security Council Resolution 687 (1991) addressed to the President of the Security Council," S/1998/767,12 August 1998. See also United Nations Security Council, "Letter dated 5 August 1998 from the Chargé D'Affaires A. I. of the Permanent Mission of Iraq to the United Nations addressed to the President of the Security Council," S/1998/718, 14 August 1998.

37. UNSC, "Letter dated 5 August 1998 from the Chargé D'Affaires A. I. of the Permanent Mission of Iraq . . . to the President of the Security Council."

38. United Nations Security Council, "Letter dated 30 November 1998 from the Executive Chairman of the Special Commission established by the Secretary-General pursuant to paragraph 9 (b) (I) of Security Council Resolution 687 (1991) addressed to the President of the Security Council," S/1998/1127, 30 November 1998.

39. United Nations Security Council, "Letter dated 15 December 1998 from the Secretary-General addressed to the President of the Security Council," S/1998/1172,15 December 1998.

40. Ibid.

41. United Nations Security Council, "Letter dated 27 March 1999, from the

Chairman of the Panels Established Pursuant to the Note by the President of the Security Council of 30 January 1999 (S/1999/100) addressed to the President of the Security Council," S/1999/356, 30 March 1999.

42. United Nations Security Council Resolution 1284, 1999.

43. For further information on UNMOVIC see its website at www.un.org/Depts/unmovic/index.htm.

44. Christopher Wren, "UN Inspector Tells Council Work in Iraq Could Be Fast," *New York Times* (22 March 2002).

45. United Nations Security Council Resolution 1134, 23 October 1997.

# V

# THE BIOLOGICAL WEAPONS CONVENTION

# 12

## Geopolitical Origins

*Susan Wright*

On August 6, 1968, the United Kingdom tabled a working paper in the Eighteen-Nation Disarmament Committee in Geneva proposing elements of a future convention banning possession of biological weapons, a move followed in July 1969 with a proposal for the convention itself. Understanding the United Kingdom's interests in proposing what would become the first disarmament treaty in the second half of the twentieth century, and the conditions that shaped these interests, is important for understanding the political substructure of the 1972 Biological Weapons Convention (BWC) and the role it was designed to play in international relations.

Until recently, the history of the BWC was known mainly through the records of the negotiations in the Eighteen-Nation Disarmament Committee (ENDC) between 1968 and 1972, occasional tantalizing reminiscences of insiders in the participating governments, and a few enterprising journalists who have managed to give us glimpses of the reasons for government policies despite the wall of secrecy that surrounded questions of chemical and biological warfare (CBW). Now the archival records of the United Kingdom and the United States, two governments that played key roles in the BWC negotiations, are becoming available, and we can begin to examine the calculations that were accessible at the time only to political elites, and even then, because of the secrecy that constrains information flows within and between governments, only partially accessible. These documents provide rich insights into the military and political constraints that defined the limits of what was deemed politically and militarily possible for the control of chemical and biological weaponry, and what was, therefore, possible as a response to growing public and international pressures for chemical and

313

biological disarmament. A primary purpose of this chapter is to explore these limits in the case of the BWC. A further purpose is to emphasize the difference between what was known to those with access to the most secret levels of government and what was provided through the media to the attentive public in the United Kingdom and the United States.

In the late 1960s, the extensive use by the United States of anti-personnel and anti-plant chemical weapons in Vietnam focused attention on issues of chemical and biological warfare in the United Nations, the United States and the United Kingdom, and elsewhere. In the United Nations, criticism of American policy came not only from the Soviet Union and the Eastern bloc but also from prominent nonaligned and non-Western countries. In November 1966, Hungary submitted to the UN a draft resolution designed to condemn the United States for violating the 1925 Geneva Protocol. The resolution demanded "strict and absolute compliance" with the Protocol, condemned actions aimed at the use of chemical and biological weapons, and declared the use of those weapons for the purpose of destroying human beings and the means of their existence "an international crime." The United States successfully maneuvered to replace the resolution with a much weaker version that could be taken to apply only to lethal chemicals, not riot control agents used for "humanitarian purposes" or herbicides, and that was eventually adopted.[1] Nevertheless, international pressure on the United States continued to intensify.

In both the United States and the United Kingdom, concern about the use of chemicals in war expanded to encompass larger questions about the purposes of their largely secret chemical and biological warfare establishments and the policies guiding them. In the United States, critical actions spanned a range from petitions to protests. Members of the U.S. scientific establishment took actions that found niches of support within the administration of President Lyndon Johnson. A well-publicized letter to the president called for an end to the use of anti-personnel and anti-crop chemical weapons in Vietnam, a study of government policy regarding chemical and biological weapons, and a U.S. commitment to a no-first-use policy for those weapons. The cover letter, signed by four eminent scientists, also proposed U.S. accession to the Geneva Protocol. These were moderate proposals in the sense that they did not directly accuse the United States of violating the Geneva Protocol or attack the programs responsible for producing the weapons. Such actions contrasted with the forceful tactics of antiwar activists who took both to the streets and to scientific meetings to stage demonstrations demanding an end to the chemical and biological weapons programs and to the complicity of science in them.

British dissent was similarly varied. Although Britain was not involved in the Vietnam War, it was known that the British CBW establishments were linked to CBW work in the United States. The records of the British Foreign Office show a beleaguered bureaucracy, anxiously attempting both to track and to respond to meetings, conferences, pointed Parliamentary Questions, letters from bishops and representatives of the YWCA, and television programs about the British chemical and biological warfare establishments. Questions were raised not only about the British government's own CBW policies but also about the precise nature of its CBW collaboration with the United States. Harold Wilson's Labour government, elected in 1964, was especially sensitive to criticism since much of it came from within its own ranks.

As this account will show, the principled public criticism of government support for CBW, which expressed abhorrence toward the use of chemicals in Vietnam and more generally toward the continued existence of CBW programs, contrasted with the political calculations and tough pragmatism that characterized CBW discussions within the UK and U.S. foreign policy and military establishments. Such governmental postures were all the more inflexible for being largely shielded from full public scrutiny. Newly available documents, many once secret, now reveal that the British and American publics were allowed to see only the tips of various military and political icebergs, if that. Much governmental understanding of the real purposes of foreign and military policies and the nature of the chemical and biological warfare programs to which they applied was either kept secret or distorted by evasions and lies.[2]

## THE U.S. AND UK CHEMICAL AND BIOLOGICAL WARFARE PROGRAMS IN THE 1960s

While criticism of the American and British CBW programs continued to intensify in the late 1960s, thinking about chemical and biological warfare and disarmament within their military establishments continued to be dominated by the Cold War and, more immediately for the United States, by the Vietnam War. Any analysis of British CBW policies must begin by considering those of the United States, Britain's closest and most powerful ally. In important respects, American military policy set limits on how far the British government felt it could move toward chemical and biological disarmament. The large U.S. chemical and biological weapons programs of the late 1960s resulted from a post–World War II expansion fueled by Cold War fears of the Soviet Union. This expansion had brought the U.S. stockpile of poison gas to some 42,000 tons; had stimulated military interest in developing novel binary nerve gas weapons; had led to stockpiling of at least ten different biological and toxin weapons; and had generated a huge, mostly secret research and development establishment. The United States had also secretly deployed lethal chemical weapons in West Germany as part of the chemical deterrent agreed upon by the member states of NATO, news of which emerged, partially, in 1969.[3]

Beyond developing lethal chemicals, the United States was also actively pursuing development of "riot control" agents also used for domestic purposes, "incapacitating agents" (a designation reflecting military claims that casualties would be nonfatal), and herbicides for destruction of vegetation. Thousands of tons of these substances were being used in Vietnam.[4] American officials contended publicly that riot control agents were being used for "humanitarian purposes," to save the lives of innocent civilians used as human shields. But in secret they acknowledged that these gases were being used in conjunction with artillery and small arms fire and air-delivered ordnance in ways that increased enemy casualties "while reducing U.S. and friendly casualties"—uses that were "inconsistent with [the] 'humanitarian' purposes rationale."[5] When U.S. and UK arms-control officials met in October 1967, the participants knew that the use of tear gas to force soldiers to break cover and expose themselves to other weapons was "against the commonly accepted rules of war."[6]

The policies for use of chemical and biological weapons were characterized by considerable secrecy and uncertainty. The United States had signed but had never ratified the 1925 Geneva Protocol, which banned the use of "asphyxiating, poisonous or other gases, and of all analogous liquids, materials or devices" as well as "bacteriological" weapons, although many countries had weakened that ban by reserving the right to retaliate in kind. In effect, the Geneva Protocol banned *first* use of chemical and biological weapons. From the mid-1960s onwards, U.S. officials began to state that national policy proscribed the first use of *lethal* chemical and biological agents but that riot control agents were not covered by the Protocol.[7] However, there was no assurance that the United States was formally bound by such promises. Indeed, a proposal originating in the U.S. Arms Control and Disarmament Agency (ACDA) for an official no-first-use policy for "permanently injurious CBW agents" went nowhere.[8] The uncertainty surrounding U.S. CBW policy in this period is confirmed by a secret letter from U.S. Secretary of Defense Robert McNamara to Secretary of State Dean Rusk in 1966 concerning a draft National Security Action Memorandum, stating that "the President does not now expect to authorize first use of lethal CB weapons."[9]

Furthermore, since "lethal chemicals" were deemed by the United States not to include tear gases, incapacitating agents, and herbicides, the U.S. intention clearly was to leave open its military options for these. McNamara so advised Rusk, "until we have better information concerning specific incapacitating agents, their effectiveness, and the political consequences of their use."[10] As a top secret 1967 British report stated, one of the reasons for the U.S. refusal to be bound by a "*formal* no-first-use commitment on CBW" was that "research may turn up non-lethal C or B agents both humane and unprecedentedly effective."[11] In effect, despite occasional official utterances that the United States would not be the first to use lethal chemical or biological weapons, there was no *formal* change of policy until President Nixon's extensive review of the chemical and biological warfare policies in 1969 and the issuance of National Security Decision Memorandum 35.

The U.S. commitment to keeping its options open with respect to its use of riot control agents and incapacitants in Vietnam guided its responses to public and international pressures for compliance with the Geneva Protocol, interpreted broadly as banning use of *all* chemical and biological agents in war. The Hungarian UN resolution of November 1966 posed a dilemma for the United States: Opposing it would play into the hands of the Eastern Bloc and the view that the United States was violating international law in Vietnam. And in any case it was doubtful that the United States could count on Western support. But supporting the resolution, with its clear implication that the United States was violating the Geneva Protocol, was out of the question. Thus the United States, in conjunction with Italy, Canada, and the United Kingdom, maneuvered to develop amendments that eliminated any implication that the Geneva Protocol applied to anti-personnel and anti-plant agents. Flurries of telegrams went back and forth between the British Foreign Office and the British mission in New York recording the U.S. effort, with the assistance of the United Kingdom, Canada, and Italy, to develop an acceptable amendment to the Hungarian text.[12] The operative lines of the amended text simply called for "strict observance" of the Protocol and invited all states to accede to it, thereby deftly sidelining the crucial question of what the Protocol did or did not cover. The text was eventually passed on December 5, 1966, by ninety-one to zero with four abstentions, and the United States and the West, except for France, voting for it. American Ambassador James Nabrit explained his vote, using the rationale developed by Washington's arms controllers, that although the United States was not a party to the Geneva Protocol, it would in no circumstances use poison gas unless it was used first by an adversary. But he emphasized that the United States did not accept the claim that the Geneva Protocol covered "the use in combat, against an enemy, for humanitarian purposes, of agents that Governments around the world commonly use to control riots by their own people." Similarly, the Protocol did "not apply to herbicides, which involve the same chemicals and have the same effects as those used domestically in the United States."[13] The interest of the U.S. military in developing more powerful incapacitating agents, and its understanding that tear gases were being used in Vietnam in conjunction with other weapons to lethal effect, remained secret.[14]

Like its closest ally, the United Kingdom maintained important interests in chemical and biological warfare in the postwar years. Its policies were linked to those of the United States at several levels. Under a tripartite agreement, the United States, the United Kingdom, and Canada shared information from their research programs; under a quadripartite agreement that also included Australia, the United Kingdom shared details of its chemical weapons program (and its "offensive capability"), presumably on a reciprocal basis.[15] The records show that American and British officials met frequently in London, Washington, Geneva, and elsewhere. British officials were allowed to share most secret documents with their American counterparts with the exception of those classified as "Top Secret—UK Eyes Only," one of the highest levels of secrecy.[16]

The American and British policies were also closely linked through their acceptance of NATO strategic doctrine. In December 1967, the NATO countries agreed secretly that they would rely principally on their conventional and nuclear forces for deterrence. However, they also anticipated military confrontations with the Soviet Union that would be deemed less than major aggression even though they might involve chemical weapons. For these reasons, it was agreed that NATO countries should possess a CW capability for retaliation only and also defensive measures for both chemical and biological warfare. Only the United States was known to have deployed chemical weapons in Europe, however.[17]

British officials accepted the American view that the most immediate CBW threat was posed by the Soviet Union, but with an important difference. Although they agreed with their American counterparts that the Soviet Union posed a substantial CW threat—British intelligence reported that the Soviets maintained a large lethal chemical capability on the Warsaw Pact front—British assessments of the Soviet BW threat were more tentative. A detailed intelligence report in 1967 concluded that although the Soviet Union had an extensive BW defense program, there was no direct evidence of offensive deployment of biological weapons, although the report argued that a BW defense "would almost certainly involve an offensive capability."[18]

At the same time, British military and arms-control analysts began to argue that chemical and biological weapons might present a strong military temptation for nonnuclear powers. According to a highly classified military analysis in 1966, "minor powers might find it relatively easy, particularly with help from advanced allies, to produce [virulent] agents in usable quantities, and in consequence we may be facing a more serious situation in actions overseas than was previously believed."[19] A lengthy draft report from the Arms Control and Disarmament Research Unit (ACDRU) of the Foreign Office expressed the same view: "While for the nuclear powers CB weapons are unnecessary, for non-nuclear powers they represent a destabilizing temptation—to exploit their killing and surprise potential if they acquire the weapons first, or to pre-empt if they suspect their opponents of acquiring them."[20] Meetings in Washington among British, Canadian, and American arms-control specialists in June 1967 underscored this view. The chief of the Political Affairs Division stated that "[w]e are very much concerned about the problems of CBW . . . since there is a danger that some countries may decide that this type of activity is a cheaper and easier alternative to having weapons of mass destruction than acquiring nuclear weapons." As a Foreign Office official summarized the British position at a further meeting with American arms controllers held in October 1967: "The CBW question has tended to be discussed too exclusively on a Great Power basis: the problem may lie just as much at the other end of the scale."[21] American and British understanding that Egypt had used poison gas in Yemen in 1967 reinforced this belief.[22]

Despite these shared threat perceptions, British CBW positions differed in important ways from those of its ally. In contrast to the United States, the British government emphasized chemical and biological defense rather than offensive capabilities, although in the 1960s the British military establishment pressed for the latter. Harold Macmillan's Conservative government had authorized limited production of a lethal chemical retaliatory capability and, assuming one could be found, an incapacitating capability as well.[23] But according to a Ministry of Defence (MoD) memorandum in 1965, this directive was "not implemented in concrete terms."[24] While the British Chiefs of Staff continued to argue for both a lethal and incapacitating tactical CW capability, a decision on authorization of a lethal CW retaliatory capacity was deferred by the Secretary of State for Defence, Denis Healey, after consultation with Prime Minister Harold Wilson.[25] The United Kingdom continued without an offensive CW capability, although this lack of a chemical weapons stockpile was kept secret even from its NATO allies until 1968, when it was leaked to the press.[26] Without a chemical weapons stockpile, the United Kingdom's sense of dependence on the United States was reinforced. As one of the most detailed secret appraisals of this period put it, Britain would need "to continue to enjoy any military benefits (as well as risks) flowing from the CBW capability of its senior Ally."[27]

Nor did the United Kingdom maintain a biological weapons stockpile. In assessing the likely course of a confrontation with the Soviet Union, a report of the chiefs of staff written in 1965 considered that chemical weapons would be more effective and that escalation would likely proceed to nuclear weapons. After such an event, in the chilling language of these military planners, "attack with [biological weapons] would be irrelevant."[28] A secret Foreign Office report reinforced this view from a different perspective: "For biological weapons, all uses remain speculative in default of realistic test facilities." Whereas the most plausible uses were thought to be small-scale covert actions and aerosol attacks, single-strike coverage of vast continental areas was deemed "less practicable than once thought." In general, "uncertainties connected with viability during dispersal, susceptibility of target populations, and possible mutation of the agents, render them more speculative than perhaps any other weapon category."[29] More bluntly, though in harmony with these appraisals, the MoD's chief scientific advisor, Sir Solly Zuckerman, was reported to have said that, within the MoD, "it was more or less accepted . . . that the bacteriological side of Porton [the British chemical and biological warfare research establishment at Porton Down] was a pain in the neck and of no military value."[30] Consequently, the British government did not produce biological weapons although, as the ACDRU draft report observed, a pilot plant at Porton Down "will always enable its owner to create an offensive BW capability in a relatively short time period provided samples, however small, of suitable pathogens are kept in stock."[31]

At the research and development level, the British government remained active, pursuing offensive as well as defensive goals. British military planners shared the American interest in developing a nonlethal chemical incapacitant, deploying some forty scientists for this purpose (as opposed to ten on lethal chemicals).[32] A detailed, highly classified review written for the Defence Research Committee in 1966 noted the "high potential" of incapacitants as "weapons of the future, particularly in relation to counter insurgency and limited warfare." The report went on to extol the advantages of "attain[ing] a military objective with far less effort and casualties on our own side and far less death and destruction to the enemy than would be the case with conventional weapons." At the same time, the report acknowledged that a "perfect" incapacitant was an impossibility. It was a matter of weighing the "scientific problem" of achieving an effective agent against the "political acceptability" of a certain percentage of fatalities.[33] However, military enthusiasm did not in this instance easily become reality. A Foreign Office report written in 1967 noted the considerable problems with the American-developed incapacitant BZ, which caused fatalities, and with LSD and its derivatives, which did not produce "reliably predictable effects even in laboratory conditions, let alone warfare." The prospects for developing incapacitating agents appeared to be "discouraging." Nevertheless, the search continued.[34]

A liaison program between the MoD and major drug and chemical firms such as BDH, ICI, Parke Davis, Lilley, Twyford Laboratories, Horlicks Pharmaceuticals, Reckitt and Sons, John Wyeth & Brother, and Organon Laboratories provided an important route of discovery of novel CW agents. The program collected secret commercial information concerning a wide range of new drugs that were screened for properties that might be of military interest. A similar industrial liaison program existed in the United States.[35]

With respect to BW, while British military planners emphasized defense, they also argued that research into *offensive* dimensions was essential. A Chiefs of Staff report in 1965 argued for the need to investigate "the offensive possibilities of BW . . . in order to ensure that defensive means are adequate, and so as to be aware of any likely breakthrough which might increase the potential effectiveness of BW." At the same time, *effective* biological defense was seen as a dubious proposition. A report of the MoD's deputy chief scientific advisor in 1967 noted that although respirators could provide a defense against airborne BW agents, they presented the problem of knowing "when to use them and when it is safe to take them off." And even though vaccination was feasible, it protected only against specific agents and "we can never be sure just what biological agents or strains the enemy may choose to employ." Moreover, vaccination presented major logistical problems: "The troops would have to be vaccinated against as many diseases as possible, and the vaccinations would have to be repeated from time to time. It is extremely difficult to detect a BW attack in time to take protective measures against it, and although there are some lines of research, both in this country and in the USA, which show promise as a means of detection and identification, there is nothing yet which suggests that this can be done in time to do anything more than choose the correct remedial treatment of the casualties."[36] Further military appraisals acknowledged divided opinion among military analysts about the likelihood of a BW attack on the United Kingdom, and therefore about the emphasis that should be given to BW research and development.

The lack of chemical and biological weapons stockpiles underscored two important characteristics of the British military posture. First, it increased reliance on American deployment of chemical weapons in Europe; second, it underscored Britain's reliance, in worst-case scenarios, on its own nuclear weapons, the most fundamental feature of British strategic thinking. Military planning documents refer repeatedly to nuclear weapons as both the ultimate deterrent and the ultimate means of reprisal. As Defence Minister Denis Healey stated in a closed parliamentary hearing in July 1968, the UK government had not felt it necessary to develop a CW capability because "we have nuclear weapons, and obviously we might choose to retaliate in that way if that were the requirement."[37]

American and British CBW interests had much in common and were linked at multiple levels through the sharing of secret military information and their acceptance of NATO CBW policy, but there were also important differences. Most significantly, the United Kingdom was formally bound by the terms of the 1925 Geneva Protocol, whereas the United States was not. At the time of ratification, the British secretary of state for foreign affairs stated that tear gases and shells producing poisonous fumes were prohibited under the Protocol. A similar position was taken by the United Kingdom in a memorandum to the Preparatory Commission for the Disarmament Conference in 1930.[38]

However, in the 1960s, as American use of tear gas in Vietnam became a prominent international concern, the United Kingdom's public position on the Geneva Protocol reflected its loyalty to, and perhaps more important, its dependence on, its ally, rather than any strict adherence to its original position. Legal opinion within the British Foreign Office shifted to the view that the extent to which the use of tear gas in war was unlawful was "uncertain."[39] The British delegation in New York supported the successful American effort to dilute the Hungarian resolution on the Geneva Protocol in November 1966 and said little about the Protocol beyond referring to the United Kingdom's adherence to it.[40] Meanwhile, in the British Parliament, the secretary of state for foreign affairs was advised by his civil servants to dodge questions about the use of "chemical weapons" in Vietnam by stating that he knew of no use of "lethal" weapons by American forces. The secret discussion within the Foreign Office of the fact that tear gases and incapacitating agents could kill in a war context did not emerge in public.[41] Neither did the concern that American use of irritant agents in Vietnam might leave the United Kingdom vulnerable: States that interpreted the Geneva Protocol comprehensively (including the entire Communist bloc) might retaliate with lethal chemical agents against the United Kingdom following the use of tear gas by an ally, even though the United Kingdom had not used tear gas itself.[42]

## THE DEVELOPMENT OF THE UK WORKING PAPER ON BIOLOGICAL DISARMAMENT, 1966–1968

### The Bull Report, 1966–1967

As public concern about the CBW question continued to rise in Britain, the Foreign Office launched a detailed "top-secret" study, "The Arms Control Implications of Chemical and Biological Warfare," drafted in 1966–1967.[43] The study was directed by the head of its Arms Control and Disarmament Research Unit (ACDRU), Hedley Bull, who joined ACDRU from academia in 1965, leaving in 1967 to become a professor of international relations.

Bull's elaborate exposition of the political and military dimensions of chemical and biological arms control was detailed to the point of being arcane. It was clearly both informed and constrained by military and political thinking within the government and marked by a tough realist understanding of international relations. Although specific aspects of his analysis would be debated, and indeed some of his recommendations would eventually be dropped, the fundamental assumptions that guided his approach to the CBW question were widely shared. They were simply part of the conceptual furniture of the linked worlds of military planning and arms control.

In the first place, it is clear from the context that Bull assumed, in line with MoD thinking, that the United Kingdom would retain its nuclear deterrent. For nuclear powers, he questioned whether use of chemical or biological weapons would be best deterred by an ability to retaliate in kind: "Both chemical and biological agents are poor candidates for the deterrent role, particularly the latter, and especially poor for contributing to stable mutual deterrence" (21). For nonnuclear powers, however, he acknowledged that the likelihood of reliance on chemical or biological weapons "would presumably depend on the lead which either side could convincingly show that it had acquired over the other" (20). The attraction of these weapons in such circumstances was therefore open to greater debate.

Bull recognized, however, that the conditions of general lack of interest in CBW could change, especially if moves toward *nuclear* disarmament proved successful. And with this possibility there entered a further assumption: that the long-term threat of chemical and biological warfare might be posed not so much by the major powers as by "under-developed" states:

> Interest in CBW possibilities is now overshadowed by the nuclear question, but every success in exorcising the nuclear threat must revive interest in other means of mass destruction, and every advance in biological knowledge in the under-developed countries will hasten their ability to make them; neither development is one that we would, or could, obstruct; so we must forestall their likely side-effects. (58)

Furthermore, "what is true now may not be true soon; and the time to strike is now, when those who can make CBW weapons have no need for them, except for mutual deterrence; while those who would like them are still ashamed to say so and cannot make them anyway" (58). Thus the basic rationale for immediate action on chemical and biological arms control was less the need to prevent use by industrialized countries than the need to prevent their spread before they became objects of interest in less-developed countries.

A third assumption, clearly supported by the MoD, was the need to maintain secrecy where chemical and biological warfare was concerned. Countering a call from the nongovernmental organization (NGO) Pugwash for transparency with respect to chemical and biological warfare activities, Bull expressed skepticism that the proposal of the "Pugwash publicists" could be effective in reducing the CBW threat. "Opening Porton Down [the British CBW establishment] to day-trippers" was, he opined, "based on exceedingly frail assumptions about the cosmopolitanisms of scientists, about the impracticability of military exploitation of existing knowledge, and about the implications of commercial secrecy with which so much microbiological work in the West is tied up" (57).

In defense of secrecy, Bull echoed the views of military planners:

No one can guarantee the permanence of our disinterest in a BW offensive capability . . . [furthermore,] even aspects of research that appear purely 'defensive' could assist an enemy's offensive plans, e.g. the findings of BW field tests could tip off an enemy about the viability of the pathogens used, and about our own detection abilities. (57)

Bull concluded that at least until strict international controls on CBW activities were achieved "some degree of secrecy in our BW defence research seems inevitable" (57).

There were further obstacles to a British chemical and biological arms-control initiative: The United States, with its large, diversified, and secretive CBW program and ongoing use of "nonlethal" chemical weapons in Vietnam, would resist any Geneva initiative that might open it up to criticism. Bull recognized that any British initiative for chemical or biological arms control would likely elicit either American resistance or accusations of U.S. violations of the Geneva Protocol from the Eastern and nonaligned blocs.

Furthermore, military and commercial interest in secrecy in the major states entailed problematic limits on verification of compliance through inspection of facilities. Bull's argument turned both on the likely demand of developing countries for inspection of industrialized countries and on the likely response, from the West as well as the East:

[S]ince . . . a system of inspection would have a greater impact on less developed and non-nuclear countries with fewer objects to inspect and with more potential interest in CB weapons, they would inevitably demand at least equivalent degrees of self-exposure by advanced countries with known CBW capabilities. The chances of agreement on this, in turn, would seem to be nil at present because of the Soviet attitude to what would need to be fairly intrusive inspection—even supposing the West could wholeheartedly accept e.g. the commercial secrecy difficulties. (cover note, 5)

Thus, while the mutual inspections envisaged by the NGO Pugwash might work for nonpossessor states, an inspected treaty regime could be only "a distant goal" for those states with major known defense programs, and for the states that Bull called "the major suspects" (cover note, 5).

Given such formidable obstacles to CBW arms control, Bull concluded that the most that could be achieved for CW arms control was to replace the existing practice of reservations to the Geneva Protocol's ban with a formal no-first-use agreement. Moreover, given the certainty of American insistence on exempting nontoxic chemicals, he proposed that the Protocol should be revised to achieve this. For biological weapons, however, he held that additional restrictions might be politically feasible. After all, he opined, in the case of an attack with biological weapons, "reprisal in kind is unnecessary and globally undesirable" (cover note, 6). In contrast to chemical weapons, use of biological weapons might be banned unconditionally. Thus Bull's analysis introduced a distinction that would prove influential: Because biological weapons were deemed less effective and were also not being seriously contemplated for use by powerful states, stricter controls than those for chemical weapons might be developed for them. This idea amounted to little more than a formal clarification of the status quo. It would have shocked sectors of the British public pressing for a comprehensive ban on chemical and biological weapons, had they known.

The Bull report was soon shared with U.S. ACDA officials.[44] At a meeting between British and American officials in October 1967, the latter made it clear that even though the United States was unwilling either to ratify the Geneva Protocol or to consider any modification of it, the CBW question was, nevertheless, "an area in which the Russians might very well play ball with us." The participants agreed that "the military in both the West and Russia might well be glad to see the whole subject eliminated." At best, biological and chemical weapons were "the poor man's deterrent." While the U.S. officials held that "the time was not yet ripe for a political initiative on CBW on the part of either the U.K. or the United States," it was also agreed that, given the possibility of initiatives by other states, it was desirable to explore, at least at a research level, the possibility of a new international instrument for controlling chemical and biological weapons. At this point, the American officials appear to have been thinking about a nonproliferation treaty similar to the nuclear nonproliferation treaty then being negotiated. But they highlighted the secrecy of biological facilities as a potential problem: Inspections might be obstructed by "the strict secrecy imposed by certain civil 'B' plants, at any rate in the U.S.A., on their commercial activities."[45] Given the industrial liaison programs that linked research in U.S. pharmaceutical companies and the Department of Defense, secrecy was important to protect not only work on patentable materials such as drugs but also information concerning novel substances deemed to be of potential military value.

For the next half year or so, while negotiations for the nuclear nonproliferation treaty (NPT) took center stage in the United Nations, the question of controlling chemical and biological weapons remained in the background.[46] An appraisal of future prospects for disarmament by the new head of the Disarmament Department of the Foreign Office, Ronald Hope-Jones,[47] anticipated that after completion of the NPT the next target for negotiations would be a comprehensive nuclear test ban. New CBW controls were viewed pessimistically, given likely American opposition and the difficulties of verification of compliance in a field rife with secrecy in both the East and the West.[48] The subject was put on the back burner pending feedback from the MoD and completion of the NPT negotiations later in the year.[49]

Meanwhile, public criticism of the British CBW programs intensified.

Conferences, letters to politicians, Parliamentary Questions, a petition from leading scientists, and media coverage continued to focus public attention on the programs and on the larger question of British complicity in America's use of chemicals in Vietnam. Prime Minister Harold Wilson was being pressured to address these issues from within his own party.[50] Foreign Office documents show civil servants drafting ministerial responses to awkward questions concerning British policy on the use of anti-personnel agents, the nature of research at Porton Down, and the extent to which results of this research were shared with the U.S. CBW programs. They would say as little as possible about the precise boundaries Britain drew between legal and illegal use of tear gases under the Geneva Protocol and the precise nature of the secret information shared by the two countries.[51]

### "Yes Minister?"

As late as June 10, 1968, Foreign Office officials anticipated slow movement on the CBW question. In a detailed memorandum, "The Next Steps for Disarmament," intended for Minister of State for Foreign Affairs Fred Mulley, Ronald Hope-Jones emphasized moves toward nuclear disarmament following successful approval of the Nuclear Non-Proliferation Treaty. While he also acknowledged that further steps toward controlling chemical and biological warfare "would be timely and would certainly have a good deal of internal political appeal,"[52] he anticipated only going so far as to raise this question at a meeting of NATO experts the following fall. But Mulley had other ideas, which apparently took Foreign Office officials and their opposite numbers in Washington completely by surprise. A headline story in *The Observer* on June 16—"Britain Seeks World Pact to Ban Germ Warfare"—announced that Mulley hoped to submit proposals for "a new convention to forbid use of chemical and biological weapons." Telegrams flew back and forth across the Atlantic as civil servants in London and Washington scrambled to discern Mulley's intentions.[53]

In fact, Mulley still had no specific plan regarding the ENDC. When American embassy officials in London met with the British minister on June 19 to attempt to clarify his intentions, Mulley told them that he was under "great pressure" to respond to public concern about CBW and that he was considering a revised Geneva Protocol on the use of chemical and biological weapons. The American officials, for their part, indicated that the United States was "probably not . . . in a position to take an initiative on biological and chemical weapons at the present time." The substance of the meeting was immediately relayed by telegrams to the State Department and to the United Kingdom's Washington embassy.[54]

Foreign Office officials immediately turned to drafting a revised protocol that would formalize the American status quo on chemical weapons (no first use of lethal chemicals; exclusion of riot control agents) but would ban all use of biological weapons. However, these efforts were quickly overtaken by Washington's response: On June 25, 1968, the U.S. State Department sent secret guidance to the American Embassy in London, specifying the American position to be conveyed to the British. In the truncated language of the telegram:

> US not yet prepared to discuss specifics on updating or revision of Protocol and for this reason would prefer that UK not rept not press for formal detailed consideration such proposal at next session ENDC . . . Mindful of consideration above, US believes Mulley proposal should be treated as illustrative of possible approaches to CBW and not rpt not be accorded undue priority. Accordingly, US suggests that UK avoid specifics as to timing and ways of revising Protocol. In particular, US would not rpt not want possible UK redraft of Protocol introduced next session ENDC.

The telegram went on to suggest that the Embassy remind the British of Soviet resistance to revising the Protocol on the grounds that this would be "tantamount to recognition of 'loopholes'" in the treaty. In other words, a British revision of the Geneva Protocol would receive a cool reception from both superpowers. The telegram indicated that these and other subjects would be fully discussed with Mulley during his visit to Washington the following week.[55]

According to a later Hope-Jones memorandum, both he and Mulley "became convinced" between June 25 and 29 that "progress would only be possible if we separated CW and BW entirely and went for a Convention that dealt only with the latter." Hope-Jones did not elaborate on the reasons for this shift, but almost certainly, given his close contact with the American embassy, a communication from there played a decisive role. On the weekend before his Washington visit, Hope-Jones drafted a working paper proposing a ban not only on use of biological weapons but also on their possession. Mulley read the paper en route to Washington for his meeting with State Department officials on July 2.[56]

This first draft provided the basic model for each subsequent draft. It began by listing weaknesses the British saw in the Geneva Protocol: the right of retaliation, the disagreement over its coverage, the fact that it banned neither manufacture nor retaliatory use, and so forth. It went on to propose that the CBW problem would be made "less intractable" if the problems posed by chemical and biological weapons were considered independently and, given the reluctance of some states to forego the right to produce and stockpile chemical weapons without "adequate verification," if biological weapons were addressed first. On that basis, the essence of the British proposal was that states would undertake, first, "never to engage in biological warfare, even if biological weapons were used against them"; second, to

destroy all BW agents in their possession, "which have no independent
peaceful justification," and not to produce any BW agents or assist any
other state in their production; and third, to put research "of potential BW
significance" under the central control of their civil authorities and to publish the results of this work."[57]

Regarding chemical weapons, the draft proposed only a study of the
"nature and probable effects of existing chemical weapons and of the implications of their use" to be pursued under the auspices of the UN Secretary-
General.[58] Therefore, as the United States wished, action on the CW problem would be postponed.

## The First Anglo-American Discussion of a Biological
## Weapons Convention, July 2, 1968

Participants at the Washington meeting included, on the American side,
the director of the U.S. ACDA, William Foster, ACDA Assistant Director for
Science and Technology Herbert Scoville, and George Bunn, ACDA general
counsel, and on the British side, Mulley, and Hope-Jones.[59] Mulley argued
that British public opinion required a response from the government but
acknowledged that revising the Geneva Protocol was not possible for the
Americans. He portrayed the ban on both the use and possession of biological weapons as a compromise that avoided the difficult questions surrounding chemical weapons. The proposal met with a blunt American response.
Foster allowed that a focus on biological weapons was advantageous as "a
diversionary tactic to distract attention from Soviet propaganda [about
American use of anti-personnel agents in Vietnam]," but he warned that if
the British government tabled the text of a convention, the U.S. government
"would have no alternative but to attack it." On the other hand, a working
paper for further study would be acceptable.

Discussion of the content of Mulley's proposal was characterized by two
themes that would resonate strongly in the 1990s: the difficulty of verification and the need for corporate secrecy. Foster emphasized that the Pentagon would see "an unverified agreement" as "an extremely bad precedent
for future disarmament measures." Herbert Scoville expressed concern over
the proposal for openness on the part of companies: American and probably
British companies would "not be anxious to publish reports of their vaccine
research." Both sides agreed that corporate openness could be a "real
problem."

By the end of the meeting, an understanding on a compromise had
emerged. On BW, Mulley would release only a working paper at the ENDC
that summer, but with the understanding that the text of a BW convention
would be tabled in the ENDC the following year. On CW, the British would
accept that the Geneva Protocol "was as good as we could get in present

circumstances" but that study of chemical warfare's effects should be pursued.

## The Evolution of the Working Paper Proposing a Biological Weapons Convention

Revision of the working paper began immediately upon the return of Mulley and Hope-Jones to London. As head of the Disarmament Department of the Foreign Office, Hope-Jones was responsible for seeing successive drafts through an elaborate process of consultation with other government departments, particularly the MoD, the Ministry of Health, and the office of the Chief Scientific Advisor to the Government (a cabinet-level position). Major steps in this process were, first, a meeting of the cabinet's Defence and Oversea Policy Committee (OPD) chaired by Prime Minister Harold Wilson (July 12); second, meetings of a Working Group on Chemical and Biological Warfare chaired by Chief Scientific Advisor Sir Solly Zuckerman (July 17 and 19), where civil servants from the key government units—Defence, Health and the Foreign Office—discussed details of specific problems; third, a meeting of the cabinet's Subcommittee on Disarmament, chaired by Sir Edward Peck; and finally, the second OPD meeting on July 26, at which final agreement on the working paper was reached. Hope-Jones was influential in this process, participating in both the Working Group and the Subcommittee on Disarmament; briefing Fred Mulley for the cabinet meetings; overseeing the drafting process; and perhaps as important as anything else, communicating with the Americans. Higher-level civil servants, notably Deputy Under Secretaries for Foreign Affairs Sir Edward Peck and Lord Samuel Hood, were much less involved in the minutiae of drafting but were influential in shaping the process. Harold Wilson's forceful scientific advisor, Sir Solly Zuckerman, was also key, notably in coping with the response of the MoD.

Substantial resistance to the idea of a biological weapons ban came from the British military establishment and Defence Secretary Denis Healey. But despite this resistance from within and the American resistance from outside, the minutes of these meetings convey a sense of inevitability that the proposal would go ahead. By early July, momentum was already building in the Foreign Office for Mulley to announce Britain's intention to table a working paper proposing a biological weapons ban at the opening of the summer session of the ENDC in mid-July.[60]

The first cabinet meeting, held only ten days after Mulley's meeting with ACDA officials in Washington, is a case in point.[61] This discussion is also representative of the nature of much of the subsequent debate within the British government. Mulley, briefed by Hope-Jones, presented the case for proposing a ban on the "use, production and research of agents of biological warfare" in the ENDC in much the same terms as he had in Washington, with an added political rationale for Washington's future support: Although the Americans did not support the proposal due to its lack of verification machinery, they also understood that a verification system for BW was "impossible to devise" and that "by concentrating on biological warfare attention would be diverted from chemical warfare on which they were vulnerable to criticism." Given the problems in addressing chemical disarmament—notably their "past use (and current use in Vietnam)," it would be best to address chemical weapons separately, in a UN study of the nature and probable effects of chemical weapons. Mulley also noted that his proposal would allow research on defenses against biological weapons.

A strong counterpoint came from Healey. Surprisingly, Healey began by seeming to emphasize the defense requirements of nonnuclear nations. It was "unrealistic" to expect nonnuclear nations to welcome a proposal that biological weapons could not be used in retaliation; the British had nuclear weapons for countering or deterring attacks, whereas they did not.[62] Furthermore, the production of biological agents for agricultural and veterinary uses meant that many countries would inevitably have some "military capability" for biological warfare. Placing defensive research under civilian authorities would "provide no safeguard in communist countries where the problems of verification were most acute." Plants for producing biological agents were easily disguised. In a phrase that still resonates today, Healey also argued that there would be difficulties in inspecting "commercial . . . establishments, who fear industrial espionage."

But Mulley found support from other cabinet members, for political reasons. As the minutes record, it was felt that "there were great advantages in a British initiative in view of the mounting public and Parliamentary interest in these weapons." Furthermore "if we did not table proposals of this kind, others undoubtedly would; we could not afford to wait until a later stage in the ENDC session."

Harold Wilson's summation at the end of the meeting left little doubt that the prime minister shared that view. Mulley should make a statement to the ENDC "declaring our intention to submit proposals on biological and chemical warfare during the current session," said Wilson. And the proposals should "be prepared urgently by an interdepartmental committee of officials, which would need to seek the advice of appropriate scientific experts," and which would also report back to the cabinet within two weeks. Despite Healey's strong reservations, Wilson clearly wanted immediate action on the BW question.

The job of refining Mulley's proposal and responding to the various issues that had surfaced was given to Chief Scientific Advisor Sir Solly Zuckerman. Within a week Sir Solly had assembled a working group composed of civil servants from the Foreign Office, MoD, and the Ministry of Health, and two meetings had been held. At the first meeting (July 17), the most difficult and contentious questions concerned the related issues of the ambiguity of biological activities, verification of compliance with a BW ban, and disclosure of military information concerning defenses, as the following passages from the minutes show.

On ambiguity:

It would be impossible to differentiate between the many BW agents and the materials required in the production of vaccine for medical research and use. . . . Even when research was entirely defensive in nature it was in general necessary to produce a poison before its antidote could be developed. Potential agents for 'peaceful' uses could not be qualitatively distinguished. All conceivable BW agents tended to occur naturally somewhere in the world and their production in advanced countries could be defended on grounds of necessity for developing aid to under-developed countries.

On verification:

Facilities necessary to produce BW agents could be so widespread as to prevent any effective method of verification of a ban. . . . It was impossible to eliminate work which had no offensive application, and sufficient quantities of BW agent (a bacteria) to attack an area ten miles by ten miles, for example, could be produced in about one week, in the sort of small manufacturing plant widely available in advanced countries.

On protecting research at Porton Down:

The United Kingdom has nothing to fear from allowing inspection of biological research work at Porton or anywhere in this country . . . No one [is] likely to disclose information which would facilitate an attack by a potential enemy. This applied to potential agents that might be used, to the means of delivering them and the state of readiness to meet any particular BW threat. Even if it were possible on an unclassified basis to carry out future BW research in the light of our present knowledge of BW agents and delivery systems, there would remain the possibility that some future development would restore the need for classification.[63]

Thus both suspicion concerning the reliability of other states and the understanding that Britain itself would wish to conceal, to some extent, its own BW defensive effort underscored the intractable nature of the verification problem. In the words of one MoD official at the meeting, "One could 'drive a coach and horses' through any proposals of the kind now being discussed."[64]

Despite continued friction with the MoD, revision of the Foreign Office working paper proceeded. After the second meeting of the Working Group (July 19), and further resistance from MoD officials, the paper went to the

Disarmament Subcommittee of the Cabinet Defence and Oversea Committee, chaired by Deputy Under Secretary at the Foreign Office Sir Edward
Peck, and a revised version was discussed by the cabinet on July 26.[65] MoD
officials felt strongly enough about the problems with a BW ban that they
submitted their own paper outlining their difficulties with the Foreign Office
draft.[66] "There is one joker in the pack," Peck wrote to his colleague Lord
Hood (with a copy to Hope-Jones) in connection with the MoD paper. "I
hope this joker will not come up to bother you and I have ascertained that
Sir Solly Zuckerman is strongly against allowing it to go forward at this
juncture."[67]

Clearly neither Sir Edward nor Sir Solly wanted the MoD objections to
stall the working paper. Sir Solly wrote in a strongly worded memorandum
to Harold Wilson that "[i]ts general tone disregards any possible advantages
of a Convention against microbiological warfare and is based on the underlying concept that 'technological development in the future could prove BW
to be a militarily effective weapon.'" Even the MoD's claim that the proposals "would likely be opposed by the Americans, whose goodwill was essential to us politically and economically, and in the field of defence including
that of disarmament" was dismissed by Zuckerman: "The implication of a
'special relationship' is vastly overemphasized."[68] In the meeting, the subcommittee was reminded that "the tabling of the proposal for proscribing
microbiological weapons was politically of vital importance." Moreover,
"the impossibility of effective verification did not bar the proposed initiative
which was a matter for the political and moral judgement of the Government." A compromise duly emerged in which a revised working paper
would go forward to the cabinet with the MoD critique attached as an
annex.[69]

When Fred Mulley presented the revised working paper to the cabinet on
July 26, it was clear that the objections of the MoD and its defence secretary
would not derail the plan for Mulley to present the paper to the ENDC later
that summer.[70] Nevertheless, the MoD's position marked the text.[71] In the
final version drafted by Ronald Hope-Jones, the difficulty of devising an
effective system of verification was acknowledged, along with the rationale
for proceeding: "In this field, the choice lies between going ahead with the
formulation of new obligations and doing nothing at all—in which case the
risks and fears of eventual use of microbiological methods of warfare will
continue and intensify indefinitely." In addition, the basic prohibition was
formulated as a ban on production for "hostile purposes," which, as Hope-
Jones noted to a colleague, made it "clear that production of such agents
for defence research is not prohibited";[72] the ban was also formulated in
two alternative ways that equally allowed defense research to continue. And
finally, the paper's call for defense research "to be open to international
investigation if so required and . . . to public scrutiny" was limited to "the

maximum extent compatible with national security and the protection of industrial and commercial processes." Transparency would only go so far. By July 30, the working paper proposing elements of a future biological weapons convention was finally ready for presentation in Geneva. That same day, Hope-Jones visited the American Embassy to present an outline of the paper. At this point, despite Hope-Jones' residual worry that MoD resistance might still scuttle the paper, he confided in the Americans that Mulley was so " 'gung ho' on the BW issue that [Foreign Office] views would prevail."[73] Apparently they did: Hope-Jones announced later that day to the British ambassador to the ENDC, Ivor Porter, that "the text of our paper will be in tomorrow evening's bag."[74]

## CONCLUDING APPRAISAL: THE GEOPOLITICS OF THE BIOLOGICAL WEAPONS CONVENTION

Fred Mulley's presentation of the British working paper to the ENDC on August 6, 1968, initiated difficult and lengthy negotiations that would lead eventually to the completion of the BWC in 1971. Initially, the British proposal faced resistance from all sides: West, East, and nonaligned. Moreover, sectors of the public that had pressed for controls on both chemical and biological weapons saw the exclusive focus on the latter as a deep compromise that allowed, first, continued American use of anti-personnel agents and herbicides in Vietnam, and second, continued secret British CBW research and development arrangements with the United States. Progress toward the British goal of a ban only on biological weapons became possible only when the United States renounced its biological weapons program in November 1969, the Soviet Union in spring 1971 reversed its expressed commitment to a treaty banning both chemical and biological weapons, and the nonaligned countries gave up hope of a comprehensive ban.

Of course the text of the proposed ban evolved as every word was subjected to scrutiny by the member states of the ENDC (later the Conference of the Committee on Disarmament). Nevertheless, the fundamental assumptions that had motivated the initial proposal persisted. Perhaps the most influential of these—one of the least obvious to the public—was the sense, so evident in the secret military and foreign policy documents discussed here, that arms-controls proposals were limited by calculations concerning the maintenance of military and strategic advantage. This fundamental requirement was never questioned. Although public pressure for chemical and biological disarmament was principled in nature, and some members of the Labour cabinet and civil servants in the Foreign Office may have shared those principles, the military requirements of NATO and of the U.S–UK alliance loomed inescapably over the biological disarmament discussion. The ultimate reliance of the West on nuclear weapons for deterrence, the most fundamental element of NATO doctrine, was never questioned.[75]

In addition, despite Sir Solly Zuckerman's dismissal of the significance of the UK–U.S. relationship, it was taken for granted that the alliance placed limits on just how far the British could press the question of chemical and biological disarmament. No one, not even Sir Solly, questioned the desirability of continuing military collaboration on BW and CW research, or the strong interests of both the British and American military establishments in developing more effective chemical incapacitating weapons. Every stage in the development of the British proposal for the BW ban demonstrated British sensitivity to American conditions and responses. Although the British took the initiative on BW and went further than Washington desired, the initiative itself tacitly incorporated a major compromise: a ban on chemical weapons was out of the question.

Moreover, in Britain there was a strong perception that biological weapons had significant military drawbacks: their time delay in acting, their mutability, their susceptibility to climatic conditions, and lack of control. As shown previously, the chief scientific advisor, himself a biologist, dismissed them as "a pain in the neck." Even if the military did not entirely agree with that appraisal, other weapons—especially chemical and nuclear—were deemed far more effective. As Ronald Hope-Jones pointed out to American officials during his visit to the London embassy on July 30, 1968: "In forgoing BW, major powers would be giving up nothing since they had much more effective weaponry readily available and would not rationally contemplate using [biological weapons] against each other, for fear of nuclear retaliation."[76] The appraisal within the U.S. government, particularly after Nixon's election in 1968, was similar. As Nixon confided to his speech writer, William Safire, "We'll never use the damn germs. So what good is biological warfare as a deterrent? If someone uses germs on us, we'll nuke 'em."[77] As public criticism of the British and American CBW programs intensified in the late 1960s, biological weapons were seen by the British government not only as the obvious but also as the only choice for renunciation. Consequently, as both Hope-Jones's and Nixon's statements imply, the move toward biological disarmament effectively reinforced the role of nuclear weapons as the ultimate deterrent.

Furthermore, as Hope-Jones also reminded American officials during his presentation of the British working paper, while "the basic premise of [the] UK approach to [the] BW issue was that development of biological weapons was of little interest or utility to well-armed major powers," such weapons "might have considerable attraction for smaller powers because of the cheapness and potential for off-setting in some degree [the] monopoly of nuclear powers enshrined in the NPT."[78] In other words, the basic problem associated with BW was defined not as that of the large BW stockpiles of the superpowers but rather as the future acquisition of biological weapons as force equalizers by developing countries. The move toward biological disarmament was justified by the British government to the United States as a way to protect military advantage rather than as a step toward general and complete disarmament.

As mentioned previously, verification of biological disarmament was acknowledged as a serious if not insoluble problem by both the British and the Americans. It was not simply that verification in this case was recognized to be technically difficult because of the dual-purpose nature of biological activities and the ease of hiding them, nor that the British and the Americans could anticipate that the Soviet Union would reject on-site verification measures. It was *also* understood that highly intrusive verification measures were undesirable from a *Western* perspective. British and American officials understood the strong reluctance of both their own governments to reveal secrets concerning their defenses and of pharmaceutical companies to reveal commercial secrets and research covered by military-industrial liaison agreements. Proposals like those of the NGO Pugwash to open military laboratories were seen by British officials as naïve, as Hedley Bull had argued at some length. As Defence Minister Denis Healey had argued at the second cabinet meeting on July 26, 1968, "it was important that we should not forfeit our exchanges of information on biological and chemical warfare with the United States." Nor should "the knowledge available at Porton [the British chemical and biological warfare research establishment] of the particular forms of microbiological warfare to which we were vulnerable . . . become public."[79] Such understanding was rarely, if ever, aired in public, however. Both technical difficulties and the recalcitrance of the Soviet Union could be relied on as arguments against the feasibility of verification. The final text of the UK working paper simply stated that "verification, in the sense in which the term is normally used in disarmament negotiations, is not possible in either the chemical or the microbiological field," leaving the reasons to the reader's imagination.[80]

Finally, the argument of the MoD that there could be no clear distinction between offensive and defensive military research, development, and production was accepted by the Foreign Office and the cabinet as a fundamental condition for any prohibition of biological warfare. As the MoD officials argued in their critique of the draft working paper that emerged from Sir Solly Zuckerman's working group, "the Convention would not debar research into BW methods to the extent necessary to confer the ability to adopt effective measures of defence at need; and this research could be applied simply, rapidly and covertly to the construction of an aggressive capability." This military requirement meant that any prohibition on biological weapons had to be written to encompass the offense/defense overlap. All three formulations proposed in the working paper did so. As Hope-

Jones had observed of one formulation, production of BW agents for defense research would not be prohibited.[81] Of course, this ambiguity at the heart of the proposed convention entailed a further major difficulty for verifying compliance. Military unwillingness to accept restrictions on preparations for BW defense meant that it was impossible to draw a clear line between permissible and impermissible BW research, or, for that matter, between permissible and impermissible development and production.

These conditions—the search for military advantage, deference to the requirements of the superpower, the reliance of powerful Western states on nuclear weapons for deterrence, the assumption of powerful Western states that the BW problem is posed primarily by certain non-Western states, the secrecy in which commercial and military biological activities are enshrouded, and the fundamental ambiguity at the heart of the ban on biological warfare—remain largely unacknowledged or even unseen today. They, rather than the technicalities of negotiations for a Protocol, are the fundamental reasons why the search for "strengthening" the BWC is proving so elusive.

## NOTES

Special thanks to Romica Singh and Joseph Brunner for their assistance with research for this chapter and to Rosemary and Thomas Hill for their generous hospitality during visits to the Public Record Office in Kew.

1. Stockholm International Peace Research Institute, *The Problem of Chemical and Biological Warfare*, vol. 4, *CB Disarmament Negotiations 1920–1970* (Stockholm: Almqvist and Wiksell, 1971), 238–43.

2. In references to government documents, I indicate the level of secrecy applied at the date of the document and subsequently until it was publicly released following a twenty-five-year (United States) or thirty-year (United Kingdom) rule. Of course, many documents, particularly those held by military and intelligence agencies, may be withheld for much longer periods of time.

3. The United States attempted to ensure that the locations of lethal chemical weapons stores in West Germany, maintained as part of the NATO chemical deterrent, would remain secret. See, for example, U.S. Department of State, Telegram 127265 to U.S. Embassy Bonn, 30 July 1968, classified "top secret," RG 59, Pol 27–10, Box 2879, National Archives.

4. Arthur Westing, *Ecological Consequences of the Second Indochina War* (Stockholm: Almqvist and Wiksell, 1976), 24–45.

5. U.S. Ambassador Nabrit, statement to UN General Assembly, 5 December 1966, UN Doc. A/PV.1484; U.S. State Department telegrams #169507 (classified "secret"), 23 May 1968 and #169508 (unclassified), to U.S. Embassy Paris, 23 May 1968, RG 59, Pol 27–10, Box 2879, file 2, National Archives.

6. U.K. Foreign Office, Record of Informal Talks between British and United States Officials on Arms Control Prospects for Biological and Chemical Weapons,

Foreign Office, London, 12–13 October 1967; FCO 10/179 (classified "secret"), Public Record Office.

7. Stockholm International Peace Research Institute, *The Problem of Chemical and Biological Warfare*, vol. 2, *CB Weapons Today* (Stockholm: Almqvist and Wiksell, 1973), 196–97.

8. U.K. Foreign Office, Arms Control and Disarmament Research Unit, "Arms Control Implications of Chemical and Biological Weapons: Analysis and Proposals," (ACDRU(66)2, 2nd Draft, classified "top secret," 4 July 1966), p. 44.

9. Robert McNamara to Dean Rusk, 17 November 1966, classified "secret."

10. RG 59, POL 27–10, Box 2879, NA. A State Department memorandum of 20 February 1967 indicates that policy for herbicides and riot gases was similarly excluded from policies on lethal chemicals: Foy D. Kohler to Katzenbach, 20 February 1967, classified "secret," RG 59, POL 27–10, Box 2879, NA.

11. U.K. Foreign Office, Arms Control and Disarmament Research Unit, "Arms Control Implications of Chemical and Biological Warfare," 3 February 1967, Annex B, p. 5; classified "top secret," FCO10/184, Public Record Office.

12. U.K. Foreign Office, FO 371/187448, Public Records Office.

13. Stockholm International Peace Research Institute, *The Problem of Chemical and Biological Warfare*, vol. 4 (Stockholm: Almqvist and Wiksell, 1971), 238–43; UN Doc A/PV.1484, 21.

14. Similar reasoning was contemplated in a draft response by State Department officials to the scientists' petition to President Johnson on 1967, although apparently the letter was never sent: "Draft Presidential Statement, attached to Walt Rostow to Secretary of State, Secretary of Defense, Director of ACDA, 10 March 1967," classified "secret," RG 59, Pol 27–10, Box 2879, NA.

15. U.K. Foreign Office, Arms Control and Disarmament Research Unit, "Arms Control Implications of Chemical and Biological Warfare: Analysis and Proposals," ACDRU(66)2 (2nd Draft), classified "top secret," 4 July 1966, 31, 60, 62, FO 371/187448, PRO.

16. U.K. Foreign Office, Record of informal talks between British and United States officials on arms control prospects for biological and chemical weapons, held at the Foreign Office, London, October 12–13, 1967, 15 November 1967, classified "secret," FCO 10/179, PRO.

17. U.K. Foreign Office, Arms Control and Disarmament Research Unit, "Arms Control Implications of Chemical and Biological Warfare: Analysis and Proposals," ACDRU(66)2 (2nd Draft), classified "top secret," 4 July 1966, 31–32, FO 371/187448, PRO; U.K. Ministry of Defence, Chiefs of Staff Committee, "United Kingdom Military Requirements for Chemical and Biological Warfare Capabilities," classified "top secret—U.K. Eyes Only;" Annex A to Report No. COS 124/67 (15 December 1967), A-5, DEFE 19/97, PRO; M.O'D.B. Alexander to D. Benest, "Chemical and Biological Warfare: NATO Aspects," classified "top secret," 8 July 1968, FCO 10/184, PRO.

18. U.K. Ministry of Defence, Defence Intelligence Staff (Directorate of Scientific and Technical Intelligence), "Soviet Measures for Biological Warfare Defence," DSTI Report No. 289 (November 1967), classified "secret," FCO10/182, PRO.

19. U.K. Ministry of Defence, Defence Research Committee, "Review of CW and

BW Research Programme," DR/P(66)42, 1 December 1966, classified "top secret–UK eyes only," 9, DEFE11/660, PRO.

20. U.K. Foreign Office, Arms Control and Disarmament Research Unit, "Arms Control Implications of Chemical and Biological Warfare: Analysis and Proposals," ACDRU(66)2 (2nd Draft), classified "secret," 4 July 1966, covering note, 3–4, FO 371/187448, PRO.

21. U.S., Arms Control and Disarmament Agency, "Chemical and Biological Warfare," record of meeting between U.S. ACDA official Robert Kranich and Canadian arms control official, 21 June 1967, classified "secret," RG 59, Pol 27–10, Box 2879, File #1, NA; U.K., Foreign Office, I. M. H. Smart to R. E. Lloyd, 21 June 1967, record of meeting with U.S. ACDA official Robert Kranich, classified "confidential," FCO 10/179, PRO; U.K. Foreign Office, telegram from U.K. Foreign Office to (British Embassy) Washington, "Poison Gas in Yemen," undated, c. 1967, classified "secret," FCO 10/179, PRO.

22. E.g., U.S. Department of State, Leonard Meeker (Legal Advisor), Memorandum for Walt Rostow, "Consideration of UAW Gas Warfare," classified "secret," 20 May 1967, RG 59, Pol 27–10, Box 2879, NA.

23. RG 59, Pol 27–10, Box 2879, NA, 29; U.K. Foreign Office, M.O'D.B. Alexander to D. Benest, Memorandum, "Chemical and Biological Warfare: NATO Aspects," classified "top secret," 8 July 1968, FCO 10/184, PRO.

24. U.K. Ministry of Defence, memorandum, "Policy on Gas," classified "top secret," c. 1965, PREM13/221, PRO.

25. U.K. Ministry of Defence, Dennis Healey to Prime Minister, "Biological and Chemical Warfare," classified "top secret," 10 November 1965, DEFE 11/660, PRO.

26. U.K. Ministry of Defence, Chiefs of Staff Committee, Defence Planning Staff, "Chemical and Biological Warfare," DP.52/65 (Final), 3 September 1965, classified "top secret," A-6, DEFE 11/660, PRO; U.K. Foreign and Commonwealth Office, "Biological and Chemical Weapons," Guidance Note 155, classified "confidential"; FCO 10/183, PRO; U.K. Foreign Office, R. C. Hope-Jones to K. T. Nash, MoD, 9 July 1968, FCO 10/181, PRO.

27. U.K. Foreign Office, Arms Control and Disarmament Research Unit, "Arms Control Implications of Chemical and Biological Warfare: Analysis and Proposals," classified "top secret," 2d draft, 4 July 1966, 63, FO 371/187448, PRO.

28. U.K. Ministry of Defence, Chiefs of Staff Committee, Defence Planning Staff, "Chemical and Biological Warfare," DP.52/65 (Final), 3 September 1965, classified "top secret," A-3, 8, DEFE 11/660, PRO.

29. U.K. Foreign Office, Arms Control and Disarmament Research Unit, "Arms Control Implications of Chemical and Biological Warfare," report written by Hedley Bull, ACDRU (67)1 (Final), 3 February 1967, classified "top secret," Annex C, 3, Annex D, 2, FCO 10/184, PRO.

30. U.K. Foreign Office, R. Hope-Jones to Moss, 4 July 1968, FCO 10/181, PRO.

31. U.K. Foreign Office, Arms Control and Disarmament Research Unit, "Arms Control Implications of Chemical and Biological Warfare," 2nd draft, 4 July 1966, 30, FO371/187448, PRO. The American position on this claim may have been that

it would take considerably longer to reconstruct an offensive BW program after termination.

32. U.K. Ministry of Defence, A. H. Cottrell, "DRC Review of Research Programme—Biological Warfare and Chemical Warfare," AHC/305/66, classified "top secret—UK Eyes Only," 14 July 1966, 2, DEFE 11/660, PRO.

33. U.K. Ministry of Defence, Defence Research Committee, "Review of CW and BW Research Programme, Note by the Defence Research Staff" (DR/P(66)42), classified "top secret—UK Eyes Only," 1 December 1966, 6, DEFE 11/660, PRO.

34. U.K. Foreign Office, Arms Control and Disarmament Research Unit, "Arms Control Implications of Chemical and Biological Warfare," report written by Hedley Bull, ACDRU (67)1 (Final), 3 February 1967, classified "top secret," 2 and Annex C, 2; ACDRU (66)2 (2nd Draft), 4 July 1966, classified "top secret," 31; FCO 10/184 and FCO 371/187448, PRO.

35. On the UK industrial liaison program, see U.K. Ministry of Defence, Defence Research Committee, "Chemical Defence Experimental Establishment: Research Program 1969–70," DR 22/69, classified "secret," 7 May 1969, DEFE 11/672; on the U.S. program, see SIPRI, *Problem of Chemical and Biological Warfare,* vol. 2, 282–84.

36. U.K. Ministry of Defence, "Research Programme on Chemical and Biological Warfare," AHC/72/67, classified "top secret," 8 February 1967, 3–5, DEFE 11/660, PRO.

37. U.K. Ministry of Defence, Chiefs of Staff Committee, Defence Planning Staff, "Chemical and Biological Warfare," DP.52/65 (Final), 3 September 1965, classified "top secret—UK eyes only," A-6–A-8, DEFE 11/660, PRO; U.K. Ministry of Defence, Chiefs of Staff Committee, "The United Kingdom Requirements for Chemical and Biological Warfare Capabilities," Annex A to COS 124/67, 15 December 1967, classified "top secret—UK eyes only," A-5; U.K. House of Commons, Select Committee on Science and Technology, Testimony of Denis Healey, 18 July 1968, 459. On UK nuclear policy, one of the most important documents from this period is U.K. Ministry of Defence, Review of British Arms Control and Disarmament Policy February 1967, classified "secret—UK eyes only," Draft III, 4 January 1967, D.DS2/3:49/9/3, FCO 10/, PRO.

38. U.K. House of Commons, *Hansard,* 18 February 1930, col. 1169; U.K. Foreign Office, H. G. Darwin, "Use of Tear Gas in Vietnam," 26 March 1965, classified "confidential"; and H. G. Darwin, "Legality of the Use of CS Gas in War," 12 April 1965, classified "confidential," FCO 10/182, PRO.

39. U.K. Foreign Office, H.G. Darwin, "Legality of the Use of CS Gas in War," 12 April 1965, classified "confidential," FCO 10/182, PRO.

40. U.K. Foreign Office, Telegram, U.K. Mission, New York to Foreign Office, 11 November 1966, classified "confidential," FO 371/1874448, PRO.

41. U.K. Foreign Office, "Notes for Supplementaries (follow-up questions to Parliamentary Questions from Mr. Tim Dalyell and Mr. Philip Noel-Baker), 11 July 1968; FCO 10/181, PRO. The SIPRI account from this period does not mention the problems that British officials debated behind closed doors; see SIPRI, *Problem of Chemical and Biological* Warfare, vol. 2, 201.

42. U.K. Foreign Office, Arms Control and Disarmament Research Unit, "Arms

340 *Susan Wright*

Control Implications of Chemical and Biological Warfare," report written by Hedley Bull, ACDRU (67)1 (Final), 3 February 1967, classified "top secret," 5; MoD, Defence Research Committee, Minutes of Meeting, 20 December 1966, 6.

43. U.K. Foreign Office, Arms Control and Disarmament Research Unit, "Arms Control Implications of Chemical and Biological Warfare," report written by Hedley Bull, ACDRU (66)2 (2nd Draft), 4 July 1966, classified "top secret," FO 371/187448. This second draft was more detailed and considerably more frank about British military dependence on the United States than the final version issued in February 1967 (ACDRU (67) 1 (Final)), which appears to have been designed for sharing with the U.S. arms controllers.

44. U.K., I. M. H. Smart (British Embassy, Washington) to Major-General R. E. Lloyd, Deputy Head, Arms Control and Disarmament Research Unit, U.K. Foreign Office, 21 June 1967, FCO 10/179, PRO.

45. U.K. Foreign Office, M. F. Cullis, "Discussion with Americans on Arms Control Aspects of Chemical and Bacteriological Weapons," 27 October 1967, classified "secret," FCO 10/179, PRO; U.K. Foreign Office, "Record of Informal Talks Between British and United States Officials on Arms Control Prospects for Biological and Chemical Officials held at the Foreign Office, London, 12–13 October 1967," 15 November 1967, classified "secret," FCO 10/170, PRO.

46. A NATO meeting of disarmament experts held early in 1968 confirms this view. The minutes indicate that participants were thinking in terms of prohibiting use of chemical and biological weapons, not production. U.K. Foreign Office, Extract, Meeting of Disarmament Experts, 27 February–1 March, 1968, FCO 10/180, PRO.

47. Hope-Jones was appointed head of the Disarmament Department in 1967.

48. U.K. Foreign Office, Ronald Hope-Jones to I. F. S. Porter, U.K. Mission, Geneva, 25 January 1968, covering "Future Prospects for the Disarmament Negotiations," FCO 10/3, PRO.

49. Ronald Hope-Jones to Mr. Moss (secretary to the Minister of State for Foreign Affairs, Fred Mulley), 10 July 1968.

50. Anon., "Nightmare Logic of Germ Warfare," *The Times* (23 February 1968); John Davy, Andrew Wilson, and Roland Huntford, "The Porton Dilemma," *The Observer* (16 June 1968).

51. For examples of parliamentary questions in 1967 and 1968 and the briefing notes for answers prepared in the Foreign Office, see U.K. Foreign Office, files FCO 10/179 and FCO10/180, PRO.

52. U.K. Foreign Office, Ronald Hope-Jones, "The Next Steps in Disarmament," 10 June 1968, FCO 10/4, PRO.

53. U.S. Embassy, London to Secretary of State, Washington, 17 June 1968 (London 9967), POL 27–10, Box 2879, NA; U.K. Foreign Office to Certain Missions, 19 June 1968 (Guidance No. 155) and 19 June 1968 (Guidance No. 156), FCO 10/183, PRO.

54. U.S. Embassy, London to Secretary of State, Washington, 19 June 1968 (London 10073), classified "secret," RG 59, POL 27–10, Box 2879, NA; U.K. Foreign Office to U.K. Embassy, Washington, 20 June 1968, classified "confidential," FCO 10/181, PRO.

55. U.S. State Department to American Embassy, London, 25 June 1968, no. 192587, classified "secret," RG 59, POL 27–10, Box 2879, NA.

56. Ronald Hope-Jones to Mr. Moss, 10 July 1968, annotated "seen by Mr. Mulley." Hope-Jones gives a detailed account of the events leading up to the drafting of a working paper proposing a convention banning biological weapons but does not refer to an interaction with officials from the American embassy in London. That connection remains to be made, although given the urgency of the State Department's communication with the latter, it seems almost certain that an exchange would have taken place. "Chemical and Biological Warfare," 1 July 1968, U.K. Foreign Office, FCO 10/4, PRO.

57. U.K. Foreign Office, "Chemical and Biological Warfare," 1 July 1968, FCO 10/4, PRO.

58. Ibid.

59. U.K. Foreign Office, Record of a Conversation between the Minister of State for Foreign Affairs and the Director of the United States Arms Control and Disarmament Agency, Washington, 2 July 1968, FCO 10/4, PRO.

60. Mulley's presentation to the ENDC was made on 16 July 1968. FCO 10/28, PRO.

61. U.K. Cabinet, Defence and Oversea Policy Committee, Minutes of a Meeting Held at 10 Downing Street, S.W.1, 12 July 1968, OPD(68), CAB 148/35, PRO.

62. In fact, nonnuclear nations would turn out to be the strongest supporters of a comprehensive ban on chemical as well as biological weapons.

63. U.K. Cabinet, Working Group on Chemical and Biological Warfare, 1st Meeting, 17 July 1968 (MISC 214(68)), CAB 130/389, PRO.

64. U.K. Cabinet, Office of the Chief Scientific Advisor, "Brief for MISC 214 Meeting (2nd) on Friday, 19 July 1968; Foreign Office Working Paper on Biological Warfare," Handwritten, nonverbatim account, CAB 168/125, PRO.

65. The Sub-committee on Disarmament was composed of civil servants drawn from the Foreign Office, the Ministry of Defence, and the Cabinet Office. Among them were Ronald Hope-Jones, Sir Solly Zuckerman, and Kenneth Nash from the Ministry of Defence, who appears to have been responsible for the MoD's critique of the draft proposal from the Foreign Office.

66. U.K. Ministry of Defence, "Disarmament—Proposed Initiative on Biological Warfare: Ministry of Defence Points," 23 July 1968, FCO 10/182, PRO.

67. U.K. Foreign Office, Sir Edward Peck to Lord Hood, copied to Ronald Hope-Jones, 22 July 1968, FCO 10/182, PRO.

68. U.K. Cabinet Office, Sir Solly Zuckerman to Harold Wilson, 25 July 1968, CAB 168/125, PRO; U.K. Ministry of Defence, "Disarmament—Proposed Initiative on Biological Warfare: Ministry of Defence Points."

69. U.K. Defence and Oversea Policy (Official) Committee, Subcommittee on Disarmament, Minutes of Meeting, 23 July 1968, CAB 148/71, PRO; see also Sir Solly Zuckerman to Michael Stewart, 26 July 1968, CAB 168/125, PRO.

70. A further criticism made at this meeting by the minister of health was that vesting responsibility in the World Health Organization for investigating allegations of noncompliance was contrary to the articles of the WHO. The final version of the working paper proposed to invest responsibility for investigations in an expert group appointed by the United Nations.

71. U.K. Foreign Office, U.K. Working Paper on Chemical and Biological Warfare for Tabling at the Eighteen Nation Disarmament Committee, 30 July 1968, FCO 10/182, PRO. This paper is the final version that was tabled at the ENDC by Minister of State for Foreign Affairs Fred Mulley on 6 August (United Nations document ENDC/231 (6 August 1968)). The three formulations of the ban on "production of microbiological agents" proposed in this paper are (1) "on a scale which had no independent peaceful justification," (2) for hostile purposes, and (3) "in quantities that would be incompatible with the obligation never to engage in microbiological methods of warfare in any circumstances."

72. U.K. Foreign Office, Ronald Hope-Jones to Mr. Moss, "Microbiological Warfare," 24 July 1968, FCO 10/182, PRO.

73. U.S. Department of State, American Embassy, London to Secretary of State, Washington, "UK Working Paper on Biological Weapons," 30 July 1968, classified "secret," RG 59, Pol 27–10, NA.

74. U.K. Foreign Office, Ronald Hope-Jones to His Excellency, Mr. I. F. Porter, 31 July 1968.

75. U.K. Ministry of Defence, Chiefs of Staff Committee, "Chemical and Biological Warfare," classified "top secret, U.K. Eyes Only," 15 December 1967, COS 124/67, A-5-A-7; U.K. Foreign Office, M.O'D. B. Alexander to Derek Benest, "Chemical and Biological Warfare: NATO Aspects," 8 July 1968, classified "top secret," FCO 10/184, PRO.

76. U.S. American Embassy, London to Department of State, Washington, "UK Working Paper on Biological Weapons (BW)," 30 July 1968, classified "secret," RG 59, Pol 27–10, NA.

77. William Safire, "On Language: Weapons of Mass Destruction," *New York Times* (19 April 1998), section 6, 22.

78. U.S. Department of State, American Embassy to State Department, 30 July 1968, telegram London 11305, "UK Working Paper on Biological Weapons (BW)," 30 July 1968, classified "Secret," RG 59, POL 27–10, Box 2879, NA.

79. U.K. Cabinet, Defence and Oversea Policy Committee, Minutes, Meeting, 26 July 1968, classified "secret," CAB 148/35, PRO.

80. Disarmament Conference document, ENDC/231.

81. Ronald Hope-Jones pointed directly to the achievement of this ambiguity in the ban in his memorandum, "Microbiological Warfare," 24 July 1968, FCO 10/182, PRO.

# 13

## The Compliance Protocol and the Three Depository Powers

*Oliver Thränert*

When the Biological Weapons Convention (BWC) entered into force in 1975, three depository states took on special responsibilities for this treaty: the United States, the United Kingdom, and the Soviet Union, whose responsibilities have since been taken over by the Russian Federation. The BWC restricts the development, production, and stockpiling of biological weapons, but it does not include effective verification provisions. Following a special conference of all the member states (states parties) in 1994, it was decided to establish an Ad Hoc Group (AHG) open for all parties to negotiate a legally binding protocol to the convention to, inter alia, introduce effective compliance provisions.

This chapter analyzes the positions taken by the three depository states in the AHG negotiations in light of the following conditions:

1. As depositories, all three countries bear a special responsibility with regard to the implementation of the convention.[1]
2. All three countries have considerable experience with offensive biological warfare (BW) programs, since each pursued such programs before the BWC entered into force. The former Soviet Union was the only country of the three depositories to the BWC that continued an offensive BW program even after 1975, and there are serious claims that parts of this program continued after the end of the Cold War.[2]
3. In an attempt to clarify the status of the Soviet/Russian BW program, the United States, the United Kingdom, and Russia established a trilat-

eral process in 1992. The three states agreed, inter alia, to the following procedure: "Visits to any non-military biological site at any time in
order to remove ambiguities, subject to the need to respect proprietary
information on the basis of agreed principles. Such visits would
include unrestricted access, sampling, interviews with personnel, and
audio and video taping. After initial visits to Russian facilities there
will be comparable visits to such U.S. and U.K. facilities on the same
basis."[3] In addition, plans were made to set up working groups to create provisions for visits to military facilities. In doing so, the three
depository states made it clear that they were prepared to accept a special responsibility for the implementation of the BWC.

4. All three countries continue to conduct extensive BW defense programs.
5. Without agreement among the United States, the United Kingdom,
   and Russia as the "big players" in the AHG negotiations, a BW protocol seems politically inconceivable.

Analysis of the positions taken by the three countries provides insight into
the politics of the BWC protocol negotiations. In particular, it shows the
political differences between the West and Russia on the one hand, and
within the Western Group itself on the other. The following questions are
central to this analysis: What positions did the United States, the United
Kingdom, and Russia take in the course of the AHG negotiations? How did
these positions develop? What were the basic contradictions among the
positions taken by the three countries? And finally, how likely, against the
background of these contradictions, is the possibility of effective verification
procedures for the BWC being instituted? This analysis focuses on the most
important issues associated with the compliance/verification measures of the
BWC, namely, definitions and thresholds, declarations, and visits and investigations. Three main sources of information have been used: documents of
the AHG, including procedural reports, the Rolling Text, and working
papers introduced by BWC members into the AHG negotiations; secondary
literature, including articles published by members of delegations; and interviews with members of delegations and other experts.[4] This chapter covers
in detail the period of AHG negotiations up until the nineteenth AHG session, which took place in March 2000. By this stage, the positions of the
three depository states were largely defined. The final part of the chapter
analyzes more recent events in 2001, when the United States finally rejected
the Protocol entirely.

## THE UNITED STATES

From the very beginning of the discussions about introducing compliance
measures into the BWC regime, the United States took a very reluctant

stance. At the third Review Conference to the BWC in 1991, where states parties established an Ad Hoc Group of Governmental Experts on Verification Measures (VEREX), members of the U.S. delegation expressed their view that, given the nature of BW, on-site inspections would reveal nothing. They would therefore be inappropriate and would only create a false sense of confidence in the convention.[5]

This position continued to be expressed during the VEREX meetings in 1992 and 1993. It produced fundamental disagreement between members of the European Union and some other Western countries on the one hand and the United States on the other about the feasibility of an effective verification regime for the BWC. Whereas the U.S. delegation claimed that effective verification of the BWC would be impossible due to the dual-use character of the pathogens, toxins, and equipment needed for a BW program, delegates from other Western states disagreed, arguing that declarations, visits, and investigations would result in more transparency. Most important, these delegates argued, an improved BWC would give a clear signal to the international community that care is being taken to strengthen the norm against biological weapons. Not surprisingly, the latter wanted to make proposals for verification while the United States wanted only an evaluation of possible compliance measures. American influence was evident in the final VEREX report in September 1993. The report identified and evaluated possible compliance measures, both on-site and off-site, but did not include any specific verification recommendations.[6]

At the request of the majority of the parties to the BWC, a Special Conference was convened in September 1994 to discuss the VEREX report and to decide on further measures. While many Western countries aimed at a mandate for another Ad Hoc Group to negotiate intrusive verification provisions, the United States still was not convinced that effective verification of the BWC was possible. Therefore, the U.S. delegation tried to water down the mandate of the new Ad Hoc Group so as to seek a "compliance" rather than a verification protocol. However, at the end of the Special Conference, a compromise was agreed upon. The mandate of the AHG stated that the group should consider, inter alia, "appropriate measures, including possible verification measures, and draft proposals to strengthen the Convention, to be included, as appropriate, in a legally binding instrument, to be submitted for the consideration of the States Parties."[7]

During the first four substantial meetings of the AHG in 1995 and 1996, the U.S. delegation did not put forward any specific ideas for effectively enhancing the BWC. The United States seemed to be prepared—as were the majority of the parties taking part in the AHG—to accept both declarations of military and civilian facilities and sites and investigations in cases of noncompliance as part of a future protocol to the BWC. But more detailed views were not laid out. In particular, the United States gave no indication of its position on inspections designed to appraise declarations according to some modality to be determined. The reason for this was that the U.S. delegation in Geneva lacked clear instructions, due to an ongoing struggle in Washington between the Department of Commerce and the Department of Defense on one side and the White House and the State Department on the other.

The Department of Commerce was mainly concerned with protecting the proprietary and commercial information of civilian industry. This emphasis reflected the views of the member companies of the Pharmaceutical Research and Manufacturers of America (PhRMA). The Pentagon for its part argued that the United States was running the world's largest and most expensive BW defense program and that it therefore had no interest in putting secret military information concerning these activities at risk in the course of international on-site visits/inspections as part of BWC verification. The military also argued that the U.S. BW defense program served the purpose of protecting not only U.S. soldiers against biological warfare waged by hostile states but also the civilian population against BW terrorist attacks. Again, it would be necessary to keep such programs secret so as to make sure that terrorists could not learn about the weaknesses of the U.S. BW defense program. In contrast, the White House and State Department emphasized the need to create an effective diplomatic instrument to address what the United States had defined as the central BW problem: proliferation. They were also more inclined to make the diplomatic effort to enhance the BWC a success story in disarmament. Because of this conflict, the National Security Council, which was the leading agency in the decision-making process, was not capable of formulating a compromise that satisfied the conflicting interests of all agencies involved.[8]

Awareness of BW as a problem existed at the highest political level in the United States. President Clinton made this clear in a speech before the UN General Assembly on September 24, 1996, in which he stated that "we must better protect our people from those who would use disease as a weapon of war, by giving the Biological Weapons Convention the means to strengthen compliance, including on-site investigations when we believe such weapons may have been used, or when suspicious outbreaks of disease occur. We should aim to complete this task by 1998."[9]

Coming on the eve of the fourth Review Conference to the BWC, which took place in November and December 1996, the presidential statement was timely. But in spite of this statement, the U.S. delegation did not show more effective leadership, or even flexibility, at the AHG. There was a common feeling in Washington that an improved BWC was needed to deal with the threat of BW proliferation, but there was no agreement about how exactly this should be achieved.

By June 1997, negotiations in the AHG became more focused when the first "Rolling Text" was prepared by the chairman, Ambassador Tibor Toth. As a result, discussions in the AHG, especially concerning compliance measures, became more substantial. The main compliance-related issues were, first, the question of the modalities for conducting either random or routine inspections (also known as visits), and second, the nature of investigations (also known as "challenge inspections") conducted in response to suspicion of noncompliance.

The United States very strongly opposed an approach promoted by some Western delegations, whereby annual declarations of both military BW defense programs and facilities and civilian facilities with certain characteristics would be checked through routine on-site inspections. It was argued by the U.S. delegation that such inspections (or visits) would not be accepted by the biotechnology and pharmaceutical industries, because they would interfere with the protection of commercial and proprietary information.[10] To the military, such on-site activities could jeopardize national security since potential opponents could use them to identify weaknesses in U.S. biological defense capabilities.

Moreover, such visits would mainly take place in the United States, the state with the largest number of facilities and sites to be declared. Since the United States would need to cover some 20 percent of the budget of a future BWC organization, it was not willing to support inspections that would focus on its own territory. Finally, the U.S. delegation argued that random visits would not be capable of deterring noncompliance. It would be necessary to conduct random visits on very short notice since otherwise a facility would be cleaned up before the visiting team arrived. Such short-notice provisions would not be possible to agree upon in the AHG, because they would be acceptable neither to the United States nor to other delegations. Therefore, random visits would not efficiently enhance the BWC but would be a burden for U.S. industry and costly for U.S. taxpayers.

The United States not only opposed random visits, it also wanted to make on-site investigations more difficult to pursue. Under the Chemical Weapons Convention (CWC), a three-quarters majority vote is required to stop an investigation (a procedure known as a "red-light" approach). For the Biological Weapons Convention, in contrast, the United States proposed a "green-light" approach according to which a simple majority vote would be required to approve an investigation. The United States argued that a "green-light" approach was needed to prevent frivolous and unfounded investigation requests. At the same time, this move would also dramatically lower the efficacy of investigations, as it would be critical (as the United States itself had noted in the context of random visits) to conduct such investigations on very short notice.

Later in the negotiations, the United States attempted to dilute the instrument of challenge investigations even further, using the U.S. national legislation for implementing the CWC as a model. The U.S. negotiators took the position that samples taken during investigations could only be analyzed in special laboratories within the country under inspection as in the CWC national legislation. There were also indications that the United States wanted a further provision of that legislation adapted for the BWC Protocol according to which the U.S. president could deny a challenge inspection if he deemed it a threat to U.S. national security.[11]

In contrast, the United States moved to strengthen the draft Protocol in other respects. For example, the United States insisted that investigations should be possible in cases of unusual outbreaks of disease. That position was based on experiences with noncompliance related to the former Soviet Union. In 1979, an anthrax outbreak occurred in the city of Sverdlovsk (now Ekaterinburg). This outbreak raised suspicions in the West that it might have been caused by an accident in a BW facility. Soviet officials denied it, but after years of investigation it is now clear that this was indeed the case.[12] Because this incident is well known in the United States, it would be difficult to obtain the needed ratification of the BWC protocol unless it were possible to investigate similar cases in the future.

The ongoing interagency discussions still prevented an American leadership role in Geneva. The division noted previously persisted. One school of thought, whose supporters were mainly drawn from the Defense, Energy, and Commerce Departments with strong backing from the U.S. pharmaceutical industry, still held that the BWC would in essence be unverifiable and, moreover, that on-site activities could endanger both military secrets and commercial proprietary information. Accordingly, nonchallenge visits to check declarations were strongly resisted and challenge investigations were required to be held only under very strict conditions (the aforementioned "green-light approach"). The other school of thought, supported mainly by members of the National Security Council and the Department of State, favored a more intrusive approach for a BWC compliance regime. This included some nonchallenge on-site activities and a less restricted challenge investigation regime that allowed investigations to proceed more easily.[13] Members of this group did not see a "green-light" approach as appropriate.

By January 1998, an interagency group had produced a compromise position:

- Annual declarations to a BWC implementing organization of facilities and activities potentially related to BW, for instance those equipped with certain types of aerosol test chambers;
- "Voluntary" visits to address questions under the BWC or the Protocol, where all decisions concerning access would be made by the visited party;
- Nonchallenge, "clarification" visits whose purpose was to clarify ambi-

guities, anomalies, omissions or other issues related to annual declarations; and

- Challenge investigations subject to a "green-light filter."[14]

Although Washington now accepted nonchallenge clarification visits, it still opposed random visits. This was one aspect of the new U.S. position that would not meet with the approval of some other Western delegations, particularly that of the United Kingdom. The other was the endorsement of a green-light filter for challenge investigations. Furthermore, the United States still did not come forward with detailed proposals concerning declarations; generally, many aspects of the U.S. proposals remained vague. However, for some in Washington, mostly in the Pentagon and the Department of Commerce, even the proposed provisions for clarification visits went much too far.

One problem with the January 1998 compromise was that the National Security Council, where the text had been formulated, had—in the eyes of PhRMA—not sufficiently consulted the U.S. pharmaceutical industry. As a result, an antagonistic relationship between the Clinton Administration and the industry, represented by PhRMA, emerged. PhRMA remained very critical of clarification visits in particular, on the grounds that a company's reputation might be seriously damaged by an unfounded clarification request.[15]

Some believe that PhRMA had no "natural" faith in a Democratic administration. In fact, mistrust between PhRMA and the Clinton Administration goes back to an international inspection undertaken as part of the U.S./ U.K./Russia trilateral process in 1993. At that time, a PhRMA company was visited in a way which left it quite dissatisfied with the behavior and activities of the visitors.[16] However, while PhRMA represents the majority of U.S. pharmaceutical companies, dissenting views were also expressed in the industry. For instance, executives of one biotechnology firm strongly supported a strengthened BWC and declared their willingness not only to accept clarification visits but even random inspections.[17]

Presumably to meet PhRMA concerns, in July 1998 the U.S. delegation in Geneva tabled a working paper concerning clarification visits. Before a clarification visit could be initiated, the Technical Secretariat and the party to be visited would try to solve the issue through written correspondence and meetings in the party's capital. A clarification visit could only take place if such measures did not resolve the situation. This visit would be limited to the relevant portion of the facility that was generating concern, use managed access procedures, and not take more than two or three days. Sampling would only be allowed if permitted by the visited state party. Visits would also be possible at undeclared facilities, following the same procedure. But for these cases, if written exchanges or consultations in the capital of the relevant party did not resolve the situation, the Executive Council of the BWC organization would be required to decide on a clarification visit under a red-light silence procedure. Under that procedure, a three-quarters majority of the Council could stop a proposed visit.[18]

When the director of the U.S. Arms Control and Disarmament Agency, John D. Holum, addressed the AHG in October 1998, he identified four principles on which the U.S. position was based:

- Legally binding, mandatory declarations to provide transparency about activities of potential relevance to the Convention.
- On-site investigations in cases of suspected noncompliance. These could concern possible use of BW, suspicious outbreaks of disease, or locations where these is concern that activities in violation of the BWC are being conducted.
- Means to ensure that declarations are complete and accurate.
- A professional organization to implement the protocol.

Holum did not mention visits at all in his speech. His ambiguous reference to "means" caused some speculation that the United States would not accept visits at all. Nevertheless, by the summer of 1999, the United States apparently had decided to support clarification visits. Later in the year, it issued a paper proposing that these should be made not only to declared sites but also to undeclared ones.[19] At the same time, random visits remained unacceptable, mainly because—as one diplomat put it—U.S. industry would hate them.

Whether the United States would contemplate nonchallenge visits other than voluntary and clarification visits remained unclear. In that regard, the issue of "transparency visits," proposed by Germany in the summer of 1999, gained some importance.[20] Such visits would be randomly selected, and their main purpose would be to familiarize members of the future BWC Technical Secretariat with a facility rather than the far more intrusive purpose of confirming the accuracy of declarations. A visit to a designated facility would consist mainly of a three-hour briefing tour encompassing a general description of declared activities and conducted in the least intrusive manner possible, without managed access procedures and without sampling. In essence, in this type of visit, information would be provided only at the discretion of the visited party, with full protection for commercial proprietary and national security information.

The United States vacillated in response to this proposal. Whereas some U.S. diplomats suggested that the concept of transparency visits might be acceptable on the condition that the visits would not probe commercial or military secrets, Secretary of Commerce William Daley rejected it on the grounds that it would not offer any national security benefits. Transparency visits, Daley opined, had "virtually no chance of discovering biological weapons activities."[21] In spring 2000, consequently, the U.S. position on transparency visits remained unclear.

The U.S. position on declarations also caused considerable dissension within the Western Group. Although there was agreement that past offensive and defensive BW programs as well as current defensive BW programs and BW-related activities should be declared, the U.S. position contained concerns about both categories. The United States feared that it would not be possible to declare past activities accurately enough, so that new incidents or investigations could lead to embarrassing situations. With regard to current activities, the United States wanted to reduce the number of facilities/sites to be declared in the country as far as possible, since the United States possesses by far the largest BW defense program and the largest number of civilian biotech/pharmaceutical facilities. Otherwise, a future BWC organization would be overwhelmed by declarations coming from the United States and other Western countries which, according to the United States, did not pose any BW compliance concern. At the same time, however, the United States wanted to make sure that even the smallest BW-related activity in countries it deemed to be of concern would be declarable.

As a result, in October 1998 the United States put forward proposals for declarations that were not entirely acceptable to the rest of the Western Group or to a number of other AHG delegations:

1. The United States wanted to differentiate between governmental and nongovernmental activities in declarations. This position meant that most European governments would need to declare even the smallest biodefense project at a university, since most European universities are completely financed by the state. In contrast, since many of the top American research universities are private, only projects undertaken at public universities in the United States would be declarable. Later in the negotiations the United States showed some flexibility on this point.

2. The United States wanted site-based declarations of current biodefense projects. This would imply that sites rather than facilities would be declared, so that many small biodefense projects in the United States, often aimed at coping with the chemical/bioterrorism threat, would not be declarable.[22] Along the same lines, a minimum declaration requirement proposed by the United States implied that a country with large defense activities would only need to declare large projects, whereas a country with only small-scale activities would need to declare all of its projects, even the smallest ones.

3. The United States wanted research and development in current biodefense projects to be declared only when they were aimed at producing

a biodefense product. In the eyes of many Europeans, this made these declarations extremely weak, as it is practically impossible to define when research and development result in biodefense products.

4. The United States did not want to include work with genetically modified microorganisms on the list of agents required to be declared. Moreover, the U.S. delegation wanted previously agreed lists of animal and plant pathogens and toxins to be reduced. The United States was also the only country participating in the AHG that did not believe that criteria for lists of pathogens and toxins should be set up in an annex to the BWC Protocol. The purpose of such criteria is to enable the Executive Council to update lists of declarable pathogens and toxins in light of new discoveries, adding new substances if they seemed potentially useful for BW applications. Having definite criteria set out would give the Executive Council clear guidelines for whether a new substance should be included on lists of declarable agents. In an attempt at compromise, the United States put forward a proposal for using commercial as well as technical and scientific criteria. This meant that the commercial value of certain items would be a factor in deciding whether they would appear on the list, so that U.S. interests would play an important role in this decision process.

Clearly, these proposals were influenced by the U.S. civilian industry and military. In attempting to protect these interests, Washington neglected the interests of its allies. Moreover, the attempt to institute a regime under which a country with large BW defensive programs would not need to declare smaller parts of its program could be seen as an invitation to cheat. If a potential violator wished to run an offensive or other illegitimate BW program without attracting suspicion, it could simply do so in its smaller facilities, hiding behind its larger, declared ones.

In sum, the position ultimately taken by the United States was greatly influenced by its biotechnology and pharmaceutical industries and its military. As a result, the U.S. delegation tried to create rules governing declarations that would significantly reduce their scope within its own territory and make on-site activities, whether visits or investigations, in the United States as unlikely as possible. By summer 1999, the U.S. delegation in Geneva was not in a position to provide leadership in the negotiations since the country was seen as more concerned with the protection of its own interests than with making the BWC an effective tool to prevent BW proliferation. With the presidential elections approaching, the U.S. delegation in Geneva was unwilling to speed up the process of negotiations. As a result, by spring 2000 no compromise on any of the still unresolved issues was in sight.

## THE RUSSIAN FEDERATION

Like the United States, from the very beginning of the attempt to strengthen the BWC, the Russian Federation adopted a hesitant position both with respect to compliance measures in general and on-site activities in particular. But Russia's motivations came from different sources. Russia's main problem was its offensive BW program, which it inherited from the Soviet Union.

This program involved dozens of laboratories and institutes, an open-air test range, and thousands of employees. Most parts of this program were conducted in the framework of a system called *Biopreparat*. It included institutes that did research and development on pathogens and toxins for both military and civilian purposes.[23] There are also allegations that *Biopreparat* stockpiled weaponized strains of anthrax, smallpox, and other sorts of plague. Since the collapse of the Soviet Union, *Biopreparat* has been transformed into a joint stock company, and there have been attempts to convert many of its laboratories into civilian facilities. But since conversion of offensive biological research, development, and even production facilities is not irreversible, international inspectors might conclude that activities that did not comply with the BWC were still being pursued at *Biopreparat* facilities. Moreover, it seems likely that the Russian military still controls *Biopreparat* to a certain extent, since its present director holds the rank of general and previously worked in the Soviet offensive BW program. As a result, it is extremely difficult to distinguish civilian from military programs in Russia.[24]

Furthermore, Russia clearly intends to continue a BW defense program. Naturally, it wants to make use of institutes that previously pursued offensive BW work. In a BWC compliance/verification regime, evidence from visits or inspections might easily be taken as indications that the work in inspected facilities still violated the BWC, since—as noted—almost nothing in a biological facility is irreversible.

Finally, many in the West believe that Russia may still be pursuing an offensive BW program.[25] Although this may or may not be the case, requests for visits and inspections in Russia seem especially likely. Against this background, the Russian Federation wanted to make sure that it would not be accused of violating the BWC as a result of international activities in the framework of a BWC compliance/verification protocol.

Consequently, from the very beginning of discussions on strengthening the BWC, Russia insisted that such a process should be based on clear definitions of terms used in the BWC itself or in the protocol. However, the BWC generally avoids clear definitions of central terms. For example, the

BWC does not include a definition of a biological weapon, or the research, development, or production that lead to it.

Western governments take the view that the formulation of article I of the BWC is designed to avoid loopholes in the convention through the broad prohibition of all biological activities except those justified for "prophylactic, protective or other peaceful purposes." This means that any attempt to define the term "biological weapon" would necessarily be incomplete, as would be a list of potential BW agents. If biological weapons are defined too strictly, the argument goes, a state intent on violating the BWC might use precisely those pathogens or toxins not mentioned in the definition and argue that its undertakings were not in violation for this reason. Western delegations also argued that defining the terms used in the BWC would mean amending the convention, which would exceed the mandate of the AHG.[26]

The view taken by the Russians could not have stood in starker contrast to this Western position. Without precise definitions of important terms, they argued, it would not be possible for inspectors or visitors to draw objective conclusions. The issue of definitions would ultimately determine the character of any BWC compliance protocol. Without clear definitions, such a protocol would imply that parameters would need to be discussed on a case-by-case basis during inspections. Consequently, the views of politically more powerful states, with more bargaining power, would be unfairly privileged against those of less powerful states. Vague criteria would also give the international media more power over the process, in that they could raise the pressure on certain countries after investigations resulting in vague conclusions were made public. Therefore, it was desirable to agree on definitions of important terms before putting a compliance protocol into force, so that judgments in the course of investigations could be objective. After all, the purpose of an inspection is to verify facts, not intentions.

According to the Russian view, definitions would be needed for such terms as "biological weapon," "hostile intentions," and "national program of biological defense." Although clear definitions of terminology should be seen as an essential element of a BWC protocol, simplistic approaches that could limit the scope of article I of the BWC should be avoided. The regime should furthermore include a certain amount of flexibility, so that definitions could be adjusted against the background of new developments in biotechnology.[27]

How seriously the question of the definition of terms was taken by the Russian Federation was illustrated by the fact that as early as the second session of the AHG (which was the first substantial one), Russia tabled a working paper on the definition of terms. In this paper, the Russian Federation aimed at definitions of many basic terms, such as "bacteriological (biological) and toxin weapons" and "bacteriological (biological) agents and toxins."[28] Apart from some support provided by the delegation from Ukraine,[29] Russia's proposals on definitions were opposed by most, if not all, other delegations in Geneva. Consequently, Russia became increasingly isolated on the definitions issue.

Related to the issue of definitions was that of so-called threshold quantities. In an effort to ensure that work in Russian biological facilities would not be perceived by international inspectors as in breach of the BWC, Russia argued that parties should be allowed to store maximum quantities of listed biological agents and toxins at facilities engaged in BW defense. Such thresholds should be defined for each listed agent.[30] Russia had already taken this position during the VEREX meetings. In a working paper dated December 1992, Russia had suggested a maximum quantity of 5 kg of biological material as sufficient for evaluating means of protection against BW. According to Russia, such an amount could not support an effective offensive operation.[31]

Since then, not much has changed in the Russian position on thresholds. In a working paper of September 1996, the Russian delegation reiterated the usefulness of thresholds and put forward a more detailed scientific analysis of how such thresholds could be calculated for certain pathogens or toxins.[32] Furthermore, Russia put forward the language for an article in the Protocol to deal with thresholds, which went into the "Rolling Text."[33] Although Russian experts agreed that it would be difficult to define such threshold quantities precisely in ways which would be acceptable to all parties, they continued to insist that thresholds would be necessary to make sure BW defense work could be clearly differentiated from offensive BW programs.[34] But this proposal specified much lower levels than those of the 1992 working paper.

The impasse over thresholds continued, with the Russian proposal supported only by Ukraine,[35] and the Western delegations completely opposed. The West continued to argue that thresholds would not be useful for strengthening the convention and that they would moreover undermine the provisions of article I. Thresholds for work in defense programs could be used to camouflage offensive programs, because microorganisms replicate in short periods of time. Furthermore, in some cases very small amounts of agents or toxins could be of military significance and therefore violate the purpose of the convention.[36]

In an effort to bridge Eastern and Western positions, Western delegations proposed combining threshold amounts with annual declarations on the production of relevant pathogens or toxins. But Russia opposed this idea, reinforcing suspicions on the part of many Western delegations that Russia wanted to keep BW agents for purposes not permitted under the convention.

Russia also wanted to make on-site activities on its own territory, such as visits or investigations, as unlikely as possible. Toward that end, the Russian delegation argued that the BWC already included provisions for a compliance request in article VI. According to this provision, such a request should be dealt with in the United Nations Security Council, which could decide to launch an investigation as it saw fit. Therefore, the AHG needed only to define the details of such a procedure. These could include a request to the Security Council, which might refer it to a technical body to analyze the request and assist with bilateral and multilateral consultations. A politically representative body might decide with a two-thirds majority to conduct an investigation.

Russia argued that for such a procedure, a special BWC organization would not be needed. The establishment of such an organization would be counterproductive as it would undermine the authority of the UN Security Council to investigate noncompliance requests. It would also undermine the political effectiveness of the United Nations in general.[37] But it was clear that Russia was not concerned exclusively or even primarily with the reputation of the United Nations. It was far more important to make sure that it would have a veto in the UN Security Council, in case of an allegation against Russia.

By 1999, the Russian delegation had changed its position to the extent of accepting a special BWC organization. However, it continued to make proposals that made on-site visits or investigations in Russia extremely unlikely. With regard to visits, Russia argued that omissions, anomalies, or a lack of precision in declarations could be resolved through clarification processes such as consultations or voluntary visits agreed upon by state parties on a bilateral or a multilateral basis. Any other type of visit, whether clarification or random, would not be needed.

Moreover, Russia opposed all on-site field investigations related to outbreaks of disease, arguing that such events should not be seen as falling under the convention since they occurred naturally. Rather, an analysis of such outbreaks would fall under the competence of national authorities or the World Health Organization. By the summer of 1999 there was some speculation that Russia might accept field investigations in principle if they were clearly connected to compliance concerns. Unusual outbreaks of disease alone, however, would not be sufficient to justify investigation. In addition, the Russians did not want to allow field investigations to lead into facility investigations, an idea promoted by the British delegation. Rather, Russia insisted that facility investigations would need their own trigger mechanism.

Together with virtually all delegations, Russia held that requests for facility investigations in cases of well-founded noncompliance concerns should be considered by the Executive Council of a future BWC organization. But Russia proposed a "green-light" filter that was even stronger than that of the United States, one that required a two-thirds majority of the Council to approve an investigation and made on-site inspections on Russian territory extremely unlikely.[38]

In sum, the Russian position was even more restrictive than that of the United States. Russia supported even greater limitations on visits and investigations. And through the introduction of clear definitions of terminology and threshold quantities, Russia wanted to avoid the possibility of the politically much more powerful United States using the BWC Protocol to accuse Russia of breaching the convention.

## THE UNITED KINGDOM

Unlike the United States and the Russian Federation, the United Kingdom showed an intense interest from the very beginning of the AHG negotiations in contributing to efforts to bring about an effective BWC protocol. The United Kingdom government sees the BWC as British-inspired and therefore feels a special responsibility for it. This view is rooted in the history of negotiations in the Conference of Disarmament. In July 1969, the United Kingdom tabled the first draft of a convention designed to prohibit biological weapons.[39] It was used as one of the basic documents during the BWC negotiations, which were completed in 1972.

When the question of BWC verification began to be addressed in the 1990s, the British delegation took the position that a verification regime could not simply copy that of the 1993 Chemical Weapons Convention, largely because of the self-replicating character of pathogens. Because small colonies of many pathogens can be grown so rapidly, a quantitative, "bean-counting" approach aimed only at measuring amounts of agents or numbers and capacities of fermenters would not be appropriate. Furthermore, the British argued that it would be necessary not to overburden the pharmaceutical and biotechnology industry and to make optimal use of the limited resources available for BWC verification. For all these reasons, a future BWC protocol could not function properly on the basis of the extensive routine inspections being used in the context of the CWC and other arms control regimes.

On the understanding that a BWC verification regime would be unique in that it could not copy existing arms control treaties, the British aimed for an integrated regime consisting of mandatory declarations, mandatory visits, challenge inspections, investigations of alleged use, and a professional inspectorate to operate the regime. Visits would not be made on a routine basis but would be conducted randomly. They would serve the following purposes:

- To facilitate transparency,
- To validate declarations,
- To provide an understanding of national safety mechanisms,
- To facilitate a working relationship between the state parties and the future BWC organization,
- To encourage state parties to make accurate declarations, and
- To contribute to deterring potential proliferators.

A verification system that only included declarations and challenge inspections was deemed highly unsuitable by the British, on the grounds that it would be ineffective.[40] This view on the need for random visits clearly distinguished the United Kingdom's position from those of the United States and Russia. The British further claimed that visits should deter potential violators from cheating and that they therefore would need to be undertaken at short notice, a view that was strenuously resisted by both Washington and Moscow. In their views, such visits would come much too close to routine inspections, which both wanted to avoid.

Support for the British position in the AHG mostly came from delegations such as Canada, Australia, New Zealand, and South Africa, as well as from Sweden and the Netherlands in the European Union. According to Canada, the BWC protocol should be a "living document" for all state parties:

> Non-challenge visits would provide a means of demonstrating that all take their obligations seriously throughout the year and they are not just placed on a shelf collecting dust until the time that an annual declaration needs to be made. The reason is simple: preparation for the possibility of non-challenge visits will require that appropriate national authorities interact with industries, laboratories and defense establishments, and allow for the possibility that an international authority may also interact with them.[41]

Later in the negotiations, the differences between the British-led group of delegations and the United States and Russia, as well as most nonaligned countries, focused on the scope of declarations and the issue of who would have the right to initiate visits. The British preferred more detailed declarations that would cover not only biological defense facilities but also nearby facilities at the same site. Furthermore, the United Kingdom argued that not only states parties but also the future BWC organization would have the right to request clarification visits. Both positions were opposed by a majority of the AHG delegations, including the United States, Russia, and most nonaligned countries.[42]

Given the widespread rejection of its proposals for intrusive inspections, by the end of 1998 the British delegation had begun to change its position, shifting closer to the less ambitious concepts being advanced by the German delegation.[43] An important consequence was that the "friend of the chair" responsible for drafting the section of the "Rolling Text" on measures to promote compliance, the British diplomat Richard Tauwhare, moved the requirements for visits from the chapter of the "Rolling Text" that also addressed investigations to the chapter on declarations. This subtle change in the text meant that visits would be seen as nonchallenge undertakings, clearly different in intent from investigations.[44] It also meant that visits would no longer be seen as instruments for deterring noncompliance, undertaken at short notice, but only as means for following up on declarations in a manner that would be far less intrusive than originally envisioned by the British and some other delegations. By this point, the British had retreated from their original emphasis on the use of visits to enhance transparency and deterrence.

Furthermore, as a result of consultations among the United Kingdom, France, Germany, Japan, South Africa, and the United States, the British delegation accepted the view that clarification visits would only take place after a clarification procedure. This would consist of written correspondence between and consultation between representatives of the party concerned and the Technical Secretariat. Moreover, it was agreed that clarification procedures could only be initiated by a party, not by the Technical Secretariat. After the written exchanges, the requested state party could offer a voluntary visit. Finally, the party receiving the request would have the right to decline a clarification visit if it considered that it had made every reasonable effort to resolve the matter through the clarification process. In such a case, the Executive Council would consider the matter at its next regular session and only then decide whether an investigation of compliance would be initiated.[45]

Thus, by the end of 1998, the British proposals for clarification visits approached those of the United States. They also took into consideration the Russian position, at least to the extent that voluntary visits would be handled as part of a clarification process and could be denied by the party receiving the request. The differences between the voluntary visits proposed by Russia and the right to deny clarification visits proposed by the United Kingdom appeared to be marginal.

The British still saw clarification visits as insufficient and therefore did not give up entirely the idea of randomly selected visits. However, although the United Kingdom still held that such visits would serve the purposes of enhancing the transparency of declared facilities and activities, promoting accuracy of declarations, and ensuring that the Technical Secretariat acquired comprehensive understanding of declared facilities and activities, it accepted the U.S. position that visits would not be designed to deter treaty violations and would allow the visited party considerable discretion in determining limits to the visit. In December 1998, the United Kingdom proposed that randomly selected visits would be announced five working days in advance, that a visiting team would consist of not more than four participants and would stay at the facility for not more than two days, that a team would have the right to tour all areas within the declared facility containing information relevant to the declaration, that all other access would be at the discretion of the visited state party and the visited facility, that sampling would only be possible if permitted by the visited state party, and that samples could not be removed from the facility.[46]

In sum, in 1998–1999 the United Kingdom abandoned its earlier proposals for achieving transparency through an integrated system of declarations, mandatory visits, and investigations, and moved closer to the far weaker proposals for clarification and transparency visits proposed by the United States and Germany. That it did so despite the surprise and disappointment expressed by smaller Western nations was no doubt a measure of the influence of its closest (and far larger) Western ally.[47] As the negotiations proceeded it became increasingly important to the British delegation to aim at a protocol that would be acceptable to the United States. The United Kingdom argued that it would be politically unwise to have a protocol that the United States would not implement.

## ENDGAME

By fall 2000, the work of the AHG had stopped almost entirely. The U.S. delegation did not provide any input to the negotiations because of the presidential elections scheduled for November 2000. To overcome this stalemate, on March 30, 2001, Tibor Toth, chairman of the AHG, issued a draft protocol to the AHG delegations.[48] This draft protocol consisted of the following key elements:

- An Organization for the Prohibition of Biological Weapons (OPBW);
- Declarations;
- Three types of visits: randomly selected transparency visits, clarification visits, and voluntary visits;
- Investigations; and
- Provisions for export controls.

Toth's goal was a draft that would be acceptable as a compromise to all parties even if it would not completely satisfy any single delegation. The protocol, had it been implemented, would not have provided opportunities for finding "smoking guns" since its provisions had been relatively weak, particularly compared to the CWC. Visits would have been much less intrusive than the routine on-site inspections of the CWC, and challenge inspections would have been much more difficult to launch due to complicated "green-light" and "red-light" procedures. On the other hand, the draft protocol had three essential advantages:

- In cases of compliance concern it would have been possible to conduct investigations.
- Through declarations and randomly selected transparency visits it would have been possible to gain more transparency particularly in states of concern.
- The protocol would have provided a strong political signal that the international community took the norm against biological weapons very seriously.

The draft protocol led to various reactions. The United Kingdom and its partners in the European Union welcomed the draft protocol, at least in principle. Russia remained almost silent, but the Russian delegation made clear that it could not accept all elements of the proposed text. The U.S. delegation did not actively take part in the discussions during the AHG meeting following Toth's presentation of the draft protocol on the grounds that the new administration would need some time for a policy review.[49] However, the Bush administration from the beginning adopted a critical attitude. In the summer of 2001, during congressional hearings, U.S. officials identified three major criticisms of the draft protocol:

- The draft protocol would weaken national export controls.
- Through the on-site activities included in the draft protocol, sensitive information both in private industry and in national defense programs would be endangered.
- The draft protocol would provide nothing to improve the verification of the BWC.[50]

When the AHG reconvened in July 2001 for its final meeting prior to the fifth Review Conference to the BWC scheduled for November 19, 2001, there was hope that progress could be achieved and that the draft protocol would at least be accepted as the basis for ongoing negotiations. But the presentation by the U.S. head of delegation, Ambassador Donald A. Mahley, destroyed those hopes.[51] From the very beginning, Mahley maintained that the draft protocol would be unacceptable for the United States even if it were modified. Neither declarations nor on-site activities such as visits would be useful instruments to enhance the BWC. The entire approach that had been used in the case of the CWC would simply not fit with the BWC. Moreover, Mahley claimed that both completely peaceful private companies as well as important and sensitive national defense programs would suffer as a result of on-site activities. Finally, Mahley insisted that export controls are national obligations that cannot be subordinated to an international regime. In sum, the BWC could not be enhanced through the proposed protocol. To strengthen the norm against biological weapons, "out-of-the-box" thinking would be needed.

In essence, with this statement the United States returned to the position taken at the very beginning of the process of enhancing the BWC: that the BWC would be unverifiable. But to give all other delegations something to bite, in a press conference right after his presentation in the AHG, Mahley identified some measures that could be taken:

- Greater universality and adherence to the BWC;
- Improved instruments to generate more information about situations that might be of concern to the BWC—outbreaks of diseases, for example;
- Improved work of the Australia Group; and
- Improved BW defense programs.[52]

Although some of these measures would indeed be helpful, Mahley's proposals did nothing to revive the AHG negotiations. The other two depository nations were also unable to provide the negotiations with a strong impetus. Russia maintained that it still supported the idea of a BWC protocol in principle, but at the same time stated that compromise on a number of serious issues had not been reached. The United Kingdom together with other European Union members supported Toth's draft protocol in principle. But given the U.S. position, concrete work on the draft protocol was impossible. In the end, the AHG did not even produce a working report. On the morning of August 18, 2001, the AHG finished its work without any result.[53]

On the occasion of the fifth Review Conference to the BWC, which took place in Geneva from November 19 to December 7, 2001, the United States went a step further. After three weeks of intense debate on complicated issues such as noncompliance and possible follow-up procedures to the Review Conference, on the afternoon of the final day of negotiations, the U.S. delegation presented a proposal that not only came as a surprise but shocked essentially all other delegations present. As Ambassador Donald Mahley stated, the Review Conference should take note of the work of the AHG and should decide that its work and mandate were terminated and replaced by a process of expert group meetings that would have no mandate to negotiate measures but only to examine possible steps to strengthen the Convention and to provide a report.

The message was clear: The U.S. delegation was not interested in proceeding with negotiations in the AHG on any protocol. Just to prevent the Review Conference from complete failure, delegates decided to adjourn its proceedings and to reconvene at Geneva from November 11 to 22, 2002. However, there is no hope that the AHG can be revived.[54]

## CONCLUSION

Neither the United States nor Russia as depository states to the BWC played a constructive role in the AHG negotiations. For very different reasons, both countries wanted to avoid on-site activities on their respective territory: the United States because it wanted to protect the interests of its civilian industry and its military; Russia because it had inherited an offensive BW program and wanted to make sure that visits to facilities that were part of the former offensive BW program would not prove to be embarrassing. In contrast, the United Kingdom initially held that the BWC could only be strengthened by requiring substantial transparency generated by an integrated regime of mandatory declarations, visits, and investigations.

Ironically, the interests of the United States and Russia encouraged the two countries to adopt quite similar positions on key elements of the protocol, notably visits and investigations, even though they took diametrically opposed positions on other issues, especially definitions and field investigations. Both countries aimed for procedures that would effectively generate little transparency under the protocol. Both rejected the early British proposal for random visits. Whereas the United States was apparently prepared to accept clarification visits as part of a clarification procedure, Russia accepted only voluntary visits. In addition, both Russia and the United States wanted to introduce a "green-light" filter for investigations of suspected noncompliance, making such investigations relatively unlikely. Given the resistance of the United States, Russia, and a number of nonaligned countries, London was forced to drastically reduce its initial vision. By 1999 it had accepted that random visits—if they were used at all—would be restricted both in purpose and scope.

In the end, due to the rejection of the draft protocol by the U.S. delegation, the negotiations of the AHG ended without any result. The burden is clearly on the United States, which decided that the proposed protocol would not be in its interest. But it is more than questionable that Russia would have played any constructive role in the AHG endgame, given its reluctance concerning on-site activities. Against the background of attitudes taken both by Washington and Moscow, a successful outcome of any multilateral efforts to enhance the BWC is very unlikely.

## NOTES

1. The responsibilities of the depository states are laid out in the BWC. They include, inter alia, that instruments of ratification and instruments of accession shall be deposited with the governments of the depositary states (the United States, the United Kingdom, and the Soviet Union (now Russia)) as defined in article XIV of the BWC. The Convention entered into force after the deposit of instruments of ratification by twenty-two governments, including the depository states. Furthermore, the depository states must promptly inform all signatories and acceding states of the date of each signature, the date of deposit of each instrument of ratification or of accession, the date of entry into force of the Convention, and of the receipt of other notices. The BWC was registered by the depository governments pursuant to Article 102 of the Charter of the United Nations. The BWC is deposited in the archives of the depository governments. Certified copies are to be sent by the depository governments to the governments of the signatory and acceding states.

2. See chapter 5.

3. U.S. Department of State, Office of the Assistant Secretary, Statement by Richard Boucher (Spokesman), Joint U.S./U.K./Russian Statement on Biological Weapons, 14 September 1992, 1.

4. Interviews are most effective when interviewees know that their names will not be cited in any publication. This is particularly the case with respect to the AHG negotiations, as this is an ongoing process and negotiators do not want to make their respective positions public. Therefore, part of what is sometimes the most interesting information cannot be documented.

5. U.S. Policy Information & Texts No. 122, "U.S. Opposes Biological Weapons Verification Regime," 11 September 1991, 39–40. Michael Moodie, who was at that time assistant director of the U.S. Arms Control and Disarmament Agency, Bureau of Multilateral Affairs and deputy head of the U.S. delegation to the third BWC Review Conference, told a news briefing in Geneva: "Given the nature of the biological weapons production process, we know of no way to effectively verify that convention."

6. Edward J. Lacey, "Tackling the Biological Weapons Threat: The Next Proliferation Challenge," *The Washington Quarterly* 17(4), 53–64; BWC/CONF.III/VEREX/9.

7. BWC/SPCONF/L.4 of 28 September 1994, Final Report of the Special Conference of the States Parties to the BWC, 2 of the Final Declaration; Jonathan B. Tucker, "Strengthening the Biological Weapons Convention," *Arms Control Today* (April 1995), 9–12.

8. Marie Isabelle Chevrier, "Preventing Biological Proliferation: Strengthening the Biological Weapons Convention—An American Perspective," in *Preventing the Proliferation of Weapons of Mass Destruction: What Role for Arms Control?* ed. Oliver Thränert (Berlin/Bonn: Friedrich-Ebert-Stiftung 1999), 85–98.

9. U.S. Information & Texts, Clinton Address to U.N. General Assembly, 25 September 1996, 2.

10. At the fourth Review Conference to the BWC in 1996, PhRMA presented a paper entitled "Reducing the Threat of Biological Weapons—A PhRMA Perspec-

tive," which included the following paragraph: "Routine inspections, and any inspections other than challenge, have the potential to inflict more harm to the site than benefit, due to the potential loss of confidential business information, inspection cost, and adverse publicity. These costs can be substantial for a large company and potentially devastating for a smaller biotech company. PhRMA does not support these types of inspections or visits."

11. Chemical Weapons Implementation Act of 1998, H.R. 4328.

12. Ken Alibek with Stephen Handelman, *Biohazard: The True Story of the Largest Covert Biological Weapons Program in the World—Told from the Inside by the Man Who Ran It* (New York: Random House, 1999), 70ff.

13. Jonathan B. Tucker, "Strengthening the BWC: Moving Toward a Compliance Protocol," *Arms Control Today* (January/February 1998), 20–27.

14. U.S. White House, Office of the Press Secretary, Fact Sheet: The Biological Weapons Convention, Washington, D.C., 27 January 1998.

15. Tucker, "Strengthening the BWC."

16. Amy A. Smithson, "Man versus Microbe: The Negotiations to Strengthen the Biological Weapons Convention," in *Biological Weapons Proliferation: Reasons for Concern, Courses of Action,* ed. Amy A. Smithson (Report No. 24 (Washington, D.C.: Henry L. Stimson Center, 1998), 112–13.

17. Thomas Monath and Lance Gordon, "Strengthening the Biological Weapons Convention," *Science* 282 (20 November 1998), 1423, cited in Chevrier, "Preventing Biological Proliferation," 96.

18. See BWC/AD HOC GROUP/WP.294 of 9 July 1998, Working Paper submitted by the United States of America, Proposed Elements of Clarification Visits.

19. BWC/AD HOC GROUP/WP. 410 of 10 December 1999, Working Paper submitted by the United States of America, Proposed Changes to Clarification Visits.

20. BWC/AD HOC GROUP/WP.380 of 29 June 1999, Working Paper submitted by Germany, Follow-up after Submission of Declarations.

21. Chevrier, "Preventing Biological Proliferation," 95–97.

22. BWC/AD HOC GROUP/WP. 319 of 2 October 1998, Working Paper submitted by the United States of America. Declarations of sites would include several facilities at one site, so that single small facilities would not be declarable.

23. An interesting inside view on the work of *Biopreparat* and the Soviet offensive BW program in general is provided by Alibek and Handelman, *Biohazard*; see also chapter 5.

24. Anthony Rimmington, "Fragmentation and Proliferation? The Fate of the Soviet Union's Offensive Biological Weapons Program," *Contemporary Security Policy* 20(1) (April 1999), 86–110.

25. Paul Quinn-Judge, "The Breeding of Death," *Time* (16 February 1998), 22–24. A DOD Report, *Proliferation: Threat and Response*, November 1997, mentions that "Russia may be continuing some research related to biological warfare"; available online at www.defenselink.mil/pubs/prolif97/html.

26. Susan Wright, "Cuba Case Tests Treaty," *The Bulletin of the Atomic Scientists* (November/December 1997), 18–19; Jonathan B. Tucker, "Strengthening the BWC"; BWC/AD HOC GROUP/ 13 of 10 July 1995, Working Paper submitted by France/Germany, Compilation of Questions for the Item "Definitions of Terms and Objective Criteria."

27. Alexander V. Vorobiev, "Working on the Compliance Regime for the BWC," *Chemical Weapons Convention Bulletin* (Quarterly Journal of the Harvard Sussex Program on CBW Armament and Arms Limitation), No. 31 (March 1996), 2–4; Oleg Ignatiev and Vladimir Novokhatsky, "Regarding the Role of Obligatory Declarations and Lists of Biological Agents and Toxins in Strengthening the Biological Weapons Convention," in *Enhancing the Biological Weapons Convention,* ed. Oliver Thränert (Bonn: Dietz Verlag, 1996), 140–46, especially 142.

28. BWC/AD HOC GROUP/15 of 11 July 1995; see also BWC/AD HOC GROUP/WP.381 of 29 June 1999, Working Paper submitted by the Russian Federation, Article II, Definitions and Criteria.

29. BWC/AD HOC GROUP/WP.352 of 25 January 1999, Working Paper submitted by Ukraine, Criteria for biological agents and toxins; BWC/AD HOC GROUP/WP.386 of 8 July 1999, Working Paper submitted by Ukraine, Article II. Definitions; BWC/AD HOC GROUP/W.P.411 Of 20 January 2000, Working Paper submitted by Ukraine, Proposal—Article II—Definitions.

30. See the language in the "Rolling Text" on thresholds, BWC/AD HOC GROUP/45 (Part I), Annex I, 34.

31. See BWC/CONF.III/WP.93 of 4 December 1992, Russian Federation, "On Determining the Quantity of Microorganisms and Toxins Required for Protective Purposes."

32. BWC/AD HOC GROUP/WP.99 of 16 September 1996, Working Paper submitted by the Russian Federation on Threshold Quantities.

33. BWC/AD HOC GROUP/WP. 290 of 2 July 1998, Working Paper submitted by the Russian Federation, Proposed language: Article III—C [Thresholds].

34. Ignatiev and Novokhatsky, "Regarding the Role of Obligatory Declarations," 145.

35. BWC/AD HOC GROUP/WP. 315 of 28 September 1998, Working Paper submitted by Ukraine, Thresholds for Agents and Toxins.

36. See the language in the "Rolling Text," BWC/AD HOC GROUP/45 (Part I), Annex I, 34.

37. BWC/AD HOC GROUP/WP.181 of 22 July 1997, Working Paper submitted by the Russian Federation, Basic Principles and Procedures for Consideration of Requests Relating to Alleged Violations of the Convention on the Prohibition of Biological Weapons.

38. BWC/AD HOC GROUP/WP. 341 of 12 January 1999, Working Paper submitted by the Russian Federation, Some Aspects of the Establishment of the Organization for the Implementation of the Protocol.

39. Revised Draft Convention for the Prohibition of Biological Methods of Warfare, in Department of State Bulletin, 15 December 1969, 542–43.

40. BWC/AD HOC GROUP/21 of 13 July 1995, Working Paper submitted by the United Kingdom, The Role and Objectives of Information Visits.

41. Gordon Vachon, "Verifying the Biological Weapons Convention: The Role of Inspections and Visits," in Thränert, *Enhancing the Biological Weapons Convention,* 147–53, especially 151. At the time of this writing Gordon Vachon was deputy director and head of verification research, Department of Foreign Affairs and International Trade, Ottawa, Canada. BWC/AD HOC GROUP/WP.193 of 28 July 1997,

Working Paper submitted by Canada, Canadian views on Non-Challenge Visits; BWC/AD HOC GROUP/WP.178 of 22 July 1997, Working Paper submitted by Australia, Austria, Canada, Netherlands, New Zealand, Sweden and Switzerland, Non Challenge Visits.

42. Tucker, "Strengthening the BWC."

43. BWC/AD HOC GROUP/WP.330 of 2 December 1998, Working Paper submitted by Germany, Follow-up after Submission of Declarations. In Germany, implementation of the CWC apparently played a significant role in regard to the formulation of Germany's position, particularly on visits, in the AHG. There was widespread disappointment that U.S. industry did not come forward with CWC declarations and that as a result there were also no industry inspections. Germany's pharmaceutical and biotech industry wanted to avoid being in the same situation with respect to the implementation of the BWC protocol, where German industry would need to declare and to accept visits while U.S. industry would avoid taking on the same responsibility.

44. BWC/AD HOC GROUP/45 (Part I) of 14 April 1999, Annex I, 47 ff.; Graham S. Pearson, Progress at the Ad Hoc Group in Geneva, Quarterly Review No. 6, Department of Peace Studies, University of Bradford, UK; available online at www.brad.ac.uk/acad/sbtwc/prgeneva/prgen6.htm.

45. BWC/AD HOC GROUP/WP.347 of 19 January 1999, Working Paper submitted by the United Kingdom of Great Britain and Northern Ireland

46. BWC/AD HOC GROUP/WP.326 of 2 December 1998, Working Paper submitted by the United Kingdom of Great Britain and Northern Ireland, Random Visits—Proposed New Protocol Text.

47. BWC/AD HOC GROUP/WP.380 of 29 June 1999, Working Paper submitted by Germany, Follow-up after Submission of Declarations, Transparency Visits Proposals to amend the current text; see also Volker Beck, "Preventing Biological Proliferation: Strengthening the Biological Weapons Convention," in Thränert, *Preventing the Proliferation of Weapons of Mass Destruction.*

48. Seth Brugger, "Executive Summary of the Chairman's Text," *Arms Control Today* 31(4) (May 2001), 11–13.

49. See Jenni Rissanen, "Hurdles Cleared, Obstacles Remaining: The Ad Hoc Group Prepares for the Final Challenge," *Disarmament Diplomacy* (April 2001), 1627.

50. See Donald A. Mahley, Special Negotiator for Chemical and Biological Arms Control, Department of State, Testimony before the House Government Reform Committee, Subcommittee on National Security; Veterans Affairs and International Relations: The Biological Weapons Convention: Status and Implications, 5 June 2001; Edward J. Lacey; Principal Deputy Assistant Secretary of State for Verification and Compliance, before the Subcommittee on National Security, Veterans Affairs, and International Relations, Committee on Government Reform, U.S. House of Representatives, July 10, 2001; see also Barbara Hatch Rosenberg, "Allergic Reaction: Washington's Response to the BWC Protocol," *Arms Control Today* 31(6) (July/August 2001), 3–8.

51. Donald Mahley, Statement on Biological Weapons Protocol, 25 July 2001; available online at usinfo.state.gov/products/pdq/pdq.htm (16 November 2001).

52. See transcript of Mahley News Conference on Biological Weapons Protocol, Washington File 25 July 2001; available online at usinfo.state.gov/products/pdq/ pdq.htm (16 November 2001).

53. Jenni Rissanen, "AHG Stumbles on Its Report—More Struggle Predicted," *Disarmament Diplomacy* (20 August 2001), online: www.acronym.org.uk/bwc/ bwc10.htm (16 November 2001).

54. Jenni Rissanen, "Left in Limbo: Review Conference Suspended on Edge of Collapse," *Disarmament Diplomacy*, No 62 (January/February 2002), online: www.acronym.org.uk/dd/dd62/62bwc.htm; Susan Wright, "U.S. Vetoes Verification," *Bulletin of the Atomic Scientists* (March/April 2002), 24–26.

# 14

## Secrecy in the Biotechnology Industry

### *Implications for the Biological Weapons Convention*

*Susan Wright and David A. Wallace*

Secrets do not develop in a social vacuum. Rather, the construction of a web of secrecy is a social process that defines relationships between those inside and those outside the web, the conditions under which secrets are wholly or partially revealed, and the conditions of access and denial. Probably more often than not, those conditions are formed and perpetuated through extended overt or covert political conflict. To fully understand the social construction of secrets, we must ask how these relations are formed and by whom, how contests of secrecy develop, by what means, in what settings, and with what effects.

The evolution of biotechnology is particularly interesting in this respect because its origins were remarkably transparent. The field evolved from what was once a purely academic discipline, molecular biology. Although actual behavior of individual scientists did not always measure up to the traditional norms of scientific inquiry, nevertheless, those norms were influential, supporting not only the (more-or-less) free exchange of research results but also broad public discussion of the social implications of the field.

After the commercial potential of genetic engineering, gene sequencing, and other techniques that provided the basis for biotechnology began to be demonstrated in the late 1970s, however, two main developments combined to veil the new field in secrecy: first, the transformation of biotechnology from a field with largely academic connections to one with strong corporate connections; and second, the U.S. Supreme Court's establishment, in *Diamond v. Chakrabarty*, of intellectual property rights for life forms and the subsequent increase in secrecy within academic biotechnology research. This chapter examines these developments, especially the ways in which they supported the replacement of the old norm of transparency in the parent field of molecular biology with a new norm of secrecy, and argues that promotion of this new norm has had a major impact on the international effort to strengthen the 1972 Biological Weapons Convention (BWC) through a turn from requirements for transparency to protection of opacity with respect to the biotechnology industry.

## THE SOCIAL TRANSFORMATION
## OF BIOTECHNOLOGY

The early development of genetic engineering (a key technique of biotechnology) is unusual for a new technology because it took place in sites to which the public had considerable access—namely, university research laboratories supported by government grants. As a result, the interests and goals of genetic engineering's pioneers—Peter Lobban (the graduate student at Stanford University who was the first to conceive of a form of genetic engineering that worked effectively), Paul Berg, Stanley Cohen, Herbert Boyer, and Robert Helling—are known through public documents, such as a thesis proposal, grant proposals to the National Institutes of Health, and a proposal to the University of Michigan for a sabbatical.[1]

This norm of transparency continued for some years as development of the techniques of genetic engineering proceeded. One expression of the persistence of traditional academic norms of research was the willingness of leading researchers to present their proposals for future research to the committee appointed by the National Institutes of Health to advise on possible hazards of genetic engineering. Detailed protocols specifying the genes to be transferred, the means for transferring them, and the recipient organisms were widely circulated not only to peers in the field but also to the larger public.[2]

At the same time, industrial applications were widely anticipated and efforts to demonstrate the potential for using genetic engineering as the basis for a new industry in which microbes would be used as "factories" for making novel proteins were widely pursued. By 1976, two genetic engineering companies—Cetus and Genentech—had started up and were embracing a vision of a commercial future for gene-splicing. "We are proposing to create an entire new industry, with the ambitious aim of manufacturing a vast and important spectrum of wholly new microbial products using industrial micro-organisms," proclaimed a Cetus report circulated to potential investors in 1975.[3] That this vision was not entirely an effect of public relations hype is suggested by other events in this period. Stanford University applied for a patent for the method of inserting foreign DNA into a bacterium developed by two of the pioneers of the field.[4] And by the fall of 1976, at least six transnational corporations—Hoffman-La Roche, Upjohn, Eli Lilly, SmithKline, Merck, and Miles Laboratories—had initiated small research programs in genetic engineering.[5]

Nevertheless, at this stage, industrial investments in the field were small. Although the pharmaceutical industry was certainly alert to the potential of the new field, a key technique of genetic engineering was missing. From an industry standpoint, it was not enough to be able to transfer DNA from a higher organism into a bacterium. It was deemed essential that the foreign DNA could reprogram the bacteria to synthesize the products encoded by the DNA. As late as the mid-1970s, it was not clear that this was feasible.[6] Consequently, investors were wary. Conceivably, Cetus's vision could turn out to be nothing but hype. In any case, for the moment, large corporations were content to watch developments in the universities and start-up companies like Cetus from the sidelines.[7]

A turning point in industry perceptions of genetic engineering was reached in the fall of 1977 when Herbert Boyer (of the University of California, San Francisco, and vice president for research at Genentech) and Keiichi Itakura (of the City of Hope Medical Center in Duarte, California) demonstrated that the DNA encoding a small human brain hormone could be used to program bacteria to make the hormone.[8] This achievement, proclaimed by the president of the National Academy of Sciences as "a scientific triumph of the first order," was announced at a congressional hearing and attended by substantial publicity.[9] From that point on, the technique was used repeatedly to demonstrate the bacterial synthesis of insulin, growth hormone, interferon, and other proteins normally made only by higher organisms. The trickle of investments in genetic engineering turned into a torrent as venture capitalists and transnational corporations raced to position themselves in the field. The transformation of genetic engineering from an area of academic research to an industrial technology was under way. Investments climbed steeply after 1977. By 1980, equity investments in small genetic engineering firms had reached $600 million. They would grow even more rapidly as front-runners like Genentech and Cetus entered the stock market in the early 1980s.[10]

Start-up genetic engineering companies moved quickly to lure scientists from universities with competitive salaries and stock options. Transnational corporations began to complement their investments in start-up firms with investments in university research. Between 1981 and 1982 alone, they invested some $250 million in biological research in universities and research institutes. These investments were supported by a most congenial economic and political climate shaped by legislation passed by the Carter and Reagan administrations that fostered university-industry cooperation, provided substantial tax credits for research and development, and allowed universities and small businesses rights to patents arising from federally supported research.[11]

The torrent of investments in genetic engineering from the late 1970s onwards encouraged practitioners to form a variety of new affiliations with the private sector. Scientists, formerly cloistered in academe, became equity owners, corporate executives, members of scientific advisory boards, and industry consultants. By the early 1980s, it was said to be difficult to find a genetic engineer who did not have a corporate connection.

Considerable evidence shows that these roles introduced new norms for the practice of science. Following the Supreme Court decision on *Diamond v. Chakrabarty* in 1980 (described below), the interest of genetic engineering firms and transnational corporations in securing patent coverage for their inventions produced confidentiality arrangements under which employees agreed not to disclose proprietary information or share materials. The start-up Biogen informed investors in 1983 that "in its relations with universities, Biogen seeks to maintain the maximum degree of openness consistent with reasonable protection of proprietary information," and the company also noted that "trade secrets and confidential know-how may be important to Biogen's scientific and commercial success."[12] Universities implicitly supported this new norm by encouraging researchers to seek patent protection for their results. Symptomatic of these changes were the contradictions that began to embroil university research and teaching from the late 1970s onwards. Complaints of researchers' unwillingness to share ideas and materials were aired. As genetic engineering pioneer Paul Berg, himself a member of the scientific advisory board to the company DNAX, told *Newsweek* in 1979: "No longer do you have this free flow of ideas. You go to scientific meetings and people whisper to each other about their companies' products. It's like a secret society."[13] Legal struggles over ownership of cell lines flared up. Although some universities issued guidelines to minimize conflicts of interest, these measures neither hindered the formation of corporate links with university research nor affected the basic conditions under which these links were formed. As Donald Kennedy, president of Stanford University, summarized the social relations of molecular biology and its commercial offspring in 1980: "What is surprising and unique in the annals of scientific innovation so far is the extent to which the commercial push involves the scientists who are themselves responsible for the basic discoveries—and often the academic institutions to which they belong."[14]

In the 1980s, a survey of university-industry research relationships in biotechnology by researchers at Harvard University confirmed what a growing body of anecdotal evidence suggested: that corporate linkages in biotechnology were growing and that these linkages were affecting the norms and practices of research in this field.[15] Most notable was the extent of the practice of secrecy of biotechnology, not only in corporations but also in universities. In 1986, the Harvard researchers concluded that "biotechnology faculty with industry support were four times as likely as other biotechnology faculty to report that trade secrets had resulted from their university research."[16] Furthermore, 68 percent of biotechnology faculty who did not receive industry support and 44 percent of those who did considered that university-industry linkages ran a risk of undermining intellectual exchange and cooperation.[17] Follow-up studies in the 1990s indicated that secrecy in this field continued to grow.[18]

If the extent of the industry linkages with university researchers were low, such results might be of minor interest. However, a further study by researchers at Tufts University in 1985–1988 demonstrated that the percentage of faculty members with industry affiliations in university departments pursuing research in areas related to biotechnology was high, peaking at 31 percent for MIT's department of biology.[19] Taken together, the Harvard and Tufts studies indicate a major shift in the social relations of biotechnology, specifically, the formation of strong linkages between academic research in biotechnology and industry.

## INTELLECTUAL PROPERTY RIGHTS FOR LIFE FORMS

Despite claims that the issue of patenting life is solely one of law and technology, it is important to remain cognizant of the fact that it also invokes a deep interplay of economics, social values, and access to information.[20] In 1980, the U.S. Supreme Court very narrowly (5 to 4) ruled in *Diamond v. Chakrabarty* that a patent could be obtained for a laboratory-created genetically engineered bacterium—that a "live, human made micro-organism is patentable . . . [as it] constitutes a 'manufacture' or 'composition of matter'" under Section 101 of the U.S. Patent Law.[21] The court argued that the genetically engineered bacterium under dispute qualified for patent protection because it was not "nature's handiwork" that produced the organism, but rather it was a "non-naturally occurring . . . product of human ingenuity" that fell within the wide scope of patentability contemplated by the Congress.[22] Prior to this decision, all that could have been obtained was a patent for the process that used the microorganism, but not for the organism itself, the established norm at the time being that life was not patentable.

The Court received ten amicus curiae briefs in advance of their decision on this case, nine in favor of the patent and one opposed. A sample of four of these briefs (three pro-patent, Pharmaceutical Manufacturers Association (PMA), Genentech, Inc., and the American Society for Microbiology (ASM); and one anti-patent, The Peoples Business Commission (PBC)) reveals alternative perspectives on the patent's consequences for openness of information.

Pro-patent briefs argued that patents would increase public knowledge and the exchange of scientific information, because the Patent Act was in part an information disclosure statute.[23] Meeting the public reporting requirements for biotechnological inventions, however, is more complex than for other types of patents. Microorganisms and other patentable life forms cannot always be adequately represented by written documents alone. To ameliorate this potentially negative consequence of patented biological entities, one pro-patent brief argued that the depositing of organisms within authorized national culture repositories would help satisfy U.S. Patent and Trademark Office (PTO) public reporting requirements.[24]

More specifically to the point of secrecy, two pro-patent briefs claimed that in the absence of patent protections, commercialization of biotechnological inventions would instead be shielded by trade secrecy, which has no public reporting requirement.[25] The anti-patent brief argued that the quest for patent rights to life forms had already inhibited the creation of federal safety standards to regulate genetic engineering experimentation and implied that oversight of any such standards would be further hampered by corporate claims of protection of proprietary information.[26]

The degree to which patenting life invoked a public interest represents an interesting split in the Supreme Court's thinking from that time. The majority stated that the public interest was not an issue appropriately related to the *legal* question of whether microorganisms were patentable. They argued that the Court was not the proper arena for challenging the patentability of life forms on the grounds that genetically altered life forms posed "potential hazards."[27] The Court's dissenting minority, four of the nine justices, held the opposite position. They believed that in this instance it was Congress's and not the Court's role to determine "whether and how far to extend the patent privilege into areas where the common understanding has been that patents are not available." This was deemed especially so when the subject "uniquely implicates matters of public concern."[28]

The decade following the Court's ruling saw a broad expansion of the scope of patentable subject matter. By 1987, the PTO considered "nonnaturally occurring nonhuman multicellular living organisms, including animals, to be patentable."[29] Currently, patentable subject matter includes natural, recombinant, and synthetic genes and other DNA; cells and cell lines; gene and cell products like proteins and antibodies; as well as novel and preexisting biological "agents," such as plants and animals, and specific parts of plants and animals.[30]

Since the Court's decision over twenty years ago, the growth of the biotechnology industry has been impressive. Presently, there are nearly 1,300 biotechnology companies in the United States, employing more than 150,000 workers. In 1998, these companies spent over $9.9 billion on research and development (R&D). The industry relies heavily on private investment seeking high returns and believes that "patents are among the first and most important benchmarks of progress in developing a new biotechnology medicine."[31] The successful commercialization of a biotechnology patent requires years of development and an average $300 million investment.[32] Between FY 1994 and FY 1997, the biotechnology industry entered over 48,000 patent applications (at 12,000 per annum). This is startling when compared to the fact that in 1978 only 30 biotechnology patents were requested and in 1988 just 500. As the biotechnology industry matured, the availability of patent information to the public began to evidence tensions in two areas: depository requirements and researcher secrecy.

In the Supreme Court case discussed previously, one of the pro-patent briefs suggested that depository requirements would help biotechnology patents meet the law's public reporting requirements. However, granting patents on life forms raises thorny questions regarding how and under what circumstances actual biological specimens should be handled in the patenting process and what role authorized bioculture repositories could play in storing the items.

The Patent Act states that reporting requirements for a specification must contain a written description of the invention and the process for making and using it. It must describe the "best mode contemplated by the inventor of carrying out his invention."[33] It is the specifics concerning what exactly satisfies the "best mode" requirement and its relationship to depositing patented entities that has proved to be problematic. A December 1989 Bureau of National Affairs report on biotechnology law noted that

> [for] lower organisms, such as microorganisms, cell lines, and even plants, it is sometimes necessary to meet the enablement and best mode requirements through the deposit of the organism itself or some part thereof, such as seeds, in special depositories to which the public has free access after the patent [is issued.] This procedure has been held to place the invention in the hands of the public, which is the policy underlying the written description, enablement, and best mode requirements.[34]

However, the report goes on to highlight the challenges presented by deposits, noting that they have created "substantive and administrative problems for patentees and would-be patentees."[35] The patentee who makes a deposit of a microorganism provides considerably more detail on the patent than a patentee who merely submits a written description. On this point, the

Bureau of National Affairs report argues that the depositor "in essence turns over the critical machinery to anybody, including his competitors who may be in countries where intellectual property receives limited or no protection, by turning over the living reproducing entity that makes the product."[36] This argument is supported by 1990 PTO rules on the deposit of biological materials for patenting purposes. The law does not aggressively require deposits, and the PTO makes determinations on a case-by-case basis, the argument against them being that deposited cultures are easy prey to infringement given that they are self-replicating entities.[37]

In 1992, at a symposium on legislative and legal issues in biotechnology, patent attorney Albert P. Halluin reviewed recent legal decisions that depositing a bioculture in a registered and authorized culture depository was not necessary to fulfill the "best mode" requirement of a patent specification. In one specific case, *Amgen, Inc., v. Chugai Pharmaceutical Co. Ltd.,*[38] a federal circuit court determined that Amgen did not violate the "best mode" disclosure requirement when it did not deposit cells it had created. The court reasoned that those skilled in the art could adequately reproduce Amgen's patented cells via its identification and description of its characteristics and that this information provided adequate disclosure.[39] Some fear that requiring a deposit for all biological patents would result in more disclosure than is necessary for obtaining a patent, and that if inventors were required to provide more than is necessary, they would opt for trade secret protection rather than the protection afforded by patenting.[40] Halluin, however, argues that such a decision "breaks the patent bargain" whereby inventors get exclusive monopoly rights to their inventions for seventeen years in exchange for public reporting of the details of that invention into the flow of scientific information, and that, by not having to make deposits, inventors will receive the benefits of both trade secrecy and patent protection simultaneously.[41]

Although the matter of university researcher secrecy did not receive attention from either the Supreme Court or the amicus curiae briefs in 1980, it has developed into a major issue.[42] Privatization of biological knowledge engendered by the patent development process has hindered the sharing of such knowledge. Such withholding can actually undermine innovations in biotechnology, as it limits reporting of research results. Some university-based researchers have become averse to freely sharing samples, and they delay publication of their research findings until after their patents are awarded.[43]

A 1994 survey by Blumenthal found that 90 percent of 210 life science companies conducting life science research, including biotechnology firms, had a relationship with an academic institution, and that over half of these relationships resulted in "patents, products, and sales" as a direct result of this relationship. A majority of these companies sometimes require academics to maintain the confidentiality of information during and after the filing of a patent application, often for three times longer than recommended by the National Institutes of Health. Withholding information in this manner was seen by Blumenthal and his coauthors as potentially denying other researchers the opportunity to conduct peer review that repeats and confirms or disconfirms prior work. Blumenthal concludes that the previous decade's interaction between universities and industries "may pose greater threats to the openness of scientific communication than universities generally acknowledge."[44]

A related 1997 survey, also authored by Blumenthal, of over 2,000 life science faculty, found that nearly one out of every five faculty members reported delaying the publication of results for at least six months; half of this group reported doing so because of patent applications. Faculty who were engaged in the commercialization of their research were found to be more likely to deny access to their research results and were three times more likely to delay publication for at least six months than those whose research was not targeted toward commercialization.[45] A more recent study by Blumenthal found that over half of some 1,000 university scientists who admitted receiving gifts from drug or biotechnology companies stated that these donors expected some influence over their work, ranging from patent rights to prepublication review.[46]

Although unforeseen at the time of the Supreme Court ruling, the patenting of life has generally negatively affected openness in terms of both the scope of patent reporting and the dissemination of research results. The largely unforeseen complications associated with depository requirements, and the increases in academic reluctance to share research results in a timely fashion, are shifting norms away from the traditional transparency that has long been associated with scientific inquiry.

## EFFECTS OF SECRECY ON NEGOTIATIONS TO STRENGTHEN THE 1972 BIOLOGICAL WEAPONS CONVENTION

The strong interests of the U.S. pharmaceutical and biotechnology industries in shrouding genetic engineering inventions in secrecy quickly found expression in public policymaking. Soon after the U.S. National Institutes of Health assumed responsibility for developing controls for genetic engineering in the United States in 1975, representatives of the pharmaceutical industry sought, and eventually achieved, a major change in the procedures for review of genetic engineering projects that allowed companies to appraise the hazards posed by industrial-scale biotechnology processes at the local level, by committees appointed by the companies themselves.

Details of these projects were therefore protected from public scrutiny.[47] More recently, from the mid-1990s onwards, industry interests in secrecy have seriously affected international arms control negotiations aimed at strengthening the BWC.

The BWC, which bans the development, production, stockpiling, and transfer of biological and toxin weapons, was negotiated in 1969–1972. With the important exception of the high levels of secrecy attached to research and development within biological warfare programs, this was a period when biological research was generally governed by traditional norms of openness, at least in the civilian sector.[48] This is not to say that the pharmaceutical industry at that time was uninterested in secrecy. Even in 1966, a British Foreign Office report referred to "the commercial secrecy with which so much microbiological work in the West is tied up," dismissing the calls for openness at that time from nongovernmental organizations such as Pugwash as "based on exceedingly frail assumptions about the cosmopolitanisms of scientists."[49] "Commercial secrecy" in this context may have referred as much to the secrecy of Britain's military-industrial liaison programs as to trade secrecy (see chapter 12).

In the 1960s, the proprietary interests of pharmaceutical corporations focused on products and processes, not genes, cells, and organisms. Furthermore, since molecular biology in this period was almost exclusively an academic field, attempts to patent the results of "basic" research in molecular biology would have been seen as anachronistic and probably also as a barrier to the "freedom" of scientific inquiry. Harvard molecular biologist Matthew Meselson, who is often credited as an influence on President Richard Nixon's decision to dismantle the U.S. biological weapons program and to support negotiations leading toward a universal ban on such weapons, has been, over the past three decades, a constant advocate of transparency with respect to biological research, of openness as the route toward strengthening the BWC.[50] During the BWC negotiations, when the Soviet Union and other members of the Eastern bloc proposed, in March 1971, a draft convention that included an article committing parties to the "fullest possible exchange of equipment, materials, and scientific and technological information for the use of bacteriological (biological) agents and toxins for peaceful purposes,"[51] not a single country objected. Indeed, the proposal was so uncontroversial that the chief American negotiator, James Leonard, recalled that it provoked no discussion at all.[52]

Today, some thirty years after the completion of the BWC, the emergence of strong norms of secrecy in the civilian sector is having a significant impact on the further elaboration of the BWC, and particularly on efforts to strengthen the convention by negotiating a legally binding protocol with compliance and verification provisions. At the end of the Cold War, such an instrument was seen, particularly by some Western states and by some nongovernmental organizations, as a promising route to "strengthening" the convention. This view also gained momentum from the progress being made at that time toward completion of the Chemical Weapons Convention (CWC) and the Soviet Union's general reversal of its previous opposition to on-site inspections. Despite reservations aired by the United States in particular, development of a verification protocol received qualified support at the third Review Conference in 1991, and following the work of an expert group and a special conference of the state parties in 1994, the negotiation of a protocol by an Ad Hoc Group comprising delegations from the state parties began in 1995.

From the outset, it was recognized by many BWC member states, as well as by leaders of the biotechnology and pharmaceutical industries, that verification in the BWC context posed particularly difficult technical problems. Unlike chemical warfare agents, biological agents can be relatively easily produced and also easily destroyed. Quantities of biological agents, therefore, are not significant markers of the presence or absence of a bioweapons program. They may also occur naturally in the environment. Consequently, biological verification poses difficult problems of interpreting both false positives and false negatives. Furthermore, both equipment and agents are largely dual-purpose in nature and cannot therefore be used as unambiguous indicators of the presence or absence of a bioweapons program.[53]

Beyond these technical problems, the boundary between permitted and prohibited activities defined by the BWC itself introduces a further and serious ambiguity. The treaty as written does not draw a sharp boundary between defensive and offensive research and development, or even, in limited quantities, production. Furthermore, by the fall of 1995, the experience of the UN Special Commission on Iraq (UNSCOM) had shown that even highly intrusive, no-notice inspections might raise strong suspicions but were unlikely to produce definitive evidence of violations if the inspected party was intent on hiding evidence of bioweapons activities (see chapter 11).

In response to these problems, supporters of verification proposed high levels of transparency in the biological sciences and biotechnology. According to an early and influential proponent of verification, "Full disclosure is the only guarantee of defensive intent. . . . If a verification regime is to provide security, it must require and enforce total openness; at the same time, it will obviate the need for secrecy by constituting a better deterrent than any secret defense program."[54] It is doubtful that any of the states parties would have endorsed such a call for complete openness. Nevertheless, the United Kingdom and several other state parties (including Australia, Canada, New Zealand, South Africa, the Netherlands, and Sweden), recognizing the major challenges of BWC verification, initially called for a high degree of transparency. In the words of a UK working paper, what was needed was "an integrated and balanced package of measures" comprising wide-ranging declarations, on-site inspections (known in this context as "visits"), challenge inspections and investigations of alleged use designed to uncover violations, and implementation by a professional inspectorate. Certainly this early vision of verification suggested that the regime would need to be even more intrusive than that of the CWC if it was to function effectively in deterring violations and enabling states to provide reassurance about their biological defense activities.[55]

From the beginning of the negotiations for the BWC Protocol, however, the U.S. biotechnology and pharmaceutical trade associations opposed development of an intrusive verification regime and pressed the U.S. government and all of the other parties to the Convention to support their position. At the forefront of this effort were the Pharmaceutical Research and Manufacturers of America (PhRMA), representing the country's leading research-based pharmaceutical and biotechnology companies, and the Biotechnology Industry Organization (BIO), representing some 1,400 biotechnology firms. Foremost among the industry's concerns was the risk of loss of intellectual property through information acquired by international inspectors during visits to industrial facilities.[56]

Loss of intellectual property was also an important concern for the chemical industry during the negotiations leading up to the CWC. However, the growth of the biotechnology industry was dynamic, with revenues tripling from 1992 to 2002.[57] Industry leaders argued that this young industry was more vulnerable to loss of proprietary information than the well-established chemical industry. In a detailed paper sent to the U.S. State Department in 1995, the trade associations PhRMA and BIO argued that "the sensitivity to loss of proprietary information is much greater in the pharmaceutical and biotechnology industries than in the basic and fine chemical production industries where numerous non-proprietary intermediates and catalysts are often used. Any implementation of a declaration and verification protocol under the BWC must protect proprietary information for the pharmaceutical and biotechnology industries where the U.S. is the undisputed world-leader." In an analysis of the various off-site and on-site measures being considered at that time in Geneva as part of a verification package, the trade organizations emphasized that all on-site measures, such as sampling, interviewing, identification of key equipment, and continuous monitoring as well as auditing off-site, were of greatest concern to the industry.[58]

PhRMA and BIO repeatedly pressed the U.S. Department of Commerce and the U.S. State Department to respond to their interests in protecting their proprietary information. In June 1996, the president of PhRMA, Gerald Mossinghoff, wrote to former Secretary of Commerce Mickey Kantor expressing concern that "the U.S. may not be able to take a forceful leadership role in formulating a protocol that achieves the objectives of strengthening the BWC while protecting U.S. businesses' legitimate proprietary interests." The U.S. government was urged to "play a positive role in these negotiations and not stand by while other countries develop an international norm that could prove inimical to our national interests." And it was also reminded that "the pharmaceutical industry is one of the few remaining U.S. industries with a positive trade balance that has been maintained for over ten years. We are relying on the U.S. Government to help us maintain this position as the BWC is negotiated."[59]

Rather than an extensive and intrusive regime aimed at transparency, the U.S. trade associations pressed for drastically limiting the reach of such a regime with respect to information concerning industrial processes, equipment, and facilities. In a policy statement circulated to the BWC parties at the fourth Review Conference of the Convention held in 1996, PhRMA proposed the following conditions:

- No routine inspections of any kind;
- On-site inspections limited to investigations of noncompliance;
- Allegations aimed at an investigation of noncompliance to be subjected to a strong "green-light" filter requiring a vote of three-quarters of the members of an Executive Council of representatives of the state parties to a protocol in order to proceed; and
- Nongovernmental inspected facilities to have the right to make the final determination of materials and equipment to be shielded from inspectors because of their proprietary nature.[60]

Similar positions were advocated by BIO and by the Materials Technical Advisory Committee, a group of senior executives drawn from U.S. industry and academia.[61] The positions taken by the European trade associations, the European Federation of Pharmaceutical Industries and Associations (EFPIA), and the Forum for European Bioindustry Coordination (FEBC) in 1998 were less specific and somewhat more flexible than that of their American counterparts but nevertheless aired the same concerns. In a position paper circulated in 1998, EFPIA resisted the idea of site visits other than investigations of noncompliance and similarly urged that proprietary information remain under the full control of an inspected company.[62] FEBC specifically rejected routine inspections.[63]

These positions contrasted with the support of the chemical industry for the CWC regime. The chemical industry, like its biotechnology counterpart, was certainly sensitive to the need to protect proprietary information.[64] Nevertheless, leaders of the chemical industry accepted such measures as routine visits to declared sites, sampling, and investigations of charges of noncompliance with a "red-light" filter. With a red-light filter, challenge investigations are carried out unless three-quarters of the members of the

Executive Council vote against proceeding. They are therefore more likely to take place than with a green-light filter. Industry leaders were also, apparently, satisfied with the procedures for protection of confidential information provided in the "Annex on the Protection of Confidential Information" to the CWC. In contrast, measures to protect proprietary information proposed for the BWC protocol have not so far reassured leaders of the biotechnology industry. The reasons for the differences in the behaviors of the two industries are beyond the scope of this chapter to analyze in depth, and they are no doubt complex. The CWC was completed at the end of the Cold War, in a different negotiating climate; the chemical industry is an older, more established, less dynamic industry, and patent data suggest that it is less dependent on cutting-edge techniques; and industry representatives also claimed that they were concerned about the negative public image that resistance to the CWC might yield.

What is clear is that, in the absence of other, overriding factors, concerns about protection of trade secrets have so far haunted the collective consciousness of the biotechnology industry, and have influenced national policy, particularly that of the United States. The effects of industry pressure on the U.S. position were evident in a brief White House statement issued in January 1998 that adopted a "green-light" filter for investigations of noncompliance. In addition, the White House paper dropped any requirement for routine inspections aimed at confirming the accuracy of declarations, proposing only "voluntary" visits where access as well as the visit itself would be controlled by the visited party, and "non-challenge clarification visits" designed to clarify ambiguities in declarations.[65] Since a "green-light" filter requires such a large majority vote to be pursued, it is likely to be very difficult to achieve in practice except in the most extreme circumstances. Thus the Clinton proposal amounted to not much more than a system of declarations plus a few clarifying visits.

Even so, the U.S. pharmaceutical and biotechnology industry was not satisfied. In March 1998, PhRMA chairman Sidney Taurel of the huge pharmaceutical corporation Eli Lilly wrote to National Security Advisor Samuel Berger and Secretary of Commerce William Daley to express the continuing concern of the industry about "possible adverse impacts on biomedical innovation through harm to our companies' intellectual property, reputations, and confidential business information." Specifically, Taurel cited the industry's "[worries about] non-challenge inspections and our skepticism whether any 'voluntary' visit will truly be voluntary."[66] A U.S. working paper tabled in Geneva in July 1998 appeared designed to meet PhRMA's concerns halfway. The paper proposed that clarification visits would be undertaken only after stringent efforts to address issues in other ways and only under conditions that allowed the visited party to protect proprietary information and to decide on access to samples. Furthermore, when the director of the U.S. Arms Control and Disarmament Agency addressed the Ad Hoc Group in October 1998, his statement was remarkable for its complete silence on the question of visits.[67]

In summary, the desire of the U.S. pharmaceutical and biotechnology industries to maintain the secrecy of their projects clearly influenced the U.S. negotiating position on requirements affecting declarations and inspections for a BWC compliance regime. Despite resistance from some Western states, the United States pressed for and achieved a remarkable dilution of the original goal of transparency for these activities.[68] As a composite text, proposed by the chair of the Ad Hoc Group and reflecting compromises among the positions of the states parties, expressed this dilution in March 2001: "[With respect to visits to facilities,] the nature and extent of all access inside the facility . . . shall be at the discretion of the visited state party. . . . [States parties] have the right to take measures to protect national security and commercial proprietary information."[69]

Over twenty years ago, before the change in the norms of biological research addressed in this chapter had taken place, the Swedish diplomat Alva Myrdal wrote: "Openness is the primary tool for verification of disarmament. . . . Immediately accessible to verification by the international community are scientific and technological data available through publications and other media." Myrdal called for even greater openness, arguing that "the key to control of disarmament is the construction of universal confidence based on the cumulative process of shared information."[70] The U.S. biotechnology industry's desire for protection of industry secrets is on a collision course with the requirement of a compliance or verification regime for high levels of transparency. PhRMA and BIO do not represent every single biotechnology company and pharmaceutical corporation. (To this point, one or two have dissented from the trade association position.) But they represent some of the most influential members of a huge industry. It is doubtful that a verification system with the kinds of restrictions proposed by PhRMA could provide either reassurance about a country's intentions or evidence of a violation since a prohibited activity could be hidden under the guise of protection of trade secrets. But the industry's position may yet evolve if it can be persuaded that support for a strong verification regime is in its best interests.[71] To this point, however, the evidence suggests that the change in norms of transparency in biotechnology has had the effect of seriously diluting present efforts on the part of governments and nongovernmental organizations to strengthen this regime.

## CONCLUSION

In the post–Cold War world of the 1990s, there was a general trend toward increased transparency by governmental bodies. Although it was true that much "sensitive" information continued to be closely guarded, there was a clear trend toward opening classified archives and developing a richer understanding of U.S. governmen decisions and actions. Ironically, at the same time that the public sector is generally making more information available about itself, both private industry and academia have witnessed increases in secrecy. However, the events of September 11, 2001, have reintroduced an invigorated information security mindset within the government akin to the changes documented above in private industry and academia. Thus, the increased secrecy currently evolving collectively within government, academia, and the biotechnology industry portends a new era of excessive information security that will produce negative consequences for an open democratic society.

The allowance of patents for biotechnology discoveries has negatively affected traditional norms of scientific inquiry, typified by openness of research and timely access to the results of research. The quite expensive race to obtain patents in the highly competitive biotechnology industry has resulted in narrowing public access not only to the contents of actual patents but also to the research undergirding the patents. Although intellectual property rights serve as an incentive to investments in and commitments to scientific innovation, the reduction of scientific investigations to largely commercial endeavors whose rewards are largely contingent on obtaining patents will continue to erode informed public and academic discourse. Concerns over securing intellectual property have already driven and will continue to drive researchers into nondisclosure and other secrecy commitments with private firms, thus severely limiting timely access to emerging scientific knowledge. And unless there are radical changes in position on the part of the biotechnology industry, these same concerns are likely to thwart progress in other important policy areas, remote from the initial sphere of action, such as biological disarmament.

In conclusion, secrets are political creatures not only because they define relations in which knowledge is withheld from the public or another country but also because they articulate a set of relative gains and losses to the actors involved. The secrets of the biotechnology industry are no exception. Since its inception in the mid-1970s, when the new field of genetic engineering was extraordinarily transparent, this study shows that the industry has exerted considerable influence to close routes of access to knowledge concerning the nature of the organisms in use, the genes they carry, the techniques of modification, and the industry's intentions for future technical developments. Such a trend poses substantial barriers to informed public policy discussion on the advisability and safety of life forms that are appropriated as "intellectual property." Furthermore, the industry's demand for secrecy has seriously undermined the negotiations for the BWC compliance protocol, producing a turn from requirements for transparency to protection of opacity with respect to biotechnology and other biological processes, equipment, and production.

## NOTES

We thank the participants in the Cornell University Conference on Secrecy in 1998 for a stimulating discussion of the issues, Judith Reppy for generative editorial suggestions, and the three anonymous reviewers for *Politics and the Life Sciences* for stimulating critiques. Earlier versions of this chapter were published in Judith Reppy, ed., *Secrecy and Knowledge Production* (Ithaca, N.Y.: Cornell University Peace Studies Program, 1999), 107–33 and *Politics and the Life Sciences* 19(1) (March 2000), 33–45.

1. Susan Wright, *Molecular Politics: Developing American and British Regulatory Policy for Genetic Engineering, 1972–1982* (Chicago: University of Chicago Press, 1994), chapter 2.

2. These practices continued until the late 1970s, when controls for genetic engineering were progressively weakened. By 1982, the responsibility for most decisions on genetic engineering precautions was delegated to local biosafety committees and public circulation of protocols for new research was, therefore, restricted. See Wright, *Molecular Politics*, chapters 9–10.

3. Cetus Corporation, "Special Report," unpublished document, c.1975.

4. U.S. patent no. 4,237,224, granted to Stanley Cohen and Herbert Boyer and assigned to Stanford University, December 1980.

5. Nicholas Wade, "Guidelines Extended but EPA Balks," *Science* 194 (1976), 304.

6. John Atkins, "Expression of a Eucaryotic Gene in *Escherichia coli*," *Nature* 262 (1976), 256–57.

7. For details, see Wright, *Molecular Politics*, 83.

8. Keiichi Itakura, "Expression in *Escherichia coli* of a Chemically Synthesized Gene for the Hormone Somatostatin," *Science* 198 (1977), 1056–63.

9. U.S. Congress, Senate Committee on Commerce, Science, and Transportation, Subcommittee on Science, Technology, and Space, *Hearings: Regulation of Recombinant DNA Research*, 95th Cong., 1st sess., 2, 8, and 10 November 1977, testimony of Philip Handler, President of the U.S. National Academy of Sciences, 13–14.

10. For details, see Susan Wright, "Recombinant DNA Technology and Its Social Transformation," *Osiris* 2 (1986), 303–60; Sheldon Krimsky, *Biotechnics and Society: The Rise of Industrial Genetics* (New York: Praeger, 1991), 21–42; Wright, *Molecular Politics*, 83–105.

11. David Dickson and David Noble, "By Force of Reason," in Thomas Ferguson and Joel Rogers, eds., *The Hidden Election: Politics and Economics in the 1980 Presidential Election Campaign* (New York: Pantheon, 1981), 260–312.

12. Biogen, N.V., *Prospectus* (14 October 1982), 14.

13. Paul Berg, quoted in Sharon Begley, "The DNA Industry," *Newsweek* (20 August 1979), 53.

14. Donald Kennedy, "Health Research: Can Utility and Quality Co-exist?" speech given at the University of Pennsylvania, December 1980.

15. David Blumenthal et al., "Industrial Support of University Research in Biotechnology," *Science* 231 (17 January 1986), 242–46; David Blumenthal et al., "University-Industry Research Relationships in Biotechnology: Implications for the University," *Science* 232 (13 June 1986), 1361–66.

16. Blumenthal, "University-Industry Research Relationships in Biotechnology," 1364.

17. Ibid.

18. David Blumenthal et al., "Participation of Life Science Faculty in Research Relationships with Industry," *New England Journal of Medicine* 335(23) (5 December 1996), 1734–39; David Blumenthal et al., "Relationships Between Academic Institutions and Industry in the Life Sciences—An Industry Survey," *New England Journal of Medicine* 334(6) (8 February 1996), 368–73; David Blumenthal et al., "Withholding Research Results in Academic Life Science: Evidence from a National Survey of Faculty," *Journal of the American Medical Association* 277(15) (16 April 1997), 1224–28.

19. Sheldon Krimsky et al., "Academic-Corporate Ties in Biotechnology: A Quantitative Study," *Science, Technology, and Human Values* 16(3) (Summer 1991), 275–86.

20. For a discussion of some of these issues, see Daniel J. Kevles, "Ananda Chakrabarty Wins a Patent: Biotechnology, Law, and Society, 1972–1980," *HSPS: Historical Studies in the Physical and Biological Sciences* 25(1) (1994), 111–36.

21. *Diamond v. Chakrabarty,* 447 U.S. Slip Opinion I–II. (1980). Inventions patentable under 35 U.S.C. §101 include discoveries of any "new and useful process, machine, manufacture, or composition of matter, or any new and useful improvement thereof."

22. Ibid., 4–7.

23. 35 U.S.C. §112 states that the patent "specification shall contain a written description of the invention, and of the manner and process of making and using it, in such full, clear, concise, and exact terms as to enable any person skilled in the art to which it pertains, or with which it is most nearly connected, to make and use the same, and shall set forth the best mode contemplated by the inventor of carrying out his invention."

24. *Diamond v. Chakrabarty,* Brief on Behalf of the American Society for Microbiology, Amicus Curiae, undated, 9–11.

25. *Diamond v. Chakrabarty,* Brief on Behalf of Genentech, Inc., Amicus Curiae, 23 January 1980, 5–6, 14–15; *Diamond v. Chakrabarty,* Brief on Behalf of the Pharmaceutical Manufacturers Association, Amicus Curiae, undated, 12–14.

26. *Parker v. Bergy* and *Parker v. Chakrabarty,* Brief on Behalf of the Peoples Business Commission, Amicus Curiae, 13 December 1979, 20.

27. *Diamond v. Chakrabarty,* 447 U.S. Slip Opinion 2, 11 (1980).

28. *Diamond v. Chakrabarty,* 447 U.S. Dissent 1–2, 4 (1980).

29. U.S. Congress. Office of Technology Assessment, *New Developments in Biotechnology: Patenting Life—Special Report* (1989), 93.

30. Ned Hettinger, "Patenting Life: Biotechnology, Intellectual Property, and Environmental Ethics," *Environmental Affairs* 22 (1995), 277–78.

31. Reported by the Biotechnology Industry Organization (BIO), *Introductory Guide to Biotechnology;* available online at www.bio.org/aboutbio/guidetoc.html (5 September 1999); *1997–1998 BIO Editor's and Reporter's Guide to Biotechnology;* available online at www.bio.org/library/welcome.dgw (1 April 1998). BIO derived these statistics from Kenneth B. Lee Jr. and G. Stephen Burrill, *Biotech '97 Alignment: An Industry Annual Report,* 11th ed. (Ernst & Young, 1997). BIO is the biotechnology industry's most important trade and lobbying organization, representing over 700 biotechnology companies, academic institutions, state biotechnology centers, and other entities in over forty-seven states and twenty countries.

32. James Nurton, "Biotechnology Patents: Biotechnology's Winning Formulas," *Managing Intellectual Property* (June 1997), online: www.lawmoney.com/public/contents/publications/MIP/mip9706/mip9706.7.html (27 March 1998).

33. 35 U.S.C. § 112. See note 23.

34. Bureau of National Affairs, *Biotechnology Law for the 1990s: Analysis and Perspective* (Washington, D.C.: Bureau of National Affairs, 1989), 18.

35. Ibid.

36. Ibid.

37. U.S. Patent and Trademark Office, "Deposit of Biological Materials for Patent Purposes: Final Rule," 37 *Code of Federal Regulations,* Part I, Section 1801, 1 January 1990.

38. 18 U.S.P.Q.2d 1016 (Fed. Cir. 1991).

39. I. P. Cooper, *Biotechnology and the Law, 1999 Revision* (St. Paul, Minn.: West, 1999), 5-52.66–5-52.67.

40. R. M. Mescher, "Patent Law: Best Mode Disclosure: Genetic Engineers Get Their Trade Secret and Their Patent Too," *University of Dayton Law Review* 18 (1992), 214–15.

41. Rudy Baum, "Knotty Biotech Issues Receive Attention," *Chemical and Engineering News* (27 April 1992), 30–31.

42. In particular, see Sheldon Krimsky, *Biotechnics and Society: The Rise of Industrial Genetics* (New York: Praeger, 1991); and Henry Etzkowitz, Andrew Webster, and Peter Healey, eds., *Capitalizing Knowledge: New Intersections of Industry and Academia* (Albany: State University of New York Press, 1998).

43. A. J. Lemin, "Patenting Microorganisms: Threats to Openness," in *Owning Scientific and Technical Information: Values and Ethical Issues,* ed. Vivian Weill and John Snapper (New Brunswick, N.J.: Rutgers University Press, 1989). Cited in Hettinger, "Patenting Life," (1995), p. 293.

44. David Blumenthal, Nancyanne Causino, Eric Campbell, and Nancy Seashore Louis, "Relationship between Academic Institutions and Industry in the Life Sciences—An Industry Survey," *The New England Journal of Medicine* 334 (6) (8 February 1996), 368–73.

45. David Blumenthal, Eric Campbell, Melissa Anderson, Nancyanne Causino, and Karen Seashore Louis, "Withholding Research Results in Academic Life Science: Evidence From a National Survey of Faculty," *JAMA: Journal of the American Medical Association* 277(15) (16 April 1997), 1224–28.

46. "Corporations Swap Gifts for Influence Over Scholars," *New York Times* (1 April 1998). Two out of every three recipients of these gifts, which ranged from

388   *Susan Wright and David A. Wallace*

pieces of DNA to lab equipment to money, stated that the gift was important or very important to their research.

47. For details, see Susan Wright and David A. Wallace, "Varieties of Secrets and Secret Varieties: The Case of Biotechnology," *Politics and the Life Sciences* 19(1) (March 2000), 33–45.

48. Activities in military contexts were an entirely different matter. The United States terminated its highly secret BW program in 1969 but the policy guiding its continuing biological defense program (National Decision Memorandum 35, 25 Nov. 25 1969) was silent on the question of secrecy. The former Soviet Union also conducted a secret BW program that began in the 1920s and underwent a substantial expansion in the 1970s. For a detailed account of the latter, see chapter 5.

49. U.K. Foreign Office, Arms Control and Disarmament Research Unit, "Arms Control Implications of Chemical and Biological Warfare: Analysis and Proposals," ACDRU(66)2 (2nd draft, 4 July 1966), p. 57, FO371/187448, Public Record Office, United Kingdom.

50. See, e.g., Matthew Meselson, Martin Kaplan, and Mark Mokulsky, "Verification of Biological and Toxin Weapons Disarmament," *Science and Global Security* 2 (1991), 235–52; Matthew Meselson, "Implementing the Biological Weapons Convention of 1972," *UNIDIR Newsletter* 4(2) (June 1991), 10–13.

51. Bulgaria, Czechoslovakia, Hungary, Mongolia, Poland, Romania, and Union of Soviet Socialist Republics, "Draft Convention on the Prohibition of the development, production and stockpiling of bacteriological (biological) weapons and toxins and on their destruction," 30 March 1971 (CCD/325).

52. Susan Wright, interview with James Leonard, August 1996.

53. United Kingdom, "The Role and Objectives of Information Visits," 13 July 1995, BWC/AD HOC GROUP/21.

54. Barbara Rosenberg and Gordon Burck, "Verification of Compliance with the Biological Weapons Convention," in S. Wright, ed., *Preventing a Biological Arms Race* (Cambridge, Mass.: MIT Press, 1990), 304.

55. United Kingdom, "The Role and Objectives of Information Visits," 13 July 1995, BWC/AD HOC GROUP/21. For further analysis of the British position, see chapter 13.

56. The documents supporting this view were obtained by one of the authors (David Wallace) through a request under the Freedom of Information Act filed in 1998.

57. For discussion of these points, see Biotechnology Industry Organization, "Guide to Biotechnology: Biotechnology Industry Statistics," online: www.bio.org/er/statistic.asp (23 July 2002).

58. U.S. Pharmaceutical and Biotechnology Industries White Paper on Strengthening the Biological Weapons Convention (n.d.; sent by A. Goldhammer, BIO, to U.S. State Department, 23 June 1995), 2 and appendix 2.

59. Gerald Mossinghoff to Michael Kantor, 12 June 1996.

60. Pharmaceutical Research and Manufacturers Association, Reducing the Threat of Biological Weapons: A PhRMA Perspective, 25 November 1996, circulated at the Fourth Review Conference of the Biological Weapons Convention, 25 November–6 December, 1996. For a detailed discussion of these requirements, see

William Muth, "The Role of the Pharmaceutical and Biotech Industries in Strengthening the Biological Disarmament Regime," in Susan Wright and Richard Falk, eds.,
Symposium: "Responding to the Challenge of Biological Warfare: A Matter of Contending Paradigms of Thought and Action," *Politics and the Life Sciences* 18 (1999),
92–97.

61. Alan Goldhammer, BIO, to William Reinsch, Under Secretary for Export
Administration, U.S. Department of Commerce, 3 July 1997; Alan Hart, Chairman,
Materials Technical Advisory Committee and R&D Director, Advanced Materials,
Dow Chemical Company, to Steven Goldman, Office of Chemical and Biological
Controls and Treaty Compliance, U.S. Department of Commerce, 27 June 1997.

62. European Federation of Pharmaceutical Industries and Associations (EFPIA),
Statement on the Biological and Toxin Weapons Convention (n.d.; c. March 1998).

63. Forum for European Bioindustry Coordination, Position on a Compliance
Protocol to the BTWC, Draft, 30 June 1998, cited in Muth, "Role of the Pharmaceutical and Biotech Industries."

64. See, for example, Detlef Mannig, "At the Conclusion of the Chemical Weap-
ons Convention: Some Recent Issues Concerning the Chemical Industry," in Benoit
Morel and Kyle Olsen, eds., *Shadows and Substance: The Chemical Weapons Con-
vention* (Boulder, Colo.: Westview Press, 1993), 145–46; John Gee, "A Strengthened
BWC: Lessons to be Learned from the Chemical Weapons Convention," *UNIDIR
Newsletter,* No. 33/96 (1996), 75–80; Ettore Greco, "Protection of Confidential
Information and the Chemical Weapons Convention," in M. Bothe et al., eds., *The
New Chemical Weapons Convention: Implementation and Prospects* (The Hague:
Kluwer Law International, 1998), 365–70.

65. U.S. Office of the Press Secretary, the White House, "Fact Sheet: The Biological Weapons Convention," 27 January 1998.

66. Sidney Taurel (Eli Lilly), Chairman, PhRMA to Samuel Berger (Assistant to
the President for National Security Affairs) and William Daley (Secretary, Department of Commerce), 9 March 1998; see also Jonathan B. Tucker, "Strengthening
the BWC: Moving Toward a Compliance Protocol," *Arms Control Today* (January/
February 1998), 20–27.

67. United States, Working Paper: Proposed Elements of Clarification Visits, 9
July 1998, BWC/AD HOC GROUP/WP.294; United States, Statement of John
Holum to the Biological Weapons Convention Ad Hoc Group Session XII, 6 October 1998. For a detailed analysis of the evolution of the U.S. negotiating position,
see chapter 13.

68. For accounts of these effects from 1999 to 2001, see the reviews of the ses-
sions of the Ad Hoc Group in the bulletin, *Disarmament Diplomacy,* of the Acronym Institute; available online at www.acronym.org. In particular, see Henrietta
Wilson, "Strengthening the BWC: Issues for the Ad Hoc Group," *Disarmament
Diplomacy,* No. 42 (December 1999); and Jenni Rissanen, "Hurdles Cleared, Obstacles Remaining: The Ad Hoc Group Prepares for the Final Challenge," *Disarmament
Diplomacy,* No. 56 (April 2001).

69. United Nations, Ad Hoc Group of the States Parties to the Convention on
the Prohibition of the Development, Production and Stockpiling of Bacteriological
(Biological) and Toxin Weapons and on Their Destruction, "[Draft] Protocol,"
BWC/AD HOC GROUP/CRP.8 (3 Apr. 2001), 31.

70. Alva Myrdal, *The Game of Disarmament* (New York: Pantheon Books, 1976), 302–4.

71. If such a reversal were to happen, we might then learn more about the positions of a further sector interested in secrecy: the military agencies around the world responsible for biological warfare programs.

# 15

# The Global Patent Regime

## *Implementing Article X*

*Biswajit Dhar*

One of the significant transformations underway in the emerging global trade regime is within the realm of technology. The key processes of generation and diffusion of technologies are undergoing far-reaching changes that could increase international disparities in technological capabilities, especially between developed and developing countries. Central to these changes is a regime of intellectual property protection, particularly recent requirements related to the most important form of intellectual property, patents. The new patent regime was formalized at the conclusion of the Uruguay Round of negotiations of the General Agreement on Tariffs and Trade (GATT) in the Agreement on Trade Related Aspects of Intellectual Property Rights (TRIPS) and seeks to redefine the basic tenets of the international patent system that has been in place since the end of the nineteenth century. Two multilateral institutions—the World Trade Organization (WTO) and the World Intellectual Property Organization (WIPO)—are currently implementing these sweeping changes.

These changes in the global patent regime are likely to have several cross-sectoral implications, including for the implementation of Article X of the Biological Weapons Convention (BWC). This article provides for the transfer of the biological sciences and biotechnology to the BWC's members in a manner that promotes the peaceful use of these fields. This was seen by the parties as the appropriate means to provide "compensation" in exchange for accepting the binding commitments under the Convention.

The BWC review conferences and the recent negotiations for a protocol

391

to monitor compliance with the convention have attempted to define conditions and mechanisms for implementing article X. Since compliance with the requirements of an inspection regime would be particularly onerous for developing countries to implement, arrangements for technology transfer under article X may be seen as providing incentives for member states from the developing world to comply and to have the technology necessary to do so. This dimension of the BWC is particularly important given that one of the more contentious North–South debates in recent decades has centered on the transfer of technology to the South on terms that it can afford.

This chapter examines critically the possibility of effective implementation of Article X of the BWC. The possibility of successful exchange of scientific and technological information and equipment will be questioned, given the parallel developments taking place under the auspices of the WTO and the WIPO that will likely restrict the access of developing countries to new technologies. The changes in the regime of intellectual property protection that are now underway and, indeed, gaining momentum raise serious doubts about the possibility of favorable transfers of technology under Article X.

The first part of this chapter examines the principal elements of Article X and the positions taken by the member states on its implementation. The second part discusses key elements of the regime of intellectual property protection introduced by TRIPs and their likely implications for the implementation of Article X. It addresses the expansion of the scope of patenting and the possible weakening of the arrangements for technology transfer. In this connection, recent claims that the Convention on Biological Diversity can provide a vehicle for technology transfer are examined. The third part examines the likely implications for the implementation of Article X of the proposed treaty for protection of nonoriginal databases that is being negotiated under the WIPO. This treaty's significance lies in the fact that during the past few years creation of global databases has been suggested as one way to share information under Article VII of the BWC protocol.

## ARTICLE X AND STRENGTHENING OF THE BWC

It has been argued that efforts to strengthen the BWC hinge critically on progress made towards the proper implementation of some of the key articles of the Convention, among which Article X holds an important place. Under Article X, the "States Parties . . . undertake to facilitate, and have the right to participate in, the fullest possible exchange of equipment, materials and scientific and technological information for the use of bacteriological (biological) agents and toxins for peaceful purposes." Furthermore, Article

X requires parties to the Convention who are in a position to do so "to cooperate in contributing individually or together with other States or international organizations to the further development and application of scientific discoveries in the field of bacteriology (biology) for prevention of disease, or for other peaceful purposes."

In the 1990s, the BWC parties emphasized the need to implement Article X as part of the overall process of strengthening the Convention. Successive review conferences of the Convention indicated that an effective compliance regime for the Convention should aim, first, to simultaneously strengthen its disarmament and deterrence elements, and second, to provide explicit incentives for the peaceful use of and international cooperation in the biosciences.[1]

The importance of Article X was brought out quite cogently by the third Review Conference of the Convention in its final declaration in 1991:

> The Conference emphasizes the increasing importance of the provisions of Article X, especially in light of recent scientific and technological developments which have vastly increased the potential for cooperation between States to help promote economic and social development, and scientific and technological progress, particularly in the developing countries, in conformity with their interests, needs and priorities. The Conference . . . notes with concern the increasing gap between the developed and the developing countries in the field of biotechnology, genetic engineering, microbiology and other related areas. The Conference urges . . . the developed countries possessing advanced biotechnology to adopt positive measures to promote technology transfer and international cooperation on an equal and non-discriminatory basis, in particular with the developing countries, for the benefit of all mankind.[2]

Clearly, the parties saw promotion of technology transfer in emerging fields of biotechnology such as genetic engineering as an important purpose of Article X.

The Special Conference of the States' Parties to the BWC held in September 1994 specifically mandated that the Ad Hoc Group of the state parties established by the conference develop measures not only to strengthen compliance with the treaty's prohibition of biological weapons but also to consider:

> Specific measures designed to ensure effective and full implementation of Article X, which also avoid restrictions incompatible with the obligations undertaken under the Convention, noting that the provisions of the Convention should not be used to impose restrictions and/or limitations on the transfer for purposes consistent with the objectives and the provisions of the Convention of scientific knowledge, technology, equipment and materials.[3]

The fourth Review Conference held in 1996 reinforced this mandate, specifically noting the need to promote scientific and technological development in developing countries and drawing attention to two specific needs. First, the Conference proposed that existing institutions and mechanisms should be developed further "in order to promote international cooperation in peaceful activities in such areas as medicine, public health and agriculture."[4] This can be considered a significant message from the fourth Review Conference, coming as it did during a phase when the market for technology was being subjected to stringent rules resulting from the strengthening of the laws governing intellectual property protection. Second, the parties indicated their support for strengthening the exchange of scientific and technical information in the biological sciences. To facilitate this process, the Conference suggested establishment of a worldwide data bank. Although the Conference did not dwell on the institutional framework for the database, the intention was clearly to make the database freely available to all rather than to establish control by a specific interest group.

During the negotiations for the BWC Protocol in the 1990s, the BWC parties considered in detail how such proposals might be implemented. The draft protocol of February 2001 included language committing parties not to "maintain among themselves any restrictions, including those in any international agreements, which would restrict or impede trade and the development and promotion of scientific and technological knowledge . . . in the fields of . . . microbiology, biotechnology, genetic engineering, and their industrial, agricultural, medical, pharmaceutical applications, and other related areas for peaceful purposes."[5] If taken in an unqualified sense, such a condition would have placed the BWC beyond the limitations that the framework of intellectual property protection adopted by the World Trade Organization (WTO) imposes through the Agreement on TRIPs. (This argument is addressed in the following section.)

Whereas developing countries repeatedly emphasized the need to effectively implement Article X as part of the overall process of strengthening the Convention,[6] developed countries drew attention to their progress toward implementing Article X. Prominent among the countries that submitted these progress reports were the United States, France, the Netherlands, Australia, and Ireland, which reported on collaboration between the European Community and developing countries.[7]

Although these reports, and the protocol negotiations in general, anticipated progress toward the general goals of Article X, the prospects for achieving these goals appear quite bleak. This pessimism is based on an understanding of the adverse impact of a host of initiatives for strengthening the global intellectual property regime that have been taken over the past decade in several multilateral forums.

## THE TRIPS AGREEMENT: CHANGING
## THE NORMS AND STANDARDS OF
## PATENT PROTECTION

One of the most far-reaching agreements to emerge from the Uruguay Round of multilateral trade negotiations under the GATT was that concerning protection of intellectual property. This issue was included for the first time in the GATT negotiating mandate and assumed importance primarily because it addressed a problem at the very heart of the North–South debate, namely, control over the market for technology. The developed countries, the protagonists for inclusion of intellectual property rights (IPRs) in the negotiations, argued that inadequate standards of intellectual property protection (IPP) worldwide encouraged unauthorized use of technology by developing countries, and that this in turn encouraged a proliferation of trade in counterfeit and pirated goods. The developed countries saw a strong system of IPP that would be enforced by GATT and give increased control to the owners of technology as an effective solution to this problem.

The Agreement on Trade Related Aspects of Intellectual Property (TRIPS) gave substance to the arguments of the developed countries and was aimed at strengthening the norms and standards of intellectual property protection worldwide. In particular, the agreement has a major impact on patent protection, unmistakably the most important form of intellectual property protection. It covers the industrial sector in all countries, and in the United States it covers agriculture as well.

The stronger system of patent protection introduced by the TRIPS agreement has considerable significance for the implementation of Article X of the BWC for two main reasons. First, the scope of protection available under the new patent regime has been expanded to include biotechnological inventions. Second, transfer of technology between the technologically advanced developed countries and the developing countries would be restricted by the TRIPs regime. Thus, while Article X of the BWC emphasizes the need to introduce mechanisms that can improve exchange of scientific and technological information in the area of biotechnology, the patent regime seeks to enhance the control of the owners of technology through the heightened monopoly power.

### Changes in the Definition of Patentable Subject Matter

All fields of technology are now covered by the TRIPS agreement, including the branches of biotechnology that alter living things. Thus, while Article 27.1 of the Agreement provides that "patents shall be available for inventions, whether products or processes, in all fields of technology," Articles 27.2 and 27.3 provide limited exceptions.[8] More significantly, Article

27.3(b) of the TRIPS agreement stipulates that microorganisms can be patented. For more than a decade before the TRIPS agreement came into formal existence in 1995, there was considerable debate on the issue of extending patent protection to the inventions of biotechnology, a debate that was initiated by the landmark U.S. Supreme Court decision, *Diamond v. Chakrabarty*, in 1980 (see chapter 14).

There are two views on the likely impact of extending patent protection to areas that were hitherto not covered by the patent laws in developing countries. The first is that developing countries would benefit from increased participation by large corporations in their economies as corporate interests find effective protection for the technology they have developed. However, the empirical basis for this argument has generally been found to be quite thin.[9]

The second view is that countries in early stages of development tend to benefit from lower standards of patent protection. This position is supported by substantial evidence, both from the historical experiences of several industrialized countries and from the more recent experiences of developing countries like India. The lower standards of protection support greater dissemination of technology and thus facilitate the development of a broad base for the process of industrialization.[10] Furthermore, defining microorganisms as patentable subject matter worldwide will likely reinforce the monopoly control of corporate interests in the area of industrial biotechnology, including the pharmaceutical sector.

A critical issue in extending patent protection to microorganisms is what constitutes a microorganism. This issue has engaged the attention of policymakers in several developing countries, including countries such as India, which have a relatively advanced biotechnology sector. Developing countries have tended to limit the definition of "microorganism" by not including genes or gene sequences, thus limiting the range of protection.[11] In contrast, in the United States, gene fragments (expressed sequence tags, or ESTs)[12] have also been brought under patent protection after considerable hesitation on the part of the U.S. Patent and Trademark Office (USPTO). Such broad protection could affect developing countries like India by forcing them to broaden the scope of patentability.

In this connection it may be useful to recall developments in the United States and Europe, two of the leading proponents of the patenting of microorganisms. Until 1980 in the United States, patents on microorganisms were generally granted only in cases where the patentable subject matter was an organism combined with a carrier or where the organism contributed to a process. The first patent of this kind appears to have been granted to Louis Pasteur in 1873 for a form of yeast free from germs of disease.[13] However, the USPTO did not grant patents to living things themselves until the U.S. Supreme Court overruled an earlier decision by the U.S. Patent and Trademark Office and granted a patent on a genetically engineered bacterium in *Diamond v. Chakrabarty*. In granting the patent, the Supreme Court stated that "Congress . . . recognized that the relevant distinction was not between living and inanimate things, but between products of nature, whether living or not, and human-made inventions."[14]

In contrast to the U.S. position, Europe has excluded living things, with the exception of microorganisms, from patent coverage. The European position originates in the Convention on the Unification of Certain Points of Substantive Law on Patents for Inventions, signed in 1963 at Strasbourg (the "Strasbourg Convention"). The Convention provided criteria for distinguishing between patentable and nonpatentable inventions on living things.

Article 2(b) of the Strasbourg Convention stated that the contracting states would not be bound to provide patents on "plant and animal varieties or essentially biological processes for the production of plants and animals," but specified that the provision did not apply to microbiological processes and products. This position was also adopted by the European Patent Convention (EPC) in Article 53(b).[15]

It has been suggested that there were at least two reasons for excluding these areas by the EPC. First, the protection of plant varieties, animal varieties, and essentially biological processes by the patent system did not interest the chemical and pharmaceutical industries. Second, commercial interests in the area of plant breeding were adequately addressed by the International Convention for the Protection of New Varieties of Plants, known as the UPOV Convention, signed in 1961.[16] The UPOV Convention defined breeders' rights for protected varieties. These were strengthened in 1991 to require both farmers who propagated protected varieties on their own holdings and researchers who used these varieties to pay royalties to breeders.

Two decades after the Strasbourg Convention was adopted, the TRIPS agreement required essentially the same intellectual property protection both for microorganisms and for plants. With respect to plants, Article 27.3(b) requires that protection be provided "either by patents or by an effective *sui generis* system or by any combination thereof."[17] So far, the common interpretation of this requirement is that countries must introduce plant breeders' rights.[18]

This system of granting plant breeders rights, which was established when farmers were increasingly displaced by commercial breeders, is now being extended to developing countries where the former continue to play their traditional roles as conservers and breeders of new varieties. Introducing intellectual property protection for agricultural plants and thereby encouraging corporate monopolies to emerge in agricultural systems dominated by farming communities raises the vital issue of sustainability of traditional farmers in developing countries. Since a large majority of these farmers operate at subsistence levels, any threat to their sustainability could endanger their food security.

## Technology Transfer and the TRIPS Agreement

Extending intellectual property protection to microorganisms and plant varieties raises critical issues about the dissemination of biotechnology, especially the forms used in the pharmaceutical industry and agriculture. These issues arise from the nature of control that the owners of technology can exercise in the market as they strengthen their IPRs. For developing countries, one of the most important areas where control can be exercised is technology transfer.

Historically, patent systems included provisions for "working the patent" that were designed to facilitate technology transfer. Working the patent in the country of grant—that is, using the patent for commercial exploitation—was the only obligation that the patent system imposed on the patent holder. The main aim of this requirement was to prevent foreign patent holders from using their patents only to protect their markets in the countries granting them patent rights and denying the invention to the domestic industries of these countries. Protection of this kind could, in turn, result in a retardation of domestic industrial development, particularly when the patent is taken in a technologically underdeveloped country. Advocates of industrialization were interested in domestic production and they therefore opposed the system that gave protection to importers rather than domestic producers.[19] Remedy for this type of situation was found through the introduction of compulsory working provisions in the patent laws of several present-day industrialized countries.

Before the Agreement on TRIPS came into existence, the Paris Convention for the Protection of Industrial Property provided the global standards of patent protection. The Paris Convention contained a provision through which an effort was made to ensure that every product that is patented could also be produced commercially in the country of grant. It was argued by the members of the Convention that patent laws should not only provide protection to the inventor but should also provide a way for society at large to benefit from the invention if the patent holder is unable to exploit it commercially. To ensure the working of a patent, the Convention introduced the mechanism of compulsory licensing: The patentee should provide a license to produce the patented product to anyone interested in its commercial exploitation if the patentee did not work the patent within a set period. Under the Convention, this period was four years from the date of application, or three years from the grant of patent protection, whichever was longer.

If the patent holder was unable to provide a license within the stipulated period or the holder did not work the patent, the patent right could be forfeited. The compulsory licensing mechanism thus ensured that dissemination of technology took place. However, patent holders could avoid forfeiting their rights if they could justify not working the patent. This provided patent holders with a way to retain their monopoly rights over products, and it appears from the manner in which compulsory licensing has worked in different countries that, in most cases, patent holders were able to deny compulsory licenses, thus depriving society of the benefits of the invention through the dissemination of the technology.[20] Given this record of implementation, the Diplomatic Conferences on the revision of the Paris Convention held in the 1980s discussed the need to make the compulsory licensing provisions more effective.[21]

In contrast to the emphasis of the Paris Convention on ensuring the working of patents, the TRIPS agreement abandons the requirements of working almost completely. Article 31 of the TRIPS agreement, defining the requirements of working, has a curious title that underscores the spirit of the agreement: "Other Use Without Authorization of the Patent Holder." No grounds are explicitly given under which a compulsory license can be issued. But the spirit of this agreement rules out compulsory licensing as a measure against abuse of monopoly rights conferred by a patent or to ensure working of the patent within the patent-granting country, for which it has been used before. Thus, "working a patent" under the TRIPS agreement is tantamount to unauthorized use of the patent. Under these circumstances, no manufacturers will come forward to seek an authorization and take the risk of "working" the patent when they do not know if the circumstances under which the authorization was issued will continue or not.[22]

Furthermore, the rights of the patent holder are extremely broad and apply whether or not products are imported or locally produced (Article 27.1). For example, the agreement allows the patent holder the right to prevent the use of a patent for production aimed at the export market (Article 31(f)). This condition gives substance to the tendency of multinational corporations to provide technology to developing countries only for the exploitation of their local markets and to prevent export of goods manufactured through the license by imposing restrictive clauses.

Substantial dilution of the compulsory licensing provisions effected by the TRIPS agreement would foreclose all possibilities of technology dissemination and would provide absolute monopoly rights to the patent holder. In the experiences of several countries, including India, the mechanism of compulsory licensing was not very effective in ensuring technology dissemination. Nonetheless, it was the only means by which the patent holder could be forced to share the benefits of the invention with society. In a situation where transnational corporations dominated patenting activity the world

over, it was important from the perspective of developing countries to introduce a more effective mechanism for compulsory licensing.

The outcome of recent trade disputes shows that the TRIPS agreement
generally supports the interests of developed countries in opposing compulsory licensing. The most significant dispute has been that between the
United States and Brazil over the provision in the Brazilian industrial property law of 1996 that seeks to ensure "local working" of inventions patented in Brazil through the grant of compulsory licenses. To the WTO, the
United States contended that article 68 of Brazilian law violated Articles 27
and 28 of the TRIPS agreement since the "'local working' requirement for
the enjoyment of exclusive patent rights can only be satisfied as per the Brazilian law by the local production and not the importation of patented subject matter."[23] This action against Brazil came after the U.S. trade
representative had for years been threatening to take action against countries by invoking section 301 of its Trade Act for not providing the level of
protection of intellectual property that the United States deemed appropriate. Support for the U.S. position was provided by the Pharmaceutical
Research and Manufacturers of America (PhRMA), the trade association
representing the leading U.S. pharmaceutical and biotechnology companies.[24]

In summary, the Agreement on TRIPS has introduced major changes in
the global patent regime that increase the control of the owners of patented
technologies over the market for technology. Besides broadening the scope
of patenting, which now includes a substantial proportion of biotechnology
inventions, the TRIPS patent regime enhances the powers of patent holders
to control technology transfer.

## Provisions for Technology Transfer in the Convention on
## Biological Diversity

Some analysts have implied that the emphasis of developing countries
that are parties to the BWC on encouraging scientific and technological
exchanges under Article X are misplaced, since support for developing the
biological sciences and biotechnology is being encouraged by other international agreements.[25] Foremost among these is the Convention on Biological
Diversity (CBD). It is therefore important to examine the implications of the
CBD's requirements for technology transfer.

A key feature of the CBD is its recognition of the ever-increasing exploitation of genetic resources that has followed the commercial development of
biotechnology. Hailed as the technology of the future, biotechnology has
brought about a transformation in the use of genetic resources, generating
in the process a wide range of products that could fundamentally alter
human existence. But many of these technologies are being developed in the

research laboratories of the industrialized world, which are controlled and financed by transnational corporations. The resulting large-scale privatization of these biotechnologies means that the question of access to these technologies has become extremely contentious, especially from the perspective of developing countries.

The CBD addresses this issue of access to biotechnologies in relation to developing countries that are the main suppliers of genetic material. In the first place, it provides that every contracting party of the CBD must make efforts to develop and carry out scientific research based on genetic resources provided by other contracting parties with the full participation of, and to the extent possible, within the countries supplying the genetic material. This provision, contained in Article 15.6, is intended to ensure that developing countries are able to participate in the process of technology generation when the technologies utilize their genetic resources. The significance of this provision needs to be understood in the context of the ongoing discussions in several multilateral fora, which have emphasized that improving the technological competence of the developing countries is a sine qua non for ensuring economic development. Previous collaborative programs between the developing and the developed countries intended to improve the scientific and technological competence of the former have failed to achieve a broad impact, mainly because the private sector in the industrialized world that is at the vanguard of the technology-generating processes did not participate. These initiatives were also voluntary in nature and therefore did not receive the critical minimum support that could have generated meaningful results.

The CBD departs from these past initiatives by introducing a binding commitment for countries to undertake collaborative research ventures in the area of biotechnology, in Article 15.6. However, the provisions of Article 15.6 leave a possible window for industrialized countries not willing to collaborate, by adding a qualification. But this only indicates that the implementation of the CBD would have to be carried out in such a manner that the spirit of the article under discussion is not diluted.

The objectives of Article 15.6 are elaborated in Article 19, which specifies requirements for the handling of biotechnology and the distribution of its benefits. The article provides for the adoption of legislative, administrative, or policy measures by every CBD contracting party to ensure the "effective participation in biotechnological research activities by those Contracting Parties, especially developing countries, which provide the genetic resources for such research, and where feasible in such Contracting Parties." Not only does Article 19 insist that the developing countries should participate in biotechnological research, it also emphasizes that the research centers should be established in the developing countries. Article 19.2 provides for equitable sharing of benefits arising out of use of biotechnologies between the countries developing the technologies and those that make the genetic resources available for the development of such technologies. The article is singularly important insofar as it explicitly recognizes the economic value of the genetic resources held by countries.

As mentioned previously, the nonparticipation of the private sector in past initiatives has hindered technology transfer. So also has the dominant technological paradigm established by the TRIPS agreement that allows corporations effectively to hold technology close. These problems are addressed in Article 16, which contains crucial proposals on access to and transfer of technology.

Article 16.1 requires the signatory states "to provide and/or facilitate access for and transfer to other Contracting parties of technologies that are relevant to the conservation and sustainable use of biological diversity or make use of genetic resources and do not cause significant damage to the environment." Furthermore, Article 16.2 addresses the problems that developing countries have experienced in obtaining technologies that they require to advance their developmental objectives. The article requires that developing countries have access to technologies on "fair and most favourable terms, including on concessional and preferential terms where mutually agreed." Such terms are extremely significant since the major impediment in developing countries' access to technology has been the unaffordable terms on which transnational corporations agree to license their technologies. As discussed previously, the monopoly power provided by the patents and other forms of intellectual property protection has seriously undermined North–South technology transfer.

However, Article 16.2 goes on to add that in the "case of technology subject to patents and other intellectual property rights, such access and transfer shall be provided on terms which recognize and are consistent with the adequate and effective protection of intellectual property rights." Clearly, this second condition could help in maintaining the status quo in the market for technology.

A response to this provocative problem is provided in Article 16.3, which requires each signatory to put in place appropriate legislative, administrative, or policy measures that can be used to ensure that organizations involved in the technology generation processes, including the private sector, can be called upon to make technologies based on genetic resources of developing countries available to the countries supplying the resources at terms that are affordable. The last mentioned objective is sought to be realized by introducing the added proviso that technology transfer shall take place on "mutually agreed terms."

The problems in the area of technology transfer arising out of the exercise of market control by the private sector are specifically addressed in Article 16.4, which requires each signatory to "take legislative, administrative, or policy measures, as appropriate, with the aim that the private sector facilitates access to, joint development and transfer of technology . . . for the benefit of both governmental institutions and the private sector of developing countries."

Although Article 16 of CBD addresses the issue of technology transfer quite comprehensively, questions arise about the possibility of implementing the relevant provisions. The most significant impediment to effective implementation of Article 16 could be posed by the intellectual property regime based on the TRIPS agreement. As emphasized previously, the structure of the patent system that the TRIPS agreement has put in place strengthens the rights of the patent holders, which, in turn, could adversely affect the terms of technology transfer for the recipients of technology. Articles 27 and 31 of the TRIPS agreement impinge on the possibilities of technology transfer by providing several mechanisms of control to the owners of patented technologies. The response of the global community to these possibilities has taken the form of the Doha Ministerial Declaration on TRIPS and Public Health, which grants some degree of flexibility in the use of compulsory licenses in case of medicines. Nevertheless, the owners of the patented technologies would still be able to decide the terms on which the licenses can be issued. This could run contrary to the spirit of Article 16.2, which provides that developing countries could access technologies on "fair and most favourable terms." In situations where a clear conflict between the provisions of the CBD and those of the Agreement on TRIPS is perceived, the latter would be given precedence since countries that do not comply with their obligations under the TRIPs Agreement may face trade sanctions authorized by the WTO.

## THE PROPOSED SUI GENERIS PROTECTION OF DATABASES

The most recent in the series of initiatives to strengthen the regime of intellectual property protection is a WIPO proposal for strengthened protection of databases.[26] Protection of databases is currently provided by the copyright laws of each country, which are in turn governed by the Berne Convention. In 1991, the U.S. Supreme Court in *Feist Publications Inc. v. Rural Telephone Services Co.* defined the limits of this protection in the United States. The court ruled that Rural Telephone Services' database was not entitled to copyright on the basis of "industrious collection" alone. In response, corporate database producers argued that national copyright laws provide little or no protection to databases against piracy. In 1996, a European Union Directive on database protection supported such arguments by prohibiting extraction of any substantial part of a database representing a significant investment.[27] The EU initiative was followed later the same year by the WIPO proposal for the sui generis protection of databases, the main elements of which are considered in the following subsections.

## Scope of Protection

The scope of protection is defined in Article 1, which proposes to protect any database that represents substantial investment in the collection, assembly, verification, organization, or presentation of the contents of the database. Such protection is proposed regardless of the form or the medium in which the database is embodied and regardless of whether or not the database is made available to the public. The resulting scope of protection fundamentally alters the principles on which the system of intellectual property protection would be established. By their very nature, intellectual property rights should entail protection of products of human ingenuity and not physical investment, as proposed in the databases treaty. Certain standards are required for any form of intellectual property to qualify for statutory protection, but in this case, these standards have been ignored. Thus, while databases can be protected under the national copyright laws only if the claimant has been able to provide a compilation of data that displays a degree of originality and creativity, the proposed WIPO treaty would protect a mere collection or assembling of information provided that the claimant could demonstrate a substantial investment in the database. At the outset, therefore, the proposed treaty makes it abundantly clear that what it seeks is investment protection rather than intellectual property protection.

A further departure from the established principles of intellectual property protection is that protection could be granted even in cases where databases are not made available to the public. One of the cornerstones of intellectual property protection is adequate disclosure of the subject matter that is given statutory protection. In fact, in those forms of intellectual property where possibilities of secrecy do arise—for example, in the case of industrial property covered by patents—the rights of the patent holder are generally tempered by an obligation to disclose the invention to the public in a clear manner.[28] These principles underlying the intellectual property regime have, however, been diluted by the inclusion of trade secrets as one of the seven forms of intellectual property that the agreement on TRIPS recognizes. The databases treaty strengthens this move toward increasing the rights of the owners of so-called intellectual property without any consideration of the benefits of access by the public.

## Rights Conferred

The WIPO proposal gives owners of databases comprehensive rights. The rights holder would be free to authorize or prohibit the extraction or utilization of the contents of databases. Furthermore, parties to the proposed treaty are allowed to provide only limited exceptions to rights that the database owner would enjoy, subject to these exceptions not affecting the legitimate interests of the rights holders. This could imply, in other words, that the fair use provisions of national copyright laws that allow use of copyrighted material for personal, educational, research, and journalistic purposes and that have previously protected the public interest could be taken out of the purview of the database treaty.

## Term of Protection

The term of protection of databases has been defined so that the owner of a database can extend the protection in perpetuity. This would be achieved through a three-tiered period of protection. Effectively, any database can enjoy a period just less than fifteen or twenty-five years of protection while undisclosed and a further period of fifteen or twenty-five years after disclosure.[29] But what makes the period of protection run into perpetuity is a third level of protection according to which any "substantial" change to a database can qualify for its own form of protection. "Substantial" changes may include those resulting from "the accumulation of successive additions, deletions, verifications, modifications in organization or presentation, or other alteration, which constitute a new substantial investment." This provision implies that periodic revision of protected databases, which can be seen as constituting a "substantial change" to their original form, would require a further term of fifteen or twenty-five years that can be rolled over into perpetuity. In this way, the proposed treaty seeks to provide an absolute monopoly over any collection of information, a move that is completely antithetical to the efficient functioning of the markets.

## Application in Time

This provision complements the term of protection by proposing to extend the provisions of the treaty to all existing databases. Databases that were available to the public at large before the treaty's adoption would qualify for protection once the treaty is in place. Here again, the treaty departs from the established norms of intellectual property protection. When any invention or literary work enters the public domain, protection cannot be extended to such intellectual property in the same form as in the past. In contrast, the databases treaty would eliminate this requirement. The rights of database owners would be enhanced further by limiting the operation of entities that may have been involved in reproducing these databases while they were not protected. Reproduction would be allowed only for two years after the databases have been brought under protection.

The implications of protection of databases through the sui generis protection proposed by WIPO could have far-reaching implications for the implementation of the BWC. Effective compliance under the Convention has been deemed critically dependent on the extent to which members can be provided with incentives under Article X. The proposed database treaty will seriously impede the free flow of information, especially information related to biotechnology, for which use of databases—on genomes, for example—is becoming increasingly important. This proposed form of intellectual property rights, coupled with the extension of patent protection to areas such as microorganisms, would most certainly not facilitate effective compliance under the BWC.

## CONCLUSION

The global regime of intellectual property protection initiated by the Uruguay Round of the GATT, which continues to be strengthened today, means that attempts to implement Article X of the BWC will almost certainly face irreconcilable problems. The Agreement on TRIPS, the most potent of the instruments influencing the global market for technology, undermines the ability of developing countries to gain access to new technologies. The TRIPS Agreement considerably strengthens the control of the owners of patented technologies, enabling them to exercise their monopoly power and to prevent the transfer of new technology to developing countries on affordable terms.

The protection of nonoriginal databases proposed by WIPO will constitute a further barrier to technology transfer. Such protection would allow any enterprise that collects a certain mass of data on which it has made substantial investments in a database to prevent access to the information it contains. The treaty proposed by WIPO would effectively bar the smooth flow of scientific information that forms one of the cornerstones of Article X.

The problems that the developing countries could face in the area of technology transfer can hardly be ameliorated by the implementation of the CBD. The key consideration here would be the regime of intellectual property protection, which, as defined by the Agreement on TRIPS, strengthens the rights of the patent owners. This is primarily because the CBD refers to the recognition that must be accorded to the regime of intellectual property protection in case of technologies that are protected by patents or other forms of intellectual property rights.

The growing dominance of the private sector in biotechnology and the corresponding decrease in the role of the government sector is likely to make the intellectual property regime all the more compelling.[30] It follows that the governments of developed countries, which would be making the commitments to implement the provisions of Article X, would not have the vehicles necessary for the effective implementation of these critical provisions because of the changing structures of the biotechnology industries in their countries. The private sector, whose interests are protected by the strengthened patent regime, will be in a position to dictate the terms of technology transfer, much against the spirit of Article X. Despite the fact that the review conferences of the BWC have strengthened the conceptual basis of Article X by indicating the need for such measures as institutions to facilitate technology transfer and to establish a worldwide data bank, such goals are highly unlikely to be realized within the present global trade regime.

In conclusion, efforts to implement Article X of the BWC and efforts to extend and enhance the global intellectual property regime are on a collision course. The first attempts to transfer technologies to developing countries on terms that they can afford. The second seeks to ensure that the owners of technologies have the ultimate control over the technology market, in which they alone set the terms of commercialization of new technologies. It seems impossible to strengthen Article X in any meaningful way unless this fundamental contradiction is addressed.

## NOTES

1. Graham Pearson, "Implementing Article X of the BTWC: Avoiding Duplication," *Chemicals Weapons Convention Bulletin*, No. 32 (June 1996), 1–6.

2. United Nations, Third Review Conference of the Parties to the Convention on the Prohibition of the Development, Production and Stockpiling of Bacteriological (Biological) and Toxin Weapons and on Their Destruction, Final Declaration, Final Document, BWC/CONF.III/23, Geneva, 1992.

3. United Nations, Special Conference of the States Parties to the Convention on the Prohibition of the Development, Production and Stockpiling of Bacteriological (Biological) and Toxin Weapons and on Their Destruction, Final Report, BWC/SPCONF/1, Geneva, 1994.

4. United Nations, Fourth Review Conference of the Parties to the Convention on the Prohibition of the Development, Production and Stockpiling of Bacteriological (Biological) and Toxin Weapons and on Their Destruction, Final Declaration, Final Report, BWC/CONF.IV/9, Geneva, 1996.

5. United Nations, Ad Hoc Group of the States Parties to the Convention on the Prohibition of the Development, Production and Stockpiling of Bacteriological (Biological) and Toxin Weapons and on Their Destruction, Procedural Report, Annex I, Rolling Text of a Protocol to the Convention, Article VII, BWC/AD Hoc Group/55-1, 1 March 2001, 155–56.

6. See, for example, working papers by India and China submitted during the sixth negotiating session of the BWC Ad Hoc Group (March 1997): India, "Measures to Strengthen Implementation of Article X of the BTWC," BWC/AD HOC

GROUP/WP.131, 10 March 1997; China, "Specific Measures to Strengthen the Implementation of Article X of the BTWC," BWC/AD HOC GROUP/WP.135, 11 March 1997.

7. For details see U.S. Agency for International Health Activities, non-paper submitted by the United States of America, BWC/AD HOC GROUP/CRP.4, 12 July 1995; France, "1972 Convention—Implementation of Article X," BWC/AD HOC GROUP/WP.19, 30 November 1995; The Netherlands, " Implementation of Article X of the BWC," BWC/AD HOC GROUP/WP.45, 7 December 1995; Australia, "Measures to promote cooperation in biotechnology and related fields," BWC/AD HOC GROUP/WP.74, 18 July 1996; Ireland, "European Community Collaboration with Developing Countries in the Field of Biotechnology," BWC/AD HOC GROUP/WP.75, 18 July 1996.

8. Excluded from patentability are diagnostic and therapeutic methods and plants and animals.

9. United Nations, *Determinants of Foreign Direct Investment: A Survey of the Evidence* (New York: United Nations, 1992).

10. Biswajit Dhar and Niranjan Rao, "Trade Relatedness of Intellectual Property Rights: Finding the Real Connections," *Science Communication* 17(3) (March 1996), 304–25.

11. Biswajit Dhar and Sachin Chaturvedi, "Intellectual Property Rights and the Development of Biotechnology: Evidence from India," Report, UN Conference on Trade and Development (forthcoming).

12. Els Torreele, "From Louis Pasteur to J. Craig Venter: When Biomedical Scientists Become Bio-Entrepreneurs," *Drugs for the Neglected Diseases Working Group Working Paper;* available online at www.neglecteddiseases.org/thedndwg.shtml (2000).

13. Joseph Strauss, Industrial Property Protection of Biotechnological Inventions: Analysis of certain basic issues, Geneva WIPO, 1985 (Document BIG/281), 56.

14. *Diamond v. Chakrabarty*, 447 U.S. 303 (1980).

15. Article 53(b) allowed member countries in their national laws to exclude from the definition of patentable subject matter "plant and animal varieties or essentially biological processes for the production of plants and animals, except microbiological processes or the products thereof."

The term "essentially biological" was further clarified in the guidelines for the examination spelled out by the European Patent Office:

> The question whether a process is 'essentially biological' is one of degree depending on the extent to which there is technical intervention by men in the process; if such intervention plays a significant part in determining or controlling the result it is desired to achieve, the process would not be excluded. To take some examples, a method of crossing, inter-breeding, or selectively breeding, say, horses, involving merely selecting for breeding and bringing together those animals having certain characteristics would be essentially biological and therefore unpatentable. On the other hand, a process of treating a plant or animal to improve its properties or yield or to promote or suppress its growth, e.g., a method of pruning a tree, would not be essentially biological since although

a biological process is involved, the essence of the invention is technical; the same could apply to a method of treating a plant characterized by the application of a growth stimulating substance of variation. The treatment of soil by technical means to suppress or promote the growth of plants is also not excluded from patentability. (From WIPO, Committee of Experts on Biotechnological Inventions and Industrial Property, "Industrial Property Protection of Biotechnological WIPO, Committee of Experts on Biotechnological Inventions and Industrial Property, "Industrial Inventions," Report Prepared by the International Bureau, Geneva, BioT/CE/11/2 (1985), 44.)

16. F. K. Beier and Joseph Strauss, "Genetic Engineering and Industrial Property," *Industrial Property* 11 (November 1986), 454.
17. The literal meaning of sui generis is "of its own kind." In the present context, sui generis means a system of protection that is distinct from all the existing forms of intellectual property protection.
18. Plant breeders' rights provide a lower degree of protection than patents. This difference is primarily due to the exceptions that the former system of protection have historically provided to the farmers and researchers.
19. Fritz Machlup, "An Economic Review of the Patent System," Study for the Sub-Committee on Patents, Trademarks, and Copyrights, Committee on the Judiciary, United States Senate.
20. India has been among the countries that had strong compulsory licensing provisions in its Patents Act enacted in 1970, but whose record of implementation was hardly encouraging.
21. WIPO, 1983, *Diplomatic Conference on the Revision of the Paris Convention*, Geneva, PR/SM/3.
22. For further discussion of the TRIPS restrictions on conditions for working patents, see Biswajit Dhar and Sachin Chaturvedi, "The Patent Regime and Implementing Article X of the BTWC: Some Reflections," *Politics and the Life Sciences* 18(1) (March 1999), 103–8.
23. WTO, "Brazil—Measures Affecting Patent Protection: Request for Consultations by the United States," WT/DS199/1,G/L/385, IP/D/23 (2000).
24. See, for example, Pharmaceutical Research and Manufacturers of America (2000), Submission of PhRMA for the "Special 301" Report on Intellectual Property Barriers, 18 February 2000; available online at www.phrma.org/policy/aroundworld/special301.
25. See, e.g., Pearson, "Implementing Article X of the BTWC."
26. WIPO, Basic Proposal for the Substantive Provisions of the Treaty on Intellectual Property in Respect of Databases to be Considered by the Diplomatic Conference, CRNR/DC/6 (1996).
27. European Union, The Database Protection Directive 96/9/EC, 11 March 1996.
28. For discussion of the problems surrounding disclosure under U.S. patent law in the case of biotechnology patents, see chapter 14.
29. The period of protection remains one of the few issues that would have to be negotiated.
30. According to the UN Food and Agriculture Organization, private-sector

agricultural research in the Organization for Economic Cooperation and Development countries is now in excess of $7 billion and accounts for half the world's entire agricultural research investment. See United Nations, *Sustainable Agriculture and Rural Development: Report of the Secretary-General, Commission on Sustainable Development* (February 2000), para. 33.

# VI

## CONCLUSION

# 16

# Rethinking Biological Disarmament

*Susan Wright and Richard Falk*

At the beginning of the twenty-first century, concerns about biological warfare in the United States are greatly elevated, associated with fears of international terrorism and of attacks using weapons of mass destruction. This sense of threat, which intensified during the later years of the Clinton administration, has of course been powerfully reinforced by the September 11 attacks. The arguments found in this book elucidate a strong tendency in the West to reduce this problem to one of "proliferation," with "non-Western states and substate actors as proliferants" as the subtext of this discourse. In the United States in the 1990s, a further narrowing of the perceived danger to one posed exclusively by "rogue states and terrorists" became entrenched in security thinking. Although the list of such states varied depending on the context, states that are seen as hostile to the United States or to its close ally in the Middle East, Israel, are regularly included. The confident claim of arms control and security specialists that "today's threat of chemical and biological weapons comes from rogue states—states that refuse to join the CWC or BWC, or that join and cheat—and from non-state terrorist groups" became the starting point for analysis of the BW problem in the United States and an important consideration elsewhere in the West.[1] This formulation of the BW problem recurred in public proclamations as clear and indisputable fact, part of the furniture of geopolitical relations.

This sense of threat from the Other was prominent in American reactions to the September 11 attacks. The anthrax-laced letters that followed, even though it became evident that their origin was almost certainly domestic not foreign, reinforced fears that international terrorists could deploy weapons

of mass destruction. Osama bin Laden joined Saddam Hussein as embodying the general BW threat to the United States. As President George W. Bush
stated on November 1, 2001: "Since September 11, America and others
have been confronted by the evils [biological] weapons can inflict. This
threat is real and extremely dangerous. Rogue states and terrorists possess
these weapons and are willing to use them."[2]

A primary purpose of this book has been to show how this discourse,
which reduces the BW problem to a single kind of threat to U.S. security,
distorts its multiplicity, obscuring its complex relations with the histories,
political relations, security interests, and roles in regional politics of states
that are regularly accused of developing and possessing biological and other
weapons of mass destruction. It also distracts attention from the problems
posed by BW programs elsewhere in the world, especially in Russia, Israel,
and the United States, and by possession of nuclear weapons. In other
words, the American perspective should not be understood as a global perspective.

The chapters of this book demonstrate the importance of an alternative
approach to the BW problem. No monofocal understanding will adequately
deal with its complexity. What follows examines the book's varied discussions of the multifaceted character of the BW problem, first, by considering
the cognitive difficulty of assessing BW claims, and second, by addressing
the geopolitical contexts in which BW problems emerge. On the basis of this
appraisal, new approaches to the problem and to strengthening the regime
of prohibition of biological warfare are proposed.

## COGNITIVE PROBLEMS OF WESTERN
## VIEWS OF THE BW PROBLEM

The uncertainty concerning claims about the BW intentions of states is
related to the serious difficulty of appraising the threat. Many of the major
states of the world pursue what are claimed to be "biological defense" programs. But there are technical and political factors that make assessment of
the real purposes and characteristics of these programs highly conjectural
and unreliable. In the first place, there is the well-known "dual use" problem. Virtually all work with microorganisms and toxins has peaceful as well
as military application. Thus the production even of recognized BW agents
is not in itself evidence for or against a weapons program but must be linked
to the form of production and other activities such as evaluation, stockpiling, and association with weapons systems that would unambiguously rule
out peaceful or defensive interests.

Compounding this problem is the ambiguity that characterizes the Biological Weapons Convention's basic prohibition on biological weapons,

which is restricted to biological agents and toxins "that have no justification for prophylactic, protective, or other peaceful purposes." This formulation fails to define a clear and unambiguous boundary between prohibited and permitted development, production, and stockpiling of biological agents and toxins, thus allowing a wide range of biological warfare activities as long as they can be justified for defense. And much development of "defensive" measures, other than general defenses such as protective clothing, demands the production of "offensive" agents. To this point, for example, no state party has questioned the development of genetically modified pathogens, even extremely harmful strains, as long as this can be justified for defense. This major loophole is there not as a result of a drafting or negotiating oversight but by intention and design. The earliest formulations of the BW prohibition by the British government in 1968 were drafted so as to allow all forms of defensive research to continue (see chapter 12), and later negotiations had the effect of expanding the loophole to include development, production, and even stockpiling.

Finally, biological weapons activities are relatively easy to hide, not only for technical reasons (the relative ease of production and destruction) but also because of the secrecy that surrounds activities in the military and commercial spheres. Also, it is never clear what really drives secret programs that are hidden in the dark recesses of governmental and private sector bureaucracies. Often political leaders are unaware or only dimly aware of such activities, and their real operational direction is under the control of nonaccountable and obscure administrative officials.

These arguments are not intended to deny that states may have interests in developing biological weapons but rather to emphasize the cognitive problem of knowing and defining these interests. Given the uncertain boundary between permitted and prohibited activities drawn by the BWC, states may develop interests in biological weaponry that fall below the threshold at which a consensus on violation could be reached. Or states may be interested in creating an option to develop biological weapons— developing the means to produce large quantities of biological agents (permissible for peaceful purposes), and studying the characteristics of biological weapons and of routes of delivery (permissible for defensive purposes)—without actually putting these components together (a violation of the BWC). Indeed, civil servants in the British government understood this possibility as they deliberated on the advantages and disadvantages of proposing a ban on biological weapons in 1968 (see chapter 12).

With such uncertain boundaries, it is not surprising that even the strongest claims of the U.S. government on the question of "proliferation" are notably vague on specifics. An important example is the Pentagon's proliferation report of 1997. A covering message from former Secretary of Defense William Cohen opens with an ominous view of the spread of weapons of mass destruction to irresponsible Third World states, ruthless terrorists, and irrational religious cults wielding "disproportionate power" through the use of biological and other weapons of mass destruction. Cohen portrays proliferation of such weapons as a "chronic disease" that must be countered as soon as the first symptoms erupt.[3] However, this metaphor breaks down as one looks for evidence in this detailed report. With the exception of Iraq, the report provides no specific, unqualified evidence to back its claim for a single country labeled as a "proliferant state." Yet such documents have been cited repeatedly as primary sources on the "BW proliferation threat" by Western politicians, defense intellectuals, and nongovernmental organizations focusing on arms control to justify their positions for strengthening defense, export controls, and the BWC.

These cognitive barriers to accurate appraisal of BW activities mean that, in the absence of either extremely intrusive verification measures or first-hand information from reliable defectors, technical assessments are unlikely to provide precise information concerning states' BW intentions. "Facts" about interests in BW may well be malleable up to the point where the nature and scale of BW activities can only be interpreted as a program aimed at developing a weapons capability. That point was clearly reached by the former Soviet Union and Iraq; each country produced tons of biological weapons as well as delivery and dissemination technologies (see chapters 5 and 11). But the terms of the Biological Weapons Convention leave open the question of precisely where the point of violation is reached.

Given such indeterminacy and the absence of detailed evidence concerning BW activities in countries labeled by the West as "proliferants," the accusations made about these activities might equally be directed at Western biological defense programs. The United States, for example, has a huge BW infrastructure (the result of its expansion from the 1980s onwards) and possesses quantities of relevant agents. Furthermore, it is known to have pursued projects that, at the very least, pushed the legal limits of permissible research and development in the late 1990s and early years of the twenty-first century.[4] From the perspective of a threatened state, it might be seen as pursuing programs that could support a future offensive effort. In effect, evidence concerning national BW efforts functions as a geopolitical Rorschach test that defines the level of trust: If the country in question is seen as friendly, its biological warfare program is generally treated as "defensive." If, on the other hand, a country is seen as hostile, its program is almost certain to be regarded, at least by the U.S. government, as "offensive." And dangerous.[5]

In effect, the United States, in accusing non-Western states of developing biological weapons, has capitalized on the uncertainty of the evidence and the ambiguity that complicates the BWC's prohibition of biological weaponry. Its arguments seem far more calculated to rouse emotions rather than to aid dispassionate appraisal. Their present emotional impact is further heightened by their recent conflation with Osama bin Laden's brand of terrorism.

The chapters of this book indicate the importance of an alternative approach to the BW problem. Instead of treating the problem as a monolithic phenomenon, it is essential to understand it by reference to the political and military characteristics of individual states as well as by taking account of non-Western perspectives. Only then may we perceive the varied geopolitical and strategic dynamics that both sustain and distort anxieties about biological weaponry.

## THE GEOPOLITICS OF THE BW PROBLEM

Four distinct political contexts frame questions concerning biological warfare: first, the legacy of the huge biological weapons program pursued by the former Soviet Union during the Cold War; second, the Middle East as a crucible of conflict that includes weapons of mass destruction (WMD); third, the new threat of bioterrorism; and finally, the direction being taken by large Western biological defense programs, especially that of the United States.

Superimposed on questions about BW arising in each of these contexts is the understanding that continuing innovation in the biological sciences and biotechnology seems to yield a double-edged power over living things. The sequencing of the entire human genome accomplished in 2001, increasing understanding of the mechanisms of the immune system and its regulatory mechanisms, and rapid gene shuffling techniques are examples of developments that are both hailed for their potential medical uses and feared for their application to novel biological weapons. Partly because of uncertainties concerning the future evolution of the fundamental paradigm of molecular biology, both sets of scenarios are characterized by radical uncertainty. [6] Nevertheless, the results of the Soviet BW program and unexpectedly harmful results reported occasionally from civil research laboratories[7] underscore the dangers, if military establishments probe the weapons applications of these technologies even at a research level.

### The Legacy of the Biological Weapons Program in the Former Soviet Union

The present American focus on BW as a problem posed by non-Western states and terrorist organizations obscures the origins of biological weapons in industrialized states and their development by the two archrivals of the Cold War. Whereas the United States had decided by 1969 that it was to its advantage to deprive nonnuclear states of a cheap mass-destruction option by supporting a universal ban on biological weapons, the former Soviet Union continued its offensive BW program despite its status as an original signatory to the Biological Weapons Convention (see chapters 5 and 12). The Russian program expanded in the 1970s and 1980s to become the largest biological weapons effort the world has ever known, larger by an order of magnitude than the American program at its peak and dwarfing the Iraqi effort. It is now known that the Soviet program not only weaponized many microbes that are lethal for humans, animals, and plants but also went further, using genetic engineering to construct hybrid microbes even more harmful than those occurring naturally.

Since Boris Yeltsin's decree terminating the program in April 1992, the challenge for supporters of biological disarmament has been to ensure that the huge biological weapons establishment left over from the Cold War would be dismantled or redirected into peaceful projects. The support and cooperation of Western states has been important, and perhaps crucial, for facilitating this decommissioning. In particular, funds from the U.S. Cooperative Threat Reduction Program have been aimed at stemming a Russian "brain drain" in which former biological weapons scientists would take their expertise abroad.[8]

Nevertheless, the remnants of the former Soviet program still pose problems. First, some facilities apparently remain closed, with no information available about the work pursued in secret.[9] Second, there is the problem of ensuring that the knowledge and techniques generated by the Soviet program are never used. Western concerns focus on the diffusion of knowledge, materials, and expertise to Middle Eastern states and international terrorist organizations. In addition, much expertise remains in Russia. In 1997, researchers at an institute in Obolensk known to have been earlier involved in the Soviet biological weapons program constructed a genetically modified form of anthrax that could overcome the protection of a vaccine. The researchers published their results in a British journal, claiming that the work was pursued for public health reasons.[10] Nevertheless, the result raised serious concerns elsewhere both about Russian motives and about the implications of the result itself. Finally, substantial parts of the knowledge and know-how concerning biological weaponry have been transferred to the West, notably to the United States—an aspect of bioweapons proliferation to which the West itself has been oblivious. One prominent biological weapons specialist, Ken Alibek, was debriefed by military and intelligence agencies for some five years. Alibek's detailed account of the Soviet BW program for the U.S. government is highly classified, and the government has not revealed its use of his information, although Alibek published his own version of his experience.[11]

A third problem is that of ensuring that former biological weapons facilities are fully converted to peaceful purposes. An example is the conversion of the Central Asian Scientific-Research Institute of Phytopathology in Tashkent, which developed plant fungi as biological weapons during the Cold War (see chapter 5). With funding from the United States and the United Kingdom, the same facility, now renamed the Institute of Genetics, received a contract from the UN Drug Control Program to develop a fungal pathogen to attack the opium poppy.[12] As the nongovernmental organization (NGO) the Sunshine Project has argued, without the consent of the people in rural areas affected by drug crop eradication programs, the use of biological agents to attack drug crops amounts to a "hostile" purpose that is prohibited by the Biological Weapons Convention.[13]

## The Biological Weapons Problem in the Middle East

In the Middle East, the BW problem takes a very different form, one that is linked to the tensions among states in the region as well as to the presence of Israel's nuclear weapons. One expression of the continuing problem is the pronounced pattern of nonadherence to the BWC as well as to the Chemical Weapons Convention (CWC) (although, despite this pattern, several Middle Eastern states have signed and ratified all of the major disarmament treaties). Egypt, Israel, Syria, Sudan, and the United Arab Emirates have not ratified the BWC. (Iraq agreed to do so only as part of the cease-fire agreement (Resolution 687) at the end of the Gulf War.) Middle Eastern states are unlikely to acquiesce in BW or CW disarmament as long as nuclear weapons are present in the region. There is no sign that the Israeli formula, that Israel will not be the first to introduce nuclear weapons into the region, can reassure its neighbors.[14] The problem is aggravated by Israel's secret biological and chemical facility at Ness Ziona and its unwillingness to join any of the major disarmament treaties. It is further aggravated by unresolved tensions between other Middle Eastern states, particularly Iran and Iraq,[15] as well as the overall tension and turmoil throughout the region.

But nonadherence is a symptom, not a root cause, of the deeper security problems that plague relations among Middle Eastern states. Neither proposals for linking universal chemical and biological disarmament to nuclear disarmament nor proposals for regional disarmament by establishing a WMD-free zone (WMDFZ) in the Middle East have succeeded. As Avner Cohen points out, while Arab states have defined such proposals as a first step toward achieving peace in the region, Israel insists that such proposals should be seen as the last stage of an arms control process (chapter 7). For example, in the 1990s, a WMDFZ in the Middle East was proposed by President Hosni Mubarak of Egypt. With Egyptian influence, the concept was also incorporated into the UN Security Council's cease-fire Resolution 687 at the end of the Gulf War.[16] But Israel's response—broached by Israeli Foreign Minister Shimon Peres at the ceremony that opened the CWC for signature in January 1993—was to make a similar proposal conditional on achieving peace in the Middle East.[17]

Banning WMD in the Middle East would require addressing a whole complex of security problems, including territory, recognition, and conventional and unconventional weapons, involved in interactions among the Middle Eastern states. Fundamental differences in worldview seem critical in understanding these problems. Israel perceives and presents itself as struggling over the decades to maintain its existence while surrounded by hostile states and deems nuclear weapons important if not essential for its long-term security, both as deterrent and as ultimate survival weapon.[18] Consequently, Israel makes progress in arms control in general, and nuclear, chemical, and biological disarmament in particular, conditional on normalization of Israel's relations with neighboring states (see chapter 7). On the other hand, Arab states are threatened by what they perceive to be Israeli aggression against Arab territory and (in the case of the Palestinians) Arab rights. They see Israel as seeking not its own defense through deterrence but regional hegemony.[19] They view Israel's nuclear weapons as destabilizing the entire region, generating security concerns on the part of neighboring states which, as Abdulhay Sayed has argued, "could reasonably translate into more proliferation."[20] Consequently, Arab states tend to see normalization of relations with Israel as one of the last moves in the long road toward peace and disarmament, and conditional on withdrawal from the occupied territories and guarantees of mutual security, possibly including a WMDFZ. As Avner Cohen points out, this has been the general pattern of Arab–Israeli interactions over Israel's undeclared nuclear weapons since Iran and Egypt first called for a nuclear-weapon-free zone in the Middle East in 1974 (chapter 7). Of course, rivalries between various Arab states and between Arab states and Iran, and the influence of the United States in the region, including its strong support for Israel, further complicate this picture, but such tensions were completely overshadowed in 2002 by the escalating Palestinian/ Israeli conflict and the collapse of efforts to bring peace to the region.

The Arms Control and Regional Security (ACRS) talks initiated after the end of the Gulf War in 1991 were an important attempt to find ways to move beyond these diametrically opposed positions. Multilateral talks on arms control were run concurrently with bilateral talks on territorial questions between Israel and each of its neighbors (Israel–Palestinians, Israel–Syria, Israel–Lebanon, Israel–Jordan).[21] Although the ACRS negotiations eventually broke down in 1996, they made clear some conditions for progress on arms control in the Middle East. First, they provided important evidence that progress in arms control and disarmament in the Middle East is conditioned on progress in the bilateral negotiations; in the absence of territorial agreements between Israel and its immediate neighbors, the confidence needed to embark on arms control seems unlikely to develop.[22]

Moreover, if territorial agreements were to be achieved, normalization of relations might be possible as the next step, and this in turn would support the willingness of parties to negotiate a range of broader security issues, including arms control. For example, the Israel–Jordan peace treaty, signed in October 1994, included a joint pledge by the two countries "to work as a matter of priority . . . for the creation of a Middle East free from weapons of mass destruction, both conventional and nonconventional, in the context of a comprehensive, lasting, and stable peace."[23]

Second, the talks underscored the need to involve all states in the region. The exclusion of Iran, Iraq, and Libya, and the absence of Syria and Lebanon, limited what could be achieved or even discussed.[24] Third, it was emphasized repeatedly by Egypt that any discussion of biological (or for that matter chemical) disarmament is intertwined militarily and politically with discussion of nuclear and other forms of disarmament. As Laura Drake has argued, it is unrealistic to expect major states in the region to agree to one form of disarmament if other major weapons systems (conventional as well as unconventional) are not addressed (chapter 6).

Despite the understanding of the dynamics of WMD interests in the Middle East, the United States and, to an extent, other Western states, continue to accuse certain Arab states and Iran of pursuing biological weapons programs while maintaining a virtual silence on the question of Israel's possession of WMD. For example, the head of the American delegation to the BWC's fifth review conference named, in addition to Iraq, Iran, Libya, Syria, and Sudan as states "engaged in biological weapons activities."[25] However, these claims were framed in vague terms that might equally have applied to the United States itself. Given the ambiguities and lack of precision that characterize the BWC, claims that a state "may be capable of producing small quantities of [BW] agent[s]," or that it "has probably produced and weaponized BW agents" do not lead definitively to a conclusion that state X is actively violating the treaty. Even asserting that a state has "weaponized" a BW agent does not necessarily mean that it has violated the BWC since there are certain legitimized defensive reasons for producing a weaponized agent.

Activities related to biological warfare on the part of Middle Eastern states may well mean that states are responding to perceptions of a dangerous environment rather than seeking to threaten other states. For example, close studies of Iran's activities related to WMD may indicate such interests.[26] Furthermore, Iran's modest military budgets suggest a prudence that is far removed from the American mainstream media's image of an Iran that is aggressively moving to develop biological and other WMD.[27] Iran may well perceive serious threats to its security from Israel, a future Iraq (which used chemical weapons against it during the Iran–Iraq war), and indeed from the United States, which has supplied its Gulf allies with billions of dollars' worth of armaments.[28]

In summary, Western-style attacks on "rogues" or "proliferants" do not solve the BW problem in the Middle East. In fact, they aggravate it, by reinforcing the double standard that has so often been applied to security problems in the region: silence on Israel's WMD programs, nuclear, chemical, and biological; a posture of suspicion and accusation with respect to those of Arab states and of Iran. What are needed, if territorial agreements in the region can ever be reached, are regionwide talks, and eventual security arrangements, that include all Middle Eastern states, including Iraq.

## The BW Problem and Iraq

The beginning of the twenty-first century has seen no resolution of the impasse over Iraq's BW activities. A discredited monitoring agency (which left Iraq in December 1998) is denied reentry and resumption of its responsibilities; a low-intensity, undeclared war against Iraq authorized by neither the U.S. Congress nor the UN Security Council is pursued by the United States and the United Kingdom; and sanctions that are killing hundreds, if not thousands, of Iraqi children each month through disease and malnutrition continue. Moreover, despite the lack of any evidence linking Iraq to the September 11 attacks, the Bush administration and the American media have been moving steadily to create a public climate of expectation and support for a war launched against Iraq with the goal of removing Saddam Hussein from power. The allegation that Saddam Hussein continues to seek, and may possess, biological weapons and other weaponry of mass destruction has played a major role in the buildup designed to legitimate such recourse to war. There is much resistance mounting to this American plan, especially among Arab countries, as U.S. Vice President Dick Cheney learned during his visit to the Middle East in March 2002.[29]

In the 1990s, the West, especially the anglophone West, concentrated on Iraq as the archetypal rogue state. Saddam Hussein not only possessed a declared chemical weapons arsenal and used chemical weapons against Iran and the Kurdish people in Northern Iraq, pursued nuclear weapons, and secretly developed biological weapons, but also attempted to conceal major parts of these programs from UNSCOM inspectors during implementation of the UN cease-fire Resolution 687 (see chapter 11). But displaying Saddam Hussein as a ruthless leader intent on gaining power at the expense of neighboring states and his own people can distract attention from Washington's permissive treatment of his roguish behavior in the 1980s. In particular, Washington tilted toward Saddam during the Iran–Iraq war, even after his use of chemical weapons against Iran and the Kurds in northern Iraq.[30] Today, the United States clearly adheres to one standard of tacit acceptance for Israel's nuclear weapons and secret chemical and biological warfare programs and another, highly punitive standard of explicit disallowance for Iraq's demonstrated interest in WMD (chapter 6).

Whatever the justification for the policies adopted toward Iraq by the UN Security Council at the end of the Gulf War and pursued through implementation of Resolution 687, it should be clear that these policies no longer function and need to be replaced (see chapter 10). The UNSCOM inspections, although largely successful until 1998 in closing down Saddam Hussein's WMD programs, were ultimately undermined not only by Iraqi resistance to the inspections but equally if not more so by Washington's use of UNSCOM to facilitate espionage against Saddam Hussein's regime, a fact not ultimately denied by Washington.[31] Furthermore, military actions against Iraq taken by the United States and the United Kingdom that have not been approved by the UN Security Council, particularly the enforcement of the "no-fly" zones in northern and southern Iraq and the bombing raids on Baghdad, have only intensified Iraq's resistance to inspections under Resolution 687.

The economic sanctions against Iraq applied under Resolution 661 (August 6, 1990) to back the UNSCOM investigation have also failed. Far from motivating Saddam Hussein to demonstrate to UNSCOM's satisfaction that the chemical and biological weapons (CBW) programs have been terminated, these sanctions have essentially held the Iraqi population captive, dramatically lowering their living standards and causing over one million deaths, especially among infants and the elderly. According to one analysis, "economic sanctions may well have been a necessary cause of the deaths of more people in Iraq than have been slain by all so-called weapons of mass destruction throughout history."[32] The huge reparations Iraq pays Kuwait compound the disaster. No limit has been set on the total amount Iraq will be required to pay, and no allowance has been made for Iraq's domestic crisis.[33]

Although the United States and the United Kingdom blame the suffering of the Iraqi people on the refusal of Saddam Hussein to use available resources to improve the conditions of life in Iraq, convincing evidence points to the devastation of Iraq's agricultural, medical, and social infrastructure by the Gulf War; Iraq's financial inability to rebuild this infrastructure (which requires far more capital than that supplied by the UN Oil for Food Program); and delays for approval of urgently needed "dual-purpose" materials and equipment imposed by the UN Sanctions Committee responsible for administering the provisions of Resolution 661.[34] Sanctions have increased the dependence of the Iraqi population on the Ba'ath regime for food and medicine, crippling political opposition to the regime.[35] Paradoxically, coercive disarmament has had long-term effects that are diametrically opposed to the declared goal, a lesson the West painfully learned in relation to the punitive peace imposed on Germany after World War I, and now apparently unlearned in relation to Iraq.[36]

Whether or not the original policy of coercive disarmament of Iraq was justified, the cumulative evidence of the suffering of the Iraqi people and the impasse over the inspections demonstrate that this policy has now failed. The time is long overdue to seek alternative approaches and above all to find a solution that provides immediate relief for the Iraqi people and ensures that this relief is permanent. However, the United States in 2002 moved in exactly the opposite direction. Not only did the U.S. government plan to invade Iraq, it also pressed for and eventually succeeded in persuading the UN Security Council to adopt a resolution (1409) implementing so-called smart sanctions claimed to distinguish between civilian and military imports.[37] This arrangement leaves in place a long list of dual-purpose items needed to rebuild essential civil infrastructures as well as the procedures that have been responsible for the dismal failure of coercive disarmament. It has little chance of being accepted by Iraq. As Amin Saikal argues, a new approach is needed that provides both immediate relief from the existing sanctions as well as a mechanism for negotiation of a clear end-game for the inspection of Iraq's WMD (see chapter 10).

## Bioterrorism

The grievous assaults on September 11 on the world's dominant military and economic power exposed the darkest side of the globalizing trends that are rendering borders porous and distances irrelevant in the post–Cold War era. As Stanley Hoffman has noted, the terrorists' organization depended on the ability to transfer money and resources around the world regardless of state boundaries: "The weapons of economic and military warfare (including for mass destruction) are now available not merely to states but to the peoples of the world."[38] Furthermore, Osama bin Laden possessed the financial resources, management skills, and fanatical commitment to exploit such structures and the charismatic leadership to persuade others to collaborate in a terrorist war against the United States.

The attacks may also indicate a stark change in the nature of terrorism.[39] Before September 11, the conventional wisdom was that "terrorists want a lot of people watching and a lot of people listening and not a lot of people dead."[40] Bin Laden and the al Qaeda network demonstrated that such thinking drastically underestimated their intentions. No longer could it be claimed that "terrorists were more interested in publicity than killing and therefore had neither the need nor interest in annihilating large numbers of people."[41]

This new perception has reinforced fears of "catastrophic terrorism" using weapons of mass destruction that were vigorously anticipated by military and intelligence officials and defense intellectuals during the Clinton administration (see chapters 1 and 3). Doubts that organizational and technological difficulties would frustrate all but state-sponsored BW attacks were shrugged off in the blitz of media coverage of bioterrorist scenarios at that time.[42] Arguably, the terrorism of al Qaeda was not of this exotic, "high-end" type, having turned the power of a peaceful technology into a vicious weapon with nothing more than "low-end" box cutters.[43] Such a horrifying transformation suggested that future terrorists would more likely aim for nuclear power plants or chemical factories rather than directly use weapons of mass destruction.

Nevertheless, no government could afford to ignore the possibility of bioterrorism, given evidence suggesting al Qaeda's interest in WMD.[44] At the same time, the vast expansion of bioterrorism defense presently underway in the United States is hardly justified. As chapters 3 and 4 explain, there can be no technical fix for biological warfare since a determined adversary can always circumvent specific defenses such as vaccines. Moreover, part of this expansion generates its own dangers by increasing access to sources of novel and weaponized pathogens.[45] In the long run, the only solutions to the bioterrorism problem are political in nature.

## The Emerging American Dimension of the BW Problem: Straining the Limits of the Permissible

The main threat of the biological weapons programs of the former Soviet Union and Iraq was that the BW arsenals of those two countries would be used as strategic weapons, producing large numbers of civilian casualties and almost certainly provoking massive retaliation. The danger posed by the large American biological defense program (and possibly the programs of other Western states) lies elsewhere, namely, in loosening the constraints of the BWC by defining loopholes in the treaty through which novel weapons development may pass.

In the early 1980s, former U.S. Secretary of Defense Caspar Weinberger implied a right under the BWC to develop and test novel genetically engineered pathogens to design defenses against novel pathogens that the former Soviet Union was suspected (correctly, as is now known) of developing.[46] But Defense Department moves in this direction were resisted by the public and by Congress in the 1980s and there is little evidence that such biological defense projects were pursued.[47] In the 1990s, however, with rising claims that the United States faced a new threat from "rogue states" and "terrorists," political resistance faded. Funding for biological defense in the United States skyrocketed over that decade, growing from some $80 million in FY1990 to over $1 billion in FY 2000 (chapters 3 and 4). Limits on biological defense activities were loosened. Although much of the work funded in the 1990s focused on defensive measures such as emergency response and preparedness, detection and diagnostic systems, vaccines and therapies to protect against naturally occurring pathogens, there was also support for projects whose purposes went considerably beyond these standard defensive goals. Among the most provocative are the following:

- A CIA-supported project, "Clear Vision," to test a mock biological warfare bomb to study its dispersion capability.
- A Defense Department project to construct a mock biological warfare factory at its nuclear test site in the Nevada desert.
- A Defense Intelligence Agency project being pursued at the Battelle Memorial Institute in Columbus, Ohio, to genetically engineer a strain of anthrax capable of resisting the protection provided by vaccination against anthrax. The rationale for this project was to reproduce the Russian vaccine-resistant strain of anthrax to design a defense against it.[48]
- Projects for developing so-called nonlethal biological weapons such as microbes engineered to attack oil and lubricants and anti-personnel biochemical weapons.[49]
- Projects for developing plant pathogens such as *Pleospora papaveracea* and *Fusarium oxysporum* to attack drug crops.[50]

These projects are likely to provoke both skepticism concerning the constraints on biological weapons development defined by the Biological Weapons Convention and desires on the part of military establishments elsewhere to pursue similar kinds of work. They also demonstrate the continuity between the Clinton administration, which launched them (apparently without presidential consent) and the Bush administration, which has continued them.[51] The first project—the bomb test—would seem to be a direct violation of the BWC, which bans without qualification the development, production, and stockpiling of equipment and means of delivery. But all of these projects are so close to the gray area between prohibited and permitted activities that fine legal distinctions hardly matter.

Attempts to construct genetically altered pathogens are particularly troubling. One of the earliest nightmare scenarios accompanying the emergence of genetic engineering was the idea of modifying a pathogen against which there would be no protection. Fears of such uses by military agencies provoked a call for banning any such projects in 1975.[52] Furthermore, justifying them by claiming that vaccines could be designed to protect against such modified organisms is illusionary; nature provides too many pathogens with too many genes that can be altered for a single vaccine to provide an effective defense. According to Richard Novick, a New York University microbiology professor who heads a committee to study research for biological defense, there is no "imaginable justification for changing the antigenicity of anthrax as a defensive measure."[53] Furthermore, the rationale for this project—to design a defense against the genetically modified strain of anthrax constructed in Russia—demonstrates precisely how military work of this kind could proliferate.

Each such project lifts the lid further from the Pandora's box of genetically altered pathogens. Other states are likely to emulate such work. Once such work is seen as normal, skepticism about the boundaries set by the BWC will result. A frightening irony is that pursuit of such work in the name of defense might unleash novel pathogens far more damaging than the weaponized natural pathogens stockpiled by Saddam Hussein.

The problems posed by the U.S. biological defense effort parallel those of the national missile defense system (see chapters 3 and 4). Each program uses a threatening adversary for its justification; each runs a grave risk of producing the very response it is claimed to counter; and each system, given the ability to overcome the inherent limitations of its defensive technology, is doomed to failure.[54]

Such observations are not intended to question legitimate defense activities on the part of the United States or any other state. Governments are fully justified in taking precautionary measures to protect their populations against a possible BW attack. Planning emergency responses, stockpiling vaccines and therapies, and developing rapid detection devices and other forms of protection are necessary in the present context. But beyond such prudential measures, we need to take account of the negative political impact of these provocative and dangerously ambiguous components of the American and other biological defense efforts.

## APPRAISAL

No less than during the height of the Cold War in the early 1980s, the Biological Weapons Convention is encountering serious pressure, beset by geopolitical problems that call for urgent action. In that earlier period, the problems confronting the BWC were generated by the arms race between the two superpowers. Today, threats to the BWC have a more complex origination, encompassing programs left over from the Cold War in Russia, unresolved tensions between a nuclear-armed Israel and neighboring states in the Middle East, international terrorism, a renewed concern that the United States is considering recourse to nuclear weapons in situations other than deterrence and self-defense, and the emergence of a unilateralist posture on the part of the world's most powerful state that legitimates use of the most sophisticated forms of biotechnology in the name of defense.

Several conditions support the continuing persistence and intractability of the BW problem. In the first place, a major condition that blocks international cooperation is the determined division of the world into two camps, and the unilateralism that this division legitimates, on the part of the world's most powerful state. As various chapters of this book relate, the Western reduction of the BW problem to one posed by "rogue states and terrorists" has a long history, one that is closely intertwined with the development of the BWC itself. The original reasoning of the United Kingdom in the late 1960s was that the West had almost nothing to lose by renouncing biological weapons and much to gain by preempting a cheap mass destruction option on the part of nonnuclear states, especially those seen as hostile to Western interests. Long before non-Western states showed any interest in biological weaponry, their *potential* interests were cast as a crucial reason for developing a universal prohibition on biological weapons (chapter 12).

Subsequent Western policies based on the concept of WMD "proliferation," and more specifically on the American concept of the "rogue" state, have deepened this division. The secret Soviet program, which had at its peak some 65,000 employees, vast facilities, huge stockpiles, and research programs aimed, ominously, at producing genetically engineered organisms, including smallpox, constituted the most egregious violation of the BWC (chapter 5). The Iraqi efforts are rudimentary in comparison. Yet the United States, cognizant of the Soviet Union's BWC violations by 1991, chose not to accuse the Soviet Union publicly.[55] To date, there has been no reassurance that the former Soviet BW program has been completely terminated (chapter 5). Yet Russia figures far less prominently than certain Arab states, Iran, and North Korea on lists of "rogues" or "proliferants." Indeed, the primary Western response to the transgressions of the former Soviet Union has been to develop cooperative measures that aim to keep former bioweaponeers usefully employed on civilian projects.[56] Similarly, Israel's unacknowledged BW program at Ness Ziona and Israel's nonadherence to the Biological Weapons Convention has provoked no serious Western pressure for change. By contrast, the American response to suspicions of biological weapons interests on the part of other Middle Eastern states has been vociferously critical and punitive. In particular, the coercive disarmament of Iraq has been one of the most punitive treatments of any modern defeated state in history. Under strong Western influence, the UN Security Council decided that there would be no economic carrots for Saddam Hussein's "rogue" state.[57]

The term "rogue," which legitimates this double standard, has been viewed with skepticism even in the West.[58] As the French foreign minister, Hugo Vedrine, commented in 2000: "It's not a geopolitical category we use. It is difficult for Europeans to imagine one of these states attacking the United States."[59] Even in the United States, use of the term has fluctuated. In the last year of the Clinton administration, as Iran held democratic elections, North Korea moved closer to rapprochement with South Korea, and Syria negotiated with Israel, the pariah term "rogue" was temporarily morphed into the more moderate formulation "states of concern."[60] However, as earlier chapters have noted, the term is again ascendant in the

George W. Bush administration, which now routinely divides the world into "responsible" states that are assumed to respect and adhere to arms control agreements and "irresponsible rogues" that are assumed to violate these agreements by secretly pursuing programs to acquire WMD in some form.

This dichotomy is used to justify an extreme unilateralism that rejects multilateral arms control on the grounds that responsible states do not need it, whereas irresponsible states will cheat and are not suitable partners for arrangements relying on some measure of reliability and trust. Hence the "Bush doctrine" promoted by national security advisor Condoleezza Rice: reject multilateralism pursued for its own sake and deal unilaterally, if necessary, with perceived threats, including holding other states responsible for all who violate international law.[61]

The September 11 attacks have reinforced these unilateralist tendencies within the Bush administration, despite its effort to form an international coalition to fight terrorism. The damaging impact of such thinking was evident at the fifth BWC review conference in 2001 when the United States insisted, against the advice of close allies, on naming and accusing six "rogue" states of violating the BWC and attempted to terminate the seven-year-old multilateral effort to strengthen the Convention. As Under Secretary of State for Arms Control and International Security Affairs John Bolton justified the American position: "The United States will simply not enter into agreements that allow rogue states or others to develop and deploy biological weapons."[62] George Bush's accusation of North Korea, Iran, and Iraq as an "axis of evil" was a frightening application of the rogue state logic, made the more so as it was expressed in the form of a warning about the extension of the war against terrorism beyond Afghanistan.

One serious consequence of this embrace of polarizing unilateralism is that it will undermine international searches for strengthening existing arms control agreements and make new, constructive, and needed agreements all but impossible. Indeed, as several chapters of this book relate, the fifth review conference witnessed the Bush administration's complete rejection of almost seven years of efforts to add a verification component to the BWC in the form of a protocol. The administration's attempt to terminate the ongoing negotiations left representatives of virtually every other treaty party in a condition of shock, anger, and dismay (see chapters 8, 9, and 13).

A second condition supporting the intractability of the BW problem is the continuing reliance of powerful states on nuclear weapons for their security. The readiness of the United Kingdom and the United States (and no doubt also the former Soviet Union) to renounce biological, and later, chemical weapons was premised on nuclear deterrence (see chapter 12). Generally, this continuing reliance has established nuclear deterrence rather than disarmament as the *primary* basis for national security of nuclear weapons states. All international prohibitions of weapons of mass destruction are weakened as a result (see chapter 2). At present, this weakening of restraints on weapons of mass destruction is especially clear in the Middle East where the presence of nuclear weapons has provided the conditions for the emergence of the BW problem in one of its most intractable forms.

However weak, previous U.S. nuclear policies built in some restraints on use. While the United States has never had a no-first-use policy, it pledged not to use nuclear weapons against signatories to the Nuclear Non-Proliferation Treaty. But in March 2002, a secret U.S. Department of Defense report leaked to the press revealed the names of seven countries—China, Russia, Iraq, Iran, North Korea, Libya, and Syria—on a nuclear strike list for contingencies going far beyond use of nuclear weapons. These situations include attacks against stocks of biological, chemical, and other weapons of mass destruction; an attack on an ally (Iraq against Israel; North Korea against South Korea; China against Taiwan); and "surprising military developments."[63]

Thus biological weapons in the hands of "rogues" have become a source of legitimation for a turn from mutually assured destruction to "unilaterally assured destruction" to a Strangelovian embrace of the bomb as the ultimate key to security.[64] Such planning for *lack* of nuclear restraint fundamentally destabilizes *all* restraints on weapons of mass destruction, including the Biological Weapons Convention. Threatened states may well conclude that their only defense is to develop their own weapons of mass destruction.

A third condition supporting the continued intractability of the BW problem is the secrecy that enshrouds biological activities in industry and in the military. As has been noted previously in this chapter and by other authors, such secrecy takes a variety of forms and characterizes the activities of virtually all states (chapters 2 and 14). Long before the difficulties of detecting Iraq's BW program were confronted, the study conducted by Hedley Bull in 1966–1967 for the British Foreign Office concluded that the prospects for detecting offensive BW activities through inspections were dim.[65] Bull dismissed a proposal from the NGO Pugwash for completely opening BW defense activities as naïve, and not primarily because of concern that other states would not reciprocate but because the British military establishment would resist revealing the nature of its defenses on the grounds that doing so would undermine them. Furthermore, Bull argued that private corporations would also desire secrecy both for commercial reasons and for protection of techniques and products that might be transferred to the military through British and American military-industrial liaison programs.[66]

Since Bull's appraisal over thirty years ago, the emergence of biotechnology and the establishment of a strict intellectual property regime have enveloped this field in a thick shroud of secrecy (see chapters 14 and 15). Concurrently, military development of the newer techniques of biotechnology has had parallel effects in the military sphere. For example, the development of a genetically engineered strain of anthrax by the U.S. Defense Intelligence Agency was revealed to the American public only as a result of the vigorous investigation of three journalists.[67] These overlapping interests in commercial and military secrecy have shaped the BW problem in at least two significant ways: first, by undermining commitments to levels of transparency concerning military intentions with respect to the biological sciences; and second, by undermining the positive dimension of the BWC that encourages the transfer of the biological sciences and technologies for peaceful purposes and thereby provides incentives to states to comply with the BWC's requirements (chapters 13 and 15).

Finally, at the most general level, the poor and war-torn regions of the world provide conditions under which terrorism can flourish. While potential epidemics spread by imagined biological weapons preoccupy the West, the poor countries of the world already face diseases of epidemic proportions. Tuberculosis infects eight to ten million people each year, mainly in developing countries. Other major killers are AIDS, malaria, and childhood infections. In a report issued in December 2001, the World Health Organization commission estimated that health spending in developing countries would need to rise from the present $13 per person to about $38 per person per year to address these diseases and protect future generations.[68] Yet at the present time there is a net outflow of capital from the developing countries of the South to the developed countries of the North.[69] Furthermore, the intellectual property regime established by the Uruguay Round trade deal of 1994 has ensured that new technologies invented in the North are largely unaffordable by the developing countries of the South. Arguably, the Uruguay Round's requirement that strict patent standards should be universal undermines the implementation of article X of the BWC, according to which parties to the convention undertake to facilitate the fullest possible exchange of biological science and technology for peaceful purposes (see chapter 15). For example, intellectual property protection for pharmaceutical drugs and agricultural seeds increases the costs of medical and agricultural products, driving peasant farmers from their land and consequently exacerbating poverty and disease to crisis levels.

As World Bank president James Wolfensohn argued shortly after September 11, although there is no direct connection between terrorism and poverty, the struggle for survival that poverty generates is a key condition of war. In turn, conflict-ridden countries "become safe havens for terrorists." If developed countries wish to find long-term solutions to the threat of terrorism, including biological terrorism, then, as Wolfensohn concludes, "our common goal must be to eradicate poverty, to promote inclusion and social justice, to bring the marginalized into the mainstream of the global economy and society."[70] Immediately addressing the epidemic diseases of poor countries and ensuring that biological technologies are available at prices these countries can afford are two major steps that should be taken by the world's rich countries and that would also fulfill their commitments under article X.

It needs emphasis that nowhere in the world is violence currently more acute and more intertwined with military interest in WMD than in the Middle East. The pattern of random terror and retaliatory assassination which the Israel/Palestine conflict has exhibited increases the dangers of regional warfare and of international terrorism, both of which could involve weapons of mass destruction. Resolving this conflict is arguably the most urgent aspect of the "BW problem."

## CONCLUSION

At the beginning of the twenty-first century, the conditions described in this chapter are generating a series of major crises: international frameworks for removing the causes of war and improving the lives of all human beings are deteriorating, secrecy is breeding misunderstanding and suspicion that further undermine these frameworks, rich countries are arming themselves with increasingly fearful weapons, war and poverty are ravaging developing countries, and terrorism flourishes. In many respects, the crises of the Middle East are only the most acute examples of the larger crises looming over the future of the world as a whole. Particularly given the present military and diplomatic unilateralism of the United States, a feeding frenzy of violence seems likely to follow. Signs of this grim future are all too apparent.

Averting this future requires a restored cooperative internationalism committed to achieving nothing less than peace and disarmament on the one hand and the elimination of poverty and disease on the other. With respect to the biological warfare problem, cooperative internationalism means action at several levels: strengthening prohibitions against all weapons of mass destruction, removing levels of military and commercial secrecy that prevent successful monitoring of compliance, immediate actions to prevent terrorist attacks by ensuring that individuals and organizations in all countries are bound by laws that implement the prohibitions of the BWC and, most fundamentally, strenuous efforts to achieve a peaceful and just resolution of the Middle Eastern conflict.

It is clearly important that parties to the BWC renew their efforts and their commitments to strengthening the BWC both by interpreting article I strictly to exclude genetic modification of pathogens for defensive as well as offensive purposes and by completing the protocol to strengthen compliance. Strong requirements for providing transparency of biological activities through declarations and routine inspections and rigorous challenge inspections conducted at short notice and an effective, well-financed organization to oversee and staff these functions could go a long way toward increasing confidence in the BWC. Weak requirements, on the other hand, would do the opposite.

There can be no illusion that achieving a strong BWC protocol will be easy, especially in view of the dual-use dimensions of virtually all biological agents, the large numbers of biological facilities that are potential candidates for inspection, and the trends over the past decade toward increasing commercial and military secrecy. There must be willingness on the part of the pharmaceutical and biotechnology industries and a will on the part of legislatures to reverse these trends in the industrial and military sectors. Even under optimum conditions, verification of compliance will be difficult. Nevertheless, the benefits of such a regime would go considerably beyond the ability to detect cheating. They would encourage transparency, they provide a means for reassurance, and they allow the parties to the BWC to act cooperatively both to respond to suspected violations and to encourage peaceful application and transfer of the biological sciences and biotechnology.

In the long run, however, these actions, ambitious though they may appear, are insufficient. Nothing less than breaking out of the twin downward spirals of violence and poverty is required to address international terrorism. It needs to be appreciated that terrorists are likely to adapt their tactics to strike at the new vulnerabilities associated with a diplomacy of reckless unilateralism.

These challenges point strongly in the direction of a final, overarching conclusion: Governments of the most militarily powerful states and their bureaucracies, left to their own devices, are not going to be able to meet this looming challenge of biological warfare. The only hopeful path is one based on the heightened mobilization of global civil society, in collaboration with small and moderate states, to address the ominous implications of complacency with respect to the various facets of policy bearing on all categories of weaponry of mass destruction. The effective avoidance of a biological arms race and buildup can only be achieved on the basis of a more humanistic outlook combined with civil society/state collaboration of the sort that worked so successfully to produce the anti-personnel landmines treaty. It is essential to find paths of political action that are able to break free from realist obsessions with regard to sovereignty, security of the state, and a total war mentality. Genuinely reliable regimes of prohibition for BW can only be established and maintained by pressures associated with morality and the rule of law. We should have no illusions; such a path has obstacles of its own and is likely to involve many twists and turns over a long period. It presupposes a willingness, not now visible on the horizon of global policy, of the strong to restrict their options to an extent comparable to that of the weak, and to agree to systemic norms of prohibition that apply by stages to categories of weaponry of mass destruction.

Perhaps the most promising efforts at this stage would be to deemphasize intergovernmental approaches and instead focus on civil society. A first step would be to encourage the resolve of those associated with work on weaponry of mass destruction to dissociate themselves from activities that seem related to the commission of crimes of state. Such crimes would involve war preparations or avoidance of existing treaty obligations. This ethos of a law-oriented professionalism would need to be strengthened in the course of specialized education and training and reinforced by national legislation that protected whistleblowing activities and punished complicity with illegal activities.

It would be beneficial to tie this effort to the wider concept of individual responsibility embedded in the "Nuremberg Principles." The eventual goal is to influence the behavioral code of the national security establishment and place some unconditional limits on its activities undertaken for the sake of state interests. In the end, the only reliable path to prohibition of biological weaponry involves a transformed ethos of responsible power by those entrusted with authority to uphold the security of the political communities that exist on the planet, implying a widespread, serious process dedicated to demilitarization, disarmament, and war prevention, which would involve the development of effective mechanisms for the peaceful settlement of international disputes and for achieving peaceful change. Of course, such efforts may seem utopian from the vantage point of the present, but no more so than to suppose that the current legal/moral framework is capable of containing geopolitical opportunism, or more specifically, of preventing over time recourse to weaponry of mass destruction, given the logic of realpolitik; the uneven circumstances and perceptions of states around the world; and the persistence of ideas that nothing is as important, even human survival, as the pursuit of strategic national interests.

It should be appreciated in the overall context of world politics that the great majority of states today are committed to the struggle to abolish all categories of weapons of mass destruction and have acted responsibly for many years by foregoing the option to develop WMD of their own. Without these commitments there would be an even more dangerous global situation. The nub of the problem has been, and remains, the unwillingness of the dominant states to act responsibly in relation to WMD by joining the demilitarizing consensus that has existed, especially among the countries of the South, since the end of World War II. A mobilized transnational civil society movement has the best prospect of overcoming this resistance of dominant states, which includes opposition to an effective regime of biological weaponry and necessarily related moves toward nuclear disarmament. In effect, the peoples of the world through their representatives, in the spirit of global democracy, need to work with as many governments as possible and within international institutions to invalidate the prerogative of any political actor, including the United States, to establish a regulatory regime for the world that leaves it free to deploy, develop, and threaten mass destruction while at the same time setting itself as the arbiter of who else may be permitted to retain a WMD option.

This imperative with respect to global security is not only a matter of elemental survivalist prudence, it also relates to the priorities affecting the resources of the world. With poverty and human suffering so widespread in Africa, Asia, and Latin America, the time has come to challenge the huge continuing expenditures on weaponry and military approaches to conflict resolution. There is a growing acknowledgment that poverty creates conditions that can lead to various forms of terrorism and that a more secure world would exist if there were not such massive concentrations of poverty that generate crime and violence. A demilitarizing process is also necessary to safeguard the planet and protect future generations against a deteriorating environment, including potentially disastrous forms of human-induced climate change. The wider implication of these challenges is that ultimately for the survival of humanity, we must think of security as "human security" rather than "national" security. This thinking applies as much to the problem of biological warfare as it does to other aspects of an increasingly militarized world.

## NOTES

1. Jan Lodal, *The Price of Dominance: The New Weapons of Mass Destruction and Their Challenge to American Leadership* (New York: Council on Foreign Relations Press, 2001), 98.

2. U.S. White House, Office of the Press Secretary, Statement of President George Bush, 1 November 2000.

3. U.S. Department of Defense, Proliferation: Threat and Response (1997), "Message of the Secretary of Defense," 1–2; available online at www.defenselink .mil/pubs/prolif97/message.html.

4. Judith Miller, Stephen Engelberg, and William Broad, *Germs: Biological Weapons and America's Secret War* (New York: Simon & Schuster, 2001); "The Emerging American Dimension of the BW Problem," below.

5. William Broad, personal communication, 24 May 2001. On the ambiguity of the U.S. biological defense program in the 1980s, see Charles Pillar and Keith Yamamotot, *Gene Wars: Military Control Over the New Genetic Technologies* (New York: Beech Tree Books, 1988).

6. Evelyn Fox Keller, *Century of the Gene* (Cambridge, Mass.: Harvard University Press, 2000).

7. A recent result that has generated great concern was the construction of a virus that attacked the immune systems of mice; see William Broad, "Australians Create a Deadly Mouse Virus," *New York Times* (23 January 2001), A6.

8. The Cooperative Threat Reduction Program began with the Nunn-Lugar

Amendment to the Conventional Forces in Europe Treaty Implementation Act of 1991. See James Clay Moltz, "Introduction: Assessing US Nonproliferation Assistance to the NIS," *The Nonproliferation Review* 7(1) (Spring 2000); and Amy Smithson, "Toxic Archipelago: Preventing Proliferation from the Former Soviet Chemical and Biological Weapons Complexes," Henry L. Stimson Center Report No. 32 (December 1999).

9. Smithson, "Toxic Archipelago," 76, 88.

10. A. P. Pomerantsev et al., "Expression of Cereolysine AB Genes in *Bacillus anthracis* Vaccine Strain Ensures Protection Against Experimental Hemolytic Anthrax Infection," *Vaccine* 15(17/18) (1977), 1846–50.

11. Tim Weiner, "Soviet Defector Warns of Biological Weapons," *New York Times* (25 February 1998), A1; Richard Preston, "The Bioweaponeers," *New Yorker* (9 March 1998), 52–65; Ken Alibek, *Biohazard* (New York: Random House, 1999). This is not the first transfer of illegal bioweapons knowledge to the West. At the end of World War II, the results of the illegal Japanese biological weapons program were transferred to the United States in exchange for a grant of immunity to the head of the program, General Shiro Ishii. See Sheldon Harris, *Factories of Death: Japanese Biological Warfare 1932–1945 and the American Cover-up* (New York: Routledge, 1995), 203, 221.

12. The Sunshine Project, "Risks of Using Biological Agents in Drug Eradication," Backgrounder Series No. 4 (February 2001), 2.

13. The language of the Biological Weapons Convention does not exclude the use of biological agents for law enforcement purposes from its prohibition. Thus BWC's prohibition of development, production, and stockpiling for "hostile purposes" extends to use of biological agents that are opposed by local populations. The phrase "hostile purposes" was originally intended by the United Kingdom to apply to situations beyond declared wars between states.

14. See, for example, the exchanges between Arab and Israeli participants at a conference organized by the UN Institute for Disarmament Research in Cairo in April 1993, recorded in *Conference of Research Institutes in the Middle East,* ed. Chantal de Jonge Oudraat (New York and Geneva: United Nations, 1994). For discussion of the nuances associated with Israel's commitment "not to be the first to introduce" nuclear weapons into the Middle East, see Avner Cohen, *Israel and the Bomb* (New York: Columbia University Press, 1998), 337–38.

15. It should be noted, however, that tensions between Iran and Iraq have eased to a considerable extent in recent years.

16. Resolution 687 noted that the actions required of Iraq "represent steps towards the goal of establishing in the Middle East a zone free of weapons of mass destruction and all missiles for their delivery and the objective of a global ban on chemical weapons."

17. David Makovksy, "FM to Meet Boutros-Ghali, Peres to Seek Mutual Verification of Arms Ban with Arabs," *Jerusalem Post* (13 January 1993); Savita Pande, "Nuclear Weapons Free Zone in the Middle East," *Strategic Analysis* 32(9) (December 1998), 1369–79, online: www.idsa-india.org/an-dec8–8.html.

18. Gerald Steinberg, "Deterrence and Middle East Stability: An Israeli Perspective," *Security Dialogue* 28(1) (1997), 51–52.

19. Abdulhay Sayed, "The Future of the Israeli Nuclear Force and the Middle East Peace Process," *Security Dialogue* 28(1) (1997), 35.

20. Ibid.

21. Peter Jones, "Arms Control in the Middle East," *Security Dialogue* 28(1) (1997), 57–70.

22. On this point, compare Laura Drake's position in chapter 6.

23. Bruce Jentleson, "The Middle East Multilateral Arms Control and Regional Security (ACRS) Talks: Progress, Problems, and Prospects," *CIAO Working Papers* (September 1995), online: www.ciaonet.org/wps/jeb01/ (March 9, 2002).

24. Ibid.

25. John Bolton, Under Secretary of State for Arms Control and International Security, Statement to the Fifth Review Conference of the Biological Weapons Convention, 19 November 2001; available online at www.acronym.org.uk/bwc/revconus.htm (March 3, 2002).

26. Middle East Institute, Policy Briefs, Summary of two lectures by Peter Jones, "Iran's Arms Control Policies and Weapons of Mass Destruction," Washington, D.C., April 16–17, 2001; available online at www.mideasti.org/briefs/jonesb.html (March 9, 2002).

27. Daniel Byman et al., *Iran's Security Policy in the Post-Revolutionary Era* (Washington, D.C.: RAND, 2001), 100.

28. Shebonti Ray Dadwal, "Iran and the US: In the Shadow of Containment," paper presented at the annual meeting of the International Studies Association, Chicago, February 2001.

29. Robert Fisk, "Arab States United in Rejecting Attack on Saddam," *The Independent* (18 March 2002).

30. Gary Sick, "Trial by Error: Reflections on the Iran–Iraq War," *Middle East Journal* 43(2) (Spring 1989), 230–45. For discussion of and references to transfers of dual-purpose materials and arms to Iraq from the United States, see Stephen Shalom, *Imperial Alibis: Rationalizing U.S. Intervention After the Cold War* (Boston: South End Press, 1993).

31. Barton Gellman, "U.S. Spied on Iraqi Military Via U.N.," *Washington Post* (2 March 1999), A1; Barton Gellman, personal communication, 2000.

32. John Mueller and Karl Mueller, "Rethinking Sanctions on Iraq," *Foreign Affairs* (May/June 1999), 51. For surveys of the decline in health standards in Iraq in the 1990s, see UNICEF and Government of Iraq Ministry of Health, *Child and Maternity Mortality Survey 1999: Preliminary Report* (Baghdad: UNICEF, 1999); available online at www.unicef.org; WHO Resource Center, *Health Conditions of the Population in Iraq Since the Gulf Crisis* (Geneva: WHO, 1996); available online at www.who.int. For further analysis, see Peter L. Pellett, "Sanctions, Food, Nutrition, and Health in Iraq," in *Iraq Under Siege: The Deadly Impact of Sanctions and War,* ed. Anthony Arnove (Boston: South End Press, 2000), 151–68.

33. Alain Gresh, "Oil for Food: The True Story," *Le Monde Diplomatique* (October 2000); available online at www.globalpolicy.org/security/sanction/iraq1/oilforfood/00gresh.htm.

34. Denis Halliday, "Why I Resigned My UN Post in Protest of Sanctions," speech at Harvard University, 5 November 1998.

35. *Iraq Under Siege*, 11–12.

36. Gresh, "Oil for Food: The True Story."

37. For discussion of the advantages and disadvantages of "smart sanctions," see David Cortright, Alistair Millar, and George Lopez, "Smart Sanctions: Restructuring UN Policy in Iraq," Fourth Freedom Forum, Goshen, Indiana, April 2001; David Cortright, "A Hard Look at Iraq Sanctions," *The Nation* (3 December 2001), and responses to Cortright's proposals by Denis Halliday and Phyllis Bennis and others, "Killing Sanctions in Iraq," *The Nation* (21 January 2002). On UN Security Council Resolution 1409, see Ewen MacAskill, "UN Agrees Long-Awaited Smart Sanctions for Iraq," *The Guardian* (15 May 2002).

38. Stanley Hoffman, "On the War," *New York Review of Books* (1 November 2001), 4–6.

39. See Bruce Hoffman, "Rethinking Terrorism in Light of a War on Terrorism," Testimony, U.S. House of Representatives, Permanent Select Committee on Intelligence, Subcommittee on Terrorism and Homeland Security, 26 September 2001.

40. Brian Jenkins, "International Terrorism: A New Mode of Conflict." in *International Terrorism and World Security,* ed. David Charlton and Carlo Schaerf (London: Croom Helm, 1975), 15, quoted in Hoffman, "Rethinking Terrorism in Light of a War on Terrorism," 4.

41. Hoffman, "Rethinking Terrorism," 3.

42. For example, disseminating biological weapons meant overcoming the substantial problem of producing "weaponized" forms of natural pathogens that could survive climatic conditions and diffuse efficiently in an environment.

43. Hoffman, "Re-thinking Terrorism"; compare Bruce Hoffman, "Change and Continuity in Terrorism," Lecture, Conference on "Terrorism and Beyond: The 21st Century," co-sponsored by Oklahoma City National Memorial Institute for the Prevention of Terrorism and the RAND Corporation, 17 April 2000.

44. See, e.g., Alan Cullison and Andrew Higgins, "A Computer in Kabul Yields a Chilling Array of Al Qaeda Memos," *Wall Street Journal* (31 December 2001), 1; Anthony Loyd, "Scientists Confirm Bin Laden's Weapons Tests," *The Times* (29 December 2001).

45. David Johnston and William Broad, "Anthrax in Mail Was Newly Made, Investigators Say," *New York Times* (23 June 2002), 1.

46. U.S. Secretary of Defense Caspar Weinberger to Senator James Sasser, 20 November 1984. For further discussion, see Susan Wright, "Evolution of Biological Warfare Policy," in *Preventing a Biological Arms Race,* ed. Susan Wright (Cambridge, Mass.: MIT Press, 1990), 53–54.

47. Miller, Engelberg, and Broad, *Germs*, 92–93, 288–89. But see also Meryl Nass, "The Labyrinth of Biological Defense," *PSR Quarterly* 1 (March 1991), 24–30.

48. Details of these projects are given in Miller, Engelberg, and Broad, *Germs*, chapter 12.

49. Sunshine Project, News Release, The Destabilizing Danger of 'Non-Lethal' Chemical and Biological Weapons in the War on Terrorism, 19 September 2001; available online at www.sunshine-project.org. On bacteria to degrade weapons systems, see Steven Aftergood, "The Soft-Kill Fallacy," *The Bulletin of the Atomic Scientists* (September/October 1994), 40–45.

50. Sunshine Project, "Risks of Using Biological Agents in Drug Eradication," Backgrounder Series No. 4 (February 2001).

51. Miller, Engelberg, and Broad, *Germs*, 308–10.

52. Royston C. Clowes et al., "Proposed Guidelines on Potential Biohazards Associated with Experiments Involving Genetically Altered Microorganisms," 24 February 1975, Recombinant DNA History Collection, MC100, Institute Archives, MIT Libraries, Cambridge, Massachusetts, USA. For discussion, see Susan Wright, *Molecular Politics: Developing American and British Regulatory Policy for Genetic Engineering, 1972–1982* (Chicago: University of Chicago Press, 1994), 151.

53. Personal communication, December 2001.

54. For discussions of the problems posed by biological defense programs, see Jonathan King and Harlee Strauss, "The Hazards of Defensive Biological Warfare Programs," in Wright, *Preventing a Biological Arms Race*, 120–32; Laura Reed and Seth Shulman, chapter 3; and Victor Sidel, chapter 4.

55. The BWC review conferences completed (in 1991 and 1996) since the end of the Cold War are remarkable for the *absence* of Western comment on the Soviet violations. As Miller, Engelberg, and Broad have argued, at the end of the Cold War in 1991, the United States had political reasons for not weakening Soviet Chairman Mikhail Gorbachev's position in the Soviet Union; see *Germs*, 125–26. Similarly, in 2001, the Bush administration had important political reasons for not embarrassing Vladimir Putin.

56. Smithson, "Toxic Archipelago."

57. Stephen Black, chapter 11; Amin Saikal, chapter 10; Tareq Y. Ismael and Jacqueline S. Ismael, "Cowboy Warfare, Biological Diplomacy: Disarming Metaphors as Weapons of Mass Destruction," *Politics and the Life Sciences* 18(1) (March 1999), 70–78.

58. The term leans heavily on its use in such phrases as "rogue elephant" to refer to an animal that is deranged in its antisocial behavior.

59. Steven Mufson, "Threat of 'Rogue' States: Is It Reality or Rhetoric?" *Washington Post* (29 May 2000), A1.

60. Christopher Marquis, "U.S. Declares 'Rogue' Nations Are Now 'States of Concern'," *New York Times* (20 June 2000); Steven Mufson, "A 'Rogue' Is a 'Rogue' Is a 'State of Concern'," *Washington Post* (20 June 2000), A16.

61. Dana Milbank, "Bush Would Update Germ Warfare Pact," *Washington Post* (2 November 2001), A16.

62. Statement of the Honorable John R. Bolton to the Fifth Review Conference of the Biological Weapons Convention, Geneva, Switzerland, 19 November 2001.

63. Paul Richter, "U.S. Works Up Plan for Using Nuclear Arms," *Los Angeles Times* (9 March 2002), A1; Michael Gordon, "U.S. Nuclear Plan Sees New Targets and New Weapons," *New York Times* (10 March 2002), A1; John Cushman, "Rattling New Sabers," *New York Times* (10 March 2002), A1.

64. These descriptions are John Cushman's; see Cushman, "Rattling New Sabers."

65. U.K. Foreign Office, Arms Control and Disarmament Unit, "Arms Control Implications of Chemical and Biological Warfare: Analysis and Proposals," ACDRU(66)2 (2nd Draft), 4 July 1966, classified "top secret," 49, FO371/187448, PRO.

66. U.K. Foreign Office, Arms Control and Disarmament Unit, "Arms Control Implications of Chemical and Biological Warfare," 56–57. Bull does not explain the reasons for commercial secrecy, but there are references to the British and American military-industrial liaison programs elsewhere. See, e.g. U.K. Ministry of Defence, Defence Research Committee, "Chemical Defence Experimental Establishment, Research Programme 1969–70: Note by the Army Department," 7 May 1969, DR 22/69, Classified "secret," Annex B, 6.

67. Miller, Engelberg, and Broad, *Germs*, 309–10.

68. WHO Commission on Macroeconomics and Health, *Final Report: Macroeconomics and Health: Investing in Health for Economic Development* (2001); available online at www.cmhealth.org.

69. Philip Bowring, "From Poor to Rich: Capital Is Flowing in the Wrong Direction," *International Herald Tribune* (12 December 2001), 8.

70. James Wolfensohn, "Rich Nations Can Remove World Poverty as a Source of Conflict," *International Herald Tribune* (6 October 2001), 6.

# 17

## Proposals for the Future
### Strengthening Global Commitments to Biological Disarmament

*Susan Wright*

The proposals presented here draw on earlier statements designed to strengthen commitments to biological disarmament on the part of states, transnational organizations, nongovernmental organizations (NGOs), and individuals. These statements include the Pledge Against Military Use of Biological Research, endorsed and circulated by the Council for Responsible Genetics in 1989, and proposals for the Hague Appeal for Peace Conference in 1999, to which several of the authors of this book—P. R. Chari, Richard Falk, Amin Saikal, Victor Sidel, and Susan Wright—contributed. The inclusion of these proposals in this book does not imply endorsement by all of the contributors.

### INTERNATIONAL AND NATIONAL LEVELS

To achieve a durable international commitment to biological disarmament, a cooperative internationalism that treats all states, whether viewed as close allies or even as potential enemies, as having equal status under international law, must be nurtured. Particularly needed are commitments to do no harm to innocent civilians and approaches that use the wealth of the West to empower developing countries to combat poverty and disease.

## The Biological Weapons Convention and the Chemical Weapons Convention as Precedents for the Abolition of All Weapons of Mass Destruction

- Governments and NGOs are urged to support a comprehensive regime of prohibition of *all* weapons of mass destruction (WMD). The Biological Weapons Convention and the Chemical Weapons Convention must be seen as part of a global effort to abolish all WMD and, more generally, as steps toward general and complete disarmament. All states should sign and ratify these conventions, and nuclear weapons states should pursue in good faith negotiations leading to nuclear disarmament, as the International Court of Justice ruled in 1996. Moves on the part of some nuclear states to use these conventions as counterproliferation measures that rely for their effectiveness on resort to the threat, or even to the use, of nuclear weapons must be challenged and resisted.

## The Biological Weapons Convention and the Responsibilities of States Parties

- It must be recognized that the BWC is not reliable in its present form to achieve its purpose of banning possession of biological and toxin weapons and that action to strengthen its scope and implementation are urgently needed.
- To provide reassurance about their intentions both to other states and to their own citizens, and to ensure the effectiveness of the BWC, all states and relevant substate organizations should, at the continuation of the Fifth Review Conference in November 2002, make strong commitments to negotiating as a matter of urgency a Compliance Protocol that supports high levels of transparency through declarations, visits to verify the accuracy of declarations, and challenge inspections.
- To avert the possibility of a "qualitative" biological arms race proceeding under the guise of research, development, and production for defense, the development of novel biological agents that do not have unambiguously peaceful purposes should be prohibited. Inspections to ensure that military and civil organizations comply will be required.
- The parties to the BWC should state that so-called nonlethal biological weapons, including biological agents intended for use against drug crops, are prohibited under article I of the BWC, which bans all biological agents and toxins of types and in quantities that have no justification for "prophylactic, protective, or other peaceful purposes."
- Relevant commercial organizations and military establishments should acknowledge that transparency for verification purposes should override secrecy for commercial and security reasons.

- States that have pursued biological weapons programs in the past should acknowledge and declare them and explain the steps they have taken to dismantle their programs and to destroy their stockpiles.
- States should develop strong national legislation that implements the BWC without qualification and that includes criminal penalties for violations by individuals and organizations. No state should take executive or legislative action that dilutes implementation of the Convention.
- States should develop legislation to protect and reward whistleblowers and investigate the information they provide, rather than proceed against these individuals for providing the information.
- States that are in compliance with the BWC should receive equal treatment with respect to trade in dual-purpose agents and equipment covered by the Convention. For states that are in compliance, the present export controls coordinated by the Australia Group, a private organization of some thirty-four Western and Western-oriented states, should be replaced by international export control standards to be negotiated and accepted by all parties.
- Sacrifices made by developing countries to join and implement the BWC should be recognized and compensated through a new framework developed under article X, according to which states undertake to share biological knowledge, materials, and technologies for peaceful purposes. This framework should provide formal recognition of the needs of developing countries to develop indigenous forms of technology under their own intellectual property laws. Such an arrangement would require modification of the present global intellectual property regime.

## Criminalization of Biological Weapons Development, Production, and Use

To the extent that it is legally possible, the requirements of the BWC should be applied not only to states but also to individuals under the jurisdiction of states.

- Under article IV of the BWC, each state should enact domestic legislation applying the requirements of the Convention to all individuals and organizations under its jurisdiction and defining violation of these requirements as a criminal act.
- All scientific organizations and individual scientists should be informed of their responsibilities under the BWC and the domestic legislation of their countries.
- The prohibitions of the BWC apply primarily to the actions of states, and not all state parties to the BWC have adopted domestic legislation

that applies the requirements of the BWC to individuals under their jurisdiction. Furthermore, the requirements enacted by a state under its domestic legislation do not apply to noncitizens on its territory who develop, produce, acquire, or use biological weapons in other states. Closing this loophole is closely related to two broader legal problems that have been brought into prominence by the September 11 attacks: first, addressing the development, acquisition, and use of *all* weapons of mass destruction by individuals and nonstate organizations; and second, addressing terrorism, understood as the "targeting or killing of civilians in armed conflict of any kind, for any purpose."[1] At present, treaty-based international law applicable to terrorism comprises thirteen separate conventions applying to such acts as hijacking, the taking of civilian hostages, and use of nuclear weapons. These laws rely for their enforcement on a web of bilateral treaties on such questions as extradition.[2] So far, there has been no international effort to develop a comprehensive international legal response to terrorism, including forms of terrorism that employ biological or other WMD. The first step toward considering an international legal response to bioterrorism should be an investigation leading to a report by an international organization of legal experts, such as the International Law Commission, followed by a decision either to develop a comprehensive convention on terrorism that would encompass possession and use of biological weapons or to continue to enlarge the present set of conventions addressing specific categories of harm to civilians.[3]

## REGIONAL LEVEL: MIDDLE EAST

Although developing and strengthening the international prohibition against biological weapons is essential, the Middle East is a special case where regionwide adherence to the BWC (and also to the CWC) seems out of the question unless disarmament with respect to *all* weapons of mass destruction is addressed. Furthermore, it seems unlikely that any such agreement is possible until the major territorial disputes are resolved and the Israeli state is recognized by all regional states. However unlikely the steps below may appear at the present time, they are necessary to pursue if the present pattern of nonadherence to the BWC is to end:

- Resolution of the Israeli–Palestinian conflict;
- Resolution of other outstanding territorial disputes between Israel and neighboring states;
- Regionwide peace agreement and recognition of Israel and a Palestinian state; and
- Negotiation of a WMD-free zone in the Middle East.

## IRAQ

The humanitarian crisis in Iraq and the devastation of its civil infrastructures call for immediate changes in the present policies based on the sanctions that have been in place since the UN Security Council approved Resolution 661 in August 1990:

- An emergency program to rebuild critical civilian infrastructures such as hospitals, water purification plants, and agricultural production should be initiated immediately.
- Sanctions on dual-purpose materials and equipment should be lifted immediately.
- Iraq should agree to join the Chemical Weapons Convention, to submit to inspections by the Organization for the Prohibition of Chemical Weapons, and to accept a future inspection regime for biological weapons. The future inspection regime for biological weapons should be the responsibility of a UN commission under the UN Secretary-General and supported by the United Nations. There must be strong procedural safeguards against the misuse of information by national governments.
- There should be a clear end-game for the UN inspections, after which sanctions would end.
- These steps should be explicitly framed in terms of UN Security Council Resolution 687, paragraph 14, according to which the steps taken by Iraq to achieve nuclear, chemical, and biological disarmament represent steps toward the goal of establishing in the Middle East a zone free from WMD and all missiles and the objective of a global ban on chemical weapons.

## CIVIL SOCIETY

Renunciation of biological warfare can only be achieved by the mobilization of citizens and NGOs throughout the world to press for government action on the various dimensions of the biological disarmament and its relation to the disarmament of other WMD and to generate a law-oriented professionalism that is committed to upholding all facets of the BWC's prohibition on biological weaponry:

- Scientists, professional societies, research organizations, industries, and educational institutions should pledge not to engage knowingly in research or teaching that furthers the development or use of biological (or chemical) weapons.
- Furthermore, scientists, professional societies, research organizations,

industries, and educational institutions should pledge not to develop novel biological and chemical agents that do not have unambiguously peaceful purposes, even if these activities are promoted for defensive purposes.

- Corporations, research organizations, and individual scientists are urged to pledge not to engage in any military activities related to biological (and chemical) warfare that could be seen either as a direct violation of the BWC or as extending the limits of legality defined by the Convention.

- Citizens and NGOs should organize to encourage wide understanding of the relevance of the Nuremberg Principles, and in particular, the responsibility to uphold international legal obligations even if inconsistent with official policies, government orders, and laws at the national level (legal obligations to maintain secrecy, for example).

## NOTES

I thank P. R. Chari, Richard Falk, and Victor Sidel for valuable suggestions and comments that have added substantively to these proposals.

1. Anne-Marie Slaughter and William Burke-White, "An International Constitutional Moment," *Harvard International Law Journal* 43(1) (Winter 2002), 1–21.

2. M. Cherif Bassiouni, "Legal Control of International Terrorism: A Policy-Oriented Assessment," *Harvard International Law Journal* 43(1) (Winter 2002), 83–103.

3. Proposals for criminalizing biological and chemical weapons have been made by the Harvard Sussex Program on CBW Armament and Arms Limitation and by Professor Barry Kellman, DePaul University, "Draft Convention on the Prevention and Punishment of the Crime of Developing, Acquiring, Stockpiling, Retaining, Transferring or Using Biological or Chemical Weapons, and accompanying editorial," *The CBW Conventions Bulletin* 42 (December 1998), 1–5; available online at fas-www.harvard.edu/~hsp/crim01.pdf; Barry Kellman, "Controlling Biological Weapons—A Criminal Law Enforcement Approach" (undated, c. 2001).

# Index

# About the Contributors

**Stephen Black** was Historian to the United Nations Special Commission from 1993 to 1999. He also served as deputy chief inspector, inspector, mission planner, operations officer, and report coordinator on fifteen UNSCOM chemical and biological weapons inspections in Iraq.

**P. R. Chari** is a former member of the Indian Administrative Service and served two spells in the Ministry of Defence. He is currently director of the Institute of Peace and Conflict Studies. He is the author of *Indo-Pak Nuclear Standoff: Role of the United States* (1995) and coeditor of *Working Towards a Verification Protocol for Biological Weapons* (2001).

**Avner Cohen** is senior research fellow at the Global Security and Disarmament Program and the Center for International and Security Studies at the University of Maryland. He is author of many works on the spread, control, and political and moral implications of weapons of mass destruction. His books include *The Nuclear Age as Moral History* (1989) and *Israel and the Bomb* (1998).

**Giri Deshingkar** (deceased) was a noted scholar specializing in Chinese history and civilization, apart from having a general interest in strategic issues. He was a former Director of the Institute of Chinese Studies and the Centre for the Study of Developing Societies.

**Biswajit Dhar** is senior fellow, Research and Information System for the Non-Aligned and Other Developing Countries, a policy research organization based in New Delhi, India. His research addresses economic dimensions of technology and development, focusing on the evolving global regime of intellectual property rights and its impact on developing countries.

**Laura Drake,** adjunct professor at the American University in Washington, D.C., specializes in Middle East strategic affairs. Her research addresses the political-military aspects of the Arab–Israel/Palestine–Israel conflict, U.S. strategy against Iraq and Iran and their responses, and the issue of unconventional weapons proliferation in the Middle East.

**Richard Falk** is professor emeritus of international law at Princeton University and currently visiting distinguished professor of global studies, University of California at Santa Barbara. His most recent books are *Predatory Globalization* (1999), *Human Rights Horizons* (2000), and *Religion and Humane Governance* (2001). He was a member of the Human Rights Inquiry Commission for the Palestinian Territories established by the UN Human Rights Commission in 2000.

**Laura Reed** is assistant director of the Peace and World Security Studies Program at the Five Colleges of Western Massachusetts and a visiting scholar in the Security Studies Program at MIT.

**Anthony Rimmington** is senior research fellow at the Centre for Russian and East European Studies, European Research Institute, University of Birmingham. He is the author of numerous books and papers on the biological weapons programs and the civil biopharmaceutical industry of the Soviet Union and its successor states, including *Technology and Transition: A Survey of Biotechnology in Russia, Ukraine, and the Baltic States* (1992).

**Amin Saikal** is director of the Center for Middle Eastern and Central Asian Studies and professor of political science at the Australian National University. He is the author and coeditor of numerous works on the Middle East, Central Asia, and Russia, including *The Middle East: Prospects for Settlement and Stability?* (1995) and *Lebanon Beyond 2000* (1997).

**Seth Shulman** is a journalist and author who has covered biological warfare issues in the United States for the past decade. He is the author of *The Threat at Home, Confronting the Toxic Legacy of the U.S. Military* (1992), *Owning the Future* (1999), and *Unlocking the Sky* (2002), the story of Glenn Curtiss and the race to invent the airplane in the early 1900s.

**Victor W. Sidel,** professor of social medicine and public health in New York City, is past president of the American Public Health Association, of Physicians for Social Responsibility, and of the International Physicians for the Prevention of Nuclear War. He is coeditor of *War and Public Health* (2000) and of *Terrorism and Public Health* (2002).

**Oliver Thränert** is head of the Research Unit on Security Policy at the German Institute for International and Security Affairs in Berlin. He specializes

About the Contributors

in arms control, including problems of proliferation of weapons of mass destruction and missile defenses. He is the editor of *Enhancing the Biological Weapons Convention* (1996) and *Preventing the Proliferation of Weapons of Mass Destruction: What Role for Arms Control? A German-American Dialogue* (1999).

**David A. Wallace** is assistant professor at the School of Information, University of Michigan. His current research interests include the implications of electronic records for the U.S. Freedom of Information Act and government secrecy. He is coeditor of *Archives and the Public Good: Accountability and Records in Modern Society* (2002).

**Susan Wright** is a research scientist specializing in the history and politics of biotechnology at the Institute for Research on Women and Gender, University of Michigan. She is the author of *Molecular Politics: Developing American and British Regulatory Policy for Genetic Engineering, 1972–1982* (1994) and coauthor of *Preventing a Biological Arms Race* (1990).

**Zou Yunhua** is senior research fellow on arms control issues at the General Armaments Department of China. From 1983 to 1996 she was a member of the Chinese delegation to the Conference on Disarmament. She participated in the CTBT negotiations and the Review and Extension Conference of the Parties to the NPT in 1995. She was a visiting fellow at the Center for International Security and Cooperation, Stanford University, in 1997–1998.